CONTEMPORARY AUDITING

Larry P. Bailey, Ph.D., C.P.A.
TEMPLE UNIVERSITY

HARPER & ROW, PUBLISHERS
New York   Hagerstown   Philadelphia   San Francisco   London

In memory of Robert and Louise

Sponsoring Editor: Bonnie K. Binkert
Project Editor: Penelope Schmukler
Designer: Rita Naughton
Senior Production Manager: Kewal K. Sharma
Compositor: Monotype Composition Company, Inc.
Printer and Binder: Halliday Lithograph Corporation
Art Studio: Danmark & Michaels, Inc.

Contemporary Auditing
Copyright © 1979 by Larry P. Bailey

All rights reserved. Printed in the United States of America. No part of this book may be used or reproduced in any manner whatsoever without written permission except in the case of brief quotations embodied in critical articles and reviews. For information address Harper & Row, Publishers, Inc., 10 East 53rd Street, New York, N.Y. 10022.

Library of Congress Cataloging in Publishing Data
Bailey, Larry P.
   Contemporary auditing.

    1.   Auditing.   I   Title.
HF5667.B235   657'.45   78-25647
ISBN 0-06-040446-9

Contents

Preface *xi*

Chapter 1 **AN OVERVIEW OF THE AUDIT PROFESSION** *1*

A BRIEF HISTORY *1*
Prior to the industrial revolution *1/*
Industrial revolution to 1900 *2/* 1900–1930 *3/*
1930 to present *3*
TYPES OF AUDITS *4*
Compliance audits *4/* Operational audits *5*
THE INDEPENDENT CPA *6*
The audit objective *6/* Business form *7/*
Internal structure *7/* Functional division *9*
THE AUDITOR'S REPORT *10*
The unqualified report *11*
REPORT MODIFICATION *13*
Accounting deficiency *14/* Scope deficiency *15/*
Uncertainty *15*
SUMMARY *16*
   Questions and problems *16*
   Multiple choice *24*

Chapter 2 **THE AUDIT FUNCTION** *26*

THE ROLE OF AUDITING IN SOCIETY *26*
ECONOMIC JUSTIFICATION OF THE AUDIT FUNCTION *27*
FILLING THE ROLE OF THE AUDITOR *28*

iv
Contents

SOCIETAL CONTROLS *29*
Institutional controls *30/* Other controls *34/*
Interpretations of auditing standards *44/*
Monitoring auditing standards in a firm *45*
CONCLUDING REMARKS *46*
Questions and problems *46*
Multiple choice *56*

Chapter 3 **THE CODE OF PROFESSIONAL ETHICS** *58*

PROFESSIONAL ETHICS *58*
THE CODE OF PROFESSIONAL ETHICS *59*
Concepts of professional ethics *59/*
Rules of conduct *60/* Enforcing professional ethics *78/*
SEC and ethics *79*
CONCLUDING REMARKS *80*
**APPENDIX: SUMMARY OF AICPA'S STATEMENTS ON RESPONSIBILITIES
IN TAX PRACTICE** *80*
Exercises and problems *83*
Multiple choice *96*

Chapter 4 **LEGAL LIABILITY** *98*

COMMON LAW LIABILITY *99*
Common law liability to clients *99/*
Common law liability to third parties *101*
FEDERAL STATUTE AND THIRD-PARTY LIABILITY *103*
Securities Act of 1933 *103/*
The Securities Exchange Act of 1934 *105*
SIGNIFICANT LEGAL CASES *106*
Civil cases *107/* Criminal cases *110*
SEC SANCTIONS *113*
LEGAL LIABILITY AND UNAUDITED STATEMENTS *114*
1136 Tenants Corporation *115/* Engagement letters *116*
PROFESSIONAL RESPONSE TO RECENT LITIGATION *116*
Education and training *116/* Peer review *118/*
Defensive auditing *118*
CONCLUDING REMARKS *119*
Exercises and problems *119*
Multiple choice *133*

Chapter 5 **EVIDENCE: COLLECTION AND EVALUATION** *134*

EVIDENCE *134*
The general sources of evidence *134/* Competency of

evidence *135/* Types of evidence *137/* Sufficiency

V
Contents

of evidence *140/* Evidence-gathering techniques *142*

AN INTEGRATED AUDIT APPROACH *147*
Environmental conditions *148/* Evaluation of internal
control *151/* Compliance tests *152/*
Substantive tests *153*

DOCUMENTATION OF EVIDENTIAL MATTER *153*
Permanent file *155/* Current file *156/*
Review of working papers *163*

CONCLUDING REMARKS *164*
Exercises and problems *164*
Multiple choice *175*

Chapter 6 INTERNAL CONTROL: SYSTEMS EVALUATIONS *176*

INTERNAL CONTROL DEFINED *176*
Administrative controls *177/* Accounting controls *178*

THE INTERNAL CONTROL MODEL *179*
Plan of organization *179/* System of authorization and
accountability *183/* Accounting structure *186/*
Personnel policies *188/* Internal audit staff *190/* Audit
committee *191/* Limitations of the internal control system *193*

STUDY OF THE INTERNAL CONTROL SYSTEM *193*
Understanding the system *194/* Evaluation of the
system *203/* Internal control recommendation letter *204/*
Communication of material weaknesses *206*

CONCLUDING REMARKS *207*
Exercises and problems *207*
Multiple choice *215*

Chapter 7 AUDITING AND EDP *217*

THE EDP INTERNAL CONTROL MODEL *217*
General controls *218/* The plan of organization *219/*
Hardware controls *222/* Access controls *222/*
Other data and procedural controls *223/*
Application controls *223*

THE STUDY AND EVALUATION OF THE EDP SYSTEM *226*
Preliminary review *227/* Assessment of preliminary review *233/*
In-depth review *234/* Assessment of in-depth review *236/*
Tests of compliance *236/* Evaluation of the system *239/*
The audit of EDP service centers *239*

CONCLUDING REMARKS *240*
Exercises and problems *240*
Multiple choice *248*

vi
Contents

Chapter 8 · SAMPLING IN AUDITING · *250*

JUDGMENT SAMPLING · *250*
STATISTICAL SAMPLING · *251*
Frequency estimation (attribute sampling) · *252*/ · Documentation: frequency estimation · *263*/ · Variable estimation (mean per unit) · *263*/ · Documentation: variable estimation · *271*/ · Discovery sampling · *273*/ · Ratio and difference estimates · *273*/ · Stratification · *273*/ · Identifying and controlling risk · *274*
CONCLUDING REMARKS · *276*
APPENDIX: A REVIEW OF STATISTICAL TERMS AND CONCEPTS · *276*
Exercises and problems · *281*
Multiple choice · *288*

Chapter 9 · THE AUDIT APPROACH: A SYSTEMS ORIENTATION · *289*

A SYSTEMS APPROACH · *289*
COMPLIANCE TESTS · *290*
Timing of procedures · *291*/ · Nature of procedures · *292*/ · Extent of procedures · *292*/ · The audit approach · *293*/ · EDP impact on the compliance tests · *296*
SUBSTANTIVE TESTS · *297*
Timing of procedures · *298*/ · Extent of procedures · *298*/ · Nature of procedures · *299*/ · Nature, timing, and extent: internal audit function · *301*/ · The audit approach · *302*/ · Impact of EDP on the substantive tests · *305*
CONCLUDING REMARKS · *307*
Exercises and Problems · *307*
Multiple choice · *313*

Chapter 10 · AUDIT OF THE CASH SYSTEM · *315*

CASH RECEIPTS SYSTEM · *315*
INTERNAL CONTROL MODEL: CASH RECEIPTS · *315*
Plan of organization · *316*/ · System of authorization and accountability · *317*
STUDY AND EVALUATION OF THE CASH RECEIPTS SYSTEM · *319*
Understanding the system · *319*/ · Evaluation of the system · *321*
COMPLIANCE TESTS: CASH RECEIPTS · *321*
Universe definition · *326*/ · Sample selection · *327*/ · Results of the compliance tests · *328*
CASH DISBURSEMENTS SYSTEM · *328*
INTERNAL CONTROL MODEL: CASH DISBURSEMENTS · *328*
Plan of organization · *329*/ · System of authorization and accountability · *329*

STUDY AND EVALUATION OF THE CASH DISBURSEMENTS SYSTEM *331*
COMPLIANCE TESTS: CASH DISBURSEMENTS *331*
Universe definition and sample selection *332*
SUBSTANTIVE TESTS: CASH IN BANK *334*
Existence *335/* Cutoff and existence *335/* Valuation, classification, and disclosure *338/* Substantive test: extended procedures *341/* Substantive procedures: other cash items *341/* Substantive tests results *345*
Exercises and problems *345*
Multiple choice *357*

Chapter 11 **AUDIT OF THE CREDIT SALES SYSTEM** *359*

CREDIT SALES SYSTEM *359*
INTERNAL CONTROL MODEL: CREDIT SALES *360*
Departmental autonomy *360/* System of authorization and accountability *361*
STUDY AND EVALUATION OF THE CREDIT SALES SYSTEM *363*
COMPLIANCE TESTS: CREDIT SALES *364*
Universe definition and sample selection *364/*
Results of compliance tests *373*
SUBSTANTIVE TESTS: ACCOUNTS RECEIVABLE *374*
Existence *374/* Valuation *383/* Cutoff *384/* Classification and disclosure *385/* Confirmation at an interim date *385/* Notes receivable *385*
Exercises and problems *387*
Multiple choice *398*

Chapter 12 **AUDIT OF THE INVENTORY SYSTEM** *401*

THE INVENTORY PURCHASE SYSTEM *401*
INTERNAL CONTROL MODEL: INVENTORY PURCHASE SYSTEM *402*
Plan of organization *402/* System of authorization and accountability *403*
STUDY AND EVALUATION OF THE INVENTORY PURCHASE SYSTEM *406*
COMPLIANCE TESTS: INVENTORY PURCHASES *406*
Results of compliance tests *413*
SUBSTANTIVE TESTS: INVENTORY *415*
Existence *415/* Valuation *424/* Valuation-Manufacturer *425/* Cutoff *429/* Classification and disclosure *429*
Exercises and problems *430*
Multiple choice *442*

viii
Contents

Chapter 13 **AUDIT OF LONG-TERM ASSETS** *445*

Part I. Audit of Property, Plant, and Equipment *445*

PROPERTY, PLANT AND EQUIPMENT *445*
INTERNAL CONTROL MODEL: FIXED ASSETS *445*
Plan of organization *446/* System of authorization and accountability *446*
STUDY AND EVALUATION OF THE FIXED-ASSET SYSTEM *449*
COMPLIANCE TESTS: FIXED ASSETS *449*
SUBSTANTIVE TESTS: FIXED ASSETS *449*
Existence *450/* Valuation *454/* Cutoff *456/* Classification and disclosure *456*

Part II. Audit of Investments *457*

INVESTMENTS *457*
INTERNAL CONTROL MODEL *458*
Substantive tests *458/* Existence *458/* Valuation *461/* Consolidated basis *463/* Cutoff *464/* Classification and disclosure *464/* Review of related accounts *464/* Other investments *465*
Exercises and problems *465*
Multiple choice *477*

Chapter 14 **AUDIT OF LIABILITIES: CURRENT, CONTINGENT, AND LONG-TERM** *478*

ACCOUNTS PAYABLE *478*
Substantive tests *479/* Existence *479/* Existence, valuation, and cutoff *481/* Valuation *482/* Classification and disclosure *483*
ACCRUED LIABILITIES *483*
Accrued wages *484/* Accrued warranty costs *484/* Accrued utility costs *485*
CONTINGENT LIABILITIES *485*
Existence and cutoff *485/* Valuation, classification, and disclosure *489*
LONG-TERM LIABILITIES *490*
INTERNAL CONTROL MODEL *490*
Plan of organization *491/* System of authorization and accountability *491*
STUDY AND EVALUATION *494*
COMPLIANCE AND SUBSTANTIVE TESTS *494*
Existence and cutoff *494*

VALUATION *497*
DISCLOSURE *498*
    Exercises and problems *499*
    Multiple choice *510*

Chapter 15   AUDIT OF STOCKHOLDERS' EQUITY *511*

INTERNAL CONTROL MODEL *511*
Plan of organization *511/*   System of authorization and accountability *512*

STUDY AND EVALUATION *514*

COMPLIANCE AND SUBSTANTIVE TESTS *514*
Existence and valuation *515/*   Existence and cutoff *519/*
Disclosure *521*

RETAINED EARNINGS *521*
Net income (loss) *523/*   Prior period adjustments *523/*
Cash and other dividends *524/*
Appropriated retained earnings *526*
    Exercises and problems *526*
    Multiple choice *531*

Chapter 16   AUDIT OF NOMINAL ACCOUNTS *532*

NOMINAL VERSUS PERMANENT ACCOUNTS: A CONTRAST *532*
Consistency of data *535/*   Evaluation of internal controls *535/*
Test of transactions (compliance tests) *535/*
Detail test of nominal accounts *537*

INTERNAL CONTROL MODEL: PAYROLL *538*
Plan of organization *538/*   System of authorization and accountability *540*

STUDY AND EVALUATION OF THE PAYROLL SYSTEM *543*

COMPLIANCE TESTS: PAYROLL *543*
Universe definition and sample selection *543/*   Validation of authorization *548/*   Review of clerical accuracy *548/*
Test of payroll summarization *549*

SUBSTANTIVE TESTS: PAYROLL *549*
Review of balance sheet allocations *549*

SUMMARY *551*
    Exercises and problems *551*
    Multiple choice *562*

Chapter 17   THE AUDIT REPORT *564*

COMPLETING THE AUDIT *564*
Review of subsequent events *564/*

x
Contents

Review of all evidential matter *571/* Independent review *572/*
Illegal acts by clients *572*

FORMULATING AN OPINION *573*

Unqualified report *573/* Report modifications *574/*
Accounting circumstances *578/* Scope circumstances *582/*
Uncertainty circumstance *585/* Emphasis of a matter *586/*
Piecemeal opinions *587/* Negative assurances *587*

CONCLUSION *587*

APPENDIX: AUDIT REPORT ILLUSTRATIONS *588*

Exercises and problems *597*
Multiple choice *612*

Chapter 18 ADDITIONAL ASPECTS OF THE AUDIT REPORT AND OTHER REPORTS *615*

Reports on comparative statements *615/* Other data in financial
reports *617/* Unaudited financial statements *618/*
Special reports *623/* Reports on internal control *626/*
Long-form reports *627/* Evaluation of the audit report *627*

Exercises and problems *629*
Multiple choice *640*

INDEX *643*

Preface

OBJECTIVE

Contemporary Auditing provides an introduction to the practice of public accounting and may be used in an undergraduate or graduate auditing class. It may also be used by public accounting firms in their professional development programs for new staff members. Finally, it may be used by an individual preparing for the auditing section of the CPA examination.

This book is not intended to be a handbook of auditing, and certain topics have been deliberately omitted. The premise of the approach adopted is that it is better to prepare the student for a variety of audit engagements and circumstances with a broad background rather than attempt to smother an eager student with numerous audit steps to memorize. This basic philosophy is recognized in the organization of the book which can be divided into four major sections.

ORGANIZATION AND COVERAGE

The first section (Chapters 1 through 4) deals with the audit environment and professional responsibility. To appreciate auditing and place the attest function in a proper perspective, a student must understand the role of the profession in society. This broad perspective is developed in the first part of the book so that subsequent chapters can be better understood. Societal and professional controls are the dominant themes of this section.

What might be referred to as basic audit methodology is developed in the second section (Chapters 5 through 9). General procedures for the collection, evaluation, and documentation of evidence are introduced in Chapter 5. The importance of the internal control system in the conduct of an engagement is discussed in Chapter 6. The next two chapters are devoted to the impact of statistical sampling and electronic data processing on the collection of audit evidence. The final chapter of this section, Chapter 9, emphasizes the integrated audit approach. The elements of this approach consist of (1) evaluation of the client's environmental conditions, (2) evaluation of the internal control system, (3) performance of compliance test procedures and, (4) performance of substantive tests. In addition, this general audit approach provides the basis for the discussion in the next major section.

The third section (Chapters 10 through 16) uses the general audit methodology developed in the previous section as a basis for the audit of specific accounting systems and balances that appear on the financial statements. Although only selected systems and accounts are discussed, the discussion encompasses typical audit situations encountered by the beginning staff auditor.

Finally, the fourth section consists of two chapters that present an in-depth analysis of the auditor's report. Chapter 17 illustrates the standard auditor's report and typical report modifications. Chapter 18 is concerned with special reports, limitations of the audit report, and possible alternative forms of the auditor's report.

SPECIAL FEATURES

In addition to the pedagogically sound approach of its basic structure, *Contemporary Auditing* has several other characteristics. It introduces and emphasizes, wherever possible, professional standards. These include codifications of generally accepted accounting principles, the professional code of ethics, Securities Exchange Commission promulgations, and especially, statements on auditing standards. This provides the student with a strong introduction to the professional literature so that, whenever an auditing problem is encountered, it can be researched and evaluated in the context of professional standards. Also, and not incidentally, exposure to these publications is a vital part of a student's preparation for the CPA examination.

Another feature of this book is the development of a general audit approach in Chapters 5–9 and the organization of Chapters 10–16 in a manner consistent with the general audit approach. This is important because it appears that many students are unable to understand the significance of an audit procedure. For this reason, this book avoids the listing and discussion of audit procedures in a mechanical fashion. Thus Chapters 10–16 are organized so that the general audit approach is reinforced, resulting in the enhancement of why audit procedures are applied in specific situations.

The organization of the material in this book allows the professor a considerable amount of flexibility in the course. If the textual material is considered too long for a particular course, a variety of chapter combinations can be adopted. The basics, that is, the minimum coverage, of auditing are discussed in Chapters 1 through 6, Chapter 9, and Chapter 17. From this point the professor can mold the course to the specific needs of the students or the program. For example, readings from professional standards, completion of an auditing practice set, or readings from professional periodicals may be added to the assignment of chapters from the textbook.

Exercises and problems at the end of each chapter have been carefully selected to illustrate the fundamental concepts presented. Many problems require the student to analyze a situation and construct a reasonable audit approach rather than parrot answers directly from the body of the text. Finally, questions from the CPA examination have been used in each chapter to introduce the student to the rigors of that examination (the author would like to thank the AICPA for allowing the use of these questions from the CPA examinations). Included in this group are multiple-choice questions, which have become an increasingly important part of the CPA examination, especially in the auditing section.

In writing an auditing textbook, more so that any other accounting textbook, it is always necessary to balance the conceptual framework with the applied aspects of the discipline. This book strives to present a solid foundation of the role of the auditor and the fundamental concepts of auditing itself. On the other hand, it is assumed that the reader is, or will be, involved in the conduct of a professional audit. Thus it would have been imprudent to avoid the practical aspects of auditing in the writing of this book. Fortunately, in the final analysis the discussion of both the conceptual approach and practical aspects of auditing reinforces one another, and neither should be slighted. It is hoped that this textbook has found that elusive blend of the two.

A special word of thanks is in order to my wife, Nancy, who proofread the first draft of the manuscript. A good deal of family cooperation is needed to complete such a project, and in addition to my wife's patience, I would like to commend my children, Kim and Scooter, for their understanding and maturity.

I would also like to thank the following reviewers for their helpful suggestions: Raymond S. Chen, California State University, Northridge; George R. Hawkes, California State University, Northridge; Russell F. Briner, University of Mississippi; Joseph F. Guy, Georgia State University; Paul A. Janell Northeastern University; David M. Dennis, University of South Florida; Park E. Leathers, Bowling Green State University; Gary John Previts, The University of Alabama; Howard Godfrey, The University of North Carolina at Charlotte; Andrew P. Barowsky; A. Barbara Byers, The University of Texas at Arlington; Duane R. Milano, Texas Christian University; Robert W. Koehler, Pennsylvania State University.

I would further like to thank Stephen L. Fogg, Temple University, for working the problems and solutions and for developing the accompanying audit case, IMPERIAL SPORTSWEAR.

Finally, no textbook is complete or without ambiguities. The author welcomes comments from anyone who has suggestions for improvement.

Larry P. Bailey

CHAPTER 1

An overview of the audit profession

A BRIEF HISTORY

The precise origin of auditing is unknown; however, there is enough information to provide a brief history. A knowledge of this past will help the reader to better understand the role of auditing in society today and to realize the potential for changes in the future. Like every profession, auditing changes as significant events occur in the environment in which it exists. While the nature of these future changes is uncertain, the probability of change is assured, especially as our society becomes even more complex as each element of society becomes increasingly interdependent. It should be noted that the emphasis at this point is focused on events and pressures that are external to the profession. It is not suggested that the profession does not stimulate or nurture change internally; however, its role usually involves refinement of the changes imposed by external factors. A significant portion of auditing literature is devoted to such refinement, and much of this literature is incorporated in this text.

Prior to the industrial revolution

Figure 1-1 is a brief summary of the history of auditing, dividing this history into four time periods. While the time periods are somewhat arbitrary, they provide a framework for relating the occurrence of external events to their subsequent impact on auditing.

Prior to the Industrial Revolution in England and the United States, auditing was not a formally recognized profession; nonetheless, there are several examples of the audit function. For example, it is known that ancient rulers used two scribes, working independently of one another, to ensure that the ruler was not defrauded and to provide a basis for determining the accountability of those in his employment. Since each scribe recorded every transaction, and the results of their work were subsequently compared, the audit approach was characterized

2
An overview of
the audit
profession

Figure 1-1

An outline of the history of auditing*

TIME PERIOD	AUDIT APPROACH	AUDIT OBJECTIVE	INTERESTED PARTY (USER GROUPS)
Prior to the Industrial Revolution	100 percent testing	Detection of fraud and stewardship	Owners
Industrial Revolution to 1900	100 percent testing	Detection of fraud	Stockholders and creditors
1900–1930	100 percent testing (with some smaller percentage testing)	Certification of the correctness of the balance sheet and income statement	Stockholders, creditors, and the government
1930 to present	Sampling of financial data	Formulation of an opinion as to the fairness of the financial statements	Stockholders, creditors, the government, unions, Congress, consumers, and other groups

* For a more detailed analysis see R. Gene Brown, "Changing Audit Objectives and Techniques," *Accounting Review*, October 1962, pp. 696–703.

by a 100 percent testing or verification. In addition, seafaring nations created an entrepreneurial group that financed explorations to new lands, making it necessary to employ auditors. Once again, the objective of the audit was to determine the accountability of those in the service of the owners and to prevent fraud.

Industrial revolution to 1900

The audit approach and audit objective did not change significantly during the period from the Industrial Revolution to 1900, but there were developments during this period that provided the impetus for subsequent changes in both. The very essence of the Industrial Revolution was the expansion of production capacity through the utilization of capital and organization of a production line. This meant that a business firm had to have significant financial resources to begin operations, resulting in a minimum size of operations. The firm began to replace the small village shop. With such growth, there was a need to develop and implement an accounting system that could process an increasing number of routine transactions. Eventually this growth made it uneconomical for an auditor to review every transaction, therefore forcing the use of a sampling approach of less than 100 percent verification. However, it was several decades before this method dominated the audit approach in the United States.

This period witnessed another development that would shape the audit profession in years to come. At this time the separation of management and ownership began to occur. As the ownership group became less involved in the day-to-day affairs of a business, it was obvious that some method of review to determine stewardship and to ensure against the possibility of fraud had to be created. It soon became apparent that such a review function required someone with special skills and someone independent of the business firm. In Great Britain this need for a professionally trained independent auditor was formalized with the passage of the Companies Act of 1862. This act required that an independent audit be performed for stock companies and was probably the genesis of today's modern audit profession, although auditing has developed its own unique characteristics in each country in which it is recognized as a profession.

1900–1930

The next significant event in the history of auditing occurred during the first third of the twentieth century. This period was again characterized by the growth and concentration of resources of business enterprises. There was also a growth in the user groups interested in the well-being of a typical business. With this expansion of the user group, there was a change in the objective of an audit. The detection of fraud and the determination of stewardship no longer satisfied stockholders and others who were more interested in the financial condition and the profitability of a firm. These groups demanded that the auditor certify the correctness of the financial statements, and the audit profession responded accordingly. The word "certify," or "certificate," is still used today, although most auditors try to avoid it because it implies a degree of precision not achieved by today's audit. Finally, this period witnessed introduction of the testing of accounting data, but the dominant audit approach retained the 100 percent review of data.

1930 to present

The real maturation of the audit profession has occurred during the last 50 years. Today's auditor recognizes that a business concern must have an adequate internal accounting system which he or she must evaluate to determine its effectiveness. The degree of effectiveness determines the extent of testing the auditor employs in examining the financial statements. This change in the audit approach is not due to developments within the profession but rather to the growth and complexity of businesses. Along with the change in the audit approach there has been a change in the audit objective. Prior to 1930, there was a strong inference that the auditor certified the penny accuracy of the financial statements; however, the current objective of an audit emphasizes a much broader approach to the review of financial statements.

It should also be noted that the user group has grown dramatically over the past few years. This has forced the auditing as well as the accounting profession into a much higher degree of visibility. Thus there is an undeniable recognition by society of the importance of the profession, but it also means that new demands are placed on it.

4
An overview of
the audit
profession

TYPES OF AUDITS

As suggested in the preceding discussion, the objective of an audit has evolved over many years. This discussion of an audit has been restricted to the external financial audit, but it would be erroneous to think of auditing as encompassing only this type. Modern auditing involves compliance audits, both financial and procedural, and operational audits. In addition, these audits are performed by individuals who work as independent certified public accountants (CPAs), internal auditors, and government auditors. It is almost an impossible task to describe the entire audit profession in a few pages, but it is instructive to generalize about it so that both the variety of auditing and the importance of auditors can be appreciated.

Compliance audits

The performance of a *compliance audit* is dependent upon the existence of established criteria which are promulgated by a recognized authority. This norm provides the basis for measuring compliance or the lack of compliance by the audited entity. In addition to established rules, there are other elements that must be present to ensure the successful performance of a compliance audit. These additional components include (1) an auditor capable of performing the audit, (2) proper documentation of the work accomplished by the entity, and (3) a method of communicating the results of the compliance audit. Compliance audits can be classified as financial compliance audits and procedural compliance audits.

This book is devoted almost exclusively to the *financial compliance audit*. The criteria that provide the basis for such an audit are generally accepted accounting principles as defined in part by the promulgations of the Financial Accounting Standards Board (FASB) (1973 to the present), the Accounting Principles Board (1959–1973), and the Committee on Accounting Procedure (1939–1959). In addition to these formal rules, there are other conventions, rules, and procedures that are generally accepted that are not formally codified. The auditor who meets certain requirements established by each state, such as passing a written examination and completing a minimum number of years of experience, is licensed to perform such audits. The financial records and the accounting system provide in part the documentation which is subject to audit. Finally, the auditor's report, which is discussed in more detail later in this chapter, is the method by which the independent CPA communicates with the users of the financial statements.

There are numerous illustrations of other types of financial compliance audits. Auditors employed by the Internal Revenue Service (IRS) perform such audits. The authoritative sources are the laws passed by Congress, the Internal Revenue Code, and judicial rulings. The IRS agent or auditor is hired and trained by the government to review the tax records of individuals, businesses, and nonprofit organizations. The results of the tax audit are communicated to the company in the form of a revenue agent report. Other financial compliance audits include reviews performed by bank examiners, the Defense Contract Audit

Agency and the General Accounting Office (GAO), as well as internal auditors of a company.

Another form of a compliance audit is that which focuses on the observance of policies and procedures established by a recognized authority. This is a *procedures compliance audit,* and it differs from a financial compliance audit in that it is not concerned with the reporting of financial data. Generally the objective of such an audit is to determine if an entity follows certain policies and procedures. These rules may be established internally by the entity, or they may be imposed externally by federal or state law or by an association to which the entity belongs. Again the auditor must be well versed in the established rules, and the entity's records must be kept in a manner conducive to an audit. The results of the audit are communicated in a manner prescribed by the business firm or the external authority. For example, an audit of a local housing authority may consist of a review to determine (1) if housing applicants are being discriminated against, (2) if local building codes are being observed before approval is granted, and (3) if applicants meet certain financial and nonfinancial criteria.

Often a compliance audit is both financial and procedural in scope. In fact, the audit approach and audit results may be interrelated; however, it is useful to differentiate between the two compliance audits.

Operational audits

Especially since the end of World War II, an additional type of audit has emerged which is significantly broader in scope than the compliance audit. Unlike the compliance audit, the operational audit does not have an authoritative source to provide the criteria for the basis of the audit. This is true because the *operational audit* is concerned with the effectiveness and the efficiency of an organization. *Effectiveness* is a measure of how successful an entity is in achieving its stated goals or objectives. On the surface this may appear to be an easy audit task; nonetheless, many organizations have found it difficult to relate broad objectives to variables that can be measured as adequate indicators of the degree to which goals are being attained. *Efficiency* is concerned with how well an organization uses its resources at a particular level of activity. This part of an operational audit is somewhat easier to measure as well as to perform.

While operational auditing is performed by a variety of auditors, the GAO is one of the leaders in this area. The GAO is the investigative agency of Congress, and it has been commissioned by Congress to perform a variety of audits, both compliance and operational. The diversity of its activities is well illustrated by its definition of auditing, which emphasizes operational auditing in its last two parts.

Financial and compliance: Determine (a) whether financial operations are poorly conducted, (b) whether the financial reports of an audited entity are presented fairly, and (c) whether the entity has complied with applicable laws and regulations.

6
An overview of the audit profession

Economy and efficiency: Determine whether the entity is managing or utilizing its resources (personnel, property, space, and so forth) in an economical and efficient manner and the causes of an inefficient or uneconomical practice including inadequacies in management information systems, administrative procedures, or organizational structure.

Program results: Determine whether the desired results or benefits are being achieved, whether the objectives established by the legislature or other authorizing body are being met, and whether the agency has considered alternatives which might yield desired results at a low cost.[1]

Because of the broad nature of operational auditing, a variety of experts is often part of an operational audit team. The group may consist of accountants, economists, electronic data processing (EDP) specialists, statisticians, lawyers, and engineers. In addition, the audit report takes a variety of forms in order to match this diversity. A consideration of operational auditing is beyond the scope of this book.

THE INDEPENDENT CPA

The previous section described a variety of audits that may be conducted. This textbook is concerned with the type of audit performed by an independent certified public accounting firm. For brevity, this group is referred to simply as the auditor. Before the details of the audit approach are discussed, it is useful to describe the audit firm in terms of its audit objective, business form, internal structure, and functional division.

The audit objective

At this point it is sufficient to describe the *audit objective* as follows:

The objective of the ordinary examination of financial statements by the independent auditor is the expression of an opinion on the fairness with which they present financial position, results of operations, and changes in financial position in conformity with generally accepted accounting principles.[2]

In addition to this unique objective and responsibility, the independent auditing profession possesses other characteristics that have a significant impact on the practice of public accounting.

---

[1] Comptroller General of the United States, *Standards for Audit of Governmental Organizations, Programs, Activities and Functions,* (Washington, D.C.: U.S. General Accounting Office, 1972), p. 2.

[2] "Codification of Auditing Standards and Procedures," *Statement on Auditing Standards No. 1* (New York: AICPA, 1973), p. 1.

Business form

The independent auditor can practice as a sole proprietor, as a partner with another CPA, or as a member of a professional corporation. Many CPAs begin their practices as sole proprietors but subsequently merge with other CPAs to form a partnership. This is usually advantageous, because it often becomes necessary for an auditor to specialize in a particular area. Also, it affords an individual an opportunity to seek the counsel of fellow professionals when difficult decisions must be made. Since the opportunity to become a part owner of the business is usually an important factor in attracting and retaining auditors, often a practice grows to a point where it is almost impossible to operate as a sole proprietorship. These are some of the reasons why the partnership form of business dominates the public accounting profession.

In 1969, the American Institute of CPAs (AICPA) allowed public accountants to form professional corporations in states with enabling legislation. Because of the nature of a professional practice, whether it be that of a medical doctor, engineer, or public accountant, there were certain stringent rules established by the AICPA to protect the public from potential abuse which may result from the incorporation of practitioners. These requirements are listed in Figure 1-2. This form of business or organization was encouraged by members of the profession who wanted to take advantage of certain tax regulations concerning deferred-compensation plans. At the present time most medium-sized and large public accounting firms have not changed from the partnership form to the professional corporation form.

Internal structure

Like any business organization, a public accounting firm must design an organizational structure that defines the lines of authority and responsibility which form the hierarchy of the firm. The size and complexity of a firm have a significant impact on the firm's internal structure. Since public accounting firms range from local firms with two partners to international firms with over 2500 professional auditors, a few hundred partners, and over 100 offices scattered throughout the world, it is difficult to generalize about an organizational structure. Figure 1-3 depicts the very simple organization of a medium-sized accounting firm and includes a description of the duties and approximation of the experience requirements for each role.

To progress in a public accounting firm requires a considerable amount of dedication and hard work—a commitment expected in any professional endeavor. The work is demanding, but one author has captured the essence of a professional in stating that "the true test of a profession is the love of the drudgery it involves."[3] Empirical research has been performed in this area to try to identify the characteristics required of an individual who aspires to become a partner in

[3] Richard Ney, *The Wall Street Gang* (New York: Praeger, 1974), p. 134.

8
An overview of the audit profession

Figure 1-2

AICPA requirements for a professional corporation

The following resolution of the council was approved at the spring meeting of the council on May 6, 1969:

RESOLVED, that members may be officers, directors, stockholders, representatives or agents of a corporation offering services of a type performed by public accountants only when the professional corporation or association has the following characteristics:

1. *Name.* The name under which the professional corporation or association renders professional services shall contain only the names of one or more of the present or former shareholders or of partners who were associated with a predecessor accounting firm. Impersonal or fictitious names, as well as names which indicate a specialty, are prohibited.

2. *Purpose.* The professional corporation or association shall not provide services that are incompatible with the practice of public accounting.

3. *Ownership.* All shareholders of the corporation or association shall be persons duly qualified to practice as a certified public accountant in a state or territory of the United States or the District of Columbia. Shareholders shall at all times own their shares in their own right, and shall be the beneficial owners of the equity capital ascribed to them.

4. *Transfer of Shares.* Provision shall be made requiring any shareholder who ceases to be eligible to be a shareholder to dispose of all of his shares within a reasonable period to a person qualified to be a shareholder or to the corporation or association.

5. *Directors and Officers.* The principal executive officer shall be a shareholder and a director, and to the extent possible, all other directors and officers shall be certified public accountants. Lay directors and officers shall be certified public accountants. Lay directors and officers shall not exercise any authority whatsoever over professional matters.

6. *Conduct.* The right to practice as a corporation or association shall not change the obligation of its shareholders, directors, officers and other employees to comply with the standards of professional conduct established by the American Institute of Certified Public Accountants.

7. *Liability.* The stockholders of professional corporations or associations shall be jointly and severally liable for the acts of a corporation or association, or its employees—except where professional liability is carried, or capitalization is maintained, in amounts deemed sufficient to offer adequate protection to the public. Liability shall not be limited by the formation of subsidiary or affiliated corporations or associations each with its own limited and unrelated liability.

In a report approved by the council at the fall 1969 meeting, the board of directors recommended that professional liability insurance or capitalization in the amount of $50,000 per shareholder or officer and professional employee to a maximum of $2 million would offer adequate protection to the public. Members contemplating the formation of a corporation under this rule should ascertain that no further modifications in the characteristics have been made.

SOURCE: *Code of Professional Ethics* (New York: Copyright 1973 by the American Institute of Certified Public Accountants, Inc.), pp. 27–28.

a public accounting firm. Figure 1-4 lists the personal characteristics and executive skills considered prerequisites for attaining partnership in a large public accounting firm. This ranking was based on a survey of new partners of the "big eight" accounting firms for 1973.[4] The survey concluded "that to achieve success (partnership status) in a national accounting firm, an individual must be a technically proficient, self-motivated, intelligent, stable leader."

[4] The "big eight" accounting firms are: Arthur Andersen and Company; Ernst and Ernst; Haskins and Sells; Coopers and Lybrand; Peat, Marwick, Mitchell and Company; Price Waterhouse and Company; Touche Ross and Company; and Arthur Young and Company.

Figure 1-3

Organizational structure of a public accounting firm

		RESPONSIBILITY	YEARS OF EXPERIENCE
	Partner	Client relations	
		Signing of auditor's report (commitment of partnership)	12 and more
		Establishment of fee structure	
		General review of audit work papers	
	Manager	Coordination and staffing of several audits simultaneously	
		Review of all work papers	6 to 12
		Resolution of most technical disagreements between client and firm	
Staff accountants:	*Senior*	Day-to-day contact and fieldwork responsibility	
		Detailed audit of accounts	2 to 6
		Supervision and review of junior accountant's work	
	Junior	Detailed audit of assigned accounts	0 to 2

Figure 1-4

Perceived characteristics needed to progress in large accounting firms

PERSONAL CHARACTERISTICS (IN ORDER OF IMPORTANCE)

1. Motivation toward achievement
2. Native intelligence
3. Stability under pressure
4. Adaptability
5. Pleasing personality
6. Personal grooming and dress
7. Physical appearance

EXECUTIVE SKILLS (IN ORDER OF IMPORTANCE)

1. Technical proficiency
2. Leadership and supervision
3. Client relations
4. Decision making
5. Oral communication
6. Written communication*

* Although ranked last, the respondents to the questionnaire considered English to be *by far* the most important nonaccounting college course contributing to professional development.

SOURCE: Hans V. Johnson, "A Survey of New Partners," *Journal of Accountancy*, July 1975, pp. 87–90.

Functional division

While the main objective of a public accounting firm is to perform a financial compliance audit that culminates in issuance of an auditor's report on the financial statements, most medium-sized and large accounting firms have subdivided

10
**An overview of
the audit
profession**

themselves along functional lines to facilitate operations. Usually this functional division results in three or possibly four operational sections of an accounting firm which have considerable autonomy in the establishment of policy as well as directing day-to-day operations.

Audit Section

- The work of this section consists of performing financial audits of profit and nonprofit organizations and formulating a professional opinion as to whether the financial statements are presented in accordance with generally accepted accounting principles.

Tax Section

- The work of this section consists of preparing federal, state, and local tax returns for both audit and nonaudit clients. In addition, members of the tax department may represent clients before the IRS, perform tax planning, and generally be available for consultation on complex tax questions that may be raised by members of the audit staff or clients.

Management Advisory Services Section

- The work of this section consists of making recommendations to a client on a variety of special projects. These may range from the suggested design of a cost accounting system to the recruitment of high-level corporate executives. Much of the work described as operational auditing earlier in this chapter is often performed by this department. For this reason, the department usually consists of accountants as well as a variety of other experts.

Small Business Section

- While this section is not as predominant as the other three, it is often a separate unit and appears to be growing in importance, especially among large firms. The work of this section consists of a combination of financial statement preparation (write-up work) rather than audit, tax preparation, and, in general, business advice for small firms. In effect, it is a consolidation of the other three areas to meet the demands of a fairly unsophisticated client who needs professional service.

For the most part, the remainder of this textbook emphasizes the work of the audit section in its attesting to the fairness of the financial statements.

THE AUDITOR'S REPORT

The audit process culminates in the issuance of an *audit report* which discloses the auditor's opinion as to whether the financial statements are presented in accordance with generally accepted accounting principles. Although the report is the final phase of the audit process, it is useful to introduce briefly the report at this point so that each phase of the audit process as discussed in subsequent chapters can be better appreciated. The auditor's report is again discussed with a more technical orientation in Chapters 17 and 18.

The unqualified report

While the audit report accompanies the basic financial statements, the auditor technically has absolute control over the content in the report. The financial statements and the footnotes to these statements are the primary responsibility of management. The auditor recommends adjustments and additional disclosures and changes in financial statement format, but it is ultimately management's decision as to whether these recommendations are followed. If management chooses not to heed the auditor's suggestions, then the auditor notes these areas of disagreement in the audit report. These are referred to as *report modifications*, which are discussed more fully later in this chapter.

If the auditor, after the performance of an audit, is satisfied that the financial statements are presented in accordance with generally accepted accounting principles, he or she issues an *unqualified opinion*. The AICPA has recommended the following wording when an unqualified opinion is warranted:[5]

The Board of Directors and Stockholders
The Bluefield Company

     We have examined the balance sheet of The Bluefield Company as of December 31, 19xx, and the related statements of income and retained earnings and changes in financial position for the year then ended. Our examination was made in accordance with generally accepted auditing standards, and accordingly included such tests of the accounting records and such other auditing procedures as we considered necessary in the circumstances.

     In our opinion, the aforementioned financial statements present fairly the financial position of The Bluefield Company at December 31, 19xx, and the results of its operations and the changes in its financial position for the year then ended, in conformity with generally accepted accounting principles applied on a basis consistent with that of the preceding year.

March 3, 19x1   Calfee, Porterfield & Company
                                     Certified Public Accountants

The auditor's report is highly structured, and each element of this report conveys or attempts to convey very definite information.

THE ADDRESSEE

The report is prepared by the auditor and is addressed to the group or individual that hired the auditor. Usually the appointment is made by the board of directors; however, if the appointment is made by the board and approved by the stockholders, the report may be addressed to both, as illustrated above.

---

[5] "Codification of Auditing Standards and Procedures," *Statement on Auditing Standards No. 1* (New York: Copyright 1973 by the American Institute of Certified Public Accountants, Inc.), p. 81.

12
**An overview of
the audit
profession**

THE SCOPE PARAGRAPH

The first paragraph is referred to as the *scope paragraph* and is concerned with the audit work performed by the auditor. This paragraph describes the auditor's basis for formulating an opinion (the second paragraph). The second sentence states that the audit was performed in accordance with "generally accepted auditing standards." These standards form the foundation of auditing and are discussed in detail throughout the remainder of this book. At this point, it should be emphasized that generally accepted auditing standards must be followed and achieved if the auditor is to perform a successful professional audit. Also contained in this sentence is a reference to the "tests of the accounting records." Earlier in this chapter the evolution of testing as an audit approach was discussed. It can be seen that this approach has been accepted by incorporating such a reference in the auditor's report. It should be noted that the auditor issues an opinion on the financial statements, but the evidence that supports such statements includes the accounting records (the general ledger, journals, work sheets, etc.) as well as corroborating evidence (bank statements, vendor invoices, etc.). The scope paragraph concludes with a reference to the amount of auditing which is "considered necessary in the circumstances." Auditing is for the most part an art and is therefore heavily dependent on the auditor's judgment. Determining the amount of testing necessary for the auditor to formulate an opinion on the financial statements is but one area where professional judgment must be exercised.

THE OPINION PARAGRAPH

In the second paragraph, the auditor makes a definite statement as to the fairness of the financial statements. Because "fairly stated" is a subjective phrase, not unlike "truth" and "beauty," this phrase has been the basis of much disagreement within the profession. The AICPA has attempted to resolve this problem by providing an operational definition of fairness.[6] In this promulgation, it was suggested that the fairness of the statements is to be based upon the auditor's judgment as to whether,

1. the accounting principles selected and applied have general acceptance,
2. the accounting principles are appropriate under the circumstances,
3. the financial statements, including the related notes, are informative of matters that may affect their use, understanding, and interpretation,
4. the information presented in the financial statements is classified and summarized in a reasonable manner, that is, neither too detailed nor too condensed, and
5. the financial statements reflect the underlying events and transactions in a manner that presents the financial position, results of operations, and change in financial position stated within a range of acceptable limits, that is, limits that are reasonable and practicable to attain in financial statements.

The second paragraph emphasizes the nature of a financial compliance audit by referring to generally accepted accounting principles as the criteria for determining compliance. The AICPA prohibits a member from expressing an un-

[6] The Meaning of "Presents Fairly in Conformity With Generally Accepted Accounting Principles" in the Independent Auditor's Report," *Statement on Auditing Standards No. 5* (New York: AICPA, 1975), pp. 2–5.

qualified opinion on the financial statements, except under unusual circumstances, if the accounting principles employed are a departure from those accounting principles issued by the body designated by the council of the AICPA.[7] Presently, the council has designated the FASB as the body with such power. The final phrase is concerned with the application of generally accepted accounting principles on a basis consistent with the previous year. The purpose of this statement is to ensure that financial statements of one year are comparable to statements from the prior year.[8]

SIGN-OFF DATE

The auditor dates the report based upon the last day of fieldwork, that is, the last day that significant audit work is performed. During the period from the date of the financial statements to the sign-off date, the auditor is responsible for disclosing significant events that require adjustments to financial accounts or footnote disclosures. After this date, except with respect to certain SEC requirements, the auditor is not required to continue auditing.

SIGNATURE

With the signature of the sole proprietor or a partner of the independent accounting firm, the reputation of the firm is committed to a particular audit report. Only after a complete review of the work papers and resolution of all material problems may a partner or proprietor sign the report.

REPORT MODIFICATION

When a user reviews the financial statements and the unqualified auditor's report or opinion discussed above, there are certain inferences that can be drawn. It can be assumed that:

- The financial statements are prepared in accordance with generally accepted accounting principles, which encompasses full disclosure.
- The generally accepted accounting principles have been consistently applied in the preparation of the current financial statements.
- There are not unusual uncertainties that exist which cannot be reasonably estimated.
- The independent auditor has not had to restrict the audit in a manner that would reduce the auditor's ability to formulate an opinion on the financial statements concerning the above three assumptions.

There are of course circumstances that may make the issuance of an unqualified opinion inappropriate. These circumstances occur when certain deficiencies exist. It is useful to identify these deficiencies and the resulting report modification so that the alternative actions which can be taken by the auditor in certain instances are identified before the audit process is discussed.

Figure 1-5 summarizes the types of deficiencies an auditor may encounter and the impact of these deficiencies on the auditor's report.

[7] Op. cit., *Code of Professional Ethics*, p. 20.

[8] See *Accounting Principles Board Opinion* (*APB*) No. 20, ''Accounting Changes'' (New York: AICPA, 1971), for what constitutes a change in accounting principles.

14
An overview of
the audit
profession

Accounting deficiency

Accounting deficiencies can result from (1) failure to prepare the financial statements in accordance with generally accepted accounting principles, (2) inconsistent application of generally accepted accounting principles, or (3) a lack of full disclosure. It should be recognized that the effect of the deficiency on the auditor's report is a function of the materiality of the deficiency. In almost every audit, the auditor discovers some examples of immaterial departures from the application of generally accepted accounting principles. For example, it is probable that a medium-sized company has a policy of capitalizing only expenditures for fixed assets that exceed $1000, an obvious violation of the matching principle in accounting. However, since this violation results in a minimal impact on the financial statements, the auditor issues an *unqualified opinion* on the financial statements.

On the other hand, if the accounting deficiency is material, the auditor must make a professional decision as to whether, overall, the financial statements may be relied upon. Again, materiality is the key factor in making this distinction. For example, recording marketable securities at market value where market is materially greater than cost is a violation of generally accepted accounting principles. However, the deficiency is isolated, and it is possible that all other items in the financial statements are correct. In this case the auditor issues a qualified opinion stating, in part, in the opinion paragraph that the financial statements are prepared in accordance with generally accepted accounting principles "except that marketable securities are reported at an amount above cost." In a middle paragraph, which is discussed in Chapter 17, the auditor describes the nature and the extent of the deficiency.

The accounting deficiency may be so material and pervasive that the financial statements cannot be relied upon and are, therefore, misleading. In this case, the auditor must issue an *adverse opinion,* which states that the financial statements are not fairly stated and are not prepared in accordance with generally

Figure 1-5

Impact of deficiencies on the auditor's report

		DEGREE OF DEFICIENCY	
	IMMATERIAL	MATERIAL (OVERALL FINANCIAL STATEMENTS CAN BE RELIED UPON)	MATERIAL (OVERALL FINANCIAL STATEMENTS CANNOT BE RELIED UPON)
DEFICIENCY	APPROPRIATE REPORT	APPROPRIATE REPORT	APPROPRIATE REPORT
1. Accounting Generally acceptable accounting principles	Unqualified	Qualified	Adverse
Disclosure	Unqualified	Qualified	Adverse
Consistency	Unqualified	Qualified	N/A
2. Scope	Unqualified	Qualified	Disclaimer
3. Uncertainty	Unqualified	Qualified	Disclaimer

accepted accounting principles. If a company uses current replacement cost **15**
rather than historical cost as the underlying principle in the preparation of the Report modification
financial statements, the auditor would issue an adverse opinion describing in
a middle paragraph the significance of the accounting deficiency. It should be
apparent that determining the degree of deficiency is no easy task and is not
subject to hard and fast rules. The auditor must make a professional judgment
in each situation.

Scope deficiency

The second major deficiency, as depicted in Figure 1-5, with which the auditor
must be concerned is that of scope. *Scope* refers to the amount of audit work
performed by the auditor in the examination of the financial statements. It has
already been suggested that the auditor cannot review every transaction and
must test the accounting data. Thus if the scope limitation is immaterial, for
example, the auditor could not count petty cash at a branch office as of the
balance-sheet date, an unqualified opinion is still appropriate.

A *qualified opinion* is issued if the amount of auditing is limited to an extent
that not enough evidential matter is collected and evaluated to form an opinion
on some component of the financial statements. If this occurs, the auditor must
describe the limitation in the scope paragraph and the effect of the limitation in
the opinion paragraph. Because of the technical nature of scope deficiencies, no
examples are suggested at this point, but a full discussion is offered in Chapter
17.

If the scope of the audit has been limited to such an extent that an overall
opinion on the financial statements is not applicable, then the auditor issues a
disclaimer of opinion. In effect, a disclaimer results from the auditor not collecting
enough evidence upon which to base an opinion and, logically, no professional
opinion can be offered.

Uncertainty

Finally, an auditor may be faced with a deficiency resulting from the uncertainty
of the outcome of an event that may have an impact on the current financial
statements. There are items presented in the financial statements and covered
by the auditor's report that are subject to future developments that cannot be
anticipated by the auditor. Because the auditor is in no better position than the
average person to predict future events, a reporting problem for the auditor
arises.

In some cases the outcome of an uncertainty problem might be of such grave
consequences that it is incumbent upon the auditor to inform the financial-report
user that the financial statements taken as a whole should not be relied upon. In
this case the auditor issues a disclaimer of opinion stating the nature of the
uncertainty problem. Usually this situation arises when the going concern concept is in question for a particular company. For example, a company that is in
a development stage, perhaps a real estate venture, has an almost insatiable need
for capital because of certain start-up costs. If such a firm is unable to prove to

16
An overview of the audit profession

the auditors that continued finances are available, through a line of credit or the like, then the continuance of the company as a going concern is very much in question. Since the auditor cannot predict the future finances of this company, a disclaimer of opinion may be issued.

On the other hand, the auditor may encounter a situation where the uncertainty is important but the financial statements are not misleading. For example, the client may be the defendant in a lawsuit where the outcome is uncertain at the date the financial statements are issued. In this case the auditor would issue a qualified opinion stating that the financial statements are fairly presented "subject to" the outcome of the pending lawsuit.

SUMMARY

The first part of this chapter provided a brief introduction to the history of auditing, the types of audits performed, and the organizational structure of independent CPA firms. The latter part of the chapter introduced the objective of a modern day audit conducted by such a firm and the types of problems the firm may encounter in the conduct of the engagement.

The following chapter provides a more in-depth analysis of the audit function by looking carefully at the role of the attest function in society and how society holds auditors accountable for the work they perform.

QUESTIONS AND PROBLEMS

1-1. Explain why the audit objective prior to the Industrial Revolution differs from the present-day objective.

1-2. Is the need for an audit unique to a capitalistic society? Explain.

1-3. Prior to 1900 the basic objective of an audit was the detection of fraud. Some individuals believe that such an objective is appropriate today. Do you agree with them?

1-4. Distinguish between a compliance audit and an operational audit.

1-5. Comment on the following statement:

An independent CPA, because of his or her background in auditing, is the logical person to perform an operational audit of a government agency.

1-6. An auditor for the Federal Election Commission would perform a compliance audit or an operational audit?

1-7. How does the work of an auditor differ from that of an accountant?

1-8. Refer to the GAO's definition of auditing on page 5. For each of the three categories, give an example of the GAO's work.

1-9. List the personal characteristics that you believe are necessary to succeed as a student. Compare your list with the characteristics presented in Figure 1-4.

1-10. There is a movement in the legal profession to recognize formally specialization in such areas as criminal law, tax law, bankruptcy and insolvency, and personal injury litigation. Do you believe such an approach is appropriate for public accounting firms?

1-11. What is the objective of an audit conducted by an independent CPA?

1-12. If an auditor issues an unqualified opinion on a company's financial statements, does this mean the company is probably well managed?

1-13. Name and explain the purpose of each element of the auditor's report.

1-14. The auditor's report refers to the phrase "fairly stated." What does this phrase mean?

1-15. Comment on the following statement:

In any audit, there is no reason for there to be a deficiency (accounting, scope, and uncertainty) in the engagement since the auditor is free to perform whatever procedures he or she considers necessary and to make any adjustments to the financial statements.

1-16. Give an example of

a. An accounting deficiency
b. A scope deficiency
c. An uncertainty deficiency

1-17. Differentiate between an adverse opinion and a disclaimer of opinion.

1-18. Why would it be inappropriate to issue a disclaimer of opinion when an accounting deficiency exists?

1-19. Refer to the auditor's report in this chapter and read it carefully. Are there any terms in the report whose meaning you are uncertain of? Do you think a lay person can understand the report?

1-20. Can you identify a future development in society that might change the objective of the current-day audit and/or the auditor's report?

1-21. In designing the standard audit report, should the profession consider the sophistication of the reader?

1-22. You have performed an examination, in conformity with generally accepted auditing standards, of the financial statements of the Boller Manufacturing Corporation for the year ended December 31, 1979. These statements, together with those for 1978 in comparative form, are presented here:

The Boller Manufacturing Corporation
Balance Sheet
December 31, 1978 and 1979

ASSETS	1979	1978	INCREASE (DECREASE)
Current assets:			
Cash	$ 36,000	$ 20,000	$16,000
Accounts receivable (net of allowance for bad debts of $3,000 and $2,500)	78,000	60,000	18,000
Inventories	149,000	122,000	27,000
Prepaid expenses	3,200	4,000	(800)
Total	266,200	206,000	60,200
Fixed assets (at cost):			
Land .... (officers' estimate of current value—$50,000)	20,000	20,000	

18
An overview of the audit profession

Building (net of accumulated depreciation of $8,000 and $6,000)	42,000	44,000	(2,000)
(officers' estimate of current value—$75,000)			
Machinery and equipment (net of accumulated depreciation of $24,000 and $18,000)	79,000	85,000	(6,000)
Total	141,000	149,000	(8,000)
Other assets:			
Goodwill	30,000	30,000	
Total	$437,200	$385,000	$52,200

LIABILITIES AND STOCKHOLDERS' EQUITY

Current liabilities:			
Accounts payable	$ 48,200	$ 35,000	$13,200
Accrued liabilities	39,000	15,000	24,000
Total	87,200	50,000	37,200
Stockholders' equity:			
Capital stock, $100 par value, 3,000 shares authorized and outstanding	300,000	300,000	
Capital contributed in excess of par value.........................	65,000	65,000	
Deficit	(15,000)	(30,000)	15,000
Total	350,000	335,000	15,000
Total	$437,200	$385,000	$52,200

The Boller Manufacturing Corporation
Statement of Income and Retained Earnings
For the Years Ended December 31, 1979 and 1978

	1979	1978	INCREASE (DECREASE)
Sales	$980,000	$920,000	$60,000
Cost of sales	720,000	685,000	35,000
Gross profit	260,000	235,000	25,000
Selling and administrative expenses	235,000	220,000	15,000
Profit from operations	25,000	15,000	10,000
Other income and (deductions), net	(10,000)	(5,000)	(5,000)
Net income	15,000	10,000	5,000
Deficit, January 1	(30,000)	(40,000)	10,000
Deficit, December 31	$(15,000)	$(30,000)	$15,000

This is your first audit of the company, and you satisfied yourself regarding the opening inventory and the consistency of the application of accounting principles. Your working papers contain the following notes:

1. In the prior year, 1978, the company changed its method of costing inventories

from the average-cost method to the last-in-/first-out (LIFO) method. The average-cost method had been used consistently in prior years. The following information was developed:

19
Questions and problems

	CALENDAR YEAR		
	1977	1978	1979
Ending inventories on LIFO method	$ —	$122,000	$149,000
Ending inventories on average-cost method	$141,000	$158,000	$173,000
Net income (loss) for period under average-cost method (estimate for 1978 and 1979)	$ (5,000)	$ 46,000	$ 39,000

2. A new highway will be constructed through the general area in which the company's building is located. The exact route of the highway will not be established for six months, and highway officials refuse to disclose their current plans other than that the building might be in the path of the highway. The officers' estimate of the value of the land and building is the amount for which they expect to sell the property to the highway department. Because of the indefinite location of the highway there have been no recent sales of property in the general area, and real estate appraisers are not in agreement on the value of the property.

3. The intangible asset is the total cost of the company's institutional advertising campaign that took place in 1974, when the company began doing business. The officers believe that the company is continuing to benefit from the goodwill developed by the campaign, and they intend to write off the asset when it becomes reasonably evident that it is worthless.

4. An analysis of the deficit account follows:

1974 Loss	$(55,000)
1975 Income	5,000
1976 Income	15,000
1977 Loss	(5,000)
1978 Income	10,000
1979 Income	15,000
Total	$(15,000)

No entries have been posted to the deficit account other than the above results of operations which are in agreement with the income tax returns. The tax returns have not been examined. Management has decided that reporting the value of the carry-forwards loss in the balance sheet would not be conservative. Management prefers not to change the financial statements in any way but will consider adding footnotes. The income tax rate that has been in effect is 50 percent.

Required

1. Prepare the footnotes you would suggest for the financial statements.

2. Assuming that the suggested footnotes will be adopted, prepare your auditor's report for the current-year financial statements. (You need not include a scope paragraph.) Include any comments in your report that you consider necessary. If your report is in any way modified or qualified as to opinion, give a full explanation.   (AICPA Adapted)

1-23. CPAs must comply with generally accepted auditing standards of reporting when they prepare opinions on clients' financial statements. One of the reporting standards relates to consistency.

20
**An overview of
the audit
profession**

Required

1. Discuss the statement regarding consistency that the CPA is required to include in an opinion. What is the objective of requiring the CPA to make this statement about consistency?

2. Discuss what mention of consistency, if any, the CPA must make in an opinion relating to his or her first audit of the financial statements of the following companies:

a. A newly organized company ending its first accounting period
b. A company established for a number of years

3. Discuss whether the changes described in each of the following cases require recognition in the CPA's opinion as to consistency. (Assume the amounts are material.)

a. The company disposed of one of its three subsidiaries that had been included in its consolidated statements for prior years.
b. After two years of computing depreciation under the declining-balance method for income tax purposes and under the straight-line method for reporting purposes, the declining-balance method was adopted for reporting purposes.
c. The estimated remaining useful life of plant property was reduced because of obsolescence. (AICPA Adapted)

1-24. A congressional report prepared by the Subcommittee on Reports, Accounting, and Management (Metcalf Committee) made the following recommendation:

The Federal Government should itself periodically inspect the work of independent auditors for publicly-owned corporations. Such a mandatory inspection program should be designed to provide assurance to the public and Congress that independent auditors are performing their responsibilities competently in accordance with proper standards of conduct. Periodic quality review could be conducted by the General Accounting Office, the SEC, or a special audit inspection agency.

Required

1. How would a proponent of the recommendation justify such a proposal?

2. How would an opponent of the recommendation argue against such a proposal?

3. Why does the recommendation refer only to publicly owned corporations?

4. How would you classify such an "audit of the auditors"?

5. Is there a precedent in other professional or regulated activities for such an approach?

1-25. The Martin Company signed a royalty agreement with Electric Motors, Inc. Electric Motors agreed to pay the Martin Company a royalty of $50 for each engine manufactured and sold during the year. The contract was signed late in 1978, and Electric started manufacturing the motors early in 1979. During 1979 Electric reported periodically the number of engines started in production for the quarter, the number of engines finished during the quarter, and the number of engines in process at the end of the quarter.

On January 15, 1980, the Martin Company received a check from Electric Motors for $887,500 for "the number of engines manufactured and sold during 1979 per our agreement." Based on the periodic production reports, the Martin Company was concerned about the amount of the check, since it believed the amount should have been approximately $1 million. The president of the Martin Company called its independent auditors and invited a representative of the firm to lunch, to discuss the matter.

During the luncheon the president of the Martin Company explained that she would like to present the matter to the executive committee of the company for possible action. At this point the president asked the independent auditor if an audit or review of the records of Electric Motors could be made which would result in some type of auditor's report.

21
Questions and problems

Required

1. Using the following criteria explain fully under what conditions the above situation would be the basis for the performance of a compliance audit.

a. A norm for measuring compliance exists.
b. The independent auditor has the expertise required by the engagement.
c. An adequate system of documentation exists.
d. An appropriate audit report can be prepared to communicate the auditor's findings.

2. Assume a compliance audit is performed and no irregularities on the part of Electric Motors are discovered. What might be the explanation for the apparent understatement of the royalty fees?

3. Assume a compliance audit is performed and the auditor believes the agreement is being followed. Prepare the auditor's report.

1-26. The complete opinion included in the annual report of The Modern Department Store for 1979 is reproduced here:

Auditors' Certificate
Doe & Doe
New City, New State

To whom it may concern:

In our opinion, the accompanying balance sheet and statement of income and retained earnings present fairly the financial position of The Modern Department Store and the results of its operations. Our examination of these financial statements was made in accordance with generally accepted auditing standards and accordingly included such tests of the accounting records and such other auditing procedures as we considered necessary, except that we did not confirm accounts receivable, but instead accounted for subsequent collections on the accounts, and we did not observe the taking of the physical inventory because it was taken prior to our appointment as auditors.

Required: List and discuss the deficiencies of the auditors' certificate prepared by Doe & Doe. (AICPA Adapted)

1-27. Client Corporation (whose fiscal year ends December 31, 1979) informs you on December 18, 1979, that it has a serious shortage of working capital because of heavy operating losses incurred since October 1, 1979. Application has been made to a bank for a loan, and the bank's loan officer has requested financial statements.

Required: Indicate the type of opinion you would render under each of the following independent sets of circumstances. Give the reasons for your decision.

1. Client Corporation asks that you save time by auditing the financial statements prepared by Client's chief accountant as of September 30, 1979. The scope of your audit would not be limited by Client in any way.

2. Client Corporation asks that you conduct an audit as of December 15, 1979. The scope of your audit would not be limited by Client in any way.

22
An overview of
the audit
profession

3. Client Corporation asks that you conduct an audit as of December 31, 1979, and render a report by January 16. To save time and reduce the cost of the audit it is requested that your examination not include circularization of accounts receivable or observation of the taking of inventory.

4. Client Corporation asks that you prepare financial statements as of December 15, 1979, from the books and records of the company without audit. The statements are to be submitted on plain paper without your name being associated in any way with them. The reason for your preparing the statements is your familiarity with the proper form for financial statements. (AICPA Adapted)

1-28. A young accountant read with interest the following statement from the FASB's *Tentative Conclusion on Objectives of Financial Statements of Business Enterprises:*

... financial accounting and financial statements should provide information that helps investors and creditors assess the enterprise's prospects of obtaining net cash inflows through its earnings and financing activities.

The accountant, as an employee of Barnes Company, had just spent a considerable amount of time in preparing the operating and capital budgets for the company for the next fiscal year.

Knowing the independent auditors would be visiting the company's offices in three weeks, the young accountant decided to do something about meeting the users' needs as described in the FASB publication. Specifically the accountant performed an "audit" and prepared a report on the *pro forma* financial statements. The report appears below:

I have examined the *pro forma* balance sheet of Barnes Company as of December 31, 1979, and the related *pro forma* statements of income and changes in financial position for the year ended. My examination included a review of (1) revenues and variable expenses which were determined by regression analysis, (2) fixed operating expenses which were approved and reviewed by the finance committee and budgetary officers of the company, (3) capital expenditures which were approved by the executive committee, and (4) expected short-term and long-term finance arrangements which were determined by the treasurer's department and are reasonable based upon comments received from financial institutions that are expected to participate in the proposed financial plans.

In my opinion, these *pro forma* financial statements present fairly the expected financial position of the company at December 31, 1979, and the expected results of their operations and the changes in their financial position for the year then ended.

When the independent auditors arrive, the Barnes' accountant gives them a copy of the report on the *pro forma* financial statements.

Required

1. Assume that the audit procedures performed by the company's accountant were performed by the independent auditor. Do you believe the independent auditor should issue such a report?

2. Comment on the criteria that provide the norm for determining whether compliance has been achieved.

3. Is the company's documentation for the preparation of the *pro forma* financial statements a proper basis for the performance of an audit?

4. Is more judgment on the part of the client and the independent auditor demanded in this audit situation as opposed to the conventional audit?

1-29. Conventional auditing requires a modification of the auditor's report if material uncertainties exist. An example of the appropriate report to be issued under these circumstances is presented here:

23
Questions and problems

CALLAHAN MINING CORPORATION
Auditors' Opinion

To the Board of Directors and Shareholders of
Callahan Mining Corporation:

We have examined the consolidated balance sheet of Callahan Mining Corporation and subsidiaries as of December 31, 1974, and the related statements of income and retained earnings and of changes in financial position for the year then ended. Our examination was made in accordance with generally accepted auditing standards, and accordingly included such tests of the accounting records and such other auditing procedures as we considered necessary in the circumstances. We previously examined and reported upon the financial statements for the year 1973.

The company's investment in the Caladay project is carried at cost, the recovery of which is subject to the success of the project which cannot be forecast at this time, as described in note 2 to the consolidated financial statements.

In our opinion, subject to the effects on the financial statements of the ultimate realization of the carrying value of the investment in the Caladay project, the aforementioned consolidated statements present fairly the financial position of Callahan Mining Corporation and subsidiaries at December 31, 1974 and 1973, and the results of their operations and the changes in their financial position for the years then ended, in conformity with generally accepted accounting principles applied on a consistent basis.

Notes to Financial Statements

2. At December 31, 1974, the company's investment in the Caladay project aggregated $3,265,000, including $247,000 representing the cost of property contributed by Callahan and $980,000 representing the net book value of buildings and equipment. The recovery of this investment is subject to the success of the project which cannot be forecast at this time. See page 4.

(Page 4)
Caladay Project

The Caladay project, which adjoins the Galena mine on the east, remained on a care-and-maintenance basis during 1974. Escalating costs have made reactivation of the proposed deep-shaft exploration program unattractive at present in light of the geologic risks involved. Discussions continue on a less costly alternative approach under which initial exploration of this property may be carried out from one or more of the lower levels of the Galena mine.

In the interest of increased public awareness of mining activities in the district and elsewhere, the Caladay tunnel and un-

24
**An overview of
the audit
profession**

derground workings were made available during Expo 74 for underground tours by some 15,000 visitors to the area.

The role of the auditor is to determine if financial statements are prepared in accordance with generally accepted accounting principles. The audit report does not comment on whether a company is well managed or a sound investment.

Required

1. Is it the duty of the independent auditor to evaluate the impact of future events that may result from general business risks?

2. If a future event is likely to occur, but is nonetheless indefinite, is it appropriate to issue a report similar to the one issued on the Callahan Mining Corporation's financial statements?

3. Is it possible that the reader of the audit report presented above may misinterpret the meaning of the report? In what ways may this occur?

1-30. The AICPA Commission on Auditors' Responsibilities made the following statement in its "Report of Tentative Conclusions":

One effect of using a standard report is that as a person becomes familiar with its words, he tends to stop reading each time he sees it. He relies on his memory of what it says and his impression of what it means and merely glances to see that it is included and that it does not contain a departure from the usual language, that is, an exception. The entire report comes to be interpreted as a single, although complex, symbol that is no longer read.*

Required

1. What does the above comment mean when it refers to the report as a symbol?

2. Should the profession attempt to remove or reduce the report's symbolism?

3. How can the profession remove or reduce the report's symbolism?

4. Does the name of a particular CPA firm have an impact on the report as a symbol?

MULTIPLE CHOICE

1. Which of the following criteria is unique to the auditor's attest function?

a. General competence.
b. Familiarity with the particular industry of which his or her client is a part.
c. Due professional care.
d. Independence.

2. Pickens and Perkins, CPAs, decide to incorporate their practice of accountancy. According to the AICPA code of professional ethics, shares in the corporation can be issued

a. Only to persons qualified to practice as CPAs.
b. Only to employees and officers of the firm.

---

* *The Commission on Auditors' Responsibilities: Report of Tentative Conclusions* (New York: The Commission on Auditors' Responsibilities, 1977), p. 73.

c. Only to persons qualified to practice as CPAs and members of their immediate families.

d. To the general public.

25
Multiple choice

3. No matter how competent a CPA may be, her opinion on financial statements will be of little value to those who rely on her unless she:

a. Issues an unqualified opinion.
b. Maintains a program of continuing education.
c. Serves her clients with professional concern for their best interests.
d. Maintains her independence.

4. Assuming that none of the following have been disclosed in the financial statements, the most appropriate item for footnote disclosure is the

a. Collection of all receivables subsequent to year end.
b. Revision of employees' pension plan.
c. Retirement of president of company and election of new president.
d. Material decrease in the advertising budget for the coming year and its anticipated effect upon income.

5. An exception in the auditor's report because of the lack of consistent application of generally accepted accounting principles most likely would be required in the event of

a. A change in the rate of provision for uncollectable accounts based upon collection experience.
b. The original adoption of a pension plan for employees.
c. Inclusion of a previously unconsolidated subsidiary in consolidated financial statements.
d. The revision of pension plan actuarial assumptions based upon experience.

(AICPA Adapted)

CHAPTER 2
The audit function

In the previous chapter the audit function was described as a process of reviewing financial statements and reporting the results of the review to interested parties. At this point it is necessary to define the auditing and reporting process in a more technical manner.

Auditing is a systematic process of objectively obtaining and evaluating evidence regarding assertions about economic actions and events to ascertain the degree of correspondence between those assertions and established criteria and communicating the results to interested users.[1]

Attestation is a communicated statement of opinion (judgment), based upon convincing evidence, by an independent, competent, authoritative person, concerning the degree of correspondence in all material respects of accounting information communicated by an entity (individual, firm, or governmental unit) with established criteria.[2]

In this chapter these expanded definitions are the basis for describing the audit and report functions as they relate to society as a whole.

THE ROLE OF AUDITING IN SOCIETY

Present-day society is dominated by large organizations that have a significant impact on almost every aspect of modern life. Because of their pervasiveness these organizations must be held accountable to society by keeping interested external parties informed of their actions. To monitor the actions of these organizations it is necessary to devise a mode of communication between the entity and the external parties. One method of communication, but only one method, is the dissemination of economic data. Typically the external group is

---

[1] "A Statement of Basic Auditing Concepts," *Studies in Accounting Research No. 6* (Sarasota: American Accounting Association, 1973), p. 2.

[2] Ibid., p. 6.

unable individually to verify the accuracy of this information. Therefore in order to ensure that the data are presented in an unbiased manner, it is necessary for the external parties collectively to audit or review such data.

While the above describes the audit function in general, this book discusses the audit function in the context of a profit-seeking organization. Recall that, in addition to public accounting, the focus of this book, auditing, encompasses internal auditing and government auditing of both profit and nonprofit organizations. In the case of profit-seeking businesses there are parties external to the organization that are referred to as users of financial statements, and these users must make economic decisions concerning this entity. This user group consists in part of investors, creditors, government agencies, employees, and the general public.

Figure 2-1 shows the relationship of the business entity, the user group, and the auditor. The business entity makes assertions concerning its activities, and these assertions are communicated to the users through the financial statements it prepares. The auditor reviews these assertions to determine if the statements fairly present the financial events of the entity. The auditor communicates the results of the audit through the preparation of an auditor's report. These financial statements and the auditor's report in part provide information that facilitates economic decisions that must be made by the user. An informed user evaluates these data with the understanding that there are inherent limitations in financial statements. These limitations are fully discussed in financial accounting courses. In addition, the audit and the auditor's report have certain limitations which are discussed throughout this book.

ECONOMIC JUSTIFICATION OF THE AUDIT FUNCTION

While the above discussion indirectly described the economic justification of the audit function, it is useful to describe this justification in a more rigorous

Figure 2-1

The Audit Function Structure

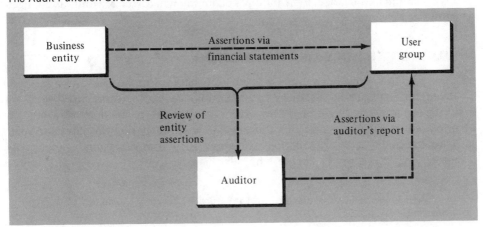

28
The audit function

manner. *Economics* can be defined as the study of the allocation of scarce goods and services. Our nation's economic structure is based upon the principles of capitalism or modified capitalism in which price structure is used to determine the allocation of scarce resources. One of the characteristics of capitalism is the presence of buyers and sellers who have complete information upon which to make their economic decisions. If this condition exists, along with other prerequisites, the allocation of goods and services based upon the pricing structure will provide an optimum solution to society's objective of maximizing the well being (utility) of the members of the economy.

On the other hand, if the economic data upon which the participants base their decisions contain material errors or omissions, there will not be an optimum allocation of resources according to classical economics. For example, if a business entity consistently reports erroneous data concerning earnings per share, it will attract capital that should be allocated to other segments of the economy. The role of the auditor is to monitor this economic data as reported in the financial statements to ensure that it is presented in accordance with financial reporting standards established by society. This is the auditor's contribution to society, and it is essential to the free enterprise system.

As a profession, accounting and auditing are more important and therefore more visible today than at any previous time. This increased visibility is not without problems and challenges, since the promulgation of accounting principles and procedures by the FASB has and will continue to have an impact on the financial information presented in the financial statements. As suggested above, the data will in part be the basis for the allocation of resources. Since accounting is an art, the selection of accounting rules is somewhat subjective, with many segments of the economy attempting to influence the FASB's decision process. Obviously, a great deal is at stake when these rules are selected, and such power has not gone unnoticed by Congress. Some accountants have suggested that the FASB in particular, and the profession in general, should respond to this challenge by expanding research endeavors to encompass the potential impact of accounting rules on the nation's economy.[3] Earlier in Chapter 1 it was suggested that the profession has responded to external events in a positive manner; this increased visibility and importance in the nation's economy will foster continuous changes in the profession.

FILLING THE ROLE OF THE AUDITOR

Figure 2-1 identifies and defines the role of the auditor in the attest function, but it does not suggest who in society should fill this role. Furthermore, the discussion of the economic justification of the auditor emphasizes the need for accurate and unbiased information, but again there is no recommendation for filling the role. Thus the audit or attest function exists and is vital in our economy, but it is necessary for society to decide who fills this role.

[3] Prem Prakash and Alfred Rappaport, "The Feedback Effects of Accounting," *Business Week,* January 12, 1976, p. 12.

There are several alternative groups that could perform the audit function.

- A government agency, at the national or state level, could perform the audit (either with a mandatory fee or without a fee).
- Private accounting firms hired and paid by the government could perform the audit.
- Private accounting firms hired and paid by the business entity could perform the audit.

It is of course no surprise that society has selected the last-mentioned group to act as the auditor. This solution has worked well, although not without some significant exceptions, but any of the three alternatives would present the audit profession and society with problems. Some of the problems of the present-day structure of the public accounting profession are discussed in this book, and they cannot be viewed as trivial. In fact, the breadth of difficulties facing the audit profession today is enumerated by an AICPA commission whose mission was described as follows.

> The Commission on Auditor's Responsibilities will study the role of independent auditors in society to identify auditors' responsibilities in relation to the needs and reasonable expectations of users of financial statements and to recommend actions that the profession should take to assure that independent auditors discharge those responsibilities adequately.[4]

In its final report issued in 1978, the commission made recommendations in eleven major areas ranging from the independent auditor's role in society to the specific mechanism needed to promulgate statements on auditing standards.[5]

Again it is emphasized that the above discussion does not suggest the demise of the present audit structure but rather a recognition of certain audit problems and a willingness on the part of the profession to resolve these problems internally. On the other hand, it cannot be naively assumed that there are no other viable solutions to the present audit structure. In fact, some critics of the auditing profession question the fundamental relationships between the accounting firm and the business entity. With government intervention in the private sector growing in almost every area of the economy, the possibility of an alternative solution cannot be viewed as remote.

SOCIETAL CONTROLS

In effect society has granted to part of the private sector, the independent auditor, a monopoly in the audit of financial statements. With the granting of this monopoly, society must establish a variety of control mechanisms that attempt to ensure that society as a whole benefits from this situation. The general problem is not unique to the auditing profession; however, the nature of the public

---

[4] *Statement of Issues: Scope and Organization of the Study of Auditors' Responsibilities* (New York: The Commission on Auditors' Responsibilities, 1975), p. 73.

[5] *The Commission on Auditors' Responsibilities: Report, Conclusions, and Recommendations* (New York: The Commission on Auditors' Responsibilities, 1978), pp. xvii–xxiv.

30
The audit function

accounting profession does generate some unique problems as well as unique controls. These controls are divided into two broad areas. The first area is concerned with institutions that provide a form of control over the individual public accountant, and the second area deals with standards established by the public accounting profession as well as standards and laws established by society as a whole. The combination of these two areas forms the mechanism by which the auditing profession is controlled and is held accountable by society.

Institutional controls

Some of the institutions that have an impact upon the accounting profession have already been mentioned. At this point a more thorough discussion of three institutions that play a vital role in the public accounting profession is required.

AICPA

Prior to the organization of the FASB, the AICPA had the responsibility of promulgating accounting principles. However, the AICPA's designation of the FASB as the rule-making body only partially reduces its role in financial reporting. The AICPA's Accounting Standards Executive Committee researches accounting problems and presents its position on accounting issues before the FASB.

In addition, the AICPA's Auditing Standards Executive Committee* is the sole determinant, with the exception of the SEC, to be discussed later, of professional auditing standards. The failure of a CPA to observe these standards can result in disciplinary action taken by the AICPA ranging from a reprimand to expulsion from the organization. The AICPA is unique in that it has no legislative power to determine who can practice as a CPA; nonetheless, its influence cannot be underestimated. Although each state has the legal authority to license CPAs, the AICPA is the moving force in the public accounting profession.

FASB

In 1972, the Wheat Commission recommended that accounting principles be determined by an organization independent of the AICPA with representation broader than that of members of the institute. The FASB was established for this purpose with the blessing of the AICPA. The articles of incorporation creating the FASB require that a seven-member board be selected; four of its members must be practicing CPAs, and the other three members must be highly qualified in the field of financial accounting but not necessarily CPAs. The council of the AICPA required that its members follow the pronouncements of the FASB and passed the resolution reproduced in Figure 2-2. More is said about this resolution in the discussion of the code of ethics in Chapter 3. A careful reading of this resolution is suggested, because it provides an operational definition of generally accepted accounting principles.

SEC

The SEC, an independent regulatory agency of the federal government, was created in 1934 to administer the Securities Act of 1933 and the Securities

* In 1979, the Committee's name was changed to the Auditing Standards Board.

Figure 2-2

AICPA's resolution concerning the promulgation of accounting principles

The following resolution of Council was approved at the spring meeting of Council on May 7, 1973:

WHEREAS in 1959 the Council designated the Accounting Principles Board to establish accounting principles, and
WHEREAS the Council is advised that the Financial Accounting Standards Board has become operational, it is
RESOLVED, that as of the date hereof the Financial Accounting Standards Board, in respect of Statements of Financial Accounting Standards finally adopted by such Board in accordance with its Rules of Procedure and the bylaws of the Financial Accounting Foundation, be, and hereby is, designated by this Council as the body to establish accounting principles pursuant to Rule 203 of the Rules of Conduct of the American Institute of Certified Public Accountants; provided, however, any Accounting Research Bulletins, or Opinions of the Accounting Principles Board presently issued or approved for exposure by the Accounting Principles Board prior to April 1, 1973, and finally adopted by such Board on or before June 30, 1973, shall constitute statements of accounting principles promulgated by a body designated by Council as contemplated in Rule 203 of the Rules of Conduct unless and until such time as they are expressly superseded by action of the FASB.

SOURCE: Reprinted with permission of the AICPA from the *Code of Professional Ethics* (New York: AICPA), Appendix B, p. 26. Copyright © 1973 by the American Institute of Certified Public Accountants, Inc.

Exchange Act of 1934. Prior to the creation of the commission, the 1933 act was administered by the Federal Trade Commission. In addition to these two laws, the SEC is responsible for administration of the (1) Public Utility Holding Company Act of 1935, (2) Trust Indenture Act of 1939, (3) Investment Company Act of 1940, and (4) Investment Advisers Act of 1940. While the independent auditor has to attest to certain data required to be filed by each one of the above laws, with the exception of the Trust Indenture Act of 1939, the discussion in this book is limited to the 1933 and 1934 acts. The commission also has a role in the administration of the (1) National Bankruptcy Act (Chapter X), (2) Bretton Woods Agreements Act, (3) Internal Revenue Code of 1954 (Section 851), and (4) Securities Investor Protection Act of 1970.

The basic objective of the 1933 and 1934 acts is to protect those who purchase securities by requiring a company to disseminate information that is not materially incorrect or that has no significant omission of data. Specifically the 1933 law requires a company to register its securities with the SEC before these securities can be initially sold to the public. Through the preparation of a registration statement to be filed with the SEC, a company must fully disclose information considered necessary to inform a potential purchaser fully about the securities. Financial statements form a vital part of the registration statement and typically include:

- Financial statements of the registrant
- Consolidated financial statements
- Financial statements of unconsolidated subsidiaries and 50% owned companies
- Financial statements of affiliates whose securities are pledged as collateral

32
**The audit
function**

- Special provisions in connection with:

  (a) Reorganization of the registrant
  (b) Succession to other businesses
  (c) Acquisition of other businesses

- Filing of other financial statements in certain cases
- Historical financial information
- Summary of earnings
- Line of business information[6]

Most of the financial data included in the registration must be covered by the independent auditor's opinion which in turn is included as part of the registration statement.

While the 1933 act is primarily applicable to securities to be sold to the public by an issuing company, the 1934 act is concerned with the subsequent trading of these securities on national stock exchanges. If a company has not registered its securities under the 1933 act prior to trading on a national securities exchange, it must go through a registration process similar to that described above. Upon the registration of these securities, the financial information must be periodically updated by additional filings required by the SEC. Although a variety of forms may be required, the principal forms are:

- *Annual Report* This report is usually filed on Form 10-K and must include a balance sheet, income statement, statement of change in financial position, statement of retained earnings, and a statement of changes in other capital accounts. These financial statements must be certified by an independent auditor.

- *Interim Report* This report is filed on Form 10-Q and must be filed quarterly. The information to be filed in this report is not as comprehensive as that required on Form 10-K and does not have to be certified by an independent auditor. At the present time interim reports are the subject of much debate within the profession as to what should be included in the interim reports and what degree of responsibility, if any, the independent auditor should assume. The general area of unaudited financial statements and recent developments in this area are discussed in Chapter 18.

- *Current Report* This report provides a certain amount of flexibility in the SEC's reporting requirements by requiring a company to file significant events that have occurred and should be brought to the attention of the commission as well as interested third parties. These events are to be filed on Form 8-K, and such events as a material default on senior securities and the results of material legal proceedings are but two examples of events that should be disclosed. In 1971 an additional item,

---

[6] Louis H. Rappaport, *SEC Accounting Practice and Procedure,* 3d ed. (New York: Ronald Press, Copyright ©1972 by The Ronald Press Company, New York, 1972), p. 5–9.

changes in a registrant's independent auditor, was added as a significant event and this requirement is discussed in more detail in Chapter 3. The information contained on Form 8-K is not subject to review by the independent auditor.

The role of the SEC in financial reporting is greater than that of requiring certain financial data to be filed on a timely basis. If the commission, after reviewing the required filings, believes that significant information has been omitted or that material errors have been made, it can require that the information be changed accordingly. If the commission's requests are not followed, it has the authority to suspend trading of the securities. In performing its duties, the commission rules on whether a registrant has complied with the requirements established or adopted by the SEC and does not approve or disapprove the investment quality of the securities. It is up to the commission to require full disclosure of information, but the investment decision of the potential purchaser of the securities is an individual decision based on one's risk preference. It would of course be impossible as well as undesirable for a government agency to attempt to vouch for the investment worthiness of securities. Those who violate the securities acts are subject to civil and criminal prosecution, which is discussed in Chapter 4.

The SEC has the legislative authority, granted to it by Congress in the 1934 act, to promulgate generally accepted accounting principles. Even with this authority it has repeatedly stated that it relies upon the public accounting profession to perform the task. As suggested above, the FASB now has this responsibility, but it would be inaccurate to describe the SEC's role in determining accounting principles as passive. There is constant communication on an informal basis between the SEC and the FASB concerning accounting principles and reporting problems. Furthermore the SEC has let it be known that, if the public accounting profession cannot resolve either specific reporting problems or the general problem of promulgating accounting principles, it will not hesitate to take on this responsibility. Some have suggested that, if the FASB should fail in its endeavors, it would be the last time the public accounting profession would be allowed to establish accounting principles. A likely candidate to fill this vacancy, should it materialize, is the SEC.

Similar to the promulgation of accounting principles is the SEC's legislative authority to prescribe auditing standards and procedures to be followed by the independent auditor. However, the commission has, for the most part, relied upon the public accounting profession to establish these rules, but again with the understanding that if the commission is not satisfied with the auditing standards and procedures it will recommend changes or decide to promulgate its own auditing rules. The latter course of action has not been followed by the commission except in special circumstances. Thus at the present time, the AICPA's Auditing Standards Executive Committee promulgates auditing procedures. The commission's opinions and announcements concerning auditing matters, as well as accounting matters, are published as *Accounting Series Releases* which appear in the *Federal Register* and are reprinted by commercial services.

Finally all businesses in this country do not come under the jurisdiction of the SEC and therefore do not have to abide by its regulations. Generally speaking, only securities traded in interstate commerce are subject to control by the federal government. However, the determination of which companies must file with the SEC is far more complex. For example, an offering of securities for sale must be a public offering rather than a private agreement between the issuer and a single third party or group of individuals. In addition certain offerings that are small can be exempted by the SEC, and companies without assets that exceed a certain dollar threshold and whose shares are not widely held are not required to file. Of concern today is the exemption by law of municipalities, states, and state agencies from registration requirements. Because of the financial difficulties in which some of these government units find themselves and the charge of a lack of full disclosure on their part, there are various amendments pending in Congress to eliminate this exemption or to create new legislation requiring a greater degree of financial disclosure.

Other controls

In addition to the institutional controls discussed above, there are a variety of other controls that play a vital role in society's control over the public accounting profession. These control mechanisms are:

- Entry-level requirements
- Professional auditing standards
- Code of Professional Ethics
- Judicial review

The remainder of this chapter discusses entry-level requirements and professional auditing standards. Chapter 3 considers the Code of Professional Ethics, and the auditor's legal liability is discussed in Chapter 4.

ENTRY-LEVEL REQUIREMENTS

There are no national requirements to determine who has the necessary expertise to be designated as a CPA. Each state and territory has established legislation to determine who may practice as a CPA within its boundaries, and this legislation is administered by a state or territorial board of accountancy. In almost all states, only a CPA can perform the attest function, and the state board of accountancy bestows or revokes the license of a CPA. Although the requirements vary from state to state, all states require that an individual pass a written examination prepared and graded on a national basis by the AICPA.

The CPA examination is given every May and November throughout the United States and consists of four parts: (1) accounting practice, (2) accounting theory, (3) auditing, and (4) business law. A few states have added other parts to the examination. The examination is a rigorous academic exercise and for this reason should be taken reasonably soon after the completion of one's academic studies. The AICPA has suggested three requisites needed to pass the CPA examination.

- An adequate general intelligence
- The education provided by a baccalaureate degree with a major in accounting
- An intensive review for an extended period of time.[7]

As a first step in preparing for the examination, a student should read the AICPA's publication, *Information for CPA Candidates*.

Although the CPA examination is academic in nature, most states require that an individual complete from one to three years of experience working for a CPA firm before the CPA certificate is issued. The experience requirement is being reduced in many states, and the AICPA has recommended that the experience requirement be abolished and be replaced with a requirement that the candidate have five years of college training. At the present time, few states have adopted the proposal, and the profession is divided over whether the recommendation should be instituted. In some states the practical experience does not have to be with a CPA firm but may in some cases be with a government agency involved in financial compliance auditing. Information concerning specific questions about eligibility can be obtained from a particular state board of accountancy or by referring to the Commerce Clearing House loose-leaf publication, *Accountancy Law Reporter Service*.

Entry-level requirements establish a minimum level of competency; however they do not ensure that, once an individual becomes a CPA, the individual will stay abreast of current professional developments. Auditing, like any profession, is a dynamic discipline, and only through personal effort on the part of the CPA can he or she hope to stay up-to-date. To ensure that CPAs meet their professional requirements, several states or state societies of CPAs have mandated that CPAs meet certain continuing-education requirements every year. These requirements may be met through a variety of ways but normally are achieved by attending in-house professional development courses or courses sponsored by the state society of CPAs.

With the establishment of entry-level requirements and the emergence of the philosophy of continuing education, society is somewhat assured of trained professional auditors. Obviously this is only an attempt to establish a minimum level of performance. Performing as a professional is a very personal matter which depends upon individual commitment to one's work.

PROFESSIONAL STANDARDS

Another mechanism by which society controls and measures the performance of the independent auditor is through the identification of what constitutes a minimum or acceptable level of performance. While these standards have been developed within the accounting profession, they have generally been accepted by society as a standard for determining accountability. Standards of performance are discussed from a legal liability perspective in Chapter 4.

Although the professional standards are the basis for making the independent auditor accountable to society, it is helpful to view these standards as guides for

[7] *Information for CPA Candidates* (New York: AICPA, 1970), p. 14.

36
The audit function

the auditor to follow in the performance of the audit. Thus they provide the skeletal outline which gives the auditor a general direction in planning, performing, and communicating the results of the audit. These standards are of necessity broad in that only broad guidelines may be expected to provide guidance in every audit situation. Professional auditing standards are applicable to every audit engagement, but the audit flexibility is achieved through the selection of audit procedures. An independent auditor, utilizing professional judgment, employs audit procedures which are applicable to a particular audit situation. Through the recognition that each audit possesses some unique characteristics, the auditor matches the audit procedures to the circumstances, the audit objective being the attainment of professional standards. A heavy responsibility rests upon the auditor to use sound professional judgment in the conduct of each audit. This judgment is the keystone in every profession and certainly critical in the audit profession. Educational training (both general and technical), experience, and intuition provide the foundation of professional judgment.

The auditing profession, through the Committee on Auditing Procedure of the AICPA (then known as the American Institute of Accountants), began to promulgate auditing standards and procedures in 1939. A consensus of what constituted auditing standards was achieved in 1948, and this forms the basis of generally accepted auditing standards. These standards have been recodified by the AICPA's Auditing Standards Executive Committee in *SAS No. 1.* Generally accepted auditing standards are composed of ten statements: three statements on general standards, three statements on standards of fieldwork, and four statements on standards of reporting. The AICPA has recognized that the standards must be observed by an auditing firm and integrated into the firm's operational procedures. For this reason the committee issued *SAS No. 4,* "Quality Control Considerations for a Firm of Independent Auditors," to "set forth certain considerations in establishing policies and procedures that will provide the firm with reasonable assurance of conforming with generally accepted auditing standards." The ten standards in *SAS No. 1* along with the applicable guidelines from *SAS No. 4,* are discussed here; however, generally accepted auditing standards are so fundamental to the audit process that they are the basis for the discussion in the remainder of the book.

GENERAL STANDARDS

The three statements which form the general standards of generally accepted auditing standards refer to the personal characteristics of the independent auditor.

⦿ STANDARD 1: The examination is to be performed by a person or persons having adequate technical training and proficiency as an auditor.*

The first standard recognizes that there is a technical body of knowledge upon which auditing is based and that this material must be mastered as a

---

* This standard and all following quotations from the AICPA Statements on Auditing Standards (SAS) are reprinted courtesy of the AICPA.

prerequisite to performing a professional audit. Most auditors acquire this background in a typical undergraduate or graduate program in accounting at a university. This academic preparation is tested in the CPA examination, as discussed earlier. However, it should not be concluded that only a CPA can perform audit work. A subsequent standard is discussed which allows inexperienced college graduates an opportunity to perform some parts of the audit under proper supervision. In *SAS No. 4,* the AICPA formally instructed and reminded public accounting firms of their responsibility in this area with this suggestion:

(Hiring:) Policies and procedures for hiring should be established to provide reasonable assurance that those employed possess the appropriate characteristics to enable them to perform competently.[8]

While generally accepted auditing standards refer only to technical training, it cannot be concluded that the successful auditor is one who has only a mastery of the technical accounting and auditing literature. One also needs an adequate background in other business subjects, such as economics, management, finance and marketing, and liberal arts. Because of the importance of communicative skills, both verbal and written, these skills cannot be omitted from one's academic preparation.

Academic preparation as well as successful completion of the CPA examination are only a first step in mastering and applying the technical rules of auditing. Acquiring technical training is a continuing endeavor of every auditor who recognizes the dynamic nature of the profession and of the financial world in general. This point was made earlier when the concept of continuing education was discussed. Auditors who choose not to stay abreast of current developments run the risk of becoming obsolete and also violate generally accepted auditing standards.

Finally auditing expertise is more than academic preparation and continuing education. The first standard of generally accepted auditing standards recognizes this by requiring that an auditor be proficient as well as technically trained. Proficiency is the application of the technical and general knowledge of an auditor to a particular audit situation. Practical experience is the key ingredient in audit proficiency. *SAS No. 4* designates two areas that are part of ensuring that members of the professional staff develop into proficient auditors as their responsibilities increase.

Assigning personnel to engagements: Policies and procedures for assigning personnel to engagements should be established to provide reasonable assurance that audit work will be performed by persons having the degree of technical training and proficiency required in the circumstances.

Professional development: Policies and procedures for professional development should be established to provide reasonable assurance

---

[8] "Quality Control Considerations for a Firm of Independent Auditors," *Statement on Auditing Standards No. 4* (New York: AICPA, 1974), p. 4.

38
The audit function

that personnel will have the knowledge required to enable them to fulfill responsibilities assigned.[9]

The second standard of generally accepted auditing standards emphasizes the need for independence on the part of the public accountant.

STANDARD 2: In all matters relating to the assignment, an independence in mental attitude is to be maintained by the auditor or auditors. (AICPA)

Although it has become somewhat of a cliché, independence is indeed the cornerstone of the profession. The idea of independence was emphasized earlier, and it is obvious that independence is fundamental to the reliance of users upon the work of the auditor. Should management of the business entity gain control of the auditor, the framework for disseminating economic data would suffer. Ultimately, if independence is materially impaired, society may seek a different arrangement, and the private-sector auditor's role may be immeasurably altered.

In the audit environment, an auditor must be independent in fact and independent in appearance. Independence in fact is a personal trait dependent upon one's intellectual honesty. The auditor is expected to evaluate audit evidence in a frame of mind that neither favors nor disfavors the auditor's client or third parties. It is of course impossible for a third party, or anyone for that matter, to determine whether the auditor is independent in fact. Because of "real-world" considerations, most of the audit literature that deals with independence discusses it from the perspective of independence in appearance. The auditing profession has adopted a code of professional ethics which devotes a considerable amount of space to independence in appearance. For example, an auditor cannot be an employee of the client, because to a third party this would strongly suggest a lack of independence. A complete discussion of independence is offered in Chapter 3.

Again, *SAS No. 4* recognizes the need for a firm to establish procedures by which independence is to be monitored.

Independence: Policies and procedures should be established to provide reasonable assurance that persons at all organizational levels maintain independence in fact and in appearance.[10]

Due professional care is the subject of the third standard.

STANDARD 3: Due professional care is to be exercised in the performance of the examination and the preparation of the report. (AICPA)

This standard recognizes that an auditor may be technically trained and independent but still not perform an adequate professional audit. Only if an

[9] Ibid., pp. 3–5.
[10] Ibid., pp. 2–3.

independent auditor performs audit procedures and prepares the report in a manner that is understood and known to be appropriate under the circumstances can generally accepted auditing standards be achieved. A concise description is offered in *SAS No. 1:* "Every man who offers his service to another and is employed assumes the duty to exercise in the employment such skill as he possesses with reasonable care and diligence."[11]

STANDARDS OF FIELDWORK

While the general standards are personal in nature, the standards of fieldwork provide the auditor guidelines for gathering and evaluating evidence upon which to form an opinion on the financial statements.

● STANDARD 1: The work is to be planned and assistants, if any, are to be properly supervised. (AICPA)

The performance of an audit is a formidable task often requiring thousands of work-hours to complete. It is not surprising that a standard has been established that requires the auditor to allocate part of the audit budget to the planning phase. There are many facets of the planning process in auditing, three of which are discussed below.

- *Manpower requirements* To insure that an adequate audit is performed, it is necessary to study the client and the nature of that particular industry and select auditors with the appropriate skills and work experience. For example, if the accounting system is heavily computerized it is necessary to assign personnel that have an adequate computer background to the audit.

- *Timing of audit work* Some audit procedures must be conducted at certain times and offer no flexibility. It is incumbent upon the auditor to anticipate and plan for these procedures. It may be necessary for the auditor to simultaneously control and count or otherwise verify undeposited cash, cash in the bank, and negotiable securities at the balance sheet date.

- *Efficient utilization of resources* The auditor has an obligation to the audit client to conduct an adequate audit at a minimum cost. This does not mean the auditor will avoid any procedure that is costly. It does mean that the auditor has the general objective of collecting enough evidence to be able to formulate an opinion on the financial statement but this should be achieved at a reasonable cost under the circumstances. For example, the auditor can often perform many audit procedures prior to the end of the client's fiscal year. This should avoid some of the costly overtime that would otherwise be required after the balance sheet date.

As with any task, only a properly planned audit can ensure that the audit is

---

[11] "Codification of Auditing Standards and Procedures," *Statement on Auditing Standards No. 1* (New York: AICPA, 1973), p. 10.

**40
The audit
function**

performed in a professional manner with the independent auditor retaining control of the job.

The second part of the first standard of fieldwork, "assistants are to be properly supervised," was alluded to earlier. Many audits involve the utilization of several auditors, which requires that a system of communication and review be established. Part of this network involves the assistant or junior accountant role in the audit. Typically an audit program, which is a list of audit procedures designed to collect sufficient evidence to form an opinion on a segment of an audit, is the basic guide for instructing the assistant. Undoubtedly during the performance of the audit procedures, the assistant may raise questions that need to be discussed with the senior auditor. There are no hard and fast rules concerning the amount of supervision to be employed over assistants; however, the degree of supervision is a function of (1) the amount of formal education and training of the assistant, (2) the amount and type of audit experience of the assistant, and (3) the complexity of the subject matter. The review process is documented in the work papers by requiring the senior accountant or other reviewer to initial each work paper reviewed.

The review process is broader than just the review of the assistant's work paper. This point is well made in *SAS No. 4* with the statement:

Supervision: Policies and procedures for the conduct and supervision of work at all organizational levels should be established to provide reasonable assurance that the work performed meets the firm's standards of quality.[12]

This provision emphasizes the need for review from the assistant auditor level to the partner in charge of the audit. Many firms have introduced an additional review procedure with the creation of a formal audit review department. The general purpose of this group is to make sure the audit working papers provide adequate documentation to show that generally accepted auditing standards were achieved. In 1978 the AICPA issued *SAS No. 22,* which is an interpretation of the first standard of fieldwork. This Statement is discussed in Chapter 5.

In Chapter 1 there was a discussion of the change in the audit approach as modern auditing evolved. It was recognized that the size of most business entities made it impossible for the auditor to verify every financial transaction. The second standard of fieldwork describes the audit approach the auditor must take in determining the degree of testing that must be performed.

● STANDARD 2: There is to be a proper study and evaluation of the existing internal control as a basis for reliance thereon and for the determination of the resultant extent of the tests to which auditing procedures are to be restricted. (AICPA)

A system of internal control comprises all measures adopted by an organization for the purpose of safeguarding its assets, ensuring the accurancy and

[12] *SAS No. 4,* p. 4.

reliability of its accounting data, promoting operational efficiency, and encouraging compliance with the organization's policy. There is a significant number of routine transactions that must be processed by a business entity each day. An adequate system of internal control reduces the probability that the information will be processed in an improper manner. The auditor studies and evaluates the internal control system to identify its weaknesses and strengths. Through this analysis, he or she can assign a risk factor to each segment of the system under which the higher the amount of risk, the more detailed the auditing procedures must be. For example, an auditor reviews the internal control system for cash to determine the amount of audit work that must be performed. If the system is weak, the auditor might insist upon preparing all bank account reconciliations for the last month of the fiscal year, whereas if it is strong, perhaps only a review of the bank reconciliations along with other procedures may be appropriate. Thus only after the auditor studies and evaluates the internal control system of an entity can the auditor intelligently determine the extent of sampling required under the circumstances.

The internal control study and evaluation approach is basic to the systems approach described in this book. As business organizations continue to grow and to become more complex, the auditor must rely more and more on a systems approach in the performance of an independent audit. The general nature of internal control systems is discussed in Chapter 6, and the specific internal control system for each functional segment of the accounting system is discussed in Chapters 10–16.

Auditing has been defined as the process of collecting and evaluating audit evidence for the purpose of forming an opinion on the financial statements. The final standard of fieldwork formalizes this description.

- STANDARD 3: Sufficient competent evidential matter is to be obtained through inspection, observation, inquiries and confirmations to afford a reasonable basis for an opinion regarding the financial statements under examination. (AICPA)

This standard requires that before an opinion can be formed a sufficient amount of evidence must be collected. Sufficiency relates to the quantity of evidence to be acquired. What constitutes a sufficient amount of evidence is of course judgmental, but it is dependent in part upon the adequacy of the internal control system, the special characteristics of the account and, collectively, the client being audited.

The simple collection of evidence through the performance of audit procedures is only one phase of the collection process. Not only must sufficient evidential matter be collected, but evidence must be competent in nature. Competency refers to the quality of the evidence being gathered. Again professional judgment is the basis for evaluating the competency of the evidence collected. The following elements determine the quality of audit evidence:

- The relevance of the evidence
- The objectivity of the evidence

- The timeliness of the evidence
- The internal consistency of the evidence

Thus evidence of sufficient quantity and quality is collected through a variety of audit techniques such as confirmation, observation, and others. Different audit techniques are used in different degrees, depending upon the account being reviewed. Subsequent chapters on evidence (Chapter 5) and statistical sampling (Chapter 8) discuss more fully the quantity and quality of evidence required. The important point at this stage is that a considerable amount of audit work must be performed before an auditor can begin to formulate an opinion on the financial statements.

STANDARDS OF REPORTING

This group of standards provides guidelines for construction of the auditor's report. Because communication with one another in a complex society is often very difficult, the standards of reporting are more specific than the general standards or the standards of fieldwork.

● STANDARD 1: The report shall state whether the financial statements are presented in accordance with generally accepted principles of accounting. (AICPA)

Generally accepted accounting principles is defined as a "technical accounting term which encompasses the conventions, rules, and procedures necessary to define accepted accounting practice at a particular time." As discussed earlier in this chapter, these principles are promulgated by the body designated by the AICPA council.

There is of course no comprehensive list of accounting principles for each reporting situation. Each reporting entity will probably have some unique problems and characteristics which will require the independent auditor to determine if generally accepted accounting principles have been observed. After an appropriate amount of auditing, this standard requires the auditor to state in the audit report whether generally accepted accounting principles were followed. If they were not followed, the auditor must explain the impact of the lack of compliance with accounting principles.

Standards of reporting require not only that the auditor state whether the financial statements are prepared in accordance with generally accepted accounting principles but that the auditor state whether these principles have been applied in a consistent manner.

● STANDARD 2: The report shall state whether such principles have been consistently observed in the current period in relation to the preceding period. (AICPA)

The purpose of the consistency standard is to ensure that financial statements are comparable from year to year. This does not mean that management cannot change accounting principles, but rather if such a change is made then the impact is disclosed in the financial statements. Furthermore, the reason for the accounting change must be stated in the financial statements, and the auditor must note in the auditor's report whether the auditor concurs with the change. *APB Opinion No. 20* ("Accounting Changes") is devoted to the broad topic of changes in accounting principles, changes in accounting estimates, and changes in the reporting entity. These topics are discussed fully in Chapter 17.

It is recognized that the simple presentation of dollar amounts, without additional explanation of these numbers, does not provide adequate information for the users of the financial statements. The third standard of reporting addresses this problem.

● STANDARD 3: Informative disclosures in the financial statements are to be regarded as reasonably adequate unless otherwise stated in the report. (AICPA)

The general objective of full disclosure rests on the assumption that the information conveyed to the user is adequate, timely, relevant, and unbiased. To be reasonably certain that this rather awesome objective is achieved, the auditor is concerned with:

- "Numbers" presented in the financial statements
- Terminology used in the financial statements
- Form and classification scheme used in the financial statements
- Parenthetical comments
- Notes to the financial statements

What constitutes adequate disclosure for a particular event or the financial statements as a whole is a judgment that the auditor must make. However in recent years the pronouncements of the FASB and the SEC have been more specific as to what must be disclosed. Some critics have suggested that this is in reaction to the general philosophy in the profession that if there is no rule then there is no need to disclose information. This statement is arguable, but it does suggest that the auditor must make sure that full disclosure is achieved irrespective of whether a specific disclosure rule exists. Furthermore, the auditor recognizes that verbosity and adequate disclosure are not synonymous.

To the average financial statement user the critical bit of information in the auditor's report is the auditor's opinion of the financial statements. In recognition of this fact, the final standard requires that the auditor be as precise as possible in stating the auditor's opinion on the statements.

● STANDARD 4: The report shall either contain an expression of opinion regarding the financial statements, taken as a whole, or an assertion to the effect that an opinion cannot be expressed. When an over-all opinion cannot be expressed, the reasons therefore should be stated. In all cases where an auditor's name is associated with financial statements the report should contain a clear-cut indication of the character of the auditor's examination, if any, and the degree of responsibility he is taking. (AICPA)

44
The audit function

As discussed in Chapter 1, if the auditor concludes that the financial statements (1) are prepared in accordance with generally accepted accounting principles, (2) achieve full disclosure, (3) do not violate the consistency standard, and (4) do not contain material uncertainties, then an unqualified opinion can be prepared. Figure 2-3 is a reproduction of an unqualified opinion issued by a national accounting firm. Note that the second paragraph, or opinion paragraph, is a manifestation of the four reporting standards. It should also be noted that the scope paragraph is, for the most part, a reflection of the standards of fieldwork.

On the other hand, if the auditor discovers material accounting deficiencies, uncertainty deficiencies, or that the scope of the audit is limited, then an unqualified opinion cannot be issued. In this case, the auditor issues a qualified opinion, or an adverse opinion, or disclaims an opinion on the financial statements depending upon the nature of the deficiency.

Interpretations of auditing standards

STATEMENTS ON AUDITING STANDARDS
From the above discussion it is obvious that the ten generally accepted auditing standards are, for the most part, very general. It is recognized that as

---

Figure 2-3

Auditor's report

**Report of Independent
Certified Public Accountants**

To The Shareholders of
American Can Company:

We have examined the statements of financial position of
American Can Company and its Consolidated Subsidiaries as of
December 31, 1977 and 1976, and the related statements of income
and earnings reinvested in the business and changes in financial
position for the years then ended. Our examinations were made in
accordance with generally accepted auditing standards and,
accordingly, included such tests of the accounting records and
such other auditing procedures as we considered necessary in the
circumstances.

In our opinion, the financial statements referred to above
present fairly the financial position of American Can Company
and its Consolidated Subsidiaries at December 31, 1977 and 1976,
and the results of their operations and changes in their
financial position for the years then ended, in conformity with
generally accepted accounting principles applied on a consistent
basis.

January 31, 1978

---

the business environment changes, it is necessary for these standards to be interpreted in light of such developments. To provide this needed flexibility, the AICPA Auditing Standards Executive Committee issues *Statements on Auditing Standards*. The importance of these statements is illustrated by the following note which appears at the end of each statement:

> It (the AICPA) recognizes Statements on Auditing Standards as interpretations of generally accepted auditing standards, and requires that members be prepared to justify departures from such statements.

While all statements at the time of this writing are incorporated in this text, serious students of auditing must stay abreast of new pronouncements. In addition, those interested in SEC practice must stay current of new issues in Accounting Series Releases.

INDUSTRIAL AUDIT GUIDELINES

Often the *Statements on Auditing Standards* are not specific enough to provide adequate guidelines in certain financial reporting or audit areas. Generally these areas are concerned with specialized problems unique to a particular industry. To remedy the limitation of generally accepted auditing standards and *Statements on Auditing Standards* without requiring such procedures for all industries, the AICPA issues industry audit guides. The guides are the result of a special task force investigation of a problem area. A guide is usually prefaced with the following note:

> A guide is not as authoritative as a pronouncement of AUDSEC, but members should be aware that they may have to justify a departure from a guide if the quality of their work is questioned.

At the present time guides have been prepared for Medicare audits, the audit of colleges and universities, and engagements which result in unaudited financial statements, to name a few.

Monitoring auditing standards in a firm

A public accounting firm has a responsibility to see that auditing standards are being observed in each engagement. In an earlier part of this chapter relevant sections of *SAS No. 4* were discussed. This standard encourages the establishment of a system that will monitor the quality of audit engagements with the following suggestion:

Inspection: Policies and procedures for inspection should be established to provide reasonable assurance that the other procedures designed to maintain the quality of the firm's auditing practice are being effectively applied.[13]

---

[13] Ibid., p. 6.

46
The audit
function

While the specific policies and procedures differ among firms, some firms have established internal audit teams. The teams are usually made up of audit managers or very experienced senior auditors who review the audit working papers and correspondence files of clients with whom they have not worked. The objective of this approach is to determine the quality of the work being performed by the audit firm and to make recommendations to strengthen areas of the audit that are deficient. Some have suggested that this approach be expanded from an internal review approach to an external "peer review." In this case auditors from another audit firm review the work of the particular firm, or the review team may be a "pool of auditors" on loan to and coordinated by the AICPA. At the present time this latter approach is in an infancy stage and is not widespread. The SEC appears to endorse the approach and in at least a few cases has insisted upon some form of peer review.

CONCLUDING REMARKS

In this chapter an economic justification of the role of the audit or attest function has been offered. Society has recognized that certain skills are needed to fill this role effectively and has designated the independent CPA as the person who will fill this position in a complex financial and social structure. To control the independent auditor certain societal controls have been established. Two of these controls, entry-level requirements and auditing standards, were discussed. Two other controls, the professional code of ethics and judicial review, are the subjects of the next two chapters.

QUESTIONS AND PROBLEMS

2-1. Define auditing.

2-2. Define attestation.

2-3. Comment on the following statement:

> An audit by a CPA is essentially negative and contributes to neither the gross national product nor the general well-being of society. The auditor does not create; he merely checks what someone else has done. (AICPA Adapted)

2-4. What is the role of the AICPA's Auditing Standards Executive Committee in establishing professional standards?

2-5. What is the purpose of *SAS No. 4*?

2-6. Are there any alternative solutions to the present structure for "filling the auditor's role"? Name them and list the advantages and disadvantages of each.

2-7. Is the term "public accounting" a misnomer when used to describe the external audit profession?

2-8. Why is it necessary for society to grant the public accounting profession an almost complete monopoly in the attest function?

2-9. How does society monitor and control the public accounting profession?

2-10. Comment on the following statement:

To be a good auditor one must be a good accountant. To be a good accountant one need not be a good auditor.

2-11. Does the SEC have the authority to determine generally accepted accounting principles and generally accepted auditing standards for the entire financial community?

2-12. Determine the requirements for becoming a CPA in your state by writing or phoning your state board of accountancy.

2-13. Differentiate between generally accepted auditing standards and statements on auditing standards.

2-14. List each standard of fieldwork and explain the objective of each one.

2-15. Distinguish between sufficient evidential matter and competent evidential matter.

2-16. Why are the standards of reporting more specific than the other standards of generally accepted auditing standards?

2-17. Contrast statements on auditing standards and industrial audit guides.

2-18. The concept of materiality is important to the CPA in his or her examination of financial statements and expression of opinion upon these statements.

Required: Discuss the following:

1. How are materiality (and immateriality) related to the proper presentation of financial statements?
2. In what ways will consideration of materiality affect the CPA in:

a. Developing his or her audit program?
b. Performance of his or her auditing procedures?

3. What factors and measures should the CPA consider in assessing the materiality of an exception to financial statement presentation?
4. How will the materiality of a CPA's exceptions to financial statements influence the type of opinion he or she expresses? (The relationship of materiality to each type of auditor's opinion should be considered in your answer.) (AICPA Adapted)

2-19. You have been assigned by your firm to complete the examination of the 1967 financial statements of Carter Manufacturing Corporation because the senior accountant and his inexperienced assistant who began the engagement were hospitalized because of an accident. The engagement is about one-half completed. Your auditor's report must be delivered in three weeks as agreed when your firm accepted the engagement. You estimate that by utilizing the client's staff to the greatest possible extent you can complete the engagement in five weeks. Your firm cannot assign an assistant to you. The working papers show the status of work on the examination as follows:

1. Completed—cash, fixed assets, depreciation, mortgage payable, and stockholders' equity.
2. Completed except as noted later—inventories, accounts payable, tests of purchase transactions, and payrolls.
3. Nothing done—trade accounts receivable, inventory receiving cutoff and price testing, accrued expenses payable, unrecorded liability test, tests of sales trans-

48
The audit function

actions, payroll deductions test and observation of payroll check distribution, other expenses, analytical review of operations, vouching of December purchase transactions, auditor's report, internal control investigation, internal control letter, minutes, preparation of tax returns, procedural recommendations for management, subsequent events, supervision, and review.

Your review discloses that the assistant's working papers are incomplete and were not reviewed by the senior accountant. For example, the inventory working papers present incomplete notations, incomplete explanations, and no cross-referencing.

Required

1. What fieldwork standards have been violated by the senior accountant who preceded you on this assignment? Explain why you feel the work standards you list have been violated.

2. In planning your work to complete this engagement you should scan work papers and schedule certain work as soon as possible and also identify work which may be postponed until after the report is rendered to the client.

   a. List the areas on which you should plan to work first, say in your first week of work, and for each item explain why it deserves early attention.
   b. State which work you believe could be postponed until after the report is rendered to the client and give reasons why the work may be postponed.

(AICPA Adapted)

2-20. Carefully read the following comment which is concerned with the impact of inflation:

> It has been suggested that conventional accounting is deficient in that historical data are presented in the financial statements even though this data may not be useful to an investor in making economic decisions concerning an entity. This loss of utility may result from the change in the level of prices due to inflation. Such changes may distort the financial statments of most entities.

Required: Relate this statement to your understanding of the basic economic justification for the CPA function in a modified capitalistic system. (Do not evaluate the technicalities of price-level accounting.)

2-21. Mr. Brown, managing partner of the public accounting firm of Brown and Nobles, received a call from Mr. Warren, president of W & W Corporation on December 27, 1979. Warren explained to Brown that W&W had requested a loan from a local bank and that the bank had insisted that their financial statements be audited. Furthermore, Warren stated that he would like to have the audit completed by mid-January 1980, if possible. Brown and Warren discussed some general aspects of the engagement, such as hourly professional rates and the amount of cooperation that could be expected from the controller's staff in preparing appropriate analysis. Mr. Warren did not seem concerned about the audit fee and stated, "We know your firm is an honest firm, that's why we called you." Mr. Brown knew that W&W Corporation had been in operation for many years and had a fine reputation in the community for its quality products and its fair treatment of employees.

Immediately after the telephone conversation ended, Brown reviewed the firm's assignment schedule which showed all seniors and partners were completely "tied up" with other engagements. Brown decided to be responsible for the job. Also, he decided to assign Bob Davis to the job as senior in charge. Bob had joined the firm about one year before, after completing an MBA degree. Also Bob was preparing to take the CPA **49** examination in May. Although he was classified as a junior auditor, it was the general **Questions and problems** consensus of members of the partnership that Bob would be promoted to the senior level at the conclusion of the busy season.

Brown instructed Bob to begin the audit engagement on December 31, 1979, the earliest day Bob could return from an out-of-town assignment. On this date Bob was told to observe the inventory count being conducted on the last day of the fiscal year. Brown had learned from the president of W&W that there was about $2 million of inventory on hand at the plant and that one person could probably count everything in 8 to 10 hours.

On January 3, 1980, Brown's busy schedule finally allowed him to visit the client. Upon arriving at the plant, the controller stated that Bob was discussing the computer system with the head of the data processing department. After some small talk with the controller, Brown decided to review the working papers prepared by Bob which were properly filed in the inventory binder supplied by the public accounting firm. Among other working papers were the following notes concerning the inventory observation.

On December 31, 1979, I observed the inventory at the W&W Corporation manufacturing plant. The preliminary dollar estimates are summarized below:

| | LOCATED AT | | |
	PLANT	WAREHOUSE	TOTAL
Raw materials	$ 300,000	$500,000	$ 800,000
Work in process	1,400,000	0	1,400,000
Finished goods	200,000	400,000	600,000
	$1,900,000	$900,000	$2,800,000

The inventory was not observed at the warehouse, since it was taken on December 30, 1979. However, the controller states that no goods were shipped to customers until January 2, 1980. I reviewed the bills of lading and none were dated December 31. Furthermore, as an alternative procedure, I obtained the prenumbered inventory listing tickets from the controller and traced 70 percent of these tickets to the costing and summary sheets prepared by the cost accounting department. No errors were discovered.

Goods were received during the physical inventory count at the plant. These were segregated on the receiving dock and counted at the end of the day. The three receipts are listed below:

RECEIVING REPORT NO.	VENDOR	DESCRIPTION
10653	G.T. Rubber Company	150 Fan belts
10654	Warehouse	Prefabricated metal
10655	Martin Supply	200 Bran castings

In summary, all of the raw material and finished goods were subjected to a 100 percent count. It was not possible to count much of the work in process, since much of the cost represented direct labor and indirect manufacturing cost. Few errors were discovered.

Required

1. Do you believe Brown violated any generally accepted auditing standards? Be specific.

2. Do you believe Bob violated any generally accepted auditing standards?

50
The audit function

2-22. In a report prepared by the Senate Subcommittee on Reports, Accounting, and Management (Metcalf Report) the following method of establishing auditing standards and procedures was recommended:

> The Federal Government should establish auditing standards used by independent auditors to certify the accuracy of corporate financial statements and supporting records. Again, participation by all segments of the public is necessary to develop auditing standards that will restore public confidence in the integrity of corporate reports. In view of the substantial record of previously unreported corporate wrongdoing which has been revealed during the past few years, a special review of present auditing standards should be undertaken to determine their adequacy prior to considering their adoption by the Federal Government. Auditing standards could be established by the General Accounting Office, the SEC or by Federal statute.

Required

1. How are auditing standards and statements on these standards established today? Are you aware of any federal agency that has the legislative authority to make such promulgations?

2. What are the advantages and disadvantages of promulgating auditing procedures, standards, and so on, by a federal agency?

3. What are the advantages and disadvantages of promulgating auditing procedures, standards, and so on, by direct federal legislation?

4. Would it be illogical and/or inappropriate to establish accounting rules in the private sector and auditing rules in the public sector, or vice versa?

5. Do you believe the financial community is more interested in participating in the process that leads to an accounting rule or to an auditing procedure?

2-23. You are finishing your examination of the financial statements of Ash Corporation for the year ended September 30, 1979. The Corporation's report to stockholders, which will include your short-form opinion, will contain the consolidated financial statements of Ash Corporation and its substantial subsidiary, Worth Corporation. This is your third annual audit of Ash Corporation, and you find that the following changes from the prior year have occurred:

1. Worth Corporation, which is located in another state, was acquired as a subsidiary during 1979. Another independent auditor, who was engaged by the client, rendered an unqualified opinion on the Worth Corporation financial statements for the year ended September 30, 1979. While you are willing to use his report for the purpose of expressing your opinion on the consolidated statements, you are unwilling to assume responsibility for the performance of the work which served as the basis for his opinion.

You have reviewed the accounting procedures employed by the client to prepare the consolidated statements and approve of them. The corporation has appended to its financial statements a footnote that explains adequately the time of acquisition and the method of consolidation.

2. In accordance with your suggestion, on October 1, 1978, for the 1979 fiscal year Ash Corporation had begun the procedure of estimating its total social security taxes expense for the calendar year and then allocating the total to monthly costs and expenses on the basis of the proportion of total estimated annual payroll actually earned each month. In prior years this tax expense was charged to costs and expenses in the same months that the related taxable wages were paid. The unallocated social security taxes expense on taxable wages earned through September 30, 1979, amounted to $20,000 before consideration of income tax effect. (The income tax rate is 50 percent.) Worth Corporation uses the same method of accounting for social security taxes as Ash adopted.

3. For 1979 Ash Corporation changed its policy of taking a complete physical

inventory on September 30 to taking physical inventories of half of the inventory on July 31 and the other half on August 31. You were consulted on this change and approved it. Your observation of the two physical inventories and your other procedures produced no exceptions as to quantities.

4. A new customer of Ash Corporation is a retail chain-store company whose accounting system makes it unable to confirm the $56,000 balance of its account. You examined related remittances by this customer totaling $50,000 in post-balance-sheet-date audit procedures and satisfied yourself regarding the balance by examination of shipping documents with the exception that there is a $200 charge in dispute, which you considered immaterial. The $56,000 is net of a credit memorandum for $150.

5. Your post-balance-sheet-date audit procedures disclosed that Ash Corporation is considering shutting down on December 31, 1979, a division that has been a marginal operation. Because of the possible effect upon stockholder and employee relations, management prefers not to make a disclosure of its consideration of the proposed shutdown in the annual report which will probably be mailed to stockholders on November 15.

6. A number of substantial claims and lawsuits, which were given widespread publicity, were filed in 1979 against Ash Corporation for damages alleged to have resulted from the use of certain products sold in 1978. The line of products was discontinued early in 1979. The corporation's attorney is unable to predict the outcome of these claims and lawsuits. The management of the corporation believes that losses, if any, incurred in excess of the product liability insurance coverage would not have a material effect upon the company's financial position.

The scope of your examination of Ash Corporation was not limited by the client in any way. No other items of importance were uncovered by your examination.

Required

1. Prepare the additional footnotes that you would suggest that the client should append to the financial statements. (Give the exact wording of the footnotes. Do not discuss what should be included in the footnotes.)

2. For each of the listed changes that you think does not require disclosure, justify your belief in one sentence.

3. Assuming that the client adopts your recommended footnotes, prepare your short-form auditor's report (scope, opinion, and middle paragraph, if any) for your examination. (AICPA Adapted)

2-24. In an article in *Business Week* the following comment was made concerning the impact of accounting on the allocation of goods and services:

> Though one may plead for "economic reality" in accounting, every accounting description is nonetheless a description of some facet of economic reality. No accounting choice, therefore, is neutral. Each involves potential redistribution of wealth. In this sense, the accounting choice involves a social choice.[14]

The level of visibility and importance of accounting and auditing in society have increased dramatically in the last quarter of a century. The above statement recognizes this development.

Required

1. Should the auditing profession be concerned with the impact of accounting rules on an individual firm or on the economy as a whole?

[14] Prem Prakash and Alfred Rappaport, "The Feedback Effects of Accounting," *Business Week*, January 12, 1976, p. 12.

52
The audit function

2. Can you identify any developments in accounting or auditing that illustrate society's concern for the impact of accounting or auditing rules on society as a whole?

3. Is the attest function neutral? Is the audit process neutral?

2-25. You have accepted the engagement of examining the financial statements of the Thorne Company, a small manufacturing firm that has been your client for several years. Because you were busy writing the report for another engagement, you sent a junior accountant to begin the audit with the suggestion that she start with the accounts receivable. Using the prior year's working papers as a guide, the junior prepared a trial balance of the accounts, aged them, prepared and mailed positive confirmation requests, examined underlying support for charges and credits, and performed such other work as she deemed necessary to ensure the validity and collectibility of the receivables. At the conclusion of her work you reviewed the working papers that she prepared and found that she had carefully followed the prior year's work papers.

Required: The opinion rendered by a CPA states ". . . Our examination was made in accordance with generally accepted auditing standards. . . ."

List the three generally accepted standards of fieldwork. Relate them to the above illustration by indicating how they were fulfilled or, if appropriate, how they were not fulfilled. (AICPA Adapted)

2-26. The following nine questions relate to the reporting responsibilities of the independent auditor and the type of opinion he or she should give under specific circumstances. Unless otherwise indicated, you should assume that the CPA has made an examination in accordance with generally accepted auditing standards, and that financial statement presentation conforms with generally accepted accounting principles applied on a consistent basis and includes all informative disclosures necessary to prevent making the statements misleading and that all amounts involved are material.

For each of the following conditions, indicate the type(s) of auditor's opinions that should be given. Mark all the options that may be appropriate for each situation. Your answer may include one or more of the following:

a. Issue an unqualified opinion
b. Issue a qualified opinion
c. Issue an adverse opinion
d. Disclaim an opinion

1. Where the exceptions concerning fairness of presentation are so material that, in the CPA's judgment, a qualified opinion is not justified, the CPA should _____.

2. When a CPA has not obtained sufficient competent evidential matter to form an opinion on the fairness of presentation of the financial statements as a whole, he should _____.

3. When a CPA has not obtained sufficient evidence to remove substantial doubt about any material item, she should _____.

4. When a client has imposed limitations on the auditor's scope of examination in satisfying himself about consistency in a first audit of an established company, the CPA should _____.

5. When matters that an auditor believes require disclosure are omitted from the financial statements, the CPA should include the appropriate disclosures in her report and _____.

6. If a subsequent event of the type requiring adjustment or disclosure comes to the attention of the auditor after he has completed his fieldwork but before he has issued his opinion, and the statements are not adjusted accordingly, the CPA should _____.

7. When a material change has resulted from a variation between periods in terms used to express changes in financial position, the CPA should _____.

8. When a CPA believes that information essential for fair presentation has been omitted from the statement of changes in financial position, the CPA should provide the information and _____.

9. When a client has changed to a principle or practice that is not generally accepted, the CPA should _____.

2-27. Part A. The auditor's report states whether the financial statements are prepared in conformity with generally accepted accounting principles applied on a consistent basis.

Required
1. What is the purpose of requiring the auditor to determine if the consistency standard has been followed?

Part B. Auditing rules require that an auditor determine whether a change to an accounting principle is appropriate based on the circumstances surrounding the change.

Required
1. Is this a realistic requirement to impose upon the auditor?
2. How does the auditor determine the appropriateness of an accounting principle?

Part C. It has been suggested that it is not necessary for the auditor to make a statement concerning the observance of consistency in the preparation of financial statements.

Required
1. What is the rationale for the above statement?

2-28. The following is an example of a report prepared at the turn of the century:

Certificate of Chartered Accountants

New York
March 12, 1903

To the Stockholders of the United States Steel Corporation:

We have examined the books of the U.S. Steel Corporation and its Subsidiary Companies for the year ending December 31, 1902, and certify that the Balance Sheet at that date and the Relative Income Account are directly prepared therefrom.

We have satisfied ourselves that during the year only actual additions and extensions have been charged to Property Account; that ample provision has been made for Depreciation and Extinguishment, and that the item of "Deferred Charges" represents expenditures reasonably and properly carried forward to operations of subsequent years.

We are satisfied that the valuations of the inventories of stocks on hand as certified by the responsible officials have been carefully and accurately made at approximate cost; also that the cost of material and labor on contracts in progress has been carefully ascertained, and that the profit taken on these contracts is fair and reasonable.

Full provision has been made for bad and doubtful accounts receivable and for all ascertainable liabilities.

We have verified the cash and securities by actual inspection or by certificates from the Depositories, and are of opinion
that the Stocks and Bonds are fully worth the value at which they
are stated in the Balance Sheet.

And we certify that in our opinion the Balance Sheet is
properly drawn up so as to show the true financial position of
the Corporation and its Subsidiary Companies, and that the Relative Income Account is a fair and correct statement of the net
earnings for the fiscal year ending at that date.

Price Waterhouse & Co.

Required
1. Contrast the current-day auditor's report with the above report.
2. Which report does a better job in communicating the results of the audit process?

2-29. The complete set of financial statements for The Maumee Corporation for the year ended August 31, 1979, is presented here:

The Maumee Corporation
Balance Sheet
August 31, 1979
(in thousands of dollars)

ASSETS

Cash		$ 103
Marketable securities, at cost which approximates market value		54
Trade accounts receivable (net of $65,000 allowance for doubtful accounts)		917
Inventories, at cost		775
Property, plant, and equipment	$3,200	
Less: Accumulated depreciation	1,475	1,725
Prepayments and other assets		125
Total assets		$3,699

LIABILITIES AND STOCKHOLDERS' EQUITY

Accounts payable	$ 221
Accrued taxes	62
Bank loans and long-term debt	1,580
Total liabilities	1,863
Capital stock, $10 par value (authorized 50,000 shares, issued and outstanding 42,400 shares)	424
Paid-in capital in excess of par value	366
Retained earnings	1,046
Total stockholders' equity	1,836
Total liabilities and stockholders' equity	$3,699

The Maumee Corporation
Statement of Income and Retained Earnings
For the year ended August 31, 1979
(in thousands of dollars)

Product sales (net of $850,000 sales returns and allowances)		$10,700
Cost of goods sold		8,700
Gross profit on sales		2,000
Operating expenses		
Selling expenses	$1,500	
General and administrative expenses	940	2,440
Operating loss		(440)
Interest expense		150
Net loss		(590)
Retained earnings, September 1, 1978		1,700
		1,110
Dividends:		
Cash $1 per share	40	
Stock 6 percent of shares outstanding	24	64
Retained earnings, August 31, 1979		$ 1,046

Required: List deficiencies and omissions in the Maumee Corporation's financial statements and discuss the probable effect of the deficiency or omission on the auditor's report. Assume that the Maumee Corporation is unwilling to change the financial statements or make additional disclosures therein.

Consider each deficiency or omission separately, and do not consider the cumulative effect of the deficiencies and omissions on the auditor's report. There are no arithmetical errors in the statements.

Organize your answer sheet in two columns as indicated below and write your answer in the order of appearance within the general headings of "Balance sheet," "Statement of income and retained earnings," and "Other."

FINANCIAL STATEMENT DEFICIENCY OR OMISSION	DISCUSSION OF EFFECT ON AUDITOR'S REPORT

(AICPA Adapted)

2-30. Upon completion of all fieldwork on September 23, 1979, the following short-form report was rendered by Timothy Ross to the directors of the Rancho Corporation.

```
To the Directors of
The Rancho Corporation:

    We have examined the balance sheet and the related state-
ment of income and retained earnings of The Rancho Corporation as
of July 31, 1979. In accordance with your instructions, a com-
plete audit was conducted.

    In many respects, this was an unusual year for The Rancho
Corporation. The weakening of the economy in the early part of
```

56
The audit function

the year and the strike of plant employees in the summer of 1979 led to a decline in sales and net income. After making several tests of sales records, nothing came to our attention that would indicate that sales have not been properly recorded.

In our opinion, with the explanations given above, and with the exception of some minor errors that are considered immaterial, the aforementioned financial statements present fairly the financial position of The Rancho Corporation at July 31, 1979, and the results of its operations for the year then ended, in conformity with pronouncements of the Accounting Principles Board and the Financial Accounting Standards Board applied consistently throughout the period.

Timothy Ross, CPA
September 23, 1979

Required: List and explain deficiencies and omissions in the auditor's report. The type of opinion (unqualified, qualified, adverse, or disclaimer) is of no consequence and need not be discussed.

Organize your answer sheet by paragraph (scope, explanatory, and opinion) of the auditor's report. (AICPA Adapted)

MULTIPLE CHOICE

1. According to *SAS No. 1*, the auditor's responsibility for failure to detect fraud arises

   a. When such failure clearly results from failure to comply with generally accepted auditing standards.
   b. Whenever the amounts involved are material.
   c. Only when the examination was specifically designed to detect fraud.
   d. Only when such failure clearly results from negligence so gross as to sustain an inference of fraud on the part of the auditor.

2. What is the general character of the three generally accepted auditing standards classified as general standards?

   a. Criteria for competence, independence, and professional care of individuals performing the audit.
   b. Criteria for the content of the financial statements and related footnote disclosures.
   c. Criteria for the content of the auditor's report on financial statements and related footnote disclosures.
   d. The requirements for the planning of the audit and supervision of assistants, if any.

3. The general group of the generally accepted auditing standards includes a requirement that

   a. The fieldwork be adequately planned and supervised.
   b. The auditor's report state whether or not the financial statements conform to generally accepted accounting principles.
   c. Due professional care be exercised by the auditor.

d. Informative disclosures in the financial statements be reasonably adequate.

57
Multiple choice

4. When a certified public accountant who is not independent is associated with financial statements, he or she would be precluded from expressing an opinion because

a. The public would be aware of his lack of independence and would place little or no faith in his opinion.
b. She would place herself in the position of suffering an adverse decision in a possible liability suit.
c. He would be in the position of auditing his own work.
d. Any auditing procedures she might perform would not be in accordance with generally accepted auditing standards.

5. An auditor's unqualified short-form report

a. Implies only that items disclosed in the financial statements and footnotes are properly presented and takes no position on the adequacy of disclosure.
b. Implies that disclosure is adequate in the financial statements and footnotes.
c. Explicitly states that disclosure is adequate in the financial statements and foot-notes.
d. Explicitly states that all material items have been disclosed in conformity with generally accepted accounting principles.   (AICPA Adapted)

CHAPTER 3

The code of professional ethics

In Chapter 2, the elements of societal control, entry-level requirements, and professional auditing standards were discussed. In this chapter the auditor's code of ethics is the basis for discussing another method by which society controls the profession. Although the ethical rules are self-imposed, a violation of these rules can be the basis for disciplinary action either by the AICPA's trial board or by a court of law. The role of the AICPA board and state boards is discussed in this chapter, and the legal liability of the auditor is considered in Chapter 4.

PROFESSIONAL ETHICS

Society, as well as most professions, recognizes a need for the formulation and enforcement of rules of conduct in particular disciplines. It is usually impractical for the general public to be aware of the necessary skills needed in a profession and the acceptable manner of practicing these skills within the profession. For this reason, the public must be able to assume that a member is in good standing in a profession and is successfully achieving at least the minimum established standards. Furthermore, society need not know the particular rules of the profession, but it should be able to assume that the minimum level of performance established by the profession is adequate to protect the public. In recent years society has taken a far more active role in the establishment of rules of conduct for a profession. For example, the Justice Department is becoming increasingly critical of professional groups whose rules of conduct might be interpreted as restraints of trade. In an interdependent society it is crucial that a profession establish rules that are consistent with the public welfare, and that these rules be enforced.

THE CODE OF PROFESSIONAL ETHICS

59
**The code
of professional
ethics**

In general, the basic objective of formulating a code of ethics for any group is twofold. First, the code provides members of the group with guidelines for behavior in the conduct of their professional affairs. Second, the rules of conduct are used as standards to determine whether or not a member has performed in an acceptable manner. In the public accounting profession, the AICPA has established a code of professional ethics to achieve this dual objective. The code is divided into three areas: (1) concepts of professional ethics, (2) rules of conduct, and (3) interpretations of rules of conduct. The first two divisions are the basis for the organization of much of the remaining material in this chapter. The third division, interpretations of rules of conduct, consists of pronouncements issued by the Division of Professional Ethics of the AICPA to provide guidelines for the scope and application of the rules of conduct. Some of the more important interpretations are discussed in the analysis of the rules of conduct.

Concepts of professional ethics

The first part of the code is a philosophical essay on professional ethics and is not intended to formulate enforceable rules of conduct. In this section of the code two broad principles of behavior are recognized and discussed. First, the code recognizes that a viable code of ethics cannot function properly by only listing rules of conduct. It is impossible to anticipate every situation in which ethical questions will arise; therefore no code of ethics is comprehensive in this respect. Second, even if the above limitation could somehow be overcome, a set of rules tends to establish minimum levels of conduct. The profession would be better served if its members were more interested in conducting their practices in a manner that does not suggest a minimum level of conduct through the observance of detailed rules. With these objectives in mind, this section of the code suggests five broad principles that an independent auditor should use as a conceptual framework in conducting a professional practice in an ethical manner. These principles are discussed fully in the code but are summarized here:

- *Independence, integrity, and objectivity:* A CPA should maintain his or her integrity and objectivity and, when engaged in the practice of public accounting, be independent of those he or she serves.
- *Competence and technical standards:* A CPA should observe the profession's technical standards and strive continually to improve his or her competence and the quality of his or her services.
- *Responsibilities to clients:* A CPA should be fair and candid with his or her clients and serve them to the best of his or her ability with professional concern for their best interests, consistent with his or her responsibilities to the public.
- *Responsibilities to colleagues:* A CPA should conduct himself or herself in a manner which will promote cooperation and good relations among members of the profession.

60
The code
of professional
ethics

· *Other responsibilities and practices:* A CPA should conduct himself or herself in a manner which will enhance the stature of the profession and its ability to serve the public.

These five principles discussed in the concepts of professional ethics section of the code are the basis for much of the discussion in this chapter.

Rules of conduct

In the second section of the code, the AICPA identifies rules that must be followed by members of the institute. The code organizes the rules of conduct in a manner that attempts to explain the five broad principles discussed in the section on concepts of professional ethics. The organizational scheme is retained for the current discussion. Thus the first rules discussed relate to independence, integrity, and objectivity.

INDEPENDENCE, INTEGRITY, AND OBJECTIVITY

The first part of the code of ethics refers to the personal qualities of the public accountant.

● RULE 101—INDEPENDENCE: A member or firm of which he is a partner or shareholder shall not express an opinion on financial statements of an enterprise unless he and his firm are independent with respect to such enterprise. Independence will be considered to be impaired if, for example:

A. During the period of his professional engagement, or at the time of expressing his opinion, he or his firm

1. a. Had or was committed to acquire any direct or material indirect financial interest in the enterprise; or

   b. Was a trustee of any trust or executor or administrator of any estate if such trust or estate had or was committed to acquire any direct or material indirect financial interest in the enterprise; or

2. Had any joint closely held business investment with the enterprise or any officer, director or principal stockholder thereof which was material in relation to his or his firm's net worth; or

3. Had any loan to or from the enterprise or any officer; the proscription does not apply to the following loans from a financial institution when made under normal lending procedures, terms and requirements:

   a. Loans obtained by a member of his firm which are not material in relation to the net worth of such borrower.

b. Home mortgages.

c. Other secured loans, except loans guaranteed by a member's firm which are otherwise unsecured.

B. During the period covered by the financial statement, during the period of the professional engagement or at the time of expressing an opinion, he or his firm

1. Was connected with the enterprise as a promoter, underwriter or voting trustee, a director or officer or in any capacity equivalent to that of a member of management or of an employee; or

2. Was a trustee for any pension or profit-sharing trust of the enterprise.

The above examples are not intended to be all-inclusive.*

● RULE 102—INTEGRITY AND OBJECTIVITY: A member shall not knowingly misrepresent facts, and when engaged in the practice of public accounting, including the rendering of tax and management advisory services, shall not subordinate his judgment to others.

In tax practice, a member may resolve doubt in favor of his client as long as there is reasonable support for his position. (AICPA)

INDEPENDENCE

The profession has defined *independence* as the ability to act with integrity and objectivity, both of which are subjective terms. *Integrity* refers to the auditor's moral character or honesty. *Objectivity* refers to his or her ability to be unprejudiced in the conduct of an audit. Obviously both elements of independence are not subject to precise measurement, and for this reason the profession recognizes the need to differentiate between independence in fact and independence in appearance. Independence in fact can only be determined by an individual auditor as that auditor measures his or her attitudes and actions against the standards of integrity and objectivity described above.

Since an auditor's work impacts other elements of society, the personal measurement of factual independence is too limited. The general public must make decisions about independence which require that more tangible rules be constructed. Again, recognizing that every situation which may impair independence cannot be anticipated, Rule 101 designates two relationships that must be avoided.

The first part of Rule 101 describes certain financial relationships with a client that are to be avoided. If the auditor were to have a direct financial interest in a client, the appearance of independence would certainly be lost. For example,

* This quotation and all those following from the AICPA Code of Professional Ethics are reprinted by permission of the AICPA.

users of the financial statements would question whether an auditor is independent if the auditor holds common stock or bonds of the client. Rule 101(A) recognizes that certain financial relationships are reasonable and are not prohibited. Therefore the auditor may have indirect financial interest in a client as long as these interests are not material. An example of an immaterial indirect financial interest is an auditor having an investment in a mutual fund which has a relatively small holding in the voting stock of the auditor's client. In addition, Rule 101(A), Section 3, specifically refers to three additional types of financial interest that are not violations of the rules of conduct. Note that, if a firm of auditors acquires a client in which a direct financial interest or material indirect financial interest is held by one or more partners, then these partners must dispose of the interest prior to the beginning of the audit.

Rule 101(B) prohibits relationships in which an auditor in essence becomes or has been an employee or a member of management during the period covered by the financial statements. Independence in appearance and perhaps independence in fact is lost if an auditor has made or has been involved in decisions as an employee of the client. To avoid this potential problem, Rule 101 prohibits certain relationships such as serving the client as a director, officer, or employee. Furthermore, it is not sufficient to avoid these relationships on the balance sheet date or the date the engagement begins, but rather the relationship may not have existed over the period covered by the financial statements. This section has and continues to be discussed in relationship to services other than the attest service performed by an accounting firm. Does the auditor impair independence in fact and in appearance when a tax service, management advisory service, or bookkeeping service is performed for the client?

INDEPENDENCE AND TAX SERVICE

Every public accounting firm is involved to some extent in providing a professional tax service to a client. In performing a tax service, the auditor is not expected to be independent in all matters and in fact takes on the role of an advocate of the client position as it relates to tax matters. In this advocacy role the auditor is careful to recommend only courses of action rather than to make managerial decisions. In addition, the auditor may recommend or agree to such decisions only if there is reasonable support for the course of action. If management's position is not supportable or is a clear violation of tax laws, the auditor must insist that management make appropriate changes in its tax policy. As long as the auditor performs in this manner, there is no violation of the rules of conduct.

There are those who question the relationship of the auditor when the role of advocate is assumed. The auditor must attest to the tax expense as it appears on the income statement and the tax accrual on the balance sheet. In this respect the dual role of the auditor provides a basis for potential conflict. On the one hand the auditor is involved in the role of advocate of the client's tax position, and on the other hand he or she must perform an independent review of the elements of the financial statements. This uncomfortable situation is best described in an article based in part on a hypothetical cross-examination of an audit partner in a lawsuit against the partner's accounting firm. The plaintiff's lawyer asks:

> Do you still contend that in examining this particular item on the financial statements you were functioning as an independent auditor reviewing the amounts which were determined by the client and not by yourself, and applying your best judgment to what would be a fair presentation? Or were you not, at least as to this item, functioning simply as an employee of the corporation, attempting to minimize the corporation's income tax expense and put the best possible face on the corporation's financial statements?[1]

The auditing profession is very much aware of and concerned with the dual role of the auditor. In 1969, the profession responded when the AICPA began issuing *Statements on Responsibilities in Tax Practice*. The purpose of the series of statements is to provide guidelines as to what constitutes good standards of tax practice, recognizing the auditor's responsibility to the client, the public, and the taxing authority. These statements are not to be viewed as a separate code of ethics for the conduct of a tax practice but rather as a recognition of the unique problems involved in this area. At the time of this writing, the AICPA had promulgated ten separate statements. These statements cover a variety of topics, including the circumstances under which an auditor should sign a tax return and the responsibility of an auditor when it is learned that an error has been made in the preparation of a client's tax return. These statements are reproduced in the appendix to this chapter.

INDEPENDENCE AND MANAGEMENT ADVISORY SERVICE

Today the independent auditor performs a variety of tasks for clients that are classified under the broad heading of management advisory services. In the performance of these duties, independence is not an important part of the auditor's mental attitude. In fact, the public accounting firm's objective in the conduct of management advisory service is to provide advice and technical assistance which will enable the client to conduct its affairs more effectively. The profession has a long history of such service because it possesses specific skills that management recognizes as potentially beneficial. Management services are a natural extension of the talents possessed by a firm of auditors.

Potentially the performance of special services by an auditor for a client can compromise the auditor's independence unless certain precautions are taken. In general, the auditor must interpret the consulting role as that of an advisor rather than as a member of management. In this way it is hoped that the auditor will not end up auditing decisions made by the auditor or other members of the auditing firm. For example, if an auditor were to design, install, and temporarily operate a cost accounting system, it would be hard for that person or the accounting firm as a whole to review objectively the financial accounts generated by the system. On the other hand, if the auditor's role is purely that of an advisor, his or her independence in a subsequent audit is not impaired.

---

[1] William L. Raby, "Advocacy vs. Independence in Tax Liability Accrual," *Journal of Accountancy,* March 1972, p. 42.

64
**The code
of professional
ethics**

In actual practice the difference between an advisor and a management decision maker is often obscured by the characteristics of a particular engagement. If, for example, a client does not have qualified personnel to review adequately the auditor's recommendations, then the recommendation is in reality the only course of action that management may select. This may be construed as a violation of Rule 101 which precludes an auditor from expressing an opinion on the financial statements of an enterprise if he or she has served in any capacity equivalent to that of a member of management. The AICPA recognized this potential conflict and has established standards in this area through the periodic issuance of *Statements on Management Advisory Services*. Figure 3-1 is a list of eight specific standards established by these statements. Furthermore, it is suggested that the following characteristics of an engagement be present before an auditor accepts a management consulting engagement in which there is limited client participation.

- The client understands the nature and implications of the recommended course of action.
- Client management has made a firm decision to proceed with implementation based on this understanding and consideration of alternatives.
- Client management accepts overall responsibility for implementation of the chosen course of action.
- Sufficient expertise will be available in the client organization to fully comprehend the significance of the changes being made during implementation.
- When the changes have been fully implemented, client personnel have the knowledge and ability to adequately maintain and operate such systems as may be involved.[2]

Through the observance of these standards and guidelines, the auditor is capable of conducting management service activities without impairing independence in the performance of the audit. However, professional judgment is always involved, and critics continue to recommend a complete separation of the attest function and the practice of management service.

INDEPENDENCE AND WRITE-UP WORK

Public accounting firms are often asked to provide accounting services that may include the journalization of transactions, posting from books of original entry, and preparation of financial statements. These requests come from small businesses that do not have employees with adequate accounting skills. If the client is also an audit client, there exists the possibility of loss of independence on the part of the auditor. The profession is concerned with the potential conflict that might result from this dual role, since the auditor prepares and processes financial information and then must audit the same data.

Again, the AICPA recognizes the potential loss of independence by the auditor or the public's loss of confidence in the auditor in this situation and has

---

[2] *Statements on Management Advisory Service* (New York: AICPA, 1972), p. 25.

Figure 3-1

65
The code
of professional
ethics

Management advisory services practice standards

- *Personal characteristics:*   In performing management advisory service, a practitioner must act with integrity and objectivity and be independent in mental attitude.
- *Competence:*   Engagements are to be performed by practitioners having competence in the analytical approach and process and in the technical subject matter under consideration.
- *Due care:*   Due professional care is to be exercised in the performance of a management advisory services engagement.
- *Client benefit:*   Before accepting an engagement, a practitioner is to notify the client of any reservations he has regarding anticipated benefits.
- *Understanding with client:*   Before undertaking an engagement, a practitioner is to inform his client of all significant matters related to the engagement.
- *Planning, supervision, and control:*   Engagements are to be adequately planned, supervised, and controlled.
- *Sufficient relevant data:*   Sufficient relevant data is to be obtained, documented, and evaluated in developing conclusions and recommendations.
- *Communication of results:*   All significant matters relating to the results of the engagement are to be communicated to the client.

concluded that the performance of accounting services or write-up work should have no effect on the subsequent audit of this work. However, public accountants performing such services for an audit client must meet the following requirements:

- The CPA must not have any relationship or combination of relationships with the client or any conflict of interest which would impair his integrity and objectivity.
- The client must accept the responsibility for the financial statements as his own. A small client may not have anyone in his employ to maintain accounting records and may rely on the CPA for this purpose. Nevertheless, the client must be sufficiently knowledgeable of the enterprise's activities and financial condition and the applicable accounting principles so that he can reasonably accept such responsibility, including, specifically, fairness of valuation and presentation and adequacy of disclosure. When necessary, the CPA must discuss accounting matters with the client to be sure the client has the required degree of understanding.
- The CPA must not assume the role of employee or of management conducting the operations of an enterprise. For example, the CPA shall not consummate transactions, have custody of assets, or exercise authority on behalf of the client. The client must prepare the source documents on all transactions in sufficient detail to identify clearly the nature and amount of such transactions and maintain an accounting control over data processed by the CPA such as control totals and document counts. The CPA should not make changes in such basic data without the concurrence of the client.
- The CPA, in making an examination of financial statements prepared from books and records which he has maintained completely or in part, must conform to generally accepted auditing standards.

66
**The code
of professional
ethics**

· The fact that he has processed or maintained certain records does not eliminate the need to make sufficient audit tests.[3]

The last point emphasizes the difference between the public accountant's processing of accounting data and the actual conduct of an audit, which consists of gathering evidence and evaluating that evidence under the circumstances. An audit is not precluded by the auditor's performance of write-up work.

MONITORING INDEPENDENCE

In Chapter 2, it was stated that *SAS No. 4* was issued by the AICPA to "set forth certain considerations in establishing policies and procedures that provide the firm with reasonable assurance of conforming with generally accepted auditing standards." The first element of quality control discussed in that statement was:

● INDEPENDENCE: Policies and procedures should be established to provide reasonable assurance that persons at all organizational levels maintain independence in fact and in appearance.[4]

The public accounting firm must design a quality control system which is effective in communicating the importance of independence and whether or not employees and partners are following policies established by the AICPA, as well as additional internal policies. The statement promulgated by the AICPA presented examples of policies and procedures that may be adopted by a firm. These include:

· Maintaining records showing which partners or employees were previously employed by clients.
· Maintaining records showing which partners or employees have relatives holding key positions with clients.
· Notifying personnel as to the names of audit clients and their affiliates.
· Confirming periodically with personnel that prohibited relationships do not exist.
· Emphasizing independence of mental attitude in training programs and in supervision and review work.

LACK OF INDEPENDENCE AND REPORT MODIFICATION

An independent auditor who is in violation of Rule 101 is precluded from issuing an unqualified opinion, even if a comprehensive audit has been conducted. Recall that the second standard of generally accepted auditing standards requires that an auditor be independent. Thus, even though an audit is performed, it is impossible for an auditor to achieve generally accepted auditing standards. Any audit procedures that may have been performed are of dubious value if the

---

[3] *Code of Professional Ethics* (New York: AICPA, 1972), pp. 31–32. Copyright © 1972 by the American Institute of Certified Public Accountants, Inc.

[4] "Quality Control Considerations for a Firm of Independent Auditors," *Statement on Auditing Standards No. 4* (New York: AICPA, 1974), p. 2.

auditor lacks independence. This situation requires a modification of the auditor's report by the issuance of a disclaimer of opinion. The AICPA recommends the following wording for the report:

> We are not independent with respect to the Green Valley Company, and the accompanying balance sheet as of December 31, 19xx, and the related statements of income and retained earnings and changes in financial position for the year then ended were not audited by us; accordingly, we do not express an opinion on them.

In addition, each page of the financial statements is clearly and conspicuously marked, ''Unaudited—see accompanying disclaimer of opinion.'' Alternatively, the disclaimer may appear directly on the financial statements.

When preparing the disclaimer of opinion, reference is made only to the lack of independence and not to the specific reason that impaired independence. If such a reason were stated, it might encourage the user of the statement to make a personal judgment as to whether the reason was adequate justification for a disclaimer. In a similar manner, audit procedures employed by the auditor are not to be listed in the report in order to prevent the users from surmising that a partial audit was employed which may lend some credence to the financial information being reported. However, if the auditor is aware of deficiencies in the financial statements, he or she insists upon appropriate revision. If the client refuses, these deficiencies are clearly explained in the auditor's disclaimer.

COMPETENCE AND TECHNICAL STANDARDS

The next major section of the code of ethics consists of four rules of conduct concerned with the competency of the auditor and the designation of technical standards to be observed by the independent auditor.

COMPETENCY

● RULE 201—GENERAL STANDARDS: A member shall comply with the following general standards as interpreted by bodies designated by Council, and must justify any departures therefrom.

a. **Professional competence.** A member shall undertake only those engagements which he or his firm can reasonably expect to complete with professional competence.

b. **Due professional care.** A member shall exercise due professional care in the performance of an engagement.

c. **Planning and supervision.** A member shall adequately plan and supervise an engagement.

d. **Sufficient relevant data.** A member shall obtain sufficient relevant data to afford a reasonable basis for conclusions or recommendations in relation to an engagement.

e. **Forecasts.** A member shall not permit his name to be used in conjunction with any forecast of future transactions in a manner which may lead to the belief that the member vouches for the achievability of the forecast. (AICPA)

68
The code
of professional
ethics

A public accountant who renders a service to a client is of course expected to be capable of performing the assignment. The first standard of generally accepted auditing standards requires that the public accountant be trained and proficient as an auditor. Earlier in this book the standard was discussed, but the discussion focused on the general auditing expertise required. Many clients' operations are highly technical and complex. Before an auditor can form an opinion on the financial statements it is necessary for him or her to understand the operations of the business in sufficient detail to determine the impact of these technicalities on the statements. For example, if a client's operations are highly computerized, it is unlikely that a public accounting firm that has had little experience in computer systems could perform adequately; therefore a firm of auditors carefully investigates a prospective client to determine if it is reasonable to expect completion of the task in a competent manner.

Rule 201 does not imply that an accounting firm must possess absolute knowledge before the acceptance of an engagement. The acceptance of a client, knowing that additional research or consultation with others may be necessary before completion of the engagement, does not represent a lack of competence. Some accounting firms have implemented this approach when one of their long-time clients decides to "go public." Going public means a privately owned company decides to sell its privately held securities to the public. Such a decision may require the company to file with the SEC, which means the independent auditor must become familiar with SEC accounting procedures. Rather than lose this client to an accounting firm that is heavily involved in SEC practice, some small firms retain a large accounting firm on a consultant basis.

During an audit engagement, the auditor may encounter a situation in which the auditor or any member of the staff does not have a certain specialized knowledge or skill. Furthermore, it is likely that this expertise may not be possessed by specialists in other accounting firms. In this case, the auditor may have to use the work of a specialist in the evaluation and collection of evidence. These specialists may be geologists, engineers, actuaries, or others whose expertise is needed before an auditor can form an opinion on the financial statement. In 1975, the AICPA promulgated *SAS No. 11* as a guide to provide direction for auditors who must use the work of specialists. In that statement, the following examples were described to illustrate situations in which the auditor might have to use the work of a specialist.

- Valuation (e.g., works of art, special drugs, and restricted securities).
- Determination of physical characteristics relating to quantity on hand or condition (e.g., mineral reserves or materials stored in piles above ground).
- Determination of amounts derived by using specialized techniques or methods (e.g., actuarial determinations).
- Interpretation of technical requirements, regulations, or agreements (e.g., the potential significance of contracts or other legal documents, or legal title to property).[5]

---

[5] "Using the Work of Specialists," *Statement on Auditing Standards No. 11* (New York: AICPA, 1975), p. 2.

Rule 201 was modified in 1978. Prior to 1978, the rule encompassed only professional competence. This new modification broadened the rule to include due professional care, planning and supervision, and sufficient relevant data. The Institute felt that Rule 201 should be broadened so as to recognize a need for a comprehensive statement of general standards that would apply to performance of engagements in all areas of practice. Up to this point there had been some confusion by the piecemeal development of various standards of general application for each of the areas of an accounting practice.

In addition the restriction on forecasts was incorporated in this rule (Rule 204 had originally dealt with forecasting). Forecasted financial information is an integral part of financial reporting. Since the information is predictive, many external users pressured the public accounting profession to accept a stronger role in this area. The SEC at one point was on the verge of requiring forecasted information be made public under certain conditions. Because of numerous potential problems, the SEC, at the present time, has decided not to require forecasted data.

This rule does not suggest that an auditor cannot assist a client in the preparation of forecasts. However, when the auditor's name is associated with a forecast, full disclosure must be made of (1) the sources of information used, (2) the major assumptions made in the preparation of the statements and analyses, (3) the character of the work performed by the auditor, and (4) the degree of the responsibility taken by the auditor.[6]

TECHNICAL STANDARDS—AUDITING

● RULE 202—AUDITING STANDARDS: A member shall not permit his name to be associated with financial statements in such a manner as to imply that he is acting as an independent public accountant unless he has complied with the applicable generally accepted auditing standards promulgated by the Institute. *Statements on Auditing Standards* issued by the Institute's Auditing Standards Executive Committee are, for purposes of this rule, considered to be interpretations of the generally accepted auditing standards, and departures from such statements must be justified by those who do not follow them. (AICPA)

Prior to the revision of the code in 1973, there was no clear reference to generally accepted auditing standards. As suggested earlier in this book, generally accepted auditing standards are broad guidelines that must be followed in the conduct of an audit. With Rule 202, it was made apparent that a violation of these standards was a breach of the code of ethics. Furthermore, the rule recognizes the need to interpret these broad standards by issuing statements on auditing standards. The AICPA issues audit guides for specific industries when audit procedures peculiar to that industry are to be followed. However, these guides are not covered by Rule 202. As suggested in the previous chapter, each

[6] Op. cit., *Code of Professional Ethics*, p. 34.

industry guide warns that those who depart from the suggested procedures may be called upon to justify such departures.

● RULE 203—ACCOUNTING PRINCIPLES: A member shall not express an opinion that financial statements are presented in conformity with generally accepted accounting principles if such statements contain any departure from an accounting principle promulgated by the body designated by Council to establish such principles which has a material effect on the statements taken as a whole, unless the member can demonstrate that due to unusual circumstances the financial statements would otherwise have been misleading. In such cases his report must describe the departure, the approximate effects thereof, if practicable, and the reasons why compliance with the principle would result in a misleading statement. (AICPA)

The code of ethics would be violated if an auditor expressed an unqualified opinion on the financial statements when the statements were not prepared in accordance with generally accepted accounting principles. The council of the AICPA on May 7, 1973, designated the FASB as the body to establish accounting principles. This resolution was reproduced in Chapter 2. Rule 203 provides some flexibility in the observance of accounting principles by allowing a departure from generally accepted accounting principles if literal application of accounting rules results in misleading financial statements. Such a departure requires that the auditor note in the audit report the nature of the departure, describing fully the impact on the financial statements and the reason for noncompliance. The auditor must use professional judgment to determine if blind adherence to accounting rules results in meaningless information. In the vast majority of situations, the observance of generally accepted accounting principles results in meaningful data. Two events which may suggest a departure are new legislation or the evolution of a new form of business transaction.[7] Most auditors are very reluctant to suggest a unique accounting principles application, which results in very few practical examples of departures from generally accepted accounting principles.

However, there are numerous examples of financial statements being prepared not in accordance with generally accepted accounting principles but in accordance with principles unique to an industry. The Auditing Standards Executive Committee has issued *SAS No. 14,* "Special Reports," which deals in part with financial statements prepared in accordance with a comprehensive basis of accounting other than general accounting principles. The audit report is modified under these circumstances to alert the user to its uniqueness. This topic is explored in Chapter 18.

● RULE 204—OTHER TECHNICAL STANDARDS: A member shall comply with other technical standards promulgated by bodies desig-

---

[7] Ibid.

nated by Council to establish such standards, and departures there-from must be justified by those who do not follow them. (AICPA)

71
**The code
of professional
ethics**

As stated earlier, Rule 204 had originally dealt with forecasted data. The new Rule 204 was adopted to provide an opportunity for the AICPA's Council to designate at some future date that the Management Advisory Services Committee and the Federal Taxation Executive Committee would be subject to Rule 204 as well as Rule 201.

RESPONSIBILITIES TO CLIENTS

It is usually emphasized that the public accountant's primary concern should be with the user of the financial statements. This is as it should be, but does not suggest that the auditor does not have some responsibility to the client.

Confidentiality

● RULE 301—CONFIDENTIAL CLIENT INFORMATION: A member shall not disclose any confidential information obtained in the course of a professional engagement except with the consent of the client.

This rule shall not be construed (a) to relieve a member of his obligation under Rules 202 and 203, (b) to affect in any way his compliance with a validly issued subpoena or summons enforceable by order of a court, (c) to prohibit review of a member's professional practices as a part of voluntary quality review under institute authorization or (d) to preclude a member from responding to any inquiry made by the ethics division or Trial Board of the Institute, by a duly constituted investigative or disciplinary body of a state CPA society, or under state statutes.

Members of the ethics division and Trial Board of the Institute and professional practice reviewers under Institute authorization shall not disclose any confidential client information which comes to their attention from members in disciplinary proceedings or otherwise in carrying out their official responsibilities. However, this prohibition shall not restrict the exchange of information with an aforementioned duly constituted investigative or disciplinary body. (AICPA)

During the course of an engagement, an auditor has access to information that the client expects to be held in a confidential manner. Therefore it is reasonable for the rules of conduct to prohibit the disclosure of confidential information. Only if a client can expect the auditor to respect this confidentiality will a client grant the auditor access to sensitive files and reports. For example, the client expects executive payroll information to be held in confidence by the auditor. This also includes procedures that limit access to the audit work papers once they are stored at the conclusion of an audit.

The principle of confidentiality is not absolute, and Rule 301 identifies four exceptions. Two of the exceptions need further analysis. The need for silence does not apply when it infringes upon the auditor's reporting obligation to third

72
**The code
of professional
ethics**

parties. The client cannot restrict the scope of the audit in a manner that violates generally accepted auditing standards and then prohibit the auditor from disclosing this deficiency based on the confidentiality principle. Likewise, if the financial statements are not prepared in accordance with generally accepted accounting principles, a client cannot prohibit appropriate disclosure by the auditor. Generally, when the choice between service to the client or service to the financial statement user must be made, the auditor usually rules in favor of the user.

Unlike that of the medical doctor or the lawyer, privileged communication between the client and the public accountant is not recognized in a court of law. Thus, if a court so desires, it can force the auditor to testify in a case involving a client. The auditor's only alternative is to invoke the Fifth Amendment to the Constitution. A few states have passed legislation that recognizes privileged communication between the client and the auditor, but these states are exceptions.

● (RULE 302—CONTINGENT FEES:) Professional services shall not be offered or rendered under an arrangement whereby no fee will be charged unless a specified finding or result is attained, or where the fee is otherwise contingent upon the findings or results of such services. However, a member's fees may vary depending, for example, on the complexity of the service rendered.

Fees are not regarded as being contingent if fixed by courts or other public authorities or, in tax matters, if determined based on the results of judicial proceedings or the findings of governmental agencies. (AICPA)

Since the client hires and pays the independent auditor, the AICPA recognizes the need to control the method of determining the amount of the fee. Rule 302 explicitly prohibits fees that are subject to the findings of the audit or contingent on some event or the results of the audit. If, for example, the fee of the auditor is contingent upon the net proceeds of a bond offering, the pressure on the auditor to maintain independence would be significant. For this reason, the engagement fee is determined partly by the number of hours required to perform the audit, the type of personnel needed for the audit, and the complexity of the job. The auditor is not prohibited from accepting an engagement in which the fee is to be determined by a court of law or in a quasi-judicial proceeding. In this case the potential for independence impairment is removed.

RESPONSIBILITIES TO COLLEAGUES

The fourth major section of the rules of conduct refers to the relationship among members of the public accounting profession. In general, the objective of the rules relating to colleague responsibility is to promote cooperation and good relations among fellow auditors in order to advance the general good of the profession.

Encroachment

- RULE 401—ENCROACHMENT: A member shall not endeavor to provide a person or entity with a professional service which is currently provided by another public accountant except:

   1. He may respond to a request for a proposal to render services and may furnish service to those who request it. However, if an audit client of another independent public accountant requests a member to provide professional advice on accounting or auditing matters in connection with an expression of opinion on financial statements, the member must first consult with the other accountant to ascertain that the member is aware of all the available relevant facts.

   2. Where a member is required to express an opinion on combined or consolidated financial statements which include a subsidiary, branch or other component audited by another independent public accountant, he may insist on auditing any such component which in his judgment is necessary to warrant the expression of his opinion.

   A member who receives an engagement for services by referral from another public accountant shall not accept the client's request to extend his service beyond the specific engagement without first notifying the referring accountant, nor shall he seek to obtain any additional engagement from the client. (AICPA)*

As in any profession there are pressures to acquire new clients. The purpose of the encroachment rule is to prohibit the pirating of clients by a public accounting firm. Such activity fosters resentment within the profession and lessens the likelihood of fraternal cooperation among members of the profession. Rule 401 does not allow an auditor to offer services currently being performed by another auditor.

Because of the possibility of violating the constraint of trade laws, as well as for the general benefit of the public, there are two broad exceptions to the basic principles suggested in Rule 401. First, a client has the right to request the services of another public accountant if the client is dissatisfied with its current auditor. In this case, the prospective auditor is expected to consult with the previous auditor to determine the circumstances under which the change of auditor has taken place. Additional rules have been adopted by the profession to implement this idea. Basically, the profession recognizes the need of the client to select freely the auditor of its choice, but this must be balanced against the possibility of a client "shopping for accounting principles." There are cases in which a client contacts numerous accounting firms until a firm is found that is willing to issue an unqualified opinion in the area of disagreement between the client and the original auditor. When there is a change in principal auditors, the SEC requires that the client notify the SEC through the filing of Form 8-K stating the reason for the change. In addition, the former auditor is requested to furnish a letter to the SEC stating whether the firm agrees or disagrees with the client's statement in Form 8-K.

---

* On March 31, 1979, Rule 401 was repealed.

74
**The code
of professional
ethics**

The AICPA has issued *SAS No. 7* which deals with a change in auditors. The basic purpose of the statement is to provide guidance for communication between predecessor and successor auditors when a change of auditors has taken place or is in process. Unfortunately, the statement does not require disclosure of the reason for the change in auditors to the public. The guidance deals for the most part with the approach to be taken by the prospective or successor auditor. The statement suggests that the successor auditor attempt the following:

- Request the client to authorize the predecessor auditor to respond fully to the successor auditor's inquiries [to avoid a violation of Rule 301].
- Determine whether the reason for the proposed change in auditors is due to a disagreement on auditing standards or procedures.
- Determine whether the reason for the proposed change in auditors is due to a disagreement on accounting principles.
- Determine facts that might bear on the integrity of management.[8]

The second exception to the general rule of encroachment is concerned with the audit of a client composed of business segments. In the audit of many large organizations, more than one accounting firm is involved in the engagement. Due to the Continental Vending case, which is discussed in Chapter 4, Rule 401 was adopted to allow the principal accounting firm to insist upon auditing components of the organization where circumstances suggest such a request is appropriate. However, the auditor can not insist upon auditing an unreasonably large part of the components if such a request might suggest that the principal accounting firm was interested primarily in earning a larger professional fee.

In the final part of Rule 401, the auditor is encouraged to consult with other practitioners who possess specialized skills. It is recognized that an auditor is permitted to solicit the assistance of another accounting firm on a consultation basis or for a limited engagement without fear of losing the entire engagement to the other accounting firm. Such a rule encourages dialogue among firms and in general increases the quality of services rendered to clients.

Offers of employment: Prior to 1978, the Code of Ethics (Rule 402) prohibited a member from making a direct or indirect offer of employment to an employee of another public accountant on the CPA's behalf or that of the CPA's client without first informing the other public accountant. In 1978 Rule 402 was repealed so that it is no longer a violation of the Code of Ethics to make such an offer.

OTHER RESPONSIBILITIES AND PRACTICES
The fifth and final section of the rules of conduct consists of a variety of topics with the overall objective being to enhance the stature of the profession. The first four rules in this area suggest certain behavior that should be practiced by public accountants. The final rule listed in the other responsibilities and practices area refers to the form of organization that a firm can take.

---

[8] "Communications Between Predecessor and Successor Auditors," *Statement on Auditing Standards No. 7* (New York: AICPA, 1975), pp. 2–3.

DISCREDITABLE ACTS

● RULE 501—ACTS DISCREDITABLE: A member shall not commit an act discreditable to the profession. (AICPA)

Rule 501 is basic to ethical conduct and only through observance of this rule can the profession expect to win public respect and confidence. An individual auditor has the obligation to conduct his or her business and personal affairs in a manner that enhances the reputation of the profession as well as the individual. Members of the general public will, in part, formulate an opinion of the entire profession based upon the actions of the few auditors with whom they have personal contact. It is, therefore, necessary for each auditor to recognize his role as representative of the entire profession.

What constitutes an act discreditable to the profession is, of course, highly subjective. In the previous code of ethics, Rule 2.02, there was a list of acts that were considered discreditable. This list dealt with only technical standards and not with general moral conduct. In the revised code these technical standards are discussed in detail under Rules 202 and 203 and there is no attempt to be specific as to what constitutes a discreditable act. Auditors who are convicted in court of law for fraudulent or criminal deeds are obviously in violation of this rule of conduct. Other questionable action by a public accountant is to be ruled upon by the AICPA's Trial Board, which will be discussed later in this chapter.

● RULE 502—ADVERTISING OR OTHER FORMS OF SOLICITATION: A member shall not seek to obtain clients by advertising or other forms of solicitation in a manner that is false, misleading or deceptive. (AICPA)

Prior to 1978 Rule 502 expressly prohibited the obtaining of clients through solicitation and advertising. Due to recent court decisions concerning such prohibitions in other professions and pressure from the Justice Department, Rule 502 was drastically modified to allow advertising that is not "false, misleading or deceptive." To guide the practitioner in the application of this new rule, the AICPA has issued four interpretations of Rule 502. These are presented below.

● INTERPRETATION 502-1—INFORMATIONAL ADVERTISING: Advertising that is informative and objective is permitted. Such advertising should be in good taste and be professionally dignified. There are no restrictions on the type of advertising or media, frequency of placement, size, art work or type of style. Some examples of informative and objective content are:

1. Information about the member and the member's firm such as:

   a. Name, addresses, telephone numbers, number of partners, shareholders or employees, office hours, foreign language competence and date the firm was established.

76
**The code
of professional
ethics**

    b. Services offered and fees for such services, including hourly rates and fixed fees.

    c. Educational and professional attainments, including date and place of certification, schools attended, dates of graduation, degrees received and memberships in professional associations.

2. Statements of policy or position made by a member or a member's firm related to the practice of public accounting or addressed to a subject of public interest. (AICPA)

● INTERPRETATION 502-2—FALSE, MISLEADING OR DECEPTIVE ACTS: Advertising or other forms of solicitation that are false, misleading, or deceptive are not in the public interest and are prohibited. Such activities include those that:

1. Create false or unjustified expectations of favorable results;

2. Imply the ability to influence any court, tribunal, regulatory agency or similar body or official;

3. Consist of statements that are self-laudatory which are not based on verifiable facts;

4. Make incomplete comparisons with other CPAs;

5. Contain testimonials or endorsements;

6. Contain any other representations that would be likely to cause a reasonable person to misunderstand or be deceived. (AICPA)

● INTERPRETATION 502-3—OTHER FORMS OF SOLICITATION: CPAs may engage in a variety of activities to enhance their reputations and professional stature with the objective of expanding their clientele. Such indirect forms of solicitation, which include giving speeches, conducting seminars, distributing professional literature and writing articles and books, are considered to be in the public interest and are permitted. However, a direct uninvited approach by a member seeking to render services to a specific potential client is prohibited because such activity tends to promote exaggerated and unsupported claims and the use of misleading and deceptive sales techniques. Such approaches are not susceptible to monitoring, verification or control by the profession. (AICPA)

● INTERPRETATION 502-4—SELF-DESIGNATION AS EXPERT OR SPECIALIST: Claiming to be an expert or specialist is prohibited because an AICPA program with methods for recognizing competence in specialized fields has not been developed and self-designations would be likely to cause misunderstanding or deception. A member or a member's firm may indicate the services offered but may not state that the practice is limited to one or more types of service. (AICPA)

Prior to 1972, the AICPA considered competitive bidding a form of solicitation, thus prohibiting such activity. Action in court brought by the U.S. Justice Department has resulted in the removal of the rule prohibiting competitive bidding from the code of ethics. While the AICPA can no longer prevent competitive bidding, many state boards of accounting have retained such a rule and at least one state attorney general has stated that the rule will be enforced.

● RULE 503—COMMISSIONS: A member shall not pay a commission to obtain a client, nor shall he accept a commission for a referral to a client of products or services of others. This rule shall not prohibit payments for the purchase of an accounting practice or retirement payments to individuals formerly engaged in the practice of public accounting or payments to their heirs or estates. (AICPA)

As discussed above, Rule 502 prohibits an auditor from soliciting clients. Rule 503 prohibits the indirect soliciting of clients by a public accounting firm by the payment of a commission to someone who might make such a referral. For example, an accounting firm cannot have an arrangement with a local bank whereby the bank refers prospective clients to the firm for a fee. The bank can, of course, recommend the services of an auditor to a client if that recommendation is based solely on the professional reputation of the public accounting firm.

● RULE 504—INCOMPATIBLE OCCUPATIONS: A member who is engaged in the practice of public accounting shall not concurrently engage in any business or occupation which would create a conflict of interest in rendering professional services. (AICPA)

An auditor must not be engaged in another occupation which impairs the auditor's independence as it relates to audit clients. Such a relationship raises questions about whether or not the auditor can objectively review the financial statements of a client. If an auditor were to simultaneously operate a public accounting practice and an investment counselor service, the potential for impairment of independence would exist. During the course of the year the auditor might make certain investment recommendations that are subject to review at the end of the year. If the investments were not sound, the auditor might be reluctant to propose to management a write down of the investment.

● RULE 505—FORM OF PRACTICE AND NAME: A member may practice public accounting, whether as an owner or employee, only in the form of a proprietorship, a partnership or a professional corporation whose characteristics conform to resolutions of Council. (See Chapter 1).
A member shall not practice under a firm name which includes any fictitious name, indicates specialization or is misleading as to the type of organization (proprietorship, partnership or corporation).

78
**The code
of professional
ethics**

However, names of one or more past partners or shareholders may be included in the firm name of a successor partnership or corporation. Also, a partner surviving the death or withdrawal of all other partners may continue to practice under the partnership name for up to two years after becoming a sole practitioner.

A firm may not designate itself as "Members of the American Institute of Certified Public Accountants" unless all of its partners or shareholders are members of the Institute. (AICPA)

In Chapter 1, the organizational forms allowable under the code of ethics were discussed. As mentioned at that point, the formation of professional corporations is a recent addition to the form of practice allowed.

Enforcing professional ethics

The focus of this chapter has been a discussion of the AICPA Professional Code. In addition, many state societies of CPAs and state boards of accountancy have adopted their own codes of ethics, although many provisions of the AICPA code are incorporated into the state codes. This three-tier structure in the public accounting profession does not facilitate the enforcement of a professional code of ethics.

The AICPA is a voluntary organization; therefore only auditors who are members are governed by its rules of conduct. The enforcement of the AICPA's code of ethics rests with its trial board which may, after a hearing, admonish, suspend, or expel a member who is found guilty of a violation of the code of ethics. Many CPAs are members of the AICPA but are not engaged in the practice of public accounting; nonetheless, such a member must observe Rules 102 and 501 of the rules of conduct. If a member is suspended or expelled from the AICPA, it does not mean that he or she cannot practice as a public accountant. Since the AICPA has no legislative authority to license public accountants, disciplinary action results only in the personal embarrassment of a member and damage to the professional reputation of the accountant or firm. The state society of CPAs enforcement mechanism works in much the same manner as the AICPA's mechanism.

The real disciplinary power in the public accounting profession rests with the state boards of accountancy. These boards are licensed by each state and have the power to regulate the profession within a particular state. These boards have the power to revoke, either temporarily or permanently, a CPA license or CPA certificate, which means the individual cannot practice as a CPA in that state.

Many public accountants are concerned with the current enforcement mechanism and the overall results of the profession's compliance with the code of ethics. First, there are instances in which an auditor has been tried by the AICPA, the state society of CPAs, and the state board of accountancy, with different results as to guilt and the nature of punishment. Furthermore, there seems to be a lack of initiative on the part of all three bodies to investigate potential violations brought to their attention. Much of the action taken by these groups occurs after an individual has been convicted in a court of law. If a profession adopts a code of ethics with the stated objective of holding its members to a performance standard greater than that imposed by society's laws, then this lack of action by the profession makes such an objective seem hollow indeed. It should be noted that those who criticize the profession are not irresponsible dissidents. For example, the following statement was made by a former president of the AICPA:

> In my view, there is an absence of spirited enforcement of the Code of Professional Ethics throughout the profession as a whole. If such a condition were allowed to continue, the result could be gradual loss of the privilege of self-discipline without our realizing it.[9]

SEC and ethics

The SEC has relied upon the public accounting profession to establish rules of conduct for ethical behavior. This basic philosophy was illustrated in the SEC's Rule 2-01(a) of Regulation S-X which states:

> (a) The Commission will not recognize any person as a certified public accountant who is not duly registered and in good standing as such under the laws of the place of his residence or principal office. The Commission will not recognize any person as a public accountant who is not in good standing and entitled to practice as such under laws of the place of his residence or principal office.

Although the SEC has not adopted a code of ethics, this rule indirectly incorporates the rules of conduct of a particular state in which the auditor resides. If the auditor has been suspended from practice for a violation of the state's code of ethics, the auditor will be prohibited from practicing before the SEC.

While the SEC has not adopted a code of ethics, it has been very active in making pronouncements concerning the auditor's independence. The following is a continuance of Rule 2-01 of Regulation S-X:

> (b) The Commission will not recognize any certified public accountant or public accountant as independent who is not in fact independent. For example, an accountant will be considered not independent with respect to any person or any of its parents, its subsidiaries, or other affiliates (1) in which during the period of his professional engagement to examine the financial statements being reported on or at the date of his report, he or his firm or a member thereof had, or was committed to acquire, any direct financial interest or any material indirect financial interest; or (2) with which, during the period of his professional engagement to examine the financial statements being reported on, at the date of his report or during the period covered by the financial statements, he or his firm or a member thereof was connected as a promoter, underwriter, voting trustee, director, or employee, except that a firm will not be deemed not independent in regard to a particular person if a former officer or employee of such person is employed by the firm and such individual has completely disassociated himself from the person and its affiliates and does not participate in auditing

[9] *CPA Letter,* February 1971, p. 2.

80
**The code
of professional
ethics**

financial statements of the person or its affiliates covering any period of his employment by the person. For the purposes of Rule 2-01 the term "member" means all partners in the firm and all professional employees participating in the audit or located in an office of the firm participating in a significant portion of the audit.

(c) In determining whether an accountant may in fact be not independent with respect to a particular person, the Commission will give appropriate consideration to all relevant circumstances including evidence bearing on all relationships between the accountant and that person or any affiliate thereof, and will not confine itself to the relationships existing in connection with the filing of reports with the Commission.

In addition to the basic rules established in Regulation S-X, the SEC has ruled on whether an auditor was independent in a specific case in several *Accounting Series Releases*. These rulings are consistent with the basic philosophy of the AICPA's professional code of ethics, with one basic exception. The SEC believes that an auditor cannot be independent when he or she performs write-up work and subsequently audits the financial statements. The AICPA insists that no loss of independence occurs under these circumstances. There are those who offer arguments to support both the commission's and the institute's point of view; however, the AICPA's rule is probably one of necessity, since many of its members work for small accounting firms where performing such a bookkeeping service is a vital part of the professional practice.

CONCLUDING REMARKS

The public accounting profession is aware of its unique position in society. In recognizing its responsibility to society, the profession has established a code of ethics and an enforcement mechanism. This establishment of rules of professional conduct and vigorous enforcement of these rules is a critical part of the overall integrity of the auditor's role in society. Maintenance of this integrity is the responsibility of every member of the profession, as well as the institutions that collectively represent them.

APPENDIX: SUMMARY OF AICPA'S STATEMENTS ON RESPONSIBILITIES IN TAX PRACTICE

Statement on Responsibilities in Tax Practice	
No. 1. *Signature of Preparer*	A CPA should sign as preparer any federal tax return which requires the signature of a preparer if he prepares it for and transmits it to the taxpayer or another, whether or not the return was prepared for compensation.
No. 2. *Signature of Reviewer: Assumption of Preparer's Responsibility*	If the CPA is not the preparer of a federal tax return, she is not required to sign the preparer's declaration. However, at her discretion, the CPA may sign the declaration on a return prepared by the taxpayer or another if she reviews the return and, in the course of the review, acquires knowledge with respect to the return substantially equivalent to that which she would have acquired

had she prepared the return. Unless such review is made, the CPA should not sign the preparer's declaration.

No. 3. *Answers to Questions on Returns*

A CPA should sign the preparer's declaration on a federal tax return only if he is satisfied that reasonable effort has been made to provide appropriate answers to the questions on the return which are applicable to the taxpayer. Where such a question is left unanswered the reason for such omission should be stated. The possibility that an answer to a question might prove disadvantageous to the taxpayer does not justify omitting an answer or a statement of the reason for such omission.

No. 4. *Recognition of Administrative Proceeding of a Prior Year*

The selection of the treatment of an item in the course of the preparation of a tax return should be based upon the facts and the rules as they are evaluated at the time the return is prepared. Unless the taxpayer is bound as to treatment in the later year, such as by a closing agreement, the disposition of an item as a part of concluding an administrative proceeding by the execution of a waiver for a prior year does not govern the taxpayer in selecting the treatment of a similar item in a later year's return. Therefore, if justified by the facts and rules then applicable, a CPA may sign the preparer's declaration on a return containing a departure from the treatment of an item arrived at as a part of concluding an administrative proceeding regarding a prior year's return. Such departure need not be disclosed.

No. 5. *Use of Estimates*

A CPA may prepare tax returns involving the use of estimates if such use is generally acceptable or, under the circumstances, it is impracticable to obtain exact data. When estimates are used, they should be presented in such a manner as to avoid the implication of greater accuracy than exists. The CPA should be satisfied that estimated amounts are not unreasonable under the circumstances.

No. 6. *Knowledge of Error: Return Preparation*

A. A CPA shall advise her client promptly upon learning of an error in a previously filed return, or upon learning of a client's failure to file a required return. Her advice should include a recommendation of the measures to be taken. Such advice may be given orally. The CPA is neither obligated to inform the IRS nor may she do so without her client's permission.

B. If the CPA is requested to prepare the current year's return and the client has not taken appropriate action to rectify an error in a prior year's return that has resulted or may result in a material understatement of tax liability, the CPA should consider whether to proceed with the preparation of the current year's return. If he does prepare such return, he should take

82
**The code
of professional
ethics**

reasonable steps to assure himself that the error is not repeated. Furthermore, inconsistent double deductions, carryovers, and similar items associated with the uncorrected prior error should not be allowed to reduce the tax liability for the current year except as specifically permitted by the Internal Revenue code, regulations, IRS pronouncements, and court decisions.

C. Paragraph B is concerned only with errors that have resulted or may result in a material understatement of the tax liability. Moreover, that paragraph does not apply where a method of accounting is continued under circumstances believed to require the permission of the Commissioner of Internal Revenue to effect a change in the manner of reporting the item involved.

No. 7. Knowledge of Error: Administrative Proceedings

When the CPA is representing a client in an administrative proceeding with respect to a return in which there is an error known to the CPA that has resulted or may result in a material understatement of tax liability, she should request the client's agreement to disclose the error to the IRS. Lacking such agreement, the CPA may be under a duty to withdraw from the engagement.

No. 8. Advice to Clients

In providing tax advice to his client, the CPA must use judgment to ensure that his advice reflects professional competence and appropriately serves the client's needs. No standard format or guidelines can be established to cover all situations and circumstances involving written or oral advice by the CPA.

The CPA may communicate with his client when subsequent developments affect advice previously provided in respect to significant matters. However, he cannot be expected to have assumed responsibility for initiating such communication except while he is assisting a client in implementing procedures or plans associated with the advice provided. Of course, the CPA may undertake this obligation by specific agreement with his client.

No. 9. Certain Procedural Aspects of Preparing Returns

In preparing a return, the CPA ordinarily may rely on information furnished by her client. She is not required to examine or review documents or other evidence supporting the client's information in order to sign the preparer's declaration. Although the examination of supporting data is not required, the CPA should encourage her client to provide her with supporting data where appropriate.

The CPA should make use of her client's returns for prior years whenever feasible.

The CPA cannot ignore the implications of information known by her and, accordingly, she is required to make reasonable inquiries where the information as presented appears to be incorrect or incomplete.

If a CPA prepares a federal return, she should sign it without modifying the preparer's declaration.

No. 10. *Positions Contrary to Treasury Department or IRS Interpretations of the Internal Revenue Code*

In preparing a tax return a CPA may take a position contrary to Treasury Department or IRS interpretations of the Internal Revenue code without disclosure, if there is reasonable support for the position.

In preparing a tax return a CPA may take a position contrary to a specific section of the Internal Revenue code where there is reasonable support for the position. In such a rare situation, the CPA should disclose the treatment in the tax return.

In no event may a CPA take a position that lacks reasonable support, even when this position is disclosed in a return.

EXERCISES AND PROBLEMS

3-1. What is the purpose of a code of professional ethics?

3-2. Differentiate between independence in fact and independence in appearance. Give an example of each.

3-3. Can an auditor be independent if he or she performs management advisory service work for a client?

3-4. Define "write-up work." Why is a question of independence involved?

3-5. What is the purpose of Rule 203 of the AICPA code of professional ethics?

3-6. On June 30, 1979, Bob Jones was hired as a staff accountant by the firm of Ajax and Brown. Jones had been controller of Yodel Corporation for two years at the time he was hired by Ajax and Brown. If Ajax and Brown audits the Yodel Corporation, a calendar-year company, for 1979, should Jones be assigned to the engagement?

3-7. Contrast the issue of privileged communication between an auditor and a client with that between a medical doctor and a patient.

3-8. Should privileged communication between an auditor and client be protected?

3-9. Why is a contingent fee prohibited?

3-10. Comment on the following statement made by a young accountant:

> If an auditor cannot solicit business or advertise in any manner, how can I possibly build my practice?

3-11. The following cases relate to the CPA's management of his or her accounting practice.

Case 1. Tom Jencks, CPA, conducts a public accounting practice. Jencks and Harold Swann, a non-CPA, organized Electro-Data Corporation to specialize in computerized bookkeeping services. Jencks and Swann each supplied 50 percent of Electro-Data's

84
The code
of professional
ethics

capital, and each holds 50 percent of the capital stock. Swann is the salaried general manager of Electro-Data. Jencks is affiliated with the corporation only as a stockholder; he receives no salary and does not participate in day-to-day management. However, he has transferred all his bookkeeping accounts to the corporation and recommends its services whenever possible.

Required: Organizing your presentation around Jencks' involvement with Electro-Data Corporation, discuss the propriety of:
  1. A CPA's participation in an enterprise offering computerized bookkeeping services
  2. The use of advertising by an enterprise in which a CPA holds an interest
  3. A CPA's transfer of bookkeeping accounts to a service company
  4. A CPA's recommendation of a particular bookkeeping service company

Case 2. Judy Hanlon, CPA, has been engaged to prepare the federal income tax return for the Guild Corporation for the year ended December 31, 1979. This is Hanlon's first engagement of any kind for the Guild Corporation.

In preparing the 1979 return, Hanlon finds an error on the 1978 return. The 1978 depreciation deduction was overstated significantly—the accumulated depreciation brought forward from 1977 to 1978 was understated, and thus the 1978 base for declining balance depreciation was overstated.

Hanlon reported the error to Guild's controller, the officer responsible for tax returns. The controller said, "Let the revenue agent find the error." He further instructed Hanlon to carry forward the material overstatement of the depreciable base to the 1979 depreciation computation. The controller noted that this error also had been made in the financial records for 1978 and 1979 and offered to furnish Hanlon with a letter assuming full responsibility for this treatment.

Required
  1. Evaluate Hanlon's handling of this situation.
  2. Discuss the additional action that Hanlon should now undertake.

Case 3. Robin Browning, CPA, has examined the financial statements of the Grimm Company for several years. Grimm's president now has asked Browning to install an inventory control system for the company.

Required: Discuss the factors that Browning should consider in determining whether to accept this engagement. (AICPA Adapted)

3-12. As part of his or her relationship with a client, a CPA often is asked to prepare or review the latter's federal income tax return.

Required
  1. In each of the following independent cases:

  a. State the CPA's obligation, if any, with respect to signing the preparer's declaration on the federal income tax return.
  b. Explain or justify the position taken.

Case 1. The tax return of Rogers, Inc., was prepared by the company controller, a recognized expert in the field of taxation. The president of Rogers asks the independent CPA to review the return and sign the preparer's declaration.

Case 2. The CPA prepares the client's tax return, signs the preparer's declaration, and forwards the return to the client for signature. The client requests that the CPA prepare a revised return and sign the preparer's declaration; the revision involves certain changes which are unacceptable to the CPA.

85 Exercises and problems

Case 3. At his wife's request, the CPA prepares the tax return for his brother-in-law. The only compensation received for this engagement is reimbursement for secretarial typing services.

2. In the course of the preparation of a client's federal income tax return, it is discovered that certain data which must be included in the tax return are not available. These data can be estimated to complete the return.

    a. Explain and illustrate the circumstances under which the CPA may prepare federal tax returns involving the use of estimates.

    b. Discuss the CPA's responsibilities with respect to the manner of presentation and disclosure of estimates used in a tax return that he or she prepares.

(AICPA Adapted)

3-13. An auditor must not only appear to be independent; he or she must also be independent in fact.

Required

1. Explain the concept of an auditor's independence as it applies to third-party reliance upon financial statements.

2. a. What determines whether or not an auditor is independent in fact?

   b. What determines whether or not an auditor appears to be independent?

3. Explain how an auditor may be independent in fact but not appear to be independent.

4. Would a CPA be considered independent for an examination of the financial statements of a

    a. Church for which he is serving as treasurer without compensation? Explain.

    b. Women's club for which his wife is serving as treasurer-bookkeeper if he is not to receive a fee for the examination? Explain.

5. Write a disclaimer of opinion such as should accompany financial statements examined by a CPA who owns a material direct financial interest in his or her audit client.

(AICPA Adapted)

3-14. It has been estimated that over 80 percent of all corporations listed on the New York Stock Exchange and the American Stock Exchange are audited by the "big eight" accounting firms. Furthermore the Cohen Commission implied that the selection of an audit firm is dependent upon factors other than product differentiation. One factor suggested was described as follows in the commission's report:

> . . . audit fees are usually negotiated by financial officers of the corporation. The quality of the audit is of comparatively less concern to the financial manager. A "clean opinion" obtained from one reputable firm is about as valuable to the competent, honest financial manager as one from another reputable firm. On the other hand, a lower price—and possibly a more rapid audit—will improve the profits of the corporation and the position of the manager. Therefore, there are incentives for managers to be particularly price conscious, thus increasing the level of competition.

The possibility of price competition was alluded to in the Metcalf Report, and the following letter from a large, although not a "big eight," accounting firm, was offered as evidence to support this contention.

Salutation

It has been brought to my attention that Senator Metcalf, as chairman of the Senate Sub-Committee on Reports, Accounting, and Management, is making some sort of investigation as to the anti-competitive activities of some of the larger international accounting firms.

If such enquiry is being conducted, we would be interested in the status and would like to do whatever we can to encourage the Senator in this endeavor. We, as a firm of practicing CPAs have continually advised the accounting professions' senior bodies of our belief that the so-called "big 8" national firms were engaging in anti-competitive activities. We have accumulated some material to support our position.

Signature

Required

1. If the position taken by the CPA firm illustrated in the above letter is correct, what part, if any, of the AICPA professional code of ethics has been violated?

2. The letter refers to certain "anti-competitive activities." Can you give examples?

3. Are there reasons other than cost of the audit that may contribute to the "big eight" accounting firms' dominance of the audit of the nations' largest corporations?

4. Are there any other segments of the business community dominated by a few large firms? How does this relate to the accounting profession?

5. What is the potential danger of a small CPA firm auditing a large business enterprise?

3-15. Gilbert and Bradley formed a corporation called Financial Services, Inc., each one taking 50 percent of the authorized common stock. Gilbert is a CPA and a member of the AICPA. Bradley is a chartered property casualty underwriter. The corporation performs auditing and tax services under Gilbert's direction and insurance services under Bradley's supervision. The opening of the corporation's office was announced by a three-inch, two-column "card" in the local newspaper.

One of the corporation's first audit clients was the Grandtime Company. Grandtime had total assets of $600,000 and total liabilities of $270,000. In the course of his examination, Gilbert found that Grandtime's building with a book value of $240,000 was pledged as security for a 10-year-term note in the amount of $200,000. The client's statements did not mention that the building was pledged as security for the 10-year-term note. However, as the failure to disclose the lien did not affect either the value of the assets or the amount of the liabilities, and his examination was satisfactory in all other respects, Gilbert rendered an unqualified opinion on Grandtime's financial statements. About two months after the date of his opinion, Gilbert learned that an insurance company was planning to loan Grandtime $150,000 in the form of a first-mortgage note on the building. Realizing that the insurance company was unaware of the existing lien on the building, Gilbert had Bradley notify the insurance company of the fact that Grandtime's building was pledged as security for the term note.

Shortly after the events described above, Gilbert was charged with a violation of professional ethics.

Required: Identify and discuss the ethical implications of those acts by Gilbert that were in violation of the AICPA code of professional ethics. (AICPA Adapted)

3-16. An auditor's report was appended to the financial statements of Worthmore, Inc. The statements consisted of a balance sheet as of November 30, 1979, and statements of income and retained earnings for the year then ending. The first two paragraphs of the report contained the wording of the standard unqualified short-form report, and a third paragraph read as follows:

> The wives of two partners of our firm owned a material investment in the outstanding common stock of Worthmore, Inc., during the fiscal year ending November 30, 1979. The aforementioned individuals disposed of their holdings of Worthmore, Inc., on December 3, 1979, in a transaction that did not result in a profit or a loss. This information is included in our report in order to comply with certain disclosure requirements of the Code of Professional Ethics of the American Institute of Certified Public Accountants.
>
> Bell & Davis
> Certified Public Accountants.

Required

1. Was the CPA firm of Bell & Davis independent with respect to the fiscal 1979 examination of Worthmore, Inc.'s financial statements? Explain.

2. Do you find Bell & Davis' auditor's report satisfactory? Explain.

3. Assume that no member of Bell & Davis or any member of their families held any financial interests in Worthmore, Inc., during 1979. For each of the following cases, indicate if independence would be lacking on behalf of Bell & Davis, assuming that Worthmore, Inc., is a profit-seeking enterprise. In each case, explain why independence would or would not be lacking.

   a. Two directors of Worthmore, Inc., became partners in the CPA firm of Bell & Davis on July 1, 1979, resigning their directorships on that date.
   b. During 1979 the former controller of Worthmore, now a Bell & Davis partner, was frequently called on for assistance by Worthmore. He made decisions for Worthmore's management regarding fixed-asset acquisitions and the company's product marketing mix. In addition, he conducted a computer feasibility study for Worthmore. (AICPA Adapted)

3-17. Shortly before the due date Daniel Burr requested that you prepare the 1978 federal income tax return for Burr Corporation, a small closely held service corporation that he controlled. Burr placed a package on your desk and said, "Here is all the information you need. I'll pay you $300 if you prepare the return in time for filing by the deadline with no extension—and if the tax liability is less than $2000 I'll increase your fee to $500." The package contained the corporation's bank statements and paid checks, prior years' tax returns prepared on the accrual basis, and other financial and tax information. The account books were not included, because they were not posted up-to-date.

You found that deposits shown on the bank statements substantially exceeded Burr's sales figure, and that the expenses listed seemed rather large in relation to sales. Burr explained that he made several loans to the corporation during the year and that expenses just seemed to "mount up."

Required

1. What ethical issues should you consider before deciding whether or not you should prepare the federal income tax return for Burr Corporation?

   a. If you prepare this return, must you sign it? Explain.
   b. If you sign the return, what does your signature imply?

88
**The code
of professional
ethics**

2. Assume that you prepared the corporation's federal income tax return. Shortly thereafter Burr comes to your office and requests that you prepare financial statements for the corporation solely from the data on the federal income tax return you prepared. The statements are to be submitted to a creditor. Discuss the ethical implications of your preparing the financial statements on:

a. Your stationery
b. Plain paper

(AICPA Adapted)

3-18. Fowler and Fowler, CPAs, is an accounting firm located in a mid-Atlantic state. The firm was started several years ago and slowly grew to include 6 partners and about 12 other staff members by 1975.

About four years ago, in 1975, new management took over a large local bank, and shortly after that switched from an international firm to F & F for the conduct of the annual audit. Over the last few years the bank president has repeatedly complemented the local CPA firm for performing an outstanding job. The bank has such confidence in F & F that it has sent many businesses to the local firm for audit work or other accounting services. A loan officer for the bank sums up the bank's attitude toward the accounting firm with the following statement: "When I see a clean opinion from F & F on one of our client's financial statements I know that client is doing well."

The relationship with the bank has had a significant impact on F & F. By 1979, the firm's billings more than tripled. New clients, of which 90 percent were initially referred to the firm by the bank, have accounted for almost all of the growth. The firm admitted 3 staff accountants to the partnership in 1979, and the staff now numbers 20 professional members. The firm has decided to expand its office space by building a new professional building in which it will occupy about 40 percent of the space and lease the remainder to other tenants. One possible tenant is a new branch of the bank. Eventually, probably no less than three years, the managing partner of F & F believes that the firm will need the entire building to accommodate the firm's growth.

F & F realizes the importance of the bank in its future. The executive committee of the accounting firm has met on several occasions to discuss the benefits and the danger of such a relationship. At a recent meeting it was noted that all the partners and several of the staff members have a home mortgage or a car loan or both with the bank. In addition, one of the partners noted that the audit fee for the bank in 1979 was not significantly greater than the 1975 fee. Also, it was noted that the bank had itself grown in the past four years and was making quite a name for itself as a dynamic financial and community leader. At this point another partner stated that a review of the working paper revealed several new audit problems in the 1979 bank audit but was unable to verify the effects on the number of hours required in the current year.

One of the new partners of the firm then raised the possibility that they were losing control of the firm and their own destiny. Furthermore, she suggested that they invite a professor from a local university to study the problem from an objective point of view and advise the firm as to what strategy should be adopted.

Required

1. Assume you have been selected to evaluate the situation. Relying upon your knowledge of professional standards, include the code of professional ethics in identifying real and potential violations of these standards.

2. Based on your analysis in part 1, make suggestions as to how Fowler and Fowler should resolve its problem(s).

3-19. You were engaged to examine Barnes Corporation's financial statements for the year just ended. The CPA firm previously engaged declined to make the examination because a daughter of one of its partners received a material amount of Barnes Corporation common stock in exchange for engineering services rendered to the corporation. The partner in the CPA firm advises his daughter in business affairs but does not own an interest in her engineering firm and has not participated in the examination in past years. Another of the CPA firm's 15 partners would have been in charge of this engagement.

This new client wants to receive three different reports from you. In the past the stockholders have considered and discussed the corporation's annual report containing the financial statements and the auditor's opinion at their annual meeting. Because of the shortage of time before the stockholders meeting, corporation executives are willing to accept (1) your report containing unaudited statements to be used for the meeting and (2) your final report after the examination is complete. Thereafter the client would like to receive (3) a report containing a forecast of the corporation's 1978–1980 operations.

Required

1. Should the CPA firm previously engaged by Barnes corporation have declined the examination of the financial statements for the year just ended? Discuss the ethical issues involved.

2. Discuss the issues in the client's request that you render unaudited financial statements prior to rendering your final report.

3. What are the issues for a CPA in rendering a report containing a forecast of a client's future operations? Discuss. (AICPA Adapted)

3-20. Lakeview Development Corporation was formed on January 2, 1979, to develop a vacation-recreation area upon land purchased the same day by the corporation for $100,000. The corporation also purchased for $40,000 an adjacent tract of land which the corporation plans to subdivide into 50 building lots. When the area is developed, the lots are expected to sell for $10,000 each.

The corporation borrowed a substantial portion of its funds from a bank and gave a mortgage on the land. A mortgage covenant requires that the corporation furnish quarterly financial statements.

The quarterly financial statements prepared at March 31 and June 30 by the corporation's bookkeeper were unacceptable to the bank officials. The corporation's president now offers you the engagement of preparing unaudited quarterly financial statements. Because of limited funds your fee would be paid in Lakeview Development Corporation common stock rather than in cash. The stock would be repurchased by the corporation when funds become available. You would not receive enough stock to be a major stockholder.

Required

1. Discuss the ethical implications of your accepting the engagement and the reporting requirements which are applicable if you do accept it.

2. Assume that you accept the engagement to prepare the September 30 statements. What disclosures, if any, would you make of your prospective ownership of corporation stock in the quarterly financial statements?

3. The president insists that you present the 50 building lots at their expected sales price of $500,000 in the September 30 unaudited statements as was done in prior statements. The write-up was credited to contributed capital. How would you respond to the president's request?

4. The corporation elected to close its fiscal year on September 30, 1979, and you are requested to prepare the corporation's federal income tax return. Discuss the implication of signing the return and the disclosure of your stock ownership in Lakeview Corporation (disregard the write-up of the land).

90
**The code
of professional
ethics**

5. Assume that you accept the engagement to prepare the tax return. In the course of collecting information for the preparation of the return, you find that the corporation's president paid the entire cost of a family vacation from corporate funds and listed the expense as travel and entertainment. You ascertain that the corporation's board of directors would not consider the cost of the vacation as either additional compensation or a gift to the president if the facts were known. What disclosure would you make on (a) the tax return and (b) the financial statements?

6. After accepting your unaudited September 30 financial statements, the bank notified the corporation that the December 31 financial statements must be accompanied by a CPA's opinion. You were asked to conduct the audit and told that your fee would be paid in cash. Discuss the ethical implications of accepting the engagement.

(AICPA Adapted)

3-21. *Part A*. During 1979 your client, Nuesel Corporation, requested that you conduct a feasibility study to advise management of the best way the corporation can utilize EDP equipment and which computer, if any, best meets its requirements. You are technically competent in this area and accept the engagement. Upon completion of your study the corporation accepts your suggestions and installs the computer and related equipment that you recommended.

Required

1. Discuss the effect the acceptance of this management services engagement would have upon your independence in expressing an opinion on the financial statements of Nuesel Corporation.

2. Instead of accepting the engagement, assume that you recommended Ike Mackey, of the CPA firm of Brown and Mackey, who is qualified in specialized services. Upon completion of the engagement your client requests that Mackey's partner, John Brown, perform services in other areas. Should Brown accept the engagement? Discuss.

3. A local printer of data processing forms customarily offers a commission for recommending him as supplier. The client is aware of the commission offer and suggests that Mackey accept it. Would it be proper for Mackey to accept the commission with the client's approval? Discuss.

Part B. Your CPA firm decides to form a partnership with Fred Reitz, a non-CPA management consultant, which would result in a mixed partnership of a CPA and a non-CPA.

Required: Under what circumstances, if any, would it be ethically proper for a CPA to form a mixed partnership? Discuss.

Part C. Alex Pratt, a retired partner of your CPA firm, has just been appointed to the board of directors of Palmer Corporation, your firm's client. Pratt is also a member of your firm's income tax committee which meets monthly to discuss income tax problems of the partnership's clients. The partnership pays Pratt $100 for each committee meeting he attends and a monthly retirement benefit of $1000.

Required: Discuss the effect of Pratt's appointment to the board of directors of Palmer Corporation on your partnership's independence in expressing an opinion on the Palmer Corporation's financial statements. (AICPA Adapted)

3-22. *Part A*. At the beginning of your examination of the financial statements of the Efel Insurance Company, the president of the company requested that in the interest of efficiency you coordinate your audit procedures with the audit being conducted by the state insurance examiners for the same fiscal year. The state examiners audited the asset accounts of the company, while you audited the accounts for liabilities, stockholders' equity, income, and expenses. In addition you obtained confirmations of the accounts receivable and were satisfied with the results of your audit tests. Although you had no supervisory control over the state examiners, they allowed you to review and prepare extracts from their work papers and report. After reviewing the state examiners' work papers and report to your complete satisfaction, you are now preparing your short-form report.

Required: What effect, if any, do the above circumstances have on your short-form report? Discuss.

Part B. During your annual audit of the Cook Manufacturing Company your assistant reports to you that, although a number of entries were made during the year in the general ledger account, "notes payable to officers," he has decided that it is not necessary to audit the account because it had a zero balance at year end.

Required: Do you agree with your assistant's decision? Discuss.

Part C. Assume that you examined the financial statements of the Nelson Company in accordance with generally accepted auditing standards and were satisfied with your findings.

Required: Would the fact that the company had a loan (of substantial amount to the Nelson Company) payable to a loan company of which your brother was principal stockholder have any effect on your auditor's opinion? Discuss.

Part D. Your son, aged 16, owns 100 shares of the 50,000 shares of the Nelson Company common stock outstanding at the balance sheet date.

Required: Would this fact have any effect on your auditor's opinion? Discuss.

(AICPA Adapted)

3-23. Hobbs and Able, a public accounting firm, audits the financial statements of Barrow Corporation. Jane Carnes, of H & A, is the audit manager in charge of the Barrow engagement and has just completed her review of the audit working papers. At this point Carnes forwards the working papers to Rick Snow, a tax partner in the firm, for a review of the tax return and the working papers.

A few days later Snow sends a memo to Carnes suggesting there are some tax problems and asks that she, Snow, and the controller of Barrow meet in his office to discuss the matter. Carnes makes the arrangement, and the three meet.

During the meeting Snow points out that he is concerned with three items appearing on the return that may result in a future tax assessment by the IRS. These items concern: (1) the possible disallowance of interest paid on the basis that it was incurred to finance the purchase of tax-exempt securities, (2) the classification of gains as capital gains rather than ordinary gains, and (3) the payment of excessive salaries to officers of Barrow Corporation.

The problem is not confined to the current year. There are similar problems in at least two of the previous tax returns filed by Barrow Corporation, although neither have resulted in deficiencies since they have not been reviewed by the IRS.

After a lengthy discussion of the matter by all three, Carnes states that there must be an increase in the tax liability for the current balance sheet, but she is willing to classify

92
**The code
of professional
ethics**

the additional amount as noncurrent, since it is probably not payable within the next 12 months. Carnes believes that the new accrual must include the tax impact of the disallowed deductions plus an estimate of interest and penalties that might be charged.

At this point the controller of Barrow asks Snow to state his professional opinion as to the outcome of the matter. Snow concludes that he is reasonably certain that Barrow may have to pay "some" additional assessment. However, he states that he has carefully reviewed several recent cases and that there have emerged conflicting federal court decisions on the matter. Snow believes the client has a fairly strong case and advocates that the tax return not be revised. He also notes that, even if a revenue agent determines a deficiency, on the average, the federal government is usually willing to settle for 30 to 50 percent of the original assessment if the area is a controversial area.

The controller asks Snow if the following schedule is reasonable as to the possibility of an additional tax assessment:

ADDITIONAL ASSESSMENT	PROBABILITY OF ASSESSMENT	EXPECTED VALUE
0	.40	0
$ 500,000	.30	$150,000
700,000	.25	175,000
1,000,000	.05	50,000
		$375,000

Snow, after studying the schedule carefully, states that he in general agrees with the analysis.

The controller notes that Carnes had just proposed an accrual in excess of $1 million and makes the following comment:

> How can you two people, who work for the same firm, come up with totally different proposals? One wants to revise the financial statements, and the other wants to submit the tax return as originally prepared. One wants to set up an accrual in excess of $1 million, and the other one's analysis suggests an expected value of $375,000.

Required

1. Is it possible that the CPA firm will lose its independence in the above situation?
2. Why are the two proposals inconsistent?
3. Do you think the CPA firm could sign the tax return if they had prepared it originally?
4. How should this situation be reflected in the financial statements?
5. What type of auditor's report should be issued assuming the client follows the recommendation proposed in part 4?

3-24. The attribute of independence has been traditionally associated with the CPA's function of auditing and expressing opinions on financial statements.

Required

1. What is meant by "independence" as applied to the CPA's function of auditing and expressing opinions on financial statements? Discuss.
2. CPA's have imposed upon themselves certain rules of professional conduct that induce their members to remain independent and to strengthen public confidence in their independence. Which of the rules of professional conduct are concerned with the CPA's independence? Discuss.
3. The Wallydrag Company is indebted to a CPA for unpaid fees and has offered to

issue to him unsecured interest-bearing notes. Would the CPA's acceptance of these notes have any bearing upon his independence in his relations with the Wallydrag Company? Discuss.

93
Exercises and problems

4. The Rocky Hill Corporation was formed on October 1, 1978, and its fiscal year will end on September 30, 1979. You audited the corporation's opening balance sheet and rendered an unqualified opinion on it.

5. A month after rendering your report you are offered a position as secretary of the company because of the need for a complete set of officers and for convenience in signing various documents. You will have no financial interest in the company through stock ownership or otherwise, will receive no salary, will not keep the books, and will not have any influence on its financial matters other than occasional advice on income tax matters and similar advice normally given a client by a CPA.

   a. Assume that you accept the offer but plan to resign from the position prior to conducting your annual audit with the intention of again assuming the office after rendering an opinion on the statements. Can you render an independent opinion on the financial statements? Discuss.
   b. Assume that you accept the offer on a temporary basis until the corporation has gotten under way and can employ a secretary. In any event you plan to resign from the position permanently before conducting your annual audit. Can you render an independent opinion on the financial statements? Discuss.

(AICPA Adapted)

3-25. CPAs have imposed upon themselves a rigorous code of professional ethics.

Required

1. Discuss the underlying reasons why the accounting profession has adopted a code of professional ethics.

2. The CPA's code of professional ethics prohibits the direct or indirect offer of employment by a CPA to an employee of another CPA without first informing the latter.

   a. What are the justifications for this rule?
   b. What action, if any, may the employee of a CPA take should she learn that another CPA firm has an open position for which she would like to apply?

3. A rule of professional ethics adopted by CPAs is that a CPA shall not be an officer, director, stockholder, representative, or agent of any corporation engaged in the practice of public accounting. List the arguments supporting this rule that a CPA firm cannot be a corporation.

(AICPA Adapted)

3-26. *Part A.* You are approached by the president of the Hopewell Manufacturing Company to audit the company's financial statements. You have no knowledge of the company other than that it is medium-sized.

Required

1. From an ethical standpoint, what should you learn about Hopewell before you agree to accept the engagement? Discuss. (Since you have not yet been engaged, do not discuss the auditor's survey of the company's systems to determine audit programs.)

2. If you find that the Hopewell Company has been the client of another CPA, is it ethically proper for you to discuss with the president the possibility of becoming the company's CPA? Discuss.

Part B. Without prejudice to your answers to part A, assume that you have accepted the engagement. You determine that this is Hopewell's first audit and that, in past periods,

94
**The code
of professional
ethics**

unaudited statements had been submitted to a local bank that is granting a substantial line of credit to the company.

The prior periods' unaudited statements had reported fixed assets at an appraised amount with a corresponding credit to an appraisal capital account. The financial statements on which you rendered your short-form report state the fixed assets at cost, make no reference to the appraisal values, and exclude the appraisal capital account. You expressed an unqualified opinion in your report.

After your report is submitted to the bank president, he advises your client that the line of credit will be reduced substantially if your report is submitted to the bank's board of directors, because the net worth of the company in the financial statements in your report does not warrant the present line of credit. The bank president returns your report to the client and suggests that the financial statements be revised.

Your client confronts you with this situation and insists that you revise the financial statements in your report so that the line of credit will not be reduced.

Required

1. What possible courses of action are open to you so that the line of credit will not be reduced? Discuss.

2. Under what conditions, if any, may the client submit additional financial statements prepared on the same basis as the prior year statements to supplement your report? Discuss.

3. Would it be proper for the CPA to prepare and to label these additional statements "Prepared without audit"? Discuss. (AICPA Adapted)

3-27. *Part A.* CPAs have adopted rules of professional conduct that prohibit them from advertising their professional attainments or services and forbid the direct or indirect solicitation of clients.

Required

1. Discuss the reasons supporting the rule against advertising.

2. After a newly established CPA has undertaken public practice, by what ethical means can he or she obtain new clients?

Part B. Competitive bidding by CPAs for an auditing engagement is generally held to be unethical.

Required

1. List the arguments for the belief that competitive bidding by CPAs for an auditing engagement is unethical.

2. Discuss what indication of fees, if any, a CPA should give to a government body seeking an estimate of the cost of an auditing engagement in the following situations:

   a. Before the CPA is engaged for the audit
   b. After the CPA is engaged for the audit (AICPA Adapted)

3-28. As a CPA you have been asked to examine and give your opinion on *pro forma* financial statements of a client.

Required

1. Define *pro forma* financial statements.

2. List and briefly discuss the conditions necessary for giving an opinion on *pro forma* financial statements. (AICPA Adapted)

3-29. Bird and Moore, a firm of CPAs, has been contacted by Dole Manufacturing Company. Dole was organized four years ago by a group of engineers to manufacture a variety of items for coal mining companies. These items consist mostly of small items, such as mining struts, that are produced and sold in large numbers. The business has grown rapidly mainly because of the company's production of quality items and its rapid completion and delivery of parts. Relationships with its customers are excellent.

For the most part the accounting records of the company have been prepared by the wife of one of the founding engineers who had a bookkeeping course in high school. The accounting system is, for the most part, a cash system. Although the company is growing rapidly, profits do not seem to be growing. Management believes that this may be due to (1) the use of the cash basis system, (2) little physical control over inventory, (3) no system for determining the total cost of producing an item, or (4) lost production due to inventory shortages.

In an attempt to gain control of the production process, the president of Dole Manufacturing asked Bird and Moore to buy a computer for them and install the best possible cost accounting system. Bird and Moore are informed that no one in the company knows anything about accounting, so they have a free hand to design, test, and operate the system. Finally, the president of Dole states, "Our company has no intention of hiring a large accounting staff, since we believe your accounting firm can function as our controller and probably save us money."

Required
1. Assuming the accounting firm has the necessary expertise, may they accept this management services engagement?
2. Prepare an outline of comments that should be made to Dole Manufacturing by the CPA firm.

3-30. Sharon Miller, managing partner of Miller and Todd, CPAs, is concerned that the firm is not growing. She strongly believes that a modest growth rate will allow the firm to hire new junior accountants and eventually move these people into management positions with the firm. The vitality of the firm is dependent upon such strategy, and she has stated so in the firm's meeting of partners.

At the last partners' meeting one of the other partners expressed the same feeling about growth as Miller has often expressed and suggested that the firm consider buying or merging with other firms in the area or in adjacent states. This partner believes there are several small firms that would like very much to be associated with Miller and Todd because of its outstanding reputation and quality clients. All partners agreed to think about the strategy and be prepared to discuss the approach seriously at the next partners' meeting.

Miller does not like the general idea of growth through acquisition. For the next two weeks she begins to develop an alternative strategy. At the partners' meeting she explains the strategy. She believes that there is and will continue to be a considerable amount of audit work with government agencies and institutions that obtain government grants at the federal, state, and local level. She has talked to several public officials, and this has been confirmed. At this point she details her proposal as follows:

I have talked with two auditors who are managers with large accounting firms and have extensive experience in this area. They are both very interested in a partnership offer and an opportunity to build a competent team of auditors for our firm.

In our newsletter we will devote the next three issues to our intention to be involved in this new area. Instead of sending the letter to our present clientele, we will send it to companies that we know are involved in government contracts. Also, this material will be sent to government agencies with a personal cover letter from me.

I will contact several accounting firms in our immediate area and in the state capital and explain that our new expertise is available to them or their clients.

96
The code
of professional
ethics

I have obtained a list of government agencies that request proposals before awarding contracts for accounting services. I plan to send them a letter stating our interest. I am sure that at a later date we will be asked to submit bids for the engagements.

Required

1. Why do you believe Miller is opposed to growth through acquisition?
2. Comment on Miller's general strategy for growth.
3. Comment on each specific part of Miller's strategy as it relates to professional standards.

MULTIPLE CHOICE

1. Fenn & Company, CPAs, has time available on a computer which it uses primarily for its own internal record keeping. Aware that the computer facilities of Delta Equipment Company, one of Fenn's audit clients, are inadequate for the company needs, Fenn offers to maintain on its computer certain routine accounting records for Delta. If Delta were to accept the offer and Fenn were to continue to function as independent auditor for Delta, then Fenn would be in violation of

a. SEC, but not AICPA, provisions pertaining to auditors' independence.
b. both SEC and AICPA provisions pertaining to auditors' independence.
c. AICPA, but not SEC, provisions pertaining to auditors' independence.
d. neither AICPA nor SEC provisions pertaining to auditors' independence.

2. In which one of the following situations is a CPA required to sign a federal tax return?

a. The CPA types a return from a draft submitted by his client.
b. The CPA prepares a return for a local civic organization for no fee.
c. The CPA prepares a capital gains schedule and sends it to his or her client for inclusion in the tax return the client is preparing.
d. The CPA reviews the client-prepared tax return before it is filed to determine the adequacy of the provision for income taxes in his or her audit of the client's financial statements.

3. The CPA firm of Lincoln, Johnson & Grant is the auditor for the Union Corporation. Mr. Lee, president of Union Corporation, has asked the firm to perform management advisory services in the area of inventory management. Lee believes the procedures in this area are inefficient. Considering the dual engagement of the regular audit and the management services assignment, which of the following functions could impair the CPA firm's independence?

a. Identify the inventory management problem as caused by the procedures presently operative in the purchasing, receiving, storage, and issuance operations.
b. Study and evaluate the inventory management problem and suggest several alternative solutions.
c. Develop a time schedule for implementation of the solution adopted by Lee, to be carried out and supervised by Union Corporation personnel.
d. Supervise management of purchasing, receiving, storage, and issuance operations.

4. Marquis, CPA, occasionally undertakes management advisory services engagements, although his practice deals primarily with auditing services. The Keller Corporation has recently asked Marquis to make a study of the company's executive compensation

package. Marquis has no prior experience in this area. What would be the most appropriate course of action for Marquis to follow?

   a. Decline the engagement because he cannot expect to complete it without undertaking research in the area.

   b. Accept the engagement and issue a report which may lead to the belief that he vouches for the achievability of the results indicated by the recommended actions.

   c. Accept the engagement and research, study, or consult with knowledgeable experts in order to increase his competence.

   d. Accept the engagement and perform it in accordance with generally accepted auditing standards.

5. Under the AICPA code of professional ethics, the CPA is allowed to

   a. include the wording "Income tax returns prepared" on the door of his or her office.

   b. include the word "Consultant" on his business card.

   c. use his or her CPA title when engaged in sales promotion.

   d. imprint his or her firm's name on newsletters not prepared by it.

(AICPA Adapted)

CHAPTER 4

Legal liability

The public accountant plays a vital role in society. Society recognizes this role and attempts to influence it in a manner that will provide the greatest benefits for the general public. The three previous chapters were devoted to the rules and procedures adopted and administered by the profession. Such internal policing or self-regulation is an important segment of the overall control mechanism, but society would neither condone nor benefit from such a completely closed system. Thus an open system in the audit function is maintained by exposing the auditor to potential legal liability.

Prior to the mid-1960s, the number of legal suits brought against public accountants was not large. Since then, legal liability cases have become numerous, and the general topic is of primary concern to the profession. The auditor is by no means the only professional to experience an increase in the number of legal suits. The role and performance in society of all the major professions are being scrutinized and, with the increasing wave of consumerism in the United States, there is no reason to believe the trend will subside. Recent court cases have had a profound impact upon the technical rules of the profession as well as the general way in which a public accounting firm conducts its practice. It would, however, be erroneous to suggest that the comments in this chapter are absolute. Current court cases yet to be resolved and future court cases are reminders that the auditor's legal liability is still an evolving concept.

The general framework for determining the auditor's legal responsibilities is based upon two main factors. First, the legal exposure of the auditor is in part determined by the relationship of the auditor and the other party. Normally, relationships are classified as those existing between the auditor and the client and those existing between the auditor and so-called third parties. There are also other relationships, as defined by the court, which are important in determining the extent of the auditor's legal liability. Finally, the appropriate body of law that is applicable to a particular relationship is of prime importance when

98

assessing the public accountant's legal responsibilities. Specifically, the auditor must know whether common law or federal law governs a relationship.

COMMON LAW LIABILITY

The public accountant's legal responsibilities to clients and third parties may be based on common law. *Common law* is applicable to relationships not specifically defined by statutory law or administrative regulations.

Common law liability to clients

The legal relationship between an auditor and a client casts the auditor in the role of an independent contractor. The duties and responsibilities of an independent contractor differ from those of an agent or employee in that the independent contractor's performance of work is not controlled by the other party (the client). In addition, there is a contractual relationship between the public accountant and the client. These two elements form the basis for determining the legal responsibility of the auditor to the client. The basic duty of the public accountant in the realm of the attest function is to perform an engagement with due professional care.

The legal liability of the auditor to the client usually rests upon determination of whether the auditor conducted the audit in a negligent manner. Ordinary negligence implies that the auditor has failed to exercise the degree of care that a reasonable person would exercise under the circumstances. The client must prove that the auditor's action was the cause of the client's financial loss. What constitutes ordinary negligence is of course subjective and must be determined in a court of law based on the merits of the case. In general, the auditor who accepts an audit engagement is expected to have and be capable of employing the special skills and judgment usually possessed by members of the public accounting profession. In part, this recognized level of performance is mandated through issuance of AICPA pronouncements such as generally accepted auditing standards, *Statements on Auditing Standards,* and industry guides. These promulgations are usually quite broad, thus requiring expert testimony in a court case to determine whether the recognized standards of the profession have been observed.

The main defense of the auditor rests upon his or her ability to prove that professional standards and procedures dictated by the circumstances were properly employed. This defense relies heavily on adequate documentation found in the auditor's working papers. Basically the work papers must demonstrate that (1) the engagement was planned and the work of assistants was supervised and reviewed, (2) the client's internal control system was reviewed and evaluated, which was the basis for determining the extent of subsequent audit procedures, and (3) sufficient competent evidential matter was obtained to provide a basis for the auditor's opinion on the financial statements.

In addition to the above defense, the auditor's legal responsibility to a client is restricted in other ways. The auditor's performance cannot be expected to be infallible, and for this reason, in the absence of negligence, bad faith, or dishonesty, he or she is not responsible for losses suffered by a client as a result of mere errors in judgment. Also, the auditor may use the defense of contributory negligence. Generally, the client is not allowed to recover damages from the auditor if it can be proven by the auditor that the client was also negligent and that this negligence, at least in part, contributed to the client's financial loss.

DISCOVERY OF FRAUD

Most legal cases involving public accountants and clients are concerned with the discovery of fraud perpetrated by a client's employee. Generally, the public believes that an audit is conducted, at least in part, to determine whether fraud exists; however, the objective of an audit is actually to render an opinion on the financial statements. The AICPA's position on fraud detection is clear, based upon the statement:

> . . . under generally accepted auditing standards the independent auditor has the responsibility, within the inherent limitations of the audit process, to plan his or her examination to search for errors or irregularities that would have a material effect on the financial statements . . .[1]

The auditor who fails to detect fraud that would have been discovered had auditing standards been followed is held responsible for damages suffered by the client. The fraud must be material in relation to the financial statements.

During the course of an engagement, an auditor may suspect that fraud exists. In such circumstances, he or she must determine the potential impact of the fraud on the financial statements. If the auditor believes that the fraud is immaterial, he or she should refer the matter to the appropriate client personnel. If the auditor concludes that the fraud is potentially material, he or she should consult with the appropriate representatives of the client. At this point, the auditors may agree to investigate the fraud or to let the client conduct the investigation. If the latter course of action is selected, the auditor should review the approach and the findings of the client's investigation.

The above discussion assumes that nonmanagement personnel or low-level management personnel were involved in the fraudulent activity. If management fraud is involved, the auditor will probably have difficulty in discovering it. This is true because management can intervene in or circumvent normal internal control procedures, often without being detected by the auditor. However, the auditor should be alert to situations that may encourage management intervention in the internal control system or involvement in material transactions. He or she should consider economic factors and the business structure as well as other factors in evaluating the possibility of unwarranted management action.

The profession's position on the auditor's responsibilities in the detection of fraud is based on several considerations. The auditor cannot be held responsible for detecting immaterial fraud. Such an approach would be far too costly, and

---

[1] "The Independent Auditor's Responsibility for the Detection of Errors or Irregularities," *Statement on Auditing Standards No. 16* (New York: AICPA, 1977), p. 2.

no amount of auditing could allow the auditor to guarantee that there is an absolute absence of fraud. The client must rely upon an internal control system to minimize such fraud. Also, the auditor cannot always discover even material fraud if such fraud is so well concealed or clever that normal audit procedures would not expose it. If the public were to hold the auditor responsible for discovering such fraud, audit procedures would have to be expanded in every engagement. Even with such an approach, the auditor could not guarantee that financial statements are free of fraud. This basic philosophy was upheld recently by the Supreme Court which ruled that private investor lawsuits must be based on allegations of "intent to deceive, manipulate or defraud" on the part of the auditor.[2]

The logic of the above passage notwithstanding, there is much debate within the profession and the general financial community about the auditor's responsibility for the detection of fraud. As the audit function continues to evolve to meet the demands of society, the problems created do not have simple solutions. The profession recognizes both its need to be responsible to society as well as the need to analyze carefully the implications of the suggested changes. For this reason, the profession included this general topic on the agenda of a committee appointed by the AICPA to study the responsibilities of the auditor.[3]

Common law liability to third parties

In contemporary auditing, the legal responsibilities of the auditor as they relate to third parties is the most critical topic in the general area of legal liability. The importance of the user is demonstrated in the following statement which was issued by a special committee of the AICPA.

> The objective of financial statements is to serve primarily those users who have limited authority, ability, or resources to obtain information and who rely on financial statements as their principal source of information about an enterprise's economic activities.[4]

This recognition of the importance of the user or third-party must be balanced against the need to define the potential liability to which a public accountant may be exposed. Since the auditor cannot control distribution of the audited financial statements, it is impossible to determine the number of users who may rely on this information. Over the past several decades, common law rules have evolved from a doctrine restricting the auditor's liability to third parties to a doctrine expanding the auditor's legal liability in this area. The responsibilities continue to change, exposing the auditor to even more liability.

Initially, common law remedies available to a third party were based upon the fact that there was no contract between the third party and the auditor. Because there was no privity of contract, an aggrieved third party could not

---

[2] *Ernst and Ernst v. Hochfelder,* 44 LW 4451 (1976).

[3] *Scope and Organization of the Study of Auditors' Responsibilities* (New York: AICPA, 1975), pp. 14–16.

[4] *Objectives of Financial Statements* (New York: AICPA, 1973), p. 17.

102
**Legal
liability**

recover damages even though ordinary negligence on the part of the auditor could be proven. This meant that a third party had to prove that the auditor was guilty of fraud and that such fraud resulted in third-party losses. The auditor would have acted in a fraudulent manner if he or she had been involved in a deliberate scheme to deceive third parties. Fraud is usually much harder to prove than ordinary negligence. This basic philosophy was first affirmed in *Landell v. Lybrand* in 1919. In this case, a third party asserted that stock had been purchased after relying on audited financial statements. The Pennsylvania Supreme Court ruled that the third party could not recover damages suffered from the use of such statements based on the negligence of the auditor, since there was no contract between the plaintiff and the defendant accountant.[5]

The foundation for expanding the auditor's obligation to third parties was established in *Ultramares Corporation v. Touche*.[6] In this case, it was reaffirmed that a third party could not recover damages from an auditor unless fraud on the part of the auditor could be established. However, this case stated that a third party could recover damages if the auditor's action could be classified as gross negligence. *Gross negligence* is defined as a reckless departure from the normal standards of performance and is often referred to as constructive fraud. Thus fraud itself does not have to be proven, but rather the auditor's actions may be so reckless that constructive fraud is implied. Although the principle of gross negligence was enunciated in the Ultramares case, the auditor was not found guilty of such action. A few years later the principle of gross negligence was used as the basis for determining the guilt of the auditor in *State Street Trust Company v. Ernst*.[7] Even with incorporation of the concept of gross negligence into common law, third parties often found it difficult to recover damages from auditors.

In addition to the above concept of gross negligence, the Ultramares case established a concept that in practice expanded the legal liability of the auditor. Judge Benjamin Cardozo ruled that the auditor could be held liable to third parties based on negligence when the third party was a primary beneficiary of the audit. Under these circumstances, the audit must have been conducted for the primary benefit of a third party. For example, a bank may demand that a company present audited financial statements before a loan request can be considered. If the company identifies the bank to the auditor prior to the audit and discloses the purpose of the audit, the bank is considered a third-party beneficiary. Subsequently, the bank may recover from the auditor damages incurred as a result of relying on the audited financial statements if the auditor is negligent in performance of the audit.

The liability of the auditor to third parties continued to be expanded. In *Ryan v. Kanne,* the principle of primary benefit was relaxed. The court ruled that third parties must be identified to the auditor before the report is submitted, but that the primary purpose of the audit need not be for the benefit of third parties. The

---

[5] *Landell v. Lybrand,* 264 Pa. 406, 107 Atl. 783 (1919).
[6] *Ultramares Corporation v. Touche,* 255 N.Y. 179, 174 N.E. 441 (1931).
[7] *State Street Trust Company v. Ernst,* 278 N.Y. 104, 15 N.E. 2d 416 (1938).

auditors need only know that the audit report will be used for the benefit and guidance of a third party.[8] In another case, *Rusch Factors, Inc. v. Levin,* a similar finding was established. In this case, the court declared that an auditor could be held liable for negligence by a third party when the third party was actually foreseen.[9]

It can be seen that the original tenet of common law, which denied a third party the right to recover damages from an auditor based on negligence, has eroded. With the rise of consumerism, it is reasonable to expect that the auditor may eventually be held liable to third parties for negligence even when the third party was not known to the auditor.

FEDERAL STATUTE AND THIRD-PARTY LIABILITY

Prior to 1933, individual states had passed "blue-sky" laws intended to reduce some of the blatant abuses in the securities market. These abuses were most evident during the 1920s when such practices as issuing fraudulent financial statements or manipulating the prices of stocks were common. The stock market crash of 1929 and subsequent investigations made it obvious that some form of federal legislation was needed to monitor the sale of securities in interstate commerce. The Roosevelt administration and Congress responded with the proposal and enactment of the Securities Act of 1933 and the Securities Exchange Act of 1934. The basic philosophy of these two acts was that there should be full and fair disclosure of information. To help ensure this objective, the public accountant associated with such information could be held legally liable to third parties under certain circumstances as considered in the following discussion. Significantly, this legal exposure to third parties was based, for the most part, on negligence, unlike the more restrictive common law doctrine of gross negligence or fraud.

Securities Act of 1933

The objective of the 1933 act was to ensure that accurate and adequate information was disclosed for all new securities offered to the public for sale. This is achieved through the preparation of a registration statement and a prospectus. Much of the information contained in these two documents is attested to by the auditor, which provides a basis for the public accountant's legal liability. Section 11(a) of the act provides that suit may be brought against "every accountant, engineer, or appraiser, or any person whose profession gives authority to a statement made by him, who has with consent been named as having prepared or certified any part of the registration statement."

The auditor must consent in writing to inclusion of the audit report in the registration statement. With such consent the auditor is exposed to the following liability:

[8] *Ryan v. Kanne,* 170 N.W. 2d 395, Iowa (1969).
[9] *Rusch Factors, Inc. v. Levin,* 284 F. Supp. 85, D.C.R.I. (1968).

104
**Legal
liability**

1. Any person acquiring securities described in the Registration Statement may sue the accountant, regardless of the fact he is not the client of the accountant.
2. His claim may be based upon an alleged false statement or misleading omission in the financial statements, which constitutes his prima facie case. The plaintiff does not have the further burden of proving that the accountants were negligent or fraudulent in certifying to the financial statements involved.
3. The plaintiff does not have to prove that he relied upon the statement or that the loss which he suffered was the proximate result of the falsity or misleading character of the financial statement.
4. The accountant has thrust upon him the burden of establishing his freedom from negligence and fraud by proving that he had, after reasonable investigation, reasonable ground to believe and did believe that the financial statements which he certified were true and not only as of the date of the financial statements, but, beyond that, as of the time when the Registration Statement became effective.
5. The accountant has the burden of establishing by way of defense or in reduction of alleged damages that the loss of the plaintiff resulted in whole or in part from causes other than the false statements or the misleading omissions in the financial statements. Under the common law it would have been part of the plaintiff's affirmative case to prove that the damages which he claims he sustained were proximately caused by the negligence or fraud of the accountant.[10]

There are several points that should be noted from the above summarization. First, the auditor is liable only to those who purchased the securities, excluding the auditor's client from those who may bring suit under the statute. Significantly, the plaintiff need only prove that there were material errors or omissions in the financial statements. There is no requirement on the part of the plaintiff to prove that reliance on the financial statements was the reason for losses suffered by the third party. Finally, the plaintiff does not have to prove that the public accountant was negligent or fraudulent. Clearly, this act was inconsistent with United States legal doctrine in that much of the burden of proof was shifted from the plaintiff to the defendant.

In way of defense, the auditor has two courses of action under the act. The independent auditor must prove that the audit was not conducted in a negligent manner. The act refers to the auditor's need to conduct a reasonable investigation. The auditor's first line of defense is to produce working papers demonstrating that generally accepted auditing standards were followed. Alternatively, he or she can avoid or partially reduce the damage claim by showing that the third party did in fact rely upon information other than that contained in the audited financial statements.

It was stated earlier that the auditor is responsible for the fairness of the financial statement up to the sign-off date. The 1933 act extends this responsibility to the effective date of the registration statement. The effective date is the date when the SEC, after a staff review of the registration statement has been performed and all deficiencies have been corrected, declares that the registration

---

[10] Saul Levy, *CPA Handbook* (New York: AICPA, 1952), p. 39. Copyright © 1952 by the American Institute of Certified Public Accountants, Inc.

statement can be distributed and the securities offered for sale to the public. The act provides for a 20-day waiting period between the filing and the effective date of the statement. This period is flexible and may be accelerated or extended depending on the number of new securities being registered with the commission. Obviously, most registration statements become effective several weeks after the date of the financial statements subject to audit. For this reason, the auditor performs an *S-1 review* of the period after the balance sheet date in order to stay abreast of current developments. Suggested audit procedures to be employed in the review of significant subsequent events are discussed in *SAS No. 1*, Sections 560.10–560.12.

The Securities Exchange Act of 1934

The 1933 act was concerned for the most part with initial offerings of corporate securities. The 1934 act extended the basic philosophy adopted in the previous act to the trading of securities registered on national securities exchanges. Later the scope of the act was expanded to include the trading of securities in the over-the-counter markets. The 1934 act requires that audited financial statements be filed with the SEC.

The public accountant's legal liability as defined in Section 18 of the Securities Exchange Act of 1934 is:

> Any person who shall make or cause to be made any statement in any application, report, or document filed pursuant to this title or any rule or regulation thereunder or any undertaking contained in a registration statement as provided in subsection (d) of section 15 of this title, *which statement was at the time* and in the light of the circumstances under which it was made false or misleading with respect to any material fact, shall be liable to any person (not knowing that such statement was false or misleading) who, in reliance upon such statement, shall have purchased or sold a security at a price which was affected by such statement, *for damages caused by such reliance*, unless the person sued shall prove that he *acted in good faith* and had no knowledge that such statement was false or misleading. . . . [italics added]

The 1934 act differs significantly from the 1933 act in that it does not suggest that the liability of the auditor extends to the effective date of the filing with the SEC. Under this act, the independent auditor is liable for errors and omissions on the financial statements as of the date of those statements and for material subsequent events that occur on or prior to the sign-off date. However, the profession has adopted auditing procedures which should be followed when the auditor discovers, after the sign-off date, information that should have been disclosed on the financial statements. This topic is covered in *SAS No. 1*, Section 561, and is discussed in Chapter 17.

The 1934 act, unlike the 1933 act, shifts the burden of proof from the independent auditor to the aggrieved third party. The plaintiff must prove that "false and misleading" statements were contained in the filing and that relying upon such information was the proximate cause of losses suffered. By way of defense, the auditor may avoid liability if it can be shown that he or she "acted in good faith and had no knowledge that such statement was false or misleading." This has been interpreted to mean that the auditor, under the 1934 act, must be guilty of gross negligence or fraud for a third party to recover damages. This is consistent with the common law doctrine discussed above.

In 1942, the SEC adopted Rule 10b-5 which expanded the legal liability of the independent auditor under the 1934 act. This rule states:

It shall be unlawful for any person, directly or indirectly, by the use of any means or instrumentality of interstate commerce, or of the mails, or of any facility of any national securities exchange,

(a) to employ any device, scheme, or artifice to defraud,
(b) to make any untrue statement of a material fact or to omit to state a material fact necessary in order to make the statement made, in the light of the circumstances under which they were made, not misleading, or
(c) to engage in any act, practice, or course of business which operates or would operate as a fraud or deceit upon any person, in connection with the purchase or sale of any security.

The auditor's liability under this rule is still evolving. Until 1976, the courts appeared to be using the criteria of whether the "average prudent investor" was affected by the false or misleading statement. The legal defense to be taken by the auditor is unsettled. The auditor's proof that professional standards and procedures were followed may not always be sufficient. In March 1976, the Supreme Court's ruling in *Ernst and Ernst v. Hochfelder* significantly restricted the legal liability exposure for the auditor under Rule 10b-5. Many lower courts had suggested that proof of negligence on the part of the auditor was sufficient to recover damages. The *Hochfelder* case required that the auditor have knowledge of the fraud or participate in the fraud. The Supreme Court ruling was not welcomed by everyone. Currently, there are proposals in Congress to amend the securities laws to allow an individual to bring suit against an auditor for simple negligence when fraud is not detected by the auditor.

SIGNIFICANT LEGAL CASES

The practicing accountant can be subject to civil liability, criminal liability, or administrative sanctions imposed by the SEC. Under civil prosecution, he or she may be held liable for monetary damages suffered by third parties. Recently, the auditor's liability has been expanded to include criminal punishment, exposing the public accountant to possible incarceration. With the public concern for "white-collar crime," there seems to be no reason for this trend to subside. Finally, in the case of auditors who practice before the SEC, the commission can suspend or disbar accountants from this practice, censure a public accounting firm, or require a firm to submit to an outside review of its internal procedures and policies.

Significant court cases are discussed at this point, dividing these cases into civil suits and criminal cases. SEC sanctions are discussed later in the chapter.

Civil cases

107
Significant
legal cases

McKESSON AND ROBBINS

The securities of McKesson and Robbins were traded on the New York Stock Exchange and were registered under the Securities Act of 1934. The financial statements for 1937 were audited by a big eight accounting firm. Later investigation disclosed that of a total $87 million of assets, approximately $10 million of inventories and $9 million of accounts receivable were entirely fictitious. The fraud was perpetrated by the president of McKesson and Robbins and his three brothers. The case was litigated but was settled out of court with the payment of approximately $500,000 by the accounting firm.

Although the case set no legal precedent, it had significant impact upon the accounting profession. The SEC conducted an investigation of the case and made, among others, the recommendation that, where material, the auditors should confirm accounts receivable and observe or test-count inventory. The profession responded with the issuance of the first codified rules in auditing, *SAP No. 1,* "Extension of Auditing Procedure." This statement, which has been incorporated after subsequent modification into *SAS No. 1,* requires the observation of inventory and the confirmation of receivables. Slowly the profession saw the need to promulgate auditing standards and procedures in order to direct the work of the auditor as well as to provide a basis for the auditor's legal defense.

BARCHRIS[11]

The BarChris case was adjudicated under the Securities Act of 1933. Prior to this case, the auditor had not been exposed to a suit brought by a large group of investors. At the time of the trial, there were over 60 plaintiffs.

BarChris was in the business of constructing bowling centers. The company filed a registration statement under the 1933 act, which covered its 5½ percent subordinated debentures. The effective date of the registration statement was May 16, 1961, and it included audited financial statements for the year 1960. Prior to 1960, the industry, as well as BarChris, had witnessed dramatic growth, but the boom period was soon to end. By 1962, customers of BarChris began to fail, resulting in significant uncollectible accounts. BarChris soon followed the course of many of its customers and filed for bankruptcy in October 1962. Purchasers of the debentures filed suit against persons who signed the registration statement, the underwriters, and the auditors.

The case was not tried before a jury. The judge's decision in this case revolved around three questions raised by the court:

1. Did the registration statement contain false statements of fact, or did it omit to state facts which should have been stated in order to prevent it from being misleading?

[11] *Escott v. BarChris Construction Company,* 283 F. Supp. 643 (1968).

2. Were the facts which were falsely stated or omitted, if any, material within the meaning of the 1933 act?
3. If there were material errors or omissions, did the auditors establish their defense of due diligence in the performance of the audit?

Based on the testimony given, the court concluded that the financial statements were misleading. It was determined that a loan had been recorded as a sale, an improper amount of income had been accrued under the percentage of completed contract method, and an intercompany receivable had not been eliminated and had been included as a trade receivable. All these acts were in obvious violation of generally accepted accounting principles. In addition, the court determined that the recording of a sale-leaseback transaction was misleading. This is significant, since at the time of the transaction the profession had not established specific rules in this area. These deficiencies, as well as others, resulted in an overstatement of sales by 8 percent, an overstatement of net operating income of 16 percent, and an overstatement of current assets and an understatement of current liabilities which resulted in a current ratio of 1.6: 1 and not 1.9:1 as originally reported.

After determining that the financial statements were misleading, the court turned to the question of materiality. The judge used the 1933 act's definition, which describes materiality as those "matters that an average investor should know before . . . [making] an investment." It was concluded that the income statement did not contain material errors. Although the net operating income was overstated by 16 percent, the court ruled that the income was 256 percent of the previous year's income rather than 276 percent, but that the difference was not significant. Furthermore, earnings should have been 65¢ per share instead of 75¢ per share but, since both were double the previous year's figure, the court again reached the conclusion that the errors were not material. The accounting firm was not so fortunate when the judge studied the impact of the errors on BarChris's balance sheet. It was concluded that the current ratio was materially overstated.

Under the 1933 act, even though there were material errors and omissions in the financial statements, the auditor could avoid liability if it could be shown that the audit was performed with due diligence. It has already been stated that the auditor must conduct an S-1 review to determine whether any significant events have occurred, subsequent to the balance sheet date, which should be disclosed either by adjusting the financial statements or by adding a footnote to the financial statements. The audit firm had a standard audit program for the S-1 review, and the court believed that the program conformed to generally accepted auditing standards; however, the court concluded that the S-1 review "was useless" as applied by the senior auditor and stated:

> Accountants should not be held to a standard higher than that recognized in their profession. I do not do so here. Berardi's [the senior auditor] review did not come up to standard. He did not take some of the steps which Peat, Marwick's written program prescribed. He did not spend an adequate amount of time on a task of this

magnitude. Most important of all, he was too easily satisfied with glib answers to his inquiries.[12]

109
Significant legal cases

Thus the audit firm was found guilty, since due diligence could not be established.

The BarChris case, like many other landmark cases in auditing, had a subsequent effect on auditing procedures. In 1971, the AICPA issued *SAP No. 47* (since incorporated into *SAS No. 1,* Section 710) which dealt with audit procedures in the review of subsequent events for financial statements filed under the Securities Act of 1933.

YALE EXPRESS

Yale Express Systems, Inc., was a common carrier. In June 1964, Yale filed a Form 10-K report with the SEC which included audited financial statements for the year 1963. The consolidated net income was reported to be an amount in excess of $1 million. It was later determined that there was in fact a substantial net loss for 1963, and this fact was disclosed in the 1964 audited financial statements. Revision of the 1963 income was the result of insufficient write-offs of 1963 receivables and certain costs applicable to 1963 that had not been accrued. In May 1965, Yale was placed in reorganization proceedings under Chapter X of the Bankruptcy Act. Creditors and stockholders brought legal action against the independent audit firm, among others, for certifying false financial statements.

The case was complicated by the fact that the auditing firm was performing management advisory services for Yale. These special services had begun in the early part of 1964, and it was discovered from the investigation that the 1963 financial statements were incorrect. The plaintiff alleged that the auditing firm did not promptly notify the SEC or the public of its findings. Since the case was settled without a trial, certain allegations were never substantiated in court. Nonetheless, the case raised a fundamental audit question that had never been resolved. Does the auditor have any obligation to report or investigate information that comes to his or her attention subsequent to the date of the report when such information may have an impact on the audited financial statements? The audit firm's position was that there was no legal requirement and no professional requirement to report such information to users of the financial statements. In response to the Yale case, in 1969 the AICPA issued *SAP No. 41* (since incorporated into *SAS No. 1,* Section 561). The promulgation made it clear that the auditor does not have to continue auditing after the date of the report, but if the auditor becomes aware of information after this date, he or she must determine if it could have affected the report if it had been known at the time of the audit. If these facts are considered material, the auditor may have to prepare a revised report and inform the client that users of the financial statements must be notified. If the client refuses to take such action, the burden of notification rests with the auditor. The approach is more fully discussed in Chapter 17.

In addition to the above problem, the Yale case raised once again the possibility of conflict of interest when the public accounting firm performs

[12] Ibid.

services other than the attest service. Some suggested that the audit firm may have impaired its independence when in performing special services it found deficiencies in the accounting system and the financial statements. The obvious question that arises, which was not answered in the out-of-court settlement, is whether the accounting firm delayed reporting deficiencies to protect its reputation. The AICPA and the SEC did not perceive such a problem, or chose to ignore it.

Criminal cases

CONTINENTAL VENDING[13]

A national public accounting firm had audited the financial statements of Continental Vending Machine Corporation for the year ended September 30, 1962. The firm had also audited the corporation since 1956, and from 1958 to 1962 Continental had made substantial loans to an affiliate, Valley Commercial Corporation. The president of Continental Vending was Harold Roth, who owned 22 percent of the stock of Valley Commercial. During this period, Valley Commercial became a conduit used by Roth to channel the funds borrowed from Continental into personal stock transactions.

By the end of the 1962 fiscal year, the financial position of Continental Vending had deteriorated, resulting in a fall in the price of its stock. The SEC suspended trading of the stock, and eventually Continental Vending went into bankruptcy. A trustee was appointed who brought civil and criminal charges against Roth and two partners and a manager of the auditing firm.

The complaint against the auditors centered upon the disclosure in a footnote to the financial statements, which was referred to as the "Valley receivable." The footnote read:

> The amount receivable from Valley Commercial Corp. (an affiliate company of which Mr. Harold Roth is an officer, director, and stockholder) bears interest at 12 percent a year. Such amount, less the balance of the notes payable to that company is secured by the assignment to the company of Valley's equity in certain marketable securities. As of February 16, 1963, the amount of such equity at current market quotations exceeded the net amount receivable.[14]

It was charged that this footnote was an inadequate disclosure of the facts of the transaction and that it omitted the fact that Roth eventually received the loan to the affiliate and that the collateral, which consisted mainly of Continental Vending securities, was not adequately described. The government insisted that the footnote should have read:

> The amount receivable from Valley Commercial Corp. (an affiliated company of which Mr. Harold Roth is an officer, director, and stockholder), which bears interest

---

[13] *United States v. Simon*, 425 F. 2d 796 (1969).

[14] Denzil Y. Causey, Jr., *Duties and Liabilities of the CPA* (Austin: Bureau of Business Research, 1973), p. 239.

at 12 percent a year, was uncollectible at September 30, 1962, since Valley had loaned approximately the same amount to Mr. Roth who was unable to pay. Since that date Mr. Roth and others have pledged as security for the repayment of his obligation to Valley and its obligation to Continental (now $3,900,000 against which Continental's liability to Valley cannot be offset) securities which as of February 15, 1963, had a market value of $2,978,000. Approximately 80% of such securities are stock and convertible debentures of the Company.[15]

The revised footnote suggested by the government did not refer to the netting of the Valley receivable ($3,543,335) and the Valley payable ($1,029,475). The auditors agreed that the footnote should not have suggested the netting of the two, but they contended that the amount was immaterial. It should also be noted that the amounts were not actually netted in the balance sheet but rather shown as a separate receivable and payable. Thus the question of full disclosure revolved around the following issues:

- Roth's borrowing from the affiliate was not noted.
- There was no disclosure that 80 percent of the collateral for the Valley receivable consisted of Continental stock and debentures.
- There was no disclosure that the Valley receivable had increased about $400,000 after the balance sheet date but before the date of the report.

Expert testimony from several accounting firms stated unanimously that there was no violation of generally accepted auditing standards or generally accepted accounting principles. In addition, the AICPA filed briefs as an *amicus curiae,* stating that a professional person could not be held to a standard above that established by the profession. However, the judge instructed the jury to consider whether professional standards had been violated but to remember that the proof of such standards and principles was not conclusive on the issue of fraud. Even if professional standards were observed, the jury still had the duty to question whether the financial statements were fairly stated. Such reasoning is very disturbing to the profession, since it suggested that the observance of professional standards may not be a proper defense for criminal fraud.

The three auditors were found guilty, and the appellate court upheld the criminal conviction for certifying misleading financial statements. The three were fined a total of $17,000. The auditors were subsequently pardoned by the President. A civil suit against the CPA firm was settled out of court for approximately $2 million.

In addition to the precedents established concerning criminal liability and the question of the fairness of the financial statements based on a layperson's perspective, the Continental Vending case had a direct impact on professional standards. The affiliate, Valley Commercial Corporation, was not audited by Continental Vending's auditors. Had the auditors insisted upon auditing the affiliate, there would have been some question as to whether they were violating the section of the code of ethics which prohibits encroachment. The code of ethics rule in effect at the time of the audit was relaxed, and Rule 401 was issued,

[15] Ibid., p. 240.

112
Legal
liability

which permits an auditor to insist upon auditing a subsidiary, branch, or other component when combined or consolidated financial statements are being prepared.

EQUITY FUNDING

The recent Equity Funding Life Insurance Company case has been highly publicized as one of the most notorious fraud cases involving a public accounting firm. The scheme involved the fraudulent creation of $120 million of assets and the sale of $2 billion of life insurance policies to reinsurers. At the time of this writing, the case has not been completely settled, even though three of the auditors have been convicted on various counts, including criminal charges. The case is not important to the profession based on the individual actions of the auditors, for most would concede the lack of due diligence. The fraud did raise the fundamental question of whether generally accepted auditing standards are adequate, especially since the use of a computer was involved.

The AICPA responded to the Equity Funding fraud with the creation of a special committee on Equity Funding. The charge to this committee was, in part, as follows:

> *Whereas,* the Institute shares the general public concern about the Equity Funding disaster, which caused enormous losses to investors and creditors apparently by reason of massive and collusive fraud; and
>
> *Whereas,* developments in the Equity Funding matter may suggest that changes in generally accepted auditing standards are called for; and
>
> *Whereas,* identification and implementation of any such changes in generally accepted auditing standards should not await the eventual resolution of litigation or other proceedings concerned with assigning responsibility in respect of Equity Funding.
>
> *Now Therefore Be It Resolved,* that a special committee be appointed by the president of the Institute to study whether the auditing standards which are currently considered appropriate and sufficient in the examination of financial statements should be changed in the light of Equity Funding and report its conclusions to the Board of Directors and the auditing standards executive committee.[16]

After its investigation, the committee concluded that "except for certain observations relating to confirmation of insurance in force and auditing related party transactions, generally accepted auditing standards are adequate and . . . no changes are called for in the procedures commonly used by auditors."[17] In addition, the committee made the following statement concerning the role of the computer in the Equity Funding fraud.

> Much of the publicity about Equity Funding has characterized it as a "computer fraud." It would be more accurate to call it a "computer-assisted fraud." The computer was used, to a large extent, to manipulate files and create detail designed

---

[16] *Report of the Special Committee on Equity Funding* (New York: AICPA, 1975), pp. 6–7. Copyright © 1975 by the American Institute of Certified Public Accountants, Inc.

[17] Ibid., p. 27.

to conceal fraud. Much of the processing was performed by personnel from outside the EDP department who were allowed access to computer hardware, software and files.[18]

Although the Equity Funding case did not have an impact on auditing liability, it played a part in a recent promulgation. In July 1975, the Auditing Standards Executive Committee of the AICPA issued *SAS No. 6,* "Related Party Transactions." In this statement, guidance was provided to assist the auditor in identifying related party transactions and in determining the impact of these transactions on the financial statements.

SEC SANCTIONS

An auditor or audit firm is subject to sanctions other than civil or criminal penalties. As suggested earlier, the AICPA, state societies of CPAs, or state boards of accountancy can discipline members of the profession. In addition, the SEC can penalize accountants who practice before it by requesting an injunction or by suspending the privilege of practicing before the SEC. In the case of the former, the SEC can seek to enjoin a company or an individual from further violations of federal laws governing the registration and trading of securities. To obtain such an injunction, the SEC must show in court that the company or individual is likely to violate such laws if not enjoined. Rule 2(e) of the SEC's rules of practice states:

> (1) The Commission may deny, temporarily or permanently, the privilege of appearing or practicing before it in any way to any person who is found by the Commission after notice of and opportunity for hearing in the matter (i) not to possess the requisite qualifications to represent others, or (ii) to be lacking in character or integrity or to have engaged in unethical or improper professional conduct, or (iii) to have willfully violated, or willfully aided and abetted the violation of any provision of the federal securities laws . . . or the rules and regulations thereunder.

Recently, in addition to temporarily suspending an auditor or a firm from practicing before the commission, the SEC has required that auditing firms' policies and procedures be reviewed by persons external to the firm. In 1975, a national accounting firm's practice was subjected to an extensive review by another national firm. This review was the result of settlement of four SEC complaints against the accounting firm for violation of federal securities laws in the audit of the National Student Marketing Corporation, Penn Central Company, Republic National Life Insurance Company, and Tally Industries, Inc. "The concrete outcome was a carefully drafted, three-paragraph opinion letter . . . marking the first time an audit firm has formally and publicly vouched for a rival firm's overall quality."[19]

---

[18] Ibid., p. 25.

[19] "Peat Marwick Says It Got a Good Rating in Quality Review Done by Arthur Young," *Wall Street Journal,* November 24, 1975, p. 10.

114
Legal
liability

LEGAL LIABILITY AND UNAUDITED STATEMENTS

All the legal cases discussed to this point have been concerned with the auditor's legal liability in the issuing of an opinion on audited statements. In an earlier chapter, the variety of services performed by the CPA was described, and among these services was the preparation of unaudited financial statements. The last few years have witnessed increased interest in unaudited financial statements. Much of this interest can be traced directly to one legal case, the 1136 Tenants' Corporation case, but the SEC has also shown great interest in unaudited interim financial statements during the same period.

For the most part, the auditor becomes associated with unaudited financial statements as an additional service when tax returns are prepared or when a client lacks the in-house expertise to process routine transactions and make the necessary year-end adjustments. The financial statements created are unaudited, because the auditor has not examined any evidence that establishes the legitimacy of the accounting transactions. For example, it is a simple bookkeeping technique to prepare an adjusting journal entry for the depreciation of a fixed asset. However, to formulate an opinion as to the legitimacy of such an entry, the auditor would have to examine the original invoice for the purchase of the asset, determine that the asset is on the premises and functioning, and perhaps examine the canceled check or other method used to finance its purchase, to name but a few of the audit procedures used to collect corroborative evidence. The auditor is not required to collect such evidence in an engagement where an unaudited financial statement is issued.

The auditor has certain reporting responsibilities when he or she becomes associated with unaudited financial statements. An auditor is considered to be associated with unaudited statements when he or she consents to the use of his or her name in a report containing the financial statements. Additionally, the auditor is associated if he or she has prepared or assisted in preparation of the unaudited financial statements. If the auditor is deemed associated, each page of the financial statements is conspicuously marked as unaudited and a disclaimer of opinion is issued by the auditor. *SAS No. 1,* Section 516.04, recommends the following form of disclaimer when financial statements are unaudited:

> The accompanying balance sheet of X Company as of December 31, 19xx, and the related statements of income and retained earnings and changes in financial position for the year then ended were not audited by us and accordingly we do not express an opinion on them.

Although the auditor is not required to perform audit procedures, during the engagement he or she may discover instances of departure from generally accepted accounting principles. In this case, the disclaimer is modified by a direct reference to the auditor's reservations and the effect, if known to the auditor, of the reservations on the unaudited financial statements.

The subject of unaudited financial statements is explored more fully in Chapter 18. The discussion is limited at this point to providing enough information to enhance discussion of the following legal case.

1136 Tenants' Corporation[20]

The 1136 Tenants' Corporation was a cooperative apartment house managed by Riker and Company, Inc. A public accounting firm was hired in 1963 by Riker via an oral agreement to prepare a tax return and a schedule for determining the apportionment of real estate taxes to the owners of the apartment house. There was an additional duty of preparing financial statements, but there was disagreement during the trial as to whether these statements were to have been audited or unaudited financial statements. The public accounting firm continued its work for 1136 Tenants' Corporation until 1965, and during this period Riker, the managing agent, embezzled substantial funds of the cooperative. The cooperative sued the auditors for negligence, since the latter had failed to discover the fraud, and for breach of contract, alleging that an audit had been contracted for but had not been performed.

Both parties to the suit introduced evidence to substantiate their beliefs as to the nature of the engagement. The plaintiff noted that the auditors had been engaged "to perform all necessary accounting and auditing services." Furthermore, the auditor had marked the financial statements, "Subject to comments in letter of transmittal." In the letter of transmittal, the auditor stated in the last paragraph: "The following statements were prepared from the books and records of the Corporation. No independent verifications were undertaken thereon. . . ." The court ruled that the auditor was engaged to perform an audit and was therefore guilty of breach of contract.

The second major issue in the case dealt with the determination of negligence on the part of the auditor. Although the auditor unsuccessfully contended that the engagement was to prepare unaudited financial statements, which required that no audit procedures be performed, the auditor examined bank statements, invoices, and bills. The most damaging piece of evidence was the auditor's preparation of a worksheet entitled "Missing invoices 1/1/63–12/31/63," which revealed $44,000 of disbursements that did not have appropriate support. The auditor did not inform the plaintiff of these missing invoices, and no additional audit work was performed either to confirm the suspicions raised by the discovery or to clear this obvious unsettled finding. The trial court found the auditor negligent in the performance of service. The appellate court, which affirmed the lower court's finding, stated:

> Utilization of the simplest audit procedures would have revealed Riker's defalcations. Moreover *even if* defendant were hired to perform only "write-up" services, it is clear beyond dispute that it did become aware that material invoices purportedly paid by Riker were missing, and accordingly, had a duty to at least inform plaintiff of this. But even this it failed to do. Defendant was not free to consider these and other suspicious circumstances as being of no significance and prepare its financial records as if same did not exist.[21]

[20] *1136 Tenants' Corporation v. Max Rothenberg and Company,* 30 N.Y. 2d 585, 330 N.Y.S. 2d 800 (1972).

[21] Emanuel Saxe, "Unaudited Financial Statements: Rules, Risks and Recommendations," *CPA Journal,* June 1972, p. 459.

The reaction to the conviction of the auditors in the 1136 Tenants' Corporation case was immediate and substantial. The AICPA, as well as many auditors, interpreted the conviction as a need for the profession to consider promulgating minimum audit procedures in such engagements. The case was affirmed by the New York Court of Appeals, the highest state court, in March 1972, and in the same year, the AICPA appointed a special task force to study the problem. The final results of the task force were published in 1975 as an audit guide, which is discussed in Chapter 18. It has been suggested that the profession overreacted to the 1136 Tenants' Corporation decision and that to prescribe a minimum level of audit procedures may result in more confusion in this area. An alternative, obviously rejected by the AICPA, is to prohibit public accountants from being associated with any unaudited financial statements.

Engagement letters

The 1136 Tenants' Corporation decision revealed the importance of a formal written agreement between the auditor and the client. To avoid any misunderstandings the auditor should prepare and have the client sign an engagement confirmation letter. Figure 4-1 is an example of such a letter when the auditor is contracted for the preparation of unaudited financial statements.

PROFESSIONAL RESPONSE TO RECENT LITIGATION

It is erroneous to conclude that the auditor loses every court case. In fact, most court cases are dismissed or settled for minor sums; nonetheless, the profession is very concerned with many recent court decisions and is attempting to react in a manner that will minimize the number of lawsuits in the future. One result, as discussed in the above cases, has been an increase in the number of accounting and auditing rules being promulgated. If auditors can be given guidelines to follow, it is likely that fewer lawsuits will materialize. However, this proscriptive approach to auditing can go only so far. Every eventuality cannot be anticipated with a comprehensive set of rules to guide the independent accountant. Furthermore, the courts seem to be saying that the auditor who blindly applies accounting rules without considering the fairness of such rules cannot hide behind them. In addition to the rather immediate action of promulgating rules, the profession has instituted programs and made recommendations that will take many years before they will impact the legal problems of the profession but which seem to be more likely to reduce the number of court cases. Some of these are discussed below.

Education and training

Auditing firms recognize that the first line of defense against any charge of substandard work depends upon the caliber of the people hired and trained by the firm. It has already been stated that the profession has endorsed the concept of continuing education for practicing accountants. Collectively, audit firms

Figure 4-1

Engagement letter: unaudited statements

Chairman of the Board of Directors
ABC Company

This letter is to confirm our understanding of the terms of our engagement and the nature and extent of the accounting services we will provide.

Our services will not constitute an audit of the financial statements of ABC Company; consequently, we will not be in a position to express an opinion on the financial statements and will issue a disclaimer of opinion with respect to them. Our disclaimer will disclose any departure from generally accepted accounting principles of which we become aware.

We will perform the following services:

1. We will prepare without audit a balance sheet for ABC Company as at December 31, 19—, and related statements of income, retained earnings, and changes in financial position for the year then ended. These statements will be prepared from the general ledger and other information you furnish us. Before issuance, the statements will be subject to your acceptance and approval inasmuch as financial statements are the representations and the primary responsibility of company management.

2. We will discuss with the officers and directors of the company such suggestions and recommendations concerning the accounting methods and financial affairs of the company that may occur to us in the course of our work.

3. We will prepare the federal and (name of state) income tax returns of ABC Company for the year 19——, and we will advise you on income tax matters upon which you specifically request our advice.

Our engagement will not be designed, and cannot be relied upon, to disclose fraud, defalcations, or other irregularities. However, we will inform you of any matters that come to our attention which cause us to believe that such a condition exists.

Our fees for these services will be computed at our standard rates and will be billed monthly as the work progresses. Bills for services will be due when rendered.

We shall be pleased to discuss this letter with you at any time and to explain the reason for any items.

If the foregoing is in accordance with your understanding, will you please sign the copy of this letter in the space provided and return it to us.

Sincerely yours,

_____

(Signature of CPA)

Acknowledged:
ABC Company

_____

Chairman, Board of Directors

_____

Date

SOURCE: *Guide for Engagement of CPAs to Prepare Unaudited Financial Statements* (New York: AICPA, 1975), pp. 13–14. Copyright © 1975 American Institute of Certified Public Accountants, Inc.

spend millions of dollars to train and develop their employees. Currently, there is a debate over the manner in which most auditors gain their formal education in colleges and universities. A special board was appointed in 1974 by the AICPA, which consisted of members of the institute, the American Accounting Association, the American Assembly of Collegiate Schools of Business, and the National Association of State Boards of Accountancy. The purpose of the board was to investigate the need for establishing standards for professional programs in accounting. The board issued an exposure draft in early 1976 which included the following significant statement:

> The objective of these standards is to establish a level of quality in accounting education programs that would graduate an entry-level professional accountant.
> Such an objective cannot be achieved within the traditional baccalaureate program. An adequate professional education in accounting will require at least two years of pre-professional education and no less than three years of professional education.[22]

The profession recognizes the need to emphasize professional courses in the accounting curriculum. In the long run, it is believed that the quality of work performed by the profession will improve significantly. Hopefully such a development will reduce the frequency and change the nature of future legal cases.

Peer review

The concept of peer review was alluded to earlier in this chapter. The purpose of such a program is to provide an auditing firm with an opportunity to have its practice reviewed to determine if a competent, professional job is being performed in each engagement. As administered by the AICPA, the program is voluntary, and the institute does not publicize which firms participate in the peer review or the results of the review. The AICPA emphasizes that the program was not formed to punish firms that had instances of substandard work but rather to identify the areas where a firm should strengthen its practice.

Obviously, as practiced by the AICPA, the peer review concept is in its infancy. It is hoped that as the program matures the profession will see the need for mandatory peer review. If such a proposal were adopted, the profession would have a means to monitor the level of competency exhibited by an audit firm. It may be that some firms would be more diligent in their work if such firms knew their work was subject to review and that the results of any peer review could be brought before the AICPA's trial board if deemed appropriate.

Defensive auditing

Conceptually one could state that the auditor must collect and evaluate enough evidence to provide a basis for formulation of an opinion on the financial statements. However, because of the possibility of a lawsuit, which has to some

---

[22] *Board on Standards for Programs and Schools of Professional Accounting* (discussion draft) (New York: AICPA, 1976), p. 2. Copyright © 1976 by the American Institute of Certified Public Accountants, Inc.

degree the advantage of hindsight, the auditor must consider satisfying third parties and the court. With this philosophy, he or she performs audit procedures, documents work in the audit working papers, and takes other steps that will provide an adequate defense should his or her actions be subject to investigation. It is not suggested that the audit approach be dominated by this defensive philosophy, but that it should be incorporated in the approach. In addition, the degree to which the defensive approach should be emphasized is a function of the overall audit environment. For example, two authors have listed several instances that should alert the auditor to potential problems:

1. Serious weaknesses in internal accounting and administrative controls.
2. Difficulties in obtaining information or documentation.
3. Unauthorized corporate transactions.
4. Material transactions not recorded in the usual manner.
5. Highly irregular or unexplained personal conduct by management or other client personnel.
6. Confusing or suspicious confirmation replies.
7. A client's insistence on increasing an already substantial loss for the year.
8. Dealings with related parties.
9. Guarded, incomplete, or seemingly "glib" client responses.
10. Apparent obstruction of audit procedures or unexplained lack of client cooperation.[23]

If auditors become more alert to potential problem areas and react accordingly, the possibility of legal liability should be reduced.

CONCLUDING REMARKS

In this chapter, the final societal control mechanism has been discussed. The exposure to possible legal liability has probably had more of an impact on the practice of accounting than any single element in the past 15 years. Recall that society could choose another method to meet the needs of society in performance of the attest function. In a recent article, the managing partner of a national accounting firm summarized the current state of the auditor's legal liability:

> We must be prepared to give up the attitude that we are beyond challenge; we must be willing to submit to the discipline of a strong profession. Only in this way can we expect and deserve public support—and, more than ever before, such support is imperative in our efforts to resolve our litigation problems.[24]

EXERCISES AND PROBLEMS

4-1. Explain the legal relationship between an auditor and a client.

[23] Charles Chazen and Kenneth I. Solomon, "The Art of Defensive Auditing, *Journal of Accountancy,* October 1975, p. 69.

[24] Russell E. Palmer, "It's Time to Stop Talking," *Journal of Accountancy,* October 1975, p. 65.

4-2. Is an auditor responsible for detecting fraud in the examination of financial statements?

4-3. Explain the legal relationship between an auditor and third parties based on (a) common law and (b) federal statutes.

4-4. Contrast the potential legal liabilities and legal remedies available under the Securities Exchange Act of 1934 and the Securities Act of 1933.

4-5. Explain the impact of the Hochfelder case on the auditor's legal liability.

4-6. Contrast the implications for the profession of the BarChris case and the Continental Vending case.

4-7. What fundamental issue was raised in the Yale Express case?

4-8. What actions may be taken against public accounting firms by the SEC?

4-9. When is an auditor considered associated with unaudited financial statements?

4-10. What are the reporting responsibilities when an auditor is associated with unaudited financial statements?

4-11. How has the 1136 Tenants' Corporation case impacted the accounting profession?

4-12. What is the purpose of an engagement letter?

4-13. How can a comprehensive peer review program reduce the possibility of future litigation against the accounting profession?

4-14. Who should determine if professional standards have been followed? (Judge, jury, governmental agency, or a special panel of court-appointed experts?)

4-15. How does an audit firm protect itself against the possibility of legal liability?

4-16. *Part A*. Ultrasound, Inc., a closely held sound systems manufacturer, decided to offer its stock to the general public and entered into an underwriting contract in which the investment banking firm of Fairweather, Reed, and Wilson agreed to market the shares.

Fairweather later repudiated the contract when it discovered Ultrasound's true financial picture. Fairweather claimed that it had been induced to sign the contract by a misrepresentation as to the corporation's income for the current period.

The facts disclosed that Fairweather had been given unaudited, condensed income statements, prepared by Ultrasound's internal accountants, showing income of $6 million for the first 9 months and $11 million for the entire year ending December 31, 1979. Thus Fairweather was led to believe that the remarkable increase in the last quarter's income was due to the enthusiastic consumer acceptance of Ultrasound's new line of sound systems.

More complete information that became available later revealed that Ultrasound's fourth quarter income had been only $800,000 and that the $4.2 million difference was due to a write-up of the finished goods inventory to selling price that had not been disclosed in the condensed statements. Upon discovering this, Fairweather promptly repudiated the underwriting agreement.

Required: What legal problems are suggested by these facts? Explain.

Part B. Charles Worthington, the founding and senior partner of a successful and respected CPA firm was a highly competent practitioner who always emphasized high professional standards. One of the policies of the firm was that all reports by members or staff be submitted to Worthington for review.

Recently, Arthur Craft, a junior partner in the firm, received a telephone call from Herbert Flack, a close personal friend. Flack informed Craft that he, his family, and some friends were planning to create a corporation to engage in various land development ventures, that various members of the family were presently in a partnership (Flack Ventures) which held land and other assets, and that the partnership would contribute all its assets to the new corporation and the corporation would assume the liabilities of the partnership.

Flack asked Craft to prepare a balance sheet for the partnership that he could show to members of his family, who were in the partnership, and friends to determine whether they might be interested in joining in the formation and financing of the new corporation. Flack said that he had the partnership general ledger in front of him and proceeded to read to Craft the names of the accounts and their balances at the end of the latest month. Craft took the notes he made during the telephone conversation with Flack, classified and organized the data into a conventional balance sheet, and had his secretary type the balance sheet and an accompanying letter on the firm's stationery. He did not consult Worthington on this matter or submit his work to him for review.

The transmittal letter stated: "We have reviewed the books and records of Flack Ventures, a partnership, and have prepared the attached balance sheet at March 31, 1980. We did not perform an examination in conformity with generally accepted auditing standards, and therefore do not express an opinion on the accompanying balance sheet." The balance sheet was prominently marked "Unaudited." Craft signed the letter and instructed his secretary to send it to Flack.

Required: What legal problems are suggested by these facts? Explain.

Part C. Cragsmore & Company, a medium-sized partnership of CPAs, was engaged by Marlowe Manufacturing, Inc., a closely held corporation, to examine its financial statements for the year ended December 31, 1979.

Prior to preparing the auditor's report William Cragsmore, a partner, and Fred Willmore, a staff senior, reviewed the disclosures necessary in the footnotes to the financial statements. One footnote involved the terms, costs, and obligations of a lease between Marlowe and Acme Leasing Company.

Fred Willmore suggested that the footnote disclose the following: "The Acme Leasing Company is owned by persons who have a 35 percent interest in the capital stock and who are officers of Marlowe Manufacturing, Inc."

On Cragsmore's recommendation, this was revised by substituting "minority share-holders" for "persons who have a 35 percent interest in the capital stock and who are officers."

The auditor's report and financial statements were forwarded to Marlowe Manufacturing for review. The officer-shareholders of Marlowe who also owned Acme Leasing objected to the revised wording and insisted that the footnote be changed to describe the relationship between Acme and Marlowe as merely one of affiliation. Cragsmore acceded to this request.

The auditor's report was issued on this basis with an unqualified opinion. But the working papers included the drafts that showed the changes in the wording of the footnote.

Subsequent to delivery of the auditor's report, Marlowe suffered a substantial uninsured fire loss and was forced into bankruptcy. The failure of Marlowe to carry any fire insurance coverage was not noted in the financial statements.

Required: What legal problems for Cragsmore & Company are suggested by these facts? Discuss.   (AICPA Adapted)

4-17. *Part A.* Carter, Wilson, and Whipple, CPAs, were engaged to examine the financial statements of Devon Corporation for the year ended September 30, 1979. The capital stock of Devon is traded on the Pacific Coast Stock Exchange.

During the engagement it was discovered that Devon had been making large, unsecured loans on favorable terms to Carbal Corporation. All the stock of Carbal is held by a majority of the board of directors of Devon.

Required: Discuss the professional and legal responsibilities of Carter, Wilson, and Whipple.

Part B. While examining the financial statements of Fesmore Industries, Inc., for the fiscal year ended October 31, 1979, Dey & Company, CPAs, discovered that J. Parker Dilmore, executive vice president of Fesmore, was actively involved in trading Fesmore's common stock. While Dilmore has always owned at least 100,000 shares of Fesmore's common stock, he executed the following specific transactions during the year under examination.

TRANSACTION	NUMBER OF SHARES	DATE	PRICE PER SHARE ($)
Purchased	15,000	March 1, 1979	24
Sold	15,000	June 5, 1979	40
Purchased	5,000	June 7, 1979	35
Sold	5,000	September 3, 1979	30
Purchased	5,000	October 2, 1979	25

The stock sold on June 5 and September 3, 1979, was the same stock purchased on March 1 and June 7, 1979, respectively.

Required: Discuss the legal implications of the facts discovered by Dey & Company.

Part C. Barney & Company, CPAs, has been engaged to perform an examination of the financial statements of Waldo, Inc., for several years. The terms of the engagement have been set out in an annual engagement letter signed by both parties. The terms of each engagement included the statement:

> This being an ordinary examination, it is not primarily or specifically designed, and cannot be relied upon, to disclose defalcations and other similar irregularities, although their discovery may result.

Three years ago Harold Zamp, head cashier of Waldo and an expert in computer operations, devised a previously unheard of method of embezzling funds from his employer. At first, Zamp's thefts were small, but increased as time went on. During the current year, before Barney began working on the engagement, the thefts became so large that serious variances in certain accounts came to the attention of the controller. When questioned about the variances, Zamp confessed and explained his unique embezzlement scheme. Investigation revealed that Zamp had stolen $257,550. Zamp has no assets with which to repay the thefts.

Waldo submitted its claim for $257,550 to Multi-State Surety Company in accordance with the terms of the fidelity bond covering Zamp. Fulfilling its surety obligation, Multi-State paid the claim and now seeks to recover its losses from Barney.

In defense, Barney asserts, in the alternative, the following defenses:

1. Multi-State has no standing in court to sue because it was not a party to the contract (i.e., lacking in privity) between Barney and its client, Waldo.

2. Even if Multi-State had the standing to sue, its claim should be dismissed because Barney's engagements with Waldo did not specifically include the discovery of defalcations other than those which might arise in the process of an ordinary examination.

3. Even if Barney's contract had made it responsible for discoverable defalcations, it could not have discovered Zamp's defalcations with the exercise of reasonable care. Zamp's technique was so new, unique, and novel that no accounting firm could have discovered the defalcations in any event.

Required: In separately numbered paragraphs, discuss the validity of each of Barney's defenses. (AICPA Adapted)

4-18. *Part A.* Williams, a CPA, was engaged by Jackson Financial Development Company to audit the financial statements of Apex Construction Company, a small closely held corporation. Williams was told when he was engaged that Jackson Financial needed reliable financial statements which would be used to determine whether or not to purchase a substantial amount of Apex Construction's convertible debentures at the price asked by the estate of one of Apex's former directors.

Williams performed his examination in a negligent manner. As a result of his negligence he failed to discover substantial defalcations by Brown, the Apex controller. Jackson Financial purchased the debentures but would not have if the defalcations had been discovered. After discovery of the fraud Jackson Financial promptly sold them for the highest price offered in the market at a $70,000 loss.

Required

1. What liability does Williams have to Jackson Financial? Explain.

2. If Apex Construction also sues Williams for negligence, what are the probable legal defenses Williams' attorney will raise? Explain.

3. Will the negligence of a CPA as described above prevent him from recovering on a liability insurance policy covering the practice of his profession? Explain.

Part B. For several years Martin engaged Watson, a CPA, to prepare the financial statements for the construction business Martin owned and operated in her own name. Franklin is the owner of a building which Martin built on a cost plus fixed fee basis. Franklin sued Martin, alleging that Martin overcharged him by inflating the cost to construct his building. In preparing for trial, Franklin obtained a court order requiring Watson to turn over to Franklin all his (Watson's) working papers and correspondence relating to Martin's construction business.

At the subsequent trial, Franklin's attorney sought to introduce in evidence the working papers and correspondence subpoenaed pursuant to the court order. Martin's attorney objected claiming that the papers were inadmissible evidence.

Required

1. What is the legal basis for Martin's attorney's objection to admission of the papers as evidence? Explain.

2. Will the evidence be admitted? Explain.

3. Who owns the working papers prepared by Watson? Explain. (AICPA Adapted)

4-19. Bob Pratt works for a large accounting firm and is in charge of the audit of Saymor Company. Bob has worked on the Saymor engagement for the three years the company has been the firm's client. For each engagement the accounting firm had issued an unqualified opinion on the financial statements covering the years 1978 to 1980.

In June 1981, Saymor Company is unable to pay its maturing obligation and shortly afterward is declared bankrupt. The Third National Bank, which made the loan to the company in 1979, holds a note that will mature in 1984. The bank has hired a lawyer and another accounting firm to see if the financial statements it reviewed during the period were properly prepared. These statements are summarized here:

	DECEMBER 31		
	1978	1979	1980
Current assets	$100,000	$ 80,000	$ 90,000
Property plant and equipment	300,000	350,000	400,000
Other assets	100,000	120,000	110,000
	$500,000	$550,000	$600,000
Current liabilities	$ 60,000	$ 40,000	$ 50,000
Long-term liabilities—10 percent	100,000	200,000	200,000
Stockholders' equity	340,000	310,000	350,000
	$500,000	$550,000	$600,000
Gross revenue	$2,930,000	$3,120,000	$3,340,000
Depreciation	60,000	70,000	80,000
Operating expenses	2,800,000	3,000,000	3,200,000
Net income	70,000	50,000	60,000

During the trial the bank presents a summary of a noncapitalized lease. The vital points of the lease are:

Saymour entered into a 10-year lease early in 1978 for a substantial portion of its machinery. Rental payments of $100,000 were paid at the beginning of each year. The estimated life of the machinery is 12 years.

The Third National Bank argued that this lease should have been capitalized at a 10 percent rate of interest under generally accepted accounting principles. It further argued that it had been deceived, since the balance sheet did not state that a significant long-term lease was not capitalized. Also, it was pointed out that the income statement did not identify rental expense as a separate item but rather lumped it with an account called "Operating expenses—other than depreciation." The bank's lawyer stated, "Clearly this figure was material since it was on the average twice as large as net income."

The accounting firm argued that the lease commitments were fully disclosed in footnotes to the financial statements which read:

The Company is committed under a long-term lease expiring in 1988. Rental expense was $100,000 for the current year. The present value of aggregate minimum lease commitments of this non-capitalized lease does not have a material impact on net earnings for the year.

The above footnote was one of many footnotes contained in each annual report. The accountant's lawyer stated, "My client required the maximum amount of disclosure under the circumstances for the lease as well as for other transactions. If the accountant is guilty of anything it is that too much data was disclosed in the financial statements."

Required

1. Have there been errors in or omissions from the financial statements?

2. If errors and omissions do exist, were they material? Comment specifically on the bank's definition of materiality in relation to net income.

3. Do you believe the accounting firm was guilty of (a) negligence? (b) gross negligence? (c) fraud?

4. Do you believe the auditor may be able to protect against lawsuits by disclosing "everything" in the footnotes?

4-20. Mainline Securities Company was a brokerage firm and a member of a regional stock exchange. David Houston was president and majority stockholder of the firm. Over a period of several years Houston persuaded several customers of Mainline to invest funds in an escrow account that he stated would yield an attractive rate of return. Customers were told to draw their personal checks payable to Houston as to a designated bank for his account.

In fact, there were no escrow accounts and Houston diverted the funds for his own personal use. This scheme was discovered when he committed suicide and left a note describing how the customers had been defrauded. A major element of the fraud was Houston's "mail rule." This rule prohibited anyone from opening the mail of another individual if the mail was addressed to the individual or to the attention of the individual. In addition, Mr. Houston had a strict rule that no one was to open his mail in his absence, no matter how long he was out of town.

In an attempt to recover their losses, the defrauded customers stated that the CPA firm that audited Mainline Securities Company's financial statements was guilty of negligence. Specifically, they charged that the accounting firm had aided and abetted the scheme by its failure to perform an adequate audit. The plaintiffs believed that the CPA firm should have been aware of the "mail rule" and recognized it as a major weakness in the company's internal control system. Furthermore, the plaintiffs contended that such a material weakness should have been reported to the regional stock exchange. The plaintiffs did not charge the accounting firm with fraud but, rather, with inexcusable negligence.

The CPA firm's defense lawyers argued that the transactions between Houston and the defrauded customers were not recorded in the records of Mainline. Furthermore, the customers never received notice of the transaction or the balance in the accounts on a periodic basis. The transactions were not included in Mainline's filings with the SEC or the regional stock exchange.

The case was concerned with the interpretation of the accountant's liability under the Securities Exchange Act of 1934 as described in Section 10(b).

Required
1. Do you believe that the defrauded customers may have been guilty of contributory negligence? Explain.
2. Was the auditor guilty of negligence?
3. Will the auditor be convicted based upon Rule 10b-5?

4-21. *Part A.* Mio & Mio, CPAs, were engaged for several years by Famous Carpet Company, manufacturers of woolen carpets, to conduct an annual audit. Excellent Carpet Company, a competitor of Famous, now seeks to engage the Mio firm to install a more advanced accounting system and to conduct an annual audit. The officers of Excellent approached Mio & Mio because of its outstanding reputation in the community and its acknowledged expertise in the carpet industry.

Required: May Mio & Mio accept the Excellent Carpet Company as a client? Explain.

Part B. (Continuing the facts in *Part A.*) Subsequently, one of the officers of Excellent offered to pay Mio & Mio a substantial bonus if they would disclose confidential financial information about Famous' operations to permit the officer to make a comparative study of the operating performances of the two carpet companies.

126
Legal liability

Required: May Mio & Mio accept this offer? Explain.

Part C. As an accommodation to its clients, the CPA firm of Ross, Smith, and Lewis sometimes served as the agent to receive the balance of the sales price due a client at a real estate closing. The CPA firm's practice was to deposit the sums received in the firm's checking account and issue its own check to the client when notified to do so.

On September 14, 1979, the CPA firm received a $10,000 payment on behalf of its client, Rosewell, and deposited the money in its own account at the Security State Bank. On September 20, 1979, after an examination by the state banking examiners, the Security State Bank closed and indicated to its depositors that the bank had failed.

Required: Who must bear the loss resulting from the Security State Bank's failure? Explain.

Part D. The CPA firm of Bigelow, Barton, and Brown was expanding very rapidly. Consequently it hired several junior accountants, including a man named Small. Subsequently, the partners of the firm became dissatisfied with Small's production and warned him that they would be forced to discharge him unless his output increased significantly.

At that time Small was engaged in audits of several clients. He decided that, to avoid being fired, he would reduce or omit entirely some of the standard auditing procedures listed in audit programs prepared by the partners. One of the CPA firm's clients, Newell Corporation, was in serious financial difficulty and had adjusted several of its accounts being examined by Small to appear financially sound. Small prepared fictitious working papers at his home at night to support the purported completion of auditing procedures assigned to him, although he in fact did not examine the adjusting entries. The CPA firm rendered an unqualified opinion on Newell's financial statements which were grossly misstated. Several creditors subsequently extended large sums of money to Newell Corporation, relying upon the audited financial statements.

Required: Would the CPA firm be liable to the creditors who extended the money in reliance on the erroneous financial statements if Newell Corporation should fail to pay them? Explain. (AICPA Adapted)

4-22. *Part A.* The Chriswell Corporation decided to raise additional long-term capital by issuing $3,000,000 of 8 percent subordinated debentures to the public. May, Clark & Company, CPAs, the company's auditors, were engaged to examine the June 30, 1980, financial statements which were included in the bond registration statement.

May, Clark & Company completed its examination and submitted an unqualified auditor's report dated July 15, 1980. The registration statement was filed and became effective on September 1, 1980. Two weeks prior to the effective date one of the partners of May, Clark & Company called on Chriswell Corporation and had lunch with the financial vice-president and the controller. She questioned both officials on the company's operations since June 30 and inquired whether there had been any material changes in its financial position since that date. Both officers assured her that everything had proceeded normally and that the financial condition of the company had not changed materially.

Unfortunately the officers' representation was not true. On July 30, a substantial debtor of the company failed to pay the $400,000 due on its account receivable and indicated to Chriswell that it would probably be forced into bankruptcy. This receivable was shown as a collateralized loan on the June 30 financial statements. It was secured by stock of the debtor corporation which had a value in excess of the loan at the time the financial statements were prepared but was virtually worthless at the effective date of the registration statement. This $400,000 account receivable was material to the financial condition of Chriswell Corporation, and the market price of the subordinated debentures decreased by nearly 50 percent after the foregoing facts were disclosed.

The debenture holders of Chriswell are seeking recovery of their loss against all parties connected with the debenture registration.

Required: Is May, Clark & Company liable to the Chriswell debenture holders? Explain.

Part B. Meglow Corporation manufactured ladies' dresses and blouses. Because its cash position was deteriorating, Meglow sought a loan from Busch Factors. Busch had previously extended $25,000 credit to Meglow but refused to lend any additional money without obtaining copies of Meglow's audited financial statements.

Meglow contacted the CPA firm of Watkins, Winslow & Watkins to perform the audit. In arranging for the examination, Meglow clearly indicated that its purpose was to satisfy Busch Factors as to the corporation's sound financial condition and thus to obtain an additional loan of $50,000. Watkins, Winslow & Watkins accepted the engagement, performed the examination in a negligent manner, and rendered an unqualified auditor's opinion. If an adequate examination had been performed, the financial statements would have been found to be misleading.

Meglow submitted the audited financial statements to Busch Factors and obtained an additional loan of $35,000. Busch refused to lend more than that amount. After several other factors also refused, Meglow finally was able to persuade Maxwell Department Stores, one of its customers, to lend the additional $15,000. Maxwell relied upon the financial statements examined by Watkins, Winslow & Watkins.

Meglow is now in bankruptcy, and Busch seeks to collect from Watkins, Winslow & Watkins the $60,000 it loaned Meglow. Maxwell seeks to recover from Watkins, Winslow & Watkins the $15,000 it loaned Meglow.

Required
1. Will Busch recover? Explain.
2. Will Maxwell recover? Explain. (AICPA Adapted)

4-23. *Part A.* Risk Capital Limited, a Delaware corporation, was considering the purchase of a substantial amount of the treasury stock held by Florida Sunshine Corporation, a closely held corporation. Initial discussions with the Florida Sunshine Corporation began late in 1979.

Wilson and Wyatt, Florida Sunshine's accountants, regularly prepared quarterly and annual unaudited financial statements. The most recently prepared financial statements were for the year ended September 30, 1980.

On November 15, 1980, after protracted negotiations, Risk Capital agreed to purchase 100,000 shares of no-par, class-A capital stock of Florida Sunshine at $12.50 per share. However, Risk Capital insisted upon audited statements for calendar year 1980. The contract specifically provided:

> Risk Capital shall have the right to rescind the purchase of said stock if the audited financial statements of Florida Sunshine for calendar year 1980 show a material adverse change in the financial condition of the Corporation.

The audited financial statements furnished to Florida Sunshine by Wilson and Wyatt showed no such material adverse change. Risk Capital relied upon the audited statements and purchased the treasury stock of Florida Sunshine. It was subsequently discovered that, as of the balance sheet date, the audited statements were incorrect and that in fact there had been a material adverse change in the financial condition of the corporation. Florida Sunshine is insolvent and Risk Capital will lose virtually its entire investment.

Risk Capital seeks recovery from Wilson and Wyatt.

Required

1. Discuss each of the theories of liability that Risk Capital will probably assert as its basis for recovery.

2. Assuming that only ordinary negligence is proven, will Risk Capital prevail? State ''yes'' or ''no'' and explain.

Part B. Wells and White, the accountants for the Allie Corporation, provided various professional services for Allie over 15 years under annual retainer agreements. The services included tax return preparation, special costs analyses, and preparation of the corporation's audited and unaudited financial statements.

The relationship had been quite harmonious until the retirement of Roberts, the president and founder of Allie Corporation. His successor, Strong, was a very aggressive, expansion-oriented individual who lacked the competence and personal attraction of his predecessor. Two years after Roberts' retirement the unbroken record of increases in annual earnings was in jeopardy.

Strong realized that a decrease in earnings would have an unfavorable impact on his image and on his plans to merge with a well-known conglomerate. He called Wells, the senior partner of Wells and White, and demanded that the method of computing and reporting the current year's earnings be changed in a way that would preserve the upward trend in earnings.

Although the proposed method would be within the realm of generally accepted accounting principles, Wells subsequently told Strong that, in the exercise of its professional judgment, the firm could not agree to such a change. Strong promptly dismissed the firm and refused to pay the final billing of $1750 for services rendered to the date of dismissal under its agreement with Wells and White.

Wells and White have brought suit against Allie Corporation for the $1750. Allie Corporation responded by denying liability on the ground that the firm's refusal to cooperate constituted a breach of contract which precluded recovery. Allie also counterclaimed by demanding the return of all audit working papers, correspondence, duplicate tax returns, and supporting explanations pertaining to Allie Corporation.

Required

1. Is the Wells and White account receivable valid and enforceable against the Allie Corporation? State ''yes'' or ''no'' and explain.

2. Will Allie Corporation prevail on its counterclaim demanding return of the audit working papers, correspondence, and tax returns? State ''yes'' or ''no'' and explain.

Part C. (Continuing the situation described in *Part B.*) Strong was unable to find other accountants who approved of the proposed change in the method of computing and reporting earnings, so he abandoned this demand and engaged new accountants, Bar & Cross. Income continued to decrease in the next two quarters, and Strong became convinced that the cause of this was defalcations by a dishonest employee. Therefore he engaged Bar & Cross to make a special study to discover the guilty person. After several months of intensive work Bar & Cross discovered minor defalcations of $950. Of this amount, $600 had been stolen during the last two years while Wells and White were Allie Corporation's accountants. Allie Corporation sued Wells and White for the loss.

Required: Will Allie Corporation recover the loss from Wells and White? State "yes" or "no" and explain. (AICPA Adapted)

4-24. *Part A.* Henry, a wealthy industrialist, bought all the outstanding stock of the Zebra Manufacturing Company from Phillips and Vogel. In deciding to purchase the stock of the corporation and in determining the purchase price of the stock Henry relied heavily on the company's financial statements which had been examined by Charles, a CPA, who had rendered an unqualified opinion on them. At the time Charles did the audit, Henry had not approached Phillips and Vogel regarding the possible purchase of Zebra.

Several months after the sale of stock had been consummated a lawsuit for a substantial sum was brought against the Zebra Corporation. The basis for this liability had been present, although contingent, at the time the audit was performed. The financial statements of the corporation failed to disclose this contingent liability. This error was due to Charles' negligence in that he had failed to make a reasonable investigation of the claim.

A valid judgment was subsequently rendered against and paid by the corporation.

Required: Can Henry recover from Charles the loss in value of the stock attributable to the liability? Explain.

Part B. The basic facts are the same as stated in *Part A,* except that the financial statements in question were prepared for submission to the SEC in connection with a public offering of the corporation's stock pursuant to the provisions of the Securities Act of 1933. James is one of the parties who bought some of the shares of stock offered to the public.

Required: Can James recover from Charles the loss in value of the stock attributable to the liability? Explain.

Part C. Johnson, a CPA, was engaged by Frank & Company, a lending institution, to examine the financial statements of the Sare partnership. Frank & Company was considering lending the Sare partnership a large amount of money. One of the partnership's current assets consisted of $25,000 face-value negotiable bearer coupon bonds which were kept in the partnership's safe deposit box. Johnson, in performing the audit, went to the box and examined the bonds. Unfortunately the bonds were not genuine; instead they were clever forgeries which only an expert could detect. This fraud was not discovered until Sare defaulted on the loan and Frank & Company attempted to sell the bonds which had been pledged as collateral to secure the loan.

Frank & Company asserts that Johnson is liable for the loss to the extent of the value of the bonds which, if they had been genuine, would have been sufficient, along with the other Sare partnership assets, to satisfy the loan. Johnson denies liability.

Required: Is Johnson liable for the loss? Explain.

Part D. Williams, a CPA, was engaged by Andrews, the president of a small corporation, to examine the corporation's financial statements. Williams was pressed for time and decided to withdraw from the engagement. Williams, without consulting Andrews told Franklin, another CPA to whom she owed a favor, to handle the client on his own behalf. Franklin was in all respects as competent as Williams. Andrews refused to accept Franklin because he took a personal dislike to him.

Required: Is Andrews liable for breach of contract as a result of refusing to accept Franklin? Explain. (AICPA Adapted)

130
Legal liability

4-25. When an auditor is not independent, he or she must disclaim with respect to the financial statements and must state specifically that the reason for the disclaimer is lack of independence.

Required

1. How does the CPA determine whether independence is impaired?
2. If the auditor concludes that independence is impaired, is the specific reason for the lack of independence disclosed in his report? Why?
3. Are the reporting requirements, when independence has been impaired, the same for an audit engagement and write-up work?

4-26. *Part A.* Mark, a CPA, was engaged by Franklin Corporation to compute the net income attributable to the sale of certain products by the corporation for the year 1964. The purpose of this special engagement was to provide the basis for determination of the year-end bonuses payable to the sales personnel responsible for these sales. Mark was fully informed of the purpose of the engagement.

Mark was negligent in performance of the engagement. As a result several key salespeople received substantially less than the amount they were entitled to receive.

The Franklin Corporation is currently bankrupt and unable to pay the claims of the salespeople. However, in the year 1964 the corporation was solvent and could have paid the proper amounts.

Required:　Can the salespeople recover from Mark the loss they suffered as a result of his negligence? Explain.

Part B. The Federal Securities Act of 1933, which regulates the public offering of securities through the mails or in interstate commerce, included some major provisions regarding accountants' legal liability.

Required:　List and explain the major provisions affecting accountants' legal liability which were incorporated in the Securities Act of 1933.　(AICPA Adapted)

4-27. The accounting firm of Smyth, Smyth & Smith of Los Angeles, California, hired Watson as a junior. Watson was required, as a condition of employment, to agree in writing that if she left the employ of the firm she would neither establish her own firm nor work for another accounting firm on the West Coast of the United States, including Alaska, for a period of 10 years from the date of termination of employment.

Watson worked for several years for Smyth, Smyth & Smith. Subsequently, she left the firm's employ to return to her hometown, Eugene, Oregon, where she established her own accounting firm.

Smyth, Smyth & Smith seek specifically to enforce the prohibitory provision contained in Watson's written employment contract.

Required:　Will Smyth, Smyth & Smith be able to preclude Watson from engaging in the practice of accounting? Explain.　(AICPA Adapted)

4-28. Jackson was a junior staff member of an accounting firm. He began the audit of the Bosco Corporation which manufactured and sold expensive watches. In the middle of the audit he quit. The accounting firm hired another person to continue the audit of Bosco. Because of the changeover and the time pressure to finish the audit, the firm violated certain generally accepted auditing standards when they did not follow adequate procedures with respect to the physical inventory. Had the proper procedures been used during the examination, they would have discovered that watches worth more than

$20,000 were missing. The employee who was stealing the watches was able to steal an additional $30,000 worth before the thefts were discovered six months after completion of the audit.

131
Exercises and problems

Required: Discuss the legal problems of the accounting firm resulting from the above facts.

(AICPA Adapted)

4-29. As part of his examination of the financial statements of the Marlborough Corporation for the year ended March 31, 1979, Mario Romito, CPA, is reviewing the balance-sheet presentation of a $1,200,000 advance to Franklin Olds, Marlborough's president. The advance, which represents 50 percent of current assets and 10 percent of total assets, was made during the year ended March 31, 1979. It is described in the balance sheet as "Miscellaneous accounts receivable" and classified as a current asset.

Olds informs the CPA that he has used the proceeds of the advance to purchase 35,000 shares of Marlborough's common stock, in order to forestall a takeover raid on the company. He is reluctant to have his association with the advance described in the financial statements, because he does not have voting control and fears that this will "just give the raiders ammunition."

Olds offers the following four-point program as an alternative to further disclosure:

1. Have the advance approved by the board of directors. (This can be done expeditiously because a majority of the board members are officers of the company.)

2. Prepare a demand note payable to the company with interest of 7½ percent (the average bank rate paid by the company).

3. Furnish an endorsement of the stock to the company as collateral for the loan. (During the year under audit, despite the fact that earnings did not increase, the market price of Marlborough common stock rose from $20 to $40 per share. The stock maintained its $40 per share market price subsequent to year end.)

4. Obtain a written opinion from the company attorney supporting the legality of the company's advance and the use of the proceeds.

Required

1. Discuss the proper balance sheet classification of the advance to Olds and other appropriate disclosures in the financial statements and footnotes. (Ignore SEC regulations and requirements, tax effects, creditor's restrictions on stock repurchase, and the presentation of common stock dividends and interest income.)

2. Discuss each point of Mr. Olds' four-point program as to whether or not it is desirable and as to whether or not it is an alternative to further disclosure.

3. If Olds refuses to permit further disclosure, what action(s) should the CPA take? Discuss.

4. In his discussion with the CPA, Olds warns that the raiders, if successful, probably will appoint new auditors. What consideration should the CPA give to this factor? Explain.

(AICPA Adapted)

4-30. *Part A.* The partnership of Smith, Frank, & Clark, a CPA firm, has been the auditor of Greenleaf, Inc., for many years. During the annual examination of the financial statements for the year ended December 31, 1980, a dispute developed over whether certain disclosures should be made in the financial statements. The dispute resulted in Smith, Frank, & Clark's being dismissed and Greenleaf's engaging another firm. Greenleaf demanded that Smith, Frank, & Clark turn over all working papers applicable to the Greenleaf audits to it or face a lawsuit. Smith, Frank, & Clark refused. Greenleaf has instituted a suit against Smith, Frank, & Clark to obtain the working papers.

132
Legal
liability

Required

1. Will Greenleaf succeed in its suit? Explain.
2. Discuss the rationale underlying the rule of law applicable to the ownership of working papers.

Part B. Parker Products, Inc., is suing Flagstone Specialties, Inc., your client, in the state court system, alleging a breach of contract. The contract provided for Flagstone to construct a piece of highly technical equipment at Flagstone's cost plus a fixed fee. Specifically, Parker alleges that Flagstone has calculated costs incorrectly, loading the contract billings with inappropriate costs. Parker seeks to recover the excess costs.

Karen Lake, your CPA firm's partner in charge of the Flagstone account, has been subpoenaed by Parker to testify. Neither Lake nor the firm wishes to become involved in the litigation. Furthermore, if Lake testifies, some of the facts she would reveal might be prejudicial to the client.

Required

1. Must Lake testify? Explain.
2. If the cause of action had been such that the suit would have been brought in a federal court, must Lake testify? Explain.

Part C. Donald Sharpe recently joined the CPA firm of Spark, Watts, and Wilcox. He quickly established a reputation for thoroughness and a steadfast dedication to following prescribed auditing procedures to the letter. On his third audit for the firm, Sharpe examined the underlying documentation of 200 disbursements as a test of purchasing, receiving, vouchers payable, and cash disbursement procedures. In the process he found 12 disbursements for the purchase of materials with no receiving reports in the documentation. He noted the exceptions in his working papers and called them to the attention of the in-charge accountant. Relying on prior experience with the client, the in-charge accountant disregarded Sharpe's comments, and nothing further was done about the exceptions.

Subsequently it was learned that one of the client's purchasing agents and a member of its accounting department were engaged in a fraudulent scheme whereby they diverted the receipt of materials to a public warehouse while sending the invoices to the client. When the client discovered the fraud, the conspirators had obtained approximately $70,000, $50,000 of which was stolen after the completion of the audit.

Required: Discuss the legal implications and liabilities to Spark, Watts, and Wilcox as a result of the above facts.

Part D. The partnership of Porter, Potts, & Farr, CPAs, was engaged by Revolutionary Products, Inc., to examine its financial statements for the year ended June 30, 1980. The contract said nothing about the CPA firm's responsibility for defalcations. Porter, Potts & Farr performed its examination in a careful and competent manner, following generally accepted auditing standards and using appropriate auditing procedures and tests under the circumstances.

Subsequently it was discovered that the client's chief accountant was engaged in major defalcations. However, only an audit specifically designed to discover possible defalcations would have revealed the fraud. Revolutionary Products asserts that Porter, Potts, & Farr is liable for the defalcations.

Required: Is Porter, Potts, & Farr liable? Explain.

MULTIPLE CHOICE

1. As a consequence of his failure to adhere to generally accepted auditing standards in the course of his examination of the Lamp Corporation, Harrison, CPA, did not detect the embezzlement of a material amount of funds by the company's controller. As a matter of common law, to what extent is Harrison liable to the Lamp Corporation for losses attributable to the theft?

    a. He has no liability, since an ordinary examination cannot be relied upon to detect defalcations.
    b. He has no liability because privity of contract is lacking.
    c. He is liable for losses attributable to his negligence.
    d. He would be liable only if it could be proven that he had been grossly negligent.

TRUE OR FALSE

2. Kenneth Chance, a senior accountant with the partnership of South, Wall, Evers, & Company, CPAs, resigned after several years with the firm. During his employment, he had examined the financial statements of Zelex Corporation and had become a close friend of the controller and the financial vice-president of Zelex.

After establishing his own firm, Chance actively solicited the business of Zelex, even though the South firm had been engaged to perform the current year's audit. During the audit, Zelex dismissed the South firm, alleging that Chance's replacement was personally obnoxious, performed his work in a slipshod manner, and was dating one of the company's female bookkeepers. Zelex demanded the return of all of its books and records and the firm's working papers.

    a. Zelex can dismiss the South firm without liability solely upon the personality conflict that arose with respect to Chance's replacement.
    b. If Chance's replacement were negligent in performing his work, Zelex could terminate the relationship and recover damages.
    c. Zelex has the right to the return of its books and records.
    d. The South firm must turn over its working papers to Zelex.
    e. If none of Zelex's allegations are true, Zelex will be liable for breach of contract.

CHAPTER 5

Evidence: collection and evaluation

EVIDENCE

Auditing can be defined as the collection and evaluation of evidence. The third standard of fieldwork of generally accepted auditing standards demonstrates the importance of evidence in the attest function by stating:

> Sufficient competent evidential matter is to be obtained through inspection, observation, inquiries, and confirmations to afford a reasonable basis for an opinion regarding the financial statements under examination.

This standard emphasizes the relationship between the formulation of an opinion on the financial statements and the need to gather evidence which logically supports the auditor's opinion. In general, *audit evidence* is defined as any information which has an impact upon the audit decision process. It is recalled from an earlier discussion that management makes certain assertions which are expressed in the financial statements. The auditor must determine the validity of these assertions by performing an audit. During the engagement the auditor gathers evidence through a variety of techniques, to be discussed below, that will persuade the auditor either that the assertions concerning the financial statements are valid, or that they are invalid. Any information that contributes to determination of the validity of management's assertions is considered evidence. Of course, each piece of evidence is not of equal significance. Thus, to include the variety of evidence properly in the auditor's decision making process, the nature of the evidence in each unique audit environment must be understood.

The general sources of evidence

An audit is performed to determine if the financial statements are prepared in accordance with generally accepted accounting principles. While the ultimate audit decision is concerned with the financial statements, the evidence-gathering function concentrates on the mechanism that creates the financial statements.

This mechanism is the accounting system illustrated in Figure 5-1. Like any system, it is composed of an input phase, a process phase, and an output phase. The auditor reviews all three elements of the accounting system and gathers evidence to an extent sufficient for formulation of an opinion on the financial statements. This evidence can be divided into two broad sources, namely, underlying accounting data and corroborative information.

Evidence categorized as *underlying accounting data* consists of general and special journals, general and subsidiary ledgers, reconciliations, analyses allocating accounting data to the proper period, and any other records or analyses that substantiate the data appearing in the financial statements. This evidence is generated by management, which suggests that, while it is helpful to the auditor, it must be validated by him or her through the use of other sources of evidence.

Corroborative evidence provides the auditor with information to determine whether a transaction is authentic, properly processed, and properly reported. Vendors' invoices, confirmations, canceled checks, or similar documentation, and any procedures performed personally by the auditor, comprise *corroborative evidence*. Although underlying accounting data and corroborative evidence are discussed separately, in practice the two are merged, often resulting in their becoming indistinguishable.

The evidence collection function is illustrated in Figure 5-1. It is assumed that the client purchased depreciable equipment during the year, which resulted in assertions concerning the asset's book value and the depreciation expense that appears on the financial statements at the end of the year. The collection of evidential matter, which is abbreviated in the illustration, involves the auditor's review of accounting records and analyses. The processing of the data in the accounting records is substantiated by the auditor's referral to corroborating evidence, such as the vendor's invoice and the client's canceled check, and his or her own computations. There are other audit procedures that must be employed in this area, but at this point the illustration is sufficient to depict the sources of evidence and the relationship of this evidence to the audit objective.

Competency of evidence

The third standard of fieldwork refers to the competency of audit evidence. Competency is dependent upon the validity and relevancy of the evidence. The validity of evidence can be determined only by the circumstances under which the data are processed and collected; however, given this qualification, *SAS No. 1,* Section 330.08, lists the following presumptions that in part determine the validity of evidence:

- When evidential matter can be obtained from independent sources outside an enterprise, it provides greater assurance of reliability for the purpose of an independent audit than that secured solely within the enterprise.

- When accounting data and financial statements are developed under satisfactory conditions of internal control, there is more assurance as to their reliability than when they are developed under unsatisfactory conditions of internal control.

136
Evidence:
collection and
evaluation

Figure 5-1

Collection of evidential matter

	ACCOUNTING SYSTEM			
	INPUT	PROCESS	OUTPUT	
Accounting transac-tion: purchased ma-chinery for $100,-000			Financial statement assertions:	
Evidential matter Underlying ac-counting data (generated by client and re-viewed by audi-tor)		Entry in journal Posting to ledger Work sheet for depre-ciation allocation Summary of fixed assets and accumulated de-preciation Summary of deprecia-tion expense	Machinery Accumulated de-preciation Depreciation ex-pense	$100,000 5,000 5,000
Corroborative evi-dence (documen-tation reviewed or computation made by auditor)	Vendor's invoice Purchase order Receiving report Canceled check	Depreciation expense recomputed		

· Direct personal knowledge of the independent auditor obtained through physical examination, observation, computation, and inspection is more persuasive than information obtained indirectly.

Each of these three statements is logical and needs no further explanation, except the second one which refers to a client's internal control system. An *internal control system* may be described as the policies and rules adopted by a client in designing an accounting system. The purpose of the internal control system is to ensure that the financial statements are accurate and reliable and to safeguard the assets of the organization. If an organization has a well-designed internal control system, it is more likely that evidence, represented by underlying ac-counting data and documents generated by the company, will be valid. On the other hand, evidence generated under a poor internal control system is not as competent.

Also, competency is dependent upon the relevancy of the evidence. Rele-vancy is determined by examining the particular audit objective and then as-certaining whether the piece of evidence under consideration logically contrib-utes to the formulation of an audit decision. Neophyte auditors collect audit evidence that has no relevance to the audit objective when they blindly perform audit procedures without relating the audit evidence to the audit objective.

Types of evidence

There are several specific types of evidence the auditor may seek in attempting to ensure that the evidence collected is competent. Each type varies as to its degree of relevance, depending upon the accounting transaction or the account being investigated. Also, the amount of reliance an auditor places on evidence depends upon the type of evidence being evaluated. The following discussion deals with several types of evidence. Also considered is the degree of reliance the auditor places upon such evidence. No type of evidence is pervasive enough to satisfy a major audit objective. This objective must be achieved through the selection of several types of audit evidence. For example, the audit of the accounts receivable balance encompasses the collection of several types of audit evidence.

PHYSICAL EVIDENCE

One of the most persuasive types of evidence is physical evidence. The auditor's actual observation of an item validates the existence of that item. To illustrate, in the audit of inventories an auditor physically inspects the inventory to determine its existence. The fact that the client physically possesses the inventory is a major step in determining that the inventory account balance is correct. While physical evidence substantiates the existence of an item, it does not satisfy other audit objectives. Continuing with the inventory illustration, the auditor needs to be satisfied as to its ownership, cost, and saleability. For these reasons, it is necessary for the auditor to gather other types of evidence to satisfy other audit objectives.

COMPUTATIONAL EVIDENCE

Another type of evidence considered highly competent is recomputations actually made by the auditor. The financial statements are the result of numerous mathematical computations made throughout the accounting system. The auditor's recomputation of the client's original calculation is absolute proof of the accuracy or inaccuracy of the mathematical process. The auditor's recomputation provides him or her with competent evidence to achieve the audit objective of determining the accuracy of such calculations. However, the auditor's recomputation is limited only to the arithmetic process, for it does not validate the authenticity of the underlying data used in the calculation. To achieve this the auditor must gather additional evidence.

DOCUMENTARY EVIDENCE

A typical audit relies heavily upon documentary evidence to corroborate data presented in the financial statements. Documentary evidence varies considerably in reliability, depending upon the source of the document and the route it follows from its source until it is reviewed by the auditor. The four classifications of documentary evidence, in order of their validity, are:

1. Documents prepared externally and received directly by the auditor

138
**Evidence:
collection and
evaluation**

2. Documents prepared externally and received by the client
3. Documents prepared internally and circulated externally
4. Documents prepared and circulated internally

Documentary evidence received directly by the auditor from an external party is the most competent type of documentary evidential matter. If the auditor is assured that the information has come directly from a source not subjected to management intervention, the validity of the information is enhanced. For example, the auditor corresponds directly with a bank asking for the balance of the cash-in-bank account. A written statement by the bank, confirming the bank balance, represents a vital piece of evidence in the audit of cash. On the other hand, the client has a year-end bank statement containing the same balance, but this statement was received by management, which reduces its validity as evidential matter.

The next level of competent documentary evidence is that which is prepared externally but which is received by management. The auditor examines and relies upon this evidence more than on any other type of corroborative evidence. It includes vendor invoices, customer orders, documentation for securities investments, broker advices, and monthly bank statements. Although this category of documentary evidence is not as strong as evidence which originates externally and is received directly by the auditor, it is still considered highly competent. Nevertheless, the auditor is aware of this limitation and inspects such documents to see if they have been altered by the client. If the auditor becomes suspicious of the integrity of such documents, which is a reflection on the integrity of management, he or she employs audit techniques that generate external evidence not subject to management intervention.

The least competent documentary evidence is that prepared by management. The quality of this evidence is enhanced if it circulates and is validated by an external party. A canceled check is such a document. A check is prepared internally but is processed externally, validation being accomplished through endorsement by the payee and cancellation by the banking system. Such evidence is considered highly persuasive by the auditor, but once again he or she inspects such documents for possible alteration.

Documents prepared by management and circulated exclusively on an internal basis are the least convincing type of documentary evidence. This category includes a wide variety of corroborative evidence such as bank reconciliations, sales invoices, purchase orders, corporate minutes, journals, and ledgers. Such evidence plays an important role in the audit as supportive evidence rather than as primary evidence. For any particular financial account or transaction, the auditor collects a variety of evidence to support assertions on the financial statements. Documentary evidence generated and held internally must be consistent with other evidence collected.

With the exception of the first category of documentary evidence, evidence prepared externally and received directly by the auditor, the competency of evidence depends upon the adequacy of the client's internal control system.

Analysis of the internal control system is another type of evidence utilized by the auditor.

INTERNAL CONTROL EVIDENCE

An internal control system is designed by management to safeguard its assets and to ensure the accuracy and reliability of its accounting data. The auditor studies the internal control system to determine its strengths and weaknesses. The auditor's conclusions as to the adequacy of the system determine the degree of reliance placed on documents generated and processed by the system, the resulting journals and ledgers, and ultimately the financial statements. For example, an auditor investigates the accounts payable account which consists of numerous payables to vendors. To support one of these payables the auditor inspects the following documentary evidence:

- Vendor invoice (document prepared externally and received by the client)
- Receiving report (document prepared and circulated internally)
- Purchase order (document prepared and circulated internally)

All this evidential matter is subject to internal manipulation, since it is not received directly by the auditor from a third party. Yet if the auditor concludes that there exists a strong internal control system, it can be surmised that competent and sufficient evidence has been collected for this single payable. When the auditor believes the system is deficient, he or she does not rely solely on this type of evidence and corresponds directly with the vendor or performs other audit procedures to enhance the competency of the overall evidence.

The role of the internal control system in contemporary auditing cannot be overstated. A comprehensive discussion of internal controls and the audit approach in this area is deferred until Chapter 6.

ACTIVITY AND TESTIMONIAL EVIDENCE

The auditor is in constant contact with the client, whether it be the corporate president or an inventory clerk. By observing activities and asking pertinent questions of management and other personnel, the successful auditor obtains another type of evidence. In this endeavor he or she is cautious in the degree of weight placed on activity observance and oral testimony. Oral evidence is substantiated by other evidence, and the auditor evaluates responses with a certain amount of skepticism. The auditor who accepts glib answers without follow-up procedures does not meet the third standard of fieldwork.

The effectiveness of activity and testimonial evidence is more useful in directing the evidence collection approach rather than in providing competent evidential matter. By observing the actions of management and asking the right questions, the auditor can identify areas that need to be investigated. To illustrate, the auditor observes the client's count of inventory. If the auditor observes personnel who are doing a poor job or, by asking questions of the personnel, discovers resentment on the part of most of the personnel, he or she modifies the audit approach accordingly. If there are two personal characteristics needed by an auditor, they are the ability to be observant and to be inquisitive.

140
Evidence:
collection and
evaluation

Sufficiency of evidence

Competent evidential matter is collected to a degree sufficient to provide a basis upon which the auditor can form an opinion as to the fairness of the financial statements. The auditor recognizes that sufficiency is not synonymous with absolute certainty. Evidence is persuasive rather than convincing, and differentiating the two levels of sufficiency is no easy task. Professional judgment directs the auditor in each area of the audit to a subjective definition of what constitutes the threshold of audit evidence sufficiency. Each engagement is different; therefore any guidelines must be of a general nature. In addition, each auditor develops a personal feeling as what is enough evidence that allows him or her to be comfortable and confident with the amount of evidence collected. One auditor may have a tendency to be cautious and conservative, and these characteristics would undoubtedly affect the audit approach in this area. Irrespective of personal idiosyncrasies, the auditor takes several factors into consideration when the sufficiency of evidence is being determined. Among the factors considered are the (1) degree of risk, (2) cost of obtaining evidence, (3) competency of evidential matter, and (4) materiality.

DEGREE OF RISK

There is a direct relationship between the degree of risk involved and the amount of evidence collected. The more risk involved, the more evidence the auditor gathers. The auditor evaluates risk from two perspectives when determining the sufficiency of evidence needed to satisfy the audit objective. Initially he or she considers the overall risk involved by evaluating the audit environment. The maturity of the industry has an impact on the level of overall risk. A relatively young industry with an uncertain future is probably classified as a high-risk audit. In addition, the financial stability and history of earnings for a particular firm within an industry contribute to the level of risk involved. The circumstances surrounding the need for an audit are another relevant factor. For a company that needs audited financial statements to secure an important loan from a financial institution, an additional risk factor is considered by the auditor. These factors and others contribute to the auditor's attitude about risk for a particular client, and this attitude affects the amount of audit evidence that must be gathered.

The auditor also views risk from another, less broad, perspective. In the audit of each account a different amount of risk is involved, depending upon several factors. For example, the adequacy of internal control for a particular account or set of related accounts is considered. An account generated under a system of strong internal controls involves less risk than an account generated under conditions of poor or nonexistent internal controls. The auditor's comprehensive investigation of management's accounting system is the basis for assigning risk for this factor. In addition, the nature of the account under review influences the degree of risk, since some accounts are more susceptible to conversion or misstatement. Cash and other highly liquid assets are more easily converted and misappropriated than other assets, such as intangible assets. Misstatement is more likely to occur in an estimated liability account, such as a provision for future warrant cost, than for an actual liability such as accrued wages payable. Risk is apparent in each account, but it exists to a greater degree in the audit of the former rather than the latter account.

COST OF OBTAINING EVIDENCE

In collecting sufficient competent evidential matter the auditor must work within economic limits. He or she cannot collect exhaustive amounts of the most competent types of evidence, since such an approach would result in a prohibitive cost to the client and ultimately to society. This practical limitation requires that the auditor collect a sufficient amount of evidence at a reasonable cost. Generally, he or she can collect different types of evidence which vary in competency. Thus competency is not the sole guideline in collecting evidence. Many students, when asked to prepare an audit program for an account, often list procedures that are highly competent but are impractical in terms of cost. For example, an auditor may want to ensure that undeposited cash at the end of the year was in fact on hand. One alternative, using physical evidence, involves having the auditor visit the premises on the last day of the fiscal year and control the receipt of cash. The evidence is highly competent, but the procedure is costly, especially if there are several branches that receive cash. As an alternative, using documentary evidence, the auditor may review year-end bank reconciliations and cut-off bank statements, which is far less costly but less competent. In most cases, the latter audit approach is satisfactory. Thus cost is an important factor in determining the sufficiency of evidence, but the cost of auditing an account is not in itself a valid reason for omitting an audit procedure.

COMPETENCY AND SUFFICIENCY

There is an interrelationship between the competency of evidence and the sufficiency of evidence. The more persuasive a piece of evidence, the less likely that additional evidence will have to be collected. As suggested earlier, physical evidence is highly competent and satisfies the auditor more quickly than oral evidence. When an auditor rejects sources of evidence, because of cost or impracticality, it usually means that a greater amount of evidence of a less competent nature must be collected. An auditor may achieve the audit objective of determining the existence of an accounts receivable by confirming this amount directly with the customer of the client. If this proves impractical, he or she may utilize less competent evidence, such as the review of subsequent cash collections and the inspection of selling and shipping documents, to a greater degree. In essence, *competency* refers to the quality of evidence, and *sufficiency* refers to the quantity of evidence. The auditor selects the proper mixture of the two to use as a basis in forming an opinion on the financial statements.

MATERIALITY

When determining the amount of evidence to collect as well as the quality of evidence needed, no factor is more important than materiality. Materiality is fundamental to the audit approach, yet the concept is very difficult to explain

142
Evidence:
collection and
evaluation

in operational terms. In *SAS No. 1,* Section 150.04, the AICPA defines the role of materiality:

> The concept of materiality is inherent in the work of the independent auditor. There should be stronger ground to sustain the independent auditor's opinion with respect to those items which are relatively more important and with respect to those in which the possibilities of material error are greater than with respect to those of lesser importance or those in which the possibility of material error is remote.

In assessing materiality, the auditor considers the potential impact of an account or transaction on the financial statements. Items for which the audit exposure is the greatest are subjected to a greater degree of investigation. The audit exposure for the account petty cash is minimal in most audit situations. Conversely, when the client has a substantial contract with the federal government that involves significant receivables and revenue recognized under the completed contract method, the auditor is more diligent in auditing these accounts because of their potential impact on the financial statements.

To measure materiality the auditor utilizes certain reference points or bases. Most auditors evaluate the materiality of items in the context of major subgroupings on the financial statements. Among the subgroupings are total assets, total liabilities, current assets, net working capital, gross revenue, functional groupings of expense accounts, and net income. There is no literature that identifies the materiality threshold. Most auditors consider 10 percent of the above subgroupings to be material, and some suggest that the threshold is below 10 percent. It is important to recognize that each audit situation is unique, and under no circumstances is an arbitrary level of 10 percent or any other percentage to be blindly followed. Using professional judgment, the auditor selects the criteria for defining materiality and the threshold percentage.

The concept of materiality is broader than the quantitative aspect discussed above. Certain items are disclosed in the financial statements as parenthetical comments or as footnotes to the financial statements in a qualitative manner. Since these items do not affect the numbers directly, the quantitative criteria discussed above are not relevant. In the area of nonnumeric disclosures, the auditor must ask if a prudent investor needs such information to make an economic decision about the firm. When he or she believes such information is material, then sufficient evidence is collected to ensure that full disclosure in the area is achieved. This type of disclosure can be onerous for the auditor, especially when the need for full disclosure of uncertain future events has an impact on the continuance of the firm as a going concern.[1]

Evidence-gathering techniques

As suggested above, a variety of audit evidence exists. In order to collect evidence for evaluation, the auditor uses several different audit techniques. In selecting the technique to be used the audit objective and the nature of the

---

[1] See Henry P. Hill, "Reporting on Uncertainties by Independent Auditors," *Journal of Accountancy,* January 1973, pp. 55–60.

account being investigated are considered. Once the relevant technique has been identified, the auditor formulates a specific audit procedure; therefore an audit procedure refers to an act to be performed by the auditor. In fact, the auditor identifies several audit procedures, which are derivatives of the general audit techniques that may be employed, in the audit of a single account. During an actual engagement the techniques tend to overlap, but it is useful to identify the general evidence-gathering techniques and discuss them on an individual basis.

OBSERVATION

The auditor can gain personal knowledge about the existence of an asset by observation. The type of evidence gathered by employing this technique is very competent. This evidence-gathering approach is the basis of several audit procedures, such as the observation of inventory and the observation of fixed assets. When using this approach, the auditor also uses the technique of counting, which in this discussion is considered an integral part of observation. The auditor does more than just observe the inventory. It is also necessary to count the inventory to gain conclusive evidence as to the number of items on hand. In the area of asset verification, observation is not limited to achieving the sole audit objective of determining existence. Through observation the auditor determines to some extent the quality of the asset under investigation. He or she may notice that some inventory items are damaged or that plant assets are not being utilized. Such observed details impact the valuation and classification of accounts. The auditor's ability to determine the quality of tangible assets is limited, since he or she is not a professional appraiser. When the nature of the asset is such that special skills are required to identify and value the inventory, the auditor considers using an independent expert.

Observation is useful to the auditor in areas other than the review of tangible assets. He or she observes the activities of the client to consider their impact on the audit approach. During the audit, the client's personnel are observed as part of the evaluation of the internal control system. Their attitudes and work habits have a definite effect on the type and extent of subsequent audit procedures employed. The technique of observation is more universal than specific audit procedures performed as part of the audit program. The auditor stays aware of events that occur in the audit environment and continually questions whether they have audit significance. The auditor who becomes completely involved in the details of the audit irrespective of what is occurring around him or her is very likely to overlook important events that may have more significance than the detail transactions or accounts being investigated. For example, an auditor who is in the client's shipping department specifically to obtain information about bills of lading may notice the shipment of inventory that appears to be unauthorized. The latter evidence may be far more significant than the former.

CONFIRMATION

Documentary evidence is collected from outside parties by confirmation. This type of evidence is very persuasive if collected under the proper circumstances. First, the third party must be qualified to express its view on the item

144
Evidence:
collection and
evaluation

being confirmed. Then the auditor must select the information to be confirmed, control the mailing of the information, and receive the third-party response without any possibility of management intervention. If any one of these elements is violated, the integrity of the technique will be compromised and the competency of the confirmation significantly reduced. The extent of management's role in the process is authorization for the release of information by the third party, which is usually achieved by the signing of the confirmation request by a responsible member of management. For example, an auditor sends a cash balance confirmation to the client's bank, but before the bank releases such confidential information it must have proper authorization.

The use of the confirmation technique is required in the audit of accounts and notes receivable. This audit procedure is discussed at length in Chapter 11. Additionally, confirmation can be used in a variety of areas. In fact, almost every transaction processed in the accounting system can be confirmed by a third party. The following uses of the confirmation technique attest to its broad applicability in the audit:

- *Inventory:* Items held on consignment
- *Accounts payable:* Unpaid vendor invoices
- *Prepayments:* Details of contractual arrangements
- *Securities:* Items held for security or items pledged
- *Common stock:* Number of shares outstanding
- *Contingent liabilities:* Details of pending litigation

The confirmation technique is usually reserved for significant transactions. In many areas where it could be employed, the auditor relies upon less competent evidence. For example, he or she could confirm the details of the sales account but instead usually relies upon internal documentation such as sales invoices. However, when the auditor becomes suspicious of internal documentation, or the internal control system is inadequate, more reliance is placed on the confirmation technique.

VOUCHING

An alternative to using direct third-party confirmation, as suggested above, is the use of vouching. *Vouching* refers to the auditor's inspection of documents that support an accounting transaction. This approach relieves the auditor of the need to use the rather costly technique of confirmation in many areas. The authoritativeness of the evidence gathered through vouching depends upon, as stated earlier, the adequacy of the internal control system and the nature of the documentation. It has already been suggested that documentary evidence varies in competency, depending upon the source of the document and the physical route it follows.

In performing the vouching technique the auditor is usually concerned with one of two audit objectives. First, he or she must determine whether there is adequate support for a transaction processed by the accounting system. Each client establishes internal control policies and procedures that control the acceptance and processing of financial data. Only transactions that are properly supported are allowed to enter the accounting system. The auditor determines the propriety of such transactions by inspecting documents that substantiate compliance with corporate policies. For example, the payment of a trade account payable is supported by documents that show proper authorization of the purchase (a signed purchase order), receipt of the goods (a receiving report), and a request for payment from an approved vendor (a vendor's invoice). All documents must be examined carefully by the auditor to determine whether they are authentic or whether they have been altered.

The vouching process encompasses a second audit objective. An inspection of the underlying documents is made to determine whether the transaction is properly processed in the accounting system. The auditor determines if a transaction has been processed in the appropriate accounting period and if it has been processed in accordance with generally accepted accounting principles. When a client has sold merchandise on consignment, the auditor reviews such documents as the consignee's sales report and consignment invoices to determine that sales are not recorded when inventory is shipped to the consignee and that sales made by the consignee are recorded in the proper accounting period.

RECOMPUTATION

Recomputation involves the auditor's independent verification of arithmetic computations performed by a client. This procedure appears to be almost trivial, but it is an indispensable tool in the audit. The auditor does not attest to the fairness of the financial statements unless some of the fundamental arithmetic manipulations of data by the client are tested. The client may give the auditor a list of 10 inventory items which the auditor physically examines, but if the latter does not recompute simple addition and multiplication competent evidence has not been obtained. In this example the auditor must foot (add) the inventory listing and test the extension of each line item by multiplying the number of units on hand by the per-unit cost.

Evidence gathered by recomputation is very competent evidence. Earlier in this chapter it was noted that this technique validates only the mathematical process. Other audit techniques are utilized to substantiate the authenticity of the data used in the computation. For example, each set of financial statements includes a determination of the earnings per share of common stock. The auditor tests this computation as a simple problem in division, but the determination of net income, common stock shares outstanding, and perhaps common stock equivalents requires a considerable amount of investigation. This means that other evidence-gathering techniques are utilized.

INQUIRY

The audit technique of inquiry is almost always a preliminary procedure that leads to the use of a more specific audit technique. Essentially, the auditor asks questions to provide direction for the detailed audit. The verbal or oral inquiry may be of a general nature or may be very specific. An auditor may ask if the credit policy of the firm has changed from the previous year and, depending upon the response, modifies the audit approach in reviewing the allowance for

146
Evidence:
collection and
evaluation

uncollectable accounts. More specifically, he or she may ask about the policy for capitalizing fixed-asset expenditures, which may result in the vouching of items in the asset account and in the repairs and maintenance expense account. In addition, the inquiry may be more formal than an "off-the-cuff" inquiry. The completion of an internal control questionnaire is an attempt to describe the accounting system through a series of prescribed questions.

The auditor often uses an analytical technique such as scanning, which is a form of inquiry. Again, this technique is usually a prelude to a more detailed audit approach. By scanning, the auditor can review a substantial amount of detail to determine if any of the items are unusual. Items that appear unusual may be subjected to the audit technique of recomputation or vouching to substantiate their authenticity. To illustrate, an auditor may not be able to recompute manually the extensions in an inventory listing which include numerous line items. To save time, the audit may sight-test or scan each line item to determine if the extension is reasonable. An auditor might use the following technique. A single line item contains two elements, namely, the quantity and the unit cost. If the quantity is 123 and the cost is $9 per item, the result will be approximately $1200 ($120 \times \$10$). If the extended value on the listing is $11,070, the auditor will investigate the error by recomputing the problem. Such an approach can be invaluable as a time-saver for the auditor.

CONSISTENCY OF DATA

The auditor plans an audit so that areas which appear to have the greatest audit risk receive the most attention. There is no way of removing risk from an audit, but it can be reduced by the auditor's analysis of the consistency of data. This is a broad technique which ultimately results in more specific audit techniques being used. Consistency is determined in the context of the firm's economic conditions and business activity for the accounting period. It is important for the auditor to look at the qualitative as well as the quantitative factors. A company may have exactly the same volume of credit sales in one year as it did in a previous year, and initially the bad debt expense would be expected to be the same amount as for the prior year. But, if there has been a business slowdown in this particular industry, a determination of the consistency of the accounting data cannot be limited exclusively to a quantitative analysis. The auditor uses the following approaches to determine the consistency of accounting data.

- Analysis of trends and ratios
- Analysis of comparative amounts
- Analysis of interrelated accounts

In formulating an audit approach that allocates the auditor's efforts to areas which warrant the most investigation, an auditor prepares financial statement ratios and a trend analysis. Depending upon the client's specific economic environment, the auditor has definite expectations about certain accounts. When the computed ratios or analysis of trends is not consistent with the auditor's expectations, the auditor more heavily investigates the accounts that comprise the analysis. An auditor usually computes an inventory turnover ratio for each inventory product line. If the current year's ratio is significantly lower than that **147** of the previous year, the subsequent audit approach will be affected. Among **An Integrated audit approach** other procedures, the auditor is particularly concerned with the saleability of inventory and designs the audit program in a manner that determines the ability of the company to recover the cost of the inventory.

Analysis of the consistency of data includes the comparison of account balances. Again, when the qualitative factors are taken into account, the account balance is expected to increase, decrease, or remain the same, depending upon the circumstances. Any significant deviation provides the impetus for additional investigation. The analysis of comparative accounts consists of a systematic comparison of current account balances with that anticipated by reference to such items as the previous year's account balance and budgeted financial amounts. Such an approach identifies areas of potential errors or omissions. A comparison of productive assets' previous year's balance and the capital budget plan for the current year may suggest a 20 percent increase in such assets. When the increase is significantly less than 20 percent, the auditor investigates such an inconsistency. This is not to suggest that the suspicion or omissions will be confirmed. It simply identifies areas that deserve substantial audit investigation.

In the auditor's initial analytical review of financial information there is an analysis of the interrelationship of data. This consistency of data is partly a result of the duality of bookkeeping. Certain transactions that impact one account have an effect on another account. There are many such interrelationships between accounts that appear on the balance sheet and the income statement, which are affected by the same transaction. A significant increase in sales suggests a rather predictable pattern in the accounts receivable balance. The interrelationship is not limited to transactions that affect the balance sheet and the income statement simultaneously. For example, an increase in sales suggests an appropriate increase in sales commission expense. Also, there is recognition of the interrelationship of financial information and managerial decisions made during the accounting period. Such decisions, which may be identified through the inquiry technique, may have a significant effect on determination of the consistency of data. A company that introduces a product as the result of new technology may expect a significant impact on the estimated warranty liability. If the auditor finds no such increase, this is an obvious area for investigation.

The auditor's analysis of the consistency of data provides an excellent basis for determining the audit approach. However, the technique is not used only at the beginning of the audit. A successful auditor is alert to inconsistencies in quantitative and qualitative data throughout the audit, modifying the audit approach accordingly.

AN INTEGRATED AUDIT APPROACH

In the auditor's quest to gather competent and sufficient evidence, it has been shown that a variety of evidence-gathering techniques is available. In addition, the extent of evidence that may be collected is limited, which implies the testing of data rather than a 100 percent review. Also, the evidence is persuasive rather

148
Evidence:
collection and
evaluation

than conclusive, which suggests that all audits involve an unavoidable amount of risk. To enable the auditor to collect evidence that provides a basis for formulating an opinion on the financial statements (subject to the above constraints) an engagement must be well planned and properly executed. The task is made manageable by the selection of an audit approach which integrates each phase of the audit in order to maximize the efficiency of the auditor. This integrated approach consists of four major audit phases, the results of each phase having an impact on the succeeding phase. These steps, in order of performance, are:

- Investigation of client environmental conditions
- Evaluation of internal controls
- Compliance tests
- Substantive tests

Environmental conditions

The first phase of the audit is general in nature but is fundamental to the overall audit approach because it establishes the direction of the audit by indicating the type of evidence to be gathered, the extent of the evidence, and the timing of the procedures used to gather the evidence. The audit techniques used in this area consist of inquiry, observation, and analysis of the consistency of accounting data. It may be recalled that these three techniques usually provide the basis for subsequent investigation using techniques that generate more competent evidence. These techniques are most appropriate for this phase of the audit. The identification of fundamental changes that may have a significant impact on the financial statements is the primary objective of this approach. Once these potential areas have been identified, the subsequent three phases of the integrated audit approach are modified in an appropriate manner. *Environmental conditions* consist of general economic conditions, specific economic and regulatory conditions, and the firm's structure. The auditor must be aware of these environmental elements as an initial step in the audit approach.

GENERAL ECONOMIC CONDITIONS

General economic conditions establish the broad framework within which the auditor first evaluates the environmental setting of a particular client. The auditor stays abreast of the business cycle and relates these conditions to the audit. No company is insulated from the effects of external economic factors. Such factors as the availability of credit and the movement of interest rates are general business factors to be considered. Although quite broad in nature, they help develop the auditor into a well-informed individual, which enables him or her to be more inquisitive and to project an image that impresses the client. The auditor must give an impression of being genuine and not superficial and should elicit respect from management that will convince the latter of the need to cooperate. In addition, a well-informed auditor is less likely to be misled by erroneous or vague comments by management.

The basic audit technique used in gathering information about general economic conditions is inquiry. Basically, this consists of reading general and business periodicals on a continuous basis. Furthermore, personal inquiries made to external parties, such as bankers, enable the auditor to be cognizant of regional or local economic conditions that may be of audit significance.

INDUSTRIAL ECONOMIC AND REGULATORY CONDITIONS

An analysis of economic conditions in the industry provides analytical evidence for the construction of subsequent audit procedures. The industry's business cycle stage can have an impact on a firm's financial statement and required disclosure. If the industry is in a downturn, the auditor is forewarned of possible excess capacity with its attendant effect on manufacturing overhead rates or inventories that may have to be reduced below cost.

The maturing of the industry and the pace of technology are two other aspects of industrial economics that may prove relevant in the audit approach. An industry that is young and dynamic usually experiences a rash of bankruptcies on its way to maturity. Such an industry often exposes audit firms to litigation. In this case, the auditor approaches the engagement with far more skepticism than a more routine audit. Similarly, the role of technology is an important industrial factor. Rapid technological changes occurring in an industry usually suggest relatively less stable firms. Even if the individual firm appears to be stable, technology can result in an uneconomical productive capacity or obsolete product lines. The auditor who is ignorant of such developments courts disaster.

The role of government at every level is increasing. Such actions often impact the financial statements of an organization. The auditor identifies the agencies that regulate a particular industry and keeps informed of new legislation or administration regulations. Promulgations that have an impact on industrial health standards or pollution standards may be examined for possible audit implications. In addition, government policy concerning trade can mean the difference between life and death for an industry. An executive order on imports may determine whether a client will be in existence next year, and the audit impact cannot be overstated.

Again, the fundamental audit technique used to gather evidence in this area is inquiry. The auditor reads relevant trade periodicals to stay attuned to industrial changes. He or she does not in most cases have the time to become an expert in a particular field. Nonetheless, it is imperative that the auditor be conversant and be capable of asking pertinent questions, as well as comprehend the answers offered by management. In addition to trade periodicals, the minutes of the board of directors and other key committee minutes are important sources of industrial developments. The board of directors discusses such topics and establishes policy to direct the action of the corporate officers. A critical reading of the minutes is made by the auditor to identify areas of potential audit risk or to confirm suspicions generated in a preliminary audit inquiry. Information concerning government action can be obtained through the utilization of a legal letter. A *legal letter* is correspondence received directly from the client's lawyer and is concerned with pending lawsuits or other legal matters. The competency

150
Evidence:
collection and
evaluation

of the evidence contained in a legal letter has received much attention recently and is discussed in Chapter 14.

CLIENT STRUCTURE

As the audit's focal point moves from an analysis of general and industrial economic developments to an analysis of the structure of the firm, more specific evidence is sought. Basically an investigation is made of the type of organization chosen by management to achieve its objective. There must be an awareness of the fundamental organizational structure as a prerequisite to the formulation of an efficient audit approach. Management's structure can be analyzed from a functional perspective, reviewing the production, marketing, and finance areas.

For a manufacturer the production function undoubtedly has unique characteristics that the auditor needs to understand. For example, familiarity with the production process and the physical flow of inventories from the raw materials stage to the finished goods stage is needed to help ensure comprehension of the cost accounting system. To acquire this evidence the auditor uses the observation technique referred to as a plant tour. Early in the engagement the auditor tours the plant with a well-informed member of the client's staff. During the tour, the auditor is observant, asks pertinent questions, and evaluates the experience in the general framework of potential impact on the accounting system and the financial statements. On most tours, the auditor notes certain characteristics that may affect his or her subsequent observation of the inventory. Such items as problems of observing work in process on the inventory date, inventories with a significant dollar value, and inventories located off the client's premises may play an important role in the auditor's planning for the inventory observation.

The method by which a client sells its products is another vital function of an organization and is fundamental in the construction of an audit approach. Again, the auditor's understanding of the accounting system is enhanced by such a review. If a client relies heavily on consignees to sell its product, the accounting system must be designed to account for such sales in accordance with generally accepted accounting principles. In addition, consignment shipments result in inventory observation problems at the end of the accounting period. The auditor must anticipate the problem and have some idea of its dollar significance. Much of the information concerning the marketing function is acquired through inquiry. Also, the auditor's knowledge of the product line of the client in relationship to new industrial developments is explored at this stage of the investigation. This illustrates the need for the auditor to relate all the evidence gathered to a certain point in the audit and use this accumulated evidence as a basis for the next step. In this area, he or she can use ratios and trend analysis to identify possible inconsistencies in the marketing data. A significant decrease in the gross profit rate, coupled with the introduction of new products by a competitor, may suggest a need for inventory write-offs.

The financial structure of a client is studied for its potential impact on the audit approach. It has already been suggested that a company which is not financially sound alerts the auditor and makes the audit approach somewhat defensive. In addition, the financial condition of the industry as a whole is considered. When the economic signs for the firm and the industry are poor, the impact on the audit approach is pervasive. Other factors, such as a tight supply of credit, are relevant, and in an extreme case the auditor may be faced with an uncertainty deficiency, availability of credit, which may lead to a qualified opinion or a disclaimer of an opinion. In a less dramatic vein, an awareness of debt instruments is warranted. A bond agreement may contain a covenant that requires a certain level of working capital. When such a condition is not met, financial statement disclosure in the form of a footnote is required.

Considering the environmental conditions of a client is an integral part of the first standard of fieldwork which requires that "the work is to be adequately planned . . ." In 1978, the AICPA issued *SAS No. 22* to serve as a guide in achieving this standard. Specifically the statement suggested the following as representative of audit procedures to be performed in this phase of the audit.

a. Reviewing correspondence files, prior year's audit working papers, permanent files, financial statements, and auditor's reports.
b. Discussing matters that may affect the examination with firm personnel responsible for nonaudit services to the entity.
c. Inquiring about current business developments affecting the entity.
d. Reading the current year's interim financial statements.
e. Discussing the type, scope, and timing of the examination with management of the entity, the board of directors, or its audit committee.
f. Considering the effects of applicable accounting and auditing pronouncements, particularly new ones.
g. Coordinating the assistance of entity personnel in data preparation.
h. Determining the extent of involvement, if any, of consultants, specialists, and internal auditors.
i. Establishing the timing of the audit work.
j. Establishing and coordinating staffing requirements.[2]

Evaluation of internal control

The second major phase of the integrated audit approach is a continuation of the analytical review used in investigation of the client's environmental conditions. The initial analysis of the client provides a basis for evaluation of the internal control system. The internal control system is in part constructed in a manner consistent with the functional organization of the company. An understanding of the production function, as well as the other functions mentioned above, enables the auditor to identify the areas of the accounting system that are important and the areas where the audit risk is the greatest. Specifically, the objective of the systems review is to determine its strengths and weaknesses, which is the basis for guidance in performance of the compliance tests and the substantive tests. Chapter 6 is devoted exclusively to the auditor's investigation

[2] "Planning and Supervision," *Statement on Auditing Standards No. 22* (New York: AICPA, 1978), pp. 2–3.

152
Evidence:
collection and
evaluation

of the internal control system. At this point, it is simply necessary to understand the relationship of the evaluation to the other three phases of the audit approach.

Compliance tests

An evaluation of a client's accounting system does not result in the generation of corroborative evidence, since it is analytical in nature. As suggested above, the auditor interviews the client's personnel in an attempt to understand how routine accounting transitions are processed. Once he or she understands the client's internal control system, it is then necessary to (1) determine whether the accounting system functions in a manner consistent with the description provided by the client's personnel and (2) determine the nature and number of processing errors that have occurred in the system. Both objectives are concerned with the effectiveness of the internal control system, and the approach is referred to as performing the *compliance tests*.

In the first phase of the tests of compliance, the auditor determines that the system is functioning as described. He or she may inspect documents for proper approval, or tasks performed by the client's personnel may be observed. For example, the client's control procedures may require that a purchase order be prepared and signed by the purchasing agent before raw materials can be ordered. To see if this procedure is being followed, the auditor may test several purchases for the accounting period by determining if the purchases are supported by a properly executed purchase order. On the other hand, some characteristics of the internal control system cannot be validated through the inspection of documents. To illustrate, part of the control system may be based on the segregation of certain duties. For example, cash receipts may be collected and deposited in the bank by the cashier, while the accounts receivable clerk's sole responsibility is to post the cash collections based on a report from another source. Through observation and inquiry the auditor determines that the two tasks are being performed by different individuals.

In this phase of the tests of compliance the auditor is not concerned with "dollar errors" but rather with compliance errors. Dollar errors have a direct impact on the financial statements in that an account will have an incorrect balance. A compliance error does not necessarily result in a dollar error on the financial statements. For example, a purchase of inventory may not be supported by a purchase order, but the dollar amounts posted to the account may be correct. Thus a compliance error alerts the auditor to a potential problem that may result in incorrect balances on the financial statements. When these errors are discovered by the auditor, he or she evaluates them to determine the impact upon the nature, extent, and timing of subsequent audit procedures.

The second phase of the tests of compliance is concerned with specific processing errors that affect the financial statements. In this phase the auditor is more concerned with the operation of the internal control system rather than with its design. For example, the auditor tests for mathematical errors, transposition errors, coding errors, and posting errors. He or she selects sample transactions that were processed during the year and performs a variety of tests. These are often referred to as the *tests of transactions*.

Substantive tests

The auditor's opinion concerns the numerical balances that appear on the financial statements. On the surface it may appear that audit procedures need to be exclusively designed to validate these numbers. One may ask why the auditor should be concerned with the other three phases of the audit approach when the audit report does not refer to the environmental conditions, the evaluation of the internal control system, or the results of the compliance tests, but rather to the balances for cash, sales, depreciation expense, and the like. The reason is that most businesses are too large for the auditor to verify every transaction that impacted the current year's financial statements. So, to determine which transactions and balances are to be tested in detail, the auditor needs to know the environmental conditions, the weaknesses and strengths of the internal control system, and the number of errors discovered during the testing of the accounting system. With this understanding he or she is prepared to design the substantive tests.

Substantive tests are concerned with the validation or substantiation of a balance that appears on the financial statements. For example, the auditor may count petty cash, confirm an accounts receivable, or inspect all documents that support a sale. The first two procedures are concerned with balances that appear on the balance sheet, and the last one is concerned with a balance that appears on the income statement. There is an overlap between the tests of transactions, considered part of the tests of compliance, and the substantive tests. For example, during the tests of transactions the auditor may select a sales invoice for testing. The invoice may be tested for proper authorization, mathematical accuracy, and proper posting to the sales journal, and eventual summarization and posting to the general ledger. These procedures obviously validate part of the sales account balance and part of the accounts receivable balance, if the amount has not been collected at the end of the year. Such a result impacts the design of the substantive tests approach which is more fully explained in Chapters 10 through 16.

At this point, it is not important to understand the detailed procedures used in the audit approach described. However, it is imperative that the interrelationship of each step be fully understood. To facilitate comprehension of the approach, Figure 5-2 illustrates how the approach may be used. The illustration is not comprehensive, in that all procedures and all potential ramifications are not discussed; nevertheless, it should be studied before proceeding. As the illustration demonstrates, the audit approach becomes more specific as the auditor moves through the different steps of the audit approach.

DOCUMENTATION OF EVIDENTIAL MATTER

In the course of an audit, a significant amount of evidence is gathered, which suggests a need to document the audit approach taken by the auditor. This objective is accomplished by preparing audit working papers. Working papers are a fundamental tool in the planning and execution of an audit. During the course of an engagement, the auditor estimates the labor requirements of an audit, the current progress of an audit, and matters to be resolved at a later date,

154
Evidence:
collection and
evaluation

Figure 5-2

The integrated audit approach

AUDIT PHASE	EVIDENTIAL MATTER ACQUIRED	IMPACT ON SUBSEQUENT AUDIT PHASE
Client environment	Through inquiry the auditor discovers that the client has designated agents that have the authority to purchase an agricultural commodity sold through local auctions scattered throughout the southeastern United States.	The auditor must determine whether the transactions are properly controlled and accounted for in an acceptable manner.
Internal control evaluation	Through inquiry (completion of an internal control questionnaire), the auditor determines that each agent has the authority to prepare and sign the check for the amount of the bid price. Daily the agent telephones the amount of the purchase to the treasurer to prevent a cash overdraft. Each week the agent prepares a report that details all purchases. The report is mailed to the central office and is processed about 10 days after the original purchase.	The auditor is satisfied that the system is adequate, but because of potential problems of not recording the transactions in the appropriate period, the auditor decides to test the processing of the agent's report.
Compliance tests	Through inspection and vouching, the auditor selects 25 agent reports and compares the date of the transaction per the report to the date it is entered in the cash disbursement journal and purchase journal. The compliance tests reveal that the transaction is entered correctly in the purchase journal but is entered in the disbursement journal on the date the entry is made rather than the date the transaction occurred.	The compliance error results in the auditor's investigation of all agent reports for the two-week period prior to the end of the accounting period.
Substantive tests	Through vouching, the auditor compares purchase transactions listed in the agent report to the entry in the cash disbursement journal. The auditor discovers several errors and lists all errors.	The auditor proposes an adjusting journal entry based on substantive tests results: Accounts payable $0.00 Cash $0.00

to name but a few aspects of planning and execution. Only through preparation of working papers can the auditor retain control of the audit by noting what needs to be accomplished and what has been accomplished. Additionally, at the conclusion of the audit, working papers demonstrate whether the audit was performed in accordance with generally accepted auditing standards. A manager or partner reviews the staff auditor's working papers to make this determination. Should the engagement result in a legal dispute, the court examines the working papers to see if professional standards and procedures were observed.

In general, working papers should provide enough information to support the auditor's opinion on the financial statements. Since each engagement has its own unique characteristics, there can be no comprehensive list of items to be included for every engagement. In *SAS No. 1*, Section 338.05, the following guidelines are suggested:

- Data sufficient to demonstrate that the financial statements or other information upon which the auditor is reporting were in agreement with (or reconciled with) the client's records.
- That the engagement had been planned, such as by use of work programs, and that the work of an assistant had been supervised and reviewed, indicating observance of the first standard of field work.
- That the client's system of internal control had been reviewed and evaluated in determining the extent of the tests to which auditing procedures were restricted, indicating observance of the second standard of field work.
- The auditing procedures followed and testing performed in obtaining evidential matter, indicating observance of the third standard of field work. The record in these respects may take various forms, including memoranda, check lists, work programs, and schedules, and would generally permit reasonable identification of the work done by the auditor.
- How exceptions and unusual matters, if any, disclosed by the independent auditor's procedures were resolved or treated.
- Appropriate commentaries prepared by the auditor indicating his conclusions concerning significant aspects of the engagement.

The details of audit working papers vary among firms and among auditors within a particular firm. However, there are several common forms of working papers that are applicable to almost every audit. Usually, the working papers are classified as part of (1) the permanent file or (2) the current file.

Permanent file

Client information applicable to current as well as the succeeding audits is retained in the permanent file. A five-year lease agreement is obviously relevant to five annual engagements, and the auditor need obtain only one copy or abstract the relevant data once. The contents of the permanent file are reviewed each year and updated where appropriate. During this review, information no longer relevant is removed from the permanent file and placed in an inactive file or destroyed, depending upon the firm's policy for the retention of data. The following list indicates the type of information retained in the permanent file:

- Copy of the articles of incorporation and bylaws
- Internal control questionnaires
- Documentation of client's internal control system
- Chart of accounts
- Contracts (union, bond indentures, etc.)
- Analysis of permanent accounts that have little or no activity (capital stock, land, etc.)

156
Evidence:
collection and
evaluation

- Running schedule of historical analysis which is updated each year and used for comparative purposes
- Audit programs

An additional document which is part of the permanent file is the audit plan. The audit plan provides general information about the client that creates the basis for construction of the initial audit approach. Much of the evidence gathered in the first phase of the integrated audit approach, the investigation of client environmental conditions, is incorporated in the audit plan. Information such as a brief history of the client, major product lines, organization chart, special reporting requirements, unique audit problems, and areas of significant audit risk are just a few elements of the audit plan. This information provides the audit with direction. An additional advantage of a well-written audit plan is that it provides an excellent orientation for a staff auditor assigned to the engagement for the first time. Like other data in the permanent file, it must be reviewed each year to bring it up to date. New developments are considered carefully for their potential impact on the audit approach.

Current file

The current audit file includes information applicable to the current financial statements under investigation. Included in this file are working papers for procedures performed by the auditor and a clear outline of the relationship between this work and the formulation of the opinion on the financial statements. Again, the specific content of the current working papers depends upon the characteristics of the audit, but their organization and format have several common aspects.

Working papers are organized in a manner to aid the auditor in conducting the engagement and to enable supervisory personnel of the firm to review them in an efficient manner. The audit of a large corporation may result in the preparation of several hundred pages of working papers. This means that a careful plan for organizing such documentation is necessary. Most audit firms use a systematic scheme for filing working papers, depending upon the nature of the document, which is called indexing. Each major section of the audit is given a unique number or letter, and all working papers relevant to this area are assigned this designation. A firm may decide that all working papers that relate to receivables are to be labeled "D." Since many pages of working papers relating to receivables are generated in the course of the engagement, each page is assigned additional designation such as D-1, D-2, and so on.

The format of an acceptable working paper possesses several characteristics, and the working papers become an invaluable aid in conducting the audit and provide an acceptable basis for determining whether auditing standards are achieved. These attributes are:

- Each page has a proper heading, consisting of the name of the client, the date of the financial statements, and a descriptive title.
- In addition to each page being indexed, each important number or comment

relevant to the analysis on another working paper is cross-indexed to that paper. For example, the analysis of the allowance for uncollectible accounts expense may be analyzed on working paper D-12, but the credit to the allowance is also relevant to the determination of bad debt expense, which may be analyzed on R-20. To avoid duplication of effort, the relevant data on D-12 are cross-referenced by writing "To R-20" beside or beneath the number. Likewise, the data taken to R-20 are labeled on that working paper as "From D-12." The appearance of the amount on R-20 with no explanation may be misinterpreted by the auditor as an unverified piece of data.

- Each paper demonstrates clearly the audit procedures employed, the results of applying such procedures, the extent to which exceptions were cleared, and the auditor's overall conclusion as to the propriety of the account. The auditor uses "tick marks" to relate the work he or she performed to the detail that comprises the account balance. A "V" beside an individual amount that makes up a detailed analysis of the rent expense account may be explained at the bottom of the working paper as follows: "V—examined the rental invoice and the canceled check." Many firms have standard tick marks that are not explained on each working paper. A "C" could be designated by a firm to mean that an item has been confirmed.
- Each page contains the signature or initials of the auditor who performed the work.
- Each page indicates the date the actual audit work was performed.

The above guidelines are used in the preparation of a variety of working papers. The more prevalent types of working papers are considered in the following discussion.

THE WORKING TRIAL BALANCE

In the course of adjusting and closing its books, the client prepares a trial balance, which is a list of all accounts in the general ledger. For many companies, this list requires several pages. When the financial statements are prepared, there is a great deal of combining of accounts to make the report more concise and useful. The auditor asks the client to prepare a working trial balance consistent with the grouping of accounts on the financial statements. Recognizing the opportunity to keep the audit fee at a minimum, most clients are willing to prepare the working trial balance.

A partial working trial balance is illustrated in Figure 5-3. After the description of the account, the first column discloses where the detailed audit work for the account can be found. The working trial balance becomes the focal point for the audit, because it functions as a control device. Each account that appears on the audited financial statement appears on the working trial balance, and the reference column provides instruction for finding the procedures used to audit each account. In addition, every number or comment in the audit papers supporting the working trial balance is referenced, either directly or by a series of intermediate references, to the working trial balance.

Figure 5-3

A-1 R.E.B. 1/8/79

49 12½ – Buff
89 12½ – Green
42 12½ – White

Mercer Manufacturing Corporation
Working Trial Balance
December 31, 1978

Current Assets:	Workpaper Reference (1)	Per Audit Report 12-31-77 (2)	Per Books 12-31-78 (3)	Adjustments Debit (4)	Adjustments Credit (5)	Reclassification Debit (6)	Reclassification Credit (7)	Adjusted Balance 12-31-78 (8)
Cash	C	5763218	6219734 1					5577392 26
Accounts Receivable	D	8229170	75686194	⑨ 6413415				82099609
	D				⑧ 6413415			
Allowance for Bad Debts	D	⟨5943623⟩	⟨496328⟩		⑥ 396672			⟨5348990⟩
Marketable Securities	E	13617906	12129919				⑦ 4587716	7632203
Prepayments	F	31724437	3855610	② 2500000	⑥ 1326172			3994708
Inventories	G	78199613	93684933	㉓ 217110				93684933

Columns 2 and 3 disclose the account balances that appear on the previous **159** year's financial statements and the unaudited balances for the current engagement, respectively. This is useful to the auditor for two reasons. Most financial reports are prepared on a comparative basis, and having the two amounts in the working trial balance makes it a simple task to trace the numbers to the material sent to the printer by the client. More importantly, the auditor compares the two columns and makes preliminary determinations as to whether the current balance is reasonable, based on the circumstances for the year. An obvious inconsistency alerts the auditor to the possibility of spending more audit hours in this area than were required in the prior year.

The findings of the audit are reflected in columns 4 through 7. The adjustment column refers to adjustments proposed by the auditor and not to routine adjustments such as provision for depreciation expense and the like. The latter adjustments are made by the client in preparing the normal adjusted trial balance. During the engagement, the auditor accumulates potential adjustments as proposals to be discussed with management. Since the financial statements belong to management, the auditor has no authority to mandate an adjusting entry. Rather, he or she, toward the final days of the audit, confers with high-level accounting personnel of the client to determine which adjustments are appropriate. The auditor's belief that an adjustment should be made does not always prevail. He or she may have made an error in the investigation or may have misinterpreted data. In addition, management may disagree with the auditor's interpretation of the accounting principles and procedures it believes are appropriate in the area. For these reasons, an auditor must be well prepared and confident before approaching management with proposed adjustments. Inadequate preparation or timidity may completely void the diligent hours of work performed by members of the audit team and have a detrimental effect on their morale. Although management has the final say about the adoption of an adjustment, the auditor makes it clear to management what impact a refusal would have on the auditor's report. When the auditor feels the lack of an adjustment will result in a material misstatement on the financial statements, his or her opinion is appropriately modified.

Reclassification entries serve the same purpose as adjusting journal entries, but reclassification entries are neither journalized nor posted by the client. For example, part of a long-term debt may have to be classified as a current liability. Rather than require a formal entry, the auditor simply lists the reclassification entry on the worksheet after the client has agreed with the auditor's proposal.

Column 8 of the worksheet lists the audited balances of the client's financial accounts. The auditor traces these final balances to the printer's proofs of the annual report or the final report if reproduced by the auditor or the client.

LEAD SCHEDULE

Since the working trial balance is the result of combining numerous ledger accounts into broad groupings, the auditor prepares a lead schedule for each major category listing in the detail ledger accounts. Figure 5-4 is a lead schedule for the general account of prepayments. The audited financial statements show

Figure 5-4

Mercer Manufacturing Corporation
Prepayments
December 31, 1978

F

REB
1/19/79

Acct #		Workpaper Reference	Balance 12/31/78	Adjustments	Adj. Balance 12/31/78
401	Prepaid Property Taxes	F-1	839212 L	AJE⑯ (132612)	706600
402	Prepaid Insurance	F-2	2631147 L	AJE⑰ 250000	2881147
403	Prepaid Rent	F-3	308807 L	—	308807
404	Deposits with Vendors	F-4	76444 L	AJE㉒ 21710	98154
			3855610	139098	3994708
			To A-1		To-A-1

L - Traced amount to ledger card.

only the combined balance and not the individual amounts for prepaid property taxes, prepaid insurance, etc. As transactions were processed during the year, the individual accounts were impacted, so each ledger account is audited. The lead schedule provides the link between the single reported figure and the detail that supports this figure. This is obvious when it is noted that the combined total is referenced to the working trial balance ("To A-1") and the detail is referenced to the individual accounts ("To F-1," etc.).

DETAIL AUDIT SCHEDULES

The auditor performs much of the detail audit analysis and documents much of the collection of corroborative evidence in detail audit schedules. These schedules are the result of auditing a specific ledger account such as the one shown in Figure 5-5. In the upper right corner it can be seen that this schedule was prepared by the client (PBC). This client-prepared schedule is audited to determine its acceptability. The final balance is referenced to the lead schedule for prepayments ("To F"), and there is a cross-reference to the detail analysis of the amortization expense account ("To N"). The nature of the audit techniques to be used is a function of the type of account under investigation. Figure 5-5 represents a 100 percent review in the substantive tests. Alternatively, the review may be less than comprehensive, or the schedule may have been generated in the compliance tests.

MEMORANDUM

One of the most versatile forms of audit working papers is the memorandum, which is descriptive or analytical. On numerous occasions the auditor needs to provide a written description of a situation. In evaluating the client's internal control system, the auditor often writes several paragraphs to describe the system. On the other hand, a memorandum may be analytical in that it combines several audit variables which are the basis for an auditor's conclusion about a particular area. In the audit of inventories, the auditor may gather audit evidence through the use of observation, confirmation, vouching, and other techniques which are documented in several individual working papers. He or she writes a cover memorandum for the inventory account stating the audit conclusions for the account and relating these conclusions to the audit evidence gathered.

OTHER WORKING PAPERS

In general, audit working papers consist of any documentation that represents analytic or corroborative evidence. Written correspondence, such as returned confirmations and the legal letter, is the basis for construction of a working paper. However, to be complete, some notation that describes what the auditor did with the evidence is crucial. A returned customer confirmation that has no indication of what the auditor did with the confirmation is unacceptable. With the development of instant copying, some auditors tend to photocopy a variety of documents in the possession of the client. The auditor must consider the competency of such evidence, and only after the use of additional audit techniques should he or she incorporate it as part of the corroborative evidence.

Figure 5-5

Mercer Manufacturing Company
Prepaid Insurance
December 31, 1978

F-2

PBC/REB
1/24/79

Insurance Company	Policy #	Type	Amount	Balance 1-1-78	Additions	Amortization	Balance 12-31-78							
1 Commonwealth Ins. Co.	A70384	Fire	3000000 ↟	120000 ↟	156000 ↟	145000 ∧	23000 0							1
2 Independence Ins. Co.	3-1884	Bus. Interruption	500000 ↟	48000 ↟	12000 0 ↟	108000 0 ∧	60000 0							2
3 Godsafe Ins. Co.	K4166	Public liability 200,000 500,000 ↟		65000 ↟	-0-	60000 ∧	5000 0							3
4 Commonwealth Ins. Co.	197862	Water damage	800000 ↟	327361 ↟	588913 ↟	377127 ∧	539147							4
5 Keyguard Ins. Co.	FF691	Product liability	600000 ↟	315000 ↟	100800 0 ↟	441000 ∧	88200 0 Ⓐ							5
6 Liberty Valley Ins. Co.	XY417	Fidelity	500000 ↟	330000 ↟	36000 0 ↟	360000 ∧	33000 0							6
7														7
8				2222361	4716913	4308127	2631147 ₭							8
9 ↟ - cross footed				✓	✓	TₒN ✓	TₒF ✓							9
10 ✓ - footed														10

11 ↟ - Inspected policy and discussed adequacy of coverage with Insurance Dept. Supervisor.

12 ↟ - Traced to previous year's workpapers.

13 ↟ - Inspected invoice from insurance companies and cancelled checks.

14 ∧ - Amortization recomputed based on details of insurance policy.

Ⓐ Additional product liability insurance was obtained on 11/2/78 which increases
coverage to $1,000,000. Additional premium of $3,000 for one year was paid
11/2/78 and charged to Miscellaneous Expense. Proposed adjusting journal
Entry:

	Prepaid Insurance	250000		
AJE #12	Insurance Expense	50000		
	Misc. Expense		3000	
TₒF				

Review of working papers

The review of the working papers is the culmination of the evidence collection phase and the evidence evaluation phase of the audit process. To ensure proper and efficient execution of the review process, there must be sufficient planning before the audit begins. This planning may result in the use of standard audit forms, questionnaires, and checklists for each engagement. In addition, staff auditors are given adequate instructions about the nature and extent of the review process, which may include guides as to the amount of testing desired and the allocation of audit time to particular accounts or areas. The responsibilities and the expectations for each member of the audit team are well defined to ensure that accountability on the part of each auditor is determinable.

The review process itself is a two-stage approach in most audits. There is a continuous review by the auditor in charge of the day-to-day fieldwork. This auditor assigns tasks to subordinates; the timing of the review is related to the degree of experience possessed by the subordinate and the complexity of the task. As audit evidence is gathered, evaluated, and subsequently reviewed by the in-charge auditor, problems are identified and the audit approach is modified to resolve these problems. The second stage of the review process is broader and is usually conducted by the manager or partner in charge of the engagement. In this case, the auditor reviews all or practically all of the working papers to determine whether the audit opinion is a reasonable result of the evidence gathered and evaluated in the course of the audit. More specifically, the reviewer determines if generally accepted auditing standards were observed. Recent promulgations concerning auditing procedures and accounting principles may be relevant to the engagement, and the reviewer must determine if they were properly applied. Also, the reviewer makes sure that problems identified during the audit were resolved and that the manner of resolution is well documented in the working papers.

Other than oral evidence, the audit working papers are the only means of determining what the auditor accomplished. Whether in the internal review process or perhaps in a court of law, the need for complete working papers is obvious. Nonetheless, students tend to take for granted the generation of adequate working papers and dismiss this topic as necessary but not intellectually demanding. In fact, many auditors evidently disregard the need for proper documentation. This trend is illustrated by the following list of working paper deficiencies noted in the AICPA's voluntary quality review program:

- A failure to fully document the procedures performed during the engagement.
- There appeared to be a lack of formal evaluation of internal control as a basis for determining the extent of the audit procedures to be used.
- The organization of working papers did not follow any logical arrangement.
- The conclusions of the auditor responsible for a given audit area were often omitted.[3]

[3] Harold B. Minkus and Phyllis E. Peters, "Two Years of Quality Review," *Journal of Accountancy,* September 1974, pp. 105–106.

164
Evidence:
collection and
evaluation

Such an approach to the preparation of working papers is dangerous and professionally unacceptable.

CONCLUDING REMARKS

The collection and evaluation of evidence plays a crucial role in the audit process. Because of the nature of medium-sized and large corporations, an integrated audit approach to the collection and evaluation of evidence is necessary. Although each of the four stages of the approach has been described, only the first stage, investigation of client environmental conditions, was discussed in detail. The next element of the approach, evaluation of internal controls, is discussed in Chapter 6.

EXERCISES AND PROBLEMS

5-1. Explain the difference between evidence described as underlying accounting data and as corroborative data. Give two examples of each.

5-2. What is meant by the competency of evidence?

5-3. List several types of evidence and give an illustration of each.

5-4. How does an auditor determine the *validity* of documentary evidence?

5-5. Are all documents prepared and circulated internally of equal validity?

5-6. How does an auditor determine that a sufficient amount of evidence has been collected?

5-7. Explain the interrelationship of the competency and sufficiency of evidence. Which is more important?

5-8. Comment on the following statement: "There is an inverse relationship between the need to collect evidence and the materiality of the account or transaction under review."

5-9. When may the auditor use the observation technique to gather evidence in an engagement?

5-10. To generate competent evidence, what general rules must be followed when the confirmation technique is employed?

5-11. Since the confirmation of a transaction or balance generates very competent evidence, why isn't it used as the primary method of gathering evidence?

5-12. It is necessary for the auditor to stay aware of general and industrial economic conditions in the performance of an audit. How does he or she accomplish this? Why is it necessary to be concerned with such developments?

5-13. Explain the integrated audit approach.

5-14. Why does an auditor study and evaluate the client's internal control system?

5-15. List four ratios that may be computed by the auditor and state how the results of the ratio computation may impact the audit approach.

5-16. Arthur, CPA, is auditing the RCT Manufacturing Company as of February 28, 1979. As in all engagements, one of Arthur's initial procedures is to make overall checks of the client's financial data by reviewing significant ratios and trends so that he has a better understanding of the business and can determine where to concentrate his audit efforts.

The financial statements prepared by the client with audited 1978 figures and preliminary 1979 figures are presented here in condensed form.

RCT Manufacturing Company
CONDENSED BALANCE SHEETS
February 28, 1979 and 1978

ASSETS	1979	1978
Cash	$ 12,000	$ 15,000
Accounts receivable, net	93,000	50,000
Inventory	72,000	67,000
Other current assets	5,000	6,000
Plant and equipment, net of depreciation	60,000	80,000
	$242,000	$218,000

EQUITIES		
Accounts payable	$ 38,000	$ 41,000
Federal income tax payable	30,000	14,400
Long-term liabilities	20,000	40,000
Common stock	70,000	70,000
Retained earnings	84,000	52,600
	$242,000	$218,000

RCT Manufacturing Company
CONDENSED INCOME STATEMENTS
Years Ended February 28, 1979 and 1978

	1979	1978
Net sales	$1,684,000	$1,250,000
Cost of goods sold	927,000	710,000
Gross margin on sales	757,000	540,000
Selling and administrative expenses	682,000	504,000
Income before federal income taxes	75,000	36,000
Income tax expense	30,000	14,400
	$ 45,000	$ 21,600

Additional information:

- The company has only an insignificant amount of cash sales.
- The end-of-year figures are comparable to the average for each respective year.

Required: For each year compute the current ratio and a turnover ratio for accounts receivable. Based on these ratios, identify and discuss audit procedures that should be included in Arthur's audit of (1) accounts receivable and (2) accounts payable.

(AICPA Adapted)

166

**Evidence:
collection and
evaluation**

5-17. The third generally accepted auditing standard of fieldwork requires that the auditor obtain sufficient competent evidential matter to afford a reasonable basis for an opinion regarding the financial statements under examination. In considering what constitutes sufficient competent evidential matter, a distinction should be made between underlying accounting data and all corroborating information available to the auditor.

Required

1. Discuss the nature of evidential matter to be considered by the auditor in terms of the underlying accounting data, all corroborating information available to the auditor, and the methods by which the auditor tests or gathers competent evidential matter.

2. State the three general presumptions that can be made about the validity of evidential matter with respect to comparative assurance, persuasiveness, and reliability. (AICPA Adapted)

5-18. Evidential matter supporting the financial statements consists of the underlying accounting data and all corroborating information available to the auditor. In the course of an independent audit of financial statements, the auditor performs detailed tests of samples of transactions from various large-volume populations. He or she may also audit various types of transactions by tracing a single transaction of each type through all stages of the accounting system.

Required

1. What are the various audit objectives associated with a sample of transactions from a large-volume population?

2. What evidential matter does the auditor expect to gain from auditing various types of transactions by tracing a single transaction of each type through all stages of the accounting system? (AICPA Adapted)

5-19. Listed below are several audit objectives. Refer to the list of general audit techniques listed in the text and select the most appropriate technique for each audit objective. Give consideration to the time constraints imposed by the typical audit. If more than one technique is selected, rank your selections.

1. Determine that accounts receivable represent sales to the client's customers.
2. Determine that accounts receivable are collectible.
3. Determine that additions to the prepaid rent account are proper charges to the account.
4. Determine that the unamortized balance in the prepaid rent account is applicable to future periods.
5. Determine that depreciation charges to current operations are computed on a consistent basis.
6. Determine that inventories held by consignees are properly stated on the financial statements.
7. Determine that inventory units are held by the client.
8. Determine that inventory is stated at the lower of (FIFO) cost or market.
9. Determine that cash receipts on the last business day of the year were properly stated.
10. Determine that all material accounts payable were recorded at the end of the year.
11. Determine that all pending lawsuits that are material are properly disclosed on the financial statements.
12. Determine that the list of approved bank accounts is complete.

5-20. In late spring of 1979 you are advised of a new assignment as in-charge accountant of your CPA firm's recurring annual audit of a major client, the Lancer Company. You are given the engagement letter for the audit covering the calendar year December 31, 1979, and a list of personnel assigned to this engagement. It is your responsibility to plan and supervise the fieldwork for the engagement.

Required: Discuss the necessary preparation and planning for the Lancer Company annual audit prior to beginning fieldwork at the client's office. In your discussion include the sources you should consult, the type of information you should seek, the preliminary plans and preparation you should make for the fieldwork, and any actions you should take relative to the staff assigned to the engagement. Do not write an audit program. (AICPA Adapted)

5-21. You are the auditor of Star Manufacturing Company. You have obtained the following data:

- A trial balance taken from the books of Star one month prior to year end follows:

	DR. (CR.)
Cash in bank	$ 87,000
Trade accounts receivable	345,000
Notes receivable	125,000
Inventories	317,000
Land	66,000
Buildings, net	350,000
Furniture, fixtures, and equipment, net	325,000
Trade accounts payable	(235,000)
Mortgages payable	(400,000)
Capital stock	(300,000)
Retained earnings	(510,000)
Sales	(3,130,000)
Cost of sales	2,300,000
General and administrative expenses	622,000
Legal and professional fees	3,000
Interest expense	35,000

- There are no inventories consigned either in or out.
- All notes receivable are due from outsiders and held by Star.

Required: Which accounts should be confirmed with outside sources? Briefly describe by whom they should be confirmed and the information which should be confirmed. Organize your answer in the following format.

ACCOUNT NAME	FROM WHOM CONFIRMED	INFORMATION TO BE CONFIRMED

(AICPA Adapted)

168
**Evidence:
collection and
evaluation**

5-22. An auditor relies heavily upon documentation to determine whether financial statements are prepared in accordance with generally accepted accounting principles. Assume that an auditor has decided to classify all documentation by using the following scheme:

- Very reliable
- Reliable
- Unreliable

Required

1. For the following list of documents determine their ranking according to the above scheme. Explain the reason for each item ranked.

a. Vendor invoice
b. Sales invoice
c. Legal letter received from the client's legal department
d. Legal letter received from the client's lawyer
e. Bank statement for the month of May
f. Bank reconciliation for the month of May
g. Bank confirmation for the month of May
h. Voucher package (invoice, receiving report, and purchase order) to support an accounts payable
i. Vendor statement to support an accounts payable
j. Confirmation of an accounts payable
k. Sales invoice to support an accounts receivable
l. Confirmation to support an accounts receivable
m. Cash remittance advice prepared after the end of the year to support an accounts receivable
n. Minutes of the board of directors' meeting to determine if the list of bank accounts is complete
o. Minutes of the board of directors' meeting to determine the value of property received in a related party transaction

2. How does the client's internal control system impact the reliability of documentation?

5-23. In examining financial statements, an auditor must judge the validity of the audit evidence he or she obtains.

Required: Assume the auditor has evaluated internal control and found it satisfactory.

1. In the course of the examination, the auditor asks many questions of client officers and employees.

a. Describe the factors the auditor should consider in evaluating oral evidence provided by client officers and employees.
b. Discuss the validity and limitations of oral evidence.

2. An auditor's examination may include computation of various balance sheet and operating ratios for comparison to prior years and industry averages. Discuss the validity and limitations of ratio analysis.

3. In connection with the examination of the financial statements of a manufacturing company, an auditor observes the physical inventory of finished goods, which consists

of expensive, highly complex electronic equipment. Discuss the validity and limitations of the audit evidence provided by this procedure. (AICPA Adapted)

169
Exercises and problems

5-24. *Part A.* In a properly planned examination of financial statements, the auditor coordinates his or her reviews of specific balance sheet and income statement accounts.

Required: Why should the auditor coordinate the examinations of balance sheet accounts and income statement accounts? Discuss and illustrate with examples.

Part B. A properly designed audit program enables the auditor to determine conditions or establish relationships in more than one way.

Required: Cite various procedures the auditor employs that might lead to detection of each of the following conditions:

1. Inadequate allowance for doubtful accounts receivable
2. Unrecorded retirements of property, plant, and equipment (AICPA Adapted)

5-25. As part of the planning phase of an engagement, an auditor may interview a variety of client personnel. Assume the following comments were made by responsible corporate officials of a Fortune 500 client.

1. "Although new air pollution standards have been issued by the federal government, we believe our plants are exempt from the new standards."
2. "We have had a significant increase in some of our inventories but we believe we can sell these with no problems once our Western European office is fully operational, although we will have to meet some rather stiff price competition."
3. "Our sales volume has increased significantly when compared to last year. This is basically due to our willingness to adopt a more liberal credit policy. We still intend to estimate our bad debt expense at 1.3 percent of gross sales, since this has been our experience rate for the last seven years."
4. "We really made a mistake in hiring Jones as chief accountant at our corporate headquarters. During his seven-month tenure this year we have had a very high personnel turnover rate in the department. It seems that no one, from the assistant chief accountant to the cost clerks, was able to get along with him. However, we have a new person in the position now, and things have settled down."

Required: Explain how each comment may impact the design of audit programs.

5-26. As part of the broad analysis of a firm an auditor may perform a variety of ratios and trend analyses. Consider the following list:

1. Receivables turnover
2. Age of receivables
3. Number of days of sales in accounts receivable
4. Inventory turnover
5. Sales commission expense as a percentage of sales
6. Warranty expense as a percentage of sales
7. Credit sales as a percentage of gross sales
8. Inventories as a percentage of current assets
9. Quick ratio

170
**Evidence:
collection and
evaluation**

Required

1. For each of the above ratios, explain the audit significance, if any, of computing each ratio.

2. Explain how the auditor can modify the audit program for each of the ratios, assuming that during the current year a significant change in the ratio has occurred.

5-27. The concept of materiality is important to the CPA in the examination of financial statements and expression of opinion on these statements.

Required: Discuss the following:

1. How are materiality (and immateriality) related to the proper presentation of financial statements?

2. In what ways do considerations of materiality affect the CPA in

a. Developing an audit program?
b. Performance of the auditing procedures?

3. What factors and measures should the CPA consider in assessing the materiality of an exception to financial statement presentation?

4. How does the materiality of a CPA's exceptions to financial statement presentation influence the type of opinion he or she expresses? (The relationship of materiality to each type of auditor's opinion should be considered in your answer.)   (AICPA Adapted)

5-28. An important part of every examination of financial statements is the preparation of audit working papers.

Required

1. Discuss the relationship of audit working papers to each of the standards of fieldwork.

2. You are instructing an inexperienced staff member on his first auditing assignment. He is to examine an account. An analysis of the account has been prepared by the client for inclusion in the audit working papers. Prepare a list of the comments, commentaries, and notations the staff member should make or have made on the account analysis to provide an adequate working paper as evidence of his examination. (Do not include a description of auditing procedures applicable to the account.)   (AICPA Adapted)

5-29. In the examination of financial statements the CPA is concerned with the examination and accumulation of accounting evidence.

Required

1. What is the objective of the CPA's examination and accumulation of accounting evidence during the course of the audit?

2. The source of the accounting evidence is of primary importance in the CPA's evaluation of its quality. Accounting evidence may be classified according to source. For example, one class originates within the client's organization, passes through the hands of third parties, and returns to the client, where it may be examined by the auditor. List the classifications of accounting evidence according to source, briefly discussing the effect of the source on the reliability of the evidence.

3. In evaluating the quality of the accounting evidence the CPA also considers factors other than the sources of the evidence. Briefly discuss these other factors. (AICPA Adapted)

5-30. Listed here are a number of typical audit procedures performed by an auditor in the course of an engagement. For each procedure determine whether the resulting evidence is classified as analytical or corroborative. If the evidence is classified as corroborative, determine if it is usually collected as part of the tests of compliance or the substantive tests.

171
Exercises and problems

	TYPE OF EVIDENCE		IF CORROBORATIVE	
AUDIT PROCEDURE	ANALYTICAL	CORROBORATIVE	TESTS OF COMPLIANCE	SUBSTAN- TIVE TESTS
1. Review credit memo for approval.				
2. Count petty cash.				
3. Compare recorded receipts with individual deposits shown on the bank statement.				
4. Compute inventory turnover rate.				
5. Observe inventory.				
6. Request a legal letter.				
7. Interview head of R&D department concerning technological changes that have occurred.				
8. Foot the trial balance of accounts receivable.				
9. Observe the tasks performed in the accounting department.				
10. List the duties performed by the cashier.				
11. Prepare a memo describing the procedures utilized by the EDP department.				

| | TYPE OF EVIDENCE | | IF CORROBORATIVE | |
AUDIT PROCEDURE	ANALYTICAL	CORROBORATIVE	TESTS OF COMPLIANCE	SUBSTAN-TIVE TESTS
12. Test postings to detail inventory records for purchases and material requisitions.				
13. Review purchase orders for proper authorization.				
14. Obtain information from the bank concerning cash funds subject to withdrawal restrictions.				

5-31. Problem Figure 5-31 was prepared by a junior accountant. Assume that you are reviewing the working paper. Make a list of comments about the working paper to be given to the junior accountant.

5-32. A new junior accountant was assigned to test the purchases of raw materials. As part of the test, she was to verify posting to the perpetual record cards by examining the voucher package which consisted of the vendor invoice, a receiving report, and a purchase order. A sample of 75 transactions was tested in this manner and the junior accountant stated that "all amounts were recorded properly."

Assume that one of the items tested in the above sample is represented by Problem Figures 5-32(a) and (b).

Required

    1. Do you agree with the junior accountant's conclusion? Explain fully.

    2. Have any of the generally accepted auditing standards been violated?

    3. How can a CPA firm be reasonably certain that the above situation does not go unnoticed?

5-33. The preparation of working papers is an integral part of a CPA's examination of financial statements. On a recurring engagement a CPA reviews his or her audit programs and working papers from the prior examination while planning the current examination to determine their usefulness for the current engagement.

Required

    1. (a) What are the purposes or functions of audit working papers? (b) What records may be included in audit working papers?

    2. What factors affect the CPA's judgment of the type and content of the working papers for a particular engagement?

    3. To comply with generally accepted auditing standards a CPA includes certain evidence in his or her working papers, for example, evidence that the engagement was

Problem 5-31

45-606 EYE-EASE
45-706 20/20 BUFF
NATIONAL · Made - U.S.A.

Wright Retail Store
Long Term Investments - Bonds
12/31/79

	Description	Balance 1/1/79	Additions	Sales	Balance 12/31/79	Bond Interest Income
1	6% - Due 12/31/85	10 000 ⁴			10 000 C	600 ⓥ
2	8% - Due 12/31/89	40 000 ⁴			40 000 C	3200 ⓥ
3	7% - Due 6/30/95	-0-	11 200 ⓨ			350 ⓥ
4	8% - Due 12/31/89	60 000 ⁴		58 000 ⓥ	-0-	
5	Treasury Bills	30 000 ⁴	80 000 ⓨ	80 000 ⓥ	30 000 φ	-0-
6	U.S. Savings Bond	65 000 ⁴		66 000 ⓥ	-0-	1000 ⓥ
7		205 000	91 200	204 000	80 000	5150
8		✓	✓	✓	✓	✓

⁴ - Traced to previous year's working papers.
ⓨ - Cash disbursements per cash book.
ⓥ - Traced to duplicate deposit ticket.
C - Confirmed directly with First Town Bank.
φ - Inspected on 12/15/79.
✓ - All balances footed.

174
Evidence:
collection and
evaluation

Problem Figure 5-32(a)

Invoice
D&B Corporation
Any Place, U.S.A.

Sold to: Bar Manufacturers   Ship to: Same
         Some Place, U.S.A.

Customer no.	Purchase Order Number and Date	Shipping Terms	Date Shipped
88125	6145—9/1/79	FOB Sp. P.	9/3/79

Part no.	Description	Quantity	Unit	Price*	Amount
X014-P	Ball-bearing seals	100	Dozen	40.00	$4,000

*Subject to trade discount.

Problem Figure 5-32(b)

Perpetual Inventory Card

Description   X014-Ball-bearing   Measurement unit   Each

Department   Stores

Date	Receipts Price	Units	Requisitions Number	Units	Units on Hand
7-8-78	38	400			400
9-22-78			8-807	50	350
12-12-78			8-912	40	310
3/12/79			9-102	120	190
8/4/79	40	100			290
12/2/79			9-957	60	230

planned and the work of assistants was supervised and reviewed. What other evidence should be included in audit working papers to comply with generally accepted auditing standards?

4. How can a CPA make the most effective use of the preceding year's audit programs in a recurring examination?

5. What advice should a CPA give a client about discontinuing the use of records needed in an examination and how should a CPA complete the examination when it is found that records reviewed in prior examinations have been discontinued by the client?

(AICPA Adapted)

MULTIPLE CHOICE

1. Evidential matter is generally considered competent when

a. it has the qualities of being relevant, objective, and free from known bias.
b. there is enough of it to afford a reasonable basis for an opinion on financial statements.
c. it has been obtained by random selection.
d. it consists of written statements made by managers of the enterprise under audit.

2. Evidential matter is generally considered sufficient when

a. it is competent.
b. there is enough of it to afford a reasonable basis for an opinion on financial statements.
c. it has the qualities of being relevant, objective, and free from unknown bias.
d. it has been obtained by random selection.

3. The most reliable type of documentary audit evidence an auditor can obtain is

a. physical examination by the auditor.
b. documentary evidence calculated by the auditor from company records.
c. confirmations received directly from third parties.
d. internal documents.

4. Theoretically, which of the following would not have an effect on the amount of audit evidence gathered by the auditor?

a. The type of opinion to be issued
b. The auditor's evaluation of internal control
c. The types of audit evidence available to the auditor
d. Whether or not the client reports to the SEC

5. The strongest criticism of the reliability of audit evidence which the auditor physically observes is that

a. the client may conceal items from the auditor.
b. the auditor may not be qualified to evaluate the items he is observing.
c. such evidence is too costly in relation to its reliability.
d. the observation must occur at a specific time, which is often difficult to arrange.

(AICPA Adapted)

CHAPTER 6

Internal control: systems evaluations

The second step of the integrated audit approach described in Chapter 5 is concerned with the study and initial evaluation of the client's internal control system. The second standard of fieldwork requires that the auditor study and evaluate the internal control system to determine the nature, extent, and timing of audit procedures to be used during the examination of the financial statements. An audit engagement that does not encompass such a study and review violates generally accepted auditing standards, which may be interpreted as a negligent act or perhaps gross negligence.

Aside from the technical requirement to review the internal control system, current conditions make such an approach inevitable. The scope and size of modern business entities have increased dramatically over the past few decades, resulting in complex organizations. For such organizations the number of routine transactions is incredibly large, and the responsibility for initiating, approving, and processing them must be determined. Management designs an internal control system to achieve these objectives. Likewise, the auditor cannot hope to review each transaction, so he or she evaluates the internal control system to determine its weaknesses and strengths as a preliminary step in establishing the detailed audit procedures to be employed. The review of the internal control system is a continuation of the analytical review of the client, and the results of this approach are the basis for collecting corroborative evidence in the tests of compliance and the substantive tests.

INTERNAL CONTROL DEFINED

After a comprehensive investigation into the nature of internal control in 1948, the AICPA Committee on Auditing Procedure defined internal control in *SAS No. 1,* Section 320.09:

> Internal control comprises the plan of organization and all of the coordinate methods and measures adapted within a business to safeguard its assets, check the accuracy

and reliability of its accounting data, promote operational efficiency, and encourage adherence to prescribed managerial policies.

This definition suggests a broad description of an internal system whose characteristics can be classified either as administrative controls or as accounting controls. While both are essential elements of management's internal control system, the auditor is concerned only with controls that are relevant to the audit objective.

Administrative controls

Internal controls that relate to the promotion of operational efficiency and encourage adherence to managerial policies are referred to as *administrative controls*. Management's primary objective is the maximization of profits. In designing the internal control system, management selects a plan of organization, methods, and procedures that contributes to the achievement of its primary objective. Conversely, the auditor's primary objective is to determine whether management's financial statements are prepared in accordance with generally accepted accounting principles. Only internal control features that affect the financial statements are of interest to the auditor, which means that he or she must be capable of identifying administrative controls. For example, management may employ a variety of capital budgeting techniques to rank capital projects according to their profitability. This contributes to the organization's goal of profit maximization, but the auditor is not concerned with the planning of future capital projects. This is beyond the scope of the audit but of course could be part of a management advisory service engagement conducted by the accounting firm.

In any classification scheme there are items that do not fit neatly into predetermined categories. This is certainly true in attempting to differentiate between administrative and accounting controls. The auditor encounters controls which have characteristics that may suggest administrative control but which have a potential impact upon the financial statements. Such controls are relevant to the auditor's evaluation and study of the client's internal control system. In the capital budget mentioned above, the auditor is concerned with capital projects in process. He or she may use the capital budget analysis prepared by the client to monitor the project for possible cost overruns which may necessitate a write-down of the cost incurred for the project. It is advantageous for the auditor to be aware of the entire internal control system, including the administrative controls. It is not necessary for the auditor to classify the controls on a formal basis but rather to evaluate each control as to its relevancy to the audit objective. Generally, administrative controls that are potentially relevant to this objective are described in *SAS No. 1,* Section 320.27:

> Administrative control includes, but is not limited to, the plan of organization and the procedures and records that are concerned with the decision process leading to management's authorization of transactions. Such authorization is a management function directly associated with the responsibility for achieving the objectives of the organization and is the starting point for establishing accounting control of transactions.

178
Internal control:
systems
evaluations

Accounting controls

Internal controls that relate to the safeguarding of assets and the reliability of financial records are referred to as *accounting controls*. Since these controls impact the financial statements, they provide the basis for the auditor's review and evaluation of the internal control system. The accounting controls designed to safeguard assets protect the client from incorrectly accounting for the movement of assets. For example, management establishes procedures that reasonably ensure that a vendor is paid only for materials that are actually ordered and received. The auditor is concerned with these accounting controls, because several accounts are affected by the movement of assets. Improper accounting for goods received from vendors may impact the accounts of purchasing, accounts payable, inventory, and/or fixed assets. The safeguarding of assets also refers to the physical loss of assets. Thus the auditor is concerned with the accounting controls for the physical protection of cash, supplies, inventories, and other assets. A lack of accounting controls for the protection of these assets, such as a lack of a fence around inventory stored outdoors, has an impact upon the subsequent audit procedures used by the auditor.

Accounting controls concerned with the ability of the accounting system to generate reliable financial records are of prime interest to the auditor. Because of the volume of transactions being processed by many business firms, the accounting system must be designed in a manner that minimizes the possibility of errors or omissions. Controls that help to ensure the proper recording and processing of a financial event are studied by the auditor to determine their adequacy. There may be proper movement of assets to or from the firm, but this does not ensure that transactions are being processed correctly by the accounting system. For example, accounting controls are designed to safeguard the company against a loss of assets through the sale of scrap inventory by using a system of authorization. On the other hand, if procedures are not designed to ensure an initial recording of the sale of scrap, such accounts as cash, inventory, and gain or loss accounts for the disposal of assets may be in error.

Again, there is an overlapping of the operational implications of safeguarding assets and ensuring the reliability of the financial records that makes it unnecessary to distinguish between these aspects in the auditor's review of the internal control system. Often an accounting control has both the effect of protecting assets and encouraging the proper recording of transactions. In order to protect against the unauthorized shipment of goods to customers, an organization may use a copy of the sales invoice as a packing slip and proper authorization for the shipping department. This is considered the part of the accounting system devoted to safeguarding assets. Additionally, sales invoices may be prenumbered and, if all invoices are accounted for periodically by management personnel, the possibility of an unrecorded sale occurring also is minimized. Thus the auditor is concerned with the role of prenumbered sales invoices in the accounting system and is less interested in a formal classification of the accounting control.

The following is a more comprehensive description of accounting controls from *SAS No. 1,* Section 320.28:

> Accounting control comprises the plan of organization and the procedures and records that are concerned with the safeguarding of assets and the reliability of

financial records and consequently are designed to provide reasonable assurance that:

a. Transactions are executed in accordance with management's general or specific authorization.
b. Transactions are recorded as necessary (1) to permit preparation of financial statements in conformity with generally accepted accounting principles or any other criteria applicable to such statements and (2) to maintain accountability for assets.
c. Access to assets is permitted only in accordance with management's authorization.
d. The recorded accountability for assets is compared with the existing assets at reasonable intervals and appropriate action is taken with respect to any differences.

This more detailed description of accounting controls forms a basis for discussing the general characteristics that comprise an adequate system of internal control.

THE INTERNAL CONTROL MODEL

Each business enterprise is unique, at least to some degree, which makes it impossible to specify the detailed characteristics of an internal system. However, there are general or broad guidelines that provide the basis for constructing an adequate internal control system. Using these elements the auditor creates a general internal control model that serves as a standard for comparison. The auditor is aware of this abstract model as an initial step in the study and evaluation of management's internal control system. A thorough understanding of the client's actual internal control system is obtained, and the auditor compares this actual system to the general internal control model. When the broad elements of an acceptable internal control system are known, it is possible to identify the weaknesses and strengths of the client's system. Subsequently, this analysis is a foundation for the selection of audit procedures to be used in the gathering of corroborative evidence. It takes an element of creativity for the auditor to apply the general characteristics of the internal control model to a specific real-world accounting system.

Since each organization must formulate its internal control system in a manner that facilitates the achievement of its goals, the following six elements are essential in the construction of an adequate internal control system:

- A well-designed plan of organization
- An adequate system of authorization and accountability
- An adequate accounting structure
- Sound personnel policies
- An effective internal audit staff
- A competent and active audit committee

Plan of organization

The nature and size of the business enterprise have an important impact upon the manner in which it is organized. Factors such as product lines, geographical location, and the structure of operating units, such as subsidiaries or branches, are considered by management in designing the internal control system. Man-

180
Internal control:
systems
evaluations

agement is concerned with achieving its objective with a system that is both effective and efficient. The auditor's understanding and evaluation of the plan of organization focuses upon the degree to which the organizational scheme designates the responsibility for the performance of relevant functions. The autonomy of departments and the identification of lines of responsibility are two elements of a sound organizational plan.

DEPARTMENTAL AUTONOMY

The organizational independence of each department is critical to a sound system of internal control. Each department's responsibilities are identified, and the operations of the department are not subject to intervention from other departments. Departmental autonomy does not suggest that each functional unit of the business enterprise operates in a manner that isolates each department. It must be recognized that all departments strive to achieve a common set of corporate goals and to cooperate in areas that allow the achievement of such objectives. In view of the commonality of goals, departments are organized so that no department is totally responsible for the safeguarding of assets and the generation of reliable financial information for any particular transaction. Such an approach adds to the integrity of the accounting data.

The principle of departmental segregation of duties rests upon the need to separate custodial responsibility, accounting responsibility, and operational responsibility. This approach provides a system of checks on the competency and integrity of each department, because it is not possible for a single department to control a transaction without creating a basis for interdepartmental review. For example, in the area of inventory, the custody, accounting, and operational functions are separated. A warehouse supervisor has physical control of and responsibility for inventory not in production. The accounting department generates some method of inventory control, perhaps in the form of perpetual inventory cards. In addition, the operational responsibility for inventory rests with the manufacturing segment of the organization. Periodically there is a physical count of inventory, and this count is compared to the inventory records. This ability to compare the performance of the three functionally segregated units is an element of the organizational plan to ensure the safeguarding of assets as well as to determine the reliability of the accounting records. When internal control systems lack such a segregation of functional responsibilities, the auditor is less willing to rely on the accounting system, necessitating a significant expansion of the collection of corroborative evidence.

Of particular interest to the auditor is an understanding of the roles of the controller's department and the treasurer's department. It is not important what designation is given to these departments, but a thorough knowledge of the acceptable functions of each department is crucial. It is especially true in this area, because the two roles often overlap or their responsibilities are not clearly defined. The controller is responsible for maintaining an organization's accounting records. The typical accounting responsibilities of the controller are illustrated in Figure 6-1. The treasurer's responsibilities include the custodial responsibility and the operational responsibility for cash and securities. Since

Figure 6-1

Organizational Chart: Controller's Function

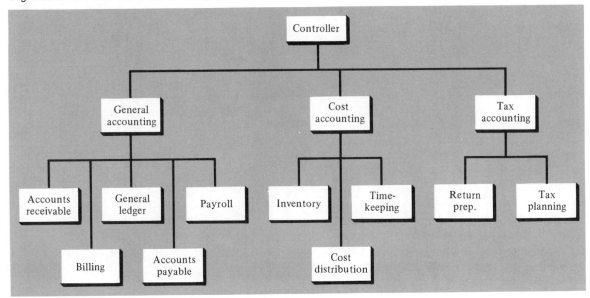

these two responsibilities are merged into the treasurer's function, appropriate accounting records are maintained in the controller's department. The typical responsibilities of the treasurer are shown in Figure 6-2. Another important role of the treasurer is responsibility for the financial planning and management of the organization. Usually this function does not have an impact on the audit, since it deals with operational efficiencies and not the reliability of accounting data.

DEPARTMENT ORGANIZATIONAL STRUCTURE

Management designs an internal control system that contributes to the goals of the organization. Certainly two of the goals of management are to safeguard assets and generate reliable economic data through the construction of an appropriate internal control system. Similar to the need for a clear delineation of departmental responsibilities, and to encourage departmental autonomy, the organizational structure within a department is an important element of management's need to define an adequate internal control structure.

Within each department the duties and responsibilities of each individual are assigned so that no one person can perpetrate or conceal unintentional or intentional errors. For this reason, no one is given the original responsibility for processing the accounting data and the responsibility for reviewing the propriety of this process through the use of control data received from an independent source. For example, the accounts payable clerk may be responsible for postings to the subsidiary accounts payable ledger, but he or she is not responsible for

Figure 6-2

Organizational Chart: Treasurer's Function

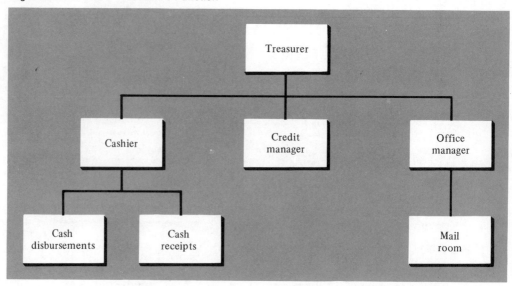

the relevant postings in the general ledger or for reconciling the detail per the subsidiary ledger cards and the control accounts payable amount in the general ledger. If these duties are not properly segregated, errors may occur and not be detected. The adequacy of an internal control system is heavily dependent upon the rule that no incompatible functions be performed by a single individual. Violations of this principle force the auditor to expand subsequent audit procedures.

By comparing the duties assigned in Figures 6-1 and 6-2, the organizational structure of departments as an important factor in the internal control model can be demonstrated. For example, cash received through the mail as a result of credit sales is opened in the mailroom, and a detailed listing of the remittances prepared. One copy of the listing and the actual cash receipts are sent to the cashier, who prepares and makes the bank deposit. Another copy of the remittance listing is sent to the accounts receivable department where the subsidiary ledger cards are updated. In addition, a third copy of the cash receipts listing goes to the cash receipts accountant for posting to the cash receipts journal. There is an independent comparison of the amount of the deposit, the summary total posted to the accounts receivable subsidiary ledger cards, and the amount posted by the general ledger accountant. If there is an error in any one of these three areas, the amounts will not reconcile and the data must be reviewed and corrected. Also, the possibility of fraud, for example, the cashier misappropriating cash, is greatly reduced through segregation of the duties of the treasurer's department and the controller's department. The custodial responsibility for cash is part of the treasurer's function, and the accounting function is exclusively that of the controller. Furthermore, the lack of incompatible duties performed by one individual within the accounting department strengthens the internal control system.

System of authorization and accountability

A modern business enterprise is too large and complex to be administered by a single individual. There must be a scheme whereby certain individuals have the authority to approve business transactions. The basic authority for the conduct of a corporation resides with the stockholders. Much of this authority is delegated to the board of directors which in turn delegates to the officers of the corporation sufficient authority to administer day-to-day operations. Even with the delegation of authority to the corporate officers and the general management group, there is additional delegation of authority down the organizational framework depending upon the nature of the business. The lower the authorization is pushed down the organization, the more specific and less broad it becomes. The board of directors possesses the power to authorize the disbursement of corporate funds, which is certainly broad and is the basis for the declaration of dividends. A clerk in a retail outlet may have the power to cash a customer's check under certain management-designated restrictions, such as the amount of the check and the type of identification offered. A proper system of authorization clearly designates the authority of each individual and matches the significance of this authority to an appropriate level in the organizational hierarchy.

Accountability is a companion to authorization in the design of an adequate internal control system. Designating an individual with the authority to approve or execute a transaction is necessary, but the actions taken by this individual must be documented in the accounting system, which provides a basis for subsequent management review. An adequate internal control system makes individuals accountable for their actions. For example, a petty cash system may be established to pay small miscellaneous expenses that need to be paid immediately, such as COD transactions. A petty cash custodian is assigned the custodial and recording functions, but his or her actions are reviewed when there is a petty cash reimbursement request. In addition, there may be a surprise petty cash count by a responsible management member. Such a system provides a reasonable degree of accountability. However, if two or more individuals are authorized to make disbursements from the petty cash fund, the accountability objective of the system is greatly reduced.

The authorization and accountability aspects of an internal control system are discussed together. In most cases, the action taken by an individual as a result of being authorized to perform certain acts results in some form of documentation which provides the basis for accountability. The board of directors declares a dividend, and its action is documented in the minutes of the meeting. The clerk who authorizes a customer's cashing of a check must initial the check. When the internal control system requires proper authorization before a transaction is executed, then only legitimate transactions enter the accounting system.

184
Internal control:
systems
evaluations

A proper system of accountability encourages those authorized to act in a manner consistent with established guidelines.

The design of an internal control system that exhibits the desired characteristics of proper authorization and adequate accountability incorporates four factors. The system must be capable of determining whether the transaction was (1) properly executed and (2) was properly recorded. In addition, there is (3) limited access to corporate assets and (4) a periodic comparison of recorded accountability with the corporate assets. These four elements are used in the definition of accounting controls on page 179.

EXECUTION OF TRANSACTIONS

The internal control system functions as a monitoring device to determine that a transaction is executed by properly authorized individuals and that the authorization is consistent with corporate policies. The nature and timing of the approval process are dependent upon the characteristics of the transaction being executed. Much of the monitoring is immediate and continuous, operating as an integral part of the internal control system. This usually occurs when a transaction must be processed in separate steps or is processed in different functional areas of the organization. For example, approval of a cash disbursement for the purchase of inventory is the result of different stages of authorization, with the authorization being reviewed for completeness and authenticity at each succeeding step. Before approving a disbursement, the accounts payable clerk reviews a purchase order signed by the purchasing agent authorizing the purchase of goods, a receiving report signed by the receiving clerk, and an invoice from the vendor. After comparing these three documents and reviewing approval notations, he or she establishes the transaction as an appropriate liability of the company. This process of authorization review strengthens the company's internal control system and is of interest to the independent auditor.

Certain actions taken by personnel which reflect their designated authorization are not subject to immediate review; nonetheless, an adequate internal control system establishes some mechanism to determine if a transaction is properly authorized. Generally, this mechanism can be in the form of occasional observation of the individual's activity or a periodic comparison of recorded transactions. For example, a credit manager is authorized to approve credit sales to customers within certain limits involving their credit rating and the size of the sale. A responsible individual or perhaps a member of the company's internal audit staff may observe the credit manager's procedures or may select a sample of credit sales approved during the year to see if corporate guidelines are being observed. The auditor is interested in such an internal control monitoring function, since its degree of effectiveness has audit implications. If the credit manager routinely approves every credit sale without reference to instructions, then the possibility of significant bad debt losses will be great.

RECORDING OF TRANSACTIONS

The execution of a transaction is followed by proper recording of it by authorized personnel. The internal control system is constructed to encourage recording of the proper amount in the appropriate accounting period and processing of the transaction in accordance with generally accepted accounting principles, which includes proper classification of the transaction amount. The method by which the accounting system monitors the recording process depends upon the nature of the transaction. One method that encourages the proper recording of transactions is the use of prenumbered forms and subsequent accounting of the forms. For example, management's review of the prenumbered sales invoices used during an accounting period determines whether all such invoices were properly recorded in the sales journal. Other procedures such as the preparation of monthly bank reconciliations, the mailing of monthly customer statements, and the use of control totals in the processing of transactions are part of the internal control structure.

ACCESS TO ASSETS

The accessibility of assets depends upon the nature of the asset and the operating characteristics of a firm. The internal control system is designed in a manner that facilitates, not obstructs, the operations of the business. In view of these constraints, the internal control system is designed to reasonably ensure that the organization's assets are utilized in an authorized manner. This accounting control may result in procedures that directly safeguard the corporate assets, such as storing inventory in a secured location where entry is controlled. In addition, the control of access to assets may be of an indirect nature. For example, raw material inventory is released to manufacturing departments only when written authorization is received by the warehouse or store clerk. At the time the goods are released to the manufacturing departments, the requisition releases the storage personnel from accountability for the goods and transfers it to the processing departments. Thus limiting access to assets encompasses control of the movement of assets in the conduct of an organization's normal business.

COMPARISON OF RECORDED ACCOUNTABILITY WITH ASSETS

Limited access to assets suggests that an individual or a group of individuals is held accountable for the assets. If the custodial responsibility and the recording functions are separated, a comparison of the recorded accountability with the asset enhances the adequacy of an internal control system. The effectiveness of the individuals responsible for each function is increased if they know there is such a comparison to determine if errors or misappropriations have occurred. A physical count of inventory and a comparison of the results with the perpetual inventory cards is an illustration of this internal control procedure. Discrepancies are investigated to determine if the errors are reasonable or unreasonable under the circumstances. If they are unreasonable, corrective action may be taken to restructure the internal control system in order to reduce the extent of the errors.

The frequency of comparing the asset count with the accounting records depends upon the nature of the asset. If the asset is susceptible to material loss, then the frequency of the use of the technique is increased. Machinery may be a material asset, but the possibility of loss or unauthorized use is relatively less

186
Internal control:
systems
evaluations

than the possibility of loss through unauthorized use of negotiable instruments. Thus an inventory of plant equipment may be conducted every two or three years, while a count of securities occurs more frequently.

Accounting structure

The presence of certain accounting features enhances the internal control system of an organization. These are specific characteristics that are often taken for granted, but their relationship to the internal control system cannot be underestimated. An appropriate plan of organization and a system of authorization and accountability are dependent upon the following elements of the accounting structure:

- Chart of accounts
- Accounting manual
- Job descriptions
- Control Accounts
- Prenumbered internal documents
- Control of data input and processing

CHART OF ACCOUNTS

The accounts used by an organization are listed in a systematic manner usually identified by a unique number or letter. The listing is referred to as a chart of accounts and is readily available as a reference source for those who process accounting data. Organizational characteristics and objectives determine the number of individual accounts used. A company that recognizes the importance of responsibility designs the accounts so that an individual's or operating segment's effectiveness can be measured. In addition, the geographical dispersion of operating units, such as the presence of numerous branches, has an impact on the design of the chart of accounts. Usually the system of accounts provides more detail than is required by the auditor. For example, the cost of goods sold may be broken down by geographical location, but this information is combined for financial reporting purposes. In general, the auditor determines if the chart of accounts provides a basis for adequate disclosure on the financial statements.

The proper design and use of a chart of accounts contributes to the internal control objectives of safeguarding assets and generating reliable accounting data. This is achieved by providing a classification scheme that categorizes similar transactions into designated accounts. In part, the safeguarding of assets is dependent upon the maintenance of accounting records that can be used as a basis for asset accountability. When the chart of accounts is deficient, then the integrity of the accounting records is reduced, forfeiting the basis for asset accountability. In a similar manner, the reliability of accounting data generated by the internal control system is dependent upon the effectiveness of a chart of accounts. For example, if similar expenses are not classified under the same account title, disclosures in the income statement may be materially deficient.

No matter how sophisticated an accounting system, its successful implementation begins with a logically designed chart of accounts.

187
**The internal
control model**

ACCOUNTING MANUAL

For a small business enterprise a chart of accounts is sufficient as a guide for the initial recording and the subsequent processing of accounting data. More complex organizations require not only a chart of accounts but also an accounting manual to ensure proper accounting for data. The purpose of the accounting manual is to ensure uniform treatment of similar transactions. To achieve this objective the accounting manual describes each account and transaction according to what is properly processed through an account and what accounts are impacted by a particular transaction. An accounting manual is of particular importance to an organization that has decentralized processing of accounting data at branches, subsidiaries, or divisions. The individual accounting statements are combined or consolidated at the end of the accounting period, and there must be a common treatment of accounting transactions in order that meaningful financial statements can be prepared.

JOB DESCRIPTIONS

Each position in an organization should have a job description that details the nature of its role in the enterprise. Although job descriptions may not be considered part of the formal accounting structure, there are implications for the internal control system that for purposes of discussion are grouped with other elements of the accounting structure. Each job description includes a list of the duties or responsibilities of the position and a complete explanation of the authority related to the position. This written description recognizes the need to have proper segregation of duties, which was discussed earlier. In addition, the job description formally documents the degree of authority held by each individual. With this approach there is a minimization of disputes over who is responsible for a particular job or who may authorize certain transactions.

CONTROL ACCOUNTS

An internal system incorporates control accounts into its structure. A control account and the use of a subsidiary ledger establish a system whereby the activities of two separate functions may be compared to determine whether errors or irregularities exist. After the processing of accounting data, a comparison is made between the amount shown in the control accounts and the aggregate totals derived from the subsidiary accounts. In an adequate internal control system, the two functions are performed by different individuals.

PRENUMBERED INTERNAL DOCUMENTS

Only properly authorized documents are processed through the accounting system, but this internal control feature is strengthened if there is a method of accounting for the documents used and not used during an accounting period. For this reason internal documents are prenumbered and periodically reviewed.

188
Internal control:
systems
evaluations

In this manner the universe of potential transactions is readily defined and easily reviewed. An accounting system may require that a sales invoice be properly authorized by the credit manager before goods are shipped to a customer. Through the use of prenumbered sales invoices, a comparison of the sales invoice copies retained by the credit manager and the copies retained by the shipping department determines if internal control procedures are being followed. This is true if the storage area releases goods to the shipping department when it receives proper authorization. If the documents are unnumbered, it becomes a more difficult task to control the processing of accounting data. Prenumbered documents may be used for receiving reports, checks, bills of lading, and purchase orders, as well as other internally created documents.

CONTROL OF DATA INPUT AND PROCESSING

The internal control system is designed so that there is immediate control of data as business transactions occur. Once input data controls are established, additional techniques are utilized to reasonably ensure that there is no loss of data as data processing progresses. As soon as data are physically possessed by a business enterprise, some means of control is established. These input controls may be in the form of sequentially numbering each piece of data, using record counts, or creating control totals. For example, customer orders received in the mail may be sequentially numbered as the mail is opened. Vendor invoices received in the mail may be counted and grouped together with a rubber band. Checks from customers may be listed individually and totaled as a means of providing data input controls. These controls are utilized each time the data are physically moved from one department to another and each time they are processed. The use of input and processing control reduces the possibility of losing data or processing only part of it.

In Chapter 7, which is concerned with the impact of computers on the audit approach, a more detailed discussion of data controls is offered. However, it should not be assumed that these controls are applicable only to EDP systems. They should be incorporated where appropriate into an internal control system utilizing manual or mechanical procedures to process data.

Personnel policies

The design of an internal control system may result in a conceptually sound system, but the system is administered by people. For this reason, adequate personnel policies are adopted and vigorously implemented by a business enterprise. These policies reasonably ensure that only capable and honest individuals become part of the employer labor force. In this vein adequate procedures in the areas of employee selection, training, and supervision are part of the internal control system.

EMPLOYEE SELECTION

Prospective employees are screened to identify those who possess the necessary skills to perform a job well. This selection process may consist of testing the individual, reviewing past job experience, or other evaluation techniques. The objective of the process is to match properly the talents of the individual with the requirements of the position. The organization is careful not to hire individuals who are obviously overqualified or underqualified for a position. Either situation is likely to result in a frustrated employee, with potentially ill effects on the internal control system.

Fidelity bonding is an important part of the selection process. Employees who are bonded are subject to investigation by the bonding company to identify those with past experiences that preclude bonding. Also, fidelity bonding discourages prospective applicants with such backgrounds from initially applying for the job. Most applicants and employees realize that a bonding company does not hesitate to prosecute an accused employee to recover losses. This has an effect not only on prospective employees but on current employees as well. Of course, fidelity bonding ultimately provides reimbursement of losses resulting from the misappropriation of assets by employees, which is an element in the system of safeguarding assets.

EMPLOYEE TRAINING

In most cases the screening process identifies individuals who are capable of performing a job after an appropriate period of training. The length of the training depends upon the technical nature of the position and the previous experience and education of the new employee. In any case the employee's training period should be sufficient to ensure that he or she can perform competently in the position.

Personnel policies in the area of employee training involve more than the training of an employee. The overall needs of the organization are studied so that employee absences do not disrupt the internal control system. This may result in training employees to do a variety of jobs so that they may fill temporary or perhaps permanent vacancies. Also, such employee training policies allow for the rotation of jobs. If an individual realizes that he or she may be transferred to another job, then it is less likely that the individual will conceal errors or perpetrate a fraud. Also, personnel policies require employees to take their vacations. Many errors and irregularities are discovered when a trusted employee is unable to perform his or her normal duties. These are discovered only by chance. An adequate internal control system formalizes these policies rather than relying on luck.

EMPLOYEE SUPERVISION

While an adequate personnel system establishes policies to select the proper employee and to provide proper training, it is also necessary to establish an adequate system of employee supervision. Supervision gives the employee an opportunity to ask for assistance when faced with an unusual transaction or situation. A capable supervisor provides a work situation that allows for on-the-job training by monitoring the work of the employee. There should be a periodic review of the employee's work to determine whether he or she is performing in a satisfactory manner, and the immediate supervisor is in the best position to

190
Internal control:
systems
evaluations

make this determination. Incompetent employees are identified as soon as possible, so that corrective action may be taken.

OTHER PERSONNEL POLICIES

There are of course numerous personnel policies that may impact the internal control system. These range from an adequate pay scale to a pleasant work environment. A thorough discussion of personnel management is beyond the scope of this book, but an auditor is cognizant of these factors because of their potential effect on the collection and processing of data.

Internal audit staff

The internal audit function is another element considered vital in an internal control system. This function is assigned to an internal audit department in most large and medium-sized enterprises, and in smaller concerns it may be the responsibility of the owner-manager or another key member of management. Internal audit is broad in scope, concerning itself with operational audits as well as financial compliance audits. In fact, internal auditing is concerned with the administrative controls of an internal control system, since the audit may be to determine if corporate policies are being observed or if operations are being conducted in an efficient manner. For the independent auditor the role of the internal auditor as it relates to the internal control system's design to safeguard the enterprise's assets and to generate reliable financial records is of interest.

The mere existence of an internal audit staff does not strengthen an organization's internal control structure. The specific role of the internal audit staff is the critical characteristic that must be determined. To be of relevance to the independent auditor's attest function, the internal audit responsibility must include a study and evaluation of the internal control system. This study and evaluation must include a review of the accounting system and tests of compliance. Although the independent auditor perceives the internal audit function as an important part of the internal control system, this function must be devoted to monitoring the internal control system rather than to functioning as part of the routine operational structure. An employee who properly authorizes a transaction is part of the operational structure, whereas the role of the internal audit staff is to review the adequacy of the accounting system and actually test transactions for proper approval as well as other relevant attributes. As stated in *SAS No. 9*, the internal audit function should "act as a separate, higher level of control to determine that the system is functioning effectively."

The internal auditor can never achieve the degree of independence achieved by the external auditor since the former is an employee of the organization. A lack of independence by the internal auditor can significantly reduce the importance of the internal audit function as an element of the internal control system. An internal audit department that is subordinate to the operating departments it must review may be ineffective. Management can avoid this situation by demonstrating its support of the internal audit department. This can be done in several ways, but one of the most important is the organizational location of the internal audit department. The internal audit department should report to a management member as far up in the organizational hierarchy as possible. Ultimately this could be the president or a vice-president of the enterprise, or the board of directors. In any case, the organizational location of the internal auditor is carefully considered by management and evaluated by the independent auditor.

In many instances the work of the internal audit staff may be used by the independent auditor in formulating an opinion on the financial statements. The circumstances that allow this relationship are discussed in Chapter 9.

Audit committee

In recent years boards of directors have been subject to the criticism that they are not performing their fundamental duty of representing the stockholders of an enterprise. In some cases the boards may be dominated by corporate officers who may not be completely candid with other board members. This situation has resulted in litigation that has often resulted in board members being held responsible for management misdeeds. A lack of full disclosure in the financial statements may result in losses to those who use this information for making economic decisions.

The legal problems encountered by boards of directors are not unlike those faced by the independent auditor. For this reason the audit committee has recently received more attention from both parties. The adoption of audit committees is being encouraged by several financial and regulatory institutions, which has in turn resulted in a dramatic increase in the number of companies, especially large ones, creating such committees.[1] Most audit committees have three to five members, and in the vast majority of cases the members are exclusively outside directors or outside directors comprise a majority of the total committee membership. Although the responsibilities of the audit committee vary among organizations, they usually consist of at least the following:

- Nominate the independent auditor
- Review the scope of the audit
- Review the results of the audit

NOMINATE THE INDEPENDENT AUDITOR

As discussed in Chapter 1, a conceptual weakness in the relationship between the auditor and the client exists because the client hires, fires, and pays the fee of the independent auditor. While most auditors may strongly argue that such an arrangement does not impede their ability to be independent, the appearance of loss of independence from the public viewpoint cannot be rationalized in the same manner. This is especially true today when every institution is being

---

[1] See *A Statement on Audit Committees of Board of Directors* (New York: AICPA, 1967); *Accounting Series Release No. 123*, "Standing Audit Committees Composed of Outside Directors" (Washington: SEC, 1972); and *Recommendations and Comments on Financial Reporting to Shareholders and Related Matters* (New York: New York Stock Exchange, 1973).

192
Internal control:
systems
evaluations

scrutinized by the public. The appearance of auditor independence can be enhanced if an outside audit committee nominates the auditor who then must be approved by the full board as well as by the organization's stockholders.

REVIEW THE AUDIT SCOPE

Prior to the actual start of an engagement, the independent auditor meets with the audit committee to discuss the scope of the audit. While the basic objective of an audit is to issue an opinion on the financial statements, other services may be rendered during the engagement depending upon the request of the audit committee. The most obvious additional service is the auditor's preparation of a management letter that deals with internal control recommendations or comments on administrative or operational procedures. Even when the audit scope is limited to the issuance of an opinion on the financial statements, the meeting between the auditor and the committee is useful, since it provides the auditor with an opportunity to discuss problems or new developments that may have audit significance. Such a meeting is part of the auditor's analytical approach of gathering evidence about the organization's environmental conditions.

REVIEW THE AUDIT RESULTS

The actual results of the audit are discussed with the audit committee. This includes a review of the financial statements and the resulting audit opinion and communication of any recommendations or problems either real or potential. In the review of the audit report, significant changes in accounting principles, unique industrial accounting practices, and similar factors are discussed. The auditor reminds the committee that the primary responsibility for the preparation of fair financial statements is that of the organization. Thus the committee must have a reasonable understanding of these reports. Finally, recommendations for improving the internal control system and other relevant topics are discussed, depending upon their importance and the initial scope of the audit.

THE COMMITTEE AS AN ELEMENT OF INTERNAL CONTROL

The audit committee is considered a desired part of an organization's internal control system. Routine transactions are processed through the internal control system, and under certain conditions the auditor can reasonably be assured that only legitimate transactions are being processed. Transactions of a nonroutine or nonrecurring basis probably do not flow through the internal control system as described above, and this may create audit problems. Often these transactions are large and have a potentially significant impact on the financial statements. Since they circumvent the normal internal accounting control system, the auditor is placed in an almost intolerable position. The auditor has responded by repeatedly stating in professional literature that he or she is not responsible for the detection of fraud if the engagement was conducted in accordance with generally accepted auditing standards. Nonetheless, if the fraud is material, the auditor runs the risk of being held responsible for not discovering it.

Although the existence of an audit committee can never eliminate corporate irregularities, it is a first step in designing an internal control mechanism that encompasses routine as well as nonroutine transactions. The internal control system is enhanced if the internal audit department reports directly to or at least has access to the audit committee. An audit committee composed of outside directors who are competent and active helps safeguard the assets of an organization and increases the likelihood that reliable financial records will be prepared. The absence of such a committee is viewed by the auditor as an internal control deficiency.

Limitations of the internal control system

The basic characteristics of an adequate internal control system provide reasonable assurance that the assets of the organization are being safeguarded and that reliable financial records are being generated. However, such a system does not provide absolute assurance that the internal control objectives are being achieved. Basic to the concept of reasonable assurance is the realization that an internal control procedure must be *cost-effective*. That is, the benefits derived from a control procedure should exceed the cost of adopting the procedure. In designing an internal control system, an organization cannot measure the cost-benefit relationship of a procedure precisely, but a reasonable analysis combined with appropriate judgment and estimates is used. In evaluating the organization's internal control system an auditor recognizes the concept of reasonable assurance.

In addition, he or she recognizes that there are inherent limitations or assumptions that further restrict the effectiveness of an internal control system. One of the fundamental principles observed in the design of an internal control system is the need to segregate properly the duties and responsibilities of departments and individuals. If collusion exists, the effectiveness of this principle may be completely invalidated. Additionally, if internal controls are circumvented by management intervention, the reliability of the system will be compromised. Other factors such as employee carelessness, misunderstanding of instructions, and errors in judgment have a similar impact on the effectiveness of the internal control system. The auditor is aware of these limitations and is alert to events that may be observed during the audit that suggest the presence of such factors. When these factors are prevalent, the auditor modifies the audit approach so that there is a lesser reliance on the internal control system, or in some cases he or she may find it necessary to withdraw from the engagement.

STUDY OF THE INTERNAL CONTROL SYSTEM

A significant portion of this chapter is devoted to a discussion of the internal control model. With an understanding of the basic principles of an adequate internal control system, the auditor can use the model, recognizing its limitations, as a framework for the study and evaluation of a specific internal accounting control system. The auditor studies the internal control system and formulates a preliminary evaluation of this system, which determines the extent and the

194
Internal control:
systems
evaluations

nature of audit procedures used in the compliance tests, which comprise the third step of the integrated audit approach. A poorly designed internal control system increases the likelihood that material errors in the financial statements will exist, and the auditor must increase the amount and type of audit procedures used to reduce this audit risk to an acceptable level.

A study of the internal control system has two important phases:

- An understanding of the internal control system
- An evaluation of the internal control system

Understanding the system

While the principles or characteristics of an adequate internal control system are relatively few, the practical application of these guides results in a significant number of accounting system procedures. The result is that accounting systems are often complex and involved, and the auditor's approach to understanding the system reflects this complexity. The study of the internal control system should be well planned, and the approach formalized and methodical. A lesser audit approach may be interpreted as inappropriate and professionally deficient.

The initial phase of comprehension of a client's accounting system is devoted to the auditor's review of materials that describe the system. The organizational chart is reviewed. A reading or review of the accounting procedures manual, chart of accounts, and job descriptions is made by the auditor. In effect, any client material that describes the elements of the internal control model is of interest to the auditor in this initial step. Much of this material is used as a reference source throughout the audit. Such material is often voluminous and difficult to integrate into a comprehensive and understandable description of the internal control system. Fortunately, the profession has developed an audit methodology that results in a manageable description of the accounting system. In applying this methodology, the auditor not only creates a comprehensible description of the system but also documents the audit approach. This documentation serves as a basis for the next phase of the study of the system, that is, evaluation of the internal control system, and, like any working paper, aids the auditor in conducting the engagement. Specifically, this is achieved through use of the following techniques:

- Preparation of internal control questionnaires
- Preparation of flowcharts
- Preparation of memoranda

The descriptive and documentary values of these techniques are discussed together.

INTERNAL CONTROL QUESTIONNAIRES

As the name implies, an *internal control questionnaire* consists of a list of questions concerning an organization's accounting system. The questionnaire is a preprinted form prepared and adopted by an individual accounting firm and is used for a variety of engagements. The questions are structured on the basic principles of the internal control model and in many firms may require 20 or more pages. The questions are grouped into categories. Figure 6-3 is a listing of questions relevant to the general characteristics of the accounting system. Other questionnaires are devoted to the cash receipts system, the payroll system, and the inventory system, to name a few. These internal control questionnaires are illustrated in subsequent chapters.

The internal control questionnaire is completed by the auditor by interviewing knowledgeable personnel such as the controller, departmental heads, or clerks responsible for particular duties. The questionnaire is structured so that either a "yes" or a "no" response can be made by the organization personnel. The questions are usually worded so that a "no" response identifies a potential weakness in the internal control system. In the case of a "no" response, the "Remarks" column is cross-referenced either to the audit program step(s), where the weakness is recognized, or to a working paper which explains the mitigating circumstances or lack of importance of the item. In addition, the questionnaire identifies the auditor who originally prepared the questionnaire and the auditor who updated it.

The internal control questionnaire is very effective if used in the proper manner. It provides an efficient method of documenting an extensive accounting control system. Furthermore, the questionnaire is comprehensive, which makes it less likely that an auditor will omit all or parts of a certain area. With well over 200 questions in some internal control questionnaires, such a structured approach is almost mandated.

On the other hand, an internal control questionnaire, like any tool or technique, can be abused or employed incorrectly. The auditor who administers the questionnaire must not view it as a perfunctory audit technique. The reading of numerous questions followed by a simple "yes" or "no" response from the client's personnel can deteriorate into a useless exchange of words rather than an effective means of communication. Also, the auditor must understand the significance of each question. Many an auditor has been embarrassed by the client asking why a question is relevant. In addition, since the questionnaire is highly structured, it has very little flexibility. Problems or unique operating characteristics may not be covered by it, resulting in a lack of review of an important segment of the enterprise. To combat this problem, many audit firms design specialized internal control questionnaires. These questionnaires may be for commercial or industrial concerns, department stores, hospitals, banks, or insurance companies. Additionally, for organizations that have a significant part of their processing computerized, the auditor utilizes an EDP questionnaire.

FLOWCHARTS

The internal control system may be described through the preparation of flowcharts for each important processing function. Before preparing the flowchart, the auditor acquires a thorough understanding of the accounting system. This understanding is gained by inquiry, by using an internal control questionnaire as well as less structured inquiry techniques, and by the auditor's observation of the system and the client's personnel. A flowchart is a graphic display of the

Figure 6-3

Internal Control Questionnaire

	Answer		Answer based on		
General	Yes	No	Inquiry	Observation	Comments
1. Does the client have a chart of organization?					
2. Does the client have a chart of accounts?					
3. Is the accounting routine set forth in accounting manuals?					
4. Do we have copies of such charts and manuals in our permanent file for this client?					
5. Does the client have – a. a controller? b. an internal auditor or audit staff?					
6. If internal auditors are employed – a. do they render written reports on the results of their exami minations? b. are they directly responsible to, and do they report to, an executive officer other than the chief accounting officer? Designate: c. have we reviewed their reports?					
7. Is the general accounting department completely separated from – a. the purchasing department? b. the sales department? c. manufacturing and/or cost departments? d. cash receipts and disbursements?					
8. Are all employees who handle cash, securities, and other valuables bonded?					
9. Are all such employees required to take regular vacations, their regular duties then being assigned to other employees?					
10. Does head office accounting control over branch offices appear to be adequate?					
11. Are expenses and costs under budgetary control?					

processing of accounting data. The starting point of the flowchart is the point where (1) financial data are received from an external source (e.g., the receipt of a vendor's invoice) or (2) the preparation of an internal document that is the initial processing step in a significant accounting transaction (e.g., the preparation of time cards and job tickets as the first step in the payroll accounting system). From this beginning point, every important processing step is described as a proper representation of the physical flow of documents through the system. The flowchart terminates with an entry in the general ledger and a description

Figure 6-4

Flowchart Symbols

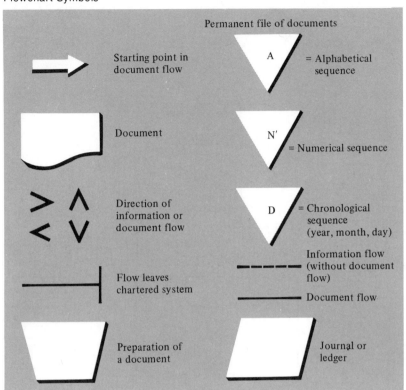

of the disposition of each document received from an external source or generated internally.

The use of flowcharts is facilitated by the use of standard flowchart symbols. In auditing there has been no codification of these symbols, and each firm must adopt an internal standardization system. Figure 6-4 is an example of a set of flowchart symbols. These symbols are the basis for the preparation of Figure 6-5, which is a description of a cash receipts system and sales system. The flowchart reads from left to right and follows the processing of the documents. The person who performs each processing step is identified. When an explanation of a process or the disposition of a document is involved, a cross-reference to a memorandum that fully describes the item is made. Also, some systems are designed so that a transaction with a unique characteristic is considered an exception and is processed in a different manner. To prevent the flowchart from becoming too detailed, these items may be described in a memorandum. For example, there is often a need to prepare a check immediately, in order to avoid an undesired delay, and a system for "quick checks" may be established.

The use of flowcharting as a descriptive and documentary technique has

Figure 6-5

Flowchart for Sales and Cash Receipts

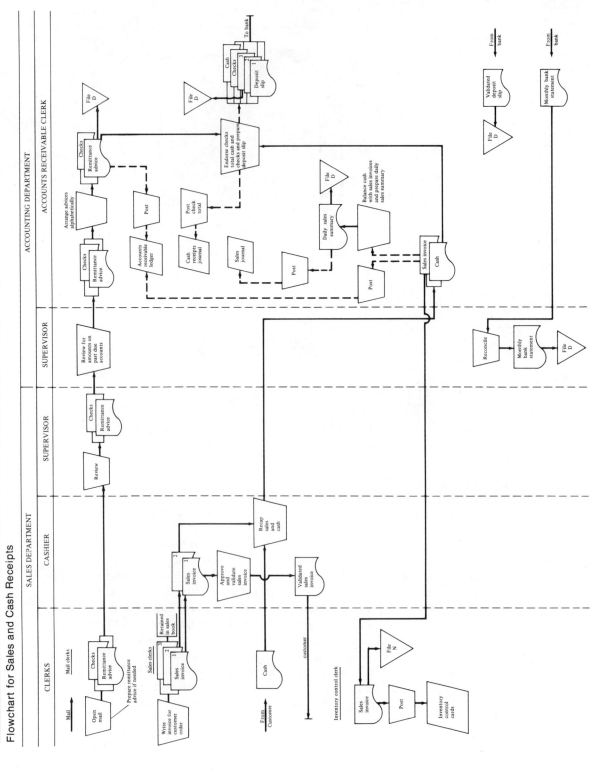

several advantages over other auditing methods. A flowchart is a visual aid which can facilitate the auditor's comprehension of an accounting system. If prepared correctly, it becomes a compact and graphic display of a complex processing system. Weaknesses in the accounting system can be readily noted by relating the processing step and the individual responsible for the process to the basic principles of the internal control model. Since the processing steps are displayed in a logical manner, it is less likely that the auditor will be unaware of a procedure. Unlike the internal control questionnaire approach, it is less likely that the auditor will acquire only a superficial understanding of the accounting system. In addition, the technique is highly flexible, since it may be adapted to any internal control system.

The preparation of flowcharts has been criticized as requiring too much time. As suggested above, a thorough knowledge of the internal control system is a prerequisite for the successful completion of this task. To convert this understanding into a legible and easily read flowchart takes additional time as well as a certain amount of creativity. However, once a set of flowcharts is prepared for a client, it is used in subsequent audits. Each year, flowcharts are reviewed and updated, if appropriate, and only if the system has changed a great deal is it necessary to prepare new ones.

MEMORANDUM

Documentation of the internal control system may be accomplished by preparation of a narrative description by the auditor. After discussing the system with the client's personnel, the auditor writes a description of the accounting procedures. Use of the memorandum technique can take the place of flowcharts to document the system. Figure 6-6, which describes the same system illustrated by the flowcharting technique in Figure 6-5, is an example of the use of a memorandum to describe an internal control system.

The main advantage of the use of a memorandum is that it is an extremely flexible method; however, it has several disadvantages. The success of the technique depends upon the auditor's ability to communicate in written form. A poorly worded or verbose memorandum hinders the subsequent evaluation process and may have to be rewritten during the following annual audit. Complex systems with involved processing characteristics can tax even auditors with strong communicative skills. Finally, the narrative form is less structured than an internal control questionnaire, which can result in the auditor omitting important processing steps.

No one technique suits the purposes of every audit engagement. In most audits, the internal control system is described through the use of a combination of questionnaires, flowcharts, and memoranda. Irrespective of use, the auditor's description is validated before a significant effort is made in the preliminary evaluation of the internal control system. To avoid the possibility of evaluating a system that exists only on paper, the auditor performs a "walk-through" of the major processing phases. He or she may select a document that has been processed, such as a canceled payroll check, and retrace it through the several procedural steps. Alternatively, the auditor may select a document that has not

Figure 6-6

Memorandum

Greenvalley Corp.
Sales and Cash Receipts System
December 31, 1978

Payment on account – The mail is opened each morning by a mail clerk in the sales department. The mail clerk prepares a remittance advice (showing customer and amount paid) if one is not received. The checks and remittance advices are then forwarded to the sales department supervisor who reviews each check and forwards the checks and remittance advices to the accounting department supervisor.

The accounting department supervisor, who also functions as credit manager in approving new credit and all credit limits, reviews all checks for payments on past due accounts and then forwards the checks and remittance advices to the accounts receivable clerk who arranges the advices in alphabetic order. The remittance advices are posted directly to the accounts receivable ledger cards. The checks are endorsed by stamp and totaled. The total is posted to the cash receipts journal. The remittance advices are filed chronologically.

After receiving the cash from the previous day's cash sales, the accounts receivable clerk prepares the daily deposit slip in triplicate. The third copy of the deposit slip is filed by date and the second copy and the original accompany the bank deposit.

Prepared by	Index No.
REB	B101
Date 2/11/79	

Figure 6-6 (Continued)

Greenvalley Corp.
Sales and Cash Receipts System
December 31, 1978

    <u>Sales</u> - Sales clerks prepare sales invoices in triplicate. The original and second copy are presented to the cashier. The third copy is retained by the sales clerk in the sales book. When the sale is for cash, the customer pays the sales clerk who presents the money to the cashier with the invoice copies.

    A credit sale is approved by the cashier from an approved credit list after the sales clerk prepares the three-part invoice. After receiving the cash or approving the invoice, the cashier validates the original copy of the sales invoice and gives it to the customer. At the end of each day the cashier recaps the sales and cash received and forwards the cash and the second copy of all sales invoices to the accounts receivable clerk.

    The accounts receivable clerk balances the cash received with cash sales invoices and prepares a daily sales summary. The credit sales invoices are posted to the accounts receivable ledger and then all invoices are sent to the inventory control clerk in the sales department for posting to the inventory control cards. After posting, the inventory control clerk files all invoices numerically. The accounts receivable clerk posts the daily sales summary to the cash receipts journal and sales journal and files the sales summaries by date.

Prepared by REB Date 2/1/79	Index No. B 102

Figure 6-6 (Continued)

The cash from cash sales is combined with the cash received on account to comprise the daily bank deposit.

Bank deposit - the bank validates the deposit slip and returns the second copy to the accounting department where it is filed by date by the accounts receivable clerk.

Monthly bank statements are reconciled promptly by the accounting department supervisor and filed by date.

Prepared by	Index No.
REB	B103
Date 2/1/79	

been processed through the system and observe it being processed. For example, an auditor may select a vendor's invoice that had just been received through the mail and follow it as it is processed through the system.

203
Study of the internal control system

Evaluation of the system

The review of the internal control system through the use of an internal control questionnaire, flowcharts, narrative memoranda, and other methods selected by the auditor is the basis for forming a preliminary evaluation of the system. The purpose of the study and evaluation of the internal control system is to provide a basis for determining the reliability of the system and the extent of the audit procedures to be employed. *SAS No. 1,* Section 320.65, describes this audit approach:

> A conceptually logical approach to the auditor's evaluation of accounting control, which focuses directly on the purpose of preventing or detecting material errors and irregularities in financial statements, is to apply the following steps in considering each significant class of transactions and related assets involved in the audit:
>
> a. Consider the types of errors and irregularities that could occur.
> b. Determine the accounting control procedures that should prevent or detect such errors and irregularities.
> c. Determine whether the necessary procedures are prescribed and are being followed satisfactorily.
> d. Evaluate any weaknesses—i.e., types of potential errors and irregularities not covered by existing control procedures to determine their effect on (1) the nature, timing, or extent of auditing procedures to be applied and (2) suggestions to be made to the client.

Steps *a* and *b* are performed after the auditor has obtained a thorough knowledge of the client's internal control system. Weaknesses are identified by describing the nature of errors or irregularities that may occur. In step c the auditor performs the compliance tests to determine how the system operates and the type and extent of errors or irregularities being generated. Once the compliance test is completed, the internal control system is again evaluated, providing a basis for determining the nature, timing, and extent of the substantive tests. Evaluation of the internal control system is discussed in the remainder of this chapter. The compliance and substantive tests are discussed in general in Chapter 9, and more specifically in Chapters 10 through 16.

DEFINING A SYSTEM WEAKNESS

Having described and documented the internal control system, the auditor uses this material to identify potential material weaknesses. A *material weakness* is an existing condition in the system that does not provide reasonable assurance that significant errors or irregularities can be prevented or detected by the accounting system. The auditor, as suggested by the above definition, differentiates between errors and irregularities. *SAS No. 16* defines these two terms:

Errors Unintentional mistakes in financial statements and includes mathematical or clerical mistakes in the underlying records and

204
**Internal control:
systems
evaluations**

accounting data from which the financial statements were prepared, mistakes in application of accounting principles, and oversight or misinterpretation of facts that existed at the time the financial statements were prepared.

Irregularities Intentional distortions of financial statements, such as deliberate misrepresentations by management, sometimes referred to as management fraud, or misappropriations of assets, sometimes referred to as defalcations.

Since an adequate internal control system reduces, but does not eliminate, the possibility of errors or irregularities, the identification of weaknesses is carefully considered by the auditor.

ANALYSIS OF A SYSTEM WEAKNESS

Consistent with the documentation approach used in describing the internal control system, each system that processes similar transactions is evaluated individually. Moreover, the evaluation is of a detailed nature, since a broad evaluation is not useful in identifying procedures to be employed in the compliance or substantive tests. For this reason the auditor reviews each procedure of the system as described in the internal control questionnaire, flowcharts, memoranda, or other documentation to determine which contributes to the occurrence of material errors or irregularities. In reviewing this documentation, the auditor (1) identifies the weakness, (2) describes the potential effects of the weakness, and (3) identifies the audit procedures to be employed to determine the actual impact, if any, of the weakness.

This three-step approach should not be an informal, unstructured analysis. It is an important step in the study and evaluation of the existing internal control system as required by the second standard of fieldwork. In addition, there is some documentation in the working papers that this analysis was performed. The preparation of a worksheet such as the one in Figure 6-7 is one method of documenting the audit approach. This worksheet shows the direct impact of a weakness on the audit procedures to be used in the compliance tests. If there are no material weaknesses in the accounting system, the auditor may prepare a memorandum or a worksheet similar to Figure 6-7 that shows how the strength of the internal control system reduces or restricts the use of some audit procedures in the compliance or the substantive tests.

Internal control recommendation letter

At the conclusion of the study and evaluation of the client's internal control system, the auditor probably has suggestions for improving the system. He or she may prepare an internal control recommendation letter or a management letter listing these suggestions. These recommendations are concerned with administrative controls as well as accounting controls. As suggested, the auditor is usually not interested in administrative controls, but during the course of the

Figure 6-7

Greenvalley Corp.
Analysis of Sales / Accounts Receivable System
December 31, 1978

Reference	Weakness	Potential Impact	Suggested Audit Procedure for Compliance Test
B-304	There is no independant procedure to determine that the accounts receivable control account is in agreement with the detail in the subsidiary ledger. The accounts receivable clerk is responsible for reconciling the balance in the control to the detail in the subsidiary ledger cards. Differences are resolved by the clerk.	There could be material errors in the subsidiary ledger cards and/or the control account that have gone undetected or have been concealed by the receivable clerk.	① Foot the sales journal and cash receipts journal for April and July and trace postings to the G/L. ② Reconcile the control account and the detail in the ledger cards for the months of April and July. ③ Select three business days at random and trace data from listing of cash remittances per listing prepared in the mail room to the subsidiary ledger cards. ④ For the same days selected in ③ trace data from copy of sales invoice to the subsidiary ledger cards.

Prepared by	Index No.
REB	B 310
Date 2/18/79	

206
**Internal control:
systems
evaluations**

engagement it is not unusual for him or her to observe administrative controls that are deficient in some manner.

Although the purpose of the audit is to form an opinion on the financial statements, it is to the auditor's advantage to consider the preparation of a recommendation letter part of the overall requirements of the audit. First, the audit task is facilitated if there is a strong internal control system. Thus the auditor has a vested interest in seeing that the client is made aware of accounting control deficiencies and that these deficiencies are corrected as soon as practicable. In addition, many clients view the audit as a necessary evil rather than as a positive endeavor. If the auditor makes suggestions that will make the system more efficient or effective, the recommendation letter will become a strong client relations tool. Hopefully, such an approach encourages the client to be more cooperative with the auditor. Finally, a strong internal control system should result in the need for less auditing, which reduces the audit fee. An inadequate system invariably requires more detailed auditing.

The internal control recommendation letter is prepared for internal use only and is not distributed to external users. On occasion, an external party may deem it desirable to have access to the auditor's evaluation of the client's internal control system. Because it is possible to misunderstand the role of an internal control system in the safeguarding of assets and the generating of reliable accounting data, an externally distributed internal control report must be carefully worded. *SAS, No. 1,* Section 640, discusses the nature and the suggested form of reports on internal control. This material is covered in Chapter 18.

Communication of material weaknesses

As suggested above, the auditor is not required to prepare an internal control recommendation letter; however, he or she is required to report the discovery of material weaknesses in the internal control system. A material weakness is defined in *SAS No. 1,* Section 320.68:

> . . . a condition in which the auditor believes the prescribed procedures or the degree of compliance with them does not provide reasonable assurance that errors or irregularities in amounts that would be material in the financial statements being audited would be prevented or detected within a timely period by employees in the normal course of performing their assigned functions.

In an actual audit engagement, differentiating between a material weakness and an immaterial weakness is a matter of professional judgment. Certainly one factor to consider is the potential dollar amount that may be in error or misappropriated. For example, controls over petty cash may be inadequate, but the degree of potential error or irregularity is limited. On the other hand, errors or irregularities that may occur because of a lack of proper segregation of duties in the processing of cash receipts are considered material in most engagements.

Once a material weakness is discovered, *SAS No. 20* requires that the weakness be disclosed to "senior management and the board of directors or its audit committee." The form of communication may be written or oral. If the weakness is communicated in oral form, the working papers should fully describe the details of the oral report. This includes (1) identification of the parties that participated in the conference, (2) the nature of the weakness, and (3) suggestions to remedy the weakness.

CONCLUDING REMARKS

The collection and evaluation of evidence in an audit can be described in a four-step approach:

1. Client's environmental conditions
2. Internal control evaluation
3. Compliance test
4. Substantive test

The first two steps were discussed in this chapter and in Chapter 5. Chapter 7 deals with the impact of a computerized system on the internal control structure of an organization, and Chapter 8 discusses sampling in auditing. After these two topics are discussed, Chapter 9 considers the final two steps of the integrated audit approach.

EXERCISES AND PROBLEMS

6-1. Explain why it is necessary for the auditor to differentiate between administrative controls and accounting controls. Give an example of each.

6-2. Accounting controls refers to the safeguarding of assets. Does this imply that the internal control system is mainly concerned with the physical protection of assets?

6-3. Why is departmental autonomy a critical element of the internal control model? Give an example to explain your answer.

6-4. What are the basic characteristics of an adequate internal control system?

6-5. In relation to the attest function, explain the role of the corporate audit committee.

6-6. What is the purpose of the auditor's understanding of the internal control model?

6-7. What methods may be used by the auditor to describe a client's internal control system? List the advantages and disadvantages of each.

6-8. In evaluating an internal control system, is an auditor generally more concerned with the possibility of an error or of an irregularity occurring? Explain.

6-9. How does the evaluation of the internal control system impact the selection of audit procedures? Give an example.

6-10. What is the purpose of the internal control recommendation letter?

6-11. The town of Commuter Park operates a private parking lot near the railroad station for the benefit of town residents. The guard on duty issues annual prenumbered parking stickers to residents who submit an application form and show evidence of residency.

208
Internal control:
systems
evaluations

The sticker is affixed to the automobile and allows the resident to park anywhere in the lot for 12 hours when four quarters are placed in the parking meter. Applications are maintained in the guard office at the lot. The guard checks to see that only residents use the lot and that no resident parks without paying the required meter fee.

Once a week the guard on duty, who has a master key for all the meters, takes the coins from the meters and places them in a locked steel box. The guard delivers the box to the town storage building where it is opened, and the coins are manually counted by a storage department clerk who records the total cash counted on a weekly cash report. This report is sent to the town accounting department. The storage department clerk puts the cash in a safe, and on the following day it is picked up by the town's treasurer who manually recounts it, prepares the bank deposit slip, and delivers the deposit to the bank. The deposit slip, authenticated by the bank teller, is sent to the accounting department where it is filed with the weekly cash report.

Required: Describe weaknesses in the existing system and recommend one or more improvements for each of the weaknesses to strengthen the internal control over the parking lot cash receipts.

Organize your answer sheet as follows:

WEAKNESS	RECOMMENDED IMPROVEMENT(S)

(AICPA Adapted)

6-12. The financial statements of the Tiber Company have never been audited by an independent CPA. Recently Tiber's management asked Anthony Burns, CPA, to conduct a special study of Tiber's internal control; this study will not include an examination of Tiber's financial statements. Following completion of his special study, Burns plans to prepare a report that is consistent with the requirements of *SAP No. 49,* "Reports on Internal Control."

Required

1. Describe the inherent limitations that should be recognized in considering the potential effectiveness of any system of internal control.

2. Explain and contrast the review of internal control that Burns might make as part of an examination of financial statements with his special study of Tiber's internal control, covering each of the following:

a. Objectives of review or study
b. Scope of review or study
c. Nature and content of reports

Organize your answer for part 2 as follows:

EXAMINATION OF FINANCIAL STATEMENTS	SPECIAL STUDY
Objective	Objective
Scope	Scope
Report	Report

d. In connection with a loan application, Tiber plans to submit the CPA's report on his special study of internal control, together with its latest unaudited financial statements, to the Fourth National Bank.

Discuss the propriety of this use of the CPA's report on internal control.

(AICPA Adapted)

209
Exercises and problems

6-13. An auditor completes an internal control questionnaire to determine if weaknesses exist in the accounting system. The following questions appear on a typical internal control questionnaire:

1. Are shipments on consignments handled separately from sales?
2. Is the signing of checks in advance of their being completely filled out prohibited?
3. Is the bank receipt for the deposit forwarded by the bank directly to a person who does not have access to cash receipts?
4. Are spoiled checks mutilated to prevent reuse and kept on file for subsequent inspection?
5. Are unmatched purchase orders and receiving reports and unvouchered vendors' invoices periodically investigated?
6. Are all incoming inventories and supplies required to pass through a central receiving department?
7. Are responsibilities for quantities of inventory fixed by assigning custody to specific individuals?
8. Are perpetual inventory cards maintained by persons other than the custodians of the inventory?

Required: Assume the answer to the above questions is "no" in each case. Explain how each response impacts the auditor's performance of subsequent audit procedures. Consider each question independently of the others.

6-14. Adherence to generally accepted auditing standards requires, among other things, a proper study and evaluation of the existing internal control. The most common approaches to reviewing the system of internal control include the use of a questionnaire, preparation of a memorandum, preparation of a flowchart, and combinations of these methods.

Required
1. What is a CPA's objective in reviewing internal control for an opinion audit?
2. Discuss the advantages to a CPA of reviewing internal control by using:

a. An internal control questionnaire
b. The memorandum approach
c. A flowchart

3. If the CPA is satisfied after completing an evaluation of internal control for an opinion audit that no material weaknesses in the client's internal control system exist, is it necessary for the CPA to test transactions? Explain. (AICPA Adapted)

6-15. An important procedure in the CPA's audit programs is his or her review of the client's system of internal control.

Required
1. Distinguish between accounting controls and administrative controls in a properly coordinated system of internal control.
2. List the essential features of a sound system of accounting control.
3. Explain why the CPA is concerned about the separation of responsibilities for operating custodianship, financial custodianship, and controllership. (AICPA Adapted)

210
Internal control:
systems
evaluations

6-16. Accounting controls comprise the plan of organization and the procedures and records concerned with the safeguarding of assets and the reliability of financial records. As part of its internal control objectives, a client designs accounting procedures to ensure reasonably that an authorized transaction is recorded as authorized. Consider the following list of authorized transactions.

1. A signed check
2. A properly executed purchase order
3. Payroll authorization for a change in the hourly rate paid to an individual
4. A deposit slip which represents the cash receipts for a given day
5. A properly completed receiving report
6. A list of cash remittances
7. A completed sales invoice

Required: For each authorized transaction identify a control procedure that can be used by a client to determine if the transaction is recorded as authorized.

6-17. A company's system of internal control (which consists of accounting and administrative controls) is strengthened by including procedures that have specific functions or purposes. For example, the system of internal control may include a voucher system that provides for all invoices to be checked for accuracy, approved for propriety, and recorded before being paid. The system reduces the likelihood that an invoice will be mislaid or the discount lost, and it provides assurance that improper or unauthorized disbursements are not likely to be made.

Required: Give the purposes or functions of each of the following procedures or techniques that may be included in a system of internal control, and explain how each purpose or function is helpful in strengthening accounting and administrative internal control.

1. Fidelity bonding of employees
2. Budgeting of capital expenditures
3. Listing of mail remittances by the mail department when the mail is opened
4. Maintaining a plant ledger for fixed assets   (AICPA Adapted)

6-18. The United Charities organization in your town has engaged you to examine its statement of receipts and disbursements. United Charities solicits contributions from local donors and then apportions the contributions among local charitable organizations.

The officers and directors are local bankers, professionals, and other leaders of the community. A cashier and a clerk are the only full-time salaried employees. The only records maintained by the organization are a cashbook and a checkbook. The directors prefer not to have a system of pledges.

Contributions are solicited by numerous volunteer workers. The workers are not restricted as to the area of their solicitation and may work among their friends, neighbors, co-workers, and so on, as is convenient. To ensure blanket coverage of the town, new volunteer workers are welcomed.

Contributions are in the form of cash or checks. They are received by United Charities from the solicitors, who personally deliver the money they have collected, or directly from donors by mail or by personal delivery.

The solicitors complete official receipts which they give to the donors when they receive contributions. These official receipts have attached stubs which the solicitors fill in with the names of the donors and the amounts of the contributions. The solicitors turn in the stubs with the contributions to the cashier. No control is maintained over the number of blank receipts given to the solicitors or the number of receipt stubs turned in with the contributions.

Required: Discuss the control procedures you would recommend for greater assurance that all contributions received by the solicitors are turned over to the organization. (Do not discuss the control of the funds in the organization's office.)   (AICPA Adapted)

6-19. During an engagement an auditor usually discovers a variety of errors. At the conclusion of the audit or at the conclusion of the study and evaluation of the internal control system, the auditor may prepare an internal control recommendation letter to encourage the client to change the accounting system so the likelihood of the occurrence of similar errors is minimized.

Assume that during your examination of the Ratcliff Company the following errors are discovered:

1. Several sales invoices were not recorded in the sales journal.
2. A significant number of sales adjustments were made because sales invoices were not properly prepared.
3. The balances in the accounts receivable subsidiary ledger cards were not a proper reflection of amounts due from customers, although the general ledger account and the detail ledger were balanced at the end of each month by an independent party.
4. The petty cash custodian could not fully account for the imprest balance of $500.
5. Several checks were used out of numerical sequence and were not recorded in the cash disbursements journal.
6. Several receiving reports were being held in the receiving department. Some of these reports were six months old.
7. Several checks stamped "Nonsufficient funds" returned by the bank were not recorded.
8. Receipts of fixtures were recorded as purchases of inventory.
9. Several expenses were not recorded, since they were paid out of the daily receipts.

Required: For each of the above errors, suggest an internal control procedure that should be adopted by the client. Consider each error independent of the other errors.

6-20. In conducting his or her examination in accordance with generally accepted auditing standards the CPA studies and evaluates the existing internal control of the client.

Required
1. List and discuss the general elements or basic characteristics of a satisfactory system of internal control.
2. List the purposes for which the CPA reviews the client's system of internal control.   (AICPA Adapted)

6-21. You are preparing an analysis of the internal control system of EKG Corporation. During your interview of the client's personnel you make the following notations for the client's credit sales system.

When an order is received from a customer, the sales order department prepares a six-copy sales invoice. Copy 2 is sent to the credit manager for approval of the credit terms and is returned to the sales order department where it is filed alphabetically. Copy 6 is sent to the customer to acknowledge the order.

Copies 1 and 3 are sent to the billing department and held in a numerical file until notification of shipment of the goods is received. Copy 4 is sent to the shipping department

212
Internal control: systems evaluations

as an authorization to accept goods from the warehouse and to ship these goods. Copy 5 is sent to the warehouse and serves as the approval to release the goods. Once the warehouse fills the order, the goods and copy 5, which is initialed, are sent to the shipping department. The shipping department matches copies 4 and 5. The goods are shipped and are accompanied by copy 4 which serves as a packing slip. Copy 5 is stamped "Shipped" and dated and is sent to the billing department. The billing department matches copy 5 with its copies and completes all copies by pricing and extending the sales invoices. Copy 1 is then sent to the customer. Copy 5 is filed alphabetically. Copy 3 for all sales that day are grouped together, and an adding machine tape of the total dollar sales is prepared in the billing department. Copy 3 is sent to the accounts receivable clerk as a basis for posting to the subsidiary ledger cards. Once posted, copy 3 is returned to the billing department where it is filed by date, and this file serves as the sales journal. The adding machine tape is sent to the general ledger clerk, accumulated for each month and posted to the appropriate accounts.

Required: The audit manager, after reading the above notes, requests that you prepare a flowchart of the sales system to facilitate the internal control study and evaluation.

6-22. Problem Figure 6-22 is a flowchart for the cash receipts system of the A-2 Corporation.

Required

1. Identify weaknesses in the system based upon your review of the flowchart.
2. Make a list of suggestions to improve the system.

6-23. You have been assigned to be the in-charge accountant for the Springfield Corporation engagement. You asked a junior accountant of your firm to complete an internal control questionnaire for the sales and shipping accounting system. Presented below is the internal control questionnaire completed by the accountant.

Required

1. For each "no" response explain the type of error that may occur.
2. For each "no" response suggest an audit procedure that should be employed by the auditor as part of the subsequent audit tests to be conducted in the tests of compliance and the substantive tests.
3. Do you believe the comments made by the junior accountant are acceptable?

Internal Control Questionnaire: Sales and Shipping Function

	ANSWER		
	YES	NO	COMMENT
1. Are sales orders approved by the credit manager?		✓	Field salespersons determine whether credit should be granted
2. Are sales prices and credit terms based on an approved price list?		✓	Salespersons enter sales prices on the customer order
3. Are prenumbered bills of lading prepared for all goods shipped?	✓		
4. Does the billing clerk receive a copy of the shipping invoice once the goods are shipped?		✓	Sales invoices are prepared and mailed as soon as a customer order is received from a salesperson

Problem 6-22

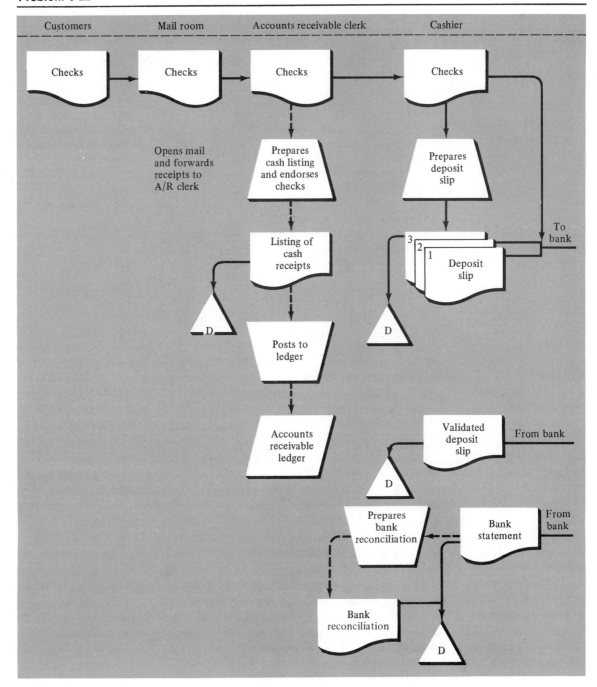

214
Internal control:
systems
evaluations

	ANSWER		
	YES	NO	COMMENT
5. Are prenumbered bills of lading accounted for on a periodic basis?	✓		Performed by shipping clerk
6. Are sales invoices prenumbered?	✓		
7. Are sales invoices accounted for on a periodic basis?		✓	However, one copy of the sales invoice serves as the sales journal
8. Are the total sales for each month reported directly to a general ledger clerk independently of the work of the accounts receivable clerk?	✓		
9. Are returned sales cleared through the receiving department?	✓		Some goods are received by salespersons.
10. Are credit memos for returned sales supported by adequate data from the receiving department?	✓		See comment in no. 9.
11. Are credit memos for returned goods approved by a responsible official?	✓		Salespersons have the authority to issue credit memos
12. Are credit memos prenumbered?		✓	
13. Are credit memos accounted for?	✓		One copy of each credit memo issued is filed with credit manager

6-24. As audit manager for the Mercer Company engagement, you are reviewing the working paper prepared by an assistant. As part of the review you note several weaknesses in the internal control system as shown by certain responses on the internal control questionnaire. You also note that your assistant has cross-referenced the weaknesses to audit procedures to be performed as part of the tests of compliance or the substantive tests.

The assistant's analysis is summarized as follows:

ANALYSIS OF SYSTEM WEAKNESS	EXTENDED AUDIT PROCEDURES
1. Although the credit manager stated that all credit sales are approved based upon guidelines used for the past several years, it is questionable whether this is correct. The business has expanded rapidly in the last six months. In addition, two people in the credit department resigned four months ago and have not been replaced. Based on my observation it appears that the normal credit analysis is not being made.	To determine if a proper credit approval of sales is being made, a random sample of 50 sales invoices is selected for testing. There is a sequential file of the prenumbered sales invoices.

2. There is a new accounts receivable ledger clerk who appears to be poorly trained for the job. Also, the controls to determine that all sales invoices are posted are weak.

3. When inventory is shipped, a pre-numbered bill of lading is prepared for each shipment. One copy of the bill of lading is sent to the billing clerk, and at this time the billing clerk prepares the prenumbered sales invoice and sends one of the copies of the invoice to the accounts receivable clerk. There is no cross-referencing between the bills of lading and the sales invoice. There is a possibility that some shipments are not being billed.

To determine if there is an unacceptable error rate in the postings to the subsidiary ledger cards, 50 postings on these cards are traced directly to the sales invoices.

To determine if goods that are shipped are not being invoiced, 50 sales invoices are selected on a random basis and traced to the appropriate bill of lading and the posting in the subsidiary ledger.

Required

1. Do you agree with the accountant's selection of extended audit procedures? Explain.

2. Suggest an alternative audit procedure for each item.

MULTIPLE CHOICE

1. What is the independent auditor's principal purpose for conducting a study and evaluation of the existing system of internal control?

   a. To comply with generally accepted accounting principles.
   b. To obtain a measure of assurance of management's efficiency.
   c. To maintain a state of independence in mental attitude in all matters relating to the audit.
   d. To determine the nature, timing, and extent of subsequent audit work.

2. The actual operation of an internal control system may be most objectively evaluated by

   a. Completing a questionnaire and flowchart related to the accounting system in the year under audit.
   b. Review of the previous year's audit workpaper to update the report of internal control evaluation.
   c. Selection of items processed by the system and determination of the presence or absence of errors and compliance deviations.
   d. Substantive tests of account balances based on the auditor's assessment of internal control strength.

3. Of the following, the best statement of the CPA's primary objective in reviewing internal control is that the review is intended to provide

   a. Reasonable protection against client fraud and defalcations by client employees.
   b. A basis for reliance on the system and determining the scope of other auditing procedures.

216
Internal control:
systems
evaluations

c. A basis for constructive suggestions to the client for improving the accounting system.

d. A method for safeguarding assets, checking the accuracy and reliability of accounting data, promoting operational efficiency, and encouraging adherence to prescribed managerial policies.

4. A responsibility that should be assigned to a specific employee and not shared jointly is that of

a. Access to the company's safe deposit box.
b. Placing orders and maintaining relationships with a prime supplier.
c. Attempting to collect a particular delinquent account.
d. Custodianship of the cash working fund.

5. When evaluating internal control, the auditor's primary concern is to determine

a. The possibility of fraud occurring.
b. Compliance with policies, plans, and procedures.
c. The reliability of the accounting information system.
d. The type of an opinion he or she will issue.   (AICPA Adapted)

CHAPTER 7

Auditing and EDP

EDP technology has had a significant impact upon the processing of business transactions. With the continued development of low-cost and small computers, this impact will become even greater in the future. In a similar manner, EDP has had a significant impact upon the audit process in many engagements, and this impact will undoubtedly expand as more businesses utilize computers in the processing of data.

The existence of computerized systems has an effect on two broad areas of the audit. First, the impact of the computer on the internal control system of an organization must be considered. Since the second standard of fieldwork requires that the auditor study and evaluate the existing internal control system, the audit approach encompasses a review and test of EDP procedures when these procedures are an important part of the organization's system of internal control. Second, the auditor can use the computer as an audit tool in the conduct of the engagement. In this case, his or her objective is to perform the audit in the most efficient manner by using current technology.

This chapter is concerned with the first aspect. In this regard, it is an extension of the previous chapter which dealt with the analysis of a client's internal control system. The discussion of the computer as an audit tool is deferred until Chapter 9.

THE EDP INTERNAL CONTROL MODEL

Regardless of whether the auditor is concerned with a manual system, a mechanical system, or an EDP system, the audit objectives are the same, namely, to determine if the system is adequately designed to protect the client's assets and to facilitate the generation of reliable financial data. However, the introduction of a computer affects the fundamental principles that comprise the internal control model as described in the previous chapter. Since there are

218
Auditing and EDP

changes in the internal control model, it is not surprising that the audit process itself is modified. An AICPA publication summarizes the impact of the introduction of a computer on the audit approach:

1. Many control procedures in manual systems leave documentary evidence of performance. Since many control procedures in computer systems leave no documentary evidence of performance, different tests of compliance may be required.

2. Information in manual systems is visible. Files and records in EDP systems are usually in machine-sensible form and cannot be read without the use of the computer.

3. The decrease of human involvement in the handling of transactions processed by computers can obscure errors that might have been observed in a manual system.

4. With proper controls in place, EDP systems can provide better reliability than manual systems because they uniformly subject all data to the same controls. Manual systems are subject to human error on a random basis.

5. To develop an understanding of a complex EDP system and to perform tests of compliance . . . and other necessary audit procedures, the auditor ordinarily must obtain specialized EDP knowledge. This may require a significant amount of training beyond what was required to cope with non-EDP systems.

6. Because of the difficulty in effecting changes after an EDP system has been implemented, the auditor may want to become familiar with the design and testing of new EDP systems at an early stage in the development process in order to anticipate possible problems in the future audits of those systems.[1]

In *SAS No. 3*, EDP internal accounting controls were classified as:

General controls

- The plan of organization and operations of the EDP activity
- The procedures for documenting, reviewing, testing and approving systems or programs and changes
- Controls built into the equipment by the manufacturer
- Controls over access to equipment and data files
- Other data and procedural controls affecting overall EDP operations

Application controls

- Input controls
- Processing controls
- Output controls

The above outline provides the basis for the following description of an adequate EDP internal accounting control model.

General controls

The general controls of the EDP internal control model refer to the organizational structure and the administrative rules applicable to the EDP area. They are concerned not with the actual activity of processing data but rather with the

---

[1] *Audit and Accounting Guide,* "The Auditor's Study and Evaluation of Internal Control in EDP Systems" (New York: AICPA, 1977), pp. 5–6. Copyright © 1977 by the American Institute of Certified Public Accountants, Inc.

administrative and physical mechanism capable of processing the data. Adequate general controls are fundamental to the construction of a sound EDP internal control system, and an absence of such controls may have a great impact on the audit approach adopted. Usually, such weaknesses are compensated for by expanding the compliance and substantive tests.

The plan of organization

As noted above, an EDP system performs many of the functions performed by a variety of individuals in a manual or mechanical system. Because of this concentration of duties in one area, the organizational structure of the EDP department is critical to the existence of an adequate internal control system. The organizational scheme must consider (1) the EDP department's relationship to user departments and (2) the internal departmental structure of the EDP group.

EDP'S RELATIONSHIP TO USERS

The basic function of the EDP department is to serve the needs of other operating departments within the organization. For this reason, it is independent of these operating departments and does not report to an operating department head. The internal control system is strengthened when the EDP departmental head reports to a high-level executive, such as the president or a vice-president in charge of operations. In many organizations, the controller is responsible for the EDP function. Such an arrangement is not ideal, since the user, the accounting department, and the EDP function may not be segregated effectively. This especially tends to be true in small companies where it may be considered uneconomical to separate EDP activities from the accounting or other user functions. Nevertheless, this is a weakness in the internal control system, and it must be recognized and evaluated for its potential effect on the overall internal control system. For example, the impact of this weakness may be mitigated by the existence of strong application controls.

Another aspect of the relationship between the EDP function and a user department involves the authorization of transactions. This authority resides with the user department, and the EDP activity is restricted to the processing of authorized data. The user department initiates processing through the preparation of data in some prescribed form and establishes a control mechanism over the data channeled to the EDP department. For example, the payroll department prepares a list of individuals who have worked during the pay period and the number of hours worked. By sending this information in a proper form to the EDP department, the processing phase is authorized. In addition, control totals, such as the number of employees to be paid, may be established in the operating department to ensure that no data were lost or errors made in the transmission, conversion, and processing of the data. (Control totals are discussed more fully under application controls.) It is important that data that are not in proper form when received by the EDP department be sent back to the operating department for correction rather than be corrected by the EDP group. If the latter makes corrections in the data, it is then responsible for the origination and authorization of transaction, an obvious violation of the need to restrict the duties of the EDP group.

The processing of authorized transactions by the EDP group may itself result in an authorized transaction in some computerized systems. Approved sales orders from the sales department may be processed by the EDP department, and the computer program may initiate a purchase order if inventory levels fall below a predetermined amount. These EDP-generated transactions are subsequently reviewed by appropriate personnel before the transaction is processed further. For example, a purchase is controlled and approved by the purchasing agent.

EDP DEPARTMENTAL STRUCTURE

An acceptable internal organizational structure of the EDP activity recognizes the need to separate certain activities within this area. Incompatible activities that may enable an individual to conceal errors or irregularities are assigned in a manner to prevent such occurrences. The following functions are considered incompatible and should be the responsibility of different individuals or groups of individuals within the EDP department:

- System analysis and programming
- Machine operation
- Library
- Control

System analysis and programming: A systems analyst is responsible for designing a system that meets the needs of a user. A programmer converts the general description provided by the systems analyst into a detailed set of instructions for operating the data processing equipment in a manner consistent with the system's objectives. In many organizations these two functions are merged with no detrimental effect on the adequacy of the internal control system. However, it is critical that this function not be merged with the machine operation function. Since the systems analyst and programmer are familiar with the programmed software controls, access to the actual running of the program affords them the opportunity to make unauthorized modifications in the program or to introduce unauthorized transactions. For this reason, access to the computer facilities, especially during processing, should be restricted and controlled.

Machine operations: The machine operator has physical control of the computerized data and the programs and the responsibility for processing routine data. The operator's knowledge and understanding of the EDP system is limited to that needed to operate the computer. If the he or she possesses such attributes and has the necessary programming skills, then the principle of segregation of duties is violated, resulting in a weakness in the internal control system. In order to protect against this occurring, computer operators are periodically, without notice, rotated from one program-operating responsibility to another. Also, a personnel policy that requires all operators to take vacations should be adopted and observed.

Library: All the benefits of proper segregation of duties within the EDP area can be negated if access to data files and programs is not limited and controlled. The librarian maintains control of the software by granting access only to individuals who are properly authorized. Some method of recording the withdrawal of material, by whom and for what amount of time, is established.

Control: The control group monitors the input, processing, and distribution of data within the EDP function. Initial monitoring occurs through the control group's acquisition of control totals generated in the user department. As data are moved from the user department to the EDP department, user control totals are communicated to the control group. These totals are reconciled with the results generated by the EDP activity. This function includes the review of error listings for items not processed and the reprocessing of data rejected during operational activity. In addition, the control group is responsible for the distribution of reports or documents generated during processing.

PROGRAM DOCUMENTATION

The presence of an adequate method of program documentation contributes to the overall strength of an EDP internal control system. From management's viewpoint it is fundamental to efficient operation of the EDP department. For the auditor it provides the basis for acquiring an understanding of the system and is a first step in evaluating whether management can control the EDP function. An inadequate system of documentation usually suggests a weak EDP internal control system.

A comprehensive discussion of EDP documentation is beyond the scope of this book. The latter part of this chapter provides a description of flowcharting as an example of an EDP documentation technique. The following is a list of the typical documentation features employed for each program in an internal control system.

Problem definition: This area encompasses a description of the need for and the objectives of the program. Approval for the program is formally documented.

Systems documentation: Included in the systems documentation is a systems flowchart that describes the processing steps of the program. Input and output documents and their attendant application controls are illustrated. Other documentation includes file descriptions and hardware requirements.

Program documentation: This documentation provides a basis for establishing control over program revisions. Program flowcharts, descriptions of file formats, and record layouts and operation instructions are examples.

Operations documentation: These are detailed instructions for computer operations concerning the setup of the program run, error or halt messages, restart, description of data files, and programs to be used and input/output data.

Adequate documentation in an EDP system is important to the auditor to avoid gaps in the audit trail. The audit trail provides the auditor with an opportunity to follow the processing of data through the accounting system. The system of documentation allows the auditor to follow input data through the accounting system processing steps to an output document. For example, an auditor must be able to trace an employee's time card through the system to an entry in the payroll journal. With the introduction of computers many auditors worried about destruction of the audit trail and the resulting impact on the audit approach. For the most part, this fear has not materialized, for two basic reasons. First, management needs to be able to trace data through the system for operational reasons. Second, the vast majority of data processing is batch processing, which makes it relatively easy to trace data through the audit trail.

Hardware controls

Although EDP equipment is very reliable, there can be malfunctions in the hardware which can result in the acceptance, processing, or transmission of inaccurate data. Computer equipment has built-in features that can be utilized to detect such malfunctions. While the auditor does not generally review these hardware characteristics, he or she does determine that management is using this error detection capability. There are a variety of techniques available which test the reliability of input, processing, and output devices. Input hardware usually employs a technique whereby the input data are read twice and then compared to determine if the device is operating properly. In the processing stage the most frequently used technique is a parity check. As data are fed into the internal storage of the computer each item is made to have an even or an odd number of bits. If, for example, an even parity check is adopted, every time data are moved or processed internally the number of bits is summed to determine if the data still have an even number of bits. When they do not, there is a possibility of hardware malfunction. Output devices are checked in much the same manner, using dual operations such as a writing of the data followed by a reading of the written data for comparative purposes.

Access controls

The personnel of EDP departments may have access to assets of the organization. This access is usually of an indirect nature in that the preparation of a document may result in the receipt or disposition of assets. For instance, a computer program may generate a purchase order authorizing the acquisition of inventory. To prevent unauthorized disposition of assets, the EDP internal control system procedures limit the access to EDP hardware, programs, and data files.

It has already been suggested that access to hardware by systems analysts and programmers is limited. The responsibility for the routine processing of transactions is assigned to machine operators. The enforcement and monitoring of this principle are accomplished through the adoption of certain control techniques. Use of the computer is scheduled, and a utilization report is maintained. Supervisory personnel review these reports to determine if there has been unauthorized usage of the equipment. In addition, EDP management routinely observes the work of machine operators to detect improper intervention by operators. If the system possesses the capability, communication between the operator and the computer is possible through the use of a console typewriter. These communications are recorded in a console log and are routinely reviewed by supervisory personnel.

Access to corporate assets through the manipulation of programs or data files is dependent upon the adoption and implementation of the library function. The librarian knows which operators have access to specific programs and data files. In addition, he or she is aware of the program scheduling, and any requests for data files or programs that are inconsistent with the routine schedule must be approved by EDP supervisory personnel.

Other data and procedural controls

An effective EDP internal control system includes controls that may not be strictly classified as accounting controls but are nonetheless important and are considered part of a comprehensive control system. Although these controls are not involved in the auditor's evaluation and study of the system, many auditors include them in the audit approach as a service to the client. Any deficiencies are discussed in the internal control recommendation letter. Among these controls are procedures that relate to the physical protection of EDP equipment and software.

Hardware protection includes controlling access to EDP equipment. From a management point of view, the investment in such equipment may represent a sizable capital expenditure and it should be subject to protective procedures appropriate for any important asset. Because of the nature of EDP equipment, it is necessary to locate these items in an environment where temperature, humidity, and the like can be controlled. Adequate insurance coverage should be obtained, and proper procedures to protect the equipment against fire and other disasters should be instituted.

EDP software presents a unique problem for an organization, and proper procedures for its protection and reconstruction are considered. Like the protection of hardware, physical protection against the possibility of destruction by fire or other disasters or climatic conditions is afforded. Such procedures can be supplemented with the storage of programs, transactions, and master files at other locations. Some organizations adopt a file reconstruction plan referred to as the *grandfather-father-son procedure*. In this approach previous data files are retained to allow the reconstruction of the current file should the latter be destroyed.

Application controls

EDP system controls that relate to specific tasks to be performed are called *application controls*. These controls are adopted to ensure reasonably that only properly authorized and complete data are received and processed. Also, these controls relate to the processing of data in a predetermined manner, and unacceptable data are rejected. Furthermore, the documents and reports generated as the result of processing data are reviewed and transmitted to the proper user department. These application controls can logically be classified in a manner consistent with the three major phases of any system, namely, input controls, processing controls, and output controls. These controls are an integral part of the EDP internal control model.

INPUT CONTROLS

The objectives of input controls are defined in *SAS No. 3:*

> Input controls are designed to provide reasonable assurance that data received for processing by EDP have been properly authorized, converted into machine sensible form and identified, and that data (including data transmitted over communication lines) have not been lost, suppressed, added, duplicated, or otherwise improperly changed. Input controls include controls that relate to rejection, correction, and resubmission of data that were initially incorrect.

The adoption of proper input controls is important, because the possibility for error in the EDP activity is greatest at the input stage. The responsibility for accurate input data rests with the user department, but the EDP department adopts procedures that test the integrity of this input data.

Application controls are established to determine whether input data are properly authorized. Data received from user departments are submitted on a standard form consistent with written instructions agreed upon by the EDP and user departments. If reasonable, these documents show approval through the use of a signature or a stamp. In instances where it is impractical or uneconomical to have the source document approved, some review of the data subsequent to processing is instituted. This review may be conducted by the control group or by responsible personnel in the user department.

As data are physically moved to the EDP area, it is necessary to establish application controls that determine if they have been lost or improperly changed. The generation of these controls occurs in the user department before the data are transferred to the EDP area. Among these controls are:

Record count: The number of documents to be processed or counted (the number of customer orders)

Control total: The total amount of items to be processed (the total number of inventory items received)

Hash total: The total of an item common to each characteristic that has no accounting significance (the sum of the vendor invoice numbers)

These controls are used each time the data are moved and are reconciled with the original control totals by the individual or department receiving the data. In addition, these totals are used in a similar manner as the data are processed by the computer.

225
The EDP internal control model

Documents prepared by the user group are converted to a machine-readable mode. This conversion may occur in the EDP department or in the user department. In either case application controls are designed to determine if the material has been properly converted without errors. These converted data are usually the result of a keying process whereby an operator copies information from a user-created document to a machine-readable version of the document. Once the data are converted, the original keying procedure is repeated and the results of the keying and rekeying are compared. This procedure is referred to as *key punch verification* when EDP cards are used, but the procedure is also applicable to key-to-tape or other methods of converting input data.

Documents received from the user department that are unauthorized, incomplete, or otherwise improper are rejected. These items are not converted by the EDP department, since this would be equivalent to initiating or authorizing a transaction. Rejected data are returned to the user department for appropriate corrections. The control group maintains a log of rejected items, which is reviewed on a timely basis. Each item should be cleared within a reasonable time, or the control group should investigate the item. It is possible that rejected data that are not initially processed may be lost, misplaced, or resubmitted for processing.

PROCESSING CONTROLS

SAS No. 3 identifies the role of processing controls in an EDP control system:

> Processing controls are designed to provide reasonable assurance that electronic data processing has been performed as intended for the particular application; i.e., that all transactions are processed as authorized, that no authorized transactions are omitted, and that no unauthorized transactions are added.

One form of processing controls is developed from input controls generated in the user department. Record counts and other batch controls are integrated into the computer program by comparing them with similar totals generated during processing. Differences in the two sets of totals suggest that all authorized transactions have not been processed or that unauthorized transactions have been added. To ensure that transactions are processed in an authorized manner, the use of the edit function is highly desirable. Basically, the computerized edit function replaces many of the duties performed by an individual in a manual system. For example, a validity check can be performed to determine if a vendor code is valid by referring to a listing of approved vendors, and a limit check can be programmed to determine if a check request exceeds a predetermined limit. Processing controls also prevent use of the wrong program or data file. The use of external labels and header labels can prevent such occurrences.

OUTPUT CONTROLS

Documents, reports, and updated files are the end result of the processing of data and are subjected to control procedures. Again, *SAS No. 3* describes the objective of output controls:

226
Auditing and EDP

Output controls are designed to assure the accuracy of the processing results (such as account listings or displays, reports, magnetic files, invoices or disbursement checks) and to assure that only authorized personnel receive the output.

Controls used in the input and processing phases can be used as an output control. If 100 check requests were made by the cash disbursement group, then 100 checks should be generated along with 100 line-item entries in the cash disbursements journal. Using these control totals, the independent control group as well as the user department reconciles these groups of control figures with computer-generated documents and other output. This reconciliation may use error listings generated during the computer run. The control group determines why the items were considered errors and returns them to the user group for correction and perhaps eventual resubmission for processing. In any event, the control group retains a copy of the error report and makes sure each item is handled in an appropriate manner.

Another important function of the control group is supervision of the distribution of EDP-generated materials. These materials are delivered to authorized personnel. For example, payroll checks are returned to the user department, the payroll department, so that this group can review the data and avoid distributing such checks in a manner that would violate the principle of segregation of duties.

THE STUDY AND EVALUATION OF THE EDP SYSTEM

The auditor is aware of the general principles or concepts of the EDP internal control model as described above. These norms are used in the study and evaluation of the system, and an understanding and knowledge of the system must be acquired by the auditor. Having achieved this knowledge, the auditor assesses the adequacy of the system by identifying its strengths and weaknesses. This analysis determines his or her willingness to rely upon the system and the extent to which audit procedures in the compliance and substantive tests may be restricted or expanded. Conceptually, the study and evaluation of an EDP internal control system is no different than in the case of a manual system. Procedurally, the differences are significant enough to warrant a separate discussion, although some of the material overlaps material presented in Chapter 6.

A prerequisite to evaluating a system is understanding the system. In actual practice evaluation and understanding is part of a single process rather than two discrete steps. In fact, as the system is evaluated the auditor's perception of it undoubtedly changes or at least is clarified.

SAS No. 3 suggests the following approach for the study and evaluation of an EDP internal control system:

- Preliminary review
- Assessment of preliminary review
- In-depth review
- Assessment of in-depth review
- Tests of compliance
- Evaluation of the system

These steps are performed in sequence to form a logical approach in the evaluation of the EDP system. Figure 7-1 is a summarization of this approach.

227
The study and evaluation of the EDP system

Preliminary review

To obtain an understanding of the EDP system, the auditor creates documents or reviews documents prepared by the client. Generally, an EDP system is better documented by a client than a manual system. This affords the auditor the opportunity to use such documentation if it is appropriate to the objective of the engagement and requires that he or she possess the necessary skills to interpret these items and to differentiate between relevant and irrelevant material. In most EDP-dominated systems the auditor utilizes the following items to acquire an understanding of the system:

- EDP internal control questionnaire
- Flowcharts
- Decision tables
- Memoranda and other documentation

EDP QUESTIONNAIRE

Through the use of a specially designed internal control questionnaire the auditor collects information concerning the general controls and application controls in an EDP installation. By interviewing knowledgeable EDP and non-EDP personnel, the internal control questionnaire is completed. Where possible, these responses are validated by the auditor's observance of the activity or by performing other audit techniques. The questions are structured so that a "no" response usually suggests a potential weakness and is evaluated by the auditor and cross-referenced to the auditor's conclusions about the weakness.

FLOWCHARTS

In a manual accounting system the auditor invariably has to prepare a system flowchart for each significant processing function. Earlier in this chapter it was noted that the documentation requirements of an adequate EDP internal control system included client-prepared flowcharts. These flowcharts may provide the auditor with an understanding of the system and should be utilized by him or her. However, a prerequisite to understanding the client's systems flowcharts is a knowledge of the symbols used in the preparation of these documents. Although each EDP installation may develop its own unique characters, Figure 7-2 illustrates the symbols adopted by the American National Standards Institute. These symbol are used in Figure 7-3, which is a system flowchart updating accounts receivable.

The illustrated system flowchart provides the auditor with a general understanding of the computer run; however, in order for him or her to evaluate the system and subsequently test it, greater detail is needed. This usually requires that the auditor review program flowcharts for each system. A program flowchart shows the detailed logic of the processing steps, which is the basis for preparation of the computer program. It may be necessary to review these flowcharts to

Figure 7-1

Study and Evaluation of EDP-Based Applications. This chart is a simplified illustration and does not portray all possible decision paths.

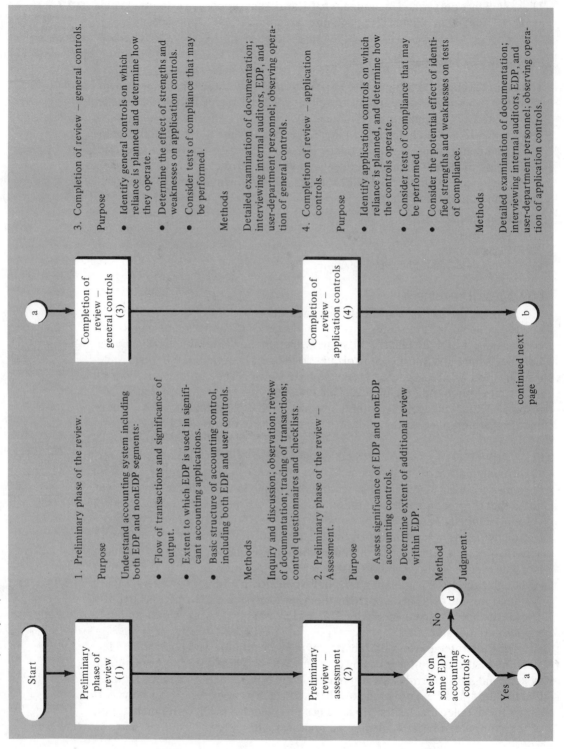

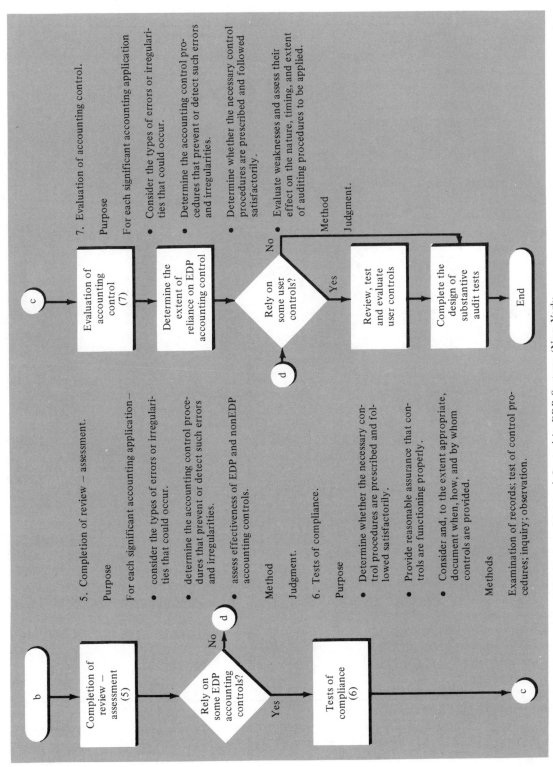

SOURCE: *The Auditor's Study and Evaluation of Internal Control in EDP Systems* (New York: AICPA. 1977). pp. 21–24.

Figure 7-2

Standard Flowchart Symbols (ANSI).

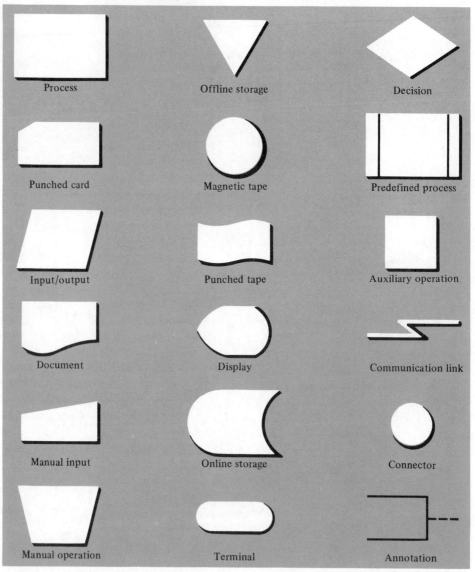

Figure 7-3

Systems Flowchart.

SOURCE: Material from the *Uniform CPA Examinations*, copyright © November 1967 by the American Institute of Certified Accountants, Inc., is reprinted with permission.

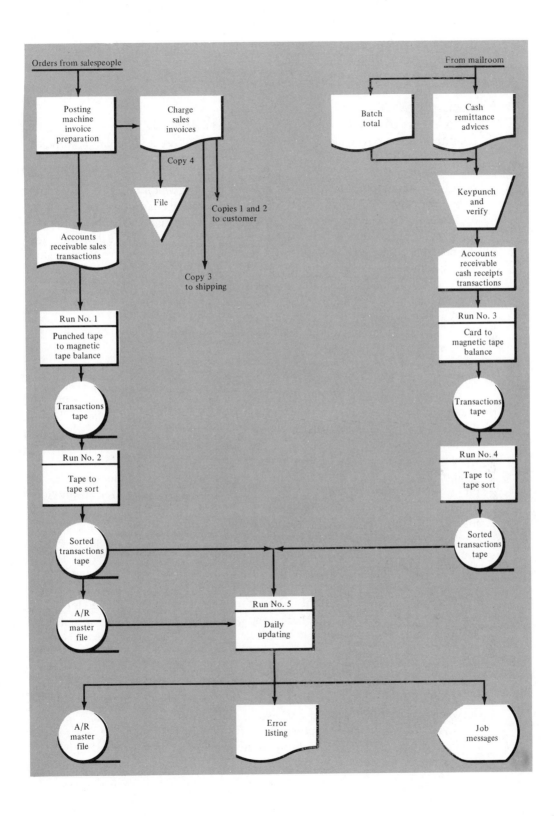

232
Auditing and EDP

determine if appropriate application controls are being utilized by the computer program. Program flowcharts can become very detailed and may require evaluation by an auditor with a strong background in EDP.

DECISION TABLES

A system or program flowchart may not be useful if there is a set of complex conditions that must be tested before specific data processing can take place. Therefore another form of graphic description of a system is the use of decision tables. A decision table has two parts—an upper portion which describes the possible conditions that occur, and a lower portion which describes the action to be taken depending upon the specific set of existing conditions. Each column of the decision table represents a rule or decision to be made when the conditions for that column are met. Figure 7-4 is an example of a decision table that illustrates the possible conditions produced by a request from a customer for a credit sale. The conditions determine whether the order will be processed, rejected, or sent to the credit manager for possible approval. For example, rule 5 describes the possible action to be taken when an order is received from a customer whose name is not on the approved customer list. When (1) the customer balance is not past due, or (2) the customer order is for an amount less than $100, then the customer order is processed.

MEMORANDA AND OTHER DOCUMENTATION

During the review of the EDP internal control system, the auditor may encounter a variety of narrative descriptions of the system. These include a description of various controls employed in EDP and related non-EDP activities. Manuals prepared by the client or the computer hardware supplier may be available, which may be helpful in understanding the system. In addition, the auditor may prepare memoranda to document interviews conducted with key employees or other procedures he or she employs. As suggested in previous chapters, this documentation approach is extremely flexible, but it must be in manageable form to be useful to the auditor.

The preliminary review must be thorough enough for the auditor to assess the role of the EDP system in the overall accounting structure of the organization. An understanding of the system includes a complete knowledge of the flow of transactions through the accounting internal control system. In effect, this review encompasses the initial step of a process function, all intermediate steps, and the output of the process which may include updated master files, output files, and reports. It is important that the EDP system not be viewed as an isolated process but rather as an integral part of the entire system. For this reason, the flow of transactions from the first step to the output includes non-EDP procedures as well as EDP procedures and their relationships to each other. In making this review the auditor develops an understanding of the division of responsibilities between the EDP department and user departments.

In addition to an understanding of the system, the preliminary review reveals the importance of the EDP structure in the processing of data. This importance can be defined in quantitative and qualitative terms. For example, some estimate

Figure 7-4

Decision Table: Customer Order Request

		RULE NUMBER								
		1	2	3	4	5	6	7	8	9
C o n d i t i o n	Request from customer on customer-approved list	Y	Y	Y	Y	N	N	N	N	N
	Customer order plus balance in receivable is less than credit limit	Y	N	Y	N	–	–	–	–	–
	Customer balance past due	N	N	Y	Y	N	N	Y	–	Y
	Customer order less than $50	–	–	–	–	Y	Y	Y	N	–
	Balance from customer less than $100	–	–	–	–	Y	N	Y	–	–
A c t i o n	Process customer order	X				X				
	Place on report to credit manager for approval consideration		X	X			X			
	Reject order				X			X	X	X

of the dollar value of computerized transactions is made. The number of functional systems and the number of transactions processed on the computer describe the importance of the EDP activity. The description is not limited to the mere collection of statistics. The types of transactions processed and the nature of the processing are considered. A client may process several million dollars of sales on the computer, but when the extent of the processing is limited to the preparation of a sales journal, then the importance of the EDP function is greatly reduced, and the auditor is more concerned with accounting controls outside the EDP area.

Assessment of preliminary review

Having performed a preliminary review of the EDP internal control system, the auditor assesses the significance of the EDP accounting controls. He or she decides whether the initial review suggests that the system may be relied upon. The auditor may decide, based on this review, that it is not appropriate to continue the study and review of the EDP system. There are several reasons why such an approach is justified.

The auditor may choose to discontinue further review and testing of the EDP system if the preliminary review reveals significant weaknesses in the EDP accounting controls. In this case, he or she may conclude that the system is too inadequate to be relied upon to safeguard the assets and to generate reliable financial information. When this approach is adopted, the EDP procedures and controls are not subjected to compliance tests. The audit approach is modified by extending the audit procedures used in the substantive tests or, if appropriate, extending them to include related accounting controls in the user departments. For example, if a client has a poor plan of organization under which EDP responsibilities and duties are not properly segregated, the auditor may conclude that no alternative controls exist that mitigate this weakness. Under these circumstances he or she cannot rely upon the EDP internal control system. Thus it is inappropriate to continue to study, evaluate, and perform tests of compliance for the EDP system.

Other circumstances exist which may be proper justification for the auditor's decision not to rely on or test the EDP accounting controls. The preliminary review may suggest that they are adequate, but the auditor is not required to complete the testing of these controls. EDP processing may be relatively insignificant or EDP controls may be duplicated in non-EDP accounting controls. There is no need to test controls that are not significant or that are redundant. Alternatively, the auditor may conclude that the audit effort necessary to test the EDP controls is not justified. The reduction in the nature and extent of audit procedures performed in the substantive tests may be less than the amount of time necessary to complete the review of the EDP control and perform tests of compliance. This conclusion is valid only if it is based on a preliminary review of the EDP system. In other words, an auditor must perform, at a minimum, a preliminary review of the EDP accounting controls.

After completing this review, the auditor may conclude that the EDP accounting controls are adequate and provide a basis for restricting the extent of the related substantive tests. Under these circumstances, he or she continues the review, completes the tests of compliance, and evaluates the system to determine the extent, if any, to which the substantive tests may be restricted. These audit steps are considered in the following discussion. During the performance of these steps, the auditor may revise the original conclusion about the adequacy of the EDP system. If, during the compliance tests, the auditor discovers that the system is inadequate or that controls are not being observed, the audit approach may be modified immediately, since the internal control system may be unreliable, insignificant, or duplicate accounting control procedures performed in other parts of the accounting system. In so doing, the auditor revises the extent and perhaps the nature of the substantive tests plan originally adopted.

In-depth review

The objective of the preliminary review is to obtain enough knowledge about the general and application controls in an EDP system to provide a basis for determining the adequacy of the system and whether it may be relied upon. From a cost perspective it is logical to limit the extent of the preliminary review, since a decision not to rely on it is based on a minimum, but adequate, amount of audit effort. When the auditor concludes that the EDP accounting system appears to be adequate, the review of the accounting controls becomes a more intensive investigation of the general and application controls.

In the in-depth review the auditor utilizes the same documentary and analytic techniques used in the preliminary review, such as the preparation or review of internal control questionnaires, flowcharts, decision tables, and the like. Whereas this documentation may have been a result of the auditor's use of the inquiry technique in the preliminary review, other techniques are used to gain a more thorough knowledge of the system. These may include observation of the operations of the EDP internal control system. Additionally, the auditor may perform a walk-through of a transaction to verify that the system operates in a manner consistent with its documentation. The inquiry technique is very much apparent in the in-depth review, and additional interviews with EDP personnel, user department personnel, and internal auditors may be conducted. The inquiry becomes more detailed, and specific questions such as the following are answered:

General Controls

- How does the organization of the data processing department provide adequate supervision and segregation of functions with EDP and between EDP and users?
- What procedures provide for control over systems development and access to system documentation?
- What procedures provide for control over program and system maintenance?
- What procedures provide control over computer operations, including access to data files and programs?
- What procedures, during the period under review, assured that file reconstruction and processing recoveries were complete?
- To what extent do internal auditors perform a review and evaluation of EDP activities?

Application Controls

- How do controls provide reasonable assurance that data received for processing by EDP have been properly authorized, converted into machine-sensible form and identified, and that data (including data transmitted over communication lines) have not been lost, suppressed, added, duplicated, or otherwise improperly changed? (Input controls include controls that relate to rejection, correction, and resubmission of data that were initially incorrect.)
- How do processing controls provide reasonable assurance that electronic data processing has been performed as intended for the particular application, i.e., that all transactions are processed as authorized, that no authorized transactions are omitted, and that no unauthorized transactions are added?
- How do output controls assure the accuracy of the processing result (such as account listings or displays, reports, magnetic files, invoices, or disbursement checks) and that only authorized personnel receive output?[2]

The responses to these questions are evaluated in the context of the fundamental concepts of the EDP internal control model.

[2] Ibid., pp. 16–17.

Assessment of in-depth review

At the completion of the in-depth review, the auditor either reaffirms the original decision to rely upon the EDP accounting controls or rejects such an approach. If the controls reasonably conform to the guidelines proposed during the earlier discussion of the EDP internal control model, the auditor proceeds with the tests of compliance. The in-depth review of the system identifies unusual strengths or weaknesses of the EDP system that affect the design of the compliance tests. On the other hand, the in-depth analysis may result in an audit decision not to rely upon the accounting controls in the EDP activity. In this case, the auditor reassesses the extent, nature, and perhaps the timing of the audit procedures to be employed in the substantive tests. Again, this approach is justified when the EDP accounting controls are inadequate, the tests of compliance may not be cost effective, or non-EDP accounting controls duplicate the EDP control and only non-EDP controls are subjected to the tests of compliance.

It is possible that the adequacy of accounting controls varies among a firm's major processing systems. The cash disbursement system may have strong controls, while the sales system may be obviously inadequate. For this reason, each system is evaluated individually, and a separate assessment is made for each at the conclusion of the in-depth review. The uniqueness of the controls is usually limited to the design of EDP application controls, and inadequacies in one system may not have an impact upon another system. However, EDP general accounting controls are pervasive, since such weaknesses usually affect all processing systems. It is possible that unusually strong application controls may somewhat offset the deficiencies in general controls, again requiring a separate evaluation of each major system.

Tests of compliance

Tests of compliance are performed if the auditor decides that the EDP accounting controls are adequate and may be relied upon. A more thorough discussion of compliance tests is offered in Chapter 9, but it is useful to complete the role of the computer in the EDP internal control at this point. Basically, the objective of the compliance tests, for either an EDP or a non-EDP internal control system, is to determine if the system is being employed in a manner consistent with the documentation in the review phase of the audit and estimate the number of errors it generates. Thus the compliance tests may reveal two distinct attributes of an internal control system. First, the system in practice may have weaknesses in design. These weaknesses may not have been discovered during the review of the system. Second, the system may be well designed, but a significant number of errors may occur because of several reasons, such as poor execution of procedures by employees. In either case, the auditor's knowledge of the system in operation, and the effectiveness of the system, are a basis for the design of the substantive tests.

In designing the tests of compliance, the auditor is confronted with two separate testing problems which vary in difficulty and have an impact on the design of the audit tests. The nature of the procedures used in the tests of **237** compliance is determined by whether an EDP accounting control is subject to manual validation. For controls subject to manual validation, the auditor constructs the audit program using the typical audit techniques of observation, vouching, and the like. For example, to determine whether a credit sale has been authorized, he or she may select individual sales listed in the EDP-produced sales journal and trace them back to a copy of a customer order initialed by the credit manager. Most EDP general controls can be tested manually. However, certain controls are not so easily tested. For example, the above illustration may be modified so that the approval of credit sales is part of the EDP program. In this case, there is no signature or initial that the auditor can inspect. Instead, he or she considers testing the program to see if the control is functioning in a manner consistent with guidelines established by the credit manager. Under these circumstances, the auditor must decide whether to audit around the computer or audit through the computer in the performance of the compliance tests.

AUDITING AROUND THE COMPUTER

As suggested by its name, auditing around the computer allows the auditor to avoid testing application controls that are computerized. It is erroneous to describe such an approach as a decision to ignore the EDP activity and to proceed with the audit as if the computer did not exist. The decision to audit around the computer is made only after the auditor has reviewed the EDP accounting controls and determined the impact of these controls on the internal control system. Often the decision to audit around the computer simply depends upon the ability to trace the source document, such as a vendor invoice, to the computer printout, such as the voucher register. This is not the sole basis for making this decision, since the auditor considers the impact of the computer on the audit trail and the nature and extent of "decisions" made by the computer.

The audit trail enables the auditor to trace a transaction from its inception through the prescribed processing steps to its eventual impact on the financial statements. One common problem encountered in a batch processing system is the grouping of data nonchronologically. A batch of sales may be processed, but the listing of these transactions may cover several days or a month and include several geographical groupings. Rather than generating a conventional sales journal, the EDP output may just list the sales amount, the customer number, and the geographical code number. If several hundred invoices are processed, the auditor may find it time-consuming to trace the source document through the processing stages to the financial statement impact. In this case the audit trail may not have been destroyed, but from an economic perspective the auditor could not justify auditing around the computer.

It has already been suggested that the EDP activity can include functions that replace personnel who may have made decisions in a manual system that is now computerized. Of course, the computer's decision-making abilities are limited to the guidelines reflected in the computer program. The impact is that the computer authorizes transactions normally subjected to testing by the auditor in a manual system. If these duties are concentrated in the EDP activity, then the auditor cannot ignore them by auditing around the computer.

When the auditor concludes, after an appropriate review of the EDP internal control system, that auditing around the computer is justified, the impact on the tests of compliance is minimal. He or she may decide not to use the computer in the test, but this does not mean that it is not utilized in the substantive tests. Chapter 9 discusses the use of the computer in this area.

AUDITING THROUGH THE COMPUTER

When the auditor decides to audit through the computer in the tests of compliance, he or she is concerned with the controls built into the computer software. The auditor is not as concerned with the processing of a particular input document as with the ability of the computer to process all transactions in this area consistent with prescribed controls. A test data approach may be used whereby the client's programs are tested for application controls. In designing the test data approach, the auditor prepares sample transactions that test the EDP controls. By reviewing EDP documentation, he or she is aware of these controls and is able to predict the outcome of a transaction. Valid as well as invalid transactions are processed. For example, a request for payment that exceeds a particular dollar limit would be expected to generate an error listing. Since the computer processes similar transactions in the same manner, the auditor need only test the control one time to substantiate that it is working properly. Additionally, in using the client's programs, he or she must be satisfied that these are the same programs that were used throughout the year. This may be accomplished by using the program to reprocess a transaction tape and comparing the new processing results with the previous processing results. In any case, the test data approach must include the testing of actual transactions processed during the accounting period and cannot be limited to a simulation.

An alternative to the use of the test data approach is the auditor's processing of data using "live" files. One variation of this approach is referred to as the integrated test facility technique:

> The ITF technique (sometimes referred to as the mini-company approach) involves establishing the capability of introducing selected input into a system simultaneously with live data, and tracing the flow of transactions through the various functions in the system. The object is to permit auditors to (1) enter an EDP system under normal operating conditions, (2) test transactions for which the results have been predetermined and (3) compare the results actually produced to the predetermined results.[3]

In using live data on files the auditor is careful not to destroy or distort the client's records.

The role of EDP in the conduct of an audit continues to evolve. As computer technology changes, new methods will undoubtedly be developed to utilize the computer to test a client's EDP system. Depending upon the pace and the nature of these changes, the audit profession will have to react, and this reaction will

---

[3] Barry R. Chaiken and William E. Perry, "ITF—A Promising Computer Audit Technique," *Journal of Accountancy,* February 1973, p. 74.

be in part dependent upon the competence of future auditors in the EDP area. Preparation for these changes through education and training is of concern to the profession. All auditors will not have to be EDP specialists, but it appears that such a specialty will be needed in significant numbers. In addition, the generalist auditor will have to have some skills in this area.

Computer audit technology should not be viewed by the auditor as a static methodology, but rather he or she must stay abreast of new changes and incorporate them into the audit approach if appropriate. One computer audit technique that has received a great deal of attention is the use of generalized computer audit programs. These software packages are best described as data file analyzers and are popular because they require little EDP training. Although they can be used in the auditor's performance of the tests of compliance, generalized computer audit programs are more useful in the substantive tests area. A few years ago, this technique was viewed somewhat as the auditor's answer to auditing the computer. Today its application is viewed in more realistic terms. This technique is discussed more fully in Chapter 9.

Evaluation of the system

Having performed the compliance tests of the EDP accounting controls, the auditor formulates a final evaluation of the internal control system. The control procedures, both EDP and non-EDP, that were tested are evaluated in relationship to their impact upon the substantive tests. When the review of the accounting controls and the performance of the compliance tests identify no material weaknesses, the auditor concludes that the internal control system can be relied upon. Disclosures of material weaknesses are analyzed as to their impact upon the nature, timing, and extent of substantive audit procedures to be employed.

The audit of EDP service centers

In some engagements the auditor may find that the client uses an EDP service center to process its financial data. When a significant amount of the client's financial transactions are processed by an outside service center, the auditor's approach must take this fact into consideration. To provide the auditor with guidance in this area the AICPA in 1974 issued an audit guide entitled *Audits of Service-Center-Produced Records*. The basic philosophy of this guide is apparent from the following quotation:

> The presence of a service center does not in any way affect the auditor's objective— *to perform an audit in accordance with generally accepted auditing standards for the purpose of expressing an opinion on financial statements.*[4]

The audit decision to include the service center in the review of the internal control system is dependent upon the importance of the duties performed by the outside group. Basically, the auditor determines whether the outside group

---

[4] *Audits of Service-Center-Produced Records* (New York: AICPA, 1974), p. 18.

240
Auditing and
EDP

processes data that may have a material impact upon the client's financial statements. He or she considers the types of data processed, the dollar volume of such data, and the types of reports produced. If it is concluded that the service center is an important element of the client's internal control system, the audit approach is broadened to include a review of the controls at the service center. The audit approach described in this chapter is used when the initial step is the preliminary review of the service center's general and application controls.

CONCLUDING REMARKS

The second step in the integrated audit approach is the review of the internal control system. This chapter discussed this step in the context of an EDP environment. The auditor's review of the internal control system is used in the design of the compliance and substantive tests. However, before the final two phases of the integrated audit approach are discussed in Chapter 9, sampling in auditing is discussed in Chapter 8. This is not a break in the continuity of the development of the four-step audit approach. The review of sampling, especially statistical sampling, provides an excellent opportunity to show the relationships of each phase of the integrated audit approach.

EXERCISES AND PROBLEMS

7-1. Why may the audit process be modified when a client converts its system from a manual system to an EDP system?

7-2. Differentiate between general controls and application controls in an EDP system.

7-3. Contrast the internal control models for a manual system and for an EDP system.

7-4. What are the objectives of (1) input controls, (2) processing controls, and (3) output controls? Give an example of each.

7-5. List and explain the six steps in the study and evaluation of an EDP-based computer system.

7-6. For what reasons may the auditor decide not to continue the study and evaluation of the EDP accounting controls after the preliminary review has been completed.

7-7. Under what conditions may the auditor test an EDP system by auditing the computer?

7-8. Differentiate between auditing around the computer and auditing through the computer.

7-9. Explain the integrated test facility technique as a method for auditing a computerized system.

7-10. What factors does an auditor consider when determining the impact of a client's use of a service center to process business transactions?

7-11. A CPA's client, Boos & Baumkirchner, Inc., is a medium-sized manufacturer of products for the leisure time activities market (camping equipment, scuba gear, bows and arrows, etc.). During the past year, a computer system was installed, and inventory records of finished goods and parts were converted to computer processing. The inventory master file is maintained on a disk. Each record of the file contains the following information:

241
Exercises and problems

- Item or part number
- Description
- Size
- Unit-of-measure code
- Quantity on hand
- Cost per unit
- Total value of inventory on hand at cost
- Date of last sale or usage
- Quantity used or sold this year
- Economical order quantity
- Code number of major vendor
- Code number of secondary vendor

In preparation for the year-end inventory the client has two identical sets of preprinted inventory count cards. One set is for the client's inventory counts and the other is for the CPA's use to make audit test counts. The following information has been keypunched into the cards and interpreted on their face:

- Item or part number
- Description
- Size
- Unit-of-measure code

In taking the year-end inventory, the client's personnel write the actual counted quantity on the face of each card. When all counts are complete, the counted quantity is keypunched into the cards. The cards are processed against the disk file, and quantity-on-hand figures are adjusted to reflect the actual count. A computer listing is prepared to show any missing inventory count cards and all quantity adjustments more than $100 in value. These items are investigated by client personnel, and all required adjustments made. When adjustments have been completed, the final year-end balances are computed and posted to the general ledger.

The CPA has available a general-purpose computer audit software package that can run on the client's computer and can process both card and disk files.

Required

1. In general and without regard to the facts above, discuss the nature of general-purpose computer audit software packages and list the various types and uses of such packages.

2. List and describe at least five ways a general-purpose computer audit software

242
Auditing and EDP

package can be used to assist in all aspects of the audit of the inventory of Boos & Baumkirchner, Inc. (For example, the package can be used to read the disk inventory master file and list items and parts with a high unit cost or total value. Such items can be included in the test counts to increase the dollar coverage of the audit verification.) (AICPA Adapted)

7-12. Georgia Beemster, CPA, is examining the financial statements of the Louisville Sales Corporation, which recently installed an off-line electronic computer. The following comments have been extracted from Beemster's notes on computer operations and the processing and control of shipping notices and customer invoices:

- To minimize inconvenience Louisville converted without change its existing data processing system which utilized tabulating equipment. The computer company supervised the conversion and provided training for all computer department employees (except keypunch operators) in systems design, operations, and programming.

- Each computer run is assigned to a specific employee who is responsible for making program changes, running the program, and answering questions. This procedure has the advantage of eliminating the need for records of computer operations, because each employee is responsible for his or her own computer runs.

- At least one computer department employee remains in the computer room during office hours, and only computer department employees have keys to this room.

- System documentation consists of materials furnished by the computer company— a set of record formats and program listings. These and the tape library are kept in a corner of the computer department.

- The company considered the desirability of programmed controls but decided to retain the manual controls from its existing system.

- Company products are shipped directly from public warehouses which forward shipping notices to general accounting. There a billing clerk enters the price of the item and accounts for the numerical sequence of shipping notices from each warehouse. The billing clerk also prepares daily adding machine tapes (control tapes) of the units shipped and the unit prices.

- Shipping notices and control tapes are forwarded to the computer department for keypunching and processing. Extensions are made on the computer. Output consists of invoices (in six copies) and a daily sales register. The daily sales register shows the aggregate totals of units shipped and unit prices which the computer operator compares to the control tapes.

- All copies of the invoice are returned to the billing clerk. The clerk mails three copies to the customer, forwards one copy to the warehouse, maintains one copy in a numerical file, and retains one copy in an open invoice file that serves as a detail accounts receivable record.

Required: Describe weaknesses in internal control over information and data flow, and in the procedures for processing shipping notices and customer invoices, and recommend improvements in these controls and processing procedures. Organize your answer sheet as follows:

WEAKNESS	RECOMMENDED IMPROVEMENT

(AICPA Adapted)

7-13. Auditing the financial statements of a client that utilizes the services of a computer for accounting functions requires the CPA to understand the operation of his client's EDP system.

Required

1. The first requirement of an effective system of internal control is a satisfactory plan of organization. List the characteristics of a satisfactory plan of organization for an EDP department, including the relationship between the department and the rest of the company.

2. An effective system of internal control also requires a sound system of records control of operations and transactions (source data and its flow) and of classification of data within the accounts. For an EDP system, these controls include input controls, processing controls, and output controls. List the characteristics of a satisfactory system of input controls. (Confine your comments to a batch-controlled system employing punched cards and to the steps that occur prior to the processing of the input cards in the computer.) (AICPA Adapted)

7-14. Roger Peters, CPA, has examined the financial statements of the Solt Manufacturing Company for several years and is making preliminary plans for the audit for the year ended June, 30, 1979. During this examination he plans to use a set of generalized computer audit programs. Solt's EDP manager has agreed to prepare special tapes of data from company records for the CPA's use with the generalized programs.

The following information is applicable to Peters' examination of Solt's accounts payable and related procedures:

1. The formats of pertinent tapes are shown in Problem Figure 7-14.

2. The following monthly runs are prepared:

 a. Cash disbursements by check number
 b. Outstanding payables
 c. Purchase journals arranged (i) by account charged and (ii) by vendor

3. Vouchers and supporting invoices, receiving reports, and purchase order copies are filed by vendor code. Purchase orders and checks are filed numerically.

4. Company records are maintained on magnetic tapes. All tapes are stored in a restricted area in the computer room. A grandfather-father-son policy is followed for retaining and safeguarding tape files.

Required

1. Explain the grandfather-father-son policy. Describe how files can be reconstructed when this policy is used.

2. Discuss whether company policies for retaining and safeguarding the tape files provide adequate protection against loss of data.

Problem Figure 7-14

Master File—Vendor Name, Master File—Vendor Address, Transaction File—Expense Detail, Transaction File—Payment Detail

Master File—Vendor Name

| Vendor code | Record type | Space | Blank | Vendor name | Blank | Card code 100 |

Master File—Vendor Address

| Vendor code | Record type | Space | Blank | Address—line 1 | Address—line 2 | Address—line 3 | Blank | Card code 120 |

Transaction File—Expense Detail

| Vendor code | Record type | Voucher number | Blank | Batch | Voucher number | Voucher date | Vendor code | Invoice date | Due date | Invoice number | Purchase order number | Debit account | Product code | Blank | Amount | Quantity | Card code 160 |

Transaction File—Payment Detail

| Vendor code | Record type | Voucher number | Blank | Batch | Voucher number | Voucher date | Vendor code | Invoice date | Due date | Invoice number | Purchase order number | Check number | Check date | Blank | Amount | Blank | Card code 170 |

3. Describe the controls that the CPA should maintain over:

   a. Preparing the special tape
   b. Processing the special tape with the generalized computer audit programs

   4. Prepare a schedule for the EDP manager outlining the data that should be included on the special tape for the CPA's examination of accounts payable and related procedures. This schedule should show the:

   a. Client tape from which the item should be extracted
   b. Name of the item of data

7-15. The Lakesedge Utility District is installing an EDP system. The CPA who conducts the annual examination of the district's financial statements has been asked to recommend controls for the new system.

Required: Discuss recommended controls over:

   1. Program documentation
   2. Program testing
   3. EDP hardware
   4. Tape files and software   (AICPA Adapted)

7-16. CPAs may audit around or through computers in examining the financial statements of clients who utilize computers to process accounting data.

Required:
   1. Describe the auditing approach referred to as auditing around the computer.
   2. Under what conditions does the CPA decide to audit through the computer instead of around the computer?
   3. In auditing through the computer, the CPA may use a test deck.

   a. What is a test deck?
   b. Why does the CPA use a test deck?

   4. How can the CPA be satisfied that the computer program tapes provided are actually used by the client to process its accounting data?   (AICPA Adapted)

7-17. You have been engaged by Central Savings and Loan Association to examine its financial statements for the year ended December 31, 1979. The CPA who examined the financial statements December 31, 1978, rendered an unqualified opinion.

In January 1979 the association installed an on-line real-time computer system. Each teller in the association's main office and in seven branch offices has an on-line input/output terminal. Customers' mortgage payments and savings account deposits and withdrawals are recorded in the accounts by the computer from data input by the teller at the time of the transaction. The teller keys the proper account by account number and enters the information in the terminal keyboard to record the transaction. The accounting department at the main office has both punched card and typewriter input/output devices. The computer is housed at the main office.

In addition to servicing its own mortgage loans the association acts as a mortgage servicing agency for three life insurance companies. In this capacity it maintains mortgage records and serves as the collection and escrow agent for the mortgagees (the insurance companies) who pay a fee to the association for these services.

Required
   1. Assume you determine that an adequate system of internal control is in effect. Prepare an audit program for examination of the mortgage accounts for which the

246
Auditing and
EDP

association acts as the mortgage servicing agency. (Do not consider computer processing of the mortgage accounts in your audit program.)

2. You expect the association to have certain internal controls in effect, because an on-line real-time computer system is employed. List the internal controls which should be in effect solely because this system is employed, classifying them as:

    a. Controls pertaining to input of information
    b. All other types of computer controls   (AICPA Adapted)

7-18. The independent auditor must evaluate a client's system of internal control to determine the extent to which various auditing procedures must be employed. A client who uses a computer should provide a flowchart of the information processing system so that the CPA can evaluate its control features. Problem Figure 7-18(a) is a simplified flowchart such as a client might provide. Unfortunately the client only partially completed the flowchart when it was requested by you.

Required

1. Complete the flowchart in Problem Figure 7-18(a). Note to student: you may check your answer by referring to page 231 of this chapter.

2. Describe what each item in the flowchart indicates. When complete, your description should provide an explanation of the processing of the data involved. Your description should be in the following order:

    a. Orders from salesman to "Run no. 5"
    b. From mailroom to "Run no. 5"
    c. "Run no. 5" through the remainder of the chart

3. Name each of the flowchart symbols shown in Problem Figure 7-18(b) and describe what each represents.   (AICPA Adapted)

7-19. When auditing an EDP system, the CPA must be aware of the different types of controls built into the equipment. These controls fall into two groups: those incorporated by the user in his or her program, and those built into the equipment by the manufacturer.

Required

1. Why are accuracy checks on system components or peripheral equipment necessary?

2. Define and give the purpose of each of the following program checks and controls:

    a. Record count
    b. Limit check
    c. Reverse multiplication
    d. Sequence check
    e. Hash total

3. Most EDP equipment manufacturers have built-in checks to ensure that information is correctly read, processed, transferred within the system, and recorded. One of these built-in checks is the parity bit.

    a. What is the parity bit?
    b. When is the parity bit control used?

Problem Figure 7-18(a)

Flowchart Symbols and Flowchart

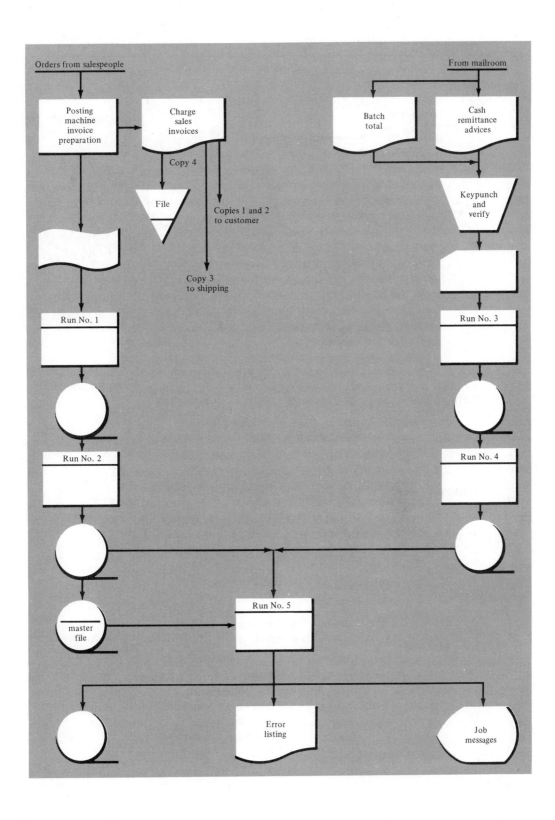

Problem Figure 7-18b.

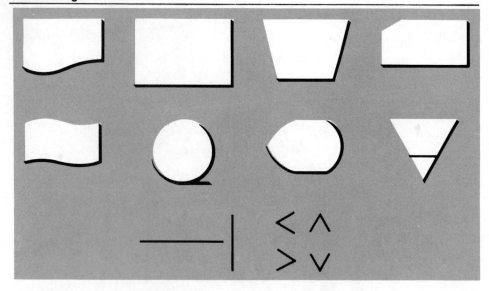

4. When computers are used, the CPA has to be familiar with the information stored on paper tape reels, magnetic tape reels, and so on. A common form of magnetic tape record retention employs the grandfather-father-son principle.

   a. Define the grandfather-father-son principle.
   b. Why are grandfather-father-son tapes usually stored at different locations?

(AICPA Adapted)

MULTIPLE CHOICE

1. The use of external labels in conjunction with magnetic tape storage is most likely to prevent errors that might be made by which of the following?

   a. A computer programmer.
   b. A systems analyst.
   c. A keypunch operator.
   d. A computer operator.

Items 2 and 3 are based on the following information:
A sales transaction card was designed to contain the following information:

CARD COLUMN	INFORMATION
1–10	Customer account number
11–30	Customer name
31–38	Amount of sale
39–44	Sales date
45–46	Store code number
47–49	Sales clerk number
50–59	Invoice number

2. If such a card is rejected during computer processing because the sales clerk **249** whose identification number appears on the record does **not** work at the store indicated Multiple choice by the numbers in card columns 45 and 46, then the error was probably detected by which of the following?

    a. A self-checking number.
    b. A combination check.
    c. A valid-character check.
    d. A limit check.

3. If the last letter of a customer's name is erroneously entered in card column 31, which of the following is most likely to detect the error during an input edit run?

    a. A logic check.
    b. A combination check.
    c. A valid-character check.
    d. A self-checking number.

4. The auditor should be concerned about internal control in a data processing system because

    a. the auditor **cannot** follow the flow of information through the computer.
    b. fraud is more common in an EDP system than in a manual system.
    c. there is usually a high concentration of data processing activity and control in a small number of people in an EDP system.
    d. auditors most often audit around the computer.

5. Control totals are used as a basic method for detecting data errors. Which of the following is **not** a control figure used as a control total in EDP systems?

    a. Ledger totals.
    b. Check digit totals.
    c. Hash totals.
    d. Document count totals.   (AICPA Adapted)

CHAPTER 8
Sampling in auditing

In most engagements the volume of evidence the auditor may collect is very large. Documents such as payroll checks, sales invoices, subsidiary ledger cards, and the like, can easily total in the thousands for a medium-sized company. The cost would be prohibitive if the auditor attempted to examine each document. For this reason he or she examines only part of the evidence available and, based on this partial review, draws inferences about the total group of documents or some other population. Contemporary auditing recognizes that such an approach involves a degree of risk. The auditor is not capable of eliminating risk in the audit engagement, but attempts to minimize the degree of risk subject to the practical cost constraint imposed. This objective is achieved through the use of two sampling approaches. These methods are popularly referred to as judgment sampling and statistical sampling. Since both methods rely upon audit judgment, they are more appropriately classified as nonstatistical and statistical sampling.

JUDGMENT SAMPLING

In determining the size of the audit sample, the auditor may rely entirely upon the subjective process. This is referred to as *judgment sampling* or *nonstatistical sampling*. Many characterize judgment sampling as capricious and inappropriate as an audit method, since the sample size is not determined in an objective manner. However, if used properly, judgment sampling is an appropriate audit tool. The application of judgment sampling requires that the auditor draw on his or her experience and the characteristics of the population being audited. Thus the size of the sample is not always arbitrarily determined when judgment sampling is employed. For example, an auditor faced with the audit objective of determining the accounting propriety of 1000 sales invoices processed during the accounting period considers the adequacy of the internal control system, audit results of similar tests in previous years for the same client, and other factors he or she considers relevant. While the size of the sample is not determined mathematically, the process cannot be characterized as arbitrary.

Almost all engagements afford the auditor the opportunity to employ both judgment sampling and statistical sampling. An auditor must be capable of using and willing to use either approach. The problem is to select the approach that best achieves the audit objective. There are no formalized guidelines that dictate the method of sampling most appropriate under the existing circumstances. However, the following situations are appropriate for the utilization of judgment sampling:

- The population is composed of relatively few items with relatively large balances.
- The population is small (probably any population less than 500, although no single number can be defended).
- The auditor is suspicious that the population has an unusual and undesirable quality, such as fraudulent documents.
- The potential audit risk is significant (this may force the auditor to review all the items in the sample).

These suggestions are illustrative and are not considered absolute guidelines. The criteria for determining when judgment sampling is appropriate are established by each auditing firm or each auditor.

Although the remainder of this chapter is devoted to statistical sampling, the length of the discussion is not to be interpreted as a means of measuring the relative importance of the methods. In fact, judgment sampling is used far more often than statistical sampling.[1] The greater attention is given to statistical sampling because this method is more susceptible to analysis and each step can be identified and explained. Furthermore, the audit factors that are applicable to statistical sampling are just as applicable to judgment sampling. The difference is that the former approach requires that the auditor quantify these factors, whereas in the latter the factors are described in subjective terms. Finally, statistical sampling represents new technology available to the auditor and deserves adequate discussion.

STATISTICAL SAMPLING

Statistical sampling enables the auditor to determine mathematically the size of the sample and the results of the audit test. This sampling approach is often described as objective, since quantitative factors determine both the sample size and the sample results. However, judgment is very much a part of statistical sampling, since the auditor uses subjective criteria as the basis for determining the quantitative factors. A discussion of statistical sampling presupposes an understanding of fundamental statistical terms and concepts. It is assumed that

[1] An article based on the results of the AICPA's quality review program concludes that "there was almost a total absence of the application of statistical sampling techniques. . . ." Harold B. Minkus and Phyllis E. Peters, "Two Years of Quality Review," *Journal of Accountancy,* September 1974, p. 105.

252
Sampling in
auditing

the reader has had such exposure. If the reader lacks this background or wishes to review the material, the appendix to this chapter should be read at this point.

Several statistical techniques may be referred to as statistical sampling methods. The methods that are likely to be employed by an auditor are:

- Frequency estimation
- Variable estimation (mean per unit)
- Discovery sampling
- Variable estimation (ratio and difference estimate)

Frequency estimation (attribute sampling)

Frequency estimation is used to determine to what extent a population exhibits a particular characteristic or attribute. This sampling method is especially useful to the auditor in performing the tests of compliance. The auditor may want to know the number of times a transaction is processed in a manner that does not conform with the company's policies, or the number of errors made during the processing of transactions. For example, he or she may want to estimate the number of times a mathematical error is made in the computation of payroll checks. This is referred to as an *error rate*. After estimating compliance rates and error rates, the auditor uses this information to determine the effectiveness of the internal control system which in turn impacts the audit procedures used in the substantive tests.

The following discussion of frequency estimation is illustrated in the context of the compliance tests. This is not to suggest that this is the only area where frequency estimation is appropriate in an audit, but it appears that it is used most often in this area. Figure 8-1 summarizes the steps taken when frequency estimation is employed.

EXPECTED ERROR RATE

In the application of frequency estimation, the auditor estimates the frequency rate or the expected error rate. This is of course what he or she wants to be able to estimate at the conclusion of the tests of compliance. Since the test results determine whether an item does or does not have a characteristic, the binomial distribution is appropriate to the audit population. The sample error of proportions is computed as follows:

$$S = \sqrt{\frac{P(1 - P)}{n}}$$

where S = standard error of the population and P = error rate of the population. As the error rate increases, the size of the sample increases, since the standard error is a measure of the variability of the population. The auditor does not compute an estimate of the standard error of the population but rather utilizes statistical tables that incorporate this parameter.

The preliminary expected error rate may be estimated by referring to the results of tests, either statistical or nonstatistical, performed in previous years. Alternatively, the auditor may select a small preliminary sample and test this

Figure 8-1

Frequency Estimation (Compliance Test)

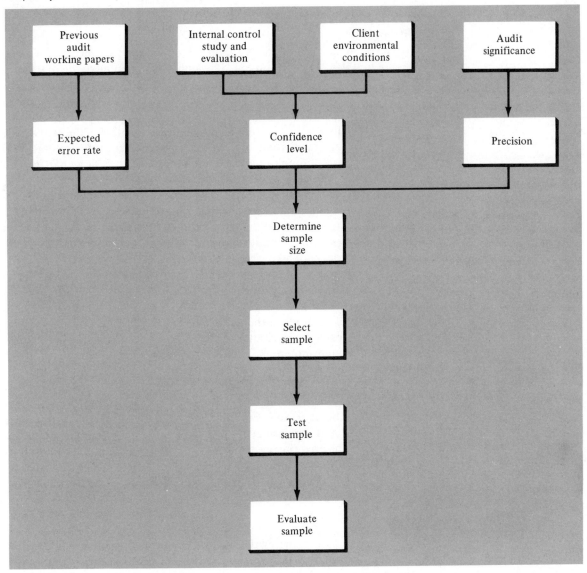

sample to establish an expected error rate. If neither approach is feasible, he or she may choose an arbitrary rate. In any case, the expected error rate is used in evaluating the sample results as described in the following discussion.

CONFIDENCE LEVEL

In addition to the expected error rate, the auditor establishes a confidence level in the application of frequency estimation. *Confidence level* or *reliability* refers to how certain the auditor wants to be that the sample drawn from the audit population is a proper representation of the population itself. This statistical factor is expressed as a percentage, such as 90 percent. With the selection of a confidence level, there is a possibility that the sample is not representative. The probability of drawing an unrepresentative sample is the complement of the confidence level. When the confidence level is established at the 90 percent level, the risk factor is 100 − 90 or 10 percent. The auditor can minimize the risk factor by selecting a higher confidence level, but as the confidence level increases the required sample size increases. This is also referred to as the alpha risk and is discussed later in the chapter.

As shown in Figure 8-1, one factor that affects determination of the confidence level is the study and evaluation of a client's internal control system. This evaluation is the result of employing such audit techniques as flowcharting and completing internal control questionnaires and the like. After these techniques have been completed, it is necessary for the auditor to formulate a preliminary judgment about the adequacy of the internal control system. This judgment is one of the two factors used to establish a confidence level. For example, when the evaluation suggests an adequate internal control system, the auditor may require a confidence level of 80 percent, whereas, when the system is weak, the required confidence level might be established at the 95 or 99 percent level. Thus the auditor is willing to assume a larger risk if the internal control system appears to be strong, since the probability of error is less. The confidence level does not refer to the degree of confidence the auditor has in the internal control system.

The second factor that contributes to the auditor's selection of a confidence level is the client's environmental conditions. As suggested in Chapter 5, these conditions encompass general economic conditions, specific economic and regulatory conditions, and the firm's structure. When they suggest a negative impact on the functioning of the organization, the auditor increases the level of confidence that needs to be achieved. For example, an auditor is likely to increase the confidence level in the compliance tests if a client has suffered a significant slump in sales since the previous year's audit. Since the environmental conditions are broad, it is difficult to establish the numerical impact of a specific factor on selection of the confidence level. This example illustrates well the point that statistical sampling requires a high degree of professional judgment.

PRECISION

The final statistical parameter the auditor establishes when employing frequency estimation sampling is precision. *Precision* refers to the degree of tolerance the auditor may accept. An auditor cannot expect to predict a single frequency or error rate but rather must be content with estimating a frequency range. Thus he or she may estimate an error rate of 3 percent with a precision of ±2 percent, which would result in a range of from 1 to 5 percent. The smaller the desired precision, the larger the required sample size.

In determining the required level of precision the auditor considers the audit significance of the attribute being tested. If a particular attribute has a potentially significant impact on the financial statements, the auditor must be more precise in estimating it, which requires a narrowing of the precision range. *SAS No. 1, Section 320B.18,* describes the criteria for the selection of a precision level:

> In considering the precision desired for compliance tests, it is important to recognize the relationship of procedural deviations to (a) the accounting records being audited, (b) any related accounting control procedures and (c) the purpose of the auditor's evaluation.

In performing the compliance tests the auditor is concerned with the degree to which established procedures are being followed. Because of the ultimate impact on the financial statements, some procedures are more important than others. This importance may be expressed in quantitative or qualitative terms. The occurrence of a particular rate of error discovered in the compliance tests does not have the same percentage impact on the financial statements. For example, 10 percent of the sales invoices may contain mathematical errors, but this frequency rate does not mean that relevant accounts on the financial statements are misstated by 10 percent. From a qualitative perspective, a very low error rate of a procedural deviation may have significant audit importance. Deliberate errors that have a low rate of occurrence are more disconcerting to the auditor than unintentional errors that have a higher occurrence rate. In selecting a precision level the auditor must evaluate the potential impact of the attribute being tested.

As suggested above, once the auditor selects an estimated error rate and the precision, the two can be grouped to form a range. For example, an expected error rate of 5 percent and a precision of ± 1 percent can be expressed as an occurrence range between 4 and 6 percent. However, the auditor is concerned with the upper precision limit of 6 percent, since this represents the greatest possibility for audit exposure. Thus, when he or she determines the sample size, the parameter utilized is the upper precision limit.

DETERMINE THE SAMPLE SIZE

Having established an expected error rate, a confidence level, and an upper precision level, the auditor determines the size of the sample by referring to specially constructed statistical tables, portions of which are reproduced in Figures 8-2 and 8-3.[2] For example, assume an auditor establishes a confidence level (reliability level) of 90 percent, an expected error rate of 2 percent, and an upper precision limit of 3 percent. By referring to Figure 8-2 it is determined that the sample size is 550. However, Figures 8-2 and 8-3 are not precise. For example, if the above illustration is changed so that the upper precision limit is 5.5 percent,

---

[2] It is often suggested that the sample size can be determined from:

$$n = \frac{P(1 - P)R^2}{E^2}$$

where n = sample size, P = expected error rate, R = the confidence coefficient (95 percent confidence level equals 1.96 confidence coefficient), and E = precision level. A recent article states that "the cited formula is not valid for the range of occurrence rates and sample sizes most often encountered in auditing." See Donald M. Roberts, "Sample Size Determination for Attributes," *Journal of Accountancy,* June 1975, pp. 46–47.

Figure 8-2

Determination of sample size—tabular form
One-sided upper precision limits

CONFIDENCE LEVEL 90.0 PERCENT

OCCURRENCE RATE

SAMPLE SIZE	0.0	.5	1.0	2.0	3.0	4.0	5.0	6.0	7.0	8.0	9.0	10.0	12.0	14.0	16.0	18.0	20.0	25.0	30.0	40.0	50.0
50	4.5			7.6		10.3		12.9		15.4		17.8	20.1	22.7	24.7	27.2	29.1		39.8	50.0	59.9
100	2.3		3.3	5.2	6.6	7.8	9.1	10.3	11.7	12.7	14.0	15.0	17.3	19.6	21.7	24.0	26.1	31.4	36.6	46.9	56.8
150	1.5			4.4		6.9		9.3		11.6		13.9	16.1	18.4	20.5	22.7	24.8		35.2	45.5	55.4
200	1.1	1.9	2.6	4.0	5.2	6.4	7.6	8.8	10.0	11.0	12.2	13.3	15.5	17.7	19.8	22.0	24.0	29.3	34.5	44.4	54.4
250	.9			3.7		6.1		8.4		10.7		12.9	15.1	17.2	19.3	21.5	23.6		33.7	43.7	53.7
300	.8		2.2	3.5	4.7	5.9	7.0	8.2	9.3	10.4	11.5	12.6	14.7	16.9	19.0	21.1	23.2	28.2	33.2	43.2	53.2
350	.7			3.3		5.7		8.0		10.2		12.3	14.5	16.7	18.8	20.9	22.8		32.8	42.8	52.8
400	.6	1.3	2.0	3.2	4.4	5.6	6.7	7.8	8.9	10.0	11.1	12.2	14.3	16.5	18.5	20.5	22.5	27.5	32.5	42.5	52.5
450	.5			3.1		5.5		7.7		9.9		12.0	14.2	16.3	18.3	20.3	22.3		32.3	42.3	52.2
500	.5		1.8	3.1	4.2	5.4	6.5	7.6	8.7	9.8	10.9	11.9	14.1	16.1	18.1	20.1	22.1	27.1	32.1	42.1	52.0
550	.4			3.0		5.3		7.5		9.7		11.8	13.9	15.9	17.9	19.9	21.9		31.9	41.9	51.9
600	.4	1.1	1.7	2.9	4.1	5.2	6.3	7.4	8.5	9.6	10.7	11.7	13.7	15.7	17.7	19.7	21.7	26.7	31.7	41.7	51.7
650	.4			2.9		5.2		7.4		9.5		11.6	13.6	15.6	17.6	19.6	21.6		31.6	41.6	51.6
700	.3		1.7	2.9	4.0	5.1	6.2	7.3	8.4	9.5	10.5	11.5	13.5	15.5	17.5	19.5	21.5	26.5	31.5	41.5	51.5
750	.3			2.8		5.1		7.3		9.4		11.4	13.4	15.4	17.4	19.4	21.4		31.4	41.4	51.4
800	.3	1.0	1.6	2.8	3.9	5.0	6.1	7.2	8.3	9.3	10.3	11.3	13.3	15.3	17.3	19.3	21.3	26.3	31.3	41.3	51.3
850	.3			2.8		5.0		7.2		9.2		11.2	13.2	15.3	17.3	19.3	21.3		31.3	41.3	51.3
900	.3		1.6	2.7	3.9	5.0	6.0	7.1	8.2	9.2	10.2	11.2	13.2	15.2	17.2	19.2	21.2	26.2	31.2	41.2	51.2
950	.2			2.7		4.9		7.1		9.1		11.1	13.1	15.1	17.1	19.1	21.1		31.1	41.1	51.1
1000	.2	.9	1.5	2.7	3.8	4.9	6.0	7.1	8.1	9.1	10.1	11.1	13.1	15.1	17.1	19.1	21.1	26.1	31.1	41.1	51.1
1500	.2		1.4	2.5	3.6	4.7	5.7	6.7	7.7	8.7	9.7	10.7	12.7	14.7	16.7	18.7	20.7	25.7	30.7	40.7	50.7
2000	.1	.8	1.3	2.5	3.5	4.5	5.5	6.5	7.5	8.5	9.5	10.5	12.5	14.5	16.5	18.5	20.5	25.5	30.5	40.5	50.6
2500	.1		1.3	2.4	3.4	4.4	5.4	6.4	7.4	8.4	9.4	10.4	12.4	14.4	16.4	18.4	20.4	25.4	30.4	40.4	50.4
3000	.1	.7	1.3	2.4	3.4	4.4	5.4	6.4	7.4	8.4	9.4	10.4	12.4	14.4	16.4	18.4	20.4	25.4	30.4	40.4	50.4
4000	.1	.7	1.2	2.3	3.3	4.3	5.3	6.3	7.3	8.3	9.3	10.3	12.3	14.3	16.3	18.3	20.3	25.3	30.3	40.3	50.3
5000	.0	.7	1.2	2.3	3.2	4.2	5.2	6.2	7.2	8.2	9.2	10.2	12.2	14.2	16.2	18.2	20.2	25.2	30.2	40.2	50.2

SOURCE: *An Auditor's Approach to Statistical Sampling*, vol. 6 (New York: AICPA, 1974), p. 95.

Figure 8-3

Determination of sample size—tabular form
One-sided upper precision limits

CONFIDENCE LEVEL 95.0 PERCENT

OCCURRENCE RATE

SAMPLE SIZE	0.0	.5	1.0	2.0	3.0	4.0	5.0	6.0	7.0	8.0	9.0	10.0	12.0	14.0	16.0	18.0	20.0	25.0	30.0	40.0	50.0
50	5.8			9.1		12.1		14.8		17.4		18.9	22.3	25.1	27.0	29.6	31.6		42.4	52.6	62.4
100	3.0		4.7	6.2	7.6	8.9	10.2	11.0	13.0	14.0	15.4	16.4	18.7	21.2	23.3	25.6	27.7	33.1	38.4	48.7	56.6
150	2.0			5.1		7.7		10.2		12.6		15.0	17.3	19.6	21.7	24.0	26.1		36.7	47.0	56.8
200	1.5	2.4	3.1	4.5	5.8	7.1	8.3	9.5	10.8	11.9	13.1	14.2	16.4	18.7	20.9	23.1	25.2	30.5	35.7	45.7	55.6
250	1.2			4.2		6.7		9.1		11.4		13.7	15.9	18.1	20.3	22.4	24.6		34.8	44.8	54.7
300	1.0		2.6	3.9	5.2	6.4	7.6	8.8	10.0	11.1	12.2	13.3	15.5	17.7	19.8	22.0	24.1	29.1	34.1	44.1	54.1
350	.9			3.7		6.2		8.6		10.8		13.0	15.2	17.4	19.6	21.7	23.6		33.6	43.6	53.6
400	.7	1.6	2.3	3.6	4.8	6.0	7.2	8.3	9.5	10.6	11.7	12.8	15.0	17.2	19.2	21.2	23.2	28.2	33.2	43.2	53.2
450	.7			3.5		5.9		8.2		10.4		12.6	14.8	16.8	18.9	20.9	22.9		32.9	42.9	52.9
500	.6		2.1	3.4	4.6	5.8	6.9	8.0	9.2	10.3	11.4	12.5	14.6	16.7	18.6	20.7	22.6	27.6	32.6	42.6	52.6
550	.5			3.3		5.7		7.9		10.1		12.3	14.4	16.4	18.4	20.4	22.4		32.4	42.4	52.4
600	.5	1.3	2.0	3.2	4.4	5.6	6.7	7.8	9.0	10.0	11.2	12.2	14.2	16.2	18.2	20.2	22.2	27.2	32.2	42.2	52.2
650	.5			3.2		5.5		7.7		10.0		12.1	14.1	16.1	18.1	20.1	22.1		32.1	42.1	52.1
700	.4		1.9	3.1	4.3	5.4	6.6	7.7	8.8	9.9	10.8	11.9	13.9	15.9	17.9	19.9	21.9	26.9	31.9	41.9	51.9
750	.4			3.1		5.4		7.6		9.8		11.8	13.8	15.8	17.8	19.8	21.8		31.8	41.8	51.8
800	.4	1.1	1.8	3.0	4.2	5.3	6.4	7.5	8.7	9.7	10.7	11.7	13.7	15.7	17.7	19.7	21.7	26.7	31.7	41.7	51.7
850	.4			3.0		5.3		7.5		9.6		11.6	13.6	15.6	17.6	19.6	21.6		31.6	41.6	51.6
900	.3		1.7	3.0	4.1	5.2	6.3	7.5	8.5	9.5	10.5	11.5	13.5	15.5	17.5	19.5	21.5	26.5	31.5	41.5	51.5
950	.3			2.9		5.2		7.4		9.4		11.4	13.4	15.5	17.4	19.5	21.4		31.5	41.5	51.5
1000	.3	1.0	1.7	2.9	4.0	5.2	6.3	7.4	8.4	9.4	10.4	11.4	13.4	15.4	17.4	19.4	21.4	26.4	31.4	41.4	51.4
1500	.2		1.5	2.7	3.8	4.9	5.9	6.9	7.9	8.9	9.9	10.9	12.9	14.9	16.9	18.9	20.9	25.9	30.9	40.9	50.9
2000	.1	.8	1.4	2.6	3.7	4.7	5.7	6.7	7.7	8.7	9.7	10.7	12.7	14.7	16.7	18.7	20.7	25.7	30.7	40.7	50.7
2500	.1		1.4	2.6	3.6	4.6	5.6	6.6	7.6	8.6	9.6	10.6	12.6	14.6	16.6	18.6	20.6	25.6	30.6	40.6	50.6
3000	.1	.8	1.4	2.5	3.5	4.5	5.5	6.5	7.5	8.5	9.5	10.5	12.5	14.5	16.5	18.5	20.5	25.5	30.5	40.5	50.5
4000	.1	.7	1.3	2.4	3.4	4.4	5.4	6.4	7.4	8.4	9.4	10.4	12.4	14.4	16.4	18.4	20.4	25.4	30.4	40.4	50.4
5000	.1	.7	1.3	2.3	3.3	4.3	5.3	6.3	7.3	8.3	9.3	10.3	12.3	14.3	16.3	18.3	20.3	25.3	30.3	40.3	50.3

SOURCE: *An Auditor's Approach to Statistical Sampling,* vol. 6 (New York: AICPA, 1974), p. 96.

258
Sampling in auditing

it can be seen that there is no entry for 5.5 percent. In this case the auditor has two alternatives. He or she may select the more conservative sample size of 100 for the upper precision limit of 5.2 percent or, through interpolation, may compute the sample size:

$$\frac{7.6 - 5.5}{7.6 - 5.2}(100 - 50) + 50 = 94$$

Finite correction factor The tables presented in Figures 8-2 and 8-3 are based on the assumption that the population being examined is infinite. Of course, in auditing populations are finite, which means that the sample size determined through the use of these tables is too large. To reduce the sample size to the appropriate number the auditor may use a formula called the finite correction factor:

$$n = \frac{n^*}{1 + (n^*/N)}$$

where n^* = sample size determined by using the tables, n = adjusted sample size taking into effect the correction due to the size of the population, and N = size of the population. The reduction in the size of the population can be significant if the sample percentage n^*/N exceeds 10 percent of the population (N).

SAMPLE SELECTION

For the results of the statistical sampling to be valid, the selection of the items to be tested must be chosen in a random manner. Random sampling means that each individual item in the total population has an equal chance of being selected, which results in an unbiased selection. The two most often used methods of random selection in auditing involve random numbers tables and systematic sampling.

Random numbers table: A random numbers table, illustrated in Figure 8-4, is a list of numbers tabulated in a random manner. To facilitate reading, the rows and columns of the table are positioned in groups of five digits. The steps to follow when selecting a sample using a random numbers table are:

1. The auditor establishes a correspondence between the audit population and the random numbers table. When a client uses prenumbered documents, the correspondence is easy to construct, since each document has a unique number and these numbers are sequential. In this case the range of valid numbers includes numbers bounded by the first and last document number used during the accounting period. For example, when the first sales invoice number used during the accounting period was 15861 and the last was 24822, only selected random numbers that fall within this range designate a sales invoice to be audited. When the audit population is not prenumbered, the auditor must be more imaginative in constructing a correspondence between the audit population and the

random numbers table. In an extreme case, he or she may have to number the entire population, but usually this is not necessary. To illustrate, the audit population may be an EDP printout of accounts receivable that is unnumbered and consists of 200 pages, each having 40 line items. In this case the auditor may construct a five-digit number in which the first three digits refer to the page number and the last two digits refer to the line-item number on the page. If the auditor finds the number 18325 in the random numbers table, it is a valid number since it refers to the twenty-fifth item on page 183. On the other hand, the numbers 42113 and 12648 are invalid, since the former is not an appropriate page number and the latter refers to an invalid line item. The auditor is careful that the concept of randomness is not violated when such a numbering scheme is used. In the above example, if some pages contain significantly more line items than other pages, each line item does not have an equal probability of being selected.

2. The auditor selects a random starting point. He or she avoids starting at the same point on the table each time it is utilized. Such an approach might introduce a degree of bias into the sample selection process. The most practical method of selecting a random starting point is to blindly point to a number on the table.

3. The auditor establishes a consistent route through the random number table. Once a random starting point has been selected, he or she moves through the table in a consistent, preestablished manner. A consistent route is part of the procedure for selecting and designating relevant numbers of the group. For example, if an auditor is interested in a four-digit number, he or she may select a five-digit number consistent with the manner in which the table is constructed and disregard the first or the last digit, as long as the procedure is followed consistently. In addition, the direction of the selection process is established. The direction may be horizontal, vertical, or diagonal, although the last-mentioned may be cumbersome.

Systematic sampling: The auditor may select a random sample through the use of systematic sampling in which every nth item is selected. To establish the interval, the size of the population is determined and then divided by the required sample size. For example, if the size of the population is 9048 items and the required sample size is 174, then every fifty-second item is selected (9048/174 = 52). A random number between 0 and 52 is selected as the starting point and is the first item selected. When 23 is the first number selected, the following numbers are 75 (23 + 52), 127 (75 + 52), and so on, until 174 items are selected.

Although systematic selection is relatively easy to apply, the auditor must be aware that such an approach may result in a biased sample selection. This could occur when the population is not random, since it may have been ordered in some manner. Ordering would occur if every fortieth item in the payroll journal represented a supervisor's pay. With the use of systematic sampling it is possible that the sample may contain a disproportionate number of salary checks for

Figure 8-4

ROW	(1)	(2)	(3)	(4)	(5)	(6)	(7)
811	53971	08701	38356	36149	10891	05178	55653
812	47177	03085	37432	94053	87057	61859	97943
813	41494	89270	48063	12253	00383	96010	41457
814	07409	32874	03514	84943	74421	86708	34267
815	03097	12212	43093	46224	14431	15065	18267
816	34722	88896	59205	18004	96431	41366	50982
817	48117	83879	52509	29339	87735	97499	42848
818	14628	89161	66972	19180	40852	91738	23920
819	61512	79376	88184	29415	50716	93393	96220
820	99954	55656	01946	57035	64418	29700	99242
821	61455	28229	82511	11622	60786	18442	36508
822	10398	50239	70191	37585	98373	04651	67804
823	59075	81492	40669	16391	12148	38538	73873
824	91497	76797	82557	55301	61570	69577	23301
825	74619	62316	80041	53053	81252	32739	65201
826	12536	80792	44581	12616	49740	86946	41819
827	10246	49556	07610	59950	34387	70013	64460
828	92506	24397	19145	24185	24479	70118	42708
829	65745	27223	22831	39446	65808	95534	03348
830	01707	04494	48168	58480	74983	63091	81027
831	66959	80109	88908	38759	80716	36340	30082
832	79278	02746	50718	90196	28394	82035	03255
833	11343	22312	41379	22297	71703	78729	65082
834	40415	10553	65932	34938	43977	39262	95828
835	72774	25480	30264	08291	93796	22281	51434
836	75886	86543	47020	14493	38363	64238	16322
837	64628	20234	07967	46676	42907	60909	73293
838	45905	77701	98976	70056	80502	68650	24469

supervisors, depending upon the selection interval and the starting point. To avoid the selection of a nonrepresentative sample, the auditor should review the population before the selection procedure is chosen. In addition, he or she should use several random starting points during the course of the sample selection as a precaution.

SAMPLE TESTING

Once the sample items are randomly selected, the auditor tests them in accordance with the compliance audit program. This step is no different from the approach used in judgment sampling. However, the auditor is usually more precise in defining an error when statistical sampling is utilized. The definition of an error is a derivative of the audit procedures listed in the audit program. Figure 8-5 illustrates this relationship. In defining errors the auditor recognizes that the listing may be modified as the actual testing is performed. The need to

Figure 8-4 (Continued)

ROW	(1)	(2)	(3)	(4)	(5)	(6)	(7)
				COLUMN			
839	77691	00408	64191	11006	39212	26862	99863
840	39172	12824	43379	57590	45307	72206	53283
841	67120	01558	99762	79752	17139	52265	97997
842	88264	85390	92841	63811	64423	50910	38189
843	78096	59495	45090	74592	47474	56157	88287
844	41888	69798	82296	09312	04150	07616	34572
845	46618	07254	28714	18244	53214	39560	68753
846	29213	42101	25089	11881	77558	72738	57234
847	38601	25735	04726	36544	67842	93937	68745
848	92207	10011	64210	77096	00011	79218	52123
849	30610	13236	33241	68731	30955	40587	45206
850	74544	72806	62226	65685	37996	00377	59917
851	76385	05431	82252	79850	31192	86315	75612
852	08059	15958	10514	86124	29817	19044	03555
853	30636	03463	50326	69684	38422	59826	47858
854	23794	51463	67574	48953	73512	46239	10953
855	01117	60216	29314	65537	84029	00741	40851
856	29527	19577	01414	35290	70174	37019	80223
857	64236	24229	17970	92022	64164	17873	41189
858	92331	30325	61918	71623	38040	51375	91127
859	93454	37190	23790	40058	03758	01774	90696
860	17101	42181	45798	68745	24190	16539	32330
861	30742	93358	95730	52535	34404	76057	21325
862	02472	01280	67106	47893	93551	76697	56598
863	80718	72187	67178	77179	06212	37409	48788
864	85406	73687	02116	57637	94701	46754	54019
865	00563	67156	88141	13491	92592	35746	72117

define new errors, a change in the definition of existing errors, and the omission of errors subsequently determined to be irrelevant are examples of audit program modifications.

SAMPLE RESULTS EVALUATION

The final step in the application of frequency estimation is evaluation of the sampling results. First, the auditor determines the actual error rate in the sample by dividing the number of errors by the number of items in the sample. Then, using Figures 8-2 and 8-3, he or she determines the upper precision limits, which many auditors refer to as the *maximum potential error rate*. For example, assume an auditor selected 200 items for audit and discovered 8 errors in the sample. The actual error rate is 4 percent (8 ÷ 200) and, if a 90 percent confidence level is selected, the maximum potential error rate is 6.4 percent. This is determined by referring to Figure 8-2, locating the 4 percent occurrence rate column and the

Figure 8-5

Partial list of audit procedures and resulting error definitions

AUDIT PROGRAM (SALES)	DEFINITION OF AN ERROR
1. Compare the information per the sales invoice to the relevant accounts receivable subsidiary ledger card.	1a. The name per the sales invoice does not agree with the name per the ledger card.
	1b. The amount per the sales invoice does not agree with the amount per the ledger card.
	1c. The date per the sales invoice differs from the posting date used on the ledger card.
2. Compare the information per the sales invoice to the relevant bill of lading.	2a. The name per the sales invoice does not agree with the name per the bill of lading.
	2b. The date per the sales invoice differs from the shipment date per the bill of lading.

row for the 200-item sample size. The matrix entry is 6.4 percent. Based on the above results it can be stated that the auditor is 90 percent certain that the maximum potential error rate in the population is no greater than 6.4 percent.

Having computed the maximum potential error rate, the auditor decides whether the error rate is acceptable. If it is acceptable, he or she retains the original evaluation of the internal control system and the timing and the extent of the audit procedures to be used in the substantive tests. However, in evaluating the results the auditor does not limit the inquiry to a simple determination of the maximum potential error rate. He or she must also be aware of the types of errors that were discovered. Errors that appear to be intentional or fraudulent indicate possible areas of audit exposure.

If the maximum potential error rate is unacceptable, several alternative courses of action may be taken.

1. The auditor may decide that the initial sample drawn was not representative of the population and draw an entirely new sample or expand the sample size originally selected. Since the complement of the confidence level (100 percent minus the confidence level) represents the probability of an unrepresentative sample being drawn, this risk cannot be eliminated. When this course of action is chosen, the new sample items are tested and evaluated in the same manner as the original sample. Obviously this is a costly alternative in terms of the auditor's time, and careful considerations are made before it is chosen.
2. The auditor, after an analysis of the errors, may identify the reason for the excessive error rate and request management to take appropriate action. For example, errors may have occurred during the training period of a new employee and may be concentrated in a period of a few weeks. The auditor may ask the client to check transactions processed during this period and make proper corrections. In this case he or she must be satisfied that this action is taken. This can be accomplished by subsequent retesting of the transactions.
3. The auditor may conclude that the internal control system cannot be

relied upon, which may require an expansion of the audit procedures to be used in the substantive tests. If it is discovered that there was a large number of errors in the accounts receivable subsidiary ledger resulting from posting errors, the auditor may decide to increase the percentage of accounts to be confirmed as part of the substantive tests, as well as adopt other procedures. Also, an excessive error rate may affect the timing of audit procedures. In the above examples it may be decided that confirmations are to be sent at the year end rather than at an interim date. Thus the timing as well as the extent of procedures may be modified.

4. The auditor may decide to change the original statistical parameters. This may be accomplished by reducing the required confidence level percentage or by increasing the acceptable upper precision limit. Such action is carefully considered before it is taken, since each of these parameters was thought to be required when the statistical sampling plan was constructed. Defending such changes either in the firm's internal review process or in a court of law may not be an easy task.

No matter which alternative is chosen, the auditor's judgment controls the course of action. In other words, he or she does not simply review the maximum potential error rate and, based only on that percentage, decide the alternative course of action. The auditor examines the nature of the errors and evaluates them in light of the audit environment. For example, only 1 error out of a sample of 200 may be discovered, but it may be the result of fraud or some other intentional error. While the error rate is low, the auditor does not automatically accept the population. He or she expands the investigation to determine the extent and significance of the irregularity.

Documentation: frequency estimation

As in any procedure utilized by the auditor, there is a need for proper documentation of the application of statistical sampling. Such documentation discloses the procedures performed, the reason such procedures were used, the results of the audit approach, and the impact upon subsequent audit procedures. Figure 8-6 is an example of a worksheet that may be used in the compliance tests where frequency estimation is used. Notice that several items on the worksheet are cross-referenced to other working papers that are not reproduced, which demonstrates the need to integrate and coordinate audit procedures used and audit decisions made in other phases of the audit.

Variable estimation (mean per unit)

Variable estimation is used to determine the estimated value of a population. Usually the auditor decides whether the book value of an account is valid. By selecting samples from the audit population and testing them in a manner prescribed by an audit program, the total value of the population is estimated. For example, the auditor may consider the inventory listing as a population.

Figure 8-6

Statistical Sampling Application

STATISTICAL SAMPLING APPLICATION

Transactions tested *Cash Disbursement Function*

Period covered *1/1/79 - 9/30/79*

Objectives of test *To determine the reliability of information generated in the cash disbursement system.*

Universe

Size *48,000*   Expected error rate *2% - See B301*

Procedures used to determine universe is intact _____

Reviewed two blocks of 100 check copies

Sample

Unit used *Individual check and voucher package*

Size *550*   How determined *Per Tables using a confidence level of 90% and a precision of ±1%*

Sampling Plan

Random Selection: Table used *Firm's Manual - Table of Random Numbers*

Starting point in table: Page *4* Line *10* Column *3*

Terminating point in table: Page *13* Line *7* Column *4*

Systematic Selection: Starting point *N/A*   Interval *N/A*

Method used in selecting start *Blind stab on table*

Other (describe): _____

Definition of Errors	Confidence Level	Max. Pot. Error	Actual Error
1. *Check not supported by voucher*	*90%*	*.4%*	*0%*
2. *Check and invoice amount differ*	*90%*	*.4%*	*0%*
3. *Check posted incorrectly to cash disbursement journal*	*90%*	*9.7%*	*8%*
4.			

Conclusions Reached

Internal control system is strong except error #3. Client has agreed to review the posting of 100 additional check postings. We will examine the results and determine the proper course.

Rather than audit each line item in the inventory, he or she selects a sample to test. The testing may consist of observing the inventory, tracing the cost of the inventory to a vendor's invoice, recomputing the inventory extension, or other procedures considered necessary.

Variable estimation is useful in performing the substantive tests. The following discussion of variable estimation is illustrated in the context of the substantive tests, which is not to suggest that this is the only phase in the audit where such an estimation method is appropriate. Figure 8-7 summarizes the steps to be taken when variable estimation is employed.

ESTIMATE STANDARD DEVIATION

As suggested earlier, the standard deviation of a population is a measurement of its variability. The greater the variability of the population, the more difficult it is to estimate its value, which results in a larger sample size. The auditor does not know the standard deviation of the population under review; therefore he or she estimates it. This estimation may be made by the selection of a preaudit sample of about 50 items. The actual computation of the standard deviation for these 50 items can be an arduous task if the auditor does not have access to a computer and the proper software packages. To overcome this obstacle he or she may use a technique that is simple although not as accurate as the direct method of computing the standard deviation. The procedure is:

- *Step 1*   Select about 50 items at random and arrange these items in groups of 6 or 7 based on their order of selection.

- *Step 2*   Determine the range for each of the groupings (range equals maximum value minus minimum value).

- *Step 3*   Determine the average range for the groupings by dividing the sum of the ranges for each group by the number of groups.

- *Step 4*   Determine the relevant d_2 factor based on the number of items that comprise the groupings.[3] A partial list of the factors is:

GROUP SIZE	d_2 FACTOR
6	2.534
7	2.704
8	2.847

- *Step 5*   By dividing the average range (step 3) by the relevant d_2 factor (step 4) the auditor can estimate the sample standard deviation.

The auditor, as noted in the following discussion, uses the estimated standard deviation of the population along with other parameters to determine the required sample size. Figure 8-8 illustrates the technique described above.

---

[3] The d_2 factor table has been compiled to facilitate estimation of the standard deviation of a population. This table is from Herbert Arkin, *Handbook of Sampling for Auditing and Accounting* (New York: McGraw-Hill, 1963), p. 423.

Figure 8-7

Variable Estimation (Substantive Test)

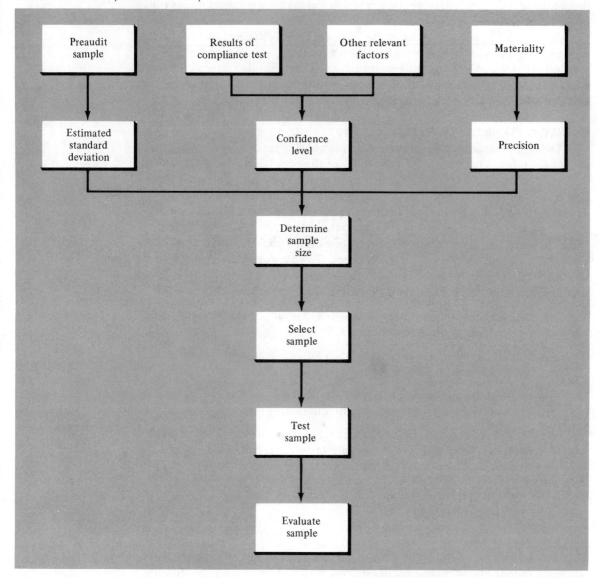

CONFIDENCE LEVEL

Before the size of the sample can be determined the auditor selects a desired confidence level. As shown in Figure 8-7, the establishment of a confidence level is based upon the results of the compliance tests and other relevant factors. The auditor determines the reliability of the internal control system after the compliance tests have been completed and then reduces the required confidence level in the substantive tests as the perceived adequacy of the internal control system increases. Thus he or she is willing to accept a higher level of risk if the internal control system is relatively strong. On the other hand, a weak internal control system suggests that the auditor should use a high confidence level, perhaps 95 or 99 percent.

Before a confidence level for the substantive tests is selected, the effect of other relevant factors is considered. These factors include any items that have an impact upon the auditor's acceptance of risk in the particular area under investigation. For example, the internal control system may have been evaluated as weak, but other client procedures may be employed to mitigate this weakness. Another example of a relevant factor is the case in which the internal control system was evaluated as weak but the auditor has made suggestions for strengthening the system and these suggestions were instituted before the year-end audit procedures were employed.

SAS No. 1, Section 320B.35, suggests the following relationship between the required confidence level in the substantive tests and the reliability of the internal control system and other relevant factors:

$$S = 1 - \frac{(1 - R)}{(1 - C)}$$

where S = reliability level for substantive tests, R = combined reliability level desired, and C = reliance assigned to the internal control evaluation and other relevant factors. The required confidence level for the financial statements (R) refers to the audit risk the auditor is willing to accept in relationship to the financial statement taken as a whole or the individual account balance being tested. For example, if R is established at a 95 percent level, the relationship between the substantive tests required confidence level and the subjective confidence level assigned to evaluation of the internal control system and other factors is:

S(SUBSTANTIVE TEST)	C(SUBJECTIVE CONFIDENCE LEVEL ACHIEVED)
90%	50%
70%	83%
30%	93%

It should be noted that the required confidence level for the substantive tests cannot be determined by using the formula. Rather the purpose is to show the conceptual relationship between the results of the evaluation of the internal control system and the required confidence level needed in the substantive tests. Also, this is an excellent example of the integrated audit approach referred to throughout this book.

PRECISION

The auditor establishes a desired precision level before the sample size is chosen. As shown in Figure 8-7, the determination of a desired precision level is based on the auditor's definition of materiality. Materiality is based upon the dollar amount of misstatement of the account balance that the auditor considers to have an impact on the fairness of the financial statements taken as a whole.

268
Sampling in
auditing

Figure 8-8

Inventory per the balance sheet on 12/31/79: $2,300,000. Number of line items contained in inventory listing on 12/31/79: 10,000. (There are 200 individual pages with 50 line items on each page.)

STEP 1		RANDOM NUMBER PAGE NO./ LINE NO.	DOLLAR VALUE PER LISTING			RANDOM NUMBER PAGE NO./ LINE NO.	DOLLAR VALUE PER LISTING
	1	14637	150 min.		25	12847	309 max.
	2	11538	193		26	08326	128 min.
	3	19050	312 max.		27	03940	181
	4	09026	164		28	08813	274
	5	07939	185		29	05810	243
Group 1	6	13841	221	Group 5	30	18642	235
	7	11306	246		31	00317	313
	8	13411	306 max.		32	11635	198
	9	08402	112 min.		33	04366	122 min.
	10	18531	197		34	08010	208
	11	12450	184		35	19033	149
Group 2	12	00502	276	Group 6	36	07033	315 max.
	13	12226	325 max.		37	17929	212 max.
	14	15046	204		38	02220	174
	15	15549	271		39	19817	153
	16	09107	236		40	13138	134 min.
	17	17322	151 min.		41	06524	178
Group 3	18	06310	215	Group 7	42	00743	160
	19	07738	311 max.		43	20041	230
	20	13505	76 min.		44	00249	274 max.
	21	07537	287		45	15723	154
	22	17229	166		46	03751	220
	23	04136	142		47	20818	112 min.
Group 4	24	11218	301	Group 8	48	13834	198

Precision can be expressed as a percentage, such as ±10 percent, or as a dollar value, such as ±$50,000. The audit determination of a materiality factor may be established as part of a firm's policy, or the partner or perhaps the manager on the engagement may establish it.

In continuing with the example shown in Figure 8-8, if materiality is defined as 5 percent, the precision range will be ±$115,000. Thus the auditor is willing to accept a misstatement of the account of $115,000 or less. Of course, if the auditor were aware of a misstatement, he or she would propose an adjusting journal entry. However, to determine the sample size an acceptable range of the account value is identified, in this case between $2,185,000 and $2,415,000. When the auditor desires a smaller range, the size of the sample is increased.

DETERMINE THE SAMPLE SIZE

Having determined the standard deviation of the sample and established a desired confidence level and precision level, the auditor can compute the required sample size using the following formula:

$$n = \frac{(RSD)^2}{P^2}$$

Figure 8-8 (Continued)

STEP 2	GROUP	MAXIMUM VALUE ($)	MINIMUM VALUE ($)	RANGE ($)
	1	312	150	162
	2	306	112	194
	3	325	151	174
	4	311	76	235
	5	309	128	181
	6	315	122	193
	7	212	134	78
	8	274	112	162
				$1379

STEP 3

$$\frac{\$1379}{8} = \$172.375$$

STEP 4

$$d_2 = 2.534$$

STEP 5

$$\frac{\$172.375}{2.534} = \$68.025 \text{ (estimated standard deviation)}$$

NOTE: A direct computation of the estimated standard deviation of the sample using the formula described in the appendix of this chapter results in an estimate of $65.28, which is not significantly different from the short-cut estimate of $68.025.

where n = sample size, R = the confidence coefficient (assume 95 percent confidence level) SD = standard deviation of the sample, and P = average precision (precision divided by the number of items in the population). For the example developed in Figure 8-7, the average precision is $11.50 ($115,000 ÷ 10,000 items). By applying the formula, the sample size is determined as follows:

$$n = \frac{(1.96 \times 68.025)^2}{11.50^2}$$

$$n = 134$$

SAMPLE SELECTION

The next step in the application of variable estimation is to select the sample items randomly. Appropriate selection methods were described in the earlier discussion of frequency estimation. The preliminary sample originally selected to estimate the standard deviation of the population is used as part of the final sample.

SAMPLE TESTING

Having selected the sample the auditor performs the appropriate audit procedures to determine the value of each sample item. The appropriateness of the audit procedures depends upon the nature of the account under investigation.

270
Sampling in auditing

For instance, when the inventory example shown in Figure 8-8 is used, the auditor audits 134 line items randomly selected from the inventory listing. Figure 8-9 illustrates only some of the audit procedures the auditor may employ to substantiate the individual line items and the results of the test. Notice that the second line item audited resulted in the discovery of an error, since the value was $136 not $193. This may have resulted from an improper quantity count, an inventory costing error, or an error in determining the extended value.

EVALUATION OF SAMPLING RESULTS

To evaluate the sampling results the auditor computes a new estimate of the standard deviation of the population based on the items in the entire sample. The method used to estimate the preliminary population standard deviation described earlier may be employed. In the inventory example, the 134 items are divided into groups of 6, resulting in 22 groupings. This accounts for 132 items (6×22). Two sample items, the last two selected, can be omitted from the computation. The average range for the 22 groupings is determined, and this average is divided by the d_2 factor 2.534. This is the revised estimate of the population's standard deviation. To continue the example, assume that the new average range is $164.71. Thus the revised estimated standard deviation of the population is $65 ($164.71 $\div$ 2.534).

In addition, the average value of the audited sample items is computed. For the example in Figure 8-8, the average audited value is equal to $220.78 ($29,585 $\div$ 134). Thus the estimated point value of the total inventory is $2,207,800 ($220.78 $\times$ 10,000 items). At this point the auditor calculates the confidence interval based on the sample results:

$$C = X^* \pm \frac{RN\,SD}{\sqrt{n}}\sqrt{1 - \frac{n}{N}}$$

where C = computed precision interval, X^* = estimated point value of the population, R = the confidence coefficient, N = size of the population, SD = standard deviation of the sample, n = size of the sample, and

$$\sqrt{1 - \frac{n}{N}} = \text{finite correction factor (optional in this example).}$$

Substituting the values determined above, the computed confidence interval is:

$$C = 2,207,800 \pm (1.96)(10,000)\frac{(65)}{\sqrt{134}}\sqrt{1 - \frac{134}{10,000}}$$

$$C = 2,207,800 \pm 109,245$$

It can be stated that the auditor is 95 percent certain that the true value of the inventory is between $2,317,045 ($2,207,800 + $109,245) and $2,098,555 ($2,207,800 − $109,245). The stated value of the inventory was $2,300,000, as shown in Figure 8-8. Since this value falls within the confidence interval computed by the auditor, the inventory value is accepted.

Figure 8-9

| | PER INVENTORY LISTING | | | |
ITEM NO.	QUANTITY (1)	COST (2)	EXTENDED VALUE (3)	AUDITED VALUE
1	50	3.00	$ 150	$ 150
2	32	6.03	193	136
3	42	7.43	312	312
.	.	.	.	.
.	.	.	.	.
.	.	.	.	.
134	22	11	242	242
Total			$30,612	$29,585

Audit procedures:
1. Quantity traced to perpetual inventory cards and inventory observed.
2. Cost traced to vendor's invoices and perpetual inventory cards based on FIFO costing method.
3. Extended value recomputed.

When the balance per the trial balance does not fall within the precision limits, one of the following alternative courses of action is selected:

1. The auditor may conclude that an unrepresentative sample was initially drawn, and another sample may then be selected. The new sample is tested in a manner similar to the audit approach used to review the original sample. Rather than draw a completely new sample, the auditor may increase the sample and evaluate the combined sample items.
2. After a review of the errors discovered the auditor may decide to expand the nature and extent of the audit procedures. This may include the decision to switch from statistical sampling to judgment sampling. At this point the auditor may conclude that the population probably contains material errors and that additional investigation is needed to obtain sufficient evidence to use as the basis for a proposed adjusting journal entry. In most cases the auditor cannot convince the client that an adjustment is needed based upon the statistical sampling results.
3. Based on the types of errors discovered, the auditor may request that the client review the entire population and make appropriate corrections. Subsequent to the client completing the review, the auditor reviews and tests the population to an extent necessary to determine that the errors have been corrected.

Documentation: variable estimation

The audit procedures employed and the statistical sampling results are properly documented in the working papers. Figure 8-10 is an example of the required documentation. There is appropriate cross-referencing in the working paper to allow for adequate comments or explanation where necessary. For example, the confidence level percentage is referenced to another working paper which explains selection of the particular percentage.

Figure 8-10

Statistical Sampling Application

CLIENT
STATISTICAL SAMPLING APPLICATION

Account tested _Inventory_

Date _12/31/79_

Objective of Test _To determine the balance in the account_

Universe Size _10,000_   Confidence Level _95%_

Desired Precision _± 5%_

Estimated Standard Deviation _Presample: $68.00 Total Sample: $65.00_

How Computed _Indirect method using a d₂ factor_

Sample Items _Line item in the inventory listing_

Sample Size _132_

How Computed _Firm Manual - Table of Frequency Estimation_

Sampling Plan
Random Selection: Table used _Firm Manual_

Starting point in table: Page _47_ Line _22_ Column _6_

Terminating point in table: Page _62_ Line _4_ Column _4_

Systematic Selection: Starting point _N/A_ Interval _N/A_

Method used in selecting start _Blind stab_

Other (describe):

Results:
Balance Per Client Records _$2,300,000_

Point Estimate _$2,207,800_

Sample Precision _± $109,245_

Confidence Limits _$2,317,045 to $2,098,555_

Conclusion Reached:

We are 95% sure that the true value of the inventory is between $2,325,248 and $2,090,352.
Inventory balance is acceptable.

Discovery sampling

In the course of an engagement an auditor is usually concerned with estimating either a rate or a dollar value. The two statistical sampling methods discussed above serve the auditor well in this situation. However he or she may be engaged to determine whether fraud or some other irregularity has occurred. One statistical sampling technique that may be used in this circumstance is discovery sampling. For example, a client might suspect that an employee is perpetrating a fraud and may ask the auditor to conduct a special investigation into the matter.

By using discovery sampling the auditor can state the probability of finding at least one irregularity if the error rate is at a particular level. To employ discovery sampling the auditor determines the size of the population and estimates the error rate in the population, and the sample size. Once these parameters have been selected, the auditor refers to specially constructed tables which state the probability of finding an error in the sample. For example, assume that the auditor determines that the size of the population is 2000 items, the sample size is 100, and the error rate is 4 percent. Under these conditions he or she can state that there is a 98.5 percent probability that at least 1 error will be found in the sample of 100 if the error rate is 4 percent. The tables are flexible so that, if the auditor wants to increase the confidence level to 99.9 percent, the sample size is increased to 200.

Ratio and difference estimates

Ratio and difference estimates are two separate statistical techniques which are examples of variable estimation techniques. The mean-per-unit variable estimation technique was illustrated earlier. The ratio estimation method or difference estimation method can be employed to test the same audit population to which the mean-per-unit estimation is applicable. The procedures used to apply these statistical methods are almost identical. When the ratio method is used, the auditor forms a fraction by dividing the audited value of the item by its book value. The ratio rather than the dollar amount becomes the definition of the sample item. When the difference method is used, the auditor determines the arithmetic difference between the audited value and the book value of the item. From this point the auditor estimates the parameters of the sample approach, such as standard deviation, and so on.

The advantage of using the ratio method or the difference method is that these sampling approaches are usually more efficient. This occurs because there is less variability in the population in the sample items, since the auditor is dealing with smaller values that result from forming ratios or determining differences. On the other hand, the auditor must know the audited value of the presample before the total sample size is determined. Since this may not be convenient or economical in some cases, these procedures may not be appropriate.

Stratification

When variable estimation techniques are employed, careful consideration is given to the possibility of dividing the total population into smaller subpopula-

274
Sampling in auditing

tions. This is referred to as *stratifying the population*. The population is segregated based upon a characteristic, usually the dollar value of the individual sample items. From a statistical perspective stratification of a population usually results in a more efficient approach, because the effects of the variability of the population are reduced. It is recalled that a population with a great degree of variability requires a large sample size. For example, the following stratified population requires a smaller sample size to achieve a particular sample reliability than it would require if unstratified:

- *Population:* Accounts receivable, range of values $450,000 to $1,500

- *Stratum 1:* $1,500 to $50,000

- *Stratum 2:* $50,000 to $200,000

- *Stratum 3:* $200,000 to $450,000

The statistical sampling procedures for the application of stratified variable estimation are tedious and are beyond the scope of this book.[4]

In addition to possibly increasing the audit efficiency, stratification provides a great deal of flexibility in the audit approach. For example, the auditor may decide that only part of the total population is to be subjected to statistical sampling. For the accounts receivable example above, the auditor may construct the following audit approach:

- *Stratum 1:* Apply statistical sampling technique.

- *Stratum 2:* Confirm 60 percent.

- *Stratum 3:* Confirm 100 percent and review subsequent cash collection on every other account.

Since judgment sampling is used in the above audit approach, the auditor is not able to make a mathematical conclusion such as that there is a 95 percent probability that the true value will fall within a certain range. However, the approach is valid, and the auditor should use the sampling approach when it appears to be the best plan under the circumstances.

Identifying and controlling risk

It was suggested earlier in this chapter that one advantage of statistical sampling was that it enables the auditor to quantify and, to some degree, control the risk factor in some phases of the audit. Specifically, the auditor is concerned with the (1) alpha risk, (2) beta risk, and (3) ultimate risk.

ALPHA RISK

In auditing, *alpha risk* refers to the probability that an auditor will reject a population that is correct. For example, he or she may draw a sample from an

---

[4] For a discussion, see *An Auditor's Approach to Statistical Sampling* Vol. 3: *Stratified Random Sampling* (New York: AICPA, 1973).

accounts receivable population, test the sample, and conclude that the computed confidence interval does not include the client's book value of the accounts receivable. Typically, the auditor's reaction to such a discovery is to perform additional audit work until the population is acceptable or enough work is done so that an adjustment can be proposed by the auditor. Thus the cost of the audit is increased, because the auditor initially rejected an acceptable population.

The auditor can reduce the alpha risk by specifying a higher degree of reliability. The alpha risk is the complement of the reliability level. Thus, if the reliability is established at 95 percent, the alpha risk is equal to 5 percent (100 percent − 95 percent).

BETA RISK

Although the alpha risk may result in the performance of unnecessary audit procedures on occasion, the auditor is most concerned with the beta risk. *Beta risk* is the probability that an auditor will accept a population as correct when in fact it is incorrect. Obviously, this could lead to a lawsuit charging that he or she erroneously stated that the financial statements were prepared in accordance with generally accepted accounting principles. The beta risk is controlled by narrowing the ratio of precision and the amount considered material by the auditor. The beta risk cannot practically be reduced to zero, since this would require an examination of every item in the population.

In most audit situations the beta risk is approximately 50 percent if materiality and precision are equated. This is of course too great a probability that the auditor will accept an incorrect population. Although a complete discussion of controlling the beta risk is beyond the scope of this book, the beta risk can be reduced to an acceptable level by defining precision as one-half of materiality. The result is that the beta risk is reduced to about one-half of the alpha risk. Unfortunately, the sample size is increased three-fold.

This short-cut approach to controlling the beta risk can be illustrated by referring to the example developed in the earlier variable estimation section. In that example, materiality was established as $11.50 per inventory item or $115,000 for the inventory of 10,000 items. By defining precision as $5.75 per item (one-half of materiality), the sample size is determined as follows:

$$n = \frac{(1.96 \times 68.025)^2}{5.75^2} = 538$$

Thus the sample size has increased about 300 percent. However, rather than having a beta risk of about 50 percent, the beta risk using the sample size of 538 is approximately 2.5 percent (the alpha risk divided by 2). Most auditors would be willing to accept a beta risk at this level.[5]

ULTIMATE RISK

In the final analysis, the auditor is concerned with the probability that he or she will not detect an erroneous population. This ultimate risk is a function of

[5] For a thorough discussion see J. Boatman and G. Crooch, "An Example of Controlling the Risk of a Type II Error for Substantive Test," *Accounting Review,* July 1975, pp. 610–615.

276
Sampling in
auditing

the adequacy of the internal control system, the beta risk, and the performance of analytical review procedures. The internal control structure has an impact on the probability of an error occurring in the first place. The stronger the internal control system, the more likely it is that material errors will not occur. As suggested above, the beta risk is the probability that the auditor will accept an incorrect balance as being correct after performing substantive audit procedures. Finally, analytical audit procedures are employed to test the overall reasonableness and internal consistency of account balances. Thus it is possible for an auditor to accept an incorrect balance after employing substantive test procedures but, because of the results of ratio analysis and other analytical procedures, question the validity of the balance. At this point the auditor conducts additional audit tests and, hopefully, discovers the material error.

There is no doubt that ultimate risk exists on an abstract basis; however, it is impossible to calculate this risk for a particular audit. There is just too much subjectivity involved in quantifying the effectiveness of the internal control system and the effectiveness of the analytical review procedures. One should be careful of any such quantification of ultimate risk. The proper approach is for the auditor to recognize the importance of each phase of an audit and evaluate these results carefully before the audit report is signed.

CONCLUDING REMARKS

Sampling, both nonstatistical and statistical, is an important part of the audit process. To apply sampling techniques successfully the auditor relies heavily upon audit judgment. There is no one statistical method that is appropriate in all audit situations. The auditor must review each situation and select the sampling method most appropriate under the circumstances.

Following the discussion of auditing methodology in Chapters 5 through 8, Chapter 9 attempts to explain fully the integrated audit approach adopted by this text. Some of the material discussed in previous chapters is introduced again in Chapter 9. This is necessary to present a complete description of the audit approach.

APPENDIX: A REVIEW OF STATISTICAL TERMS AND CONCEPTS

Population

The population or universe consists of the total collection of items or elements that have some common characteristic(s) that are of interest to the auditor.

Examples

· Sales invoices processed during the accounting period

· Accounts receivable at a particular date

Mean
The arithmetic average of all items that comprise a grouping:

$$\overline{X} = \frac{\sum_{i=1}^{N} X_i}{N}$$

where $\overline{X}$ = population mean, X_i = each element in the population starting with the first and going through the Nth or last element, N = number of elements in the population, and Σ = sum of the observations.

Example: Assume nine items in the grouping with the following values:

$$
\begin{array}{r}
40 \\
20 \\
30 \\
60 \\
30 \\
10 \\
20 \\
10 \\
\underline{50} \\
\end{array}
$$

$$\sum_{i}^{N} X_i = 270$$

Mean $= \overline{X} = 270/9 = 30$

Variability

The elements that comprise a population may be similar in value to the population mean, or they may be dissimilar. One way of measuring the composition or variability of the population is by determining the standard deviation of the population:

$$\sigma_{X_i} = \sqrt{\frac{\sum_{i=1}^{N} (X_i - \overline{X})^2}{N}}$$

where σ_{X_i} = standard deviation of the population.

Example

X	$\overline{X}$	$X - \overline{X}$	$(X - \overline{X})^2$
40	30	10	100
20	30	-10	100
30	30	0	0
60	30	30	900
30	30	0	0
10	30	-20	400
20	30	-10	100
10	30	-20	400
50	30	20	400
			2400

$$\sigma_{X_i} = \sqrt{\frac{2400}{9}}$$

$$= 16.3$$

In an audit situation the standard deviation of the population is not known, and the auditor cannot efficiently determine it. Alternatively, the auditor can determine the standard deviation of a sample:

$$SD_{x_i} = \sqrt{\frac{\sum_{i=1}^{n}(x_i - \bar{x})^2}{n - 1}}$$

where SD_{x_i} = standard deviation of the sample, x_i = each element in the sample, and n = number of elements in the sample.

Example: Assume four items are selected as a sample from the nine-element population used in the previous examples.

x	$\bar{x}$	$x - \bar{x}$	$(x - \bar{x})^2$
30	25	5	25
10	25	−15	225
40	25	15	225
20	25	−5	25
100			500

$$\bar{x} = \frac{100}{4} = 25$$

$$SD_{x_i} = \sqrt{\frac{500}{3}}$$
$$= 12.9$$

Normal Curve

The frequency distribution of a population can be plotted in the following manner:

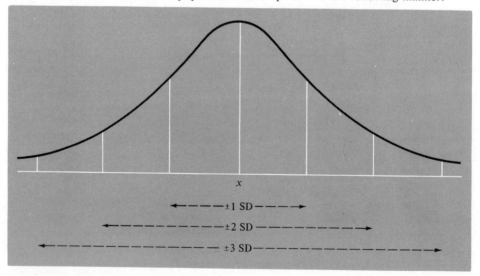

The value of each item is plotted on the horizontal axis, and the frequency occurrence of a single value is plotted on the vertical axis. When a population distribution is symmetric, the population is characterized as having a normal distribution, the apex of the distribution being the mean or average value of the population.

In a normal distribution the mean value plus or minus the standard deviation of the population can be used to estimate the probable value of an item drawn from the population. For example, the mean value ± 1.00 standard deviation repesents 68.3 percent of the area of the normal distribution. If the mean of a population were 50 and the standard deviation were 10, then there would be a 68.3 percent chance that the value of the item chosen from the population is between 40 and 60 (50 $\pm$ 10). The accompanying table summarizes some of the relationships between standard deviations and the area under the normal curve.

STANDARD DEVIATION	AREA REPRESENTED (%)
± 1.00	68.3
± 1.96	95.0
± 2.00	95.5
± 3.00	99.7

The standard deviation factor is often referred to as the *confidence coefficient*. For example, if the auditor wished to establish a 95 percent confidence level, then the confidence coefficient would be 1.96.

Accounting populations are not normally distributed but rather are skewed to the left or right. For example, an accounts receivable population may consist of a few large balances and several small balances. However, when several samples are selected and the mean computed for each and plotted, the distribution is normally distributed around the mean of the samples. In addition, this sample mean would equal the mean of the population.

From the standard deviation of the sample, the auditor can estimate the standard deviation of the mean (often referred to as the standard error of the mean).

$$SE_{\bar{x}} = \frac{SD_{x_i}}{\sqrt{n}}$$

where $SE_{\bar{x}}$ = standard error of the mean.

Example: Using the previous example, the standard error of the mean can be computed:

$$SE_{\bar{x}} = \frac{12.9}{\sqrt{4}}$$
$$= 6.5$$

Confidence Interval

The more precise an auditor must be about estimating a dollar amount, the larger the required sample size. The auditor is not interested in estimating a single dollar amount but rather is content to identify an acceptable range of values. For example, the auditor may be willing to accept the client's value for inventory if it falls between $800,000 and $750,000. To be more precise, the sample size would have to be increased.

280
Sampling in auditing

In constructing a range or confidence interval, the auditor must compute the precision of the sample results at a particular confidence level. Precision is defined as the range in which the true value of the population is expected to fall. Reliability or confidence level refers to the degree of assurance that the sample results are a proper representation of the population.

The confidence interval can be computed as follows:

Formula:

$$C = \bar{x} \pm \left[\frac{R \cdot SD_{X_i}}{\sqrt{n}} \right]$$

where

C = computed precision interval
R = confidence coefficient

Example: Using the illustration in the previous example the confidence interval is computed at the 95 percent confidence level. Thus, $R = 1.96$.

$$CI = 25 \pm (1.96 \cdot 6.5)$$
$$= 25 \pm 12.7$$
$$= 37.7 \text{ } _{TO} \text{ } 12.3$$

Thus, we can state that we are 95 percent certain that the average value of the elements in the population falls between 37.7 and 12.3. Also, it can be stated that we are 95 percent certain that the true value of the population is between 339.3 (37.7 × 9) and 110.7 (12.3 × 9).

SAMPLE SIZE

The formula for computing the precision interval can be used to determine the size of the sample. By inspecting the confidence interval formula:

$$\bar{x} \pm R \left(\frac{SD_{X_i}}{\sqrt{n}} \right)$$

it can be seen that the second part of the formula, $[(R)(SD_{X_i})]/\sqrt{n}$, is the precision factor. Thus

$$\text{precision} = R \frac{SD_{X_i}}{\sqrt{n}}$$

This formula can be manipulated so that the sample size can be determined:

$$n = \frac{[(R)(SD_{X_i})]^2}{P^2}$$

where n = required sample size and P = precision.

Example: The sample size of the illustration used in previous examples can be computed.

$$n = \frac{[(1.96)(12.9)]^2}{(12.7)^2}$$
$$n = 4 \text{ (rounded)}$$

Attribute Sampling

The previous illustrations were concerned with variable estimates (estimating dollar values). A similar approach can be developed for attribute sampling (estimating characteristics). The formula for determining the sample size for attributes (a binomial distribution) is:

$$n = \frac{R^2 p(1-p)}{\text{precision}^2}$$

where p = estimated error rate of the population. Unfortunately this formula is not accurate when p approaches zero percent. In auditing most error rates are close to zero. For these reasons the formula can not be used, but tables have been developed to take this problem into account (Figures 8-2 and 8-3).

EXERCISES AND PROBLEMS

8-1. Compare the audit decisions that must be made when judgment sampling and statistical sampling are used.

8-2. List and explain the audit decisions that must be made when the auditor decides to use frequency estimation in the compliance tests phase of the audit.

8-3. Explain how the following factor would impact the sample size, if that and only that factor were (1) increased or (2) decreased:

  a. Confidence level
  b. Precision
  c. Standard deviation

8-4. What is meant by random selection?

8-5. Explain how a random numbers table is used.

8-6. What is meant by establishing a correspondence between the audit population and the random numbers table? How is this done for a population represented by cash disbursements for the year?

8-7. Is systematic sampling an acceptable method for selecting a random sample? Explain how systematic sampling is used.

8-8. Why is the auditor more likely to employ variable estimation instead of frequency estimation in the substantive tests phase of the audit?

8-9. Given the following audit objectives, would the auditor use frequency estimation or variable estimation in each case?

  1. Determine the dollar amount in accounts receivable.
  2. Determine the number of times a credit sale was not approved.
  3. Determine the number of tons of coal stored in several coal cars.
  4. Determine the number of accounts improperly aged by the client in preparation of the aged trial balance of accounts receivable.
  5. Determine the amount of credit sales not properly approved during the year.

8-10. Why is it necessary to document the performance of work done in connection with statistical sampling?

282
Sampling in auditing

8-11. The following formula, explained in this chapter, emphasizes the relationship between reliance assigned to the internal control system of an organization and the required confidence level used in performance of the substantive tests.

$$C = 1 - \frac{(1 - R)}{(1 - S)}$$

1. Explain why S and C are related.
2. From a practical perspective, can the auditor use the above formula? Explain.

8-12. Assume that an auditor has completed the review of an audit population and that the results are unsatisfactory. What alternative actions are available?

8-13. Explain how the auditor uses discovery sampling.

8-14. Are the statistical methods referred to as ratio and difference estimation properly classified as variable estimation techniques? Explain.

8-15. Why is stratification often used when sampling is employed?

8-16. Of the following populations, which one is more likely to be stratified?

	POPULATION A	POPULATION B
Number of items	20,000	20,000
Range	$150–$800	$100–$10,000
Standard deviation	Unknown	Unknown
Total value	$10,000,000	$12,000,000
Internal control system	Weak	Strong

8-17. Are random selection and statistical sampling synonymous?

8-18. You desire to evaluate the reasonableness of the book value of the inventory of your client, Draper, Inc. You have satisfied yourself as to inventory quantities. During the examination of the pricing and extension of the inventory, the following data were gathered using appropriate unrestricted random sampling with replacement procedures.

Total items in the inventory N	12,700
Total items in the sample n	400
Total audited value of items in the sample	$38,400
$\displaystyle\sum_{j=1}^{400} (x_j - \bar{x})^2$	312,816

Formula for estimated population standard deviation

$$S_{X_j} = \sqrt{\frac{\displaystyle\sum_{j=1}^{j=n} (x_j - \bar{x})^2}{n - 1}}$$

Formula for estimated standard error of the mean. $\qquad SE = \dfrac{S_{X_j}}{\sqrt{n}}$

Confidence level coefficient of the standard error of the mean at a 95 percent confidence (reliability) level is 1.96.

Required

1. Based on the sampling results, what is the estimate of the total value of the inventory? Show computations in good form where appropriate.

2. What statistical conclusion can be reached regarding the estimated total inventory value calculated in part 1 at a confidence level of 95 percent? Present computations in good form where appropriate.

3. Independent of your answers to parts 1 and 2, assume that the book value of Draper's inventory is $1,700,000, and based on the sample results, the estimated total value of the inventory is $1,690,000. The auditor desires a confidence (reliability) level of 95 percent. Discuss the audit and statistical considerations he or she must evaluate before deciding whether the sampling results support acceptance of the book value as a fair presentation of Draper's inventory. (AICPA Adapted)

8-19. The use of statistical sampling techniques in an examination of financial statements does not eliminate judgmental decisions.

Required

1. Identify and explain four areas where judgment may be exercised by a CPA in planning a statistical sampling test.

2. Assume that a CPA's sample shows an unacceptable error rate. Describe the various actions that he or she may take based upon this finding.

3. A nonstratified sample of 80 accounts payable vouchers is to be selected from a population of 3200. The vouchers are numbered consecutively from 1 to 3200 and are listed, 40 to a page, in the voucher register. Describe four different techniques for selecting a random sample of vouchers for review. (AICPA Adapted)

8-20. An auditor is constructing the tests of compliance for the payroll system of a client. The testing period covers all payroll checks written from January 6, 1979, to September 29, 1979. The first payroll check written was numbered 15849, and the last was numbered 21663. The checks are listed in a payroll journal. For the nine-month period, the client used 120 pages in the payroll journal. Each journal page contains 50 possible lines.

Required

1. Fully describe three methods of random selection.

2. For the methods described in part 1 that utilize a random number table, list the first five sample items to be chosen. (Use Figure 8-4 and assume that the starting point is row 821 and column 4. Also, assume that you have decided to proceed down each column.)

8-21. In the examination of a particular account, the auditor must test certain items within a finite population to form an opinion of the reliability of the account as a whole. In a judgment sample he or she commonly tests most of the large dollar-amount items and a smaller proportion of the small dollar-amount items. A random stratified sample makes the same type of selection but is said to be superior to the judgment sample.

Required

1. For each of the following define the terms and explain how the selection process can be applied to a test of accounts receivable:

    a. A judgment sample
    b. A stratum in a finite population
    c. A systematic random stratified sample.

2. Explain why a random stratified sample is superior to a judgment sample.

3. Discuss sequential sampling and explain how and why this statistical technique might be more useful to an auditor than simple random sampling. (AICPA Adapted)

284
Sampling in
auditing

8-22. You are now conducting your third annual audit of the financial statements of Elite Corporation for the year ended December 31, 1966. You decide to employ unrestricted random number statistical sampling techniques in testing the effectiveness of the company's internal control procedures relating to sales invoices, which are all serially numbered. In prior years, after selecting one representative two-week period during that period and resolved all of the errors which were found to your satisfaction.

Required

1. Explain the statistical procedures you would use to determine the size of the sample of sales invoices to be examined.

2. Once the sample size has been determined, how would you select the individual invoices to be included in the sample? Explain.

3. Would the use of statistical sampling procedures improve the examination of sales invoices as compared with the selection procedure used in prior years? Discuss.

4. Assume that the company issued 50,000 sales invoices during the year and that the auditor specified a confidence level of 95 percent with a precision range of ± 2 percent.

   a. Does this mean that the auditor will be willing to accept the reliability of the sales invoice data if errors are found on no more than 4 sales invoices out of every 95 examined? Discuss.

   b. If the auditor specified a precision range of ± 1 percent, would the confidence level be higher or lower than 95 percent, assuming that the size of the sample remains constant? Why?   (AICPA Adapted)

8-23. Listed in the accompanying table are the statistical parameters that must be quantified by the auditor before the sample size is computed. Using these data and Figures 8-2 and 8-3, determine the appropriate sample size for each of the six audit situations. Interpolate and use the finite correction factor when appropriate.

POPULATION	UPPER PRECISION LIMIT (%)	POPULATION SIZE	ESTIMATED OCCURRENCE RATE (%)	CONFIDENCE LEVEL (%)
1	5	5,000	4	90
2	1.1	5,000	0	90
3	2	1,000	2	90
4	8.5	6,000	8	95
5	8	6,000	6	95
6	5	25,000	4	95

8-24. In the development of an audit program it is determined that to achieve specified precision and confidence, a sample of 436 items from a population of 10,000 is adequate on a statistical basis.

Required

1. Briefly define each of the following terms used in the above statement:

   a. Population
   b. Sample
   c. Precision
   d. Confidence

2. If the population is 10,000 and the specifications for precision and confidence are unchanged from the situation above for a population of 10,000, which of the sample sizes (436, 454, 3000, and 4360) could be expected to be statistically correct for the larger

population? Justify your answer. (Your answer should be based on judgment and reasoning rather than actual calculation.)

3. Statistical sampling techniques are being used in auditing. A sample is taken and analyzed to draw an inference or reach a conclusion about a population, but there is always a risk that the inference or conclusion may be incorrect. What value, then, is there in using statistical sampling techniques? (AICPA Adapted)

8-25. B Company asks its CPA's assistance in estimating the proportion of its active 30-day charge account customers who also have an active installment credit account. The CPA takes an unrestricted random sample of 100 accounts from 6000 active 30-day charge accounts. Of the accounts selected 10 also have active installment credit accounts. If the CPA decides to estimate with 95 percent confidence, what is the estimated percentage range for the active 30-day charge account customers that also have active installment credit accounts? (AICPA Adapted)

8-26. Summarized in the accompanying table are six situations in which the auditor has used frequency estimation.

	SAMPLE SIZE	POPULATION SIZE	CONFIDENCE LEVEL (%)	NUMBER OF ERRORS IN SAMPLE	ORIGINAL UPPER PRECISION LIMIT (%)
Situation no.					
1	800	10,000	90	16	5
2	350	4,000	90	0	8
3	200	6,000	90	20	4
4	600	12,000	95	6	9
5	650	10,000	95	65	10
6	350	5,000	95	7	13

Required

1. For each situation determine the maximum potential error rate. Use Figures 8-2 and 8-3.

2. Assume that your answer for situation 1 suggests a maximum potential error rate of 3 percent. Can the auditor state that he or she is 90 pecent certain that the error rate is 3 percent?

3. Of the six situations which ones are likely to require additional investigation? Why?

8-27. An auditor has decided to use the variable estimation technique in reviewing the accounts receivable balance.

Required

1. What audit decisions and statistical decisions must be made before the statistical procedure can be employed?

2. Assume that the auditor desires a confidence level of 99 percent, estimates the standard deviation of the population to be $15, and establishes a desired average precision of $3. What is the required sample size?

3. Refer to the data presented in part 2. Assume that the auditor decides to change the confidence level from 99 to 95 percent. What is the required sample size? Why did the size of the sample change? Explain fully.

286
**Sampling in
auditing**

4. Refer to the data presented in part 2. Assume that the auditor decides to change the average precision from $3 to $2. What is the required sample size? Why did the size of the sample change? Explain fully.

5. Refer to the data presented in part 2. Assume that the auditor's estimate of the population's standard deviation changes from $15 to $20. What is the required sample size. Why did the size of the sample change? Explain fully.

8-28. P Company asks its CPA's assistance in estimating the average gross value of the 5000 invoices processed during June 1979. The CPA estimates the population standard deviation to be $8. If a precision of $\pm$$2 with a 95 percent level of confidence is to be achieved, the auditor should draw an unrestricted random sample of what size?

(AICPA Adapted)

8-29. A CPA's client is considering the adoption of statistical sampling techniques and has asked the CPA to discuss these techniques at a meeting of client employees. In connection with this presentation the CPA has prepared the accompanying table, which shows the comparative characteristics of two populations and the samples to be drawn from each. (For example, in case 1 the variability of population 1 is smaller than that of population 2, whereas the populations are of equal size and the samples to be drawn from them have equal specified precisions (confidence intervals) and specified reliabilities (confidence levels).

	POPULATION 1 RELATIVE TO POPULATION 2		SAMPLE FROM POPULATION 1 RELATIVE TO SAMPLE FROM POPULATION 2	
	SIZE	VARIABILITY	SPECIFIED PRECISION	SPECIFIED RELIABILITY
Case 1	Equal	Smaller	Equal	Equal
Case 2	Smaller	Equal	Equal	Higher
Case 3	Equal	Equal	Wider	Equal
Case 4	Larger	Equal	Narrower	Equal
Case 5	Equal	Greater	Equal	Higher

By using the table and the technique of unrestricted random sampling with replacement, meeting participants are asked to determine the relative required sample size to be drawn from the two populations.

Required: For each of the five cases, indicate the relationship of the sample size to be selected from population 1 relative to the required sample from population 2. Select your answer from the following four alternatives:

The required sample size from population 1 is

1. Larger than the required sample from population 2
2. Equal to the required sample size from population 2
3. Smaller than the required sample size from population 2
4. Indeterminate relative to the required sample size from population 2 (AICPA Adapted)

8-30. You have decided to use variable estimation in the year-end audit of the accounts receivable of your client. The client's aged trial balance of accounts receivable shows a total amount due of $6,784,815. This balance agrees with the amount per the control account. There are 5620 accounts included in the aged trial balance. The auditor establishes an average precision of $10 per account, estimates the standard deviation of the population to be about $50, and establishes a confidence level of 95%.

The auditor determines the sample size, selects the items for review, and performs the appropriate audit procedures.

Required
1. Determine the required sample size.
2. Assume that the sample size computed in part 1 was 100 and that the total dollar value of receivables validated through appropriate audit procedures was $120,000.

    a. Calculate the point value of the accounts receivable.
    b. Calculate the computed confidence interval.
    c. Will the auditor accept the $6,784,815 balance shown on the client's financial records?

3. What was the original precision estimate? How did the auditor determine this range?
4. Compare the original precision estimate to the computed precision range. What is the role of each range in the auditor's evaluation of the sampling results?
5. Assume that the auditor's original estimate of the population's standard deviation was based on a preliminary sample of 48 items. If the auditor recomputes the population's estimated standard deviation based on a sample size of 100 and the estimate is $45, what action will be taken by the auditor?

8-31. The financial statements of the Summit Appliance Repair Company are being audited for the year ended June 30, 1979. Summit has a large fleet of identically stocked repair trucks. It establishes the total quantities of materials and supplies stored on the delivery trucks at year end by physically inventorying a random sample of trucks.

An auditor is evaluating the statistial validity of Summit's 1979 sample. The auditor knows that there were 74 trucks in the 1978 required sample. Assumptions about the size, variability, specified precision (confidence interval), and specified reliablity (confidence level) for the 1979 sample are given in each of the following five cases. You are to indicate in each case the effect upon the size of the 1979 sample as compared to the 1978 sample. Each of the five cases is independent of the other four and is to be considered separately. Possible answers are:

1. Larger than the 1978 sample size
2. Equal to the 1978 sample size
3. Smaller than the 1978 sample size
4. Of a size that is indeterminate based upon the assumptions given

• *Case 1*   Summit has the same number of trucks in 1979, but supplies are replenished more often, meaning that there is less variability in the quantity of supplies stored on each truck. The specified precision and specified reliability remain the same.

• *Case 2*   Summit has the same number of trucks, but supplies are replenished less often (greater variability). Summit specifies the same precision but decides to change the specified reliability from 95 percent to 90 percent.

• *Case 3*   Summit has more trucks in 1979. Variability and specified reliability remain the same, but with the auditor's concurrence Summit decides upon a wider specified precision.

• *Case 4*   The number of trucks and the variability remain the same, but with the

288
Sampling in auditing

auditor's concurrence Summit decides upon a wider specified precision and a specified reliability of 90 percent rather than 95 percent.

· *Case 5* The number of trucks increases, as does the variability of quantites stored in each truck. The specified reliability remains the same, but the specified precision is narrowed.

MULTIPLE CHOICE

Items 1 through 5 are based on the following information:

An audit partner is developing an office training program to familiarize his professional staff with statistical decision models applicable to the audit of dollar-value balances. He wishes to demonstrate the relationship of sample sizes to population size and variability and the auditor's specifications as to precision and confidence level. The partner prepared the accompanying table to show the comparative population characteristics and audit specifications of two populations.

	CHARACTERISTICS OF POPULATION 1 RELATIVE TO POPULATION 2		AUDIT SPECIFICATIONS AS TO A SAMPLE FROM POPULATION 1 RELATIVE TO A SAMPLE FROM POPULATION 2	
	SIZE	VARIABILITY	SPECIFIED PRECISION	SPECIFIED CONFIDENCE LEVEL
Case 1	Equal	Equal	Equal	Higher
Case 2	Equal	Larger	Wider	Equal
Case 3	Larger	Equal	Tighter	Lower
Case 4	Smaller	Smaller	Equal	Lower
Case 5	Larger	Equal	Equal	Higher

In each item 1 through 5 you are to indicate for the specified case from the above table the required sample size to be selected from population 1 relative to the sample from population 2. Your answer choice should be selected from the following responses:

a. Larger than the required sample size from population 2
b. Equal to the required sample size from population 2
c. Smaller than the required sample size from population 1
d. Indeterminate relative to the required sample size from population 2

1. In case 1 the required sample size from population 1 is
2. In case 2 the required sample size from population 1 is
3. In case 3 the required sample size from population 1 is
4. In case 4 the required sample size from population 1 is
5. In case 5 the required sample size from population 1 is   (AICPA Adapted)

CHAPTER 9

The audit approach: a systems orientation

Previous chapters were devoted to gathering evidence through the use of analytic methods. These methods were concerned with the first two phases of the integrated audit approach. In these phases the auditor investigates the client's environmental conditions and makes an initial evaluation of the internal control system. This chapter is devoted to the final two phases of the integrated audit approach, namely, performance of the tests of compliance and the substantive tests. Chapter 9 forms the foundation, and the audit approach is illustrated in Chapters 10 through 16. Furthermore, the audit approach adopted in these chapters emphasizes the need for the auditor to use a systems orientation in the audit of financial statements.

A SYSTEMS APPROACH

For the past several decades the typical financial audit performed by an accounting firm has been dominated by the so-called balance sheet approach. The objective of this approach is to substantiate or verify the ending account balances that appear on the balance sheet. Recently, such an approach has been supplemented by the auditor's verification of balances that appear on the income statement but, even with this more recent modification, the major audit effort is still directed toward balance sheet accounts.

A systems approach to auditing does not suggest that there be a change in the amount of effort devoted to the audit of income statement accounts, with an attendant reduction in the review of accounts that appear on the balance sheet. First, the approach to auditing recognizes that account balances result from financial transactions. In many instances the transaction results in a change in account balances that appear on the balance sheet as well as on the income statement. If the auditor collects sufficient evidence to be persuaded that the transaction was accounted for properly, the account balances on the two financial

289

statements will have in part been audited. For example, the credit sales system of an organization results in the following transaction analysis in a debit/credit format:

Accounts receivable	$100	
Sales		$100

When the auditor selects this single transaction for review and is able to collect sufficient evidence to establish the validity of the entry, there is a partial audit of the accounts sales and accounts receivable. It is true that the ending balance in accounts receivable may not include this $100 amount, since it may have been collected. However, the auditor also reviews the cash receipts system of an organization, and some cash inflow transactions are chosen for examination. In this way the auditor reviews the increases and decreases in an account based on current transactions, and this evidence contributes to his or her eventual formulation of an opinion on the financial statements.

The above transaction analysis is only part of the systems approach, for it is still necessary for the auditor to verify ending balances on the balance sheet. The balance sheet audit approach is not discarded, but it is recognized as only part of a much broader systems approach. Specifically, the audit approach in the review of ending or resulting balances is dependent upon the system that generated the balances. When the system is considered strong, the audit effort in the verification of balances is reduced accordingly. On the other hand, if the system is inadequate, more audit time is devoted to the verification of balances.

There may appear to be an overlap between the integrated audit approach described earlier and the systems approach described above; however, it is really not important to distinguish between the two. The integrated audit approach is often adopted in practice, but each of the four phases of gathering evidence is accomplished without relating the results of each phase to the other phases. Only if the approach integrates the steps into a systems approach will the audit be efficient as well as effective.

The remainder of the chapter considers, in general, compliance tests and substantive tests.

COMPLIANCE TESTS

Chapters 6 and 7 discussed the initial study and evaluation of a client's internal control system. The purposes of the study and evaluation are (1) to enable the auditor to understand the system fully and (2) to identify its weaknesses and strengths as a basis for the design of subsequent audit procedures.

In the study and evaluation phase the auditor's approach is somewhat passive; i.e., the system is analyzed through making inquiries and observations. Conversely, the compliance tests are characterized by the auditor's actual testing of the internal control system. The objectives of the tests of compliance are (1) to determine whether the accounting system is functioning in a manner consistent with the description resulting from the study and evaluation of the internal control system, (2) to determine the nature and number of processing errors that have occurred in the system based on tests of transactions, and (3) to provide a basis for the design of the substantive tests.

The results of the study and evaluation of the internal control system provide the basis for construction of the tests of compliance. The timing, nature, and extent of compliance audit procedures must be consistent with these results.

Timing of procedures

Many audit procedures may be undertaken at various times during the year. Compliance tests are usually performed at an interim date rather than after the close of the fiscal year. Since these tests are a review of transactions to determine if the internal control system is working effectively, the auditor is not concerned with a resulting balance on a particular date. For example, he or she may select credit sales transactions processed on March 23 of the fiscal year for review. The auditor is not concerned with the balance of sales or accounts receivable on that date but rather with the manner in which the transactions were handled. As suggested above, the results of the compliance tests provide a basis for determining procedures to be used in the substantive test phase of the audit which, for the most part, occurs after the close of the fiscal year.

Performing the compliance tests at an interim date has a practical advantage. From January through mid-April most accounting firms witness their peak work load period because of the need to prepare tax returns and because, for many business organizations, the fiscal year ends on the last day of December. A properly organized accounting firm attempts to schedule the compliance tests at an interim date, probably in September or October for a calendar-year company, in order to lighten the work load after the end of the year.

The practical considerations of scheduling the tests of compliance at an interim date do not take precedence over the audit considerations. After a proper study of the internal control system, the auditor may conclude that the accounting control procedures are so inadequate that they cannot be relied upon. Under these circumstances the compliance tests are omitted, and the audit effort is concentrated in the substantive phase. In addition, *SAS No. 1*, Section 310.55, suggests that the auditor may decide not to perform the test of transactions if "the audit effort required to test compliance with the procedures to justify reliance on them in making substantive tests would exceed the reduction in effort that could be achieved by such reliance."

Finally, the nature of the account balance affects the timing of audit procedures. An account balance composed of numerous transactions is appropriate for performance of the tests of compliance. On the other hand, an account which results from a few relatively large transactions is more likely to be part of the audit procedures conducted during the substantive tests after the close of the year. In addition, some accounts have particular characteristics requiring that an audit procedure be performed during the substantive tests in order that sufficient competent evidence be obtained. For example, certain procedures in

292
**The audit
approach:
a systems
orientation**

the audit of cash and accounts payable are performed at or after the year end, whereas under certain conditions accounts receivable may be confirmed at an interim date as part of the interim test rather than as part of the year-end test.

Nature of procedures

In the compliance tests the auditor selects audit procedures to determine if the internal control system is functioning adequately. These procedures are derived from the audit techniques discussed in Chapter 5. Of the techniques listed in that chapter, the techniques of vouching, recomputation, and observation are the most appropriate in performing the compliance tests. *Vouching* refers to the auditor's inspection of documents that support an accounting transaction. The examination of a vendor's invoice in support of a fixed-asset addition is an example of vouching. *Recomputation* involves the auditor's independent verification of an arithmetic function initially performed by the client. Finally, the auditor can gain first-hand knowledge by physically observing an event.

The nature of the compliance audit procedure is determined by the accounting control under review. The auditor verifies that there is proper segregation of duties by observing tasks performed by the client's personnel. This may include determining who makes the bank deposit or who posts credit sales to the accounts receivable subsidiary ledger. On the other hand, verification of the execution and recording of transactions relies heavily upon the auditor's use of vouching. In determining whether a transaction was executed as authorized, the auditor may vouch the transaction by reviewing documents for proper signatures, initials, or other indications of authorization. Information contained on a document may be used by the auditor to determine if the transaction was recorded in a proper manner. For example, information appearing on an invoice provides evidence of the recording of the amount, classification of the transaction, and the date of the transaction. Finally, recomputation is used in conjunction with vouching, since the auditor inspects the documents in addition to determining the mathematical accuracy of the item.

Extent of procedures

The auditor's selection of transactions for review is drawn from a population that includes all transactions processed during the accounting period, in order to have proper representation of the universe. Since the compliance tests are usually performed at an interim date, this guideline must be modified. This modification results in the auditor selecting transactions from a partial year, perhaps from January 1 through September 30 for a calendar-year organization. When the auditor returns after the close of the year, a few transactions are selected from the untested portion of the year, which in the above example is October 1 through December 31, for review. In testing the intervening transactions, the auditor is not concerned with the number of transactions tested but rather with determining whether the internal control procedures have been changed or compliance with these controls has deteriorated.

The extent or size of the sample is subjective. As suggested in previous chapters, the auditor collects sufficient competent evidential matter upon which to formulate an opinion on the financial statements. Because of cost constraints and the nature of the attest function, the audit evidence collected is expected to be persuasive rather than convincing. There are of course general guidelines which only reinforce the observation that selection of the size of the sample is highly subjective. In fact, there are no guidelines that are specific, since each audit is unique and each auditor has a different expectation about the amount of evidence that must be collected. However, the study and evaluation of the internal control system is an important factor in determining the extent of the compliance test procedures. The stronger the internal control system appears to be, the smaller the required sample size. Other factors relevant to selection of the sample size are the results of the review of the client's environmental conditions, the audit significance of the accounting control, and the expected error rate. These factors were discussed in Chapter 8.

The audit approach

One objective of the compliance tests is to determine if the internal control procedures are being observed by the client. To achieve this objective the auditor defines a population which encompasses all transactions processed in a particular system, such as the cash disbursements system. Most accounting systems generate more than a single universe. The auditor selects a universe that is accessible and that can be determined to be intact. To be accessible the individual items of the universe must be subject to identification and therefore selectable. A population that is prenumbered meets the criterion of accessibility, since each sample item is identified by a unique number. For example, prenumbered checks written during an accounting period are an acceptable universe for the cash disbursements system. On the other hand, all vendor invoices processed during the same period do not meet the accessibility criterion. Usually these invoices are stored in numerous file cabinets, and it is not possible to identify each invoice specifically. In addition, the auditor must be able to conclude that the population is intact, since the sample must be drawn from the entire population. Again, prenumbered documents facilitate this objective, since the auditor need only review the numerical sequence of the documents used. To return to the above example of invoices processed, there is no way the auditor can be satisfied that the documents in the filing cabinets represent all the invoices processed during the accounting period. However, the use of prenumbered documents is not the only basis for sample selection that meets the accessibility and intactness requirements. Usually a detailed listing, such as all entries in the sales journal, is an acceptable basis for defining a population.

Having defined the population, the auditor selects transactions from this population for review. The review procedures are necessarily dependent upon the type of transaction being tested. Nonetheless, a general audit approach is applicable to the majority of transactions. The auditor prepares an audit program that follows a transaction from initial input to its eventual impact upon the

294
**The audit
approach:
a systems
orientation**

general ledger. Figure 9-1 is a representation of this process, which shows that at each processing or summarization step, the transaction is tested by the auditor through vouching or recomputation. This approach is often referred to as following the audit trail. Figure 9-1 is a simplification of the process and does not purport to include all possible compliance test procedures that may be utilized by the auditor.

Execution of the transaction is tested by the auditor to verify that the item has been properly authorized. Initial authorization may consist of the document being prepared or signed by appropriate client personnel. For example, a purchasing agent may sign a purchase order or the credit manager may initial a sales order for a credit sale. In many cases the initial authorization document generates the preparation of additional documents. For example, the approval of a credit sale may eventually generate the preparation of a sales invoice, a packing slip, and a bill of lading. In any case, the document or documents that initiate the movement of assets or the recording of a journal entry are inspected by the auditor. If there is more than one document, the auditor compares them to determine the consistency of data. Also, during the execution of a transaction the data are likely to be processed or manipulated in some manner, such as the pricing and extension of dollar amounts on a sales invoice or the client's verification of the mathematical accuracy of a vendor's invoice. The audit program has procedures to test these processing steps, including the auditor's recomputation of additions and multiplications performed by the client in the preparation of a sales invoice.

As shown in Figure 9-1, the auditor constructs an audit approach that tests the recording of transactions as well as their execution. The documentation generated in execution of the transaction is used in substantiating the recording of the item in original-entry journals and subsidiary journals. Supportive documents of a credit sale may include a customer order, sales invoice, packing slip, and bill of lading. Information such as customer name, invoice amount, and transaction date per these documents is compared to the corresponding entry in the sales journal and subsequent posting to the accounts receivable subsidiary ledger card. At this point in the recording of the item, a single transaction is not processed on an individual basis, but rather some summary processing occurs by grouping similar transactions. The auditor follows the transaction from its initial starting point to its eventual impact on the general ledger. However, a single transaction is not posted directly to the general ledger but rather is usually totaled on a monthly basis with other transactions and then posted to the general ledger. At this point the auditor tests the mathematical accuracy of the client's summarization for one or more months. In the case of the sales transaction discussed above, the auditor may foot the sales journal for the months of March, June, and September and trace these totals to the debit column of the accounts receivable control account and to the credit column of the sales control account.

As part of the compliance tests the auditor reviews the accounting records for unusual items. An internal control system is constructed to process routine transactions. The use of specialized journals is a prime element of such an approach. However, transactions that are unusual need to be identified and

Figure 9-1

Compliance Test: A Generalization of the Audit Approach

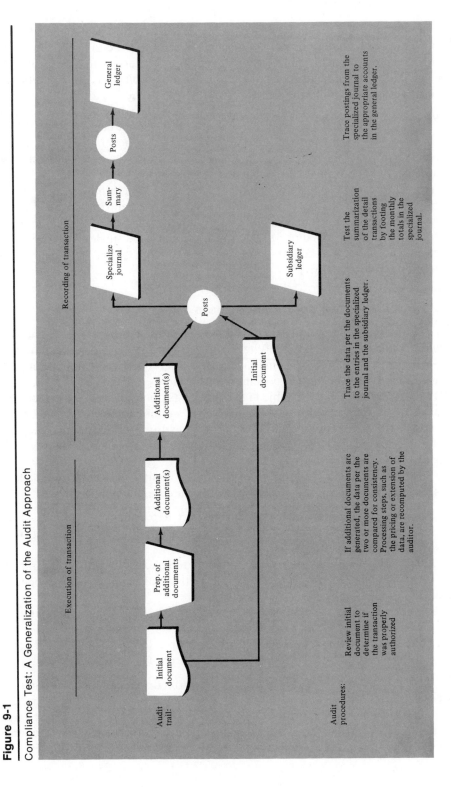

296
The audit approach: a systems orientation

usually examined on a more thorough basis. What constitutes an unusual item depends upon the nature of a client's business and the structure of the internal control system. The audit approach for identifying such items consists of scanning the accounting records for items that in the auditor's opinion require additional investigation. The ability to identify such items is gained in part through experience. However, most auditors are careful to note the source of the posting in the accounting records and the relative size of the amount being posted. When the auditor reviews the control accounts receivable ledger account, debits sources should be referred to the sales journal and, in addition, there probably should be one posting for each month of the year. A posting source other than the sales journal should be investigated. Another factor used in determining an unusual item is the size of the posting in relationship to other entries. If the client's normal transactions include sales of a few hundred dollars, an entry in the sales journal in excess of $5000 or $10,000 would probably be singled out for investigation. In general, the auditor is inquisitive, and items out of the ordinary are noted for further review.

EDP impact on the compliance tests

Chapter 7 discussed the impact of EDP on the internal control model and the auditor's study and evaluation of the client's system. It was emphasized in that chapter that the EDP controls must be tested when they are an important part of the overall internal control system. In performing compliance tests where an EDP system is involved, the objective of the tests does not change. In fact, the general audit approach does not change, because the auditor still reviews the processing of transactions from their initial execution to their ultimate impact on the general ledger. However, an EDP system presents unique problems which must be considered.

The following is a list of procedures that the auditor may perform on a test basis in an internal control system with automated equipment:

- Input control totals generated in the user department are compared to totals recorded by the independent control group upon the receipt of a batch of transactions.
- Transactions processed by the computer and chosen for review are traced to original documents to determine if the transactions were properly authorized.
- Information per the original documents is compared to computer-generated entries in journals and ledgers.
- Process control totals generated are compared to input controls and controls recorded by the independent control group.

The above audit procedures may be performed manually by the auditor. Where controls are incorporated into the computer software, the audit approach is changed. In this case the auditor prepares a *test deck* or tape of transactions to test these controls. A test deck or test tape is composed of transactions selected by the auditor to determine whether programmed controls are in operation. The transactions may include actual transactions, fictitious transactions created by the auditor, or a combination of both. With a thorough understanding of the EDP system the auditor is able to predict the results of processing the transactions. Controls in which the auditor is interested may include:

Limit checks: Transactions that exceed a certain dollar limit must have special approval.

Valid code: Transactions that are coded with an invalid number are not processed.

Missing data: Transactions that do not have complete data are not processed.

Sign test: Depending upon the nature of the transaction, only transactions with the proper mathematical sign are processed.

When errors occur in this phase of the EDP compliance testing, the auditor carefully considers the impact of such errors on the adequacy of the internal control system. With the concentration of duties in the EDP section, which are normally dispersed to other departments in a non-EDP environment, the potential effects of errors are naturally magnified.

SUBSTANTIVE TESTS

Similar to the tests of compliance, the substantive tests are used to collect corroborative evidence concerning financial transactions. *SAS No. 1,* Section 320.70, states that the purpose of the substantive tests is "to obtain evidence as to the validity and the propriety of accounting treatment of transactions and balances or, conversely, of errors or irregularities therein." Thus substantive tests are concerned with substantiating a balance that appears on the financial statements. For example, the auditor may confirm an accounts receivable, count inventory items, or inspect all the documents that support a sale. The first two audit procedures are concerned with balances that appear on the balance sheet, and the last one with a balance that appears on the income statement. As explained in Chapter 5, there is an overlap between the performance of the tests of transactions, considered part of the tests of compliance, and the substantive tests. For example, during the tests of transactions the auditor may select a sales invoice for testing. The invoice may be tested for proper authorization, mathematical accuracy, and proper posting to the sales journal and eventual summarization and posting to the general ledger. Such procedures obviously validate part of the sales account balance and part of the accounts receivable balance if the amount has not been collected at the end of the year.

Thus based on the above discussion it is technically correct to classify the tests of transactions as part of the substantive tests. However, from a practical point of view the tests of transactions are usually performed at the interim date

298
The audit approach: a systems orientation

when the tests of compliance are performed. For the purpose of this discussion the tests of transactions are considered part of the tests of compliance, and this is the approach observed in Chapters 10 through 16. Again from a practical point, the auditor performs the tests of transactions to determine the extent of the errors occurring in the processing of data. The auditor is less interested in testing a balance at this point.

Timing of procedures

The discussion of the timing of compliance audit procedures pointed out that some procedures may be performed at an interim date or after the close of the fiscal year. For example, most auditors perform the tests of transactions at the interim date. Contrarily, some procedures must be performed at or after the end of the year. Thus the practical aspects of the conduct of an audit and the nature of an account or a transaction play a dominant role in the timing of audit procedures whether they involve compliance or substantive testing. Certain tests may be performed at either an interim date or after the conclusion of the accounting period. These procedures are considered substantive tests in nature but they can be performed at an interim date.

In order to perform a year-end procedure at an interim date, the client's internal control system must be strong, and the results of the compliance tests must confirm this strength. When these circumstances exist, the auditor examines the interim account balance on the balance sheet in the same manner he or she would examine the account if it were being reviewed at the end of the accounting period. Figure 9-2 summarizes the audit approach that is taken. Once the auditor is satisfied with the account balance at the interim date, it is necessary for him or her to return to the account after the end of the fiscal year. At this time the auditor reviews the summarization, usually from a special journal, of transactions that increased and decreased the interim balance. He or she selects a few transactions and performs the compliance tests. If the results are satisfactory, it is concluded that the internal control system is still strong and that the activity after the interim date is authentic. In addition, the auditor obtains a detail listing of items that constitute the year-end balance. This listing is footed, scanned for unusual items or amounts, and compared to the detail listing audited at the interim date. Again, if the auditor finds no major discrepancies, there is no need to perform the substantive tests at year end. However, when problems are discovered, additional audit steps are performed which include the use of substantive test procedures. It should be noted that only some accounts can be audited in this manner. This approach as it relates to the audit of accounts receivable is discussed in Chapter 11.

Extent of procedures

The degree to which substantive audit procedures are employed is always a difficult problem. There are at least three major factors the auditor considers in formulating a decision. Initially the strengths and weaknesses of the internal

Figure 9-2

Performing substantive tests at an interim date

		TIME OF AUDIT PROCEDURES	NATURE OF PROCEDURES
Account balance at the interim date	$XXX	Interim	Substantive tests approach
Add: Routine transactions subsequent to the interim date that increase the account balance	XX	Year end	Compliance tests approach (tests of transactions)
Less: Routine transactions subsequent to the interim date that decrease the account balance	XX	Year end	Compliance tests approach (tests of transactions)
Account balance at year-end date	$XXX	Year end	Substantive tests approach

control system as validated by the compliance tests determine the reliability of the accounting data generated in account balances. The stronger the system, the less likely the possibility of a material error or errors occurring in the processing of the transactions. In addition, the materiality of the account balance in part determines the degree of audit exposure associated with a particular account. An account with a relatively small balance usually requires less audit effort than one with a large balance. Finally, the composition of the account balance affects the extent of audit procedures. When an account on the balance sheet is made up of numerous small items, the auditor usually tests fewer individual items than when the balance contains a few items with relatively large balances. In the final analysis the auditor examines a sufficient number of items to be satisfied that the account balance is prepared in accordance with generally accepted accounting principles.

Nature of procedures

To determine the validity and propriety of an account balance, the evidence-gathering techniques of confirmation, observation, vouching, and recomputation are especially useful. The asset being audited and the characteristics of the audit environment are two important elements in selection of the specific audit procedures to be utilized. When the balance is created based on a relationship with an independent party, the auditor may employ the confirmation technique. Examples of account balances for which the confirmation technique is applicable are confirmation of a customer's account balance and confirmation of client inventory held by a consignee. When physical evidence of an account balance exists on the premises of the client, the observation technique is employed. The observation of inventory and the observation of fixed assets are examples.

Although evidence gathered through confirmation and observation is very competent, it is seldom sufficient to substantiate a balance. Vouching is often necessary to support the evidence gained through these two techniques. For

300
**The audit
approach:
a systems
orientation**

example, an inventory item that is observed is validated as to existence but is not validated in other respects such as ownership and historical cost. By examining the supporting documentation consisting of a vendor's invoice and a receiving report, the auditor can satisfy these other audit objectives. However, the technique of vouching is not limited to a supportive role, since in some areas of the substantive tests it is the primary source of evidence. For example, in the audit of liabilities an auditor performs a search for unrecorded liabilities, which consists partly of the review of documentation. On the other hand, recomputation is entirely supportive of other audit techniques. It may include testing of the mathematical accuracy of inventory summarization sheets, bank reconciliations, or allocation of the cost of prepayments to the appropriate accounting period.

In addition to the account balance under investigation, the characteristics of the audit environment impact the nature of audit procedures used in testing balances. In this respect the auditor takes into consideration the effectiveness and efficiency of audit procedures under the circumstances. His or her primary concern is with effectiveness, since this refers to the competency and sufficiency of audit evidence. However, the auditor is willing to accept persuasive evidence, which takes into consideration the cost of obtaining evidence, rather than insisting upon conclusive evidence. A variety of methods can be employed to gather evidence, but the cost in terms of audit effort must be considered. For example, an auditor must determine the existence of accounts receivable. The utilization of mailed confirmations meets this objective but, to avoid the possibility of misunderstanding on the part of the client's customer and to validate that there is a real customer and not a phony mail drop, the auditor may call the customer on the telephone and explain the situation in detail before the confirmation is mailed. This of course significantly increases the audit effort. The question that must be answered is whether the significant increase in audit effort is justified by an equal increase in the competency of audit evidence. The auditor constantly weighs the factors of audit effectiveness and efficiency in the selection of audit procedures.

Under some circumstances an auditor may not have the expertise or appropriate experience to perform an audit procedure adequately as part of the validation of an account balance. *SAS No. 11*, Paragraph 3, lists the following as illustrations of such circumstances:

- Valuation (e.g., works of art, special drugs, and restricted securities).
- Determination of physical characteristics relating to quantity on hand or condition (e.g., mineral reserves or materials stored in piles above ground).
- Determination of amounts derived by using specialized techniques or methods (e.g., certain actuarial determinations).
- Interpretation of technical requirements, regulations, or agreements (e.g., the potential significance of contracts or other legal documents, or legal title to property).

In such cases the auditor may enlist the services of specialists, such as geologists, engineers, and actuaries, in the collection of sufficient and competent evidential matter.

In selecting the specialist, the auditor inquires into his or her background and technical competence to ensure that it is appropriate in the formulation of an opinion on the financial statements. Normally the auditor seeks a specialist who is independent of the client. When the specialist is related to the client, the auditor determines whether the findings of the specialist are reasonable and consistent with evidence gathered in other phases of the audit. Additionally, the auditor reviews and tests calculations, summarizations of data, and assumptions made by the specialist. When the auditor is not satisfied with the results or is unable to understand the process and accept its reasonableness, then an independent specialist is engaged. In some cases it may be that a consensus of an opinion among specialists and the auditor cannot be achieved, or it may be impossible for any specialist to evaluate the evidence. Under these circumstances the auditor considers modifying the audit report by issuing a disclaimer of opinion or a qualified opinion. However, when the auditor relies upon the specialist's report and is satisfied with the findings, the auditor's report is not modified. This prohibits a reference in the scope paragraph to the role of the expert in the audit.

Nature, timing, and extent: internal audit function

In Chapter 6 the role of the internal auditor in the internal control model was considered. The internal audit function was shown to be a necessary and vital part of the internal control system. In addition to this aspect of internal auditing, the auditor may use the internal auditor or the results of the internal auditor's investigation in performance of the compliance and substantive tests. For example, the independent auditor may ask the internal auditor to test a sample of sales invoices prepared during the year to determine if each invoice has been properly posted to the sales journal. Additionally, the internal audit staff may be asked to help the auditors in the observation of inventory.

As a prerequisite to use of the internal audit staff, the independent auditor determines the competence and objectivity of its members. Competence can be determined by reviewing the educational background and experience of each internal auditor. Also, through personal interview, the independent auditor can verify that the internal auditor understands the role and the needs of the independent auditor. As employees of the client, the internal audit staff is evaluated as to its ability to be objective in the review of client records and financial statements. *SAS No. 9,* makes the following comment relative to objectivity:

> When considering the objectivity of internal auditors, the independent auditor should consider the organizational level to which internal auditors report the results of their work and the organizational level to which they report administratively. This frequently is an indication of the extent of their ability to act independently of the individuals responsible for the functions being audited. One method for judging internal auditors' objectivity is to review the recommendations made in their reports.

There is an inherent limitation in the use of client personnel and, for this reason, the use of internal auditors is restricted to accounts that are only a minor part of the audit. Furthermore, accounts likely to contain numerous errors are investigated by the independent auditor. In any case, the results of the internal

302
**The audit
approach:
a systems
orientation**

audit staff's tests of transactions or test of balances is reviewed carefully by the independent auditor.

The audit approach

The specific audit procedure used in the substantive tests for each account balance is determined by many factors, including the very nature of the account itself. Depending upon the uniqueness of a particular account, the auditor selects audit procedures that provide competent evidential matter to an extent that an informed opinion can be formulated. However, it is possible to generalize about the substantive audit approach so as to describe a logical approach that can be used as a guide in the audit of account balances. This can be achieved by identifying four audit objectives that are common to the verification of a balance sheet amount. In constructing an audit program the auditor selects auditing procedures to achieve these objectives. Specifically, these audit objectives are existence, valuation, cutoff, and disclosure. In many cases the auditor's performance of a specific audit procedure partially achieves two or more of these objectives. This causes no concern, since the audit objectives are not to be envisioned as mutually exclusive but rather as elements of the overall objective to determine whether an account is presented in accordance with generally accepted accounting principles.

EXISTENCE

In the verification of assets, liabilities, and owners' equity accounts, the auditor must be satisfied that the existence of the item is consistent with assertions made in the accounting records. Although the existence objective is applicable to each balance to be substantiated, the audit approach is different, depending upon the classification of the balance as an asset, liability, or owners' equity account. In the audit of assets, the audit exposure is most apparent in the possibility that the asset amount is overstated rather than understated. For this reason the auditor focuses on the assertions made in the financial records and selects audit techniques to verify these balances. For example, in the review of the accounts receivable balance, the focal point is the trial balance of receivables, and from this listing specific balances are selected for verification. On the other hand, a liability account presents the greatest audit exposure in the event that an existing liability is not recorded. A listing and subsequent verification of the individual items in a liability account is not of prime importance. Instead, the auditor uses other audit evidence sources to determine that all liabilities have been recorded. In the case of trade accounts payable, the auditor vouches transactions processed at the beginning of the following accounting period to see if these transactions were actually liabilities of the fiscal year being audited.

Ownership is considered part of the existence objective for assets, since existence is not limited simply to the physical presence of an item. The auditor's personal observation of an item confirms its existence but does not identify its owner. To determine that the item is on the list of the client's assets requires that additional audit procedures be employed. Usually this is accomplished by reviewing documentations that may be in the form of a vendor's invoice or a more formal document, such as a deed for real estate. In some instances it may be necessary to engage the services of a lawyer to determine the ownership of an asset.

Finally, the existence objective includes the auditor's recomputation of balances or allocation. For example, this includes footing of the accounts receivable trial balance or testing of the extensions on the inventory listing sheets.

VALUATION

Valuation, as an accounting term, has a variety of meanings. Fundamentally, it refers to the concept of historical cost, which is a basic premise in modern financial accounting. Thus assets and equities are recorded in the amounts validated by an arm's-length transaction. In the case of nonmonetary assets, whose costs are eventually allocated to the income statement in the form of expenses, historical cost is reported net of the cumulative amortization or depreciation. The allocation process is validated by recomputation. However, the audit approach is complicated by the existence of a variety of acceptable allocation methods, such as the use of straight-line and accelerated methods of amortization. The valuation of some nonmonetary items is further complicated by the applicability of the lower-of-cost-or-market rule. For example, when an inventory item's cost is not recoverable, the auditor determines its replacement cost and net realizable value. In this latter case valuation assumes a definition more consistent with a layperson's interpretation.

The valuation of a monetary asset begins with a determination of its historical cost. However, the asset may be reported at lower than historical cost or net realizable value, which requires that the auditor be concerned with two valuation figures. In the case of accounts receivable he or she determines the historical cost of the account and estimates an allowance amount that reduces it to a net realizable value basis.

In a similar fashion, liabilities must be valued. Liabilities may be classified as fixed amounts, estimated amounts, and contingencies. Fixed liabilities present no real valuation problem, assuming they have been identified, since the amount is fixed by contract or other documentation, such as in the trade accounts payable or a mortgage. However, a valuation problem exists in the audit of estimated liabilities, which represent obligations that exist but the amount of the obligations is not fixed. Under these circumstances the auditor employs the ratio and trend analysis technique, allowing modifications for current changes in the client's environment. A *contingent liability* is defined in *Statement of Financial Accounting Standard No. 5,* Paragraph 1, as "an existing condition, situation, or set of circumstances involving uncertainty as to . . . possible loss . . . to an enterprise that will ultimately be resolved when one or more future events occur or fail to occur." This *Statement* requires the disclosure of "an estimate of the possible loss or range of loss or state that such an estimate cannot be made" in the case of loss contingency. The auditor collects evidence to be reasonably sure that the disclosure requirement is met.

Other valuation problems must be considered in the audit of liabilities, such

304
The audit approach: a systems orientation

as the estimated obligation under capitalized lease agreements and determination of the present value of certain liabilities where imputed interest must be recognized.

CUTOFF

The term "cutoff" refers to the general accounting control objective of recording transactions in the accounting period in which they are executed. To ensure that there is proper valuation of assets and proper measurement of income, the auditor is concerned with the client's achievement of a proper cutoff. Although cutoff accounting controls are considered part of the internal control system of a client, the auditor is not concerned with determining whether a proper cutoff is achieved at the end of each month or other interim accounting periods but rather with the quality of cutoff at the end of the year. In addition, most organizations are not concerned with implemented cutoff accounting controls as part of their normal recording routine. Thus cutoff procedures may not be comprehensive, or they may not be applied to an extent that client personnel are completely familiar with them. The auditor incorporates audit procedures into the audit plan to determine whether a proper cutoff is achieved.

The general audit approach in the test of a proper cutoff focuses on the auditor's examination of transactions recorded a few days before and a few days after the end of the accounting period. For most engagements the auditor is not able to examine every transaction that occurred during this period because of the cost involved. Therefore he or she usually draws a sample from two separate universes. One universe consists of the file or collection of documents generated by execution of the transaction. The other universe is the appropriate book or journal of original entry. These two universes are compared to determine if they are consistent. For example, in the inventory cutoff audit procedure, the auditor selects a sample of receiving reports prepared during the last five days of the year. Based on the date entered in the receiving report, he or she traces this inventory receipt to the line-item entry in the purchase journal or raw materials ledger. If the purchase was not recorded in the December journal for a calendar-year company, a cutoff error exists. The auditor uses a similar approach in tracing from the purchase journal to the appropriate receiving report. This is only part of the inventory cutoff test. A more thorough discussion is reserved for Chapter 12.

DISCLOSURE

The third standard of reporting requires that financial statements represent an adequate disclosure of information. Full and adequate disclosure in financial statements encompasses many elements including footnote disclosures, parenthetical comments, terminology, classification, and the format of financial statements. *APB Opinion No. 22*, "Disclosure of Accounting Policies," formalized the need for disclosing accounting policies and principles and specifically encouraged disclosure of the following items:

- A selection from existing acceptable alternatives.
- Principles and methods peculiar to the industry in which the reporting entity

operates, even if such principles and methods are predominantly followed in that industry.

- Unusual or innovative applications of generally accepted accounting principles (and, as applicable, of principles and methods peculiar to the industry in which the reporting entity operates).

The board recommended that this information be disclosed in a separate summary of significant accounting policies preceding the footnotes, or as the initial footnote. Recent pronouncements by the FASB and the SEC attest to a significant increase in the amount of data that must be disclosed. The auditor is aware of these disclosure requirements and sees that they are met through the client's preparation of footnotes and parenthetical comments and the selection of appropriate accounting terminology.

The classification of accounts and the format of financial accounting statements contribute to the overall accounting concept of full disclosure. Financial accounts reflect the nature of transactions that impact the account. For example, the designation "accounts receivable" implies that an account is the result of transactions between the client and its customers in the normal course of operation. For this reason, loans to officers and employees and other miscellaneous receivables are not to be included in this account balance if they are material. The summarization or grouping of accounts and their display constitute the format of financial statements. Relative to asset presentation, groupings include current assets, property, plant and equipment, intangible assets, and other investments. The auditor must be satisfied that these accounts are properly classified. Similar classification schemes are appropriate for the remainder of the balance sheet, as well as the income statement and the statement of change in financial position.

Impact of EDP on the substantive tests

Earlier in this chapter and in Chapter 7, the role of EDP was considered. The discussion focused on the impact of EDP on the general principles of the internal control model and the use of this system in the tests of compliance. This section is devoted to still another aspect of EDP—the impact of EDP on the substantive tests. In the substantive tests the auditor is concerned with the validation of balances, and in many cases he or she can use computer capabilities to assist in this phase of the audit. In this respect, the auditor is more interested in the computer as a helpful tool rather than in evaluating and testing the system.

Basically, the auditor has two alternative approaches in utilizing the computer. Special programs may be written by the client or members of the audit staff. These programs have the advantage that they are designed specifically for a client or an industry and do not present a problem of applicability or adaptability. The preparation of such programs is often costly and has limited use as far as other audit clients are concerned. To mitigate these disadvantages an alternative approach has been developed which utilizes a generalized audit software package. As the name implies, the package is general and can be used in the audit of many clients that have a variety of computer hardware configu-

306
The audit approach: a systems orientation

rations. An additional advantage of the package is that it does not require a considerable knowledge of computers in order to use it. The sofeware package is limited, since it is a packaged program and is not adaptable to every client or capable of performing every audit test an engagement may require. On balance, though, it has proven very popular, which is evidenced by the fact that many firms and the AICPA have developed their own version for utilization. The AICPA's version is available to medium-sized and small firms which find the cost of developing such a package exorbitant and redundant.

The generalized audit software package is considered in the following discussion. Many of the comments made are applicable to specially prepared audit software packages.

GENERALIZED AUDIT SOFTWARE PACKAGE

The generalized audit software package is appropriately referred to as a file analyzer. In essence, it performs many of the functions an auditor would perform if the data were in hard-copy form instead of stored electronically. Specifically, most software packages can perform the following operations:

Computational routine: The basic mathematical functions (addition, subtraction, multiplication, and division) can check the arithmetic accuracy within the file. (Example: An auditor can test the extension of every line item in the inventory summarization or perpetual inventory cards.)

Sample selection routine: Individual items contained within a data file can be sequentially selected based upon the auditor's specification. (Example: Every fourth account in the accounts receivable file can be selected for investigation.)

Stratification routine: Data can be stratified or segregated based upon a specified characteristic. (Example: Customer balances can be segregated by an absolute dollar amount.)

Comparison routine: Data from two or more sets can be compared. (Example: Inventory test counts made by the auditor can be compared to perpetual inventory records.)

Confirmation routine: Confirmation requests can be made on preprinted forms ready for mailing.

Summarize routine: Data stored at different locations within the file can be combined. (Example: Inventory listed by location, such as by branch, can be summarized by part number for all locations.)

Before data files can be analyzed by the use of a generalized audit software package, the auditor must be knowledgeable of the client's hardware and record

Figure 9-3

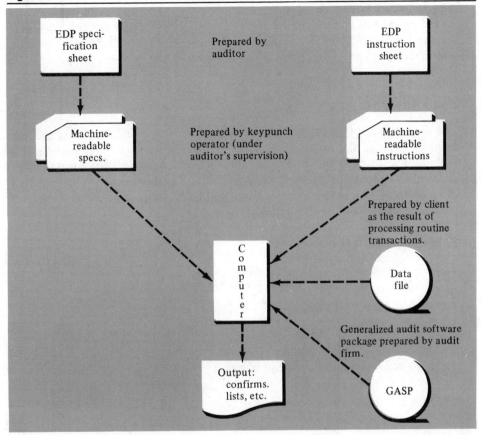

formats. Information such as file storage, magnetic tape or punched card, the storage of data in fixed or variable length, and the length of the data record must be known. This information is obtained by interviewing client personnel and is converted into a machine-readable form so that the self-contained operating system of the software package can be adapted to the client's particular EDP environment. In addition, operation specifications identify what routines are to be performed through the use of certain key words such as "foot." These key words are translated into a machine-readable form. At this point the auditor has the following elements:

1. Machine-coded specifications concerning the client's EDP system
2. Machine-coded instructions identifying the routine to be performed
3. The client's data file, a copy of the client's data file, or information abstracted from the client's data file
4. The generalized audit software package

The computer run is then performed. Output, such as printed confirmations or

308
**The audit
approach:
a systems
orientation**

certain listings, is generated by the EDP system and by the auditor. For example, the computation routine may be employed to verify the extensions on the inventory listings and to list any errors over a certain dollar amount. Based on the number of errors and the magnitude of the errors, the auditor decides whether additional audit procedures are to be employed. The process is illustrated in Figure 9-3.

CONCLUDING REMARKS

The discussion in this chapter concerned the tests of compliance and the substantive tests as the final two phases of the integrated audit approach. The material presented to this point provides the foundation for a discussion of the audit of a system and the balances generated by this system. Chapter 10 is devoted to cash systems, cash receipts and cash disbursements, and the cash balance that appears on the balance sheet.

EXERCISES AND PROBLEMS

9-1. Are the same evidence-gathering techniques generally used in the analytical stages of the audit and the corroborative stages of the audit? Explain.

9-2. What is meant by the integrated audit approach?

9-3. Why is it important that the auditor use a systems approach in the performance of an audit?

9-4. Is a systems audit approach more appropriate for a large corporation or for a small business? Explain.

9-5. Must the auditor perform the tests of compliance? Explain.

9-6. Why must the study and evaluation of the internal control system be made before performing the tests of compliance?

9-7. Comment on the following quotation from *SAS No. 1*, Section 320.56:

> In practice, auditing procedures often concurrently provide evidence of compliance with accounting control procedures as well as evidence required for substantive purposes.

9-8. In determining the sample size for the tests of compliance, what factors are considered by the auditor?

9-9. What is the audit trail?

9-10. To audit the propriety of a processed transaction, the auditor follows the transaction from input to impact on the financial stages. Discuss the typical processing phases for a transaction. Explain how the auditor verifies each phase.

9-11. Must the compliance tests performed by the auditor encompass procedures that are computerized? Explain.

9-12. To determine that depletion expense is properly computed, the auditor must be capable of reading and interpreting geological reports. Is this correct? Explain.

9-13. In the auditor's performance of the substantive tests, what are the four basic objectives?

9-14. Is a generalized audit software package more helpful to the auditor in performing the tests of compliance or in performing the substantive tests? Explain.

309
Exercises and problems

9-15. What routines can be performed by a generalized audit software package?

9-16. You are engaged in your second annual examination of the financial statements of the Claren Corporation, a medium-sized manufacturing company with 25 stockholders that manufactures optical instruments. During the audit the following matters come to your attention.

Part A. A new controller was employed six months ago. He also serves as office manager but apparently exercises little disciplinary control over his 15 subordinates, who include a cashier, two bookkeepers, a supply room attendant, and two technicians who show the company products in a factory salesroom attached to the office. The office staff seems to be continually talking about social matters, visiting, making personal telephone calls, or engaged in other private matters that are generally indicative of inefficiency. You know that the office has fallen about three weeks behind in its accounting work for the year 1965. On numerous occasions you have been unable to obtain answers to questions that arose during the audit because the person who could supply the information was out of the office.

Required
1. Discuss what you would do when you found that you were frequently unable to obtain answers to questions because the person who could supply the information was out of the office.
2. Discuss your responsibility for drawing attention to the apparent general inefficiency of office operations.
3. What steps would you take if you found numerous errors in the books?
4. What effect, if any, would the errors have upon your opinion?

Part B. The president's salary has been increased substantially over that of the prior year by action of the board of directors. Her present salary is much greater than salaries paid to presidents of companies of comparable size and is clearly excessive. You determine that the method of computing the president's salary was changed for the year under audit. In prior years the president's salary was consistently based on sales. In the latest year, however, it was based on net income before income taxes. The Claren Corporation is in a cyclical industry and would have had an extremely profitable year except that the increase in the president's salary siphoned off much of the income that would have accrued to the stockholders. The president is a substantial stockholder.

Required
1. Discuss your responsibility for disclosing this situation.
2. Discuss the effect, if any, that the situation has upon your opinion as to

a. the fairness of the presentation of the financial statements
b. the consistency of the application of accounting principles   (AICPA Adapted)

9-17. For each of the following audit procedures, determine whether the procedure is more likely part of the tests of compliance, including tests of transactions, or the substantive tests.

1. Compare the detail of the cash receipts list to the cash receipts journal.
2. Count and list the cash on hand.
3. Confirm accounts receivable.
4. Determine the adequacy of the allowance for uncollectible accounts.

310
**The audit
approach:
a systems
orientation**

5. Compare information per the bill of lading to the sales journal and sales invoice.
6. Review customer orders for credit approval.
7. Apply the lower of FIFO cost or market test to inventory prices.
8. Review the cutoff data for purchases and sales transactions.
9. For selected purchases, trace information per the vendor invoice to the subsidiary accounts payable ledger card.
10. Perform a search for unrecorded accounts payable.

9-18. In auditing the financial statements of a manufacturing company, which were prepared from data processed by EDP equipment, the CPA has found that the traditional audit trail has been obscured. As a result the CPA may place increased emphasis upon overall checks of the data under audit. These overall checks, which are also applied in auditing visibly posted accounting records, include the computation of ratios, which are compared to prior year ratios or to industrywide norms. Examples of such overall checks or ratios are computation of the rate of inventory turnover and computation of the number of days' sales in receivables.

Required
1. Discuss the advantages to the CPA of using ratios as overall checks in an audit.
2. In addition to the computations given above, list the ratios a CPA may compute during an audit as overall checks on balance sheet accounts and related nominal accounts. For each ratio listed name the two (or more) accounts used in its computation.
3. When a CPA discovers that there has been a significant change in a ratio when compared to the prior year's ratio, he or she considers the possible reasons for the change. Give possible reasons for the following significant changes in ratios:

a. The rate of inventory turnover (the ratio of cost of sales and average inventory) has decreased from the prior year's rate.
b. The number of days' sales in receivables (the ratio of average daily accounts receivable and sales) has increased over that of the prior year.

(AICPA Adapted)

9-19. In connection with an examination of the financial statements of Houston Wholesalers, Inc., for the year ended June 30, 1971, a CPA performs several cutoff tests.

Required
1. a. What is a cutoff test?
   b. Why must cutoff tests be performed for both the beginning and the end of the audit period?
2. The CPA wishes to test Houston's sales cutoff at June 30, 1979. Describe the steps that should be included in this test.
3. The CPA obtains a July 10, 1979, bank statement directly from the bank. Explain how it will be used:
   a. in a review of the June 30, 1979, bank reconciliation
   b. to obtain other audit information

(AICPA Adapted)

9-20. You have completed your examination of the financial statements of Rumson Corporation for the year ended December 31, 1979, and are prepared to render an unqualified short-form auditor's report.

The board of directors now requests that you instead render your opinion in a long-form report and proposes that it include (1) a schedule of gross profit by branches, (2) a statement of funds flow and changes in working capital for the corporation, (3) a schedule of inventories by location, and (4) the auditor's accounts receivable confirmation statistics.

The board also indicates that Rumson's northeastern branch may be sold in the near future and requests a separate report containing the balance sheet and income statement for that branch.

311
Exercises and problems

Rumson Corporation has a main office and 14 branches. Total 1979 sales aggregated $5 million for the corporation, and the sales of individual branches ranged from $200,000 to $500,000. You visited 7 branches, including the 3 largest, and conducted surprise tests of the records maintained at each, including cash on hand, accounts receivable, inventories, sales, payrolls, and certain expenses. All the branches of the corporation exercise the same degree of control over operations and maintain the same records. At the main office you conducted supplementary audit tests for all branches. The northeastern branch, which had sales of $300,000 was not selected by you for a 1979 visit, since it was visited by an internal auditor in August 1979 and your October 1979 visit revealed that the records were in good condition.

Required

1. Explain (a) why the auditor should learn the client's report requirements early in the engagement, and (b) what steps can be taken to assure that this information is received when it is timely.

2. Describe the additional audit steps or other work, if any, necessary to enable you to comply with the board's wishes for each of the following additional report requirements:

   a. Schedule of gross profit by branches
   b. Statement of funds flow and statement of changes in working capital
   c. Schedule of inventories by location
   d. Accounts receivable confirmation statistics
   e. Northeastern branch financial statements

3. Assume that the Rumson board refuses to allow you to do any additional work for inventories by location. Because this schedule must be a part of the report including your unqualified opinion on the financial statements, you will be required to explain the status of the inventory schedule above your signature in the report.

   a. Why is such an explanation necessary?
   b. List the facts you would include in the aforementioned explanation in order to conform with generally accepted reporting standards.   (AICPA Adapted)

9-21. *Part A. SAS No. 9* states that certain work of the internal auditors may be substituted for work normally performed by the independent auditor. Listed below are several audit procedures performed during an engagement.

   1. Review the year-end bank reconciliation for the payroll account.
   2. Foot the inventory listing based on the client's physical count.
   3. Evaluate the adequacy of accounting controls for the credit sales system.
   4. Test the client's aging of accounts receivable.
   5. Investigate several material-related party transactions.
   6. Vouch expenditures for the travel and entertainment account.
   7. Review cash discounts and freight allowances.
   8. Determine the number of accounts receivable confirmations to be sent.
   9. Count petty cash.
   10. Design the substantive tests audit program for property, plant, and equipment.

Required

1. For each of the audit procedures listed above, determine which can be performed by the internal audit staff.

312
The audit approach: a systems orientation

2. For audit procedures performed by the internal audit staff, what is the responsibility of the independent auditor?

Part B. Assume that the audit budget for the (1) review and evaluation of the credit sales system, (2) performance of the tests of compliance, and (3) performance of the substantive tests for accounts receivable is about 250 hours.

Required

1. What procedures in general may be performed by the internal audit staff?
2. Of the 250-hour budget, how many hours may be performed by the internal audit staff?

9-22. You have just been hired as a junior accountant for the accounting firm of Brown and Dawn. For your first assignment you have become part of the audit team performing an audit of Moore Manufacturing Company. The senior on the job instructs you to write a substantive audit program for the account entitled "Marketable Securities." The only investment in this account is represented by the following general ledger card:

INVESTMENT: 100 SHARES OF IBM COMMON STOCK

9/15/78 Purchased
100 shares $25,000

You recall from your intermediate accounting class that *Financial Accounting Standards Board (FASB) Statement No. 12* discusses the proper accounting for certain investments.

The audit opinion is to be issued on the financial statements for the calendar year ended December 31, 1979.

Required: Prepare an audit program for the investment account. After each procedure note whether the procedure is related to the (1) existence, (2) valuation, (3) cutoff, or (4) classification and disclosure objective.

9-23. In the performance of the substantive tests, a variety of audit techniques are used. Listed below are several of these procedures.

1. Confirm accounts receivable with customers.
2. Foot the accounts receivable aged trial balance.
3. Observe the physical count of inventory.
4. Trace bills of lading prepared on the last day of the fiscal year to the sales journal.
5. Inspect marketable securities on hand.
6. Compare sales prices for sales after the end of the fiscal year to amounts used to price the ending inventory.
7. Review the list of aged trial balance of accounts receivable for possible receivables from corporate officers, subsidiaries, and affiliates.
8. Compare the cost of marketable securities to quotations listed for the New York Stock Exchange.
9. Determine the quality of inventory.
10. Trace the amount listed as a deposit in transit on the bank reconciliation at the balance sheet date to the bank statement received after the end of the balance sheet date.

Required: Classify each of the above procedures as being primarily performed to achieve the existence, valuation, cutoff, or classification and disclosure objective.

9-24. In the audit of the Valare Company for 1979, you encounter problems involving the accounts receivable subsidiary ledger. During 1979, the company computerized the audit sales and cash receipts system. The data are now stored in the accounts receivable master file. For each customer the following data are on the file:

- Customer number
- Customer address
- Account balance
- Date and amount of last payment
- Sales invoice number and amount
- Total sales for year
- Total collection for year
- Credit limit

The client has stated that it can "dump" the information for each customer and convert it to hard-copy form. You have decided to try to use your firm's newly developed generalized audit software package called "Scan-A-File."

Required
1. Does it matter whether the auditor reviews the data in hard-copy form or in computerized form?
2. If the auditor decides to use the generalized audit software package, list some of the routines he or she can use in reviewing the accounts subsidiary ledger file.

MULTIPLE CHOICE

Items 1 and 2 apply to a CPA's examination of the financial statements of the Echo Corporation for the year ended December 31, 1973. An auditing procedure is described in each item, and four potential errors or questionable practices are listed as answer choices. You are to choose the error or questionable practice that has the best chance of being detected by the specific auditing procedure given.

1. The CPA analyzes the accrued interest payable account for the year, recomputes the amounts of payments and beginning and ending balances, and reconciles to the interest expense account.

    a. Interest revenue of $80 on a note receivable was credited against miscellaneous expenses.
    b. A provision of Echo's loan agreement was violated. Dividends on common stock are prohibited if income available for interest and dividends is not three times interest requirements.
    c. Interest paid on an open account was charged to the raw material purchases account.
    d. A note payable had not been recorded. Interest of $150 on the note was properly paid and charged to the interest expense account.

2. The CPA compares 1973 revenues and expenses with the prior year and investigates all changes exceeding 10 percent.

    a. The cashier began lapping accounts receivable in 1973.

314
The audit approach: a systems orientation

b. Because of worsening economic conditions, the 1973 provision for uncollectible accounts was inadequate.
c. Echo changed its capitalization policy for small tools in 1973.
d. An increase in property tax rates has not been recognized in Echo's 1973 accrual.

3. When a CPA expresses an opinion on financial statements, his or her responsibilities extend to

a. The underlying wisdom of the client's management decisions.
b. Whether the results of the client's operating decisions are fairly presented in the financial statements.
c. Active participation in the implementation of advice given to the client.
d. An ongoing responsibility for the client's solvency.

4. The major reason an independent auditor gathers audit evidence is to

a. Form an opinion on the financial statements.
b. Detect fraud.
c. Evaluate management.
d. Evaluate internal control.

5. The CPA tests sales transactions. One step is tracing a sample of sales invoices to debits in the accounts receivable subsidiary ledger. Based upon this step, he or she forms an opinion as to whether

a. Each sales invoice represents a bona fide sale.
b. All sales have been recorded.
c. All debit entries in the accounts receivable subsidiary ledger are properly supported by sales invoices.
d. Recorded sales invoices have been properly posted to customer accounts.

(AICPA Adapted)

CHAPTER 10
Audit of the cash system

In the formulation of an opinion on the financial statements, the auditor must gather evidence to determine whether the cash account is fairly stated in accordance with generally accepted accounting principles. The audit approach discussed in this book emphasizes the need to develop an investigation that is broader than just verification of the cash account. The auditor studies, evaluates, and tests two cash systems that process a large volume of transactions which produce the year-end balance in the cash account. The two systems are the cash receipts system and the cash disbursements system. The study and evaluation of the cash internal control systems is the basis upon which the nature, timing, and extent of audit procedures in the compliance and the substantive tests are initally determined. At the conclusion of the cash compliance tests, the auditor decides whether the cash substantive procedures need to be revised.

CASH RECEIPTS SYSTEM

An organization may have a variety of sources of cash, including cash sales, dividend income, and proceeds from the sale of plant assets. In this chapter the cash receipts system is discussed only as it applies to the collection of cash from credit sales. For most organizations this is the single most important source of cash. This is not to say that the other cash sources are not to be studied and evaluated by the auditor, but such a discussion is beyond the scope of this book.

INTERNAL CONTROL MODEL: CASH RECEIPTS

Chapter 6 was devoted in part to a detailed discussion of the internal control model. Several general characteristics were identified as being essential to an adequate internal control system. The auditor uses these characteristics as a norm against which to measure a client's actual internal control system. In addition, each general characteristic should be related to a particular segment

316
Audit of the
cash system

of the internal control system. In this way it is possible to identify specific internal control characteristics that comprise an adequate internal control system for cash receipts. By using these specific characteristics as a reference, the auditor determines the weaknesses and strengths of the client's cash receipts accounting system. Although the following discussion deals with fairly concrete procedures and policies, it should be recognized that each real-world system is somewhat unique, and the auditor takes such uniqueness into consideration. Nonetheless, in most situations the following characteristics should be a part of a client's internal control system.

The following discussion is consistent with the approach established in Chapter 6. Specifically, the cash receipts internal control model is discussed in the context of:

- A well-designed plan of organization
- An adequate system of authorization and accountability

Two other elements, an adequate accounting structure and an effective internal audit staff, are not considered separately but are integrated into the discussion of the above two elements. Finally, the discussion does not include the two elements characterized as sound personnel policies and a competent and active audit committee. The latter two elements are broad in nature, and their discussion would be redundant at this point.

Plan of organization

DEPARTMENTAL AUTONOMY

In the cash receipts system it is important that each department's responsibilities be identified and the operations of each department not be subject to intervention from another department. Such an identification of responsibilities recognizes the need to separate the responsibilities of cash receipts as they relate to the custodial function and the recording function. The segregation of departmental duties is summarized below:

I. Accounting department
   1. Accounting control over the receipt of cash from sales on credit
   2. Accounting control over cash in bank
   3. Maintenance of the general ledger
   4. Maintenance of the cash receipts journal
   5. Maintenance of the accounts receivable subsidiary ledger
   6. Preparation of the monthly bank reconciliation
   7. Preparation of monthly customer statements
II. Treasurer
   1. Custody control over the receipt and deposit of cash receipts from sales on credit (cashier).
III. Functions other than accounting and treasurer
   1. Authorization of bank accounts (board of directors)
   2. Discontinuance of bank accounts (board of directors)

The above plan of organization emphasizes the critical need to keep the custodial responsibility separate from the recording responsibility for cash receipts. A violation of this principle, either in design or through lack of operational autonomy, is viewed by the auditor as a major weakness in the system, and in most cases he or she forgoes the tests of compliance and extends the audit procedures employed during the substantive tests.

DEPARTMENTAL ORGANIZATIONAL STRUCTURE

An adequate plan of organization encompasses the need for a proper structure within each department. This is especially applicable to the design for the accounting department. Specifically, the internal structure of any department ensures that the duties and responsibilities of each individual are assigned so that no one person can perpetrate or conceal intentional as well as unintentional errors or misdeeds. To achieve this objective several organizational rules relating to the segregation of duties are observed.

Custodial and accounting responsibility: Individuals that have access to cash receipts are not responsible for maintaining cash accounting records. This point was made in the previous section; however, it requires elaboration. The cashier, considered part of the treasurer's department, has custodial control over cash, which includes preparation of the bank deposit and actual deposit of the cash in the bank. The accounting control over the receipts resides with the accounting department, which has no access to the asset.

Recording responsibilities within the accounting department: Within the accounting department the task of maintaining the detail accounts receivable subsidiary ledger is kept separate from that of maintaining the accounts receivable control account. If these duties are the responsibilities of a single individual, the opportunity to provide a basis for an internal check is lost. As shown in the following discussion, an independent comparison of these two sources is part of an adequate internal control system. Also, the responsibilities for posting to the cash receipts journal and the general ledger account for cash should be handled by individuals who have no other cash recording duties. If, for example, a single person has the job of maintaining the detail receivable ledger cards and the general ledger, this person could conceal errors in the detail ledger cards by making unauthorized postings to such accounts as miscellaneous expense and accounts receivable.

System of authorization and accountability

EXECUTION OF TRANSACTIONS

The internal control system for cash receipts is designed in a manner that ensures that only authorized transactions are executed and that these transactions are processed consistent with corporate policies. In several functional areas of an accounting system, authorization is explicit, such as the signing of a purchase order by the purchasing agent. No such formal authorization is required in the receipt-of-cash phase, since the very fact of a cash receipt implies that the transaction is legitimate. Nonetheless, to ensure that cash receipts are processed properly, specific rules of good internal control procedures are followed.

Daily deposits: Cash receipts are deposited promptly, at least once a day. Such a procedure minimizes the possibility of loss through misplacement or theft.

Deposits made intact: All receipts are deposited in the bank and not used to pay invoices or to meet other cash disbursement commitments. Such a procedure protects against the possibility of recording data on a net basis, which is a violation of generally accepted accounting principles. In addition, a strong internal control system segregates the cash receipts and the cash disbursements functions.

RECORDING OF TRANSACTIONS

Internal control procedures in the cash receipts area are designed to encourage recording of the proper amount in the appropriate accounting period. Basically, these procedures include the establishment of immediate control over cash receipts, which in turn forms a basis for determining whether the total cash receipts were deposited promptly and intact in the cash-in-bank account.

Independent cash receipts listing: An individual, usually the mailroom clerk, who is independent of the cash custody function and the cash recording function, prepares a listing of cash receipts. The cash receipts, along with one copy of the listing, are given to the cashier. Another copy of the listing is sent to the clerk responsible for posting to the detail subsidiary accounts receivable ledger.

Independent comparison of deposit and accounting records: Someone who has no other cash receipts duties receives a duplicate deposit slip from the bank and compares this amount to the entry in the cash receipts journal, the listing of cash receipts, and the entry in the accounts receivable control account totals.

ACCESS TO ASSETS

Since cash receipts, even in the form of a check, are easily misappropriated, procedures are adopted to limit access to the asset.

Restrictive endorsement: Checks received are endorsed by the individual preparing the cash receipts listing. The endorsement is restrictive, such as "For deposit only."

Limited access: Only the individual preparing the cash receipts listing and the cashier have access to the receipts. Until the deposit is made, the cash is kept under the control of the cashier either in a locked cash drawer or some other secure location.

COMPARISON OF RECORDED ACCOUNTABILITY WITH ASSETS

319
Study and
evaluation of the
cash receipts
system

On a periodic basis the asset is compared with the accounting records. Any discrepancies are investigated by the client and, if appropriate, the internal control procedures or personnel are changed.

Preparation of a periodic bank statement: An individual independent of other cash duties receives the bank statement directly from the bank and prepares a bank reconciliation. Unusual items or a lack of reconciliation suggests that those responsible for the recording of cash transactions or for the handling of cash receipts may have made an error. The reconciliation is made on a timely basis, probably monthly, to detect errors or defalcations as soon as possible.

Preparation of customer statements: An individual not responsible for opening mail receipts, the custodial function, or the maintenance of cash or receivable records prepares and mails periodic customer statements. In the cash receipts function this provides a needed control over the individual responsible for opening the mail and preparing the cash receipts listing. Customers with complaints are instructed to contact directly the individual responsible for preparing the statement.

STUDY AND EVALUATION OF THE CASH RECEIPTS SYSTEM

Using the basic principles of the cash receipts internal control model as a guide, the auditor employs procedures that result in a thorough understanding of the system. This phase of the engagement enables him or her to evaluate the strengths and weaknesses of the system and to determine the audit approach for the compliance and substantive tests.

Understanding the system

A thorough understanding of a fairly complex system requires that a structured audit approach be taken if the task is to be successful. Furthermore, to provide a basis for the subsequent audit step, evaluation of the cash receipts system, there must be an adequate description of the system. This is obtained through the preparation of questionnaires, flowcharts, narrative memoranda, or other documentation methods which adequately serve the needs of the auditor.

INTERNAL CONTROL QUESTIONNAIRE

The cash receipts internal control questionnaire is designed so that the fundamental principles of the cash receipts internal control model are converted into a list of questions. Figure 10-1 is an example of such a questionnaire. A yes response suggests that the established procedure does not violate the conceptual internal control model. A no response alerts the auditor to potential weaknesses in the cash receipts system, and such responses are cross-referenced to a working paper which analyzes the impact of such weaknesses on the audit procedures to be used in subsequent testing.

Figure 10-1

Internal Control Questionnaire: Cash Receipts System

Cash Receipts	Answer		Answer based on		
	Yes	No	Inquiry	Observation	Comments
1. Are cash receipts deposited intact?	✓		✓		
2. Are cash receipts deposited promptly?	✓		✓		
3. Does someone other than the cashier prepare a listing of cash receipts received through the mail?		✓	✓	✓	See comment on working paper 102 *
4. Does someone independent of the accounting department prepare a listing of cash receipts received through the mail?	✓		✓		
5. Are all checks endorsed for deposit only to the credit of the company immediately upon receipt?	✓			✓	
6. Are the duties of the cashier completely separate from duties relating to the recording of cash receipts?	✓		✓		
7. Are the following duties in the accounting department segregated:					Copy #2 of receipts listing serves as the cash receipt journal
a. Maintenance of the cash receipts journal?	✓				
b. Maintenance of the general ledger?	✓				
c. Maintenance of the detail accounts receivable ledger?	✓				
d. Reconciling the control account and the detail receivable ledger?		✓			See comment on working paper 108 *
8. Does the cashier prepare the bank deposit?	✓				
9. Does the cashier make the bank deposit?	✓				
10. Is the validated deposit ticket returned by the bank directly to a person who has no access to cash receipts?	✓	✓			
If so, is this compared to the —					
a. posting in the cash receipts journal?		✓	✓		See comment on working paper 103 *
b. control totals established over mail cash receipts?		✓	✓		
11. Are all bank debit and credit memos returned received directly by a person who has no access to cash receipts?	✓		✓		Assistant Controller
12. Do persons who have no access to cash receipts and no other cash recording responsibilities prepare a bank reconciliation?	✓		✓		
If so, is the bank statement received unopened?		✓	✓		See comment on working paper 106 *
13. Is the bank reconciliation prepared periodically and discrepancies investigated?	✓		✓		
14. Are monthly statements sent to customers by someone independent of the listing of cash receipts and the maintenance of receivable records?	✓		✓	✓	
15. Does a responsible person review the completed bank reconciliation?		✓			

FLOWCHART

The internal control system may be described by preparing a flowchart. A flowchart for a cash receipts system is shown in Figure 10-2.

MEMORANDUM

In addition to the above two techniques, the auditor may document the cash receipts system through the preparation of narrative memoranda. The same system documented in Figures 10-1 and 10-2 is reproduced in narrative form in Figure 10-3.

Evaluation of the system

Having described the system, the auditor determines the adequacy of the cash receipts internal control procedures. Weaknesses and strengths are identified to determine if audit procedures are to be restricted or extended in the test of cash receipts transactions and the resulting cash balance. When the auditor determines that the system is so weak that it cannot be relied upon, then it is inappropriate to perform the compliance tests. In this case the auditor relies entirely upon the substantive tests as a basis for formulating an opinion on the cash balance. In most cases the system is strong enough to allow the auditor to reduce the degree of test procedures employed at year-end. In this case he or she constructs the compliance tests to (1) determine whether control procedures are being followed, (2) determine if errors or misappropriations are resulting from weaknesses in the system, and (3) formulate a final evaluation on the internal control system.

In evaluating the cash receipts system, the auditor relies upon the documentation generated in the system description phase of the study and evaluation. By utilizing the cash receipts internal control questionnaire, flowchart, and memorandum, the auditor can identify strengths and inadequacies in the system. Figure 10-4 is an example of a working paper that may be prepared after the accounting system documentation has been thoroughly analyzed. At this point the auditor's understanding of the system should be complete, since misunderstandings may lead to an inappropriate audit approach either in the compliance or substantive tests.

COMPLIANCE TESTS: CASH RECEIPTS

Audit procedures selected for the tests of compliance in the cash receipts system are based on the auditor's evaluation of the system. He or she designs the audit program to determine the effects of the weaknesses and strengths of the system upon the cash substantive tests. An example of a compliance audit program is presented in Figure 10-5. In actual practice the design of this program is dictated by factors such as the specific controls in the internal control system, the operating characteristics of a particular industry, and the selection of data processing hardware. However, the procedures suggested in Figure 10-5 are typical of the tests performed in investigating a cash receipts system. It should

Figure 10-2

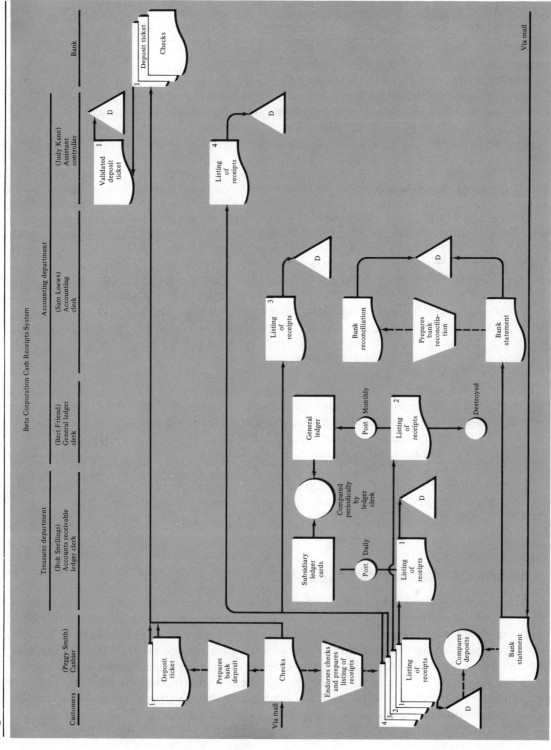

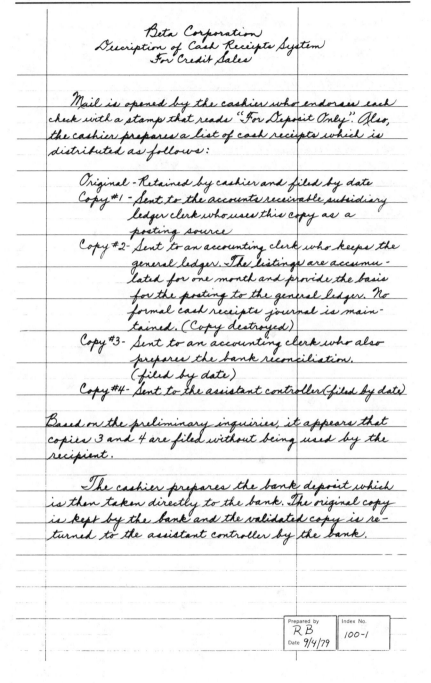

Figure 10-3

Beta Corporation
Description of Cash Receipts System
For Credit Sales

Mail is opened by the cashier who endorses each check with a stamp that reads "For Deposit Only". Also, the cashier prepares a list of cash receipts which is distributed as follows:

Original - Retained by cashier and filed by date
Copy #1 - Sent to the accounts receivable subsidiary ledger clerk who uses this copy as a posting source
Copy #2 - Sent to an accounting clerk who keeps the general ledger. The listings are accumulated for one month and provide the basis for the posting to the general ledger. No formal cash receipts journal is maintained. (Copy destroyed)
Copy #3 - Sent to an accounting clerk who also prepares the bank reconciliation. (filed by date)
Copy #4 - Sent to the assistant controller (filed by date)

Based on the preliminary inquiries, it appears that copies 3 and 4 are filed without being used by the recipient.

The cashier prepares the bank deposit which is then taken directly to the bank. The original copy is kept by the bank and the validated copy is returned to the assistant controller by the bank.

Prepared by: RB
Date: 9/4/79
Index No. 100-1

324
Audit of the
cash system

Figure 10-3 (Continued)

The assistant controller files the validated deposit ticket by date and this is the extent of its utilization.

The monthly bank statement is received by the cashier who opens it and verifies that each deposit per the cash receipts listing agrees with the amount on the bank statement. If there are no descrepancies the bank statement is sent to an accounting clerk for the preparation of a monthly bank reconciliation. The reconciliation is filed by date when completed.

Prepared by	Index No.
Date	

Figure 10-4

PROCEDURE(S) THAT VIOLATES INTERNAL CONTROL MODEL PRINCIPLES	IMPACT ON SUBSEQUENT AUDIT PROCEDURES		
	POTENTIAL IMPACT ON ACCOUNTING SYSTEM	RESULTING COMPLIANCE TESTS PROCEDURE	TENTATIVE AUDIT PROCEDURES FOR SUBSTANTIVE TESTS

1. a. Cashier prepares listing of cash receipts received through the mail.
 b. Cashier receives bank statement directly from the bank before confirmation is prepared.
 c. No independent comparison is made between the deposit ticket and
    i. the copy of the receipts listing that serves as a cash receipt journal
    ii. the control totals established over mail cash receipts.
	Mail cash receipts may not be deposited. Lapping could occur, since the accounts receivable ledger posting source is the listing prepared by the cashier.	a. Obtain a sample validated deposit slip from the file maintained by the assistant controller. Trace the detail per the deposit slip to the bank statement, the detail per the cash receipts listing (copies 3 and 4 and the original), and the detail posting to the accounts receivable subsidiary ledger.
		 b. On a surprise basis intercept the bank deposit, count it, and compare to the cash receipts listings (original and all copies) prepared for the day.
			a. For accounts receivable confirmation, (i) circulate at the year-end date, (ii) use only positive form, and (iii) increase coverage from last year by 50 percent.
			 b. For exceptions noted on the confirmation, be particularly careful to reference concerning posting delays.
			 c. Prepare the bank reconciliation at the year-end date. Notify the bank to send the bank statement directly to the auditor.
			 d. Obtain a cutoff bank statement two weeks after the year end.

2. The accounts receivable subsidiary ledger clerk reconciles the detail to the control account.	Since an independent party does not prove the detail balances to the control totals, it is possible that errors in either the control account or the detail accounts are being concealed.	a. For an interim date, 10/31, foot the accounts receivable subsidiary ledger and tie the total to the control account balance. b. Select 5 percent of the ledger balances and trace to the cash receipts listing for decreases and to the sales invoices for increases (use copy 4 of listing).	a. Request that the client have someone other than the subsidiary ledger clerk prepare a trial balance of accounts receivable at the year-end date. b. Trace 75 percent of the accounts from the trial balance to the detail subsidiary ledger. c. Trace every fourth detail ledger balance to the accounts receivable trial balance. d. Foot the trial balance and tie the total to the control account balance.
3. Copy 2 of the cash receipts listing serves as the cash receipts listing and is destroyed after posting to the general ledger.	Essential permanent accounting records are not maintained, which means that subsequent questions raised by management will have to be answered from information sources other than that which served as the original source (in effect the audit trail or management trail has been altered).	a. Obtain the three copies of the cash receipts listing. b. Foot the listings for every other month and trace to postings in the general ledger. c. Notify the client to retain the copy of the listing normally destroyed for the remaining months.	Foot the year-end cash receipts listing and trace totals to the posting in the general ledger.

326
Audit of the
cash system

Figure 10-5

Audit program: cash receipts

PROCEDURES	DATE COMPLETED	WORK PERFORMED BY
1. The universe is defined as the detail line items in the cash receipts journal. Each line entry is a sample item. Determine the size of the universe.		
2. Select every twentieth sample item for investigation.		
3. For each sample item:		
a. Compare detail to the remittance advice or listing of cash receipts.		
b. Trace detail to posting to the accounts receivable subsidiary ledger.		
c. Compare the amount to the detail on the duplicate deposit ticket.		
d. Check discounts and allowances for proper authorization in accordance with corporate policies.		
4. Randomly select 10 business days, and for each day:		
a. Obtain the appropriate duplicate deposit ticket, cash receipts listing, and bank statement.		
b. Foot the deposit ticket and the cash receipts listing.		
c. Compare the detail per the duplicate deposit ticket to the detail per the cash receipts listing.		
d. Compare the total amount per the deposit ticket and the cash receipts listing to the amount on the bank statement.		
5. For the months of March, June, and September, foot the cash receipts journal and trace postings to the general ledger.		
6. Review the cash receipts journal, the subsidiary ledger, and the general ledger accounts for unusual items.		

be noted that the following procedures are based upon the assumption that an adequate internal control system exists. For specific weaknesses or strengths in the system, the audit program is modified in the manner suggested in Figure 10-4.

Universe definition

The selection of the universe in the cash receipts compliance tests depends upon the audit objective. The objective selected for this audit program is to determine if entries in the cash receipts journal are authentic. Auditing procedures 3a through 3d in Figure 10-5 provide the auditor with enough evidence to determine if the objective has been achieved. While this is the primary objective of the cash receipts tests of transactions, most auditors perform additional procedures to determine if all cash received is being deposited and deposited intact and promptly. The latter objective is the basis for procedures 4a through 4d.

Specifically, the individual sample items in the cash receipts journal appear as:

		DEBIT		CREDITS			
			SALES	ACCOUNT	ACCOUNTS		
DATE	EXPLANATION	CASH	DISCOUNT	TITLE	RECEIVABLE	OTHER	SALES
March 4	Cash sales	10,700					10,700
	Bob Smith	392	8		400		
	Joe Fritz	320			320		

Since the cash receipts journal includes cash sales and other sources of cash, the auditor ignores these entries for the purposes of this test. These items are of course tested in other phases of the audit.

Sample selection

The size of the sample selection is dependent upon the auditor's study and evaluation of the client's internal control system. The sample must be large enough to meet the objectives of the audit. As described in Chapter 8, the objectives may be described in a quantitative manner if statistical sampling is employed, or in a nonquantitative manner if judgment sampling is utilized.

COMPARISON OF ENTRY TO OTHER RECORDS AND DOCUMENTATION

To verify that the entry in the cash receipts journal is authentic and is processed in an appropriate manner, the cash receipts listing is obtained and reviewed. The auditor determines if the amount and name on the listing agree with the information on the cash receipts journal. In addition, the date of the listing is compared to the date entered in the cash receipts journal. These data, name, date, and amount, are traced to the accounts receivable subsidiary ledger journal. If the receivables clerk has access to cash receipts, a misappropriation of cash through *lapping* may occur. Lapping involves the concealment of cash shortages by abstracting cash received from a customer and covering this shortage with subsequent cash collections from another customer. Delays in posting to the cash and receivable records and the "splitting" of a cash receipt among two or more customers are indications of lapping.

Once the auditor has compared the cash receipts journal entry with the cash receipts listing, the next step is to compare this information with the duplicate deposit ticket. Finally, cash discounts and allowances are reviewed. To test the appropriateness of a discount, the auditor refers to the payment terms listed on the sales invoice and performs a recomputation. Allowances are investigated to determine if they were approved by authorized personnel. When an allowance results from the return of goods, the auditor reviews the receiving report.

DETERMINE IF ALL CASH RECEIPTS ARE DEPOSITED

By shifting the basis of the audit inquiry from items recorded in the cash receipts journal, the auditor can determine if the cash received is properly processed. In the audit program described in Figure 10-5, the auditor randomly selects 10 business days as a starting point. Then he or she obtains the cash receipts listing for these days and traces the total receipts to the entry on the bank statement. In addition, the details of the listing and duplicate deposit ticket are compared. These two documents are footed and compared. From these procedures the auditor is able to determine if cash receipts are being deposited promptly and are deposited intact.

TESTING THE SUMMARIZATION OF THE RECEIPTS JOURNAL

The detail transactions are seldom posted directly to the general ledger account. For this reason the auditor tests the summarization step which leads to a periodic entry in the general ledger. He or she selects a few months, foots and cross-foots the cash receipts journal, and traces the postings to the appropriate general ledger account.

REVIEW OF UNUSUAL ITEMS

The auditor reviews the cash receipts journal, the subsidiary ledger, and the cash account for unusual items. The definition of an unusual item is in part dependent upon the structure of the client's internal control system. Transactions not normally processed through a ledger or account are investigated. In addition, unusual sources for a posting or an unusually large dollar amount may suggest that an item should be selected for further review. For example, the debit side of the cash account should have 12 postings from the cash receipts journal. Other sources or multiple postings from an appropriate source should be investigated.

Results of the compliance tests

Having tested the cash receipts system, the auditor reassesses the original conclusion reached at the end of the study-and-evaluation phase of the audit. For example, the compliance tests may reveal significant errors that may result in a revision of the timing, nature, and extent of audit procedures originally selected for the substantive tests.

The relevant substantive tests, that is, the tests of the year-end cash balance, are deferred until the cash disbursements system is discussed.

CASH DISBURSEMENTS SYSTEM

The cash disbursements system includes payments to vendors, employees, and a variety of creditors. In most instances disbursements to vendors for the purchase of inventory and payments to employees for services rendered to the organization constitute a significant portion of total cash disbursements. Chapter 16 discusses the payroll system, and therefore this chapter is concerned only with payments on trade accounts payable.

INTERNAL CONTROL MODEL: CASH DISBURSEMENTS

As discussed earlier in the chapter, it is necessary to discuss in more precise terms the general principles of an adequate internal control model offered in

Chapter 6. This discussion is organized around the controls associated with a well-designed plan of organization and those related to an adequate system of authorization and accountability.

329
Internal control model: cash disbursements

Plan of organization

DEPARTMENTAL AUTONOMY

Specific responsibilities which relate to the cash disbursements function are assigned to appropriate operating units of an organization. The major duties in this area are:

    I. Accounting department
       1. Review of all disbursement requests for proper authorization
       2. Maintenance of the cash disbursements journal
       3. Maintenance of a voucher register or a purchase journal
       4. Preparation of the monthly bank reconciliation
   II. Treasurer
       1. Custody control over cash
       2. Signing of checks
       3. Distribution of signed checks
  III. Functions other than accounting and treasurer
       1. Authorization for the expenditure of resources (purchasing agent)
       2. Authorization of bank accounts (board of directors)
       3. Discontinuance of bank accounts (board of directors)

This organizational structure emphasizes the need to provide an appropriate segregation of departmental responsibilities in the cash disbursements function.

DEPARTMENTAL ORGANIZATIONAL STRUCTURE

The accounting department is structured to minimize the likelihood of payment of an unauthorized disbursement request. For this reason, the responsibility for preparing vouchers requesting payments is separate from the responsibility for preparing, but not for signing, checks. In addition, the preparer of the check reviews the voucher in order to prevent the erroneous preparation of checks. This procedure is valid even though the signer of the check performs the same task, that is, reviews the voucher. In most cases this occurs only on a sampling basis.

System of authorization and accountability

EXECUTION OF TRANSACTIONS

In the area of cash disbursements for trade accounts payable, several rules are followed to ensure that a transaction is executed as authorized.

Authorization for the disbursement: The basic authorization for a disbursement is usually the result of matching three documents in the accounts payable section of the accounting function. This authorization is referred to as a voucher package and consists of a purchase order, a receiving report, and a vendor's invoice. Authority for the acquisition of inventory rests with the purchasing department, which means that only trade payables supported by a properly executed purchase order are processed. Since the preparation of a purchase order does not impact the accounting equation, another authorization, the receiving report, is prepared to verify that goods were received. These two documents are matched with the vendor's invoice, and at this point liability is established. Although this documentation is fundamental to the purchasing function, it also serves as a basis for authorization in the disbursement function, as shown in the following discussion.

Check preparation: Only disbursement requests that are properly authorized, as represented by a voucher package, result in the preparation of a check. Each check is made payable to the individual or company represented by voucher material. To avoid alteration of the payee name, the check should be made of material that readily shows signs of erasure or other alteration attempts.

Check signature: Before a check is signed, the signer reviews the voucher package to determine if the check request is proper. After it is signed the voucher material is canceled, usually by marking the documents "Paid" through a perforation process to prevent resubmission for payment. The authority to sign checks is restricted to responsible officials of the organization not involved in other cash functions. In many cases the signing may be done mechanically rather than personally. If so, the mechanical check writer is under the control of the person responsible for its use.

RECORDING OF TRANSACTIONS

Subsequent to preparing a check, accounting controls are adopted to encourage proper recording of the disbursement.

Preparation of cash disbursements journal: In most cases the cash disbursements journal simply results from the recording of checks written during the business day. To ensure that all disbursements are recorded, prenumbered checks are used, and periodically all check numbers are accounted for to determine if they are unused or recorded in the cash disbursements journal. Furthermore, unused checks are controlled, with access limited to only the individual responsible for the preparation of checks.

ACCESS TO ASSETS

Limiting access to cash in a checking account results from adopting many of the procedures discussed above. In addition, an adequate cash disbursements internal control system possesses additional characteristics.

Control of check distribution: Signed checks are mailed directly by the signer. This safeguard prevents someone who has a cash disbursement task from authorizing an improper check request, intercepting the check, and misappropriating cash in several ways.

All disbursements by check: Obviously cash is very susceptible to misappropriation, theft, and the like. To avoid having significant cash on hand, the vast majority of disbursements are made by check. In cases where it is impractical or inefficient to follow this practice, an organization can establish a petty cash fund. A practice in the cash receipts area that requires the deposit of cash intact without disbursements derives from the rule that all disbursements must be made by check.

COMPARISON OF RECORDED ACCOUNTABILITY WITH ASSETS

The basic procedure which emphasizes the need to compare the cash account balance with the actual asset results from the independent preparation of a periodic bank reconciliation. This accounting control feature was discussed in the cash receipts section of this chapter. An additional control feature is considered in the following discussion.

Review of vendor statements: On a periodic basis, usually monthly, the client's vendors mail out statements which disclose the amount owed for the purchase of inventory. Someone who does not have any cash disbursements responsibility reconciles these statements with the client's accounts payable records. Such a procedure may reveal recording errors in the cash records as well as in the liability account.

STUDY AND EVALUATION OF THE CASH DISBURSEMENTS SYSTEM

In a manner similar to the approach described earlier in this chapter, the auditor's study of the cash disbursements system begins with an understanding of the system. This understanding rests upon an appropriate description of the system obtained through the preparation of questionnaires, flowcharts, and a narrative memorandum. An internal control questionnaire for the cash disbursements function is presented in Figure 10-6.

After the internal control system for cash disbursements is understood and properly documented, the auditor evaluates its adequacy. This analysis results in the selection of specific audit procedures to be included in the tests of compliance. At this point the auditor determines the tentative approach to be taken in the substantive tests for the cash account. An analysis similar to the approach illustrated in Figure 10-4 is made. Much of the detailed documentation and evaluation of the disbursements system is deferred until Chapter 14 which considers the accounts payable and purchasing system. Since these two systems overlap, it is unnecessary to discuss the material thoroughly at this point.

COMPLIANCE TESTS: CASH DISBURSEMENTS

The compliance tests for cash disbursements are performed after the study and evaluation phase has been completed. Some of the basic procedures of the tests are illustrated in Figure 10-7 and are considered in the following discussion.

Figure 10-6

Internal Control Questionnaire: Cash Disbursements System

Cash Disbursements	Answer		Answer based on		
	Yes	No	Inquiry	Observation	Comments
1. Are all checks prenumbered and accounted for?					
2. Are unused checks adequately safeguarded?					
3. Are unused checks under the control of someone other than the person who signs the check manually or who has control of the check-signing device?					
4. Are voided checks retained and accounted for?					
5. Is the practice of drawing checks to "cash" or "bearer" prohibited?					
6. Are check signers authorized by the board of directors?					
7. Do the persons who sign the checks review the supporting check request documentation?					
8. Are the persons who sign the checks independent of —					
a. the purchasing department?					
b. those who approve vouchers?					
c. those who prepare checks?					
d. those who prepare the disbursements journal?					
e. those who prepare the voucher register?					
9. Is the signing of checks in advance prohibited?					
10. Are vouchers canceled upon the signature of the check?					
11. Are checks mailed directly by the person who signs the checks?					

Universe definition and sample selection

The auditor may define the universe as all checks prepared during the year or all line-item entries in the cash disbursements journal. Selection of the universe may appear unimportant, but it is crucial that the auditor be able to describe and have access to it. For example, the universe may be defined as all invoices paid during the period. However, such a universe definition poses practical problems, since it is not prenumbered and it is not possible to determine if it is intact. In the example presented in Figure 10-7, the checks prepared during the period provide a prenumbered universe whose intactness can be determined by reviewing groups of check copies filed by number. Also, a prenumbered universe facilitates the sample selection process, since there is a ready correspondence between the universe and a random numbers table. Of course, other selection methods may be employed.

Figure 10-7

Audit program: cash disbursements

PROCEDURES	DATE COMPLETED	WORK PERFORMED BY
1. The universe is defined as the number of prenumbered checks written during the testing period. Determine the size of the universe.	_____	_____
2. Randomly select 150 sample items by utilizing a random numbers table.	_____	_____
3. For each sample item:		
a. Trace the check to the cash disbursements journal.	_____	_____
b. Determine that the check has been signed by authorized personnel.	_____	_____
c. Trace the check to proper authorization.	_____	_____
d. Examine the check for payee endorsement.	_____	_____
e. Trace the check to the bank statement.	_____	_____
4. For the months of April and August foot the cash disbursements journal and trace postings to the general ledger.	_____	_____
5. Review the cash disbursements journal, the voucher register, and the general ledger accounts for unusual items.	_____	_____

COMPARISON OF CHECK TO CASH DISBURSEMENTS JOURNAL

For each sample check chosen for investigation, the auditor traces the check number, the check date, the payee name per the check, and the amount of the check to the pertinent data in the cash disbursements journal. The primary objective is to determine that the authorized disbursement was properly recorded in the accounting records. For example, when the check is recorded in the journal based on the date of the recording rather than on the date of the check, the auditor may modify the substantive audit approach to be assured that a cutoff problem does not exist.

CHECK IS PROPERLY SIGNED

The auditor obtains a list of individuals who have the authority to sign checks. The auditor updates this list by reviewing the minutes of the board of directors, since the latter body grants such authority. When a check bears the signature of an unauthorized signer, the auditor investigates the reason for such an incident and the extent of the irregularity.

REVIEW AUTHORIZATION FOR DISBURSEMENT

For each disbursement sampled, the auditor determines whether the item was properly authorized. This review includes inspecting the purchase order, the receiving report, and the vendor invoice. The purchase order is examined to determine if it was signed by the purchasing agent or other authorized persons in the purchasing department; the receiving report is reviewed to verify the receipt of the goods; the invoice inspection reveals discounts, allowances, and shipping terms. The auditor notes whether the vendor package was canceled. All the data per the vendor package, vendor name, and dollar amount support the data recorded on the check.

EXAMINE ENDORSEMENT

The auditor reviews the check endorsement to make sure it is consistent with the name of the company per the purchase order and vendor invoice. The auditor is especially careful of double endorsements which may suggest that the check was intercepted and cashed by client personnel. Also, the auditor investigates any check which is payable to cash or to the bearer.

TRACE TO BANK STATEMENT

The auditor traces cash disbursements to the bank statement to determine if the cash account was relieved by the authorized amount. The bank statement, since it is in the client's possession, is examined carefully for alterations. In addition, the auditor samples some of the amounts per the bank statement and traces these items back to the proper authorization. This satisfies the auditor that unrecorded checks are not being issued.

TESTING THE SUMMARIZATION OF THE CASH DISBURSEMENTS JOURNAL

The auditor traces cash disbursements from the book of original entry to the impact on the general ledger. In step 4 in Figure 10-7, the months of April and August were chosen for review.

REVIEW FOR UNUSUAL ITEMS

The accounting records impacted by a cash disbursements transaction are reviewed for unusual items. The credit side of the cash general ledger account should have 12 postings from the disbursements journal. Undoubtedly, there may be other posting sources, but these items are investigated by the auditor to determine their propriety. Other records, such as the voucher register and the subsidiary accounts payable ledger, are reviewed in a similar fashion.

With the completion of the compliance tests for the cash disbursements function, the auditor relates these testing results to the substantive audit approach. The remainder of this chapter discusses the substantive audit procedures for cash.

SUBSTANTIVE TESTS: CASH IN BANK

The timing, extent, and nature of audit procedures used in the verification of cash on deposit with banks depend upon the adequacy of the internal control system. The audit approach considered in the following discussion assumes that an adequate internal control system for receipts and disbursements exists. Also, it is assumed that the procedures are performed after the close of the fiscal year.

In the audit of cash, as for every balance sheet account, the auditor must be satisfied as to the existence and valuation of the asset at the balance sheet date. In addition, he or she must determine whether the client has recorded cash transactions in the proper accounting period, which is commonly referred to as the cutoff objective. Since financial statements must meet the standard of full disclosure, the auditor must be satisfied that the cash account is properly classified and that disclosures, if any, are made in parenthetical comments or footnotes. In practice these four audit objectives often overlap when audit procedures are selected, and it is not important to classify procedures based upon the related audit objective. However, for discussion purposes it is useful to observe this classification scheme, since it emphasizes the reason for employing a particular audit procedure. A typical audit program for cash in the bank is presented in Figure 10-8.

Existence

As a first step in determining the existence of cash in a bank account at the close of the fiscal year, the auditor obtains and reviews the client-prepared bank reconciliation. If there is an adequate internal control system, most auditors do not insist upon preparing the bank reconciliation. In this case, since the reconciliation is client-prepared, the auditor reviews the analysis. Through this review he or she verifies the existence of the cash per the client records by using data generated by the bank. Figure 10-9 is an illustration of a working paper that documents the specific audit procedures used in verifying the year-end bank reconciliation. These procedures include:

- Foot the reconciliation, including subtotals of outstanding checks.
- Compare checks returned with the year-end bank statement to the cash disbursements journal, noting payee, amount, date, signature, and endorsement.
- Compare the deposit in transit on the reconciliation with the appropriate entry in the cash receipts journal.
- Trace outstanding checks on the bank reconciliation to the cash disbursements journal, noting check number, amount, and payee.
- Investigate and obtain evidence for reconciling items other than outstanding checks and deposits in transit such as bank transfers, collection of notes, bank charges, and so on.

Cutoff and existence

A bank reconciliation is prepared because there are time lags between the recording of information by the bank and by the client. For this reason reconciling items that appear on the client's year-end bank reconciliation are recorded by the bank on the next bank statement. To take advantage of this relationship, one of the strongest audit procedures in the audit of cash is for the auditor to obtain and review a cutoff bank statement. He or she requests that the bank prepare a bank statement which includes transactions for about 10 to 12 business days after the close of the year. This cutoff bank statement is received directly from the bank by the auditor. With this data the auditor determines if the client made

336
Audit of the
cash system

Figure 10-8

Audit program: cash in bank

PROCEDURES	DATE COMPLETED	WORK PERFORMED BY
1. Review the client's bank reconciliation(s) for all open accounts.	_____	_____
2. Obtain a bank cutoff statement 10 to 12 business days after the balance sheet date for all open accounts.	_____	_____
3. Confirm the bank balance(s) at year-end with the bank for all open accounts.	_____	_____
4. Determine the proper classification and disclosure for all open accounts.	_____	_____

a proper cutoff of all cash transactions. Specifically, the auditor wants to make sure that (1) the cash receipts book was not kept open after the year end, (2) cash disbursements were recorded in the proper year, and (3) bank transfers are accounted for properly.

By keeping the cash receipts journal open after the end of the year, the client may improve its liquidity position and its results of operation for the year. Checks received through the mail a few days after the year end result in a larger cash balance and a smaller balance in trade accounts receivable, with an overall increase in the liquidity position of the company. Furthermore, cash sales for a few days after the close of the period increase the cash position and the gross sales for the year. The impact on the net income may be magnified if the client does not record the cost of goods sold for these cash sales. Of course, these collections show up on the year-end bank reconciliation as a deposit in transit. To determine if the cash book has been kept open, the auditor traces each reconciling deposit in transit to the bank cutoff statement. Furthermore, these deposits should clear within one or possibly two business days after the year-end date. This procedure is included as part of the working paper illustration in Figure 10-9.

A company may also manipulate its liquidity position at the end of the year by improperly recording cash payments. First, cash disbursements may be recorded as payments during the last few days of the fiscal year with a proper dating on the check but retained by the client and not mailed until a few or several days after the close of the year. When the current ratio before the payment is greater than 1:1, this results in an increase in the current ratio. To determine if this has taken place, the auditor reviews the checks listed as outstanding at year end and determines if these checks cleared with the cutoff bank statement. Generally, if the checks did not clear, the auditor must consider whether they were not mailed by the last day of the fiscal year. This audit procedure is not as effective as the procedure used to determine if the cash receipts book was kept open. Undoubtedly, some of the year-end outstanding checks do not clear with the cutoff bank statement, since some vendors do not deposit receipts promptly or checks may have to be processed through one or more banking systems. The auditor looks for a pattern rather than concentrating on a single check. When

Figure 10-9

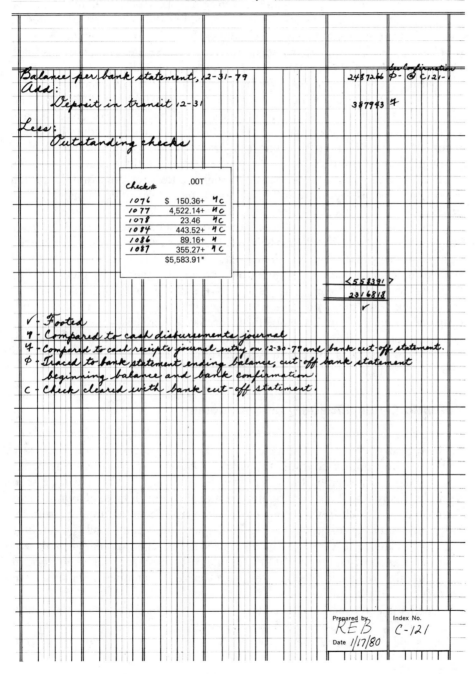

338
**Audit of the
cash system**

a block of checks does not clear the cutoff statement, additional investigation is required.

Also, checks may be written and mailed in the fiscal year and not recorded until the first month following the end of the year. This is usually a problem when the authority to sign checks is given to a variety of individuals, because of the operating characteristics of the industry, but the checks are recorded at a central location based upon a subsequent cash report. To test for such a cutoff problem, as well as for other irregularities or errors, the auditor traces each check returned with the cutoff bank statement to the cash disbursements journal, comparing check number, date, payee, signature, and endorsement.

The auditor is especially cautious about bank transfers occurring at the end of the fiscal year. The client may increase its cash position or cover a cash shortage by recording the bank transfer as an addition to one account but fail to record it as a deduction from the transferring account. This is one form of "kiting." If there are transfers at the year end, the auditor prepares a working paper detailing the movement of cash through the transfer. An example of such a working paper is presented in Figure 10-10. In this schedule, transfers a few days before and a few days after the balance sheet date are examined.

The cutoff bank statement is reviewed for poststatement events that may have an impact on the fiscal year being audited. For example, deposited checks from customers that were returned because of insufficient funds are charged against the client's account in the cutoff statement. Other items such as notes to be collected by the bank may be dishonored at the payment date. Loans or the drawing down of a credit line with a bank may show on the statement and, if significant, may require footnote disclosure since there has been a postbalance sheet increase in a liability. In general, the auditor must be satisfied that every item in the cutoff bank statement is properly recorded, and each unusual item must be investigated.

Valuation, classification, and disclosure

For the cash account, valuation is not generally a problem, since the asset is the medium of exchange. To achieve the valuation, classification, and disclosure objectives, the auditor confirms the year-end balance directly with the bank. The standard confirmation form is presented in Figure 10-11. As can be seen from this figure, the bank confirmation contains a considerable amount of evidential matter which is very competent since it is received directly from an independent source. First, the balance in the account is confirmed. The auditor uses this evidence to verify the balance used in the client-prepared bank reconciliation as shown in Figure 10-9. It should be emphasized that all authorized accounts are confirmed whether they are active or inactive or have a zero balance.

The bank confirmation also contains data which help determine the appropriate classification of the cash balance. Obviously cash is a current asset, but this classification depends upon whether the cash is subject to immediate with-

Figure 10-10

339
Substantive tests:
cash in bank

Green Valley Corp.
Schedule of Bank Transfer
December 31, 1979

Amount	Receiving Bank Account	Disbursing Bank Account	Transfer to Bank Account		Transfer from Bank Account	
			Per Books	Per Bank	Per Books	Per Bank
10000 00	General -101	General -109	12/25	12/28	12/25	12/26
11867 94	Payroll -110	General -101	12/30	1/3 φ	12/28	12/30
7800 00	General 104	General -101	1/3	1/4	1/3	1/3
9500 00	Special 100	General 101	12/30 7	1/6	1/4	1/5

φ - See payroll bank reconciliation @ C-140.

7 - See special account bank reconciliation @ C-142.

Note: Includes all transfers two weeks before and two weeks after 12/31/79.

Prepared by REB	Index No.
Date 1/25/80	C-130

340
Audit of the cash system

Figure 10-11

STANDARD BANK CONFIRMATION INQUIRY
Approved 1966 by
American Institutes of Certified Public Accountants
and
Bank Administration Institute (formerly NABAC)

DUPLICATE
To be mailed to accountant

_____ ˙19 _____

Dear Sirs:

Your completion of the following report will be sincerely appreciated. IF THE ANSWER TO ANY ITEM is "NONE", PLEASE SO STATE. Kindly mail it in the enclosed stamped, addressed envelope direct to the accountant named below.

Yours truly, _____

(ACCOUNT NAME PER BANK RECORDS)

(Bank) _____

By _____
Authorized Signature

Bank customer should check here if confirmation of bank balances only (item 1) is desired.

☐

Name of Accountant

NOTE—If the space provided is inadequate, please enter totals hereon and attach a statement giving full details as called for by the columnar headings below.

Dear Sirs:

1. At the close of business on _____ 19 ___ our records showed the following balance(s) to the credit of the above named customer. In the event that we could readily ascertain whether there were any balances to the credit of the customer not designated in this request, the appropriate information is given below.

AMOUNT	ACCOUNT NAME	ACCOUNT NUMBER	SUBJECT TO WITH-DRAWAL BY CHECK?	INTEREST BEARING GIVE DATE
$				

2. The customer was directly liable to us in respect of loans, acceptances, etc., at the close of business on that date in the total amount of $ _____ , as follows:

AMOUNT	DATE OF LOAN OR DISCOUNT	DUE DATE	INTEREST		DESCRIPTION OF LIABILITY, COLLATERAL SECURITY INTERESTS, LIENS, ENDORSERS, ETC.
			DATE	PAID TO	
$					

3. The customer was contingently liable as endorser of notes discounted and/or as guarantor at the close of business on that date in the total amount of $ _____ , as follows:

AMOUNT	NAME OF MAKER	DATE OF NOTE	DUE DATE	REMARKS
$				

4. Other direct or contingent liabilities, open letters of credit, and relative collateral, were

_____

5. Security agreements under the Uniform Commercial Code or any other agreements providing for restrictions, not noted above, were as follows (if officially recorded, indicate data and office in which filed):

_____

Yours truly, (Bank) _____

Date _____ 19 _____

By _____
Authorized Signature

Additional copies of this form are available from the American Institute of CPAs, 666 Fifth Avenue, New York, NY 10019 drawal. When there are restrictions, there is a designated space on the confirmation that the bank may use. For example, a client may have a loan outstanding with the bank and the loan agreement may call for the client to maintain a certain cash balance in the account referred to as a compensating balance. This requires disclosure in a footnote to the financial statement if the amount is material. In addition to the bank confirmation, the auditor reads the minutes of the board of directors and loan agreements to determine if the cash account is subject to other restrictions. When cash is part of a sinking fund account to pay off long-term liabilities, it should not be listed as a current asset.

As shown in Figure 10-11, the bank confirmation contains information not related to the audit of cash. Information concerning liabilities both real and contingent is very useful in other phases of the audit. These data are cross-referenced to working papers where the analysis of liabilities and interest expenses is being made.

Substantive tests: extended procedures

As suggested earlier, the audit approach described in this chapter assumes that the client has an adequate system of internal controls. When the internal control system is deficient, the auditor uses extended audit procedures. One such procedure is preparation of a proof of cash. A proof of cash is essentially an expanded bank reconciliation which consists of four columns as shown in Figure 10-12. The first column is a reconciliation of the balance per the bank statement and the balance per the books for the beginning of the period. The period covered by the reconciliation may be a year or a month or some period in between. The next two columns reconcile receipts and disbursements per the bank with cash receipts and disbursements per the client's records for the period. The final column is the normal reconciliation prepared for the end of the period.

The auditor may prepare a proof of cash at an interim date or at the balance sheet date. When the procedure is performed at an interim date, it is part of the test of transactions. On the other hand, when it is performed on the balance sheet date, it is considered part of the substantive tests. Generally speaking, the weaker the client's internal control system, the more likely it is that a proof of cash will be performed at the balance date.

Substantive tests: other cash items

Typically, the cash balance that appears on the balance sheet consists not only of cash on deposit but currency on hand, undeposited checks, perhaps at several branch locations, and petty cash funds. In addition, many companies with excess cash may invest these funds in near-cash instruments such as time deposits, treasury bills, and certificates of deposit. In many cases these cash and near-cash items are immaterial and deserve little audit effort. However, if they are material or if the client insists that the auditor test them, he or she must perform the appropriate audit procedures. These procedures are briefly considered in the following discussion.

Figure 10-12

NATIONAL 45-604 EYE-EASE / 45-704 20/20 BUFF — Made in U S A

Green Valley Corporation
Proof of Cash
12-31-79

Acct. #100

	Balance 11-30-79	December Receipts	December Disbursements	Balance 12-31-79
Balance per Bank	7823 64 ⁴	158722 0 ⁴	138400 0 ⁴	98558 4 ᶜ
Deposits-in-transit				
@ 11-30-79	1201 59 ⁴	⟨1201 59⟩ ⁴		
@ 12-31-79		685 96 ⑦		685 96 ⑦
Outstanding check				
@ 11-30-79	⟨1584 16⟩ ∅		⟨1584 16⟩ ∅	
@ 12-31-79			1711 94 ∅	⟨1711 94⟩ ∅
NSF check - December		⟨626 49⟩ #	⟨626 49⟩ #	
Service Charge				
November	15 00 ⁴		15 00 ⁴	
December			⟨15 00⟩ ⁴	15 00 ⁴
Balance per Book	7456 07	14730 08	13341 29	8844 86 ˣ
	✓	✓	✓	✓ To A1

⁴ Traced to bank statement.
⁴ Cleared bank statement on 12/3/79.
⑦ Cleared bank statement on 1/2/80.
∅ See analysis @ working paper A-11.
Cleared bank 12/19.
✓ Footed.
ˣ Cross-footed.
C See confirmation @ A-12.

REB 1/21/80

A 10

PETTY CASH

In most business it is necessary to have a cash fund on hand so that miscellaneous expenditures for postage stamps, minor supplies, and the like may be purchased and paid for immediately. Since the custodian of the petty cash fund has total responsibility for the fund, including custodial control, authority to make expenditures, and recording responsibilities, there is an obvious violation of the internal control procedures. However, the fund is small, and this limits the impact of irregularities upon the audited financial statements. The opportunity for fraud and errors is minimized if the following internal control guidelines are observed:

- All cash funds are handled on an imprest[1] basis.
- Each fund is the responsibility of only one person.
- The fund is replenished only after supporting vouchers for disbursements have been reviewed.
- Payees are required to sign vouchers for all disbursements.
- Supporting vouchers are canceled when the cash fund is replenished to prevent them from being reused.
- Employees checks cashed for accommodation are deposited promptly.
- Cash funds are subject to surprise audit by internal auditors or other responsible corporate officials.

In most audits the testing of the petty cash system is performed as part of the compliance tests. Based on the adequacy of the petty cash internal control system, the auditor selects some of the petty cash reimbursements for review by performing the following procedures:

- Foot the petty cash vouchers and compare with the reimbursement check.
- Examine vouchers for approval and payee signature.
- Determine if invoices and other supporting documents have been canceled.

Alternatively, the auditor may decide on a surprise count of the petty cash fund at an interim date. He or she counts all currency and supporting vouchers to determine if they total to the established petty cash balance. Also, vouchers and supporting documents are reviewed to determine if the expenditure was approved and is appropriate. The auditor insists upon the petty cash custodian remaining with the auditor during the count. Upon the return of the fund to the custodian, most auditors ask that the custodian sign a statement declaring that the fund was counted in the presence of the custodian and returned intact. This is for the protection of the auditor in case there is a shortage in the fund. If the auditor believes it necessary, or if the client makes the request, the petty cash count can be made on the balance sheet date. In addition, the auditor scans the petty cash reimbursements subsequent to the balance sheet date to determine if they are significant or unusually large. If so, the supporting documents are inspected to determine if the expenditures should have been recorded in the fiscal year being audited.

---

[1] An imprest petty cash fund is created by debiting petty cash and crediting cash. Periodically the fund is replenished by charging the appropriate accounts, usually expenses, and crediting cash. The petty cash account balance is not changed unless the standing balance is increased or decreased.

344
Audit of the cash system

UNDEPOSITED CASH RECEIPTS AND NEAR-CASH ITEMS

Cash receipts for the last day of the fiscal year may consist of customer checks and currency. It has already been suggested that these receipts are usually shown as a deposit in transit on the year-end bank reconciliation. The auditor traces the deposit to the cutoff bank statement to determine if the deposit cleared within one or two days of the end of the year. In certain instances such an audit approach may not be appropriate. These conditions include an inadequate cash receipts internal control system and significant cash receipts because of the nature of the client's operation, as in the case of a financial institution. The basic audit approach is to obtain control of all cash and near-cash items and to count these items simultaneously.

To gain control of cash on hand, the auditor asks the client to prepare a detailed listing of cash. This list includes checks and currency which constitute the current day's bank deposit, permanent amounts in cash registers and other cash funds, and specific investments in time deposits, certificates of deposit, and the like. From this control sheet the auditor verifies each balance and does not release the fund to the client until satisfied that the total balance is correct.

The most obvious audit procedure entails the counting of currency and checks. Again the auditor insists upon appropriate company officials being present during the count. If the auditor has a sufficient number of assistants, it may be possible to count all funds, which may be scattered throughout the company's facilities, at the same time. Each assistant is informed that the cash fund is not to be released to the client until notified. Notification is given after all funds per the control listing are verified. If the auditor is unable to assign an assistant to each fund, each one must be counted and then sealed. Again, the seals are broken only after all funds are verified. If checks are a significant part of the cash on hand, the auditor must be satisfied that they are legitimate and have not been substituted by the client to cover a shortage. In this case the auditor takes control of the bank deposit by accompanying the cashier to the bank for the deposit or observes the deposit pickup made by an armored car service. Subsequently, the auditor reviews the cutoff bank statement to determine if the checks were honored. Also, the amount of the deposit is traced to the subsequent entry in the cash receipts journal.

In many cases near-cash items are not on the client's premises but rather in a safe deposit box. An assistant may be assigned to count these items in conjunction with the count of other cash funds. When it is not practical to do this, the auditor instructs the client not to open the safe deposit box on the count date or until the auditor visits the depository. When the auditor inspects the safe deposit box, the near-cash items are verified. Also, the depository records are reviewed to make sure the client has not had access to the deposit box since the count date. Some near-cash items cannot be physically inspected or counted, and other audit procedures may be needed. For example, time deposits are confirmed directly with the financial institution.

It is acceptable to combine near-cash items with other cash accounts and present one line item called "Cash on the balance sheet." However, when these items are not subject to immediate conversion into cash or if other restrictions are imposed, this information should be adequately disclosed in a footnote or shown as a separate line item directly below the cash account.

345
Exercises and problems

Substantive tests results

After the auditor completes the substantive tests, an overall opinion on the cash balance is formulated. During the audit of cash the auditor constructs a working paper on which proposed adjusting journal entries are listed with appropriate reference to detailed analysis to support the auditor's proposal. A similar working paper for adequate disclosures, either as footnotes or parenthetical comments, is also made. At the conclusion of the audit, the auditor meets with the chief financial executives of the firm to agree on what adjustments and disclosures are to be made for the cash account as well as all items on the financial statement. If the auditor is unable to convince the client that the adjustments and disclosures should be made, his or her report may have to be something other than an unqualified report.

EXERCISES AND PROBLEMS

10-1. In the design of the cash receipts system, why is it necessary to have different individuals responsible for the receipt of cash and the posting to the accounts receivable subsidiary ledger cards?

10-2. Describe the duties of the cashier.

10-3. Why is it important to have autonomous departments for the custodial and recording responsibilities for cash?

10-4. What accounting control procedures are adopted to ensure that cash receipts are properly recorded?

10-5. In defining a universe in the cash receipts on accounts system, is it acceptable to use all deposits shown on the bank statements for the year?

10-6. What is considered an unusual item in reviewing the general ledger cash account?

10-7. How does the auditor determine if the cash receipts journal has been held open beyond the last day of the year?

10-8. What audit procedure would be adopted by the auditor if several checks were made payable to cash?

10-9. Why does an auditor review petty cash reimbursements for January and February of 1980 for the 1979 calendar-year audit?

10-10. Is it acceptable to perform the cash substantive tests at an interim date if the client has a strong system of internal controls?

10-11. Is it necessary to request a bank confirmation, obtain a bank cutoff statement, and review the year-end bank reconciliation for an inactive bank account or a bank account with a zero balance per the general ledger? Why?

10-12. What is a compensating balance and why must the auditor be concerned with such items?

346
**Audit of the
cash system**

10-13. If cash-on-hand and near-cash instruments are significant, why is it necessary to control these items simultaneously during a review?

10-14. In examining cash the CPA is watchful for signs of lapping and kiting.

Required
1. Define (a) lapping and (b) kiting.
2. List the audit procedures that would uncover (a) lapping and (b) kiting.
3. In examining financial statements the CPA evaluates the quality of the available accounting evidence. An audit procedure that may be employed in the examination of cash is to submit duplicate deposit slips to the depository bank to be authenticated.
   a. Discuss the reliability of authenticated duplicate deposit slips as accounting evidence.
   b. What additional audit procedures are available to the CPA to verify the detail of deposits? (AICPA Adapted)

10-15. You are in charge of the audit of the financial statements of the Demot Corporation for the year ended December 31, 1979. The corporation has had the policy of investing its surplus funds in marketable securities. Its stock and bond certificates are kept in a safe deposit box at a local bank. Only the president and the treasurer of the corporation have access to the box.

You were unable to obtain access to the safe deposit box on December 31 because neither the president nor the treasurer was available. Arrangements were made for your assistant to accompany the treasurer to the bank on January 11 to examine the securities. Your assistant has never examined securities being kept in a safe deposit box and requires instructions. She should be able to inspect all securities on hand in an hour.

Required
1. List the instructions you would give to your assistant regarding the examination of the stock and bond certificates kept in the safe deposit box. Include in your instructions the details of the securities to be examined and the reasons for examining these details.
2. When she returned from the bank, your assistant reported that the treasurer had opened the box on January 4. The treasurer stated that he had removed an old photograph of the corporation's original building. List the additional audit procedures required because of the treasurer's action. (AICPA Adapted)

10-16. The Varnke Company, a medium-sized manufacturer, has never been audited by a CPA firm during its 20 years of existence. During this period minor errors and irregularities have been discovered by members of the controller's staff. Most of the discoveries were the result of luck rather than by design. In fact, the internal control system is very weak, and the president of the company is concerned that there may be significant errors or frauds that have never been discovered.

The president of Varnke contracts your CPA firm, explains the problem, and asks your help in designing an effective internal control system. During your conversations with the president, the following errors and frauds are described as occurring over the past few years:

   a. Cash receipts received through the mail were taken by the mailroom clerks whose job was to distribute the mail.
   b. Several cash receipts were posted to the wrong subsidiary ledger card.
   c. Checks were prepared and mailed but were not posted to the cash disbursements journal.

d. Expenses were paid out of the current day's cash receipts. These expenses were not recorded.
e. Invoices were submitted two or more times for payment.
f. The petty cash custodian cashed personal checks of friends, which were not deposited for several months.
g. Several checks were identified as "Void" in the cash disbursements journal. However, they were actually used as payments to the clerks that prepared the bank reconciliation.
h. Personal expenses of the petty cash custodian were paid out of the petty cash fund.
i. The cashier opened an unauthorized bank account in the name of the company, made deposits to the account, and wrote checks for personal expenses on the account.
j. Bank service charges, charges for checks stamped "Nonsufficient funds," and other items were not recorded for some of the bank accounts.

Required

1. For each of the above errors or irregularities, describe accounting controls that should be adopted to prevent the likelihood of future occurrence. (Consider each problem independent of the others.)

2. Based on the types of errors and irregularities described in the above listing, would the CPA firm have any special problems if it were asked to perform an audit of the Varnke Company?

3. If your firm were asked to perform an audit of the Varnke Company, would it be responsible for discovering all the errors and irregularities for the year under review?

10-17. Jordan Finance Company opened four personal loan offices in neighboring cities on January 2, 1979. Small cash loans are made to borrowers who repay the principal with interest in monthly installments over a period not exceeding two years. Ralph Jordan, president of the company, uses one of the offices as a central office and visits the other offices periodically for supervision and internal auditing purposes.

Mr. Jordan is concerned about the honesty of his employees. He came to your office in December 1979 and stated, "I want to engage you to install a system to prohibit employees from embezzling cash." He also stated, "Until I went into business for myself I worked for a nationwide loan company with 500 offices and I'm familiar with that company's system of accounting and internal control. I want to describe that system so you can install it for me because it will absolutely prevent fraud."

Required:

1. How would you advise Mr. Jordan on his request that you install the large company's system of accounting and internal control for his firm? Discuss.

2. How would you respond to the suggestion that the new system would prevent embezzlement? Discuss.

3. Assume that in addition to undertaking the systems engagement in 1979, you agreed to examine Jordan Finance Company's financial statements for the year ended December 31, 1979. No scope limitations were imposed.
   a. How would you determine the scope necessary to satisfactorily complete your examination? Discuss.
   b. Would you be responsible for the discovery of fraud in this examination? Discuss. (AICPA Adapted)

348
Audit of the cash system

10-18. You have been asked by the board of trustees of a local church to review its accounting procedures. As part of this review you have prepared the following comments relating to the collections made at weekly services and record keeping for members' pledges and contributions:

- The church's board of trustees has delegated responsibility for financial management and audit of the financial records to the finance committee. This group prepares the annual budget and approves major disbursements but is not involved in collections or record keeping. No audit has been considered necessary in recent years, because the same trusted employee has kept church records and served as financial secretary for 15 years.

- The collection at the weekly service is taken by a team of ushers. The head usher counts the collection in the church office following each service. He then places the collection and a notation of the amount counted in the church safe. The next morning the financial secretary opens the safe and recounts the collection. He withholds about $100 to meet cash expenditures for the coming week and deposits the remainder of the collection. In order to facilitate the deposit, members who contribute by check are asked to make out their checks to "Cash."

- At their request a few members are furnished prenumbered predated envelopes in which to insert their weekly contributions. The head usher removes the cash from the envelopes to be counted with the loose cash included in the collection and discards the envelopes. No record is maintained of issuance or return of the envelopes, and the envelope system is not encouraged.

- Each member is asked to prepare a contribution pledge card annually. The pledge is regarded as a moral commitment by the member to contribute a stated weekly amount. Based upon the amounts shown on the pledge cards, the financial secretary furnishes a letter to requesting members to support the tax deductibility of their contributions.

Required: Describe the weaknesses and recommend improvements in procedures for:

1. Collections made at weekly services
2. Record keeping for members' pledges and contributions. Organize your answer sheets as follows:

WEAKNESS	RECOMMENDED IMPROVEMENT

10-19. You are reviewing the working papers for the Troy Department Store for the year ended December 31, 1979. A schedule from the working papers is reproduced in Problem Figure 10-19.

Required: Prepare a list of comments to be given the auditor that prepared the schedule.

Problem Figure 10-19

		1	2 Third State Bank	3 Comments	4
Balance per Bank			16781 22		
Deposit in Transit			1722 19	Traced to Cash Receipts Journal	
Outstanding Checks					
#2096		426 14			
#2097		381 61		Traced to Cash	
#2106		917 53		Disbursements Journal	
#1604		524 87	2250 15		
Bank Transfer to Second City Bk.			500 00	Agrees with Bank Statement	
Adjusting Journal Entry #12-84			286 14	Traced to approved journal entry	
Petty Cash Reimbursement - 1-8-80			394 76	Examined.	
			15861 88		
				RB	

Green Valley Corp.
Bank Reconciliation
12-31-79

PBC

350
Audit of the cash system

10-20. You are auditing the Alaska branch of Far Distributing Company. This branch has substantial annual sales which are billed and collected locally. As a part of your audit you find that the procedures for handling cash receipts are:

Cash collections on over-the-counter sales and COD sales are received from the customer or delivery service by the cashier. Upon receipt of cash the cashier stamps the sales ticket "Paid" and files a copy for future reference. The only record of COD sales is a copy of the sales ticket which is given to the cashier to hold until the cash is received from the delivery service.

Mail is opened by the secretary to the credit manager, and remittances are given to the credit manager for review. The credit manager then places the remittances in a tray on the cashier's desk. At the daily deposit cutoff time the cashier delivers the checks and cash on hand to the assistant credit manager who prepares remittance lists and makes up the bank deposit which he also takes to the bank. The assistant credit manager also posts remittances to the accounts receivable ledger cards and verifies the cash discount allowable.

You also ascertain that the credit manager obtains approval from the executive office of Far Distributing Company, located in Chicago, to write off uncollectible accounts, and that he has retained in his custody as of the end of the fiscal year remittances that were received on various days during the last month.

Required

1. Describe the irregularities that might occur under the procedures now in effect for handling cash collections and remittances.

2. Recommends procedures to strengthen internal control over cash collections and remittances. (AICPA Adapted)

10-21. William Green recently acquired the financial controlling interest of Importers and Wholesalers, Inc., importers and distributors of cutlery. In reviewing the duties of the employees Green became aware of loose practices in the signing of checks and the operation of the petty cash fund.

You have been engaged as the company's CPA, and Green's first request is that you suggest a system of sound practices for the signing of checks and the operation of the petty cash fund. Green prefers not to acquire a check-signing machine.

In addition to Green, who is the president, the company has 20 employees, including 4 corporate officers. About 200 checks are drawn each month. The petty cash fund has a working balance of about $200, and about $500 is expended by the fund each month.

Required: Prepare a letter to Green containing your recommendations for good internal control procedures for:

1. Signing checks. (Green is unwilling to be drawn into routine check-signing duties. Assume that you decided to recommend two signatures on each check.)

2. Operation of the petty cash fund. (Where the effect of the control procedure is not evident, give the reason for it.) (AICPA Adapted)

10-22. An essential phase of the audit of the cash balance at the end of the year is the auditor's review of a cutoff bank statement. Listed below are several objectives associated with the cash substantive tests:

1. Determine if lapping has occurred.
2. Determine if kiting has occurred.
3. Determine if the cash receipts journal was held open.
4. Determine if year-end bank transfers are properly recorded.
5. Determine if unauthorized bank accounts are being used.

6. Determine if disbursements per the bank statement can be reconciled with total checks written.
7. Determine if cash funds are subject to a compensating balance requirement.
8. Determine if the cash disbursements journal was held open.

Required

1. What is a bank cutoff statement?
2. For each item listed above explain whether the cutoff bank statement is utilized to achieve the objective.

10-23. Jerome Paper Company engaged you to review its internal control system. Jerome does not prelist cash receipts before they are recorded and has other weaknesses in processing collections of trade receivables, the company's largest asset. In discussing the matter with the controller, you find she is chiefly interested in economy when she assigns duties to the 15 office workers. She feels that the main consideration is that the work is done by people who are most familiar with it, capable of doing it, and available when it has to be done.

The controller says she has excellent control over trade receivables because receivables are pledged as security for a continually renewable bank loan and the bank sends out positive confirmation requests occasionally, based on a list of pledged receivables furnished by the company each week. You learn that the bank's internal auditor is satisfied if he receives an acceptable response on 70 percent of his requests.

Required

1. Explain how the prelisting of cash receipts strengthens internal control over cash.
2. Assume that an employee handles cash receipts from trade customers before they are recorded. List the duties that employee should not perform to withhold from him or her the opportunity to conceal embezzlement of cash receipts. (AICPA Adapted)

10-24. You are the in-charge accountant examining the financial statements of the Gutzler Company for the year ended December 31, 1979. During late October 1979 you, with the help of Gutzler's controller, completed an internal control questionnaire and prepared the appropriate memoranda describing Gutzler's accounting procedures. Your comments relative to cash receipts are:

All cash receipts are sent directly to the accounts receivable clerk with no processing by the mail department. The accounts receivable clerk keeps the cash receipts journal, prepares the bank deposit slip in duplicate, posts from the deposit slip to the subsidiary accounts receivable ledger, and mails the deposit to the bank.

The controller receives the validated deposit slips directly (unopened) from the bank. He also receives the monthly bank statement directly (unopened) from the bank and promptly reconciles it.

At the end of each month, the accounts receivable clerk notifies the general ledger clerk by journal voucher of the monthly totals of the cash receipts journal for posting to the general ledger.

Each month, with regard to the general ledger cash account, the general ledger clerk makes an entry to record the total debits to cash from the cash receipts journal. In addition, the general ledger clerk on occasion makes debit entries in the general ledger cash account from sources other than the cash receipts journal, e.g., funds borrowed from the bank.

Certain standard auditing procedures listed here have already been performed by you in the audit of cash receipts. The extent to which these procedures were performed is not relevant to the question.

352
Audit of the cash system

- Total and cross-total all columns in the cash receipts journal.
- Trace postings from the cash receipts journal to the general ledger.
- Examine remittance advices and related correspondence to support entries in the cash receipts journal.

Required: Considering Gutzler's internal control over cash receipts and standard auditing procedures already performed, list all other auditing procedures and reasons therefor which should be performed to obtain sufficient audit evidence regarding cash receipts. Do not discuss the procedures for cash disbursements and cash balances. Also, do not discuss the extent to which any of the procedures are to be performed. Assume adequate controls exist to assure that all sales transactions are recorded. Organize your answer sheet as follows:

OTHER AUDIT PROCEDURES	REASON FOR OTHER AUDIT PROCEDURES

(AICPA Adapted)

10-25. You are the senior in charge of a medium-sized audit engagement. Your assistant on the job was assigned the majority of the tests associated with the cash disbursements system and the substantive tests for cash. The assistant has completed the tests associated with the cash disbursements system and is about to begin the substantive tests.

During your preliminary review of some expense accounts, you are somewhat suspicious of a few of the disbursements. It is apparent that your assistant shares your concern, when he asks, "How can we be sure that cash disbursements are made only to authorized payees?"

Required

1. How would you respond to the question?

2. Is the problem suggested above likely to be discovered in the (a) cash compliance tests, (b) cash substantive tests, or (c) review of the nominal accounts?

10-26. Listed in the accompanying table are several bank transfers made during late December 1979 and early January 1980. The schedule was made, at your request, by the client.

TRANSACTION NUMBER	SECOND COUNTY BANK DISBURSING DATE		STATE BANK OF PRINCETON RECEIVING DATE	
	PER BANK	PER BOOKS	PER BANK	PER BOOKS
1	12/30	12/29	12/30	12/29
2	1/3	12/31	12/31	12/31
3	1/4	12/30	1/3	12/30
4	1/3	1/2	1/4	1/2
5	1/4	1/3	1/4	1/2
6	1/3	12/31	1/2	1/2

Required

1. How would you verify the accuracy of the schedule?

2. Would any of the six transfers appear on the bank reconciliation at December 31, 1979?

3. Assuming the schedule is correct, would you propose an adjusting journal entry?

10-27. The following information was obtained in an audit of the cash account of Tuck Company as of December 31, 1979. Assume that the CPA is satisfied as to the validity of the cash book, the bank statements, and the returned checks, except as noted.

1. The bookkeeper's bank reconciliation at November 30, 1979

Balance per bank statement			$ 19,400
Add deposit in transit			1,100
Total			20,500
Less outstanding checks No. 2540	$140		
1501	750		
1503	480		
1504	800		2,300
1505	30		
Balance per books			$ 18,200

2. A summary of the bank statement for December 1979

Balance brought forward	$ 19,400
Deposits	148,700
	168,100
Charges	132,500
Balance, December 31, 1979	$ 35,600

3. A summary of the cash book for December 1979 before adjustments

Balance brought forward	$ 18,200
Receipts	149,690
	167,890
Disbursements	124,885
Balance, December 31, 1979	$ 43,005

4. Included with the canceled checks returned with the December bank statement were the following:

NUMBER	DATE OF CHECK	AMOUNT OF CHECK ($)	COMMENT
1501	November 28, 1979	75	This check was in payment of an invoice for $750 and was recorded in the cash book as $750.
1503	November 28, 1979	580	This check was in payment of an invoice for $580 and was recorded in the cash book as $580.
1523	December 5, 1979	150	Examination of this check revealed that it was unsigned. A discussion with the client disclosed that it had been mailed inadvertently before it was signed. The check was endorsed and deposited by the payee and processed by the bank even through it was a legal nullity. The check was recorded in the cash disbursements.

NUMBER	DATE OF CHECK	AMOUNT OF CHECK ($)	COMMENT
1528	December 5, 1979	800	This check replaced no. 1504 that was returned by the payee because it was mutilated. Check no. 1504 was not canceled on the books.
	December 19, 1979	200	This was a countercheck drawn at the bank by the president of the company as a cash advance for travel expenses. The president overlooked informing the bookkeeper about the check.
	December 20, 1979	300	The drawer of this check was the Tucker Company.
1535	December 20, 1979	350	This check had been stamped "nonsufficient funds" and returned to the payee because the bank erroneously believed it was drawn by the Luck Company. Subsequently the payee was advised to redeposit the check.
1575	January 5, 1980	10,000	This check was given to the payee on December 30, 1979, as a postdated check with the understanding that it would not be deposited until January 5, 1980. The check was not recorded on the books in December.

5. The Tuck Company discounted its own 60-day note for $9000 with the bank on December 1, 1979. The discount rate was 6 percent. The bookkeeper recorded the proceeds as a cash receipt at the face value of the note.

6. The bookkeeper records customers' dishonored checks as a reduction in cash receipts. When the dishonored checks are redeposited, they are recorded as a regular cash receipts. Two checks stamped "nonsufficient funds" for $180 and $220 were returned by the bank during December. The $180 check was redeposited, but the $220 check was still on hand on December 31.

   Cancelations of Tuck Company checks are recorded as a reduction in cash disbursements.

7. December bank charges were $20. In addition a $10 service charge was made in December for the collection of a foreign draft in November. These charges were not recorded on the books.

8. Check no. 2540 listed in the November outstanding checks was drawn in 1976. Since the payee cannot be located, the president of Tuck Company agreed to the CPA's suggestion that the check be written back into the accounts by a journal entry.

9. Outstanding checks at December 31, 1979, totaled $4000 excluding checks no. 2540 and no. 1504.

10. The cutoff bank statement disclosed that the bank had recorded a deposit of $2400 on January 2, 1980. The bookkeeper had recorded this deposit on the books on December 31, 1979, and then mailed the deposit to the bank.

Required: Prepare a four-column reconciliation (sometimes called a proof of cash) of the cash receipts and cash disbursements recorded on the bank statement and on the company's books for the month of December 1979. The reconciliation should agree with the cash figure that will appear in the company's financial statements. (AICPA Adapted)

10-28. You have completed your examination of the cash on hand and in banks in your audit of the Hoosier Company's financial statements for the year ended December 31, 1977, and noted the following.

1. The company maintains a general bank account at the National Bank and an imprest payroll bank account at the City Bank. All checks are signed by the company president, Douglas Hoosier.

2. Data and reconciliations prepared by Donald Hume, the company bookkeeper, on November 30, 1977, indicated that the payroll account has a $1000 general ledger and bank balance with no in-transit or outstanding items, and that the general bank account had a $12,405 general ledger balance with checks outstanding aggregating $918 (no. 1202 for $575 and no. 1205 for $343) and one deposit of $492 in transit.

3. Your surprise cash count on Tuesday, January 2, 1978, revealed that customers' checks totaling $540 and a National Bank deposit slip for that amount dated December 29, 1977, were in the company safe and that no cash was in transit to the bank at that time. Your examination of the general account checkbook revealed check no. 1216 to be the first unused check.

4. Company general ledger accounts are prepared on a posting machine, and all transactions are posted in chronological sequence. The ledger card for the general bank account is reproduced on page 000.

5. The December statements from both banks were delivered unopened to you. The City Bank statement contained deposits for $1675, $1706, $1845, and $2597 and 72 paid checks totaling $7823. The National Bank statement is reproduced here:

THE NATIONAL BANK
Account: Hoosier Company (General Account)

DATE	CHARGES		CREDITS	BALANCE
Nov. 30				12,831
Dec. 1			492	13,323
Dec. 5	1,675	267 RT	496	11,877
Dec. 8	575		832	12,134
Dec. 11	1,706	654	975	10,749
Dec. 14	1,987 D	2,062	8,045	14,745
Dec. 18	6,237	1,845	9,949	16,612
Dec. 21	241 RT	546 RT	546 CM	16,371
Dec. 22	2,072 D		1,513	15,812
Dec. 26	2,597			13,215
Dec. 28	362	4 DM	1,010 CM	13,859
Dec. 29	12 DM		362	14,209
	Total charges: $22,842		Total Credits: $24,220	

Legend: OD: Overdraft   RT: Returned check   DM: Debit memo
CM: Credit memo   D: Draft

356
Audit of the
cash system

GENERAL LEDGER
GENERAL BANK ACCOUNT
(The National Bank)

REF.	DEBITS	CREDITS	BALANCE
Bal			12,405
12-1	496 ✓		12,901
1206		1,675	11,226
1207		(645)	10,581
12-6	832 ✓		11,413
1208		1,706 ✓	9,707
12-8	975 ✓		10,682
1209		2,062 ✓	8,620
1210		3,945 ✓	4,675
1211		6,237 ✓	1,562*
12-12	8,045 ✓		6,483
12-15	(9,549)		16,032
1212		1,845 ✓	14,187
RT		241 ✓	13,946
1213		350 ✓	13,596
D		2,072 ✓	11,524
12-22	1,513 ✓		13,037
1214		2,597 ✓	10,440
1215		1,739 ✓	8,701
12-29	540		9,241
12-31	942		10,183
1216		1,120 ✓	9,063
	22,892	26,234	

*Represents a negative balance.

6. Cutoff statements were secured by you personally from both banks on January 8, 1978, and the National Bank statement is reproduced here:

THE NATIONAL BANK
Account: Hoosier Company (General Account)

DATE	CHARGES		CREDITS	BALANCE
Dec 29				14,209
Jan 2	1,739	3,945	540	9,065
Jan 5	350		942	9,657

7. You determine that the bank statements are correct, except that the National Bank incorrectly charged a returned check on December 21 but credited the account the same day.
8. The $362 check charged by the National Bank on December 28 was check no. 2000 drawn payable to Hoosier Company and endorsed "Hoosier Company by Donald Hume." Your investigation showed that the amount credited by the National Bank on December 29 was an unauthorized transfer from the City Bank payroll account to the National Bank general account which had been made by the company's bookkeeper who made no related entry in the company's records. The check was charged to Hoosier Company on January 2, 1978, on the cutoff statement received by you from the City Bank.

9. Drafts charged against the National Bank account were for trade acceptances which were signed by Douglas Hoosier and issued to a supplier.
10. On December 28 a 60-day 6 percent $1000 note was collected by the National Bank for Hoosier for a $4 collection fee.
11. The $12 debit memo from the National Bank was a charge for printed checks.
12. Check no. 1213 was issued to replace check no. 1205 when the latter was reported not received by a vendor. Because of the delay in paying this account, Hoosier Company was no longer entitled to the 2 percent cash discount it had taken in preparing the original check.

Required: Prepare a proof of cash for December for Hoosier's general bank account at the National Bank. Your proof of cash should show the computation of the adjusted balances for both the bank statement and the general ledger account of the National Bank for cash in bank November 30, December receipts, December disbursements, and cash in bank December 31. The following column headings are recommended:

DESCRIPTION	NOVEMBER 30 RECONCILIATION	DECEMBER RECEIPTS	DECEMBER DISBURSEMENTS	DECEMBER 31 RECONCILIATION

(AICPA Adapted)

MULTIPLE CHOICE

1. Which of the following is a responsibility that should not be assigned to only one employee?

   a. Access to securities in the company's safe deposit box.
   b. Custodianship of the cash working fund.
   c. Reconciliation of bank statements.
   d. Custodianship of tools and small equipment.

2. One of the better ways for an auditor to detect kiting is to

   a. Request a cutoff bank statement.
   b. Send a bank confirmation.
   c. Prepare a bank transfer working paper.
   d. Prepare a bank reconciliation at year end.

3. During his examination of a January 19, 1979, cutoff bank statement, an auditor noticed that the majority of checks listed as outstanding at December 31, 1978, had not cleared the bank. This indicates

   a. A high probability of lapping.
   b. A high probability of kiting.
   c. That the cash disbursements journal had been held open past December 31, 1978.
   d. That the cash disbursements journal had been closed prior to December 31, 1978.

358
**Audit of the
cash system**

4. For good internal control, the monthly bank statements should be reconciled by someone under the direction of the

    a. Credit manager.
    b. Controller.
    c. Cashier.
    d. Treasurer.

5. For good internal control, the person who signs checks should be the

    a. Person preparing the checks.
    b. Purchasing agent.
    c. Accounts payable clerk.
    d. Treasurer.

(AICPA Adapted)

CHAPTER 11

Notes & Accts Rec.

Audit of the credit sales system

There is a variety of accounting methods that are acceptable for the recognition of revenue. These range from the percentage of completion method for long-term contracts to a modified cash basis for certain installment contracts. *APB Statement No. 4* declares that "Revenue is generally recognized when both of the following conditions are met: (1) the earning process is complete or virtually complete, and (2) an exchange has taken place." In contemporary accounting the circumstances of the transaction determine the appropriate revenue recognition method.

This chapter deals with typical methods by which revenue is recognized. For most business entities revenue is recognized when goods or services are delivered to their customers. This transaction may result in the immediate payment of cash or in the financing of the sale through the issuance of credit to the customer. Both systems, the credit sales system and the cash sales system, are discussed, although more attention is given to the credit sales system. Since this book emphasizes a systems approach, a thorough discussion of the substantive tests for accounts receivable is offered. The cash substantive procedures were discussed in the previous chapter.

CREDIT SALES SYSTEM

The credit sales system is a vital part of the overall internal control system in most organizations. This system encompasses the receipt of an order from a customer to the delivery of goods or services to that customer. The processing of credit sales transactions has a significant impact upon the financial statements of the customer. Such importance affects the auditor's design of the audit plan, and an appropriate audit effort is devoted to study and evaluation of the credit sales system. The ability to evaluate the system rests in part on the auditor's comprehension of what constitutes a sound system of internal accounting controls

359

360
Audit of the credit sales system

in this phase of the engagement. Again, it is possible to construct an internal control model that can be used as a norm for the evaluation of an accounting system.

INTERNAL CONTROL MODEL: CREDIT SALES

The features of an adequate internal control system for credit sales can be grouped as those relating to the plan of organization and those associated with the authorization of, and subsequent accountability for, a transaction.

Departmental autonomy

A plan of organization recognizes that tasks and responsibilities need to be assigned to specific departments. Once designated, these roles should not be infringed upon by other departments. In the credit sales system the following assignment of tasks and responsibilities is observed:

I. Accounting department
1. Maintenance of the sales journal
2. Maintenance of the accounts receivable subsidiary ledger
3. Maintenance of the general ledger
4. Review of sales authorization and execution
5. Review of authorization and execution of credit allowances and write-offs
6. Accounting for the numerical sequence of sales documents
7. Preparation of customer invoices
8. Preparation of monthly customer statements

II. Treasurer
1. Approval of credit sales (credit manager)
2. Initiation of bad debt write-offs (credit manager)
3. Approval of bad debt write-offs (treasurer)
4. Approval of credit allowances in conjunction with the sales department (credit manager)
5. Responsibility for collection function (credit manager)

III. Functions other than accounting and treasurer
1. Custody control over inventory (warehousing)
2. Responsibility for the receipt of returned goods (receiving department)
3. Authorization to sell goods (sales department)
4. Responsibility for the delivery of goods upon proper approval (shipping department)

A proper plan of organization segregates the elements of the selling and recording function so that no one department has complete authority over the transaction. This helps to ensure that fraudulent sales are not made and that errors are not perpetuated and concealed.

System of authorization and accountability

361
Internal control
model: credit
sales

EXECUTION OF TRANSACTIONS

In the credit sales system several authorizations take place before a transaction can be processed. The authorization is for each individual transaction and is not general in nature. For this reason, several documents are generated during the execution phase of the system.

Authorization for sale: The authority to sell an organization's goods resides in the sales department. Receipt of a customer order may take a variety of forms, including a formal customer purchase order, an order prepared by a salesperson, or a telephone order. In any case, the sales order is prepared in a manner consistent with the policies established by the sales department. After review and appropriate notation of authorization the customer order is then sent to the credit department for further scrutiny.

Authorization for credit: To act as a restraint on the sales department's natural desire to sell as much of the organization's goods as possible, the sales order must be approved by the credit manager who is usually part of the treasurer's department. Authorization generally consists of initialing or stamping the sales order. Although responsible for administration of the credit policy, the credit manager or treasurer does not unilaterally determine this policy for an organization. The general credit policies and guidelines are usually established by responsible corporation officials drawn from the sales, finance, accounting, and other appropriate functional areas of an organization. Such an approach suggests the importance of establishing and administering a credit policy. From an audit perspective, the credit policy and procedures have an impact on determination of the bad debt expense for the year and the allowance account balance at the end of the year.

Authorization for shipment: An organization carefully controls the movement of its assets. To prevent the unauthorized shipment of goods, either by mistake or by intent, the warehouse or stores department delivers goods to the shipping department only upon the receipt of appropriate instruction. The sales order approved by the credit department may serve as authorization for the movement of goods from the inventory storing area to the shipping department. After inspecting the authorization, the shipping department prepares the goods for shipment and documents the shipment by an entry in a shipping register or through the preparation of a prenumbered bill of lading.

Authorization for billing: Once the goods are shipped, the accounting department is notified so that the customer can be billed. Notification from the shipping department as to the description and quantity of goods shipped serves as authorization for the preparation of a sales invoice.

362
Audit of the credit sales system

Authorization for write-offs and credits: In the course of normal events an organization may reduce a receivable balance through the write-off of an account or the granting of an allowance. Execution of a bad debt write-off requires that the credit manager initiate a write-off request, and ultimate approval rests with the credit manager's superior, usually the treasurer. An allowance resulting from the return of goods is approved by the sales department and the credit manager. In addition, the receiving department prepares and forwards a receiving report to the accounting department to substantiate the receipt of the goods. Other allowances, such as credits allowed for advertising, are approved by the corporate official responsible for administration of the special program. Appropriate approval in the form of a document is forwarded to the accounting department for review and processing.

RECORDING OF TRANSACTIONS

The internal accounting control system includes procedures to encourage the recording of a transaction in a manner consistent with its execution. Entry in the proper accounting period, in the correct amount, and in the appropriate account are elements of the recording of transactions.

Review of documentation: Before a credit sales transaction is recorded, the documents supporting it are reviewed. An employee in the accounting department inspects and compares the customer order, sales invoice, and shipping authorization to determine the legitimacy of the sale. In addition, the sales invoice is reviewed for proper pricing and correct quantities, and extensions and footings are verified.

Accounting for prenumbered documents: Documents that are prenumbered provide an excellent basis for determining if all transactions are recorded. Internal control procedures include accounting for all sales invoices and bills of lading or shipping advices used during the accounting period. A document is either unused or is part of the documentation package that substantiates a transaction. For example, if it is determined that the first bill-of-lading number used during the accounting period was 10,600 and the last number used was 11,900, then a review of the numerical file of the used documents can satisfy the reviewer that all used prenumbered sales invoices were recorded. This review may be done by a member of the accounting department who has no other duties in the sales function or by the internal audit department. A similar approach can be used to account for shipping documents. Such procedures are part of the normal routine in a well-designed internal control system.

Consistency of data: An additional element that strengthens an internal control system is the comparison of amounts generated by two or more independent sources. In the credit sales system there is a comparison of total sales, usually on a monthly basis, to the total debits processed through the accounts receivable subsidiary ledger. In some organizations this comparison is made on a daily basis, or any time a batch of sales invoices is processed. If the amounts do not balance, an error obviously exists somewhere in the transaction recording process.

ACCESS TO ASSETS

The safeguarding of assets in the credit sales function is concerned with indirect access to inventory and accounts receivable. This objective is enhanced by the proper segregation of duties and observance of the following internal control procedures.

Access to inventory: Inventory is the custodial responsibility of the storeroom clerk or a warehouse employee. These individuals do not release inventory unless appropriate authorization is presented. Thus shipping clerks are denied access to merchandise. Conversely, only goods that are properly approved are shipped by the shipping department. In this case, the storeroom clerk is not allowed to ship material.

Access to accounts receivable: Unlike inventory, accounts receivable cannot be physically removed from the client's premises. Nonetheless, internal control measures are adopted to protect against an unauthorized write-off or credit being charged against the receivable balance. As suggested earlier, only authorized personnel can initiate and approve such charges.

COMPARISON OF RECORDED ACCOUNTABILITY WITH ASSETS

The credit sales accounting system has an impact on determining the balance in accounts receivable. Effective internal control procedures are adopted to validate the accounting records by determining the existence of the asset.

Preparation of customer statements: Someone independent of the billing and posting function prepares and mails customers' statements, usually on a monthly basis. This individual is responsible for the receipt and clearance of any complaints from customers. In some organizations the internal auditors perform this task.

Direct confirmation: In a manner similar to the above procedure, but performed less frequently, a letter is sent directly to the customer asking for verification of a balance at a specific date. Again, someone independent of the billing and posting function is responsible for the confirmation of balances and the review of responses.

STUDY AND EVALUATION OF THE CREDIT SALES SYSTEM

The study of the credit sales system is conducted so that the auditor can gain a knowledge of the accounting control procedures being utilized. As in other systems documentation procedures in the audit engagement, the auditor may prepare an internal control questionnaire, flowchart, memorandum, or a combination of the three.

364
Audit of the credit sales system

Figure 11-1 is a typical credit sales system internal control questionnaire. Again, the questions are structured so that the auditor can identify processing steps or organizational structure that violates the concepts of the internal control model. A flowchart illustrating a strong internal control system is presented in Figure 11-2.

Having studied the credit sales internal control system, the auditor forms a preliminary evaluation of it. The evaluation process provides a link between the analytic and corroborative phases of the audit. Consideration is given to the types of errors that may occur in the credit sales system. In addition, accounting controls that may prevent such errors are identified. Upon completion of the evaluation of the system, the auditor considers the nature, timing, and extent of the auditing procedures to be used in the compliance and substantive tests. For example, he or she may conclude that the credit sales internal control system is strong and therefore decide that the confirmation of accounts receivable is to be conducted at an interim date. However, the auditor's conclusions are tentative and do not become firm until the compliance tests are completed. It is not unusual for a system to look strong on paper but in actuality to operate in a manner that violates many of the concepts of adequate internal control structure.

COMPLIANCE TESTS: CREDIT SALES

The auditor's initial evaluation of the credit sales internal control system is the basis for the selection of specific audit procedures for the compliance tests. There is no general audit program that is applicable to every audit, but the one in Figure 11-3 lists the typical procedures performed when an adequate internal control system is assumed to exist.

Universe definition and sample selection

The compliance tests for the credit sales system are designed to determine if prescribed accounting procedures are being observed. More specifically, an auditor is concerned with determining whether recorded sales are authentic and that all items shipped are billed. Based on the auditor's review of the client's internal control system, the area of significant audit exposure usually dictates the identification of the universe. For example, when it is concluded that the shipping function for an organization is weak, the auditor is concerned with determining whether all inventory shipped was billed. In this example the auditor selects the shipping information, such as a file of prenumbered bills of lading, as the universe. On the other hand, when he or she is concerned with validating recorded sales, the universe consists of a collection of sales information, such as a file of prenumbered sales invoices or the sales journal. It is important that the auditor identify the audit objective and then proceed to select a universe that is consistent with this objective.

Having selected an appropriate universe, the auditor determines that it is intact. The completeness of the universe ensures that the auditor has defined the entire set of credit sales transactions that occurred during the review period. Each transaction must be part of the total universe to allow it to be selected for investigation. This is true of judgment as well as statistical sampling. If an auditor

Figure 11-1

Internal Control Questionnaire

	Answer		Answer based on		
Sales and shipping	Yes	No	Inquiry	Observation	Comments
1. Are sales orders adequately controlled?					
2. Are all orders approved by the credit manager or department before shipment?					
3. Is the credit department entirely independent of the sales department?					
4. Are sales prices and credit terms based on approved standard price lists?					
5. If so, are any deviations from standard approved — a. by an officer? b. by another? Explain.					
6. If not, are all sales prices and credit terms approved by the sales manager or in the sales department?					
7. Are prenumbered shipping advices prepared for all goods shipped?					
8. Are the quantities shown on the shipping advices double-checked in the shipping department?					
9. Does the billing clerk or some other designated employee receive the shipping advices directly from the shipping department? (If so, identify this employee.)					
10. Does this employee check the numerical sequence of shipping advices to assure that all are accounted for?					
11. Are sales invoices checked — a. as to prices? b. as to quantities? c. as to credit terms? d. as to extensions and footings? e. against customers' orders? f. against shipping advices? (Identify the department or individual responsible for the above.)					
12. Are sales invoices prenumbered?					
13. Is there a check in the arithmetic accuracy of total sales by means of a statistical or product analysis?					
14. Are total sales for the respective accounting periods (e.g., monthly) reported directly to the general ledger bookkeeper independently of the work of the accounts receivable bookkeepers?					
15. Are there adequate safeguards against understatement of sales through the suppression of sales invoices or shipping advices?					

Figure 11-1 (Continued)

Sales and shipping (continued)	Answer		Answer based on		
	Yes	No	Inquiry	Observation	Comments
16. Are returned sales cleared through the receiving department (i.e., the department receiving incoming purchased materials and supplies)?					
17. Are credit memos for returned sales supported by adequate data from the receiving department as to quantity, description, and condition?					
18. Are the following classes of sales accounted for in substantially the same manner as regular credit sales of merchandise:					
a. Sales to employees?					
b. C.O.D. sales?					
c. Sales of property and equipment?					
d. Cash sales of merchandise?					
e. Scrap and waste?					
(If the answers are in any case negative, amplify by a concise description of the procedures.)					
19. Is there an adequate check on freight allowances –					
a. by reference to terms of sale?					
b. by checking against freight bills or established and up-to-date schedule of freight rates?					
c. by other means? (If any, explain.)					

selects prenumbered sales invoices as the universe, a scanning of the sequential file and an accounting for a few blocks of invoices are employed to determine if the universe is intact.

Once the universe is defined and determined to be intact, the auditor selects a sample of transactions for audit. The selection approach involves utilization of a random numbers table, sequential sampling, or block sampling. As suggested in previous chapters, the size of the sample is dependent upon the evaluation of the credit sales internal control system, the results of previous years' tests, and the audit significance of the control under investigation. Documentation of the selection process and control of the sample items selected for investigation are two important elements of sample selection. The selection process documentation provides a basis for subsequent review by other members of the audit firm to see if the approach is justified by the audit circumstances. Once they are selected, the auditor establishes control over the sample items. The control, which may consist of recording the sales invoice numbers selected, is used as the basis for keeping abreast of what procedures have been completed and the outcome of employing the procedure. In many cases the client is asked to obtain or "pull" documents that support an item chosen for review. In the case of a sales invoice number, the relevant documents are the customer order, sales invoice, and bill of lading or other shipping authorization document. To ensure the integrity of the control sheet, the auditor does not allow the client an

Figure 11-1 (Continued)

	Answer		Answer based on		
Accounts receivable	Yes	No	Inquiry	Observation	Comments
1. Are the customers' ledgers kept by employees who have no access to cash receipts?					
2. Are the customers' ledgers balanced at least monthly and the totals agreed with the general ledger control account?					
3. Answer the following: a. Are statements of open items mailed to all customers monthly? If not, to what extent are they mailed?					
b. If so, is this done by an employee who has no access to cash and who is independent of the accounts receivable book-keepers and the billing clerks?					
c. Does this employee retain control of the statements until mailed?					
d. Are differences reported by customers routed to this same employee for investigation?					
4. Are delinquent accounts listed periodically for review by an official other than the credit manager?					
5. Are write-offs of bad debts approved by an official other than the credit manager?					
6. Are charged-off accounts kept under memo ledger control and followed up? Explain.					
7. Are credit memos approved by a responsible official?					
8. Are such credit memos under numerical control?					
9. Is approval of a responsible official required for discounts allowed after the discount date or in excess of normal credit terms?					
10. Are credits for returned goods checked against receiving reports?					
11. Are direct confirmations of notes and accounts receivable obtained periodically — a. by internal auditors? b. by other designated employees?					
12. Is the management of the credit department entirely divorced from the sales department?					
13. Is the cashier denied access to the accounts receivable ledgers?					
14. Answer the following: a. Is merchandise out on consignment recorded in a memor-andum accounts receivable ledger?					
b. If consigned merchandise is a material and/or continuing factor, outline the client's procedures in this respect on a separate page with a cross reference hereto.					
15. Are journal entries affecting accounts receivables approved by someone senior to the accounts receivable bookkeepers?					

Figure 11-2
Sales: Procedural Flowchart Shown in Relation to Organizational Chart to Portray the Control Obtained through Segregation of Functional Responsibility.

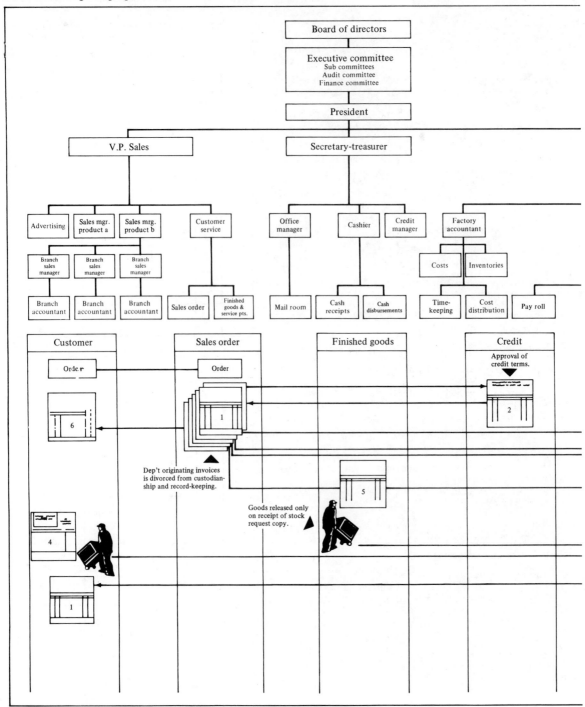

SOURCE: AICPA, "Internal Control," 1949.

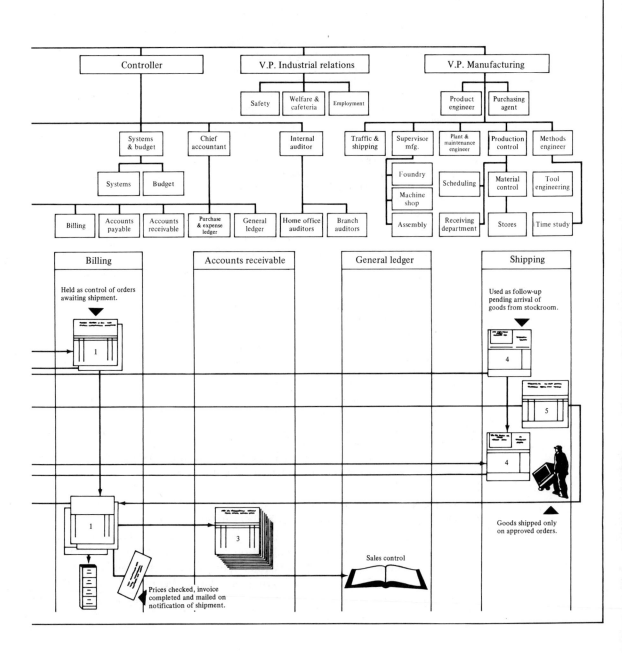

370
Audit of the
credit sales
system

Figure 11-3

Audit program: credit sales

PROCEDURES	DATE COMPLETED	WORK PERFORMED BY
1. The universe is defined as the prenumbered sales invoices used during the review period. Each invoice is a sample item. Determine the size of the universe.	_____	_____
2. Randomly select 150 sales invoices for investigation.	_____	_____
3. For each sample item:		
a. Trace authorization for the sale and the granting of credit to the customer order.	_____	_____
b. Trace authorization for shipment to the bill of lading.	_____	_____
c. Compare the information per the sales invoice, customer order, and bill of lading, noting customer name, address, and shipping instructions.	_____	_____
d. Trace authorization documents to entry in the sales journal and the accounts receivable subsidiary ledger.	_____	_____
e. Recompute footings and extensions on the sales invoice.	_____	_____
f. Trace billing prices per the sales invoice to an approved price list or other authorization.	_____	_____
4. Select 20 sales credit memos for review and perform the following procedures:	_____	_____
a. Examine the credit memo for proper authorization, including the unit price allowance.	_____	_____
b. For items returned, trace to the receiving report and note the quantity, date received, and product identification.	_____	_____
c. Recompute footing and extensions on the credit memo.	_____	_____
d. Trace authorization documents to entry in the appropriate journal and the accounts receivable subsidiary ledger.	_____	_____
5. Account for the numerical sequence of sales invoices, shipping documents, and sales credit memos.	_____	_____
6. For three months chosen at random, foot the sales journal and trace postings to the general ledger.	_____	_____
7. Review the sales journal, the subsidiary accounts receivable ledger, and the general ledger accounts for unusual items.	_____	_____

opportunity to make changes to the original listing. Figure 11-4 is an example
of the usefulness of a control sheet. The audit procedures listed in this figure are
based on the audit program illustrated in Figure 11-3.

VALIDATION OF AUTHORIZATION

The execution of a sales transaction is reviewed to determine if it is properly
authorized. In the normal sales cycle there are three stages of authorization that
are validated by the auditor. The validation process consists of obtaining a list
of employees who have the authority to execute a transaction and the auditor's
inspection of a document for a signature or other indication of approval. The
initial approval granted in the sales department for the sale of goods at a certain

Figure 11-4

371

Compliance tests: credit sales

Green Valley Corp.
Test of Sales Transaction
For 1979 FY

		Audit Procedures Sales Invoices								Audit Procedures Credit Memos			
Sample#	Sales Invoice#	3a	3b	3c	3d	3e	3f	Sample#	Memo#	4a	4b	4c	4d
1	10643	✓		✓	✓	✓	✓	1	822	✓		✓	
2	14187	✓	✓	✓	✓	✓	✓	2	629	✓	④	✓	✓
3	17703	✓	✓	✓	①	✓	✓	3	839	✓	✓	✓	✓
4	16898	✓	✓	✓	✓	✓	✓	•					
5	14742	✓	✓	✓	✓	③	✓	•					
6	12693	✓	✓	✓	✓			•					
•								18	693	✓	④	✓	✓
•								19	749	✓	✓	✓	✓
•								20	798	✓	✓	✓	✓
148	18114	✓	✓	✓	✓		✓						
149	17010	✓	✓	②	✓	✓	✓						
150	13496	✓	✓	✓	✓	✓							

✓ - Audit Procedure performed.

① - Amount per sales invoice was $475.64; amount entered in subsidiary ledger was $457.64. Appears to be unintentional.

② - Bill of lading missing. Subsequent cash collection reviewed.

③ - Two extension errors on sales invoice. Client states temporary office help was used for a 9 day period during summer vacation. Thirty sales invoices were chosen for these 3 days and math accuracy was checked. No errors discovered.

④ - Client is not prompt in posting credit memos to accounting records. These two memos were posted three weeks after issued and dated as of the date of posting. Cut-off procedures should be expanded at year-end. See audit program @ D-15.

Prepared by REB
Date 10/3/79

Index No. B-410

price, along with other mutually agreed-upon terms, may take the form of a stamped customer order or a formal contract. During the inspection of these documents the auditor not only notes that the transaction was authorized but also reviews other information contained in the document to determine if it has audit significance. For example, a contract that contains a bill-and-hold clause, whereby the client in effect functions as a warehouse for the customer, has an impact on the auditor's inventory observation procedures.

Credit authorization commits the client to a sale on account. The credit-granting process results in some form of approval notation that is inspected by the auditor for the sample items chosen for review. This review is not perfunctory, for the auditor is concerned not only with the approval process but also with any changes in the credit-granting policy and the application of the policy. For example, a client usually has a list of customers approved for credit and a maximum line of credit for each. The auditor confirms that the guidelines are being observed by comparing the balance per the subsidiary accounts receivable ledger card at the date of the credit request to the credit line amount approved. A significant deviation from the credit line guide or the granting of credit to customers not on the approved list has an impact on the determination of bad debt expense for the fiscal year.

Shipping authorization is the final approval stage in the credit sales system. In most cases a copy of the approved sales invoice or a special shipping order serves as authorization for the shipment of goods. During the shipment phase, the shipping department generates documentation that shows that the goods were shipped. This part of the execution of the transaction is documented by the completion of a bill of lading, a delivery ticket, or simply an entry in a shipping register. Whatever the form of documentation, the auditor inspects it for authenticity. If he or she has chosen prenumbered sales invoices as the universe, during the review of the documents generated in the shipping area, the auditor selects a few items from the shipment file. These items are traced to the sales journal to verify that items shipped are billed and recorded properly.

PROPRIETY OF DATA DOCUMENTED

Approval of a transaction at one point does not ensure that data originally approved have not been modified, lost, or changed in some manner. For this reason, the auditor follows the data through each execution stage to make sure they are consistent with the previous processing step. In the credit sales system, the auditor compares data contained on the customer order, sales invoice, and shipment document as to name, address, quantity, and product description. Inadequacies in this area may result in excessive sales returns which the auditor considers in planning the audit program for the year end. Special attention is devoted to preparation of the sales invoice. In addition to the review of appropriate customer, description, and item quantity, the auditor checks the propriety of the invoice price. Prices appearing on the sales invoice are traced to an approved customer price list, appropriate catalog, or amounts specified in a contract. Computations resulting from invoice extensions and summations are verified by the auditor.

COMPARISON OF DOCUMENTS TO ACCOUNTING RECORDS

Having determined that the transaction was executed properly, the auditor performs tests to see if it was recorded as executed. Utilizing the previous audit procedures, he or she substantiates the authenticity of the data appearing on the sales invoice. The sales invoice is traced to postings in the sales journal and the accounts receivable subsidiary ledger, comparing the name, address, and dollar amount. In addition, using the shipment date per the delivery document, the auditor verifies that the sale is recorded promptly. This alerts him or her to the possibility of a cutoff problem.

If the auditor chooses sample items from the sales invoices used, transactions must be traced from the books of original entry back to supporting documents. For example, he or she selects a few postings from the sales journal and the accounts receivable subsidiary ledger and validates them by reviewing the sales invoice, customer order, and bill of lading.

TEST OF THE SALES SUMMARIZATION

Sales invoices are not posted to the general ledger on an individual basis, but rather they are summarized on a monthly basis and the resulting total posted to the ledger. The auditor selects one or more months and foots the sales journal for these months, tracing the total to the appropriate account in the general ledger. At the same time he or she determines if the subsidiary ledger is balanced with the accounts receivable control account on a periodic basis. To substantiate a positive response from the client, the auditor may inspect the monthly trial balance of accounts receivable and trace the total to the general ledger amount. Also, reconciliations bringing the two accounting records into agreement may be prepared by the client and inspected by the auditor.

REVIEW FOR UNUSUAL ITEMS

A detailed review of a few sales transactions is not the extent of the audit test. The subsidiary ledger accounts, the sales journal, and the accounts receivable control account are reviewed for unusual items. The credit sales system impacts the debit side of the accounts receivable control account. Any debit to this account, other than from the sales journal, is investigated. Furthermore, unusually large sales amounts appearing in the sales or subsidiary journal are selected for further analysis by the auditor. Inquisitiveness is the auditor's best ally in the successful implementation of this procedure.

Results of compliance tests

The audit results of the tests of compliance for the credit sales system are used by the auditor to finalize the substantive tests of accounts receivable. A sound internal control structure validated by the compliance tests suggests that audit procedures may be restricted. For example, the number of accounts receivable confirmed may be reduced from the coverage achieved in the previous year's audit. The nature of the audit procedures employed may also be altered by the

374
Audit of the
credit sales
system

results of the tests of compliance. A client that has chosen to liberalize its credit policy makes it necessary for the auditor to be more concerned with the collectibility of the account rather than the existence of the balance. In the latter case, the auditor concentrates on the review of cash collections subsequent to the end of the year and the critical evaluation of the aged trial balance of accounts receivable with perhaps an attendant reduction in the circularization of receivables.

SUBSTANTIVE TESTS: ACCOUNTS RECEIVABLE

The processing of transactions through the credit sales internal control system has an impact on the balance in the accounts receivable account. In a similar fashion, the cash receipts system impacts this balance sheet account. Having evaluated these two accounting systems subsequent to the compliance tests, the auditor devises a substantive audit approach for review of the accounts receivable balance. This analysis is the basis for determining the timing, nature, and extent of the audit procedures. In the timing of the audit procedures the auditor may confirm accounts receivable at an interim date or at the balance sheet date. The following discussion assumes that the audit procedures are performed at or after the balance sheet date. Later in the chapter an interim review approach is discussed.

The nature and extent of the audit procedures are expressed in the preparation of an audit program for accounts receivable. In structuring the audit program, the auditor attempts to meet the basic audit objectives of determining the existence and valuation of the asset, as well as making sure that the client achieved a proper cutoff. Finally, the auditor must be satisfied that the resulting balance from the financial transactions is fully disclosed and classified properly in the financial statements. Figure 11-5 is an example of a typical audit program.

Existence

The first three audit procedures listed in Figure 11-5 are concerned with the existence of the amounts that comprise the accounts receivable balance. These procedures are utilized by the auditor to determine that a customer has acknowledged a debt to the client and that the debt has been properly recorded in the accounting records as to name, amount, and date.

THE AGED TRIAL BALANCE

In the review of any account or group of transactions the auditor is careful to gain control of the data before more detailed audit procedures are employed. However, it is impractical and cumbersome for him or her to control physically the accounts receivable subsidiary ledger during the audit of the account. For this reason, the client is asked to prepare a detailed listing of accounts receivable as of the balance sheet date, classifying each account by its age. An example of an aged trial balance appears in Figure 11-6.

Figure 11-5

Audit program: accounts receivable

PROCEDURES	DATE COMPLETED	WORK PERFORMED BY
1. Obtain and test the accuracy of the aged trial balance prepared by the client.		
2. Select a sample of receivables for confirmation.		
3. Review nonresponses and exceptions for confirmations mailed.		
4. Review the adequacy of the allowance for bad debt accounts.		
5. Determine the propriety of sales cutoff at the end of the year.		
6. Review receivables for proper classification and disclosure.		

Since the trial balance is prepared by the client or the internal audit staff, the auditor determines its authenticity. The trial balance is footed and cross-footed, and the total is compared to the total in the control account. In addition, the auditor selects a sample from the listing and traces it to the appropriate ledger card in the subsidiary ledger, noting the amount, name, and date. At this point the nature of subsequent audit procedures to determine the authenticity of a single balance is dependent upon the results of the auditor's compliance tests and evaluation of the internal control procedure for the cash receipts and credit sales systems. When the systems are considered weak, the auditor traces the entries in the subsidiary ledger to corroborative evidential matter such as sales invoices, shipment documents, and customer orders. On the other hand, when the systems are adequate, no additional procedures are employed. However, in either case the auditor traces data from the subsidiary ledger to the aged trial balance to make sure no items were intentionally or unintentionally omitted.

THE CONFIRMATION PROCESS

The objective of the confirmation of accounts receivable is to establish the existence of an amount owed by a client's customer. The confirmation process generates evidence that is often useful in the auditor's achieving the valuation, cutoff, and disclosure objectives. For example, through the use of confirmations the auditor may discover an account that is in dispute and unlikely to be collected. Nonetheless, the primary purpose of confirming accounts receivable is to establish the existence of a debtor, which provides the context for the following discussion. This discussion strongly implies that the auditor needs to perform other audit procedures in order to collect sufficient evidence to form an opinion on the presentation of accounts receivable and related accounts on the financial statements.

Control of the confirmation process: The initial step in the confirmation process is establishing control over all accounts receivable that will be subject to selection

Figure 11-6

Green Valley Corp.
Aged Trial Balance
12-31-79

Age of Account

Customer	Balance @12-31-79	0-30	31-60	61-90	Over 90
A. B. Plumbing	2876 42 ϕ	287642			
Brown Machinery	37 21				37 21
Carter Inc.	46581	15823 ✓		30758 ✓	
Clovis Dept. Store	114980 ϕ	114980			
Cost Construction	364419	300000	64419		
Warner Castings	78922	78922 ✓			
York Manuf.	228000	228000			
Y & Y Delivery	43891 ϕ	22569	21322		
✗	35157431	33269587	1243698	487213	156933
		✓	✓	✓	✓
	100% ϕ	94.6% ϕ	3.5% ϕ	1.4% ϕ	.5% ϕ

✗ - Cross footed and traced to G/L.
✓ - Footed.
ϕ - Calculation checked and total cross footed.
✓ - Aging tested.
ϕ - Selected for confirmation.

for confirmation. A detailed listing, such as the aged trial balance shown in Figure 11-6, provides this basis. The confirmation process results in highly competent evidential matter, since the auditor communicates directly with a third party. However, in the circularization of accounts for confirmation, he or she is careful not to destroy the integrity of the process. Initially, this is accomplished by the unbiased selection of accounts for confirmation. The client does not know before the selection which accounts are to be confirmed. Also, the client should not influence the selection process by indicating which accounts may or may not be confirmed. Having selected the accounts, the auditor retains control over the sample items during the physical preparation of the confirmation. In many instances the auditor asks the client to prepare the confirmation and type the envelope. A working paper, such as the one shown in Figure 11-6, showing the items to be confirmed may be photocopied and given to the client so that the auditor can maintain control. When the client prepares the confirmation and envelope, the auditor compares the name and amount to the control sheet and on a sample basis traces the address to the subsidiary ledger card. Once the auditor is satisfied that the confirmations are proper, the letters are placed by him or her in a U.S. Postal Service mailbox and are not sent through the client's mail system. Finally, each confirmation package contains a stamped return envelope so that the confirmation is returned to the auditor's business address or to a special U.S. Postal Service box number.

Once the auditor establishes a plan of control for the confirmation process, a sample is drawn from the total universe of accounts receivable. The sample items can be chosen through the use of a variety of techniques. If the auditor decides to employ a statistical sampling technique, a random selection method is used. Even if statistical sampling is not used, many auditors employ a random sampling method to be sure a representative sample is drawn. In many instances the auditor stratifies the accounts receivables by some characteristic, usually dollar value. For example, groups of accounts with a relatively large balance are more likely to be chosen for confirmation. No grouping of accounts is excluded from the possibility of selection, since collectively they may represent a material amount or they may disclose significant weaknesses in the internal control system. Finally, the auditor scans the entire listing for accounts that appear to be unusual. This may be reflected in the size of the account balance, the name of the customer, or other characteristics that make the auditor skeptical about the existence of the account.

Sample size: The size of the sample selected for confirmation depends on the auditor's evaluation of the client's internal control system and the materiality of the account. The structure of the internal control system, as validated by the compliance tests, provides insight into the risk that material errors may result from the processing of routine accounting transactions. When the auditor concludes that the system is weak or a significant processing error rate was discovered during the compliance tests, the size of the sample selected for confirmation is appropriately increased. In fact, the auditor may conclude that the internal control structure is unreliable and that all accounts receivable are to be confirmed.

378
Audit of the credit sales system

A more subtle factor that impacts the size of the confirmation sample is the environmental conditions of the client. As suggested in Chapter 5, the environmental conditions encompass general economic conditions, specific economic and regulatory conditions, and the firm's structure. For example, a company may be considering purchasing the auditor's client which is a closely held corporation. Since the financial statements are used by the acquiring company as a major source of information, the auditor's exposure is greater than in previous years, and the degree of testing in the accounts receivable area, as well as in other areas, is expanded.

Confirmation form: In the confirmation of accounts receivable the auditor may use a positive form or a negative form or a combination of both. The use of either a positive request or a negative request is dictated by audit circumstances. A positive confirmation asks that the client's debtor acknowledge the existence of the receivable as of a particular date. Furthermore, the debtor is requested to indicate that the balance is correct or incorrect. This confirmation is usually sent to the debtor in the form of a letter or as a specially printed form used by a particular auditing firm. An example of the letter form is illustrated in Figure 11-7. A negative confirmation asks that the debtor respond only if the balance is incorrect. Like the positive request, the negative confirmation may assume a variety of forms. If periodic customer statements are mailed by the client, the auditor may use a rubber stamp with appropriate wording as a negative confirmation form. This method is illustrated in Figure 11-8.

Positive and negative confirmations are not substitutes for one another. The auditor selects the confirmation form that is appropriate based on the characteristics of the accounts receivable population. If the accounts receivable are composed of a few relatively large balances, use of the positive confirmation form is suggested. Also, the positive form is used in circumstances in which the internal control evaluation reveals an inadequate system and there are likely to be errors or irregularities in the account balance. Both of these audit situations require the collection of highly competent evidence in the confirmation process. Where the audit risk is considered to be less, the negative confirmation form is employed. The individual account balances may be relatively small but numerous. Since no one account is material, the auditor is willing to accept less competent evidence, which suggests use of the negative confirmation. In a similar manner, a strong internal control system minimizes the risk that material errors may occur, and under these circumstances the negative confirmation form is appropriate. Finally, the negative form is selected if the auditor is reasonably certain that the debtor will respond to the request if the balance is incorrect. This determination is based upon previous experience with the debtor and the composition of the debtor group.

An accounts receivable population may be stratified by dollar value operating segment or other characteristics, and a combination of the two confirmation forms may be employed. For example, an auditor may send positive confirmations to a sample of account balances that exceed $1000 and send negative confirmations to those that have a balance of less than $1000. When the negative

Figure 11-7

379
Substantive tests:
accounts
receivable

Green Valley Corporation

Y & Y Delivery Service
One York Road
Bluefield, W. Va. 24701

Gentlemen:

 In accordance with the request of our auditors, please confirm the correctness of your account as listed below. If the amount
is correct, sign in the space provided and return this letter to our
auditor in the enclosed self—addressed envelope. If the amount is
incorrect, sign in the space provided, explain the difference on
the back of this letter, and return this letter to our auditor in the
enclosed self—addressed envelope.

 This is not a request for payment.

 Thank you for your prompt attention to this matter.

Very truly yours,

_____

Betty Coors, Controller

Account Number   18907
Account Balance $438.91
Confirmation Date: December 31, 1979

The above balance at the confirmation date is correct, except as
noted on the back of this letter.

_____

Signature

_____

Title
_____

form is chosen, the auditor sends a greater number of confirmations than would
be sent if the positive form were chosen. When positive confirmations are sent,
the auditor sends second and sometimes additional requests to customers who
do not respond. In many instances debtors do not respond to a confirmation
request because they are on a voucher system and do not accumulate unpaid
invoices by vendor name but rather by voucher number. In this case, the auditor
may consider confirming individual sales invoices that comprise an account
balance rather than the total amount due. If the response rate is not satisfactory,
even after two or more requests are mailed, the auditor employs alternative
procedures in order to collect sufficient evidential matter.

Figure 11-8

Negative confirmation request

```
                    CONFIRMATION REQUEST

    Please examine this statement carefully. If it is not cor-
rect, please notify our auditors of any differences. For your
convenience a stamped, self-addressed envelope is enclosed.

    If you do not reply to this request, it will be assumed that
the balance is correct.

    This is not a request for payment.
```

Alternative audit procedures: As suggested above, the auditor's use of positive confirmations may result in some nonresponses. In this case, he or she performs alternative audit procedures to determine the existence of the accounts chosen for confirmation but which provided no response.

The nature of the alternative procedures depends upon events subsequent to the confirmation date. An alternative procedure that results in highly competent evidence is the auditor's review of subsequent cash collection. The receipt of cash from a debtor suggests that a debt exists. However, the auditor is careful to relate the cash receipts to an invoice or contract that substantiates the debt at the confirmation date. In examining subsequent cash collections, he or she may take control of all cash receipts. This approach is justified if the internal control system is weak. On the other hand, the auditor may inspect the accounting records and the underlying documentation under conditions of an adequate internal control system. For example, entries in the cash receipts journal and the accounts receivable subsidiary ledger may be reviewed and compared to the daily list of cash receipts or remittance advices.

For nonrespondents that do not pay before the audit report date, the alternative procedures change. Initially the auditor establishes the shipment of goods by inspecting shipment documents such as the bill of lading or delivery ticket. To determine the existence of an approved sale, he or she inspects the customer order received and approved by the sales department. The actual billing of the customer is determined by a review of the sales invoice. Finally, all supporting documents are compared for internal consistency and then compared to postings in the sales journal and accounts receivable subsidiary ledger.

Confirmation exceptions: When positive confirmations are returned by debtors, a variety of exceptions is often noted. The auditor reviews the exceptions and decides whether they are to be investigated by the auditor or by the client. When the internal control system is adequate and the exceptions do not suggest a pattern of errors or irregularities, the client is asked to reconcile the differences. At the conclusion of the client's review, the auditor reviews its findings to see if the exceptions were cleared and that the differences are immaterial and require no additional investigation. Figure 11-9 is a summary of the typical exceptions

Figure 11-9

Clearing confirmation exceptions

TYPICAL CONFIRMATION EXCEPTIONS	AUDIT PROCEDURE USED TO CLEAR EXCEPTION
In-transit payment	Review cash receipts records and note posting date.
Disputed amount	Obtain the customer order, sales invoice, and shipping document and ask appropriate personnel about the propriety of the dispute. Check computations.
Goods returned	Inspect receiving report and discuss the matter with personnel responsible for authorizing the return.
Nonreceipt of goods	Obtain shipping documents and discuss the matter with personnel responsible for freight claims.
Inability to confirm because of accounting system	Employ alternative audit procedures.

encountered in the confirmation process and the methods by which they are cleared.

Summary of findings: After the confirmation process is complete, the auditor reviews all the evidence collected to determine if the audit objective of existence has been achieved. It is necessary to perform this step in a formal manner, since the confirmation approach generates a variety of audit evidence including confirmed accounts, accounts substantiated through alternative procedures, and accounts that resulted in exceptions to the stated amount. A useful technique is to summarize the audit results in a working paper similar to the one shown in Figure 11-10. Based on the evidence gathered for the sample items, the auditor draws an inference about the existence of the accounts receivable. When the evidence is not sufficient for the auditor to conclude that there is no material error in the existence of the receivables, the extent and nature of the audit procedures are modified. The auditor may expand the confirmation sample or may elect to use alternative procedures.

Limitations of the confirmation process: The confirmation of receivables results in highly competent evidence if the third party's behavior is consistent with the auditor's expectations. However, recent research has suggested that this assumption is not entirely valid.[1] Some of the preliminary findings are:

[1] See Gordon B. Davis, John Neter, and Roger R. Palmer, "An Experimental Study of Audit Confirmation," *Journal of Accountancy,* June 1967, pp. 36–44; Eugene H. Sauls, "An Experiment on Nonsampling Errors," *Empirical Research in Accounting: Selected Studies* (Chicago: University of Chicago Press, 1971), pp. 157–171; Eugene H. Sauls, "Nonsampling Errors in Accounts Receivable Confirmation," *Accounting Review,* January 1972, pp. 109–115; and Thomas D. Hubbard and Jerry B. Bullington, "Positive and Negative Confirmation Requests–A Test," *Journal of Accountancy,* March 1972, pp. 45–56.

Figure 11-10

4912 – Buff
6912 – Green
4712½ – White

Green Valley Corp.
Summary of Confirmations
12-31-79

	Dollar Value	Number of Accts.	Relative to Total Accounts Receivable		Relative to Total Confirmations Sent	
			Dollar Value	Number of accts.	Dollar Value	Number of Accts.
Total Accounts receivable	351 574.31	426				
Total Confirmations mailed	223 876.12	235	63.7%	55.2%		
Accounts Confirmed (including exceptions cleared)	184 392.13	177	52.5%	41.6%	82.4%	75.3%
Unconfirmed Accounts Verified through Alternative Procedures	36 726.75	43	10.4%	10.1%	16.4%	18.3% / 18.3%
Exceptions not cleared 1	2 757.24	15	.8%	3.5%	1.2%	6.4%
	223 876.12	235	63.7%	55.2%	100.0%	100.0%

1 – See analysis of exceptions not cleared at D104.

R.E.B.   D101
2/12/80

- It appears as though the larger the account being confirmed, the more accurate the confirmation response will be.
- Confirmation detection rates may differ significantly among different types of respondents.
- Confirmations are less likely to detect misstatements favorable to confirmation recipients than unfavorable misstatements.
- Positive confirmation response rates do not appear to differ significantly between correct and misstated confirmation requests. Although only limited evidence is available, further study may be necessary.[2]

Even though these findings are preliminary and additional research is needed, the informed auditor recognizes the potential limitation of the confirmation process and modifies the audit approach accordingly.

Valuation

In the financial statement, accounts receivable are stated at their net realizable value. The confirmation of receivables establishes the gross value of the receivable balance but is not persuasive evidence in determining the likelihood of collection. In achieving the valuation objective, the auditor reviews the analytical evidence collected in other phases of the audit. Environmental conditions, such as the business cycle of the industry, suggest whether conditions have changed in a manner that would reduce or increase the probability of collecting receivables. In addition, a change in the credit policy of the business and the effectiveness of the credit manager are evaluated. The valuation of receivables relies heavily upon ratio and trend analysis, and the auditor keeps abreast of any variables that may alter these relationships.

A variety of audit procedures may be employed in the review of accounts receivable valuation. In an engagement all procedures are employed, but the emphasis of a particular procedure depends upon the characteristics of the receivable population. The most important variable is the relative size of the individual accounts.

Accounts receivable may be made up of numerous small balances. In this case the audit focal point is the aged trial balance, as illustrated in Figure 11-6. Assuming the aged trial balance is prepared by the client, the auditor verifies that the aging is proper by tracing a sample from the accounts to the supporting sales invoice. Using the aged categories 30 to 60, 61 to 90, and so on, the auditor applies the client's write-off experience rate to the appropriate grouping. He or she is careful not to apply these percentages mechanically, but rather to consider if the client's situation has changed to an extent that requires a modification of the rates. For example, a client that has reduced its credit rating requirement will have a larger proportion of bad debts. The auditor recognizes that the aged trial balance and the historical write-off rates are a starting point but not the solution to the valuation of accounts receivable.

[2] Carl S. Warren, "Confirmation Reliability—The Evidence," *Journal of Accountancy*, February 1975, pp. 85–89.

384
Audit of the credit sales system

When accounts receivable are comprised of relatively large balances, the auditor emphasizes the review of subsequent cash collections. Where individual accounts are significant, the audit exposure of a few accounts can be large. For this reason the auditor relies less on an analytic approach ratio and trend analysis, and more on gaining corroborative evidence about each individual account. Using an aged trial balance, he or she notes the cash collections that are applicable to the year-end receivables. For accounts not collected, the status is discussed with the credit manager, and the customer correspondence file is reviewed. In addition, the auditor obtains credit reports from Dun & Bradstreet or other credit-rating services, when available.

In many instances the account balance of receivables may contain a few large and numerous small balances. In this case the auditor uses both the analytic approach and the corroborative approach. The mix of the two approaches depends upon the dominance of large account balances or small account balances.

Imputed interest and receivable valuation: *APB Opinion No. 21* identifies another facet of accounts receivable valuation if the receivable is due one year beyond the balance sheet date. The auditor determines if the stated interest rate, if any, is a proper reflection of the economic realities of the transaction. If not, a realistic interest rate is imputed. To determine such an interest rate, he or she collects evidence relative to the following:

· An approximation of the prevailing market rates for the source of credit that would provide a market for sale or assignment of the receivable.
· The prime or higher rate for notes which are discounted with banks, giving due weight to the credit standing of the client.[3]

Cutoff

A review of transactions before and after the year-end date is performed to see if a proper cutoff of sales and credit allowances was made. For sales, the auditor reviews shipping information contained on the bill of lading, delivery ticket, or other shipping document. He or she traces these items to the appropriate entry in the sales journal. Also, the entries in the sales journal are traced to the shipment documents. In both cases the critical information is the date of shipment and the recording date.

Credit allowances may be generated by the return of goods or special allowances. The auditor reviews for cutoff in these areas in a manner similar to that described above. In addition, he or she reviews the volume of allowances granted after the end of the accounting period. This procedure is concerned not only with cutoff but also with valuation, since it is possible for a client to generate sales toward the end of the year, knowing that allowances will be granted for such things as improper pricing.

[3] *APB Opinion* No. 21, "Interest on Receivables and Payables" (New York: AICPA, 1971), Paragraph 14.

Classification and disclosure

The classification and disclosure of receivables on the balance sheet is dependent upon the variety and complexity of a client's transactions. In general, accounts receivable are shown as a current asset after taking into consideration the valuation allowance for bad debts. If the amounts are not collectible within the client's operating cycle, these receivables are classified as noncurrent items. Often a client generates other receivables, such as amounts due from officers, employees, or affiliates. If material, these items are not part of the balance associated with normal trade receivables. Other aspects of the accounts receivable balance that require disclosure include the pledging, discounting, or assignment of accounts. Because of the increased emphasis on full disclosure, the auditor carefully reviews the client's data suggested for disclosure. This emphasis has been confirmed by recent promulgations by the SEC and FASB. In addition, auditors are aware that the disclosures must not only meet formal compliance rules but must adequately reflect the economic realities of the transaction. The Continental Vending case, which was concerned with the disclosure of a note receivable, vividly illustrates the wisdom of such an approach.

Confirmation at an interim date

Accounts receivable may be confirmed at an interim date if there is an adequate internal control system. The confirmation procedures are applied in the manner described in this chapter, except that the confirmation date is prior to the year end. Figure 11-11 summarizes the audit approach used in this circumstance. The starting point after the end of the year is the confirmation interim balance date. For transactions occurring after the interim date, the auditor relies upon the internal control system to process data in an acceptable manner. Summary data in the sales journal and cash receipts journal are reviewed for unusual items. In addition, the client prepares an aged trial balance at the year-end date, and the auditor reviews this analysis. During the review he or she looks for significant amounts from customers that were not listed on the interim trial balance. Other items that come to the auditor's attention are considered for confirmation.

Notes receivable

For a few businesses credit sales may be financed through the issuance of trade notes receivable. In this case the audit approach for the review of notes receivable is the same as for trade accounts receivable. Thus the internal control model discussed earlier in this chapter is applicable to the sales and notes receivable system. The audit programs for tests of compliance, Figure 11-3, and for substantive tests, Figure 11-5, are typical of the procedures performed by the auditor. In addition, two other substantive test procedures are employed.

The auditor inspects notes receivable at the balance sheet date if the notes are material. In Chapter 10 it was stated that cash and negotiable instruments are counted simultaneously to prevent them from being used to cover shortages.

Figure 11-11

Green Valley Corp.
A/R Reconciliation to Year-End
12-31-79

	1	2	3	4
A/R Balance @ 9-30-79 – See D44				43964385
Sales – October			7986434 ⁴	
– November			8433918 ⁴	
– December			9166373 ⁴	
				25586725
Receipts – October			7526984 ⁴	
– November			8294375 ⁴	
– December			8954638 ⁴	
				⟨24775997⟩
Writeoffs – October			128913 C	
– November			84675 C	
– December			197328 C	
				⟨410916⟩
A/R Balance @ 12-31-79 – See D40				44364197

4 - Traced to Sales Journal – Footed Nov. & Dec.
⁴ - Traced to Cash Receipts Journal – Footed Oct. & Dec.
C - Traced to approvals and reviewed with credit manager.
✓ - Footed.

REB
1/18/80

D41

This is also true for notes receivable. If the auditor cannot inspect the notes on the balance sheet date, he or she may seal all the notes until they can be counted. In some cases the auditor may not be able to inspect a note, since it may be held by a third party as collateral or for collection by a collection agency. The auditor sends a confirmation to the holder of the note, verifying the maker of the note, amount, interest rates, and due date. This confirmation is not a substitute for the confirmation sent to the maker of the note.

Another unique audit feature of the review of notes receivable is the need for verifying interest accounts associated with notes. Using data that appear on the note and data confirmed by the maker of the note, the auditor recomputes the amount of interest earned during the period and the amount of interest accrued at the balance sheet date. When there are several notes receivable, the data may be sample-tested.

EXERCISES AND PROBLEMS

11-1. In an adequately designed internal control system for credit sales, what tasks should be assigned to departments that are not part of the treasurer's department or the controller's department?

11-2. Why is the sales department not primarily responsible for the establishment and administration of an organization's credit policy? Is this aspect of the plan of organization relevant to the audit?

11-3. What are the essential features of an adequate internal control system for credit sales?

11-4. Why should someone in the accounting department periodically mail customer statements? Should this procedure be performed by the accounts receivable clerk?

11-5. How can an internal system be designed to ensure reasonably that all goods shipped are billed?

11-6. Comment on the following statement:

In the audit of accounts receivable the ~~only~~ important procedure is confirmation of the account balance.

11-7. When should an auditor use a negative confirmation?

11-8. If an auditor sends a negative confirmation and receives no response, what does he or she conclude?

11-9. Under what conditions may it be impractical to confirm an accounts receivable?

11-10. If an account cannot be confirmed, must the auditor issue a qualified opinion on the financial statements?

11-11. Why doesn't an auditor confirm sales as well as accounts receivable?

11-12. In the confirmation of accounts receivable is it true that the third party's behavior is consistent with the auditor's expectations?

11-13. Assume that a client has prepared the aged trial balance of accounts receivable. How does the auditor verify this schedule?

388
Audit of the credit sales system

11-14. Why is it necessary for the auditor to identify receivables that are not collectible within a year?

11-15. Does the confirmation of receivables at an interim date or at the year-end date provide the auditor with the most competent evidential matter?

11-16. A CPA accumulates various kinds of evidence from which he or she formulates an opinion on the fairness of the financial statements examined. Among this evidence are confirmations from third parties and written representations from the client.

Required

1. (a) What is an audit confirmation? (b) What characteristics should an audit confirmation possess if a CPA is to consider it valid evidence?

2. (a) What is a written representation? (b) What information should a written representation contain? (c) What effect does a written representation have on a CPA's examination of a client's financial statements?

3. (a) Distinguish between a positive confirmation and a negative confirmation in the auditor's examination of accounts receivable. (b) In confirming an audit client's accounts receivable, what characteristics should be present in the accounts if the CPA is to use negative confirmations?

4. List the information a CPA should solicit in a standard bank confirmation inquiry sent to an audit client's bank. (AICPA Adapted)

11-17. You have been engaged to examine the financial statements of the Dean Corporation for the year ended December 31, 1979, and have begun your auditing procedures.

Required: Discuss the following questions relating to your examination:

1. Several accounts receivable confirmations have been returned with the notation, "Verifications of vendors' statements are no longer possible because of our data processing system." What alternative auditing procedures can be used to verify these accounts receivable?

2. You are considering obtaining written representations from the client concerning the financial statements and matters pertinent to them.

   a. What are the reasons for obtaining written representations from the client?
   b. What reliance can you place upon written representations from (i) the client, (ii) independent experts, and (iii) debtors? (AICPA Adapted)

11-18. During your examination of the financial statements of the Dartmark Corporation, you instruct an assistant to send 150 confirmations and prepare a memo on the results of the investigation. As part of the memo the assistant lists several confirmation exceptions along with the manner in which each exception was cleared. This analysis is presented in the accompanying table.

CONFIRMA-TION NO.	COMMENT BY CUSTOMER	AUDITOR'S ANALYSIS
17	Check was mailed for this amount on 12/30/79.	Review sales invoice, customer order, and shipping document. Shipment was made on 12/31/79.
40	Goods should have been billed at 80 percent of retail price, since we received them on consignment.	In conversation with the sales department this pricing policy was confirmed.

CONFIRMA-TION NO.	COMMENT BY CUSTOMER	AUDITOR'S ANALYSIS
41	Per our agreement we will pay off the debt in $4000 installments beginning 1/1/81 and continuing through 1/1/87.	Customer correspondence file was reviewed, and several letters supported repayment plans.
63	We returned the goods on 12/3/79.	Examined receiving report for returned goods.
78	This debt has been partially canceled by our payment for local advertising.	Client agreed and has prepared an adjusting journal entry on working paper B-40.*
112	Shipment in transit at 12/31/79.	Examined bill of lading date 12/30/79. Probably had not been received by client on 12/31/79.
113	We do not owe this amount.	Reviewed sales documentation, which confirmed a posting error.
122	Per our telephone call, you agreed to reduce the price 50 percent, since some of the goods were received damaged.	Credit manager agreed but stated that the credit memo would not be issued until January, since that was the date of the telephone conversation.
138	The amount should be $950 and not $1000. Starting in December $50 was withheld from my monthly paycheck (Signed ''V.P.—Research'').	Traced to the payroll journal and amount was credited to a miscellaneous payable.

*The entry at B-40 was: Allowance for bad debts $1200
   Accounts receivable $1,200

The assistant also wrote a memo which stated, ''Since all 150 confirmation requests were returned and all exceptions were satisfactorily cleared, the gross value of accounts receivable on 12/31/79 is correct.''

Required

1. Comment on the auditor's analysis for each of the nine confirmation exceptions.
2. Based on your analysis in part 1, what adjusting journal entries would you propose?
3. Do you agree with the auditor's general conclusion concerning the gross value of accounts receivable? If not, what additional audit procedures would you suggest.

11-19. You are making an examination of the accounts of the Hardy Corporation. Accounts receivable represent a significant proportion of the total assets of the company. At the beginning of the audit you mailed out positive confirmations on a test basis. Included in your test were confirmations requested from several U.S. government departments; the confirmation requests for these accounts were returned along with the following notation:

Your confirmation letter is returned herewith without action inasmuch as the type of information requested therein cannot be compiled by this office with sufficient accuracy to be of any value.

Your test also included customers whose accounts payable systems were either decentralized or who used a voucher system which made it impossible or impractical to

390
Audit of the credit sales system

give the requested information. These customers either informed you of their inability to comply with the request or did not reply.

Required

1. Assuming the number and amount of responses to confirmation requests are unsatisfactory, what additional auditing procedures would you apply?

2. If satisfaction is obtained by these procedures, what effect, if any, would your difficulties with the examination of receivables have on your report? (AICPA Adapted)

11-20. As part of the study and evaluation of a client's internal control system, an auditor usually prepares an internal control questionnaire. Assume that you have just completed such a questionnaire in your review of the sales system. The following questions generated a negative response:

1. Are the customers' ledgers balanced at least monthly and the totals compared with the general ledger control account?
2. Are credits for returned goods checked against receiving reports?
3. Is the management of the credit department entirely divorced from the sales department?
4. Are sales prices and credit terms based on approved standard price lists?
5. Are prenumbered shipping advices prepared for all goods shipped?
6. Are sales invoices checked as to prices, extensions, and footings?
7. Are delinquent accounts listed periodically for review by an official other than the credit manager?

Required

1. For each of the seven questions, determine the audit significance of a no response.

2. What audit procedures will be adopted by the auditor based on a no response for each question?

11-21. Your examination of the financial statements of General Department Stores, Inc., disclosed the following:

1. The store has 30,000 retail accounts which are billed monthly on a cycle basis. There are 20 billing cycle divisions of the subsidiary accounts receivable ledger, and accounts are apportioned alphabetically to the divisions.
2. All charge sales tickets, which are prenumbered, are microfilmed in batches for each day's sales. These sales tickets are then sorted into their respective cycle divisions, and adding machine tapes are prepared to arrive at the total daily sales for each division. The daily totals for the divisions are then combined for comparison with the grand total daily charge sales determined from cash register readings. After the totals are balanced, the daily sales tickets are filed behind the related customer account cards in the respective cycle divisions.
3. Cycle control accounts for each division are maintained by posting the tapes of daily sales.
4. At the cycle billing date the customers' transactions (sales, remittances, returns, and other adjustments) are posted to the accounts in the individual cycle. The billing machine used automatically accumulates six separate totals: previous balances, purchases, payments, returns, new balances, and overdue balances. After posting, the documents and the customers' statements are microfilmed and then mailed to the customers.
5. Within each division a trial balance of the accounts in the cycle obtained as a by-product of the posting operation is compared with the cycle control account.

6. Credit terms for regular accounts require payment within 10 days of receipt of the statement. A credit limit of $300 is set for all accounts.
7. Before the statements are mailed they are reviewed to determine which are past due. Accounts are considered past due if the full balance of the prior month has not been paid. Past due accounts are noted for subsequent collection effort by the credit department.
8. Receipts on account and customer account adjustments are accumulated and posted in a similar manner.

Required

1. List the audit procedures you would apply in the audit of the accounts comprising one billing cycle division. Confine your audit procedures to the sales tickets and charges to the accounts and to the verification of account balances. Do not discuss the audit of cash receipts or customer account adjustments.

2. Assume that the group of accounts selected for audit in part 1 was in the cycle division billed on January 19. List the additional overall audit procedures you would apply to satisfy yourself as to the reasonableness of the total balance of accounts receivable at January 31, 1979, the fiscal year end. (AICPA Adapted)

11-22. Mary Hartke has been assigned to the audit of the Caine Corporation. As part of her responsibilities she is to study and evaluate the company's credit sales system. Mary analyzes the system through the preparation of a flowchart and completion of an appropriate internal control questionnaire. Next she performs compliance tests of the system. Based on this audit approach she concludes that there are several weaknesses in the design of the internal control system, and she discovered several processing errors when she performed the tests of compliance. All this work was performed at an interim date.

After the close of the client's fiscal year, Mary returns to the audit and is assigned the task of auditing accounts receivable at the balance sheet date. She immediately asks the client to prepare an aged trial balance of accounts receivable. The client agrees and within three days gives Mary a copy of the trial balance. Mary compares the total per the trial balance to the accounts receivable control account. The two totals agree.

Next she places a tick mark beside those accounts she plans to confirm. There are 1200 individual accounts. She decides to send negative confirmation to 240 of the customers, which represents 25 percent of the total accounts receivable balance. Another 100 positive confirmations are to be sent to customers with larger balances. These 100 customers represent 40 percent of the total accounts receivable balance. The aged trial balance with 340 customers with tick marks beside their names is given to the controller so that the appropriate confirmation letters can be prepared.

The controller reviews the customers selected for confirmations. Because some of the accounts are considered "sensitive," he asks to select 25 other customers for confirmation. Mary agrees but requests that the controller give her all the documentation and correspondence files for the sensitive accounts. These sensitive accounts represent 20 percent of the total accounts receivable balance. With these changes the controller has the accounts receivable clerk prepare the 340 confirmations, address the envelopes, and stamp and seal them. The confirmations are given to Mary, and she personally mails them at the local post office.

A few of the negative confirmations are returned, but these exceptions are cleared satisfactorily. Thirty of the positive confirmations are not returned, and second requests are sent. Of these 30, only 5 are returned. Mary then selects 25 new customers, with accounts of approximately the same dollar amount, for confirmation. These are to replace the positive confirmations not returned. All exceptions are satisfactorily cleared.

392
Audit of the credit sales system

Mary Hartke prepares a memo stating that the gross value of accounts receivable is correctly stated based on the results of the confirmation process.

Required

1. Do you believe the audit approach selected in the confirmation of accounts receivable was appropriate? List each deficiency in the audit approach.

2. For each deficiency listed in part 1, suggest a more appropriate audit procedure.

11-23. The Meyers Pharmaceutical Company, a drug manufacturer, has the following system for billing and recording accounts receivable:

1. An incoming customer's purchase order is received in the order department by a clerk who prepares a prenumbered company sales order form in which is inserted the pertinent information, such as the customer's name and address, customer's account number, quantity, and items ordered. After the sales order form has been prepared, the customer's purchase order is stapled to it.

2. The sales order form is then passed to the credit department for credit approval. Rough approximations of the billing values of the orders are made in the credit department for accounts on which credit limitations are imposed. After investigation, approval of credit is noted on the form.

3. Next the sales order form is passed to the billing department where a clerk types the customer's invoice on a billing machine that cross-multiplies the number of items and the unit price and then adds the automatically extended amounts for the total amount of the invoice. The billing clerk determines the unit prices for the items from a list of billing prices.

The billing machine has registers that automatically accumulate daily totals of customer account numbers and invoice amounts to provide "hash" totals and control amounts. These totals, which are inserted in a daily record book, serve as predetermined batch totals for the verification of computer inputs.

The billing is done on prenumbered, continuous, carbon-interleaved forms having the following designations:

    a. "Customer's copy"
    b. "Sales department copy," for information purposes
    c. "File copy"
    d. "Shipping department copy," which serves as a shipping order. Bills of lading are also prepared as carbon-copy by-products of the invoicing procedure.

4. The shipping department copy of the invoice and the bills of lading are then sent to the shipping department. After the order has been shipped, copies of the bill of lading are returned to the billing department. The shipping department copy of the invoice is filed in the shipping department.

5. In the billing department one copy of the bill of lading is attached to the customer's copy of the invoice, and both are mailed to the customer. The other copy of the bill of lading, together with the sales order form, is then stapled to the invoice file copy and filed in invoice numerical order.

6. A keypunch machine is connected to the billing machine so that punched cards are created during the preparation of the invoices. The punched cards then become the means by which the sales data are transmitted to a computer.

The punched cards are fed to the computer in batches. One day's accumulation of cards comprises a batch. After the punched cards have been processed by the computer, they are placed in files and held for about two years.

Required: List the procedures a CPA would employ in examining selected audit samples of the company's

1. Typed invoices, including the source documents
2. Punched cards

(The listed procedures should be limited to verification of the sales data being fed into the computer. Do not carry the procedures beyond the point at which the cards are ready to be fed into the computer.)   (AICPA Adapted)

11-24. An auditor performs a sales cutoff test to determine if transactions are reported in the proper accounting period. Assume the following working paper was prepared by an auditor in a review of financial statements for the year ended December 31, 1979:

INFORMATION PER SALES INVOICE		INFORMATION PER SALES JOURNAL		INFORMATION PER BILL OF LADING	
INVOICE NO.	TERMS	DATE ENTERED	AMOUNT	DATE SHIPPED	DOCUMENT NO.
1287	FOB Destination	12/30/79	$ 4,000	1/2/80	4718
1288	FOB S.P.	12/29/79	3,700	12/28/79	4714
1289	FOB S.P.	12/30/79	6,400	1/3/80	4719
1290	FOB Destination	12/30/79	4,850	12/31/79	4716
1291	FOB S.P.	12/30/79	12,000	Bill and hold	
1292	FOB S.P.	1/2/80	6,450	12/31/79	4717
1293	FOB S.P.	1/2/80	2,200	1/3/80	4720
1294	FOB Destination	1/2/80	9,500	12/31/79	4715

Required

1. How should an auditor perform a sales cutoff test?
2. Of the eight items listed above, which are accounted for improperly?
3. From the manner in which the data are listed in the above analysis, what appears to be the auditor's focal point in performance of the sales cutoff test? Do you agree with this focal point?

11-25. You have examined the financial statements of the Heft Company for several years. The system of internal control for accounts receivable is very satisfactory. The Heft Company is on a calendar-year basis. An interim audit, which included confirmation of the accounts receivable, was performed on August 31 and indicated that the accounting for receivables was very reliable.

The company's sales are principally to manufacturing concerns. There are about 1500 active trade accounts receivable of which about 35 percent in number represent 65 percent of the total dollar amount. The accounts receivable are maintained alphabetically in five subledgers which are controlled by one general ledger account.

Sales are machine-posted in the subledgers by an operation that produces simultaneously the customer's ledger card and monthly statement and the sales journal. All cash receipts are in the form of customers' checks and are machine-posted simultaneously on the customer's ledger card and monthly statement and the cash receipts journal. Information for posting cash receipts is obtained from the remittance advice portions of the customers' checks. The bookkeeping machine operator compares the remittance advices with the list of checks prepared by another person when the mail was received.

394
Audit of the credit sales system

Summary totals are produced monthly by the bookkeeping machine operations for posting to the appropriate general ledger accounts such as cash, sales, accounts receivable, and so on. Aged trial balances by subledgers are prepared monthly.

Sales returns and allowances and bad debt write-offs are summarized periodically and recorded by standard journal entries. Supporting documents for these journal entries are available. The usual documents arising from billing, shipping, and receiving are also available.

Required: Prepare in detail the audit program for the Heft Company for the year-end examination of the trade accounts receivable. Do not give the program for the interim audit.

(AICPA Adapted)

11-26. Armstrong Manufacturing Company suffered a significant decline in sales for 1978 and the first half of 1979. For this period it used about 40 percent of its capacity. In mid-1979 the officers and board of directors meet to plot a course of action that will hopefully increase the quantity of items sold during the latter half of 1979. They decide that it would be disastrous to reduce the price of their inventory, since other competitors would probably do likewise. However, they believe they can recapture part of the market by changing their credit terms. Specifically, they decide to allow a customer to buy goods on a long-term credit basis. They all agree, and the policy is immediately implemented. By the end of 1979 it appears that their decision was correct, since sales have increased significantly.

Your firm has performed the audit of Armstrong Manufacturing Company for the past five years. For simplicity assume that accounts receivable as of December 31, 1979, are represented by the following:

CUSTOMER NO.	DATE OF SALE	AMOUNT PER SALES JOURNAL AND SALES INVOICE	AMOUNT IS DUE
10465	9/1/79	$100,000	9/1/81
10744	11/1/79	250,000	11/1/84
10633	8/15/79	300,000	8/15/82
		$650,000	

Required

1. Has the corporation's credit policy resulted in an auditing problem? If so, specifically list the audit procedure to be performed by the auditor.

2. Based upon your explanation in part 1, prepare an adjusting journal entry. (You will have to make an assumption to complete this requirement.)

11-27. The customer billing and collection functions of the Robinson Company, a small paint manufacturer, are attended to by a receptionist, an accounts receivable clerk, and a cashier who also serves as a secretary. The company's paint products are sold to wholesalers and retail stores.

The following describes all the procedures performed by the employees of the Robinson Company pertaining to customer billings and collections:

1. The mail is opened by the receptionist who gives the customers' purchase orders to the accounts receivable clerk. Fifteen to 20 orders are received each day. Under instructions to expedite the shipment of orders, the accounts receivable clerk at once prepares a five-copy sales invoice form which is distributed as follows:

a. Copy 1 is the customer billing copy and is held by the accounts receivable clerk until notice of shipment is received.

b. Copy 2 is the accounts receivable department copy and is held for ultimate posting of the accounts receivable records.

c. Copies 3 and 4 are sent to the shipping department.

d. Copy 5 is sent to the storeroom as authority for release of the goods to the shipping department.

2. After the paint ordered has been moved from the storeroom to the shipping department, the shipping department prepares the bills of lading and labels the cartons. Sales invoice copy 4 is inserted in the carton as a packing slip. After the trucker has picked up the shipment, the customer's copy of the bill of lading and copy 3, on which are noted any undershipments, are returned to the accounts receivable clerk. The company does not back-order in the event of undershipments; customers are expected to reorder the merchandise. The Robinson Company's copy of the bill of lading is filed by the shipping department.

3. When copy 3 and the customer's copy of the bill of lading are received by the accounts receivable clerk, copies 1 and 2 are completed by numbering them and inserting quantities shipped, unit prices, extensions, discounts, and totals. The accounts receivable clerk then mails copy 1 and the copy of the bill of lading to the customer. Copies 2 and 3 are stapled together.

4. The individual accounts receivable ledger cards are posted by the accounts receivable clerk by a bookkeeping machine procedure whereby the sales register is prepared as a carbon copy of the postings. Postings are made from copy 2 which is then filed, along with staple-attached copy 3, in numerical order. Monthly the general ledger clerk summarizes the sales register for posting to the general ledger accounts.

5. Since the Robinson Company is short of cash, the deposit of receipts is also expedited. The receptionist turns over all mail receipts and related correspondence to the accounts receivable clerk who examines the checks and determines that the accompanying vouchers or correspondence contains enough detail to permit posting of the accounts. The accounts receivable clerk then endorses the checks and gives them to the cashier who prepares the daily deposit. No currency is received in the mail, and no paint is sold over the counter at the factory.

6. The accounts receivable clerk uses the vouchers or correspondence that accompanied the checks to post the accounts receivable ledger cards. The bookkeeping machine prepares a cash receipts register as a carbon copy of the postings. Monthly the general ledger clerk summarizes the cash receipts register for posting to the general ledger accounts. The accounts receivable clerk also corresponds with customers about unauthorized deductions for discounts, freight or advertising allowances, returns, and so on, and prepares the appropriate credit memos. Disputed items of a large amount are turned over to the sales manager for settlement. Each month the accounts receivable clerk prepares a trial balance of the open accounts receivable and compares the resultant total with the general ledger control account for accounts receivable.

Required: Discuss the internal control weaknesses in the Robinson Company's procedures related to customer billings and remittances and the accounting for these transactions. In your discussion, in addition to identifying the weaknesses, explain what could happen as a result of each. (AICPA Adapted)

11-28.

1. Refer to the data presented in Problem 11-27 and prepare a flowchart of the sales system.

2. Prepare a list of recommendations for improving the system.

396
Audit of the credit sales system

11-29. The Cowslip Milk Company's principal activity is buying milk from dairy farmers, processing it, and delivering it to retail customers. You are engaged in auditing the retail accounts receivable of the company and determine the following:

1. The company has 50 retail routes; each route consists of 100 to 200 accounts, the number that can be serviced by a driver in a day.
2. The driver enters cash collections from the day's deliveries to each customer directly on a statement form in record books maintained for each route. Mail remittances are posted in the route record books by office personnel. At the end of the month the statements are priced, extended, and footed. Photocopies of the statements are prepared and left in the customers' milk boxes with the next milk delivery.
3. The statements are reviewed by the office manager who prepares a list for each route of accounts with 90-day balances or older. The list is used for intensive collection action.
4. The audit program used in prior audits for the selection of retail accounts receivable for confirmation stated, "Select two accounts from each route, one to be chosen by opening the route book at random and the other as the third item on each list of 90-day or older accounts."

Your review of the accounts receivable leads you to conclude that statistical sampling techniques may be applied to their examination.

Required

1. Since statistical sampling techniques do not relieve the CPA of his or her responsibilities in the exercise of professional judgment, of what benefit are they to the CPA? Discuss.

2. Give the reasons why the audit procedure previously used for the selection of accounts receivable for confirmation (as given in item 4 above) would not produce a valid statistical sample.

3. What are the audit objectives or purposes in selecting 90-day accounts for confirmation? Can the application of statistical sampling techniques help in attaining these objectives or purposes? Discuss.

4. Assume that the company has 10,000 accounts receivable and that your statistical sampling disclosed 6 errors in a sample of 200 accounts. Is it reasonable to assume that 300 accounts in the entire population are in error? Explain. (AICPA Adapted)

11-30. An adequate internal control system is adopted by a client to ensure the reliability of accounting records created through the processing of transactions. The following errors may be discovered by the auditor in the test of a client's credit sales system:

1. A number of sales invoices were not recorded in the sales journal.
2. Several sales were not posted to the customers' subsidiary ledger cards.
3. Several sales invoices contain mathmatical errors and pricing errors.
4. The accounts receivable clerk prepared a credit memo so as to reduce the balance due from a friend.
5. A number of goods were shipped but were not recorded as sales.
6. The accounts receivable clerk posts from a listing of cash receipts prepared by the mail clerk. There were several errors in the listing of the dollar amounts.
7. Several customer credits were granted by the accounts receivable clerk.

Required

1. What are the audit implications of the above errors?

2. For each type of error, what audit procedures should the auditor adopt in the design of the year-end test of accounts receivable?

3. For each type of error, what internal control procedure should be adopted by the client to reduce the likelihood of the error occurring in the future?

11-31. You are a senior accountant on the staff of Marin and Matthews, CPAs. You are conducting the annual audit of the Never-Slip Corporation for the calendar year 1979.

You are now working on the audit of the accounts receivable and related allowance for bad debts accounts. The study of the internal control has been finished, and the audit program has been completely carried out.

All data and information for the setting up and completion of your working papers are summarized here:

GENERAL LEDGER

ACCOUNTS RECEIVABLE		
1979		
Dec. 31	Balance	$184,092.42

ALLOWANCE FOR BAD DEBTS							
1979				1979			
July	31	G.J.	570.00	Jan.	1	Balance	$2,712.50
Oct.	31	G.J.	954.16	Dec.	31	G.J.	2,698.10

BAD DEBTS							
1979				1979			
Dec.	31	G.J.	$2,698.10	Aug.	1	C.R.J.	$85.00

GENERAL JOURNAL

JULY 31		
Allowance for bad debts	$570.00	
Accounts receivable		$570.00
To charge off bad accounts (detail omitted)		

OCTOBER 31		
Allowance for bad debts	954.16	
Accounts receivable		954.16
Accounts charged off:		
Baker, J.A.	$110.00	
Dehner & Son	9.75	
Meek, Roger	350.00	
Wagner, James	494.41	
	$954.16	

DECEMBER 31		
Bad debts	2,698.10	
Allowance for bad debts		2.698.10
Annual charge based on ½ percent of net credit		

CASH RECEIPTS JOURNAL

On August 1 the $85 account of John Smith, previously charged off as of July 31, was collected in full. Credit was to bad debts.

398
Audit of the credit sales system

SUMMARY OF AGING SCHEDULE

The summary of the subsidiary ledger as of December 31, 1979, was totaled as follows:

Under one month	$ 92,715.60
One to three months	58,070.15
Three to six months	29,126.89
Over six months	4,624.10
	$184,536.74

Credit balances:

Dabney Cleaners	$ 16.54—O.K. Additional billing in January 1980
Britting Cafeteria	72.00—Should have been credited to Britt Motor Company*
Wehby & Son	384.00—Advance on a sales contract
	$472.54

The customers' ledger is not in agreement with the accounts receivable control. The client instructs the auditor to adjust the control to the subsidiary ledger after any corrections are made.

ALLOWANCE FOR BAD DEBT REQUIREMENTS

It is agreed that ½ percent is adequate for accounts under one month.
Accounts one to three months are expected to require a reserve of 1 percent.
Accounts three to six months are expected to require a reserve of 2 percent.
Accounts over six months are analyzed as follows:

Definitely bad	$ 416.52
Doubtful (estimated 50 percent collectible)	516.80
Apparently good, but slow (estimated 90 percent collectible)	3,690.78
	$4,624.10

*Account is in one to three months classification.

Required

1. Prepare audit working papers in reasonable detail for the accounts receivable and allowance for bad debts accounts. Introduce any new accounts or more discriminating classifications if advisable. Make appropriate cross-references by numbers in parentheses.

2. Prepare correcting entries with adequate explanations and key to the working papers. (AICPA Adapted)

MULTIPLE CHOICE

Items 1 through 4 are based on the following information:

The following sales procedures were encountered during the regular annual audit of Marvel Wholesale Distributing Company.

Customer orders are received by the sales order department. A clerk computes the dollar amount of the order and sends it to the credit department for approval. Credit approval is stamped on the order and returned to the sales order department. An invoice is prepared in two copies, and the order is filed in the customer order file.

The customer copy of the invoice is sent to the billing department and held in the pending file awaiting notification that the order has been shipped.

The shipping copy of the invoice is routed through the warehouse and the shipping department as authority for the respective departments to release and ship the merchandise. Shipping department personnel pack the order and prepare a three-copy bill of lading: the original copy is mailed to the customer, the second copy is sent with the shipment, and the other is filed in sequence in the bill-of-lading file. The invoice shipping copy is sent to the billing department.

The billing clerk matches the received shipping copy with the customer copy from the pending file. Both copies of the invoice are priced, extended, and footed. The customer copy is then mailed directly to the customer, and the shipping copy is sent to the accounts receivable clerk.

The accounts receivable clerk enters the invoice data in a sales accounts receivable journal, posts the customers' account in the subsidiary customer's accounts ledger, and files the shipping copy in the sales invoice file. The invoices are numbered and filed in sequence.

1. In order to gather audit evidence concerning the proper credit approval of sales, the auditor selects a sample of transaction documents from the population represented by the

    a. Customer order file.
    b. Bill-of-lading file.
    c. Subsidiary customers' accounts ledger.
    d. Sales invoice file.

2. In order to determine whether the system of internal control operated effectively to minimize errors of failure to post invoices to customers' accounts ledger, the auditor selects a sample of transactions from the population represented by the

    a. Customer order file.
    b. Bill of lading file.
    c. Subsidiary customers' accounts ledger.
    d. Sales invoice file.

3. In order to determine whether the system of internal control operated effectively to minimize errors of failure to invoice a shipment, the auditor selects a sample of transactions from the population represented by the

    a. Customer order file.
    b. Bill-of-lading file.
    c. Subsidiary customers' accounts ledger.
    d. Sales invoice file.

4. In order to gather audit evidence that uncollected items in customers' accounts represent valid trade receivables, the auditor selects a sample of items from the population represented by the

    a. Customer order file.
    b. Bill-of-lading file.
    c. Subsidiary customers' accounts ledger.
    d. Sales invoice file.

5. On January 15, 1974, before the Longview Company released its financial statements for the year ended December 31, 1973, Agie Corporation, a customer, declared bankruptcy. Agie has had a history of financial difficulty. Longview estimates that it will

400
Audit of the
credit sales
system

suffer a material loss on an account receivable from Agie. How should this loss be disclosed or recognized?

a. The loss should be disclosed in footnotes to the financial statements, but the financial statements themselves need not be adjusted.

b. The loss should be disclosed in an explanatory paragraph in the auditor's report.

c. No disclosure or recognition is required.

d. The financial statements should be adjusted to recognize the loss. (AICPA Adapted)

CHAPTER 12

Audit of the inventory system

Inventory is defined as goods held for resale or for use in the manufacture of goods to be sold. A major accounting objective is the valuation of ending inventory and the measurement of the cost of goods sold. This allocation process is based upon a company's utilization of either the periodic inventory system or the perpetual inventory system. Irrespective of the inventory system adopted, the auditor determines that the cost pool is a proper representation of historical product cost and that this cost is allocated between the balance sheet and the income statement consistent with generally accepted accounting principles. The discussion in this chapter is concerned with the periodic system approach; however, the use of the perpetual system requires only a slight modification in the audit approach. Specifically, the chapter deals with the purchasing accounting system, which accumulates the cost pool, and the resulting amount of ending inventory that appears on the balance sheet. The impact on trade accounts payable resulting from purchase transactions is discussed in Chapter 14.

THE INVENTORY PURCHASE SYSTEM

The appropriate accounting entries for the periodic inventory system are:

TRANSACTION	ACCOUNTING ENTRY		
Acquisition of goods	Purchases	$00	
	Accounts payable		$00
Sale of goods	Accounts receivable	$00	
	Sales		$00

The above summary demonstrates that the cost of goods acquired during the accounting period is accumulated in the purchases account. The auditor reviews this accounting system to determine if the internal control system is adequate; this determination impacts audit programming for the compliance and substantive

402
Audit of the inventory system

tests. For the other accounts generated, the auditor reviews the credit sales system, which was the topic of the previous chapter. The accounts payable balance, which is discussed in Chapter 14, is also subjected to audit.

INTERNAL CONTROL MODEL: INVENTORY PURCHASE SYSTEM

Once again the auditor is cognizant of the internal control features that provide for an adequate system. Violations of these features are analyzed by the auditor to determine if resultant audit procedures to be used are to be restricted or extended.

Plan of organization

DEPARTMENTAL AUTONOMY

The organizational structure of a company should reflect the need to segregate the authorization responsibility, the recording responsibility, and the custodial responsibility for the inventory purchase system. When departmental autonomy is not recognized in the plan of organization, the auditor has serious reservations about the reliability of accounting data generated by the system. In an extreme case he or she may conclude that the system is so weak that the compliance tests are superfluous and that the audit effort is to be concentrated in the substantive tests phase of the audit. The following segregation of duties and responsibilities is observed in the organizational plan:

I. Accounting department
1. Maintenance of the purchase journal
2. Maintenance of the accounts payable subsidiary ledger
3. Maintenance of the general ledger
4. Review of purchases authorization and execution
5. Review of documentation for receipt of goods
6. Control and responsibility for the periodic counting of all inventory
7. Responsibility for the valuation of ending inventory and cost of goods sold in accordance with generally accepted accounting principles
II. Treasurer
No specific responsibilities in the inventory purchase system
III. Functions other than accounting and treasurer
1. Responsibility for the requisition of goods (manufacturing or sales department)
2. Responsibility for approval of the purchase of goods (purchasing agent)
3. Responsibility for the receipt of goods (receiving department)
4. Responsibility for the storage of goods (warehousing or stores)

In the absence of collusion or management intervention, the above organizational scheme becomes an integral part of a strong internal control system. The auditor's review of documents generated or processed under this plan of organization results in competent evidential matter. If the above system is validated as existing and functioning adequately, it is appropriate for the auditor to restrict the extent of audit procedures utilized in subsequent tests. In addition, the nature and timing of audit procedures may be affected.

System of authorization and accountability

A contributing factor to the adequacy of the plan of organization is the established system of authorization and accountability.

EXECUTION OF TRANSACTIONS

The proper execution of a transaction in the inventory purchase system depends upon authorization for the purchase of inventory, the actual receipt of inventory, and the receipt of an invoice from the vendor. In this accounting system the client reviews documents that exhibit specific authorization to obtain reasonable assurance that a transaction is executed as authorized.

Authorization for purchase: The need to acquire inventory is initiated in the operating departments or in the inventory control area. After taking into consideration such variables as carrying cost of the inventory, discounts based on the size of the purchase, and future demands, a purchase requisition is generated and forwarded to the purchasing department. The purchasing department has the exclusive authority to purchase inventory for the organization. Additionally, it has the responsibility to purchase quality goods at minimum price. In fulfilling its responsibilities, it generates a prenumbered purchase order for each purchase, listing the quantity of items to be purchased, the price, and delivery instructions, including a delivery date or schedule of deliveries. The original purchase order is sent to the vendor, and at least three copies are usually retained for internal use. One copy, which serves as the open purchase order file, is kept by the purchasing department. The receiving department is sent a copy which serves as authorization for the receipt of the goods. This copy may be a "blind" copy which does not designate the quantity of items ordered, so that there will be an independent count of these goods when they are received. A third copy is sent to the accounting department as part of the documentation necessary for recording the acquisition.

Authorization of receipt and storage: As suggested above, an independent receiving department is notified by the receipt of a purchase order to accept goods shipped from a particular vendor. Once the goods are received, the receiving department counts, weighs, or otherwise measures the inventory received, inspects the goods to determine if they are in acceptable condition, and compares their description to the detail listed on the purchase order copy. If the shipment is satisfactory, the receiving department prepares a multicopy receiving report. The goods are forwarded to the requisitioning department or stores, and, if accepted, the acceptance is noted on the receiving report. At this point, the receiving department retains and files the original receiving report and

404
**Audit of the
inventory system**

forwards copies of it to the purchasing department and the accounting department.

RECORDING OF TRANSACTIONS

Once an inventory purchase transaction has been executed, internal control procedures are devised which reasonably ensure that the transaction is recorded in the proper amount, in the correct account, and in the appropriate accounting period. This responsibility rests with the accounting department and is dependent upon its review of authorized documents.

Matching of supportive documents: A plan of organization that incorporates the internal control principles of duties properly segregated and departmental autonomy adds integrity to internally prepared documents. Under these conditions the accounting department accumulates and matches documents to support the recording of the purchases/accounts payable entry. In addition to the internally generated documents, the accounting department receives an external document, the vendor's invoice. The information per the purchase order, the receiving report, and the invoice are compared. If the data are in agreement, the authorized transaction is recorded in the purchase journal or the voucher register.

ACCESS TO ASSETS

Adopting internal control procedures that limit the access to assets associated with the inventory purchase system is designed to safeguard the assets against improper disposition. This is achieved by controlling access to inventory on hand and by controlling documents that provide the basis for the movement of inventory.

Access to inventory: Since inventory represents a significant investment for most organizations, there is adequate justification for adopting accounting procedures that limit access to this asset. A physical barrier, such as a fence or an entire warehouse, is usually employed when goods are stored rather than displayed for sale. Access to the goods is limited to individuals who are duly authorized. In the case of inventory displayed for sale, the physical design of the display area and the number of employees assigned to it are taken into consideration. Of course, any accounting control procedure is evaluated in the context of the cost-benefit relationship of the procedure, since there is always a trade-off between the cost of a control and the benefits derived from it. Thus each situation is evaluated in light of this factor.

Accounting for prenumbered documents: To make sure that authorized transactions are recorded, a numerical file of prenumbered documents is maintained. On a periodic basis this sequential file is reviewed by someone independent of the purchasing and receiving functions. In the area of purchased inventory transactions, two files, one consisting of purchase orders processed and the other of receiving reports used, are kept. At any particular time purchase orders used during the accounting period are complete and represent a recorded transaction, canceled, or still open. On the other hand, receiving reports represent a completed transaction or are in the unmatched receiving report file in the accounts payable department. During the accounting for prenumbered documents the client reviews unused documents to make sure they are being processed in order.

Consistency of data: Accounting controls are adopted so that similar data at two or more locations can be compared. In the purchases system the total purchases as shown in the purchase journal or voucher register is compared to the total credits made in the accounts payable subsidiary ledger for a group of transactions processed.

Once an authorized shipment of goods is received, access to and responsibility for these items is maintained. In the case of a nonmanufacturing client, goods are retained in storage or at another designated source. If the client is a manufacturer, goods remain in storage until an authorized production requisition is received. At this point they are moved from the storage area to the production area and remain there until they are completed and sent to the finished goods storeroom or warehouse. The client's cost accounting system, based on responsibility accounting, follows these goods from raw materials, to work in process, and finally to finished goods. At each stage, access to the inventory is limited to individuals involved in the appropriate production or storage phase of the industrial process. In addition, those with access to the inventory at the different stages are held accountable for its physical safeguard. This accountability is based upon properly executed documents that are prepared or initialed at the completion of each stage of the movement of inventory.

COMPARISON OF RECORDED ACCOUNTABILITY WITH ASSETS

The internal control system for purchase transactions provides a basis for determining the accountability of those who control the inventory.

Periodic inventory: The significance of the segregation of the custodial and recording responsibilities is apparent when there is a comparison between the actual inventory on hand and the inventory as determined in the accounting records. Under the supervision of the controller or perhaps the chief cost accountant, a periodic inventory count is made by the client. The inventory may be counted on a single date or it may be taken in cycles throughout the fiscal year. If the client employs a periodic inventory system and the inventory is not counted at the end of the physical year, the accounting records may be inadequate for comparing the asset to the recorded amount. For these interim inventory counts, most clients use the gross profit method for estimating inventory or inventory segments, or some form of perpetual inventory cards are used even though they are not integrated with the general ledger.

The counting of inventory and the auditor's observation of this count is a critical phase of an audit. Later in this chapter, the inventory procedures employed by the client, as well as those employed by the auditor, are discussed in detail.

406
Audit of the
inventory system

STUDY AND EVALUATION OF THE INVENTORY PURCHASE SYSTEM

The initial study of the inventory purchase system is designed to provide the auditor with a thorough knowledge of the system. A partial internal control questionnaire and flowchart for this system is illustrated in Figures 12-1 and 12-2, respectively. With the use of the guidelines suggested in the discussion of the inventory purchase internal control model, the weaknesses and strengths of the system are identified. This analysis provides the basis for audit program planning at the interim date and at the year end.

COMPLIANCE TESTS: INVENTORY PURCHASES

To determine that accounting control procedures in the inventory purchases system are being applied, the auditor constructs an audit program similar to the one shown in Figure 12-3. Since the study and evaluation of the internal control system are almost entirely analytic in nature, the auditor's initial impression of it is a preliminary assessment. The compliance tests provide a more concrete base upon which to evaluate the system. At the conclusion of the compliance tests the auditor is in a position to identify specifically the timing, nature, and extent of the procedures to be utilized in the substantive tests.

UNIVERSE DEFINITION AND SAMPLE SELECTION

The auditor's test of inventory purchases is concerned with determining if purchase transactions are properly authorized and that these transactions are correctly processed through the accounting system. To achieve this objective, the auditor may select the purchase journal as the universe. With the selection of this universe, it is relatively simple to determine if the universe is intact. A review of the individual entries and the test footing of one or more months of the purchases journal is the basis for this determination. Obviously, the individual sample items, each line entry in the purchases journal, are readily accessible. It should be noted that defining the universe as purchase orders prepared during the accounting period does not satisfy the objective stated above. The preparation of a purchase order does not impact the accounting equation. Thus only purchase orders for inventory items received during the year are of interest. This definition results in a universe that is very cumbersome to work with and to control. In an audit engagement, neither condition can be tolerated.

Once the auditor is satisfied with the definition of the universe, an appropriate method of sample selection is chosen. For the sample items selected, supporting documents are obtained. The supporting documents include the purchase order, the receiving report, and the vendor's invoice. In addition, the working paper reveals the items selected for review, and this working paper usually provides the basis for the control of the sample. Control is necessary to ensure that the auditor reviews, evaluates, and draws conclusions based upon all the sample items independently chosen by the auditor. The initial selection of items for review does not preclude the auditor from expanding the size of the sample at a later date.

Figure 12-1

Internal Control Questionnaire

Purchases	Answer		Answer based on		
	Yes	No	Inquiry	Observation	Comments
1. Is there a purchasing department?					
2. If so, is it entirely independent of – a. the accounting department? b. the receiving and shipping departments?					
3. Are purchases made only on the basis of purchase requisitions signed by the respective department heads?					
4. Are all purchases (except small items purchased from petty cash) routed through the purchasing department?					
5. Are all purchases made by means of the client's purchase orders sent to the vendors?					
6. Are the purchase-order forms prenumbered?					
7. Are certain items required to be purchased subject to competitive bidding?					
8. If so, does the procedure followed indicate the result of the review of the bids received?					
9. Are purchase prices approved – a. by responsible official in purchasing department? b. If not, by any other responsible official?					
10. Is the quantity and condition of goods received determined at the time of receipt by someone independent of the purchasing department?					
11. Is the receiving department denied reference to copies of the purchase orders for authority to accept materials, etc.?					
12. Are receiving reports prepared by receiving department? a. Are such reports prenumbered?					
13. Are copies of receiving reports – a. filed permanently in the receiving department? b. furnished to the accounting department? c. furnished to the purchasing department?					
14. Is the accounting department notified promptly of purchased goods returned to the vendor?					

Figure 12-2

Procedural Flowchart: Purchases, Procedural Flowchart Shown in Relation to Organization Chart To Portray the Control Obtained through Segregation of Functional Responsibility

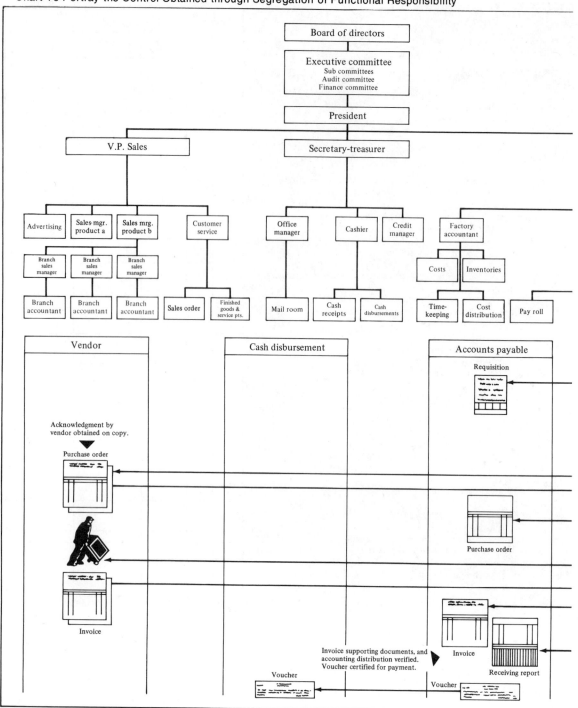

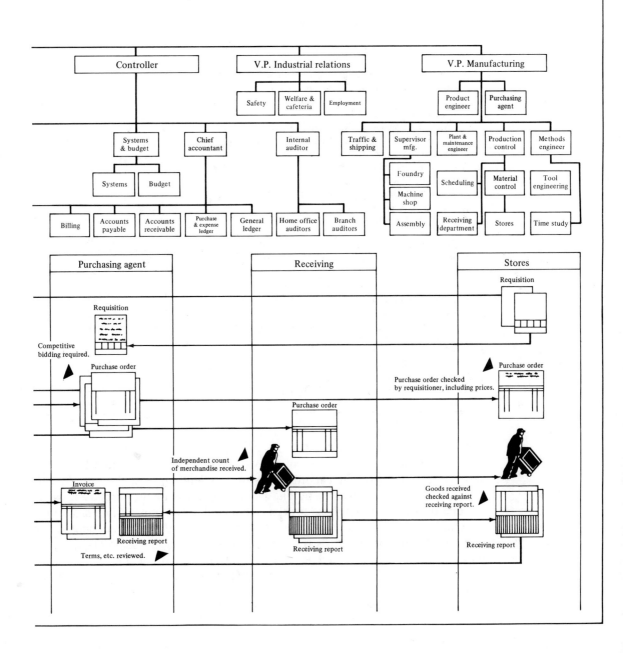

410
Audit of the
Inventory system

Figure 12-3

Audit program: inventory purchases

PROCEDURES	DATE COMPLETED	WORK PERFORMED BY
1. The universe is defined as the individual line-item entries in the purchase journal. Determine the size of the universe.		
2. Randomly select sample items from the above universe.		
3. For each sample item:		
a. Trace authorization for the purchase to the purchase order.		
b. Trace authorization for receipt of the goods and storage of the goods to the receiving report.		
c. Compare the information per the vendor's invoice to the purchase order and receiving report.		
d. Review the vendor invoice for proper pricing and mathematical accuracy.		
e. Trace the voucher package (invoice, purchase order, and receiving report) to entry in the purchase journal and the accounts payable subsidiary ledger.		
4. Select a few purchase debit memos for review and perform the following procedures:		
a. Examine the debit memo for proper authorization for return or allowance.		
b. For purchases returned, trace to shipping documentation and note quantity, date shipped, and product identification.		
c. Recompute footings and extensions on the debit memo.		
d. Trace authorization document to entry in the appropriate journal and the accounts payable subsidiary ledger.		
5. Account for the numerical sequence of the purchase orders and receiving reports.		
6. For three months chosen at random, foot the purchases journal and trace postings to the general ledger.		
7. Review the purchases journal, the subsidiary accounts payable ledger, and the general ledger accounts for unusual items.		

VALIDATION OF AUTHORIZATION

For the sample items selected, a review is made to determine if the transactions were authorized in accordance with the client's policy. The authority to commit the organization to the purchase of goods rests with the purchasing agent or department. Each purchase order is examined for an appropriate signature. In addition, the auditor determines that purchase orders are accounted for properly. He or she observes the storage of unused purchase orders to see if they are adequately protected. A review of the purchase orders filed numerically is made to see, on a test basis, if they are supported by a voucher package or are still open.

The review of authorization is completed by inspection of the receiving report and the vendor's invoice. The receiving report preparation and signature provide evidence that a certain quantity of goods was received on a specific date. Again, the auditor reviews the numerical file of receiving reports to see if they are being accounted for on a periodic basis. In an inventory purchase system, the establishment of liability depends upon the receipt of a vendor's invoice. The auditor inspects the vendor's invoice to determine that an appropriate clerk initialed the invoice to show that sufficient documentation was received to justify journalization of the transaction.

COMPARISON OF DOCUMENTS TO ACCOUNTING RECORDS

Once a transaction is determined to be properly authorized, audit procedures are employed to see if the information is recorded in the accounting records. The elements of the recording process encompass the amount recorded, the date recorded, and the classification of the entry. The validated invoice, which is the result of the utilization of procedures to determine the propriety of the dollar amount, is traced to the line-item entry in the purchases journal. The date of the receipt of the inventory, as shown in the receiving report, is used to see if the purchase is recorded in the proper month. Unusual lags in recording the transaction in the journal or numerous posting errors alert the auditor to the possibility of cutoff problems at the end of the year. Appropriate classification of the purchase depends upon the descriptions of the goods contained in the voucher package. For example, purchases of property, plant, and equipment should not be processed through the purchases journal. The ability to detect such errors is dependent upon the auditor's understanding of the client's operations. Classification also includes the proper posting to the subsidiary accounts payable ledger, if one is maintained. Again, vendor name, date of transaction, and amount are traced from the validated documents to the individual entry.

PROPRIETY OF DATA DOCUMENTED

The propriety of data contained on the purchase order, receiving report, and vendor's invoice is partially dependent upon the internal consistency of the data. For example, the numbers of items billed, the description of the items, and the document date contained on the vendor's invoice are substantiated by data appearing on the purchase order and receiving report. The inventory cost per item is validated by the auditor by referring to a contract signed by the vendor, an approved price list, or catalogs in the possession of the client. Finally, the vendor's invoice is tested for mathematical accuracy by checking the extensions and the summation of the total.

TEST OF PURCHASES SUMMARIZATION

On a periodic basis inventory purchases are summarized, and the balances transferred to the appropriate accounts in the general ledger. Figure 12-4 illustrates this approach by showing that a sample item (Klarn & Sons) is tested in detail to determine that it was properly executed and recorded in the purchase journal. At this point the auditor can trace a single transaction no farther, but rather must test the summarization of the purchases journal and the monthly

Figure 12-4

Test of Inventory Purchases Summarization

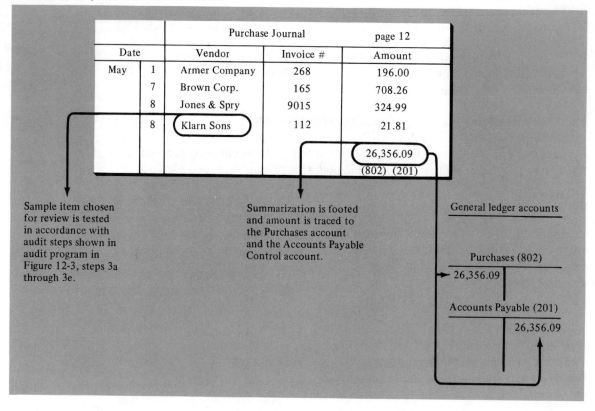

postings to the purchases account and the accounts payable in the general ledger. The auditor reviews one or more of the monthly summarizations, depending upon the adequacy of the internal control system for inventory purchases and his or her personal preferences.

REVIEW OF UNUSUAL ITEMS

An internal control system is established to process numerous routine transactions. The auditor's random selection of a relatively few transactions usually exposes him or her to a representative sample of the transactions being processed. However, there is always the possibility that some transactions are not routine, and these are obviously of interest to the auditor. To identify these items in the inventory purchases system, a review of the purchases account and the control accounts payable account is made. As suggested in earlier chapters, the source of the posting in these accounts and the amount of the posting are two elements that may describe an unusual item. The auditor inquires about any item that is not consistent with his or her understanding of the client's internal control system or the client's overall operating characteristics. For example, assume that a journal entry on August 3 increased the purchases account by $30,000.

The auditor, after additional investigations, discovers that this was part of a purchase of several items, inventory, equipment, fixtures, and so on, from a competitor that went out of business, and that a single sum was paid for all the assets. This investigation raises the audit question of how costs were allocated to the individual assets, some of which are depreciable and some of which are not. The point is that the auditor is alert to the possibility of unusual items and the audit exposure they represent.

413
Compliance tests:
inventory purchases

TEST OF PURCHASE MEMOS AND DISCOUNTS

The amount of purchases incurred during an accounting period is reduced by purchase returns and allowances and purchase discounts. In most engagements the amount is not significant; nonetheless, a review of some of these transactions is performed. For goods returned to the supplier because of damage and so on, the client generates a debit memorandum which is sent to the supplier. The auditor selects a few debit memos for the accounting period, checking for proper authorization and inspecting the shipping document to see that the goods were actually returned. For cash purchase discounts that do not require the return of goods, the auditor reviews the vendor's invoice for credit terms and the date of the subsequent cash payment. If allowances are other than for returns or cash discounts, he or she reviews the item for proper authorization, consistency with industrial practice, or perhaps a specific contract signed by the vendor and the client.

TEST OF CREDIT MEMOS

For most engagements credit memos supporting sales returns, allowances, and discounts are not material, and the audit effort is not significant. However, a few credit memos are selected to determine that they are properly authorized and recorded. An unusually large increase in the use of credit memos is investigated by the auditor to find out if such an occurrence has significance in other audit areas. For example, a large number of allowances may suggest that a line of inventory is not moving well and a inventory write-down may be justified. In any case, the auditor integrates this bit of evidence into the overall evaluation of the acceptability of the financial statements, noting its consistency with evidence collected in other phases of the audit.

Results of compliance tests

With the completion of the compliance tests for the inventory purchases system, the auditor finalizes the audit strategy for substantive tests procedures for the inventory account and the accounts payable account. The impact of the results of the tests of compliance is illustrated in Figure 12-5. The original audit approach in the substantive tests for inventory was determined after the study and evaluation of the inventory purchases system was completed. Subsequently, the compliance tests identified errors in inventory costing, as shown in Figure 12-5. Because of these errors, the auditor reassesses the adequacy of the internal control system to see if the nature, the extent, and/or the timing of the substantive

Figure 12-5
Results of Compliance Tests and Subsequent Impact on Substantive Tests

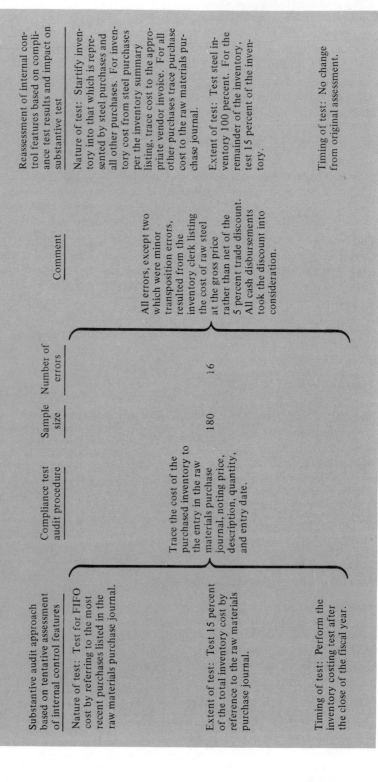

audit procedures are to be modified. A similar approach is used in the design of accounts payable substantive tests.

SUBSTANTIVE TESTS: INVENTORY

Substantive tests procedures are, for the most part, concerned with balance sheet accounts. In a periodic inventory system, the inventory account is not impacted by acquisitions and sales during the accounting period. The inventory cost pool, or goods available for sale, is the sum of the balance at the beginning of inventory and the amount of purchases for the accounting period. At the end of the period, an enterprise takes a physical inventory and assigns costs to these quantities. This ending inventory balance becomes critical in the allocation of costs on the balance sheet and the same figure is subtracted from goods available for sale to determine the cost of goods sold for the year. Through the performance of the compliances test the auditor determines whether the cost accumulated in the purchases account is reliable. The cost represented in the beginning inventory has been verified from the previous year's audit when it was that year's ending inventory. Thus it is not surprising to learn that an auditor spends a considerable amount of time on the test of the current year's ending inventory to ensure a proper cost allocation between accounting periods. The remainder of this chapter deals with the audit of inventories. A typical year-end audit program for inventories is presented in Figure 12-6.

Existence

One objective in the audit of inventories is to determine that they physically exist. This objective is achieved through the auditor's observation of the physical inventory count performed by the client. *SAS No. 1,* Section 331.09, emphasizes the importance of the procedure in the following statement:

> . . . it is ordinarily necessary for the independent auditor to be present at the time of count and, by suitable observation, tests and inquiries, satisfy himself respecting the effectiveness of the methods of inventory-taking and the measure of reliance which may be placed upon the client's representations about quantities and physical condition of the inventories.

It should be emphasized that the auditor observes the inventory rather than takes the inventory.

PRELIMINARY INVESTIGATION

The listing of inventory by the client, as well as the observation of inventory by the auditor, involve a significant amount of labor. To ensure that these tasks are performed successfully, there is extensive planning on the part of both parties. The planning involves the client's physical inventory practices and the client's detailed procedures for counting and listing all inventory. It is essential that the auditor understand the client's physical inventory procedures to see that they are adequate under the circumstances of the audit and to coordinate audit procedures he or she will use in the inventory observation.

416
Audit of the
inventory system

Figure 12-6

Audit program: inventory

PROCEDURES	DATE COMPLETED	WORK PERFORMED BY
1. Determine the client's physical inventory timing practices.	_____	_____
2. Review the client's physical inventory-taking procedures.	_____	_____
3. Obtain control of the physical inventory and counting procedures.	_____	_____
4. Observe the client's physical inventory.	_____	_____
5. Confirm or observe inventories held by others.	_____	_____
6. Test the summarization of inventory.	_____	_____
7. Test the cost assigned to inventory items.	_____	_____
8. Determine the propriety of inventory purchases at the end of the year.	_____	_____
9. Review inventories for proper classification and disclosure.	_____	_____

CLIENT'S PHYSICAL INVENTORY TIMING

The client must physically count inventory at least once during the fiscal year. The actual count may occur on the balance sheet date, before the balance sheet date, after the balance sheet date, or on a cycle basis throughout the year. Selection of physical inventory date is not a unilateral decision made by the client, since the auditor determines if the inventory-taking practice is justified under the circumstances. In most cases it is agreeable to the auditor to count the inventory on the balance sheet date, since this is the date to which his or her opinion is applicable. If the client does not count inventory on the balance sheet date, the auditor concurs only if the internal control system is strong. For this approach to be acceptable, perpetual inventory records must be kept, because the auditor observes inventory on a date other than the year-end date and then utilizes the internal control system to reconcile to the amount shown on the balance sheet date.

Professional standards recognize the need to be flexible enough to meet the legitimate demands of a business enterprise, as well as to encourage new and efficient methods of taking inventory. For example, some businesses employ statistical sampling methods to estimate inventories, while others count inventories on a cycle basis throughout the year to avoid a disruption of normal operations. In any case *SAS No. 1,* Section 331.11, identifies the broad responsibilities of the auditor when these or other techniques for counting inventories are employed by stating the following requirement:

> . . . the independent auditor must satisfy himself that the client's procedures or methods are sufficiently reliable to produce results substantially the same as those which would be obtained by a count of all items each year. The auditor must be present to observe such counts as he deems necessary and must satisfy himself as to the effectiveness of the counting procedures used.

No matter what technique is used by the client, the auditor is required to observe some of the inventory. Total reliance on the accounting records does not generate sufficient competent evidential matter. Except as noted, the following discussion assumes that the inventory observation occurs on the balance sheet date.

417
Substantive tests:
inventory

CLIENT'S PHYSICAL INVENTORY PROCEDURES

The client's detailed physical inventory procedures describe how the inventory is to be counted. Since many individuals are part of the inventory counting and listing teams, the client lists the procedures in writing and encourages its employees to read these instructions carefully. Because the custodial responsibility of the inventory rests with the store's employees or other operating personnel, the physical inventory is conducted by the controller's staff. However, this practice does not preclude the operating personnel from assisting in taking the physical inventory.

The inventory instructions typically include:

- Name of person coordinating the physical inventory
- Plans for rearranging and/or segregating inventory
- Provisions for controlling the receipt, shipment, or movement of inventory during the physical inventory
- Instructions for describing inventory as to quantities by weight, count, or other measurements
- Instructions as to the use of inventory tags or sheets and their distribution, collection, and control
- Plans for determining the amount of inventory in the possession of consignees, public warehouses, or other outside parties

The auditor reads the inventory instructions and, based upon his or her understanding of the enterprise's operations, determines if they are adequate. In addition, the auditor attends the physical inventory briefing held by the client just prior to the beginning of the inventory count to see if the instructions are understood by the client's personnel. If this phase of the preinventory count is not adequate, there is a good chance that an improper physical inventory count will be performed.

The preliminary investigation of the client's inventory listing procedures enables the auditor to plan properly for the physical inventory observation. He or she becomes aware of the number of plants, branches, and so on that have inventory, as well as the estimated dollar value of the inventory at each location. Special inventory problems, such as the need to use unique techniques to estimate raw materials or work in process, are identified. These and other elements are used by the auditor to determine the labor requirements and level of expertise required by the engagement. Completion of a successful physical inventory observation is dependent upon adequate planning in the preliminary investigation.

CONTROL OF THE PHYSICAL OBSERVATION

On the actual day of observation of the inventory, the auditor's first step is to gain control of the inventory-counting process. An understanding of the

418
Audit of the
inventory system

physical layout of the plant or store is gained through a tour of the premises. When the physical premises are complex, involving a number of buildings or several floors, the auditor obtains a map of the facilities or draws a sketch of the layout. This diagram is marked to show such things as concentration of inventory dollar values or potential problem areas.

A second element of control of the inventory-counting process is concerned with the client's methods of documenting the count. In some manner the client lists the inventory and marks it as counted. Usually, the client uses prenumbered inventory tags or prenumbered listing sheets. The auditor notes the range of the prenumbered documents, for example, from 1 to 10,000, and lists the block of numbers assigned to each inventory team. At the end of the count of the inventory, the auditor determines which documents were not used and reviews these unusued documents to make sure that one or more out of sequence is not used. During the auditor's inspection of the inventory, the used documents are completely or partially accounted for in numerical sequence. The auditor uses these procedures to make sure that only a certain block of tags or listing sheets is used and that each one could be observed by the auditor during the observation. A typical working paper illustrating this approach is shown in Figure 12-7. Document control is an easier task if the auditor obtains a copy of the document as the inventory is observed. For example, a multiple-copy inventory tag, such as the one shown in Figure 12-8, is attached to the inventory by the client's counting team and the auditor removes one of the copies as the inventory observation is conducted.

The movement of inventory during the count and during the auditor's observation is discouraged. Obviously, it is more difficult for auditors to maintain control of the inventory and ensure the integrity of the count if goods are transferred from one location to another. However, it is often. necessary for the client to continue to ship and receive goods during the physical inventory. Proper planning in the preliminary stage alerts the auditor to this problem, so that appropriate procedures can be established. The following procedures are typically used, although each engagement is evaluated and procedures are tailored accordingly:

- All goods received are placed in the receiving department area; receiving reports are prepared, and they are counted at the end of the day.
- All goods to be shipped are placed in the shipping department area prior to the beginning of the inventory count. For items shipped, appropriate bills of lading are prepared. For items not shipped at the close of the day, inventory tags are prepared.
- Any other goods that need to be moved during the count are approved by the auditor in charge.

PHYSICAL INVENTORY OBSERVATION

Once the auditor establishes a basis for control of the inventory count, the actual observation begins. Although the auditor does not take the inventory, the observation is in no way a passive endeavor. The in-charge auditor assigns an auditor the observation responsibility for several areas, depending upon the size

Figure 12-7

419
Substantive tests:
inventory

Green Valley Corp.
Inventory Ticket Control Sheet
12-31-79

Client Inventory Teams	Counting Area	Assigned Tickets	Tickets Used		
#1 - Barnes & Jones	Warehouse 1 & 5	1-500	1-416	✓	
#2 - Ford & Harris	Storeroom	501-700	501-659	✓	
#3 - Conta & Darby	Shipping & Receiving, Warehouse 2 & 4	701-1200	701-909 / 1100-1136	✓ ✓	
#4 - Smith & Hoback	Sheet steel in yard area	1201-1500	1201-1483	✓	
#5 - Vermillon & Simms	Goods in Process	1501-1600	1501-1542	✓	
Unassigned		1600-2000	1601-1618	✓	✓

✓ - All unused tickets reviewed; Used tickets accounted for numerically during observation.

✓ - 18 unassigned tickets were used for items missed during original count. Each item was observed.

Prepared by	Index No.
Date	

Figure 12-8

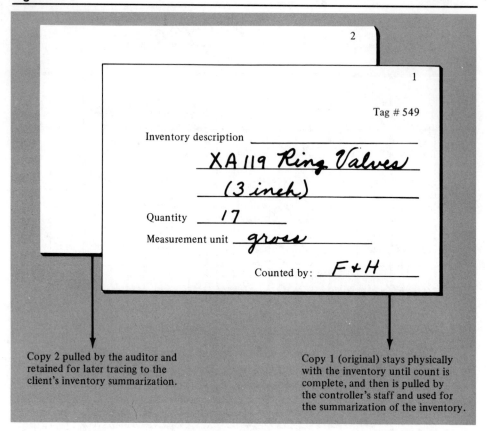

of the client, and observes the client's counting teams to determine that instructions are being followed. Initially the auditor performs a detailed count of a few items to determine that the information listed on the inventory tag or sheet is valid. Once this is determined, he or she relies more heavily on the reasonableness of the count rather than making a detailed count of each grouping. If it appears that an adequate count is not being made, the auditor contacts the client so that the problem can be resolved as early as possible.

As the auditor test-counts the inventory, some of the counts are listed for subsequent tracing to the client's inventory summarization. The data contained in this summarization are basically the same data shown on the inventory tag. The extent of items counted and listed by the auditor is dependent upon the adequacy of the client's inventory count procedures and the number of discrepancies discovered by the auditor.

The observation of inventory is more than a mechanical counting and listing approach on the part of the auditor. Inquisitiveness and common sense supplement the auditor's technical accounting background. He or she is alert for the possibility of goods being counted twice, empty containers, "hollow squares" for stacked inventory, or items not counted, such as those on top shelves. Items that appear to be damaged, obsolete, or slow-moving are of particular interest to the auditor and are listed for further investigation concerning cost recoverability. Finally, once the auditor is satisfied with the count, the control information for inventory listing documents is noted in the working papers. It is also helpful to make a last walk-through of the inventory area to make sure all aisles, shelves, and so on have been counted.

As each area is counted and observed by the auditor, the data are transmitted to the auditor in charge of the inventory observation. Each area is checked off, ticket control data are obtained, and unused tickets are reviewed for sequential order. Exceptions or problems are cleared or evaluated as to their materiality. If the auditor is satisfied with the results, the entire inventory is released, and the client is free to move the inventory or otherwise rearrange the goods.

INVENTORY HELD BY OTHERS

Inventory of the client may be held by others, such as in the case of consigned goods or goods held in public warehouses. The adequacy of the client's internal control procedures with regard to such transactions and the materiality of goods held by other parties are determinants of the audit approach. When the internal control system is adequate and the goods are not a significant proportion of current assets or total assets, direct written confirmation from the other party provides competent evidential matter. On the other hand, when the above two elements are not applicable, supplemental inquiries are made by the auditor. *SAS No. 1,* Section 331.15, describes the following steps as supplemental inquiries that may be applied by the auditor to the extent deemed necessary under the circumstances when a public warehouse is used:

- Discussion with the owner as to owner's control procedures in investigating the warehouseman, and tests of related evidential matter

- Review of the owner's control procedures concerning performance of the warehouseman, and tests of related evidential matter

- Observation of physical counts of the goods wherever practicable and reasonable

TEST OF INVENTORY SUMMARIZATION

As part of the determination of the existence of inventory, the auditor tests the summarization. In most cases the client does not list each item counted as a separate line item; rather, several counts from a variety of locations are combined to form a single total count for the inventory item. Figure 12-9 illustrates a typical summarization process that may be employed by a client. This summarization is completed a few days after the physical inventory is taken.

The objective of the test of the inventory summarization is to determine whether the physical inventory count is properly transferred to the client's final inventory summarization schedule, which becomes the basis for determining the value of the ending inventory. The auditor tests the summarization by using data gathered during the inventory observation. The audit approach is both specific and general. Since the auditor made and recorded test counts during the physical

Figure 12-9

Tag # 816

Inventory description _____

XA 119-3"

Quantity __*25*__

Measurement unit __*GR.*__

Counted by: __*C + D*__

Tag # 387

Inventory description _____

XA 119-3" Ring Valves

Quantity __*34*__

Measurement unit __*gross*__

Counted by: *Barnes + Jones*

Tag # 549

Inventory description _____

XA 119 Ring Valves (3 inch)

Quantity __*17*__

Measurement unit __*gross*__

Counted by: __*F + H*__

Line item listing in client's
final inventory summarization
schedule

Description	Qty.	Cost	Total
XA119-3 in.	76	$4.12	$313.12

Compare

Data per auditor's inventory test count working papers:

Tag #	Inventory Description	Counting unit	Quantity
549	XA 119-3" Ring Valve	Gross	17
565	O-Ring - Double 6"	CA.	43

inventory observation, these test counts are used in verifying the inventory summarization. However, these specific counts may not be traceable to a single line item in the summarization but rather to two or more inventory tags that represent the same type of inventory. In Figure 12-9 it is shown that the 76 items for the inventory unit are comprised of three separate counts. Thus the auditor traces only the information for tag no. 549 from the audit working papers to the client's combined count, which is usually just the result of stapling similar inventory tags together. Obviously, this is highly competent evidential matter for the support of the 17 items as shown on tag no. 549. The other two tags (no. 816 and no. 387) are tested in a more general manner. Ticket control data (Figure 12-7) obtained during the physical inventory observation are used to verify that the two tickets were used and that they were not added by the client. In the absence of significant errors or a pattern of errors, the auditor is reasonably certain that inventory counts recorded at the physical inventory are transferred properly to the inventory summarization schedule.

Summarization of the inventory requires a considerable number of mathematical calculations on the part of the client. Consequently, the auditor recomputes some of these calculations to verify their accuracy. This includes checking extensions (quantities times unit cost) and testing the addition of the total inventory summary sheets which may consist of several pages. The majority of these tests involve "sight-testing" for reasonableness rather than using a calculator or adding machine.

ALTERNATIVE AUDIT PROCEDURES

Under certain circumstances it may be impossible for the auditor to observe the physical inventory at the end of the fiscal year or at the time the client counts the inventory. For example, he or she may be contracted for the job after the close of the fiscal year to be audited. The need for flexibility in required auditing procedures is reflected in the following quote from *SAS No. 1*, Section 331.10:

> When the well-kept perpetual inventory records are checked by the client periodically by comparison with physical counts, the auditor's observation procedures can be performed either during or after the end of the period under audit.

Therefore the professional literature implies that alternative audit procedures are appropriate only when a client has an adequate internal control system for inventories and perpetual inventories are maintained.

If the above prerequisites are met, alternative audit procedures for determining the existence of inventory include:

- Review the client's inventory-counting and listing procedures.
- Review the inventory listing tags or sheets and trace them to the perpetual inventory cards, noting any exceptions.
- Make test counts after the end of the year and utilize the internal control system documentation (receiving reports for receipts and bills of lading for shipments) to reconcile to the number of units on hand at the year-end date.

The alternative procedures integrate the physical observation of the inventory and utilization of the internal control system. Under no conditions does the

424
**Audit of the
inventory system**

auditor rely exclusively on the internal control system to substantiate the existence of inventory. *SAS No. 1,* Section 331.12, states that

> . . . tests of the accounting records alone will not be sufficient for him to become satisfied as to quantities; it will always be necessary for the auditor to make, or observe, some physical counts of the inventory and apply appropriate tests of intervening transactions.

If the auditor is unable to obtain sufficient competent evidential matter to substantiate the existence of the inventory, a disclaimer of opinion or a qualified opinion must be issued.

Valuation

The term "valuation" is often misleading when used in accounting. Generally speaking, *valuation* is defined as the historical cost of an item rather than its value or replacement cost. In the inventory area, the lower of cost or market, for practical purposes, is the currently acceptable valuation technique. Thus ending inventory is assigned a value based on historical cost but, as stated in *Accounting Research Bulletin No. 43,* Section 5121.07–5121.08, "a departure from the cost basis of pricing the inventory is required when the utility of the goods is no longer as great as its cost . . . a loss of utility is to be reflected as a charge against the revenues of the period in which it occurs."

INVENTORY COST METHODS

Initially the auditor identifies the inventory cost method employed by the client. Acceptable costing methods include first in first out (FIFO), weighted average, last in first out (LIFO), or a variation of these three methods. Once the method is identified, the auditor traces the cost shown in the inventory summarization to the appropriate vendor's invoice(s) if the client is a nonmanufacturing entity. If FIFO is employed, the auditor reviews the most recent purchases as shown on the vendor's invoices with the cost used on the summarization. For a weighted-average method, the auditor reviews costs incurred for the current accounting period as well as the cost represented in the beginning inventory. If LIFO is utilized, the client may employ unit LIFO, dollar-value LIFO, or retail LIFO. The auditor reviews the client's computation of the LIFO inventory by referring to vendor invoices to verify the pattern of cost of inventory items for the period.

The selection of items in the inventory to be tested for proper costing is dependent upon the adequacy of the internal control system, the results of the compliance tests, and the nature of the ending inventory. The evaluation of the internal control system or the compliance tests results may identify a segment of the inventory where costing errors are probable. For example, compliance tests may have revealed an inordinate number of errors in the cost transferred to the perpetual inventory cards for a particular branch or type of inventory. In addition, the composition of the inventory impacts the selection of items for testing the cost assigned to these items. High-dollar-value items are more likely to be tested than lower-dollar-value items, for obvious reasons. Nonetheless, the auditor tests some of the lower-value items to be sure that errors are not accumulated in this segment of the ending inventory.

LOWER OF COST OR MARKET

In some cases the inventory may be costed in accordance with an acceptable method, but the market value, defined as the replacement cost, may be less than the cost. As suggested earlier, the adjustment, if material, is made in the current accounting period. The application of the rule is complicated by the establishment of a so-called ceiling and floor for market value. These terms are defined as follows:

Ceiling: Market cannot exceed the net realizable value (estimated selling price in the ordinary course of business less reasonably predictable costs of completion and disposal).

Floor: Market cannot be less than net realizable value reduced by an allowance for an approximately normal profit margin.[1]

From intermediate accounting it is recalled that the full application of the lower of cost or market subject to the ceiling and floor is extremely tedious. For this reason auditors usually do not perform such a detailed procedure but rather rely upon a broader approach which approximates the application of the rule. First, the market or replacement cost adjustment is much more likely to be needed when the FIFO inventory method is used, because of the assumption of cost flow in this method. In addition, the auditor attempts to identify segments of the inventory that are obsolete or slow-moving by being observant during the physical inventory and by determining inventory turnover rates for inventory segments. Such inventory items are prime candidates for write-downs or write-offs. Finally, the auditor reviews the client's records to determine if the normal sales price is being maintained in the subsequent accounting period. This is verified by reviewing the latest catalog and price sheets and the most recent sales invoices. In any case, the auditor attempts to identify inventory items or segments which represent costs that are not recoverable.

Valuation-manufacturer

For a manufacturing concern, determination of the propriety of the inventory valuation is more complex and time-consuming. Obviously, a manufacturer's inventory consists of raw materials, work in process, and finished goods. In addition, the cost elements includes direct material, direct labor, and factory overhead. These costs are processed through the inventory accounts and eventually become part of the cost of goods sold. The manner in which these costs are processed depends upon the cost accounting system employed by the manufacturer. A thorough understanding of the cost accounting system is a prereq-

[1]Restatement and Revision of Accounting Research Bulletins,'' *Accounting Research Bulletin No. 43* (New York: AICPA, 1961), p. 31.

426
Audit of the inventory system

uisite to the auditor's verification of the valuation of manufactured products. This understanding is gained through the study and evaluation of the client's internal control system and performance of the compliance tests. The following discussion identifies the typical audit problems and approaches associated with the review of a manufacturer's inventories. A thorough discussion of the audit of a sophisticated cost accounting system is beyond the scope of this book.

RAW MATERIALS

Since raw materials are purchased in a manner similar to the entire inventory of a retailer, the valuation audit approach described earlier is appropriate. That is, the inventory costing method is identified, and the appropriate vendor invoices are examined and compared to the cost used in the raw materials inventory summarization. Market, defined as replacement cost, is determined by looking at the most recent vendor invoices, catalogs, and market quotations for commodities and, in some cases, direct communication with vendors. With the determination of cost and market, the lower of cost or market is applied to the raw materials inventory. In addition, contracts to purchase raw materials subsequent to the balance sheet date are examined. If the contract is uncancelable and unhedged and the future price is materially greater than the replacement cost on the balance sheet date, a loss recognizing the difference is booked for the current accounting period.

WORK IN PROCESS AND FINISHED GOODS

Inventory that is in process or completed contains charges for direct materials, direct labor, and factory overhead. In most instances, the rate charge for each cost element is the same for work in process and for finished goods. That is, for a similar manufactured item the direct material rate is the same whether the goods are finished or still in process. The difference is the amount of material used for items in process. It is therefore critical for the auditor to determine the degree of completion for items in process at the close of the year. This is done during the observation of the inventory. Appropriate notations are made so that the auditor can substantiate the degree of completion as reflected in the client's subsequent costing of the work-in-process inventory. Once the auditor is satisfied with this report, the costing rates used in the finished goods and work-in-process summarization schedules are audited.

DIRECT MATERIALS

The cost verified during the testing of the raw materials inventory is used to verify the cost rate used for determining the raw material costs for work in process and finished goods. As suggested above, the auditor uses notes made during the inventory observation to ensure that an incorrect quantity of raw material units is not assigned to the items in process. For finished goods, he or she inspects the goods to obtain some idea of the physical composition of the item. In addition, the auditor utilizes engineering drawings and bills for materials to see if the direct material quantity listed is consistent with these specifications.

DIRECT LABOR

Unlike that for direct materials, the cost element assigned to work in process and finished goods is not subject to physical observation. For this reason, the auditor relies heavily upon internally generated documents to substantiate this cost. This reliance is acceptable only if the client's internal control system is adequate.

The number of client labor hours assigned to an inventory item is supported by approved job tickets and time cards in a job order cost accounting system. On a sample basis, the auditor tests the direct labor hours assigned to a specific job to obtain this documentation. In addition, a knowledgeable auditor is able to test the reasonableness of the hours by comparing this amount with similar jobs and previous years' records. For a process cost accounting system, the employee's job description and department assignment determine if the labor costs appear to be direct. The labor rate used in the cost summarization is verified by referring to the employee's personnel file to see if the rate has been approved. In the file there may also be a job rating form which is the basis for determining the labor rate if the client has a union contract.

FACTORY OVERHEAD

All manufacturing costs not identified as direct are grouped as factory overhead and allocated to the work-in-process and finished goods inventory, as well as to the cost of goods sold. Although the allocation process can be very complicated and tedious in actual practice, it can be represented by the following relationship:

$$\frac{\text{Total factory overhead}}{\text{Activity base}} = \text{factory overhead rate per unit of activity}$$

The numerator consists of manufacturing costs such as supplies consumed, indirect labor, depreciation of machinery, and utilities associated with the manufacturing process. One audit objective is to determine that these manufacturing cost elements are similar to the manufacturing cost elements included in the factory overhead account for the previous year. This determination is facilitated by preparing a working paper similar to the one illustrated in Figure 12-10. Such an analysis allows the auditor to determine if the consistency principle is violated. In addition, this comparative analysis is useful in assessing whether increases or decreases in the cost of a single line item are consistent with the activity for the period and the auditor's understanding of the fixed-cost and variable-cost pattern for the client.

Finally, the cost elements of factory overhead are vouched, or the allocation process is tested. For example, supplies expense is tested by reference to vendor invoices, observing the supplies inventory, and testing the valuation of the ending inventory. Utilities expense is traced to the appropriate invoices, but in most cases this cost is allocated to factory overhead and administrative, general, and selling accounts based on a ratio such as square footage. This allocation computation is tested by the auditor. Other costs are tested in an appropriate manner.

Figure 12-10

Green Valley Corp.
Analysis of Factory Overhead
12-31-79

Factory Overhead	FYE 1979	FYE 1978	Increase (Decrease)	
Indirect Labor	23800	21465	2335	Ⴉ
Maintenance & Repairs	4700	4256	444	Ⴉ
Utilities	43765	31876	11889	Ⴉ
Supplies	8994	7754	1240	Ⓨ
Property Taxes	4967	5765	<798>	Ⓣ
Depreciation - Machinery	17876	16792	1084	φ
Depreciation - Bldg.	12800	12800	-0-	φ
Insurance Exp.	3200	4500	<1300>	V
	120102	105208	14894	

Ⴉ Traced to time cards and labor distribution sheets on a test basis.

Ⴉ Traced to utility bills on a test basis; significant increase due to new rates instituted during the current year.

Ⓨ Traced to vendor invoices and physical inventory observed. Summarization sheets tested.

Ⓣ Traced to property tax assessment. Client was successful in its appeal for revaluation of some items of machinery.

φ Depreciation and allocation tested in accordance with audit program at S110.

V Insurance bill examined. Client decided to drop insurance coverage on machinery with little market value.

The activity base used in determining the factory overhead rate may be based on direct labor hours, direct labor dollars, machine hours, a combination of these, or other measures of manufacturing activity. Again, the auditor relies upon internal documents to substantiate the actual activity for the period. Production reports and summarizations are reviewed and tested. If predetermined rates are used during the fiscal year to estimate charges to the work-in-process, finished goods, and cost of goods sold accounts, these rates are compared to the actual factory overhead rate incurred.

429
Substantive tests: inventory

Cutoff

The inventory cutoff test procedures are constructed to determine if (1) all goods received prior to the end of the year are recorded as purchased and included in the ending inventory and (2) all goods shipped prior to the end of the year are recorded as sales and excluded from the ending inventory. During the discussion of inventory observation it was noted that the auditor controls the movement of goods during the taking of the inventory. It was suggested that these goods received from vendors be segregated in the receiving area or some other appropriate location and inventoried at the end of the business day. The auditor observes these items after they have been counted and tagged. In addition, he or she records in the working paper the last few prenumbered receiving reports used for these goods. This information is subsequently traced to an appropriate voucher package and entry in the current fiscal year's purchases journal or voucher register. A sample of receiving reports used immediately after the end of the year is traced to the following year's entry in the purchases journal or voucher register.

During the inventory observation, the auditor instructs the client to move all goods expected to be shipped during the taking of the inventory to the shipping department. Goods, if any, not shipped at the end of the business day are inventoried and observed by the auditor. He or she records the last few bills of lading or other shipping forms used by the client. This information is later traced to the customer order and sales invoice supporting the shipment. Also, the data are traced to the posting in the sales journal. A sample of shipments made after the close of the fiscal year is traced to the following year's entry in the sales journal.

Classification and disclosure

During the audit of inventories the auditor collects sufficient evidential matter to determine that the asset is classified properly and that disclosure requirements are met. Inventories are defined as goods held for resale or partially completed goods still in the process of production. Any other costs are excluded from the inventory classification. In addition, inventory costs are classified as current assets, and for a manufacturer these costs are allocated among raw materials, work in process, and finished goods. Since a variety of costing methods, ranging from specific cost to net realizable value, may be employed under certain

430
Audit of the inventory system

circumstances, the inventory method is disclosed. Finally, if the goods are pledged or otherwise encumbered, this too is disclosed.

Disclosure requirements for publicly held corporations have recently been expanded by the SEC's *Accounting Series Release No. 190*. The promulgation requires that the replacement cost of ending inventory be disclosed. In addition, the cost of goods sold is to be determined based upon the current replacement cost in effect at the time the revenue was recognized. These data are to be disclosed in an "unaudited" footnote to the financial statements; however, the auditor is to be associated with the footnote. At present the precise definition of "unaudited but associated" has not been clarified by the SEC.

SAS No. 18 was issued in 1977 as a guide for the auditor's review of unaudited replacement cost information presented in Form 10-K filed with the SEC. The suggested procedures are analytical in nature and generally do not require the collection of corroborative evidence.[2] The specific procedures to be used are discussed more fully in Chapter 13.

EXERCISES AND PROBLEMS

12-1. Why should a "blind" copy of the purchase order be sent to the receiving department?

12-2. What documents are matched by the accounts payable clerk before liability is established?

12-3. Why is a plant tour an important part of the preliminary phase of the inventory observation?

12-4. Should the auditor observe or count all the inventory items?

12-5. Why is it important for the auditor to obtain ticket control information before he or she leaves the inventory observation?

12-6. Does the observation of inventory meet all of the substantive audit objectives?

12-7. Does the auditor allow the client to move inventory during the count? Explain.

12-8. Can the auditor issue an unqualified opinion on the financial statements if he or she is unable to observe inventory on the balance sheet date?

12-9. What information does the auditor gather to perform an inventory cutoff test?

12-10. Why is it necessary for the auditor to test the inventory summarization if he or she has already observed the inventory count?

12-11. How does the auditor determine if inventories are stated at the lower of cost or market?

12-12. For certain large companies that are subject to the SEC's *Accounting Series Release No. 190*, how may the auditor determine the replacement cost of (1) ending inventories and (2) cost of goods sold? (Assume the auditor must collect corroborative evidence.)

---

[2]"Unaudited Replacement Cost Information," *Statement on Auditing Standards No. 18* (New York: AICPA, 1977), p. 3.

12-13. Part A. When a CPA accepts an engagement from a new client who is a manufacturer, it is customary for him or her to tour the client's plant facilities.

431
Exercises and problems

Required: Discuss the ways in which the observations made by the CPA during the course of the plant tour are of help in planning and conducting the audit.

Part B. In verifying the amount of the inventory, the CPA is concerned that slow-moving and obsolete items are identified in the inventory.

Required: List the auditing procedures the CPA employs to determine whether slow-moving or obsolete items are included in the inventory. (AICPA Adapted)

12-14. The Borow Corporation is an importer and wholesaler. Its merchandise is purchased from a number of suppliers and is warehoused by Borow Corporation until sold to consumers.

In conducting an audit for the year ended June 30, 1979, the company's CPA determined that the system of internal control was good. Accordingly she observed the physical inventory at an interim date, May 31, 1979, instead of at year end.

The following information was obtained from the general ledger:

Inventory, July 1, 1978	$ 87,500
Physical inventory, May 31, 1979	95,000
Sales for 11 months ended May 31, 1979	840,000
Sales for year ended June 30, 1979	960,000
Purchases for 11 months ended May 31, 1979 (before audit adjustments)	675,000
Purchases for year ended June 30, 1979 (before audit adjustments)	800,000

The CPA's audit disclosed the following information:

Shipments received in May and included in the physical inventory but recorded as June purchases	$ 7,500
Shipments received in unsalable condition and excluded from physical inventory. (Credit memos had not been received nor had charge-backs to vendors been recorded.)	
Total at May 31, 1979	1,000
Total at June 30, 1979 (including the May unrecorded charge-backs)	1,500
Deposit made with vendor and charged to purchases in April 1979 Product was shipped in July 1979	2,000
Deposit made with vendor and charged to purchases in May 1979 Product was shipped, FOB destination, on May 29, 1979, and was included in May 31, 1979, physical inventory as goods in transit	5,500
Through the carelessness of the receiving department a June shipment was damaged by rain. This shipment was later sold in June at its cost of $10,000.	

Required: In audit engagements in which interim physical inventories are observed, a frequently used auditing procedure is to test the reasonableness of the year-end inventory by the application of gross profit ratios. Prepare in good form the following schedules:

1. Computation of the gross profit ratio for 11 months ended May 31, 1979
2. Computation by the gross profit ratio method of cost of goods sold during June 1979
3. Computation by the gross profit ratio method of the June 30, 1979, inventory (AICPA Adapted)

432
**Audit of the
inventory system**

12-15. An auditor is performing a cutoff test for inventory on the balance sheet date. As part of the procedure the following data are examined:

INVOICE DATA		RECEIVING REPORT DATA		DATE ENTERED IN THE PURCHASE JOURNAL
DATE SHIPPED	SHIPPING TERMS	NUMBER	DATE RECEIVED	
12/19/77	FOB S.P.	7971	12/29/77	12/30/77
12/22/77	FOB Dest.	7972	12/30/77	12/31/77
12/26/77	FOB Dest.	7973	12/31/77	1/3/78
12/27/77	FOB S.P.	7974	12/31/77	1/3/78
12/28/77	FOB S.P.	7975	1/3/78	1/3/78
12/29/77	FOB S.P.	7976	1/3/78	12/31/77
12/30/77	FOB Dest.	7978	1/3/78	12/31/77

Required

1. After reviewing the above cutoff information, is each item properly accounted for by the client? Explain.

2. Does the cutoff data appear to be complete?

12-16. The client's cost system is often the focal point in the CPA's examination of the financial statements of a manufacturing company.

Required

1. For what purposes does the CPA review the cost system?

2. The Summerfield Manufacturing Company employs standard costs in its cost accounting system. List the audit procedures you would apply to satisfy yourself that Summerfield's cost standards and related variance amounts are acceptable and have not distorted the financial statements. (Confine your audit procedures to those applicable to materials.) (AICPA Adapted)

12-17. An auditor reviews a client's inventory instructions and observes the client's personnel to determine if their instructions are being followed. The following inventory counting procedures should be carried out by the client:

· There should be written inventory instructions.

· The inventory count should be properly supervised by the client.

· Prenumbered tags should be used and accounted for.

· Obsolete items, scrap, consigned goods, and so on should be marked accordingly on the inventory tag.

· A full description of the item should be noted on the inventory tag.

· The unit of measurement should be adequately described on each inventory tag.

· Tags should be used in sequence.

Required

1. For each of the seven procedures listed above explain how the inventory could be impacted if the procedure is not observed.

2. How can the auditor determine whether the procedure is being followed by the client's personnel?

12-18. Often an important aspect of a CPA's examination of financial statements is his or her observation of the taking of the physical inventory.

Required

1. What are the general objectives or purposes of the CPA's observation of the taking of the physical inventory? (Do not discuss the procedures or techniques involved in making the observation.)

2. For what purposes does the CPA make and record test counts of inventory quantities during his or her observation of the taking of the physical inventory? Discuss.

3. A number of companies employ outside service companies who specialize in counting, pricing, extending, and footing inventories. These service companies usually furnish a certificate attesting to the value of the inventory.

Assume that the service company took the inventory on the balance sheet date.

1. How much reliance, if any, can the CPA place on the inventory certificate of outside specialists? Discuss.
2. What effect, if any, does the inventory certificate of outside specialists have upon the type of report the CPA renders? Discuss.
3. What reference, if any, does the CPA make to the certificate of outside specialists in his or her short-form report? (AICPA Adapted)

12-19. The Warex Company counts its inventory on December 31, 1979. As a senior auditor assigned to the engagement you observe the inventory count on this date. During the inventory observation you encounter only minor problems which are cleared up to your satisfaction. On January 15, 1980, the controller for Warex informs you that the inventory summarization is complete and gives you a copy, part of which is reproduced here:

TAG NO.	DESCRIPTION	QUANTITY	PRICE ($)	EXTENDED VALUE
2683	Metal clips, X104	764	1.50 each	$ 1,146
686	Metal strips, 8″	1,264 feet	0.50 per foot	632
4822	Pipe, 3″	856 feet	3.00 per foot	2,568
43	Heavy-duty clamps, no. 4	376	0.10 each	376
776 and 2264	Air hose, 1″	98	22.00 per gross	2,156
561	Pump, heavy duty	178	4.50 each	801
2184 and 692	Metal struts, 6″	415	1.20 each	498
3421	Corner braces, no. 107	36	25.00 per box	900
1746	Inner facing, rubber	312	15.00 per doz.	4,680
5785	See listing for goods in transit			43,781
	Total inventory			$849,621*

* Other items not listed.

During the inventory observation you noted the following inventory tag control information:

COUNT TEAM	ASSIGNED TAGS	LAST TAG USED
A	1–750	609
B	751–2000	1824
C	2001–4000	3476
D	4001–5500	4926
E	5501–6000	5784

434
Audit of the
inventory system

At the inventory observation you test-counted several items and documented the following counts in your working papers:

TAG NO.	INVENTORY DESCRIPTION	MEASUREMENT UNIT	QUANTITY
561	Pump, 3″ valve	Each	178
2264	Air hose, 1″	Gross	63
4822	Pipe, 3″	Yards	856
2184	Metal struts, 6″	Each	126
5627	Corner braces, no. 107	Boxes	48
1746	Inner facing, rubber	Dozen	26

Required

1. Using the inventory listing, ticket control data, and the test counts made by the auditor identify errors in the inventory summarization.

2. Do any of the items listed in the inventory summarization require that additional audit procedures be employed? Explain fully.

12-20. Your audit client, Household Appliances, Inc., operates a retail store in the center of town. Because of lack of storage space Household keeps inventory that is not on display in a public warehouse outside of town. The warehouse supervisor receives inventory from suppliers and, on request from your client by a shipping advice or telephone call, delivers merchandise to customers or to the retail outlet.

The accounts are maintained at the retail store by a bookkeeper. Each month the warehouse supervisor sends the bookkeeper a quantity report indicating the opening balance, receipts, deliveries, and ending balance. The bookkeeper compares book quantities on hand at month end with the warehouse supervisor's report and adjusts the books to agree with the report. No physical counts of the merchandise at the warehouse were made by your client during the year.

You are now preparing for your examination of the current year's financial statements in this recurring engagement. Last year you rendered an unqualified opinion.

Required

1. Prepare an audit program for observation of the physical inventory of Household Appliances, Inc., (a) at the retail outlet and (b) at the warehouse.

2. As part of your examination would you verify inventory quantities at the warehouse by means of

a. A warehouse of confirmation? Why?

b. Test counts of inventory at the warehouse? Why?

3. Since the bookkeeper adjusts the books to quantities shown on the warehouse supervisor's report each month, what significance would you attach to the year-end adjustments if they were substantial? Discuss.

4. Assume you are unable to satisfy yourself as to the inventory on the audit date of Household Appliances, Inc. Can you render an unqualified opinion? Why?

(AICPA Adapted)

12-21. Line-Rite Manufacturing Company, Inc., is a moderate-sized company manufacturing equipment for use in laying pipe lines. It has prospered in the past, gradually expanding to its present size. Recognizing a need to develop new products, if its growth is to continue, the company has created an engineering research and development section. During 1979, at a cost of $70,000, this section designed, patented, and successfully tested a new machine which greatly accelerates the laying of small-sized lines.

In order to finance the manufacture, promotion, and sale of this new product adequately, it has become necessary to expand the company's plant and to enlarge inventories. Required financing to accomplish this has resulted in the company engaging you in April 1979 to examine its financial statements as of September 30, 1979, the end of the current fiscal year. This is the company's initial audit.

In the course of your preliminary audit work you obtain the following information:

1. The nature of the inventory and related manufacturing processes do not lend themselves well to taking a complete physical inventory at year-end or at any other given date. The company has inventory items on a cycle basis throughout the year. Perpetual inventory records, maintained by the accounting department, are adjusted to reflect the quantities on hand as determined by these counts. At year end an inventory summary is prepared from the perpetual inventory records. The quantities in this summary are subsequently valued in developing the final inventory balances.
2. The company carries a substantial parts inventory which is used to service equipment sold to customers. Certain parts are also used in current production. The company considers a part to be obsolete only if it shows no usage or sales activity for two consecutive years. Parts falling into this category are fully reserved. A reserve of $10,000 exists at present.

Your tests indicate that obsolescence of inventories might approximate $50,000. As part of your audit you must deal with each of the foregoing matters.

Required
1. With respect to inventories define the overall problem involved in this first audit.
2. Outline a program for testing inventory quantities.
3. Enumerate and discuss the principal problems involved in inventory obsolescence for the company, assuming the amount involved is significant with respect to the company's financial position. (AICPA Adapted)

12-22. During the examination of the Kappa Manufacturing Company, you ask the client to prepare an analysis of the work-in-process inventory. Kappa manufactures a limited line of furniture based on specific orders from its customers. The client uses a job order cost accounting system, charging a job number with all raw material costs when production begins, direct labor when incurred, and factory overhead as a percentage of direct labor dollars.

Problem Figure 12-22 is the analysis of goods in process prepared by the client and audited by one of your assistants.

Required
1. Is the working paper complete? If not, suggest additional audit procedures to be employed.
2. Based on the data presented in the working paper, should an adjusting journal entry be proposed? Explain.

12-23. Coil steel comprises one-half of the inventory of the Metal Fabricating Company. At the beginning of the year the company installed a system to control coil steel inventory.

The coil steel is stored within the plant in a special storage area. When coils are received a two-part tag is prepared. The tag is prenumbered, and each part provides for entry of supplier's name, receiving report number, date received, coil weight, and description. Both parts of the tag are pepared at the time the material is received and weighed and the receiving report prepared. Part A of the tag is attached to the coil, and part B is sent to the stock records department with the receiving report. The stock records

Problem Figure 12-22

Kappa Manufacturing Company
Analysis of Work-in-Process
12-31-79

Job #	Materials ᵞ	Direct Labor ᵞ	Applied ᵞ Overhead	12-31-79 Work-in Process	Expected Delivery Date	Contract Price
79-109	18746	8159	4080 C	30985	1/22/80	46000
79-111	7681	3393	1697 C	12771	2/1/80	16000
79-119	12864	8616	4308 C	25788	1/12/80	20000
79-120	16119	12984	10000 C	39103	2/1/80	③
79-121	3894	4120	2060 C	20074	1/27/80	20000
79-122	17222	11471	5736 C	34429	1/16/80	46000
79-124	9876	4918	2459 C	①<2747>	1/15/80	35000
79-125	1209	399	200 C	1808	2/12/80	6500
79-126	3818	1842	921 C	②<1419>	2/3/80	15000
				160792 ✓		204500 ✓

① Less $20,000 progress payment received 12/22/79.
② Less $8,000 progress payment received 1/8/80.
③ Cost plus 10%- Foreign government contract-Profit included in overhead

✓ - Footed.
ᵞ Cost traced to Job cards.
C - Overhead computation checked.

department files the tags numerically by coil width and gauge. The stock records department also maintains perpetual stock cards on each width and gauge by total weight; in a sense, the cards are a control record for the tags. No material requisitions are used by the plant, but as coils are placed in production, part A of the tag is removed from the coil and sent to stock records as support of the production report which is the basis of entries on the perpetual inventory cards.

When part A of the tag is received by the stock records department, it is matched with part B and part A is destroyed. Part B is stamped with the date of use, processed, and retained in a consumed file by width and gauge The coils are neatly stacked and arranged, and all tags are visible.

The balance of the inventory is examined by standard procedures, and you are satisfied that it is fairly stated.

Physical inventories are taken on a cycle basis throughout the year. About one-twelfth of the coil steel inventories are taken each month. The coil steel control account and the perpetual stock cards are adjusted as counts are made. Internal control of inventories is good in all respects.

In previous years the client had taken a complete physical inventory of coil steel at the end of the year (the client's fiscal year ends December 31), but none is to be taken this year. You are engaged for the current audit in September. You audited the financial statements last year.

Required

1. Assuming that you decide to undertake some preliminary audit work before December 31, prepare programs for:

   a. Verification of coil steel quantities previously inventoried during the current year
   b. Observation of physical inventories to be taken in subsequent months.

2. What deviation, if any, will be necessary from the standard short-form accountant's opinion because of the client's inventory practices and the audit programs you have prepared? Explain.   (AICPA Adapted)

12-24. Your CPA firm was appointed auditor for the Moorestown Pipe Company on January 26, 1980. Because the company is trying to borrow funds from a local bank it needs audit financial statements for the year ended December 31, 1979. The company is seven years old and has never been audited.

Since your firm was appointed after December 31, 1979, there was no representative from your firm present when the inventory was counted on that date. The client has informed you that it is unwilling to take another inventory for the benefit of the auditors. However, inventory tags used during the December 31, 1979, count and the inventory summarization are available for your testing. Similar data are available for the December 31, 1978, inventory count.

You assign an assistant to study and evaluate the inventory purchase accounting system and the sales system. The assistant informs you that both systems are very adequate and, based on a small sample of transactions, no errors were discovered. Also, the assistant states that the client maintains a perpetual inventory system. An example of the client's perpetual inventory cards in presented on the following page.

After reviewing the assistant's working papers concerning the study of the two systems, you tell the assistant to complete the substantive tests for the inventory account. A few hours later your assistant informs you that it will be impossible to complete the substantive tests since there are no procedures that can be employed to be certain that the inventory was really on the premises of the client on December 31, 1979.

438
Audit of the
inventory system

Part no: *1046*

Description: *Master Clamps*

TRANSACTION DATE	P.O. NO.	PRICE	QUANTITY	INVOICE	QUANTITY	BALANCE
		RECEIPTS			SHIPMENTS	
9/20/78	4413	3.00	150			150
11/ 3/78				8-309	25	125
12/22/78				8-564	80	45
3/ 9/79	6495	3.25	200			245
6/ 3/79				9-154	75	170
10/ 4/79				9-264	90	80
12/ 2/79				9-468	50	30
1/ 6/80	7816	3.30	200			230
1/17/80				0-076	85	145

Required

1. Is there any way the auditor can be certain that the client did in fact have the inventory on the balance sheet date.

2. Using the perpetual record card presented above as an example, prepare a list of audit procedures your assistant should perform for the substantive tests.

3. Do you believe your firm can issue an unqualified opinion on the financial statements for the year ended December 31, 1979?

4. How does the client restriction (no new inventory count for the auditors) impact the auditor's ability to issue an unqualified opinion?

12-25. The processing operations of the Gaylord Company, your client, require a basic raw material, colgum, which is imported and refined by several domestic suppliers. Colgum is combined with other raw materials of the same general category to produce the finished product. Gaylord Company has been disturbed by the unreliability of the supply because of the international situation and labor troubles of the suppliers and has stockpiled a large supply of colgum to ensure continued oeprations. This supply of colgum is a substantial portion of Gaylord's inventory, and you determine that it is a three-year supply. Colgum is a staple commodity widely used in manufacturing operations. Gaylord has consistently applied the lower of cost or market rule to the valuation of its total inventory. The year-end market price of colgum is less than Gaylord's cost.

Required

1. What effect, if any, would this excess supply have upon the financial statements and your report? Discuss briefly.

2. What effect, if any, would this excess supply have upon the application of the lower of cost or market rule to the valuation of individual items as against category totals in the total inventory? Discuss briefly. (AICPA Adapted)

12-26. The following is a list of several audit procedures associated with the audit of the inventory internal control system and the inventory balance.

1. Account for the numerical sequence of purchase orders.
2. Test the unit cost used in the inventory summary.
3. Trace data per the vendor's invoice to the perpetual inventory card.
4. Compare data on the purchase order, vendor's invoice, and receiving report.
5. Confirm inventory held by consignees.

6. Foot the inventory summarization.
7. Test perpetual record cards for slow-moving items.
8. Review inventory adjustments to the perpetual record cards as the result of the inventory count.

Required: For each of the above procedures determine whether the test is primarily one of compliance, including the tests of transactions, or a substantive test.

12-27. On April 6, 1980, fire completely destroyed the warehouse and all books and records of the Kramer Corporation, a wholesaler of office stationery. The Kramer Corporation had a fire insurance policy on the inventory (in addition to insurance policies on other assets) which did not require the corporation to file a monthly inventory report. The Eckner Insurance Company retained you to audit the statement of the actual cash value of the inventory fire loss of $265,000 reported by the Kramer Corporation.

The corporation began doing business on January 1, 1979, and the financial statements for 1979 were audited by the corporation's CPA who rendered an unqualified opinion. The CPA also prepared the corporation's income tax return for 1979 and, with the president's permission, has granted you access to his copy of the tax return as well as to his work papers relating to the Kramer Corporation.

Required

1. List the audit procedures you would apply to verify the amount of the inventory fire loss on April 6, 1980, claimed by the insured.

2. Assume that you are satisfied with the results of your examination and you are now preparing your report.

   a. Which, if any, of the generally accepted auditing standards pertaining to reporting apply to this report? Discuss.
   b. Describe the topics relating to your examination to which you should refer in your report. (AICPA Adapted)

12-28. Late in December 1979, your CPA firm accepted an audit engagement at Pine Jewelers, Inc., a corporation which deals largely in diamonds. The corporation has retail jewelry stores in several eastern cities and a diamond wholesale store in New York City. The wholesale store also sets diamonds in rings and in other quality jewelry.

The retail stores place orders for diamond jewelry with the wholesale store in New York City. A buyer employed by the wholesale store purchases diamonds in the New York diamond market, and the wholesale store then fills orders from the retail stores and from independent customers and maintains a substantial inventory of diamonds. The corporation values its inventory by the specific identification cost method.

Required: Assume that on the inventory date you are satisfied that Fine Jewelers, Inc., has no items left by customers for repair or sale on consignment and that no inventory owned by the corporation is in the possession of outsiders.

1. Discuss the problems the auditor should anticipate in planning for observation of the physical inventory on this engagement because of the (a) different locations of the inventories and (b) nature of the inventory.

2. (a) Explain how your audit program for this inventory would be different from that used for most other inventories. (b) Prepare an audit program for verification of the corporation's diamond and diamond jewelry inventories, identifying any steps you would apply only to the retail stores or only to the wholesale store.

3. Assume that a shipment of diamond rings was in transit by corporation messenger

440
**Audit of the
inventory system**

from the wholesale store to a retail store on the inventory date. What additional audit steps would you take to satisfy yourself concerning this jewelry?   (AICPA Adapted)

12-29. In order to issue an opinion on the financial statements of an organization many audit procedures must be employed to be reasonably certain inventories are properly stated. Listed here are potential errors that may be found in a client's inventory.

- Obsolete inventory was priced at FIFO cost.

- Inventory quantities as shown on the inventory count tag were increased after the auditor left the inventory observation.

- Raw materials were described as being of a much better quality (e.g., grade A versus grade AAA).

- Goods that were in-transit on the balance sheet date and should have been part of the client's inventory were omitted from the inventory count.

- Work in process was listed at cost on the balance sheet date, but the government subsequently disallowed part of the cost.

- Inventory in transit between two plants of the client was listed as part of both plants' goods.

- An entire product line of the client's became obsolete as a result of technological changes.

- A commodity used in the manufacturing process was stated at cost but far in excess of the balance sheet market price.

- The auditor was unable to observe inventory at a public warehouse since he was unaware of its location until several weeks after the observation date.

Required: Assume each error is material in relation to the total assets of the organization. What audit procedures should be employed by the auditor in a routine engagement to detect such errors?

12-30. On January 15, 1978, you were engaged to make an examination of the financial statements of Kahl Equipment Corporation for the year ended December 31, 1977. Kahl has sold trucks and truck parts and accessories for many years but has never had an audit. Kahl maintains good perpetual records for all inventories and takes a complete physical inventory each December 31.

The parts inventory account includes a $2500 cost for obsolete parts. Kahl's executives acknowledge these parts have been worthless for several years, but they have continued to carry the cost as an asset. The amount of $2500 is material in relation to the 1977 net income and year-end inventories but not material in relation to total assets or capital on December 31, 1977.

Required

1. List the procedures you would add to your inventory audit program for new trucks because you did not observe the physical inventory taken by the corporation as of December 31, 1977.

2. Should the $2500 for obsolete parts be carried in inventory as an asset? Discuss.

3. Assume your alternative auditing procedures satisfied you as to the corporation's December 31, 1977, inventory but that you were unable to apply these alternative procedures to the December 31, 1976, inventory. Discuss (ignoring the obsolete parts) the effect this would have on your auditor's report in (a) the scope (or middle) paragraph and (b) the opinion paragraph.   (AICPA Adapted)

12-31. In connection with his examination of the financial statements of Knutson Products Company, an assembler of home appliances, for the year ended May 31, 1979. Ray Abel, CPA, is reviewing with Knutson's controller the plans for a physical inventory at the company warehouse on May 31, 1979. Note: In answering the two parts of this question do not discuss procedures for the physical inventory of work in process or inventory pricing, or other audit steps not directly related to the physical inventory taking.

Part A. Finished appliances, unassembled parts, and supplies are stored in the warehouse, which is attached to Knutson's assembly plant. The plant will operate during the count. On May 30 the warehouse will deliver to the plant the estimated quantities of unassembled parts and supplies and ship finished appliances. However, appliances completed on May 31 will be held in the plant until after the physical inventory.

Required: What procedures should the company establish to ensure that the inventory count includes all items that should be included and that nothing is counted twice?

Part B. Warehouse employees will join with accounting department employees in counting the inventory. The inventory takers will use a tag system.

Required: What instructions should the company give to the inventory takers? (AICPA Adapted)

12-32. Renken Company cans two food commodities which it stores at various warehouses. The company employs a perpetual inventory accounting system under which the finished goods inventory is charged with production and credited for sales at standard cost. The detail of the finished goods inventory is maintained on punched cards by the tabulating department in units and dollars for the various warehouses.

Company procedures call for the accounting department to receive copies of daily production reports and sales invoices. Units are then extended at standard costs, and a summary of the day's activity is posted to the finished goods inventory general ledger control account. Next the sales invoices and production reports are sent to the tabulating department for processing. Every month the control account and detailed tabulation records are reconciled and adjustments recorded. The last reconciliation and adjustments were made at November 30, 1979.

Your CPA firm observed the taking of the physical inventory at all locations on December 31, 1979. The inventory count began at 4:00 P.M. and was completed at 8:00 P.M. The company's figure for the physical inventory is $331,400. The general ledger control account balance at December 31 was $373,900, and the final "tab" run of the inventory punched cards showed a total of $392,300.

Unit cost data for the company's two products are:

PRODUCT	STANDARD COST($)
A	2.00
B	3.00

A review of December transactions disclosed:

1. Sales invoice no. 1301, 12/2/79, was priced at standard cost for $11,700 but was listed on the accounting department's daily summary at $11,200.

2. A production report for $23,900, 12/15/79, was processed twice in error by the tabulating department.

3. Sales invoice no. 1423, 12/9/79, for 1200 units of product A, was priced at a standard cost of $1.50 per unit by the accounting department. The tabulating department noticed and corrected the error but did not notify the accounting department.

4. A shipment of 3400 units of product A was invoiced by the billing department as 3000 units on sales invoice no. 1504, 12/27/79. The error was discovered by your review of transactions.

442
Audit of the inventory system

5. On December 27 the Memphis warehouse notified the tabulating department to remove 2200 unsalable units of product A from the finished goods inventory, which it did without receiving a special invoice from the accounting department. The accounting department received a copy of the Memphis warehouse notification on December 29 and made up a special invoice which was processed in the normal manner. The units were not included in the physical inventory.

6. A production report for the production on January 3 of 2500 units of product B was processed for the Omaha plant as of December 31.

7. A shipment of 300 units of product B was made from the Portland warehouse to Ken's Market, Inc., at 8:30 P.M. on December 31 as an emergency service. The sales invoice was processed as of December 31. The client prefers to treat the transaction as a sale in 1979.

8. The working papers of the auditor observing the physical count at the Chicago warehouse revealed that 700 units of product B were omitted from the client's physical count. The client concurred that the units were omitted in error.

9. A sales invoice for 600 units of product A shipped from the Newark warehouse was mislaid and was not processed until January 5. The units involved were shipped on December 30.

10. The physical inventory of the St. Louis warehouse excluded 350 units of product A that were marked "Reserved." Upon investigation it was ascertained that this merchandise was being stored as a convenience for Steve's Markets, Inc., a customer. This merchandise, which has not been recorded as a sale, is billed as it is shipped.

11. A shipment of 10,000 units of product B was made on December 27 from the Newark warehouse to the Chicago warehouse. The shipment arrived on January 6 but had been excluded from the physical inventories.

Required: Prepare a work sheet to reconcile the balances for the physical inventory, finished goods inventory general ledger control account, and tabulating department's detail of finished goods inventory ("tab run"). The following format is suggested for the work sheet.

	PHYSICAL INVENTORY	GENERAL LEDGER CONTROL ACCOUNT	TABULATING DEPARTMENT'S DETAIL OF INVENTORY
Balance per client	$331,400	$373,900	$392,300

(AICPA Adapted)

MULTIPLE CHOICE

1. McPherson Corporation does not make an annual physical count of year-end inventories but instead makes test counts on the basis of a statistical plan. During the year Mullins, CPA, observes such counts as he deems necessary and is able to satisfy himself as to the reliability of the client's procedures. In reporting on the results of his examination Mullins

a. can issue an unqualified opinion without disclosing that he did not observe year-end inventories.
b. must comment in the scope paragraph as to his inability to observe year-end inventories, but can nevertheless issue an unqualified opinion.
c. is required, if the inventories were material, to disclaim an opinion on the financial statements taken as a whole.
d. must, if the inventories were material, qualify his opinion.

2. On June 15, 1973, Ward, CPA, accepted an engagement to perform an audit of the Grant Company for the year ended December 31, 1973. Grant Company has not previously been audited by a CPA, and Ward has been unable to satisfy herself with respect to opening inventories. How should Ward report on her examination?

a. She would have to disclaim an opinion or qualify her opinion on the December 31, 1973, balance sheet, but could issue an unqualified opinion on the income statement and the statement of changes in financial position.
b. She must disclaim an opinion on the financial statement taken as a whole.
c. She could give an unqualified opinion on the financial statements taken as a whole so long as the change in the inventories from the beginning of the year to the end of the year was not material.
d. She would have to disclaim an opinion or qualify her opinion on the income statement and the statement of changes in financial position, but could issue an unqualified opinion on the December 31, 1973, balance sheet.

3. On January 2, 1974, the Retail Auto Parts Company received a notice from its primary suppliers that effective immediately all wholesale prices would be increased 10 percent. On the basis of the notice, Retail Auto Parts Company revalued its December 31, 1973, inventory to reflect the higher costs. The inventory constituted a material proportion of total assets; however, the effect of the revaluation was material to current assets but not to total assets or net income. In reporting on the company's financial statements for the year ended December 31, 1973, in which inventory is valued at the adjusted amounts, the auditor should

a. issue an unqualified opinion provided the nature of the adjustment and the amounts involved are disclosed in footnotes.
b. issue a qualified opinion.
c. disclaim an opinion.
d. issue an adverse opinion.

4. In a company whose materials and supplies include a great number of items, a fundamental deficiency in control requirements would be indicated if

a. perpetual inventory records were not maintained for items of small value.
b. the storekeeping function were to be combined with production and record keeping.
c. the cycle basis for physical inventory taking were to be used.
d. minor supply items were to be expensed when purchased.

5. The Smith Corporation uses prenumbered receiving reports which are released in numerical order from a locked box. For two days before the physical count, all receiving reports are stamped "Before inventory," and for two days after the physical count, all receiving reports are stamped "After inventory." The receiving department continues to receive goods after the cutoff time while the physical count is in process. The least efficient method for checking the accuracy of the cutoff is to

444
**Audit of the
inventory system**

a. list the number of the last receiving report for items included in the physical inventory count.
b. observe that the receiving clerk is stamping the receiving reports properly.
c. test-trace receiving reports issued before the last receiving report to the physical items to see that they have been included in the physical count.
d. test-trace receiving reports issued after the last receiving report to the physical items to see that they have not been included in the physical count. (AICPA Adapted)

CHAPTER 13
Audit of long-term assets

PART I: Audit of Property, Plant, and Equipment

PROPERTY, PLANT, AND EQUIPMENT

Assets that form the productive capacity for an organization are often referred to as property, plant, and equipment, or fixed assets. Specifically, they include land used in the normal course of the entity's business, buildings, machinery, and tools. These assets are not acquired for resale but rather are used in the operations of a firm's business. In addition, the lives of these items may extend over several years and, with the exception of land, are subject to depreciation. This chapter is in part concerned with the audit of property, plant, and equipment. As in other chapters, an integrated audit approach is utilized. That is, the auditor studies and evaluates the fixed-asset internal control system, performs tests of compliance, and finally applies substantive audit procedures to the balances that appear on the financial statements. Again, it should be remembered that each step is not conducted in a vacuum; instead all results are related to subsequent audit steps to facilitate the auditor's formation of an opinion on the financial statements.

INTERNAL CONTROL MODEL: FIXED ASSETS

Annual commitments for the purchase of fixed assets are often a significant amount for many corporations; on a cumulative basis these items usually represent a significant percentage of the total assets of an organization. To see that they are protected and accounted for properly, an adequate internal control system is needed.

Plan of organization

DEPARTMENTAL AUTONOMY

In designing an adequate internal control system for fixed assets, it is important to separate the authorization responsibility, the recording responsibility, and the custodial responsibility. If the concept of departmental autonomy is observed, other internal control features can be added to the accounting system, resulting in an even stronger internal control system. On the other hand, a violation of the departmental autonomy concept significantly weakens the fixed-asset accounting system foundation. The following separation of duties and responsibilities is fundamental to the design of a strong internal control plan for property, plant, and equipment:

I. Accounting department
1. Maintenance of detailed plant ledger
2. Maintenance of the general ledger
3. Review of asset purchase authorization and execution
4. Review of asset disposition, authorization, and execution
5. Control and responsibility for the periodic counting of fixed assets
6. Establishment and administration of depreciation policies
II. Treasurer
1. Signing of checks for fixed assets purchased
2. Custody control over cash received from fixed assets sold
III. Functions other than accounting and treasurer
1. Responsibility for the purchase and sale of fixed assets (various departments)
2. Responsibility for the approval of fixed-asset purchases and sales (board of directors or a designated committee)
3. Custodial responsibility for items acquired (various departments)

If the above system is validated as existing and functioning adequately, it is appropriate for the auditor to restrict the audit procedures performed. Conversely, an internal control system lacking the above structure either through design or lack of operational autonomy significantly changes the audit approach. In an extreme case the auditor may decide to omit the tests of compliance and concentrate entirely on substantive audit procedures.

System of authorization and accountability

An integral part of the plan of organization of the internal control structure is the establishment of an acceptable system of transaction authorization and accountability.

EXECUTION OF TRANSACTIONS

To ensure that fixed-asset transactions are properly processed, the first step in the design of a system of authorization is concerned with controlling the purchase and disposition of fixed assets. Because of the nature of these transactions, explicit authorization for each item is required. Only transactions with proper approval are processed.

447
Internal control
model: fixed assets

Authorization for purchase: The authority to purchase fixed assets rests with the board of directors of an organization. To facilitate day-to-day operations the board usually delegates a portion of this authority to a special committee such as a finance committee or a capital projects committee. Even under these arrangements, the board reserves for itself the authority to approve major purchases, such as the acquisition of another company.

Most companies prepare a capital budget which lists in detail the purchase of long-term assets expected during the budgetary period. These expenditures are the result of a lengthy analysis in which capital budgeting techniques are used to evaluate and rank budget requests. Once the projects become part of the capital budget as approved by the appropriate committee, the basic authorization for the purchase of fixed assets has been granted. In addition, a major expenditure may be assigned a unique number, so that costs can be accumulated and assigned to the proper project. As costs are accumulated, the originally approved dollar amount for the project may be exceeded. Except for minor variations, cost overruns or expected cost overruns should be subject to the same approval process used in the initial review of the project.

Authorization for disposition: Eventually, property, plant, and equipment items are retired or sold. To make sure that these disposals are accounted for properly, adequate accounting controls must be built into the internal control structure. Like fixed-asset purchases, dispositions should be formally approved by appropriate corporate officials. This could include members of the capital projects committee, operating department heads, or other designated officials. It is important that the process be controlled so that all retirements are reported. One method may include the use of prenumbered retirement authorizations which are accounted for on a periodic basis by personnel in the accounting department. While fixed-asset acquisitions are usually subject to stringent controls, fixed-asset disposals are often not adequately controlled. The auditor designs the audit program based on this fact.

RECORDING OF TRANSACTIONS

Once the fixed-asset purchase or disposition is authorized, internal control procedures are devised to ensure reasonably that the transaction is recorded and accounted for properly in the appropriate period.

Accumulation of cost: As suggested above, the basic authorization for the purchase of fixed assets is usually incorporated into the capital budget. However, the actual purchase of a long-lived asset is subject to many of the procedures associated with the purchase of inventory. For example, (1) a purchase order is prepared, (2) the asset is inspected in the receiving department and a receiving report is prepared, and (3) the accounting department receives the vendor invoice and matches this document with the purchase order and the receiving report.

After this matching, the cost is charged to the fixed-asset account and is usually accumulated by project number if several purchases from a variety of vendors are required.

Revenue and capital expenditures: As part of the design of an adequate internal control system, an organization may adopt a formal policy concerning revenue and capital expenditures. Revenue expenditures are charged to operations in the year incurred, whereas capital expenditures are established as assets and depreciated over their estimated lives. Most companies adopt a minimum dollar figure for an expenditure to be capitalized. For example, a firm may decide that expenditures for $500 or less will be expensed. To avoid an inconsistent application of the rule, the policy should be formally adopted by the company and monitored by the company, probably through audits conducted by the internal audit staff.

The establishment of a capitalization policy is not entirely determined by management. Capitalization policies need to be consistent with generally accepted accounting principles. In general, all costs associated with putting the fixed asset in a productive stage are to be capitalized. These costs include the invoice price, transportation charges, closing costs, professional fees, and the like. In some instances, generally accepted accounting principles allow a company two or more methods for accounting for costs. For example, when a company constructs its own fixed assets, indirect manufacturing costs (1) may be assigned based on a full costing concept, (2) may be assigned on an incremental basis, or (3) may not be assigned at all to the fixed-asset account. No matter which accounting method is used, a formal policy should be adopted by management so that the approach is consistently observed.

Finally, classifying cost as a revenue or capital expenditure is subject to the general guideline that a capital expenditure must increase the utility of the asset being renovated or repaired. This may require the client to differentiate between ordinary repairs and extraordinary repairs, replacements, betterments, and additions. This is often no easy task. These expenditures should be reviewed in the accounting department by experienced personnel to ensure proper classification.

ACCESS TO ASSETS

Like any asset, property, plant, and equipment are to be protected from unauthorized use. Such procedures include (1) limited access to production areas, (2) a single exit from the company, which is guarded by security personnel, and (3) adequate security during nonproductive hours. Procedures adopted to protect fixed assets depend upon the type of asset involved and the nature of the client's operations. In general, security procedures must not disrupt the normal operations of the business, and they must be cost-effective.

COMPARISON OF RECORDED ACCOUNTABILITY WITH ASSETS

As part of the internal control system, the client should periodically compare the fixed-asset ledger with the actual fixed assets on hand. This comparison is made by members of the controller's staff. Unlike the situation with inventory, it is not necessary to count all fixed assets once a year. Most companies count a portion of their fixed assets each year, so that items may be counted every three or four years.

STUDY AND EVALUATION OF THE FIXED-ASSET SYSTEM

An understanding of the accounting system designed to process fixed-asset transactions is the first step in evaluating the system. Usually the system is documented by the auditor's completion of an internal control questionnaire and perhaps a narrative description of the system. In most companies the accounting system is not complex, so it is not necessary or useful to prepare a flowchart. A typical internal control questionnaire is presented in Figure 13-1. The results of the evaluation of the internal control system for fixed assets is the basis for the selection of audit procedures used in subsequent tests.

COMPLIANCE TESTS: FIXED ASSETS

Unlike the accounting systems discussed previously in this book, the initial purchase of property, plant, and equipment does not impact the income statement. In addition, most charges to these accounts during the year remain as part of the amount that appears on the balance sheet at the end of the year. For example, a credit sale results in an increase in accounts receivable, but it is likely that by the end of the year this amount or at least part of it will have been collected and therefore will not be in the accounts receivable balance. For these reasons the fixed-asset accounting system audit approach is slightly different from the audit approach previously described. In the audit of fixed assets there is less emphasis on differentiating between tests of compliance, including tests of transactions, and substantive tests. Consistent with this fact, this chapter combines all audit procedures in the discussion of substantive tests.

Before the substantive tests for property, plant, and equipment are described it is useful to discuss the timing of such procedures. All substantive audit procedures may be performed as year-end audit procedures. However, many accounting firms perform some of the procedures at an interim date so as to save time during the hectic year-end period. For example, an auditor may vouch all fixed-asset purchases made from January to September at an interim date, perhaps October. When the auditor returns after the year end, purchases made from October to December are reviewed. These procedures, described in the remainder of the chapter, are discussed in the context of a year-end review, but many of them can, to some extent, be performed at an interim date.

SUBSTANTIVE TESTS: FIXED ASSETS

In the performance of substantive audit procedures, the auditor is concerned with two groups of balance sheet accounts. Obviously, these two groups are those representing the fixed-asset balances and those representing the associated

Figure 13-1

Internal control questionnaire

PROPERTY, PLANT, AND EQUIPMENT	ANSWER		ANSWER BASED ON		
	YES	NO	INQUIRY	OBSERVATION	COMMENTS
1. Is prior authorization for capital expenditures required?					
2. When actual capital expenditures exceed the amount approved, is this excess properly approved?					
3. Is there a consistent policy for identifying capital and revenue expenditures?					
4. Is a detailed plant ledger kept?					
5. On a periodic basis, is an inventory of plant assets taken?					
6. Are the recording of and the accounting for capital replacements, betterments, and extraordinary repairs designed to ensure proper accounting treatment?					
7. Is there a proper system for the retirement and disposal of fixed assets?					

accumulated depreciation accounts. It is also efficient for the auditor to review simultaneously depreciation expense, since this account is related to the accumulated depreciation account. Finally, the disposal of equipment impacts the asset balance and the accumulated depreciation balance and may generate a gain or loss account. Because of the interrelationships of these accounts, they are all reviewed as part of a single audit program. A typical audit program is illustrated in Figure 13-2.

Existence

As in the review of any asset, one of the objectives is to determine if property, plant, and equipment are in existence.

SUMMARY OF FIXED-ASSET CHANGES

To gain control of the universe that represents all fixed-asset transactions that have occurred during the year and the fixed assets that remain at the end of the year, the auditor obtains a summary of activity for the year. A typical summary of fixed-asset changes is shown in Figure 13-3. This illustration is simplified, since many companies have several acquisitions and disposals during a single year, necessitating additional support schedules. The basic audit approach, as described here, would not be changed by such an increase in the volume of transactions.

Once the analysis of fixed assets is obtained, the auditor foots and crossfoots the schedule. The beginning balances in the schedule are substantiated by tracing these amounts to the ending balances in the previous year's working

Figure 13-2

Audit program: property, plant, and equipment

PROCEDURES	DATE COMPLETED	WORK PERFORMED BY
1. Obtain and audit an analysis of changes in the fixed-asset accounts during the year.	_____	_____
2. Inspect fixed-asset additions for the year and consider extending this procedure to all major items on hand at the end of the year.	_____	_____
3. Vouch fixed-asset additions.	_____	_____
4. Test fixed-asset disposals and retirements and search for unrecorded transactions.	_____	_____
5. Obtain and review an analysis of the repair and maintenance expense account.	_____	_____
6. Obtain an analysis of changes in the accumulated depreciation accounts during the year.	_____	_____
7. Test depreciation computations.	_____	_____
8. Determine if a proper cutoff of fixed-asset transactions was made.	_____	_____
9. Review fixed-asset accounts and related accounts for proper classification and disclosure.	_____	_____

papers. For each of the groupings of fixed assets, the year-end balance is traced to the detail records contained in the plant ledger. For example, delivery equipment may consist of several trucks, vans, and automobiles. Each vehicle has a separate plant ledger card which the auditor uses to verify the overall balance in the delivery equipment account. These totals are then traced to the balance in the general ledger control account.

FIXED ASSET INSPECTION

It may seem reasonable to believe that a client must count its fixed assets on an annual basis, as it counts inventory. However, professional standards do not make such a demand. It is usually suggested that the counting of fixed assets is not necessary because (1) it is costly to the client, (2) many fixed assets are large and not easily removed from the client's premises, and (3) an adequate internal control structure affords reasonable protection for these assets. These reasons do not preclude the auditor from inspecting the fixed assets to determine their existence. However, professional standards do not require the auditor to perform such a procedure. In practice, the observation of fixed assets is usually restricted to the inspection of major purchases made during the current period. When such an inspection is made, the auditor should be accompanied by the plant engineer or a similar official who is familiar with the company's plant assets and operating procedures.

The extent of utilization of the observation technique is determined by the audit situation. If the auditor is satisfied with the existence of fixed assets by an inspection limited to current additions, then the technique need not be extended. On the other hand, if circumstances are such that the limited use of this procedure does not satisfy the auditor, then the application of the procedure is broadened.

Figure 13-3

4912½ - Buff
8912½ - Green
4212½ - White

The Green Valley Corporation
Analysis of Property, Plant Equipment and Accumulated Depreciation
12/31/79

	Fixed Assets				Accumulated Depreciation			
	Balance 12-31-78	Additions	(Retirements)	Balance 12-31-79	Balance 12-31-78	Provisions	(Retirements)	Balance 12-31-79
Land	250000 ¶			250000				
Buildings	400000 √	78000 ⊬		478000	95000 √	13900 ⊄		108900
Machinery	120000 √	35000 ⊬	15000 φ	140000	36000 √	8000 ⊄	2500 φ	41500
Office Equipment	25000 ¶	8000 ⊬	3000 φ	30000	12900 ¶	2500 ⊄	1900 φ	13500
Delivery Equipment	170000 ¶	22000 ⊬	10000 φ	182000	90000 ¶	28000 ⊄	8000 φ	110000
	965000	143000	28000	1080000 X	233900	52400	12400	273900 X
	√	√	√	√	√	√	√	√

√ - Footed.
X - Crossed footed.
¶ - Traced to previous year's working papers.
⊬ - All additions vouched.
φ - Retirements reviewed for proper treatment and cash receipts, if any, traced to C.R.J.
⊄ - Depreciation computations tested - See detailed Schedules @ F101, 102, 103, and 104.

F-100
REB

For example, in the audit of a construction company, the auditor probably would not be satisfied with inspecting only new equipment, since much of the equipment is mobile and subject to theft. In this case he or she may inspect each major piece of equipment. A similar decision may be made by the auditor when the internal control system is determined to be weak.

453
Substantive tests:
fixed assets

VOUCHING ADDITIONS

As described in the section on the internal control model, major purchases must be approved by the board of directors, a designated committee, or an official. The auditor selects a sample of purchases for testing and reviews the documents granting approval. Comparison of the budgeted amount and the actual cost of the fixed asset is made, and any significant difference substantiated by appropriate corporate approval.

Vouching the actual cost of a fixed-asset purchase and determining the ownership of the item depends upon the type of asset acquired. Fixed-asset additions may represent (1) purchases of real property, (2) purchases of personal property, or (3) property constructed by the client. Real property purchases include the acquisition of land or buildings and additions or improvements to them. The existence of these items is determined by the auditor's review of deeds, contracts, or other evidence of ownership for real property additions. These may include vendor invoices or correspondence. In many instances personal property acquired, such as machinery and equipment, is evidenced by contracts, vendor's invoices, receiving reports, and purchase orders. If the items have been paid for, the disbursement is represented by a canceled check. Documentary evidence used by the auditor to establish the cost of fixed assets constructed by the client is less competent than documentary evidence supporting the purchase of fixed assets. Nonetheless, the auditor reviews such internal documents as material requisitions, work orders, and labor records. In addition, for major assets constructed, he or she determines the reasonableness of the total construction costs. This may be done by reviewing similar contract quotations, discussions with plant personnel, or the use of an independent specialist capable of estimating the asset cost.

REVIEW OF DISPOSALS AND RETIREMENTS

A major concern of the auditor is the possibility that fixed assets have been retired, sold, or abandoned but have not been accounted for properly. This is often the weakest part of any client's internal control system, simply because it is difficult to centralize retirements or other disposals of fixed assets. For this reason, the auditor is more concerned with finding transactions not journalized rather than verifying transactions that appear in the accounting records.

Fixed assets, retired or otherwise disposed of during the accounting period, are validated by the auditor's review of sales contracts, invoices, and correspondence. Proceeds from sales are traced to the cash receipts records. The accounting records are reviewed to see if the correct amounts for asset cost and accumulated depreciation are removed from the appropriate accounts and to determine if a gain or loss on disposal resulted from the transaction. If an exchange of dissimilar nonmonetary assets has occurred, *APB Opinion No. 29* requires that the asset acquired be recorded at its fair value and that the difference between the cost of the asset given up and the fair value of the asset received be recorded as a gain or loss. For such exchanges, the auditor verifies the fair value of the asset received by reviewing price lists and catalogs or, if this information is not available, the fair value may be confirmed by contacting the manufacturer or dealer.

To determine if unrecorded fixed-asset retirements or other disposals have occurred, the auditor may ask key corporate officials about assets no longer in service, major modifications to production lines, abandonment of facilities, or other significant changes. These questions are structured according to his or her knowledge of the operational characteristics of the client's business. For example, if the auditor knows that during the current year technological changes required changes in the type of product manufactured by the client, it is reasonable to expect that some fixed assets were retired, modified, or abandoned. In addition, a review of certain accounting records may result in the discovery of unrecorded retirements. The auditor reviews miscellaneous income accounts to determine if such credits represent proceeds from the disposal of fixed assets. Finally, he or she reviews current insurance appraisal reports and current property tax statements to see if these reports suggest significant fixed-asset retirements.

REVIEW, REPAIR, AND MAINTENANCE EXPENSE

In determining the existence of property, plant, and equipment items, the auditor asks the client to prepare an analysis of the repair and maintenance expense account. Major charges to this account are vouched by the auditor to determine if each item is properly classified as an expense rather than as an asset. To make this determination, the auditor reviews vendor invoices, contracts, work orders, and the like. Professional judgment is used by the auditor in evaluating each expenditure. Some expenditures may be difficult to evaluate, since the auditor must determine if an item is a repair, betterment, replacement, or extraordinary repair. For example, an overhaul of a piece of machinery, depending on the circumstances, may be treated as an ordinary repair or may be capitalized.

Valuation

The above audit procedures involve verification of the existence and the initial cost of property, plant, and equipment. Determining the value or net book value of fixed assets, reported on the balance sheet, is based on the depreciation policies of the client. Thus valuation of fixed assets is concerned with the allocation of depreciable cost over the estimated life of the assets.

ANALYSIS OF ACCUMULATED DEPRECIATION

A summary of changes in the accumulated depreciation accounts is obtained from the client. Such a summary is illustrated in Figure 13-3. The beginning balances are verified by tracing them to the ending balances in the previous year's working papers. For each major grouping, such as office equipment, the year-end balance is traced to the detail records in the plant ledger. Each piece of equipment has a separate plant ledger card which the auditor uses to substantiate the overall accumulated depreciation balance for each fixed-asset grouping. The review of entries representing retirements or other reductions to the accumulated depreciation accounts was discussed in a previous section of this chapter.

RECOMPUTATION OF DEPRECIATION

Audit verification of the provision for depreciation expense is concerned with (1) the depreciable cost, (2) the estimated life of the asset, (3) depreciation policies, and (4) the selection and application of an acceptable depreciation method.

The audit approach to substantiate the cost of property, plant, and equipment was described in a previous section of this chapter. To determine depreciable cost, an estimated salvage value is subtracted from the original cost of the asset. Since salvage value is an estimate, the auditor is concerned only with the reasonableness of the amount. Past experience and estimated disposal or dismantling costs are two factors considered by the auditor. Materiality is probably the key factor in determining the appropriateness of salvage value. Thus, as long as the salvage value is not estimated to be a significant percentage of the cost of the fixed asset, the amount of audit exposure is not great.

A second estimate, the estimated life of an asset, is an important part of the depreciation process. Again, since an estimate is involved, the auditor is concerned with the reasonableness of the estimate. In determining reasonableness the auditor refers to past experiences of the client and guidelines established by the IRS. Past experiences can be verified by discussions with plant officials and other appropriate officials and by the auditor's review of plant ledger cards for similar assets. In conventional accounting, IRS guidelines play a dominant role in the estimation of the life of depreciable property. These guidelines are presented in the IRS's *Depreciation Guidelines* and *Rules and Asset Depreciation Range System*. In many instances the auditor simply refers to these publications to verify an asset life, but he or she is responsible for recognizing circumstances where conditions preclude the use of averages recommended in these publications.

Depreciation computations made by the client are reviewed on a test basis to determine if depreciation policies are being consistently followed. Most companies adopt specific policies concerning the amount of depreciation recognized for assets purchased or sold during the current year. For example, a client may recognize no depreciation in the year of purchase and recognize a full year of depreciation in the year of sale. In addition, once a depreciation method is adopted for a particular asset, a deviation, if material, results in a consistency qualification in the auditor's report.

If the auditor is satisfied as to the depreciable cost, the estimated life, and the consistent application of depreciation policies, the final step simply involves recomputation of the mathematical process. For example, if a client uses the double-declining-balance depreciation method for an asset, the auditor doubles the straight-line rate and applies this percentage to the net book value of the fixed asset.

In addition to the above procedures, the auditor tests the reasonableness of the depreciation calculation. Such an overall test may be necessary, since he or she may actually verify only a few depreciation calculations as described above. This approach includes a comparison of the current year's depreciation with the previous year's depreciation for each class of property. Major acquisitions or retirements are considered by the auditor in evaluating the reasonableness of the depreciation provision. When assets can be easily grouped by age, the average rate (based on the weighted-average age) can be multiplied by the average asset value.

It is very likely that the client uses one depreciation method for financial accounting and another depreciation method for tax accounting. This requires the auditor to perform the above tests on both methods of determining depreciation, so that financial statement depreciation and tax depreciation can be verified. In addition, the use of different depreciation methods creates a timing difference and requires the recognition of deferred tax credits or charges. Since these deferred tax accounts are shown on the balance sheet, the auditor must be satisfied that they are properly stated. These accounts are basically audited by the auditor's review of client computations, although the review can be quite involved in some cases. A comprehensive discussion of the audit of deferred tax accounts is beyond the scope of this book.

Cutoff

To determine if the client has performed a proper cutoff of fixed-asset transactions, the auditor reviews data processed subsequent to the balance sheet date. He or she checks the fixed-asset ledger to identify these transactions and then reviews the supporting documentation to see if they are recorded in the proper accounting period. In addition, the auditor's search for unrecorded liabilities, as explained in Chapter 14, is performed as part of the cutoff test procedures for fixed-asset transactions.

Classification and disclosure

Accounting principles require that the dollar balance of major types of fixed assets, such as land, buildings, and machinery, be disclosed in the balance sheet or in footnotes to the financial statements. Accumulated depreciation must be disclosed on the financial statement as a single amount or as separate balances related to the type of fixed-asset classification. Depreciation methods must also be disclosed. If there have been changes in the methods of depreciation used during the current year, disclosures must be in accordance with guidelines established in *APB Opinion No. 20*.

In addition, the basis for fixed-asset valuation is disclosed on the financial statements or in the accompanying footnotes. Normally, cost is the only acceptable valuation method. However, if fixed assets are not being used by the

business, they should be valued at a net realizable value. In addition, companies **457**
subject to *Accounting Series Release No. 190* must disclose the replacement cost Investments
of productive capacity and the approximate effect replacement cost would have
had on the computation of depreciation expense for the year under review.

At the moment, the auditor's opinion does cover the disclosure requirements
established by *Accounting Series Release No. 190.* The data are simply disclosed
in a footnote labeled "Unaudited." Although the SEC does not require that
these data be audited, it has strongly suggested that the auditor be associated
with such data. In response, in *SAS No. 18*, the AICPA suggested that the following
procedures be carried out:

a. Inquire of management as to whether the replacement cost information has been
   prepared and presented in accordance with the requirements of regulation S-X.
b. Inquire of management as to the methods selected to calculate replacement cost
   information and the reasons for selecting them, including consideration given by
   management to (1) current replacement programs, (2) plans or expressed intentions
   concerning future replacements, (3) plans or expressed intentions not to replace
   certain inventories or productive capacity, and (4) technological changes that
   have occurred in the industry.
c. Inquire of management as to procedures used to compile the data supporting the
   replacement cost information and as to the relationship between data supporting
   the replacement cost information and data supporting the audited financial information. Examples of such inquiries follow: Are the useful lives used to calculate
   depreciation on the historical cost basis the same as those used on the replacement
   cost basis? Are inventory quantities used in the determination of inventory value
   for the historical cost financial statements the same as inventory quantities used
   to calculate the replacement cost information?
d. Inquire about the methods and basis used by management to calculate any
   supplemental replacement cost information, such as historical relationships between cost of sales and selling prices or the effect of technologically improved
   capacity replacements on operating costs.
e. If management has changed the method of calculating replacement cost information, inquire as to the reasons for using a method different from that used in
   the previous fiscal period.

The above approach is analytical in nature and requires that little, if any,
corroborative evidence be collected by the author. If, however, replacement cost
should become the basis for reporting the value of fixed assets, the conventional
audit approach would be significantly altered.

PART II: Audit of Investments

INVESTMENTS

Investments by a client may include purchases of common stock, preferred
stock, bonds, commercial paper, certificates of deposit, and the cash surrender
value of life insurance policies of which the company is the beneficiary. The first
part of this section of the chapter is devoted to common stock investments.

Common stock investments are subject to a variety of accounting standards depending upon the nature of the investment. For example, investments in the common stock of another company, the investee company, may be classified as a current asset or a long-term asset depending upon the size of the investment or the intentions of the acquiring company. Since the accounting standards vary, different auditing procedures must be used depending upon the nature of the investment. The following discussion encompasses both short-term and long-term investments in common stocks and, where appropriate, notes the unique procedures to be used for each type of purchase.

INTERNAL CONTROL MODEL

In the study and evaluation of the investment accounting system, the auditor is concerned with several procedures. An adequate system should observe the following:

- Securities transactions should be authorized by the board of directors, a special committee, or some other designated corporate official.
- All securities should be made out in the name of the company.
- Securities should be kept in a safe deposit box or in a safe place under the control of an officer. If a safe deposit box is used, access to the box should require the signature of two corporate officials.
- A detailed securities ledger should be maintained by the accounting department.
- On a surprise basis, the internal audit staff or a designated corporate official should count and inspect all securities and compare the count to the records maintained by the accounting department.

The auditor usually completes an internal control questionnaire as a basis for the study of the investment accounting system. Since the system is usually simple, a flowchart is not prepared.

Substantive tests

Generally, the investment accounting system is not characterized by numerous transactions. For this reason, the auditor normally performs combined compliance and substantive tests. This approach is the basis of the following discussion; however, many of the procedures can be performed as part of the compliance tests if the transactions are voluminous.

A typical investment audit program is illustrated in Figure 13-4. These procedures are selected to satisfy the auditor as to the existence, valuation, cutoff, classification, and disclosure in the investment balance.

Existence

SUMMARY OF INVESTMENT CHANGES

To gain control of all transactions that have had an impact on the investment account during the year, the auditor asks the client to prepare a summary of

Figure 13-4

Audit program: investments

PROCEDURES	DATE COMPLETED	WORK PERFORMED BY
1. Obtain and verify an analysis of changes in the investment account during the year.	_____	_____
2. Inspect securities on hand and in the safety deposit box as of the balance sheet date.	_____	_____
3. For securities held by others, obtain a confirmation as of the balance sheet date.	_____	_____
4. Determine if the investment account is properly valued and accounted for on a	_____	_____
a. Cost basis	_____	_____
b. Equity basis	_____	_____
c. Consolidation basis	_____	_____
5. Determine if a proper cutoff of investment transactions was made.	_____	_____
6. Review the investment account and related accounts for proper classification and disclosure.	_____	_____
7. Review the following accounts that are related to investment transactions:	_____	_____
a. Dividend income	_____	_____
b. Dividends receivable	_____	_____
c. Gain or loss on sale of investments	_____	_____

investment changes. An example of such a summary is presented in Figure 13-5, which is limited to investments in marketable securities. Once received from the client, the schedule is footed and cross-footed, the beginning balances are traced to the previous year's working papers, and the ending balance is compared to the general ledger control account. Current transactions are also verified. For example, the purchase of an investment during the year is validated by reviewing the appropriate authorization which may be expressly detailed in the minutes of meetings of the board of directors or may be given by a designated corporate official or committee. Further verification includes the auditor's examination of the broker's advice and the canceled check.

COUNT OF SECURITIES

On the balance sheet date, the auditor inspects securities held by the client. The count is made in the presence of the securities custodian, and a signed receipt for the return of the securities to the custodian is obtained. During the inspection, the auditor is careful to verify that the stock certificates are made out in the name of the client, the number of shares held, and the certificate numbers. The verification includes tracing these data to the investment summary and records maintained by the accounting department. For securities held in a safe deposit box, the auditor, along with the appropriate client personnel, visits the bank and performs the inspection in the presence of the client's employee.

Ideally, the auditor counts all securities on the balance sheet date. However, it may be impractical to do so in many cases. This may require the auditor to seal

Figure 13-5

49124 - Buff
89124 - Green
47124 - White

Green Valley Corp.
Analysis of Investments – Marketable Securities
12-31-79

Company Name		Date Acquired	Certificate #	Number of Shares	Cost Per Share	Balance 1-1-79	Purchases	Sales	Balance 12-31-79	Market Price Per Share 12-31-79	Total 12-31-79	Dividends Income	
Martin Company	✓	9/12/79	R1164	1100	13⁵⁰	-0-	14850 ✓		14850 ✓	14²⁵ Ⓠ	15675 ¢	550 ¢	
Pine Hill, Inc.	✓	6/15/75	CC109	450	18⁸⁰	8460 P			8460 ✓	17¹⁰ Ⓠ	7695 ¢	450 ¢	
Vob-True Motors		3/7/71	L-M044	900	9²⁵	8325 P		8325 ✓	-0- ✓	—	—	225 ¢	
Wallen Corp.	✓	8/4/76	86713	150	16⁴⁴	2466 P			2466 ✓	19⁵⁰ Ⓠ	2925 ¢	75 ¢	
						19251	14850	8325	25776 ✗		26295	1300	
						✓	✓	✓	✓ T		✓	T ✓	

T – Traced to the general ledger control account.
✓ – Footed.
✗ – Cross-footed.
✓ – Stock certificates inspected and counted at 1st National County Bank.
P – Balance traced to prior year's working paper.
✓ – Purchase authorization examined in Board of Director's minutes – 9/4/79.
  Broker advice and cancelled check examined.
✓ – Sale authorization examined in Board of Director's minutes – 3/5/79.
  Proceeds traced to cash receipts journal.
  Analysis of Sale:
              Sale Price   9480
              Cost   8325
              Gain on Sale   1155   To Trial Balance – B4
Ⓠ – Quotations per W.S.J. – 1/3/80.
¢ – Calculations checked.
¢ – Traced to cash receipts journal – Dividend rates verified per Standard & Poor's.

the safe containing the securities on or before the end of the year and to return to count these items at a later date. For securities held in a safe deposit box, the auditor may ask the client not to enter the box after the balance sheet date and obtain a letter from the bank attesting to nonentry during the intervening period. The auditor can then inspect the securities after the balance sheet date. The inspection of securities is carefully coordinated with the count of cash and negotiable instruments to prevent the substitution of one asset for another or the proceeds of the sale of one asset for another asset.

CONFIRMATION OF SECURITIES

On occasion, securities may not be held by the client. For example, they may be held by a broker, or a creditor may be holding them as collateral for a loan. The existence of these securities can be verified by the confirmation process. The confirmation request, prepared by the client, verifies the number of shares held, certificate number, investee name, and reason the securities are being held. As in any confirmation request, the auditor mails the letter personally and provides a stamped, self-addressed envelope to ensure direct receipt of the confirmation from the outside party. If for any reason the auditor questions the legitimacy of the holder of securities, the former may request that the securities be made available for personal inspection.

Valuation

The valuation of common stock investments is dependent upon the nature of the investment. Basically, the securities can be valued according to (1) a cost basis, (2) an equity basis, or (3) a consolidated basis. For each, the accounting rules and the audit approach are different.

COST BASIS

Investments in capital stock may be accounted for on a cost basis. Under this accounting method, the following entries are made:

TRANSACTION	INVESTOR'S ENTRY		
Investee pays a dividend	Cash	$00	
	Dividend income		$00
Investee earns a profit or loss	No entry made		

Thus earnings of the investee's company impact the investor's accounts only if a dividend distribution is made by the investee. Professional accounting standards state that such an approach is reasonable when the investor company does not exercise significant influence over operating and financial policies of the investee. *APB Opinion No. 18* states that "an investment of less than 20% should lead to a presumption that an investor does not have the ability to exercise significant influence unless such ability can be demonstrated."

Initially, capital stock investments that represent less than 20 percent of the investee's voting stock must be evaluated to determine if they meet the definition of marketable securities. Capital stock is a marketable security if the securities market price is available on a national securities exchange, such as the New York Stock Exchange, or in the over-the-counter market. Equity securities that meet this definition are subject to guidelines established by *FASB Statement No. 12*. Specifically, such securities are reported on the balance sheet at the lower of cost or market on an aggregate basis. Determining the cost of a security requires the auditor to examine the broker's advice and appropriate canceled check. Market value is verified by the auditor's review of year-end market price quotations that appear in a variety of publications, such as the *Wall Street Journal*.

When market is less than cost, the asset balance is reduced through the establishment of an allowance account. For marketable securities classified as a current asset, the reduction is recorded as a loss in the determination of the current year's net income. An allowance account is used to reduce the cost of securities to a market value basis. For noncurrent marketable securities, the reduction is not used in the determination of net income. Rather, it becomes a contra equity account.

Capital stock investments do not meet the definition established by *FASB Statement No. 12* when their market price is not quoted on established stock exchanges. In such instances, the investment is subject to the criteria established in *Accounting Research Bulletin No. 43*. This bulletin states that, "where market value is less than cost by a substantial amount and it is evident that the decline in market value is not due to a mere temporary condition, the amount to be included as a current asset should not exceed the market value."[1] This guideline presents the auditor with a problem, since it suggest that a write-off be made only if there has been a permanent reduction in the value of the asset. There are occasions when a permanent impairment of value is obvious, for example, an investee that has filed for bankruptcy. On the other hand, it is likely the auditor will have incomplete data, or even conflicting data, so that evaluation becomes very difficult. In an extreme case the auditor may issue a qualified opinion or disclaim an opinion if the investment is material to the investor company.

EQUITY BASIS

When an investment is accounted for on the equity basis, the following basic entries are made:

TRANSACTION	INVESTOR'S ENTRY		
Investee pays a dividend	Cash	$00	
	Investment		$00
Investee earns a profit	Investment	$00	
	Income		$00

APB Opinion No. 18 concluded "that an investment of 20% or more of the voting stock of an investee should lead to a presumption that in the absence of evidence

---

[1] "Restatement and Revision of Accounting Research Bulletin," *Accounting Research Bulletin No. 43* (New York: AICPA, 1961), p. 23.

to the contrary an investor has the ability to exercise significant influence over an investee." By examining the financial statements of the investee the auditor can determine if the investor owns 20 percent or more of the voting stock of the investee.

463
Internal control model

As shown above, an investee dividend and the net earnings or loss of the investee change the carrying value of the investment account. Verification of the dividend amount is made by referring to a financial data publication source, such as *Standard & Poors,* where the quarterly dividend rate is disclosed. In addition, the cash receipts journal may be examined. Ideally, audit verification of the investee's results of operations for the year is made by examining the investee's audited financial statements. When these financial statements are unaudited, the auditor must decide whether the investment is material enough to (1) require him or her to do "some" auditing of the statements or (2) request the investee's auditor to perform the audit procedures.

The audit approach becomes more difficult when there are intercompany transactions or when there is a difference between the original cost of the investment and the investor's equity in the net assets of the investee. For the former problem, intercompany profits and losses must be eliminated until realized. To determine the extent of such profits and losses the auditor reviews the supporting documents for intercompany transactions. In addition, it may be necessary to use the work of the investee's auditor to verify further the intercorporate profit or loss for very material transactions. Where there is a difference between the fair value of the investee's assets as reflected in the investment account and the book value of the assets as reflected in the investee's financial statements, the auditor must verify the fair market value estimation. In addition, there must be verification of the allocation of the cost of the investment to assets subject to amortization and those not subject to amortization. This may require the auditor to review evaluation reports prepared by the investee, investor, or some independent party. If the auditor is not satisfied with the appraisal, it may be necessary to hire an expert to make an independent evaluation.

Ultimately investments carried on the financial statements on an equity basis are subject to a write-off if there is a permanent loss in value. Again, professional judgment must be used to differentiate between a permanent loss and a temporary loss in value. Year-end market value quotations on established stock exchanges are not necessarily interpreted as a permanent loss in value. The auditor evaluates all the facts based on his or her understanding of the general economy, the industrial structure, technological developments, and other environmental conditions.

Consolidated basis

If the investor company owns more than 50 percent of the investee, consolidated financial statements generally must be prepared. The auditor reviews and verifies the consolidating work sheet. Internal documents may be used by the auditor, or it may be necessary to review documents or collect data held by the investee. The auditor may perform the audit of the investor and investee or may have to use the work of another audit firm. Chapter 17 discusses the guidelines to be followed when the investor's auditor utilizes the work of another independent auditor.

Cutoff

To determine that the client has performed a proper cutoff for the purchase and sale of investments, transactions completed after the balance sheet date are examined. By reviewing the investment ledger account, the auditor identifies these transactions. Once the transactions are identified, the auditor refers to the appropriate broker's advice.

When the investment is accounted for on an equity basis, the auditor should read the investee's interim financial statements issued prior to the date of the report.

Classification and disclosure

Investments described as marketable securities may be shown as a current or noncurrent asset. Management's intentions determine the classification. If management's objective is long-term in nature, for example, control of a company, the investment is shown as a long-term asset. On the other hand, investments that are available as working capital if so needed may be classified as current assets. It is very difficult for the auditor to question the classification, since intent is not easily audited. Thus most companies classify investments in marketable securities as current assets. In addition, the following information concerning marketable securities should be disclosed:

- Aggregate cost and market value
- Allowance for unrealized losses
- Realized gains or losses included in the income statement
- Valuation allowance (for noncurrent marketable securities) shown in the equity section

If an investment is accounted for on the equity basis, the name of each investee and the percentage of voting stock held by the investor are disclosed. Also, when there is a quoted market price for the investee's stock, the aggregate fair market value of the investment is disclosed. For an unconsolidated subsidiary, the equity method must be used by the investor company and, if significant, summarized data concerning the assets, equities, and results of operations are disclosed.

Review of related accounts

During the review of the investment account, the auditor examines related accounts. For investments sold during the period, transactions are reviewed to verify gains and losses from disposition. Canceled checks and brokers' advices are examined to establish the sale price and related costs, such as commissions. The original cost or adjusted cost of the investment is usually substantiated by a review of the auditor's working papers.

If the cost method of accounting for investments is used, there may be a **465** dividend income account and a dividends receivable account to verify. This is **Exercises and problems** accomplished by reviewing the cash receipts journal and by referring to a publication, such as *Standard & Poors*, to establish the dividend rate.

Other investments

A variety of short-term and long-term investments may be made by a client. This chapter has been devoted in part to a discussion of capital stock investments. A long-term investment in bonds presents the auditor with basically the same verification problem. For example, he or she needs to substantiate the original cost of the investment, inspect or confirm the bonds on the balance sheet date, and determine if there has been a permanent loss in the carrying value of the bonds. In addition, there may have been a discount or premium account generated when the bonds were sold. Each year it is necessary for the auditor to recompute the bond premium or discount amortization and its impact on bond interest expense.

Other investments, such as promissory notes, joint ventures, certificates of deposit, and short-term investments in bonds, may be encountered during an engagement. For these accounts, as well as other investments, the audit approach requires the auditor to be satisfied as to the existence, valuation, cutoff, and disclosure for the account.

EXERCISES AND PROBLEMS

13-1. List and explain the basic features of an adequate internal control system for property, plant, and equipment.

13-2. Does the use of a capital budget by a client enhance its internal control system?

13-3. Why is it more difficult for a client to control the disposition of fixed assets than it is to control the purchase of fixed assets?

13-4. Is it necessary for a client to account for its fixed assets on a yearly basis? Why?

13-5. How does an auditor determine that the client's selection of a depreciation method is appropriate for a particular asset?

13-6. Which of the following transactions is more difficult to verify:

Notes receivable	$50,000	
Accumulated depreciation	15,000	
Loss of disposition	10,000	
Machinery		$65,000
Discount on notes receivable		10,000
Land	$40,000	
Accumulated depreciation	15,000	
Loss of disposition	10,000	
Machinery		$65,000

13-7. Why is it necessary to analyze the repairs and maintenance expense account as part of the audit of property, plant, and equipment?

466
Audits

13-8. Assume that the accounting profession adopts current value accounting (as opposed to historical cost) as the basis for presenting fixed-asset and the related depreciation accounts on the financial statements. Refer to the audit program illustrated in Figure 13-2 and (1) identify audit procedures that would continue to be used under a current value audit, and (2) list new audit procedures that would have to be added to the audit program.

13-9. To improve the utility of the financial statements, it has been suggested that they be (1) restated based on current purchasing power (inflation accounting), or (2) restated based on current replacement costs (fair value accounting). For property, plant, and equipment restatements, which approach would be the less difficult to audit?

13-10. Why is it necessary for the auditor to control simultaneously the count of cash and all negotiable instruments?

13-11. The following investment is discovered in the ledger card of your client:

Investment in Dodd Company's common stock
10,000 shares at a cost of $50 per share: $500,000

A junior accountant inspected the securities at the balance sheet date. In addition, the cost of the securities was verified by inspecting a broker's advice. Do you believe sufficient evidential matter has been collected for this account?

13-12. Should all investments be valued at cost?

13-13. Is it possible to count securities at an interim date as part of the compliance tests?

13-14. During the inspection of securities what data should be verified by the auditor?

13-15. If all securities are inspected at the balance sheet date, is it necessary to perform any cutoff procedures for the securities account?

13-16. In connection with the annual examination of Johnson Corporation, a manufacturer of janitorial supplies, you have been assigned to audit the fixed assets. The company maintains a detailed property ledger for all fixed assets. You prepared an audit program for the balances of property, plant, and equipment but have yet to prepare one for accumulated depreciation and depreciation expense.

Required: Prepare a separate comprehensive audit program for the accumulated depreciation and depreciation expense accounts. (AICPA Adapted)

13-17. Hardware Manufacturing Company, a closely held corporation, has operated since 1969 but has not had its financial statements audited. The company now plans to issue additional capital stock expected to be sold to outsiders and wishes to engage you to examine its 1979 transactions and render an opinion on the financial statements for the year ended December 31, 1979.

The company has expanded from one plant to three plants and has frequently acquired, modified, and disposed of all types of equipment. Fixed assets have a net book value of 70 percent of total assets and consist of land and buildings, diversified machinery and equipment, and furniture and fixtures. Some property was acquired by donation from stockholders. Depreciation was recorded by several methods using various estimated lives.

Required
1. May you confine your examination solely to 1979 transactions as requested by

this prospective client whose financial statements have not previously been examined? Why?

2. Prepare an audit program for the January 1, 1979, opening balances of the land, building, and equipment and accumulated depreciation accounts at Hardware Manufacturing Company. You need not include tests of 1979 transactions in your program. (AICPA Adapted)

13-18. In connection with a recurring examination of the financial statements of the Louis Manufacturing Company for the year ended December 31, 1979, you have been assigned the audit of the manufacturing equipment, manufacturing equipment—accumulated depreciation, and repairs to manufacturing equipment accounts. Your review of Louis' policies and procedures has disclosed the following pertinent information:

1. The manufacturing equipment account includes the net invoice price plus related freight and installation costs for all the equipment in Louis' manufacturing plant.
2. The manufacturing equipment and accumulated depreciation accounts are supported by a subsidiary ledger which shows the cost and accumulated depreciation for each piece of equipment.
3. An annual budget for capital expenditures of $1000 or more is prepared by the budget committee and approved by the board of directors. Capital expenditures over $1000 which are not included in this budget must be approved by the board of directors, and variations of 20 percent or more must be explained to the board. Approval by the supervisor of production is required for capital expenditures under $1000.
4. Company employees handle the installation, removal, repair, and rebuilding of the machinery. Work orders are prepared for these activities and are subject to the same budgetary control as other expenditures. Work orders are not required for external expenditures.

Required

1. Cite the major objectives of your audit of the manufacturing equipment, manufacturing equipment–accumulated depreciation, and repairs of manufacturing equipment accounts. Do not include in this listing the auditing procedures designed to accomplish these objectives.

2. Prepare the portion of your audit program applicable to the review of 1979 additions to the manufacturing equipment account. (AICPA Adapted)

13-19. You were contacted on November 14, 1979, to perform the audit of the financial statements of the Martin Company for the year ended December 31, 1979. Previous audits had been performed by a sole practitioner who became ill during the year and was unable to conduct the audit. The predecessor auditor, with the client's concurrence, has made available the previous year's working papers. The working papers are not complete, since the internal control questionnaire, analysis of accounts, and other documents are missing or were never prepared.

The Martin Company specializes in the repair of automobile transmissions and has 47 shops spread throughout the southeastern United States. The central office, where the majority of the accounting records are kept, is located in Richmond, Virginia.

As part of your initial review of the company and its operations, you read all reports prepared by the internal audit department over the past five years. A current report notes that "at almost every location visited in 1978 we discovered that many items classified as property, plant, and equipment had been sold but the items were not removed from the plant ledger kept at the central office." The report further explained that the proceeds,

468
Audits

if any, were recorded as miscellaneous income in the cash receipts journal maintained at each location. To correct the problem the internal auditors decided to visit all the locations during September and October of 1979 and review the miscellaneous income accounts. At every location they found that between 3 and 5 percent of the gross cost of fixed assets had been disposed of during the year and improperly accounted for in the plant ledger maintained at the home office. Based on their findings, correcting journal entries were made.

You have assigned an assistant the task of auditing property, plant, and equipment. In addition, you have given the assistant a copy of the internal audit report referred to above. Specifically, you ask the assistant to look at the report and determine if the firm's standard fixed-asset audit program should be modified. (Assume that the firm's audit program is similar to the one presented in Figure 13-2.)

The following day the assistant returns and states that there is no need to modify the normal audit procedures. The assistant notes that "only about 3 to 5 percent of the total fixed assets could be overstated, and this amount has already been booked by the client and we certainly aren't worried about such an immaterial misstatement."

Required

1. Assuming the internal auditors did a competent job in their review of miscellaneous income, do you agree with their audit approach?

2. Do you agree with your assistant's conclusions? Explain.

3. Prepare any recommendations to management which you believe are appropriate concerning the disposal of assets.

13-20. In your examination of the financial statements of Gaar Corporation at December 31, 1979, you observe the contents of certain accounts and other pertinent information as follows:

	BUILDING				
DATE	EXPLANATION	LF	DEBIT	CREDIT	BALANCE
12/31/78 Balance		X	$100,000		$100,000
7/1/79 New boiler		CD	16,480	$1,480	115,000
9/1/79 Insurance recovery		CR		2,000	113,000

	ALLOWANCE FOR DEPRECIATION—BUILDING				
DATE	EXPLANATION	LF	DEBIT	CREDIT	BALANCE
12/31/78 Balance—15 years at 4 percent of $100,000		X		$60,000	$60,000
12/31/79 Annual depreciation		GJ		4,440	64,440

You learn that on June 15 the company's old high-pressure boiler exploded. Damage to the building was insignificant, but the boiler was replaced by a more efficient oil-burning boiler. The company received $2000 as an insurance adjustment under the terms of its policy for damage to the boiler.

The disbursement voucher charged to the building account on July 1, 1979, is reproduced here:

To: Rex Heating Company

List price—new oil-burning boiler
(including fuel oil tank and 5,000 gallons fuel oil) $16,000
Sales tax—3 percent of $16,000 480
Total 16,480

Less allowance for old coal-burning boiler in building—to be
    removed at the expense of the Rex Heating Company 1,480

    Total price $15,000

In vouching the expenditure you determine that the terms included a 2 percent cash discount which was properly computed and taken. The sales tax is not subject to discount.

Your audit discloses that a voucher for $1000 was paid to the Emment Company on July 2, 1979, and charged to the repair expense account. The voucher is adequately supported and is marked "Installation costs for new oil-burning boiler."

The company's fuel oil supplier advises that fuel oil had a market price of 16¢ per gallon on July 1 and 18¢ per gallon on December 31. The fuel oil inventory on December 31 was 2000 gallons.

A review of subsidiary property records discloses that the replaced coal-burning boiler was installed when the building was constructed and was recorded at a cost of $10,000. According to its manufacturers the new boiler should be serviceable for 15 years.

In computing depreciation for retirements Gaar Corporation consistently treats a fraction of a month as a full month.

Required: Prepare the adjusting journal entries you would suggest for entry on the books of Gaar Corporation. The books have not been closed. Support your entries with computations in good form. (AICPA Adapted)

13-21. You have been engaged to audit the December 31, 1979, financial statements of the Smith Equipment Corporation which was formed in 1946 and sells or leases construction equipment such as bulldozers, road scrapers, dirt movers, and so on to contractors. The corporation at year end has 50 pieces of equipment leased to 30 contractors who are using the equipment at various locations throughout your state.

The Smith Equipment Corporation is identified as the owner of the leased equipment by a small metal tag attached to each machine. The tag is fastened by screws so that it can be removed if the machine is sold. During the audit you find that the contractors often buy the equipment that they have been leasing, but the identification tag is not always removed from the machine.

The corporation's principal asset is the equipment leased to the contractors. While there is no plant ledger, each machine is accounted for by a file card that gives its description, cost, contractor-lessee and rental payment records. The corporation's system of internal control is weak.

You were engaged upon the recommendation of the president of the local bank. The Smith Equipment Corporation, which had never had an audit, had applied to the bank for a sizable loan; the bank president had requested an audited balance sheet.

You barely know Joan Smith, the principal stockholder and president of the Smith Equipment Corporation; she has a reputation for expensive personal tastes and for shrewd business dealings, some of which have bordered on being unethical. Nevertheless, Smith enjoys a strong personal allegiance from her contractor-lessees, who favor she has curried by personal gifts and loans. The lessees look upon Smith as a personal friend for whom they would do almost anything. Often they overlook the fact that they are dealing with the corporation and make their checks payable to Smith, who endorses them over to the corporation.

Required

1. List the audit procedures you would employ in examination of the asset account representing the equipment leased to the contractors.

2. Although your audit procedures, including those you described in answering part 1, did not uncover any discrepancies, you have been unable to dismiss your feeling that

470
Audits

Smith and some of the contractor-lessees may have collaborated to deceive you. Under these conditions discuss what action, if any, you would take and the effect, if any, of your feeling upon your opinion. (Assume that you would not withdraw from the engagement.)

(AICPA Adapted)

13-22. You are examining the financial statements of Morex Corporation for the year ended December 31, 1979. For the first time since it was organized, it has a preaudit loss of $250,000 which was mainly due to a significant drop in sales for the year. The sales decrease appears to be temporary, and industrial forecasts strongly suggest an upturn in activity in the second quarter of 1980.

As part of your review of the fixed assets of Morex you notice the following entries made in the machinery and related accounts late in the year.

MACHINERY			NO. 714
Balance 1/1/79	$800,000	JE no. 13	$100,000
JE no. 13	200,000	JE no. 14	160.000
		JE no. 15	50,000

ACCUMULATED DEPRECIATION—MACHINERY			
JE no. 13	$30,000	Balance 1/1/79	$200,000
JE no. 14	40,000	AJE 12/31/79	28,000
JE no. 15	40,000		

You discover that the $28,000 credit to accumulated depreciation is for the current year's depreciation expense. After appropriate recomputations you conclude that this entry is correct.

In support of journal entries no. 13, no. 14, and no. 15, you discover the following data:

JOURNAL ENTRY NO. 13:

12/31/79	Machinery	$200,000	
	Accumulated depreciation	30,000	
	Machinery		$100,000
	Cash		50,000
	Gain on exchange		80,000

Explanation: Morex exchanged several pieces of equipment with a company located in a distant state and paid $50,000 "boot."

Evidential matter: Morex's engineering department, in a report submitted to the board of directors, estimated it would cost about $200,000 to build the newly acquired machinery or have it built locally.

JOURNAL ENTRY NO. 14:

12/31/79	Notes receivable	$120,000	
	Accumulated depreciation	40,000	
	Machinery		$160,000

Explanation: Morex sold general-purpose machinery to a customer who normally buys inventory on a long-term basis. Morex usually charges 8 percent on these sales, but believes it was fortunate to sell the machinery at $120,000 and feels it is unlikely that the customer would pay any interest at this price.

Evidential matter: A non-interest-bearing note signed by the customer stating that the total amount is due at the end of three years. In addition, you send and receive back a signed confirmation from the customer.

JOURNAL ENTRY NO. 15:

12/31/79	Land	$600,000	
	Accumulated depreciation	40,000	
	Machinery		$50,000
	Cash		250,000
	Gain		340,000

Explanation: Morex acquired land which is located directly behind its present plant. Morex believes the land will be needed for expansion in the near future. Machinery and cash was the consideration given by Morex.

Evidential matter: Morex's accounting department, in a report submitted to the board of directors, estimated the value of the new land based on a recent appraisal made by an independent firm of appraisers of its present location. The per-acre figure in the appraiser's report was used to estimate the value of the newly acquired land.

Required

1. Based on the evidential matter gathered at this point, would you propose any adjusting journal entries?

2. For any of the three journal entries under investigation for which you did not propose an adjusting entry in part 1, explain (a) what problem(s) you may encounter in verifying the entries, and (b) what additional evidential matter you believe needs to be gathered. (Hint: Review *APB Opinion No. 29*.)

13-23. You are the senior accountant in the audit of the Paulsen Grain Corporation whose business primarily involves the purchase, storage, and sale of grain products. The corporation owns several elevators located along navigable water routes and transports its grain by barge and rail. Your assistant submitted the following analysis for your review.

Paulsen Grain Corporation
ADVANCES PAID ON BARGES UNDER CONSTRUCTION—a/c 210
December 31, 1980

Advances made:	
1/15/60 Ck. no. 3463—Jones Barge Construction Company	$100,000 (1)
4/13/60 Ck. no. 4129—Jones Barge Construction Company	25,000 (1)
6/19/60 Ck. no. 5396—Jones Barge Construction Company	63,000 (1)
Total payments	$188,000
Deduct cash received 9/1/80 from Eastern Life Insurance Company	188,000 (2)
Balance per general ledger—12/31/80	0

(1) Examined approved check request and canceled check and traced to cash disbursements record.

(2) Traced to cash receipts book and to duplicate deposit ticket.

Required

1. In what respects is the analysis incomplete for report purposes? (Do not include any discussion of specific auditing procedures.)

472
Audits

2. What two different types of contractual arrangements may be inferred from your assistant's analysis?

3. What additional auditing procedures would you suggest that your assistant perform before you accept the working paper as being complete? (AICPA Adapted)

13-24. In connection with his examination of the financial statements of Belasco Chemicals, Inc., Kenneth Mack, CPA, is considering the necessity of inspecting marketable securities on the balance sheet date, May 31, 1978, or on some other date. The marketable securities held by Belasco include negotiable bearer bonds, which are kept in a safe in the treasurer's office, and miscellaneous stocks and bonds kept in a safe deposit box at the Merchants Bank. Both the negotiable bearer bonds and the miscellaneous stocks and bonds are material to proper presentation of Belasco's financial position.

Required

1. What are the factors that Mack should consider in determining the necessity for inspecting these securities on May 31, 1978, as opposed to other dates?

2. Assume that Mack plans to send a member of his staff to Belasco's offices and the Merchants Bank on May 31, 1978, to make the security inspection. What instructions should he give to this staff member as to the conduct of the inspection and the evidence to be included in the audit working papers? (**Note:** Do not discuss the valuation of securities, the income from securities, or the examination of information contained in the books and records of the company.)

3. Assume that Mack finds it impracticable to send a member of his staff to Belasco's offices and the Merchants Bank on May 31, 1978. What alternative procedures may he employ to assure himself that the company had physical possession of its marketable securities on May 31, 1978, if the securities are inspected (a) May 28, 1978, and (b) June 5, 1978? (AICPA Adapted)

13-25. In late 1978 your client, Elmo Company, invested idle cash in Dare Company's common stock. The investment consisted of 10,000 shares purchased at $30 per share. This represented less than 1 percent of the voting stock of Dare.

This investment was intended to be a temporary one in Dare. Dare's stock is traded on a national stock exchange, and it would be easy to dispose of the stock at any time. Elmo would need the funds in the fall of 1979, when it expected to expand its own facilities. The investment in Dare Company's common stock was shown as a current asset on the December 31, 1978, balance sheet.

Early in 1979 the market value per share of Dare's common stock began to drop when Dare announced that it would have to suspend all dividends for an indeterminate period. On March 31, 1979, the value of the stock had dropped to $25 per share. To reflect this in its first-quarter financial statements, Elmo made the following entry:

3/31/79 Loss on revaluation of marketable securities	$50,000	
Allowance for the revaluation of marketable securities		$50,000

By the end of Elmo's second quarter of operations in 1979, the stock had fallen to $20 per share, and the loss was increased by another $50,000.

By the fall of 1979 the market value of Dare's common stock had stabilized at about $20 per share. Although funds were needed to finance the planned expansion, the board of directors decided to keep the investment in Dare's stock until it recovered to at least its original purchase price. The board realized that this might take several years. Nonetheless, it was reluctant to have to explain a real loss to its stockholders. It believed it was much easier to explain a "paper loss." In addition, a member of the board that was

an accountant stated that it would not be necessary to show even a paper loss, since the **473**
investment was now a long-term investment and reporting standards did not require that Exercises and problems
a loss be taken through the income statement.

Based on instructions from the board of directors, the controller of Elmo Company
made the following entries:

10/1/79	Allowance for the revaluation of marketable securities	$100,000	
	Loss on revaluation of marketable securities		$100,000
10/1/79	Unrealized losses—investments	$100,000	
	Allowance for the valuation of long-term investments		$100,000

The first entry was made to reverse the previous two entries made when the investment
was considered a current asset. The second entry was made to recognize a reduction in
the value of the long-term investment through a contra equity account rather than in the
determination of income for 1979.

On December 31, 1979, the market value of the stock was about $20.

Required

1. Do you believe the investment should be classified as a long-term asset on the
December 31, 1979 balance sheet?

2. Do you agree with the two entries made on October 1, 1979?

3. Assume that the market value per share of Dare's stock had dropped to $15 per
share on December 31, 1979, would it be proper to increase the contra equity account by
another $50,000?

4. Is the audit problem faced by an auditor more difficult when (a) there is a fall in
the market value of a marketable securities classified as a current asset, or (b) there is
a fall in the market value of a security listed as a long-term investment?

13-26. As part of her examination of the financial statements of the Marlborough Corporation for the year ended March 31, 1978, Maria Romito, CPA, is reviewing the balance
sheet presentation of a $1,200,000 advance to Franklin Olds, Marlborough's president.
The advance, which represents 50 percent of current assets and 10 percent of total assets,
was made during the year ended March 31, 1978. It has been described in the balance
sheet as "Miscellaneous accounts receivable" and classified as a current asset.

Olds informs the CPA that he has used the proceeds of the advance to purchase
35,000 shares of Marlborough's common stock in order to forestall a takeover raid on the
company. He is reluctant to have his association with the advance described on the
financial statements because he does not have voting control and fears that this will "just
give the raiders ammunition."

Olds offers the following four-point program as an alternative to further disclosure:

1. Have the advance approved by the board of directors. (This can be done expeditiously because a majority of the board members are officers of the company.)
2. Prepare a demand note payable to the company with interest of 7½ percent (the
   average bank rate paid by the company.)
3. Furnish an endorsement of the stock to the company as collateral for the loan.
   (During the year under audit, despite the fact that earnings did not increase, the
   market price of Marlborough common rose from $20 to $40 per share. The stock
   has maintained its $40 per share market price subsequent to year end.)
4. Obtain a written opinion from the company attorney supporting the legality of the
   company's advance and the use of the proceeds.

Required

1. Discuss the proper balance sheet classification of the advance to Olds and other appropriate disclosures on the financial statements and in the footnotes. (Ignore SEC regulations and requirements, tax effects, creditor's restrictions on stock repurchase, and the presentation of common stock dividends and interest income.)

2. Discuss each point of Olds's four-point program as to whether or not it is desirable and as to whether or not it is an alternative to further disclosure.

3. If Olds refuses to permit further disclosure, what action(s) should the CPA take? Discuss.

4. In his discussion with the CPA, Olds warns that the raiders, if successful, probably will appoint new auditors. What consideration should the CPA give to this factor? Explain.

(AICPA Adapted)

13-27. You have audited the financial statements of Torre Company for several years. On January 1, 1979, Torre Company purchased 30 percent of the voting stock of Voll Corporation for $15 million. An analysis of Voll's balance sheet at the acquisition date is presented here:

	VOLL CORPORATION	
	BOOK VALUES	FAIR MARKET VALUE
Monetary assets	$ 2,000,000	$ 2,000,000
Inventories (LIFO)	10,000,000	15,000,000
Depreciable properties (10 years remaining life)	25,000,000	30,000,000
Total	$37,000,000	$47,000,000
Current liabilities	$ 3,000,000	
Long-term debt	14,000,000	
Stockholders' equity	20,000,000	
	$37,000,000	

A condensed (audited) income statement for Voll Corporation for the year ended December 31, 1979, is presented here:

Gross revenues	$16,600,000
Expenses	15,400,000
Net income before extraordinary items	1,200,000
Extraordinary item	1,300,000
Net income	$2,500,000
Dividends, 1979	$1,000,000

You are reviewing Torre's financial statements for the year ended December 31, 1979, and find only the following disclosures on its statements concerning the investment in Voll Corporation.

Balance sheet:	
Investment—minority interest	$15,450,000
Income statement:	
Equity in investee's income	$ 750,000

Note 3 (to the financial statements): Early in the current year the company purchased a minority interest in a supplier.

Required

1. Prepare an audit program for review of the investment account.
2. Do you agree with the client's accounting for the investment? Be specific.
3. Has the client properly disclosed the investment on the financial statements and in the footnotes?
4. Does the fact that there was a difference between the book value and the fair market value of Voll's assets on the purchase date present an audit problem?

13-28. You have been engaged to examine the financial statements of the Elliott Company for the year ended December 31, 1978. You performed a similar examination as of December 31, 1977.

Following is the trial balance for the company as of December 31, 1978:

	DEBIT (CREDIT)
Cash	$128,000
Interest receivable	47,450
Dividends receivable	1,750
6½ percent secured note receivable	730,000
Investments at cost:	
Bowen common stock	322,000
Investments at equity:	
Woods common stock	284,000
Land	185,000
Accounts payable	(31,000)
Interest payable	(6,500)
8 percent secured note payable to bank	(275,000)
Common stock	(480,000)
Paid-in capital in excess of par	(800,000)
Retained earnings	(100,500)
Dividend revenue	(3,750)
Interest revenue	(47,450)
Equity in earnings of investments carried at equity	(40,000)
Interest expense	26,000
General and administrative expense	60,000

You have obtained the following data concerning certain accounts:

· The 6½ percent note receivable is due from Tysinger Corporation and is secured by a first mortgage on land sold to Tysinger by Elliott on December 21, 1977. The note was to have been paid in 20 equal quarterly payments beginning March 31, 1978, plus interest. Tysinger, however, is in very poor financial condition and has not made any principal or interest payments to date.

· The Bowen common stock was purchased on September 21, 1977, for cash in the market where it is actively traded. It is used as security for the note payable and held by the bank. Elliott's investment in Bowen represents approximately 1 percent of the total oustanding shares.

· Elliott's investment in Woods represents 40 percent of the outstanding common stock which is actively traded. Woods is audited by another CPA and has a December 31 year end.

· Elliott neither purchased nor sold any stock investments during the year other than that noted above.

Required: For the following account balances, discuss (1) the types of evidential matter you should obtain and (2) the audit procedures you should perform during your examination.

    a. 6½ percent secured note receivable
    b. Bowen common stock
    c. Woods common stock
    d. Dividend revenue
                          (AICPA Adapted)

13-29. During an engagement an auditor may encounter a variety of investment accounts. Assume you are auditing the financial statements of the Nova Company for the fiscal year ending on June 30, 1980. Two investments listed on the trial balance of the company are described as follows:

- Investment in Arn Company bonds
  Purchased January 15, 1980; maturing date December 31, 1989
  Cost $6,400,000
  Face $6,000,000
  Interest rate 8 percent (stated on the face of the bonds)
  Investment objective: To hold until maturity

- Investment in Baker Company marketable securities
  Purchased January 15, 1980
  Cost $3,800,000
  Number of shares 100,000 (represents 6 percent of Baker Company's voting stock)
     Dividend rate is currently $1.50 per share
     Investment objective: To hold for approximately nine months and then sell to meet maturing debt obligations

Required: Contrast the audit approach for each investment. Label your answer sheet (1) similarities and (2) differences.

13-30. As a result of highly profitable operations over a number of years, Eastern Manufacturing Corporation accumulated a substantial investment portfolio. In his examination of the financial statements for the year ended December 31, 1979, the following information came to the attention of the corporation's CPA:

1. The manufacturing operations of the corporation resulted in an operating loss for the year.
2. In 1979 the corporation placed the securities making up the investment portfolio with a financial institution which will serve as custodian of the securities. Formerly the securities were kept in the corporation's safe deposit box in the local bank.
3. On December 22, 1979, the corporation sold and then repurchased on the same day a number of securities that had appreciated greatly in value. Management stated that the purpose of the sale and repurchase was to establish a higher cost and book value for the securities and to avoid the reporting of a loss for the year.

Required

   1. List the objectives of the CPA's examination of the investment account.

   2. Under what conditions would the CPA accept a confirmation of the securities on hand from the custodian in lieu of inspecting and counting the securities himself?

   3. What disclosure, if any, of the sale and repurchase of the securities would the CPA recommend for the financial statements? If the client accepts the CPA's recommen-

dations for disclosure, what effect, if any, would the sale and repurchase have upon the CPA's opinion on the financial statements? Discuss. (AICPA Adapted)

MULTIPLE CHOICE

1. In the following item, two independent statements (numbered I and II) are presented. You are to evaluate each statement individually and determine whether it is true. Your answer for each item should be selected from the following responses:

a. Only I is true.
b. Only II is true.
c. Both I and II are true.
d. Neither I nor II is true.

In his or her report on financial statements, the auditor states whether generally accepted accounting principles have been consistently applied in the current period in relation to the preceding period.

I. During the year ended December 31, 1972, Abel Company, because of altered conditions, changed the estimated economic life of all its equipment from 8 to 10 years. This accounting change and the amount of its effect may be required to be disclosed in a note to the financial statements for the year ended December 31, 1972, but no comment as to consistency is required in the auditor's report.

II. During the year ended December 31, 1972, Abel Company changed from the straight-line method to the declining-balance method of depreciation for all its equipment. This accounting change had no effect on the financial statements for the year ended December 31, 1972, but is expected to have a substantial effect in later years. The change should be disclosed in a note to the financial statements for the year ended December 31, 1972, but no comment as to consistency is required in the auditor's report.

2. A CPA is completing an examination of the financial statements of the Proshek Trucking Company. The company had been depreciating its trucks over an 8-year period but determined that a more realistic life is 10 years and based this year's depreciation provision upon that life. The change and the effects of the change have been adequately disclosed in a note to the financial statements. If the CPA agrees that the change in estimated life was properly made, he should

a. Omit mention of the change in his or her report because it results from changed conditions, is not a change in accounting principles, and has been properly disclosed.

b. Recognize this change as one that involves a choice between two generally accepted principles of accounting and qualify his or her report as to consistency.

c. Render an unqualified opinion provided that comparative income statements for prior years are restated based upon the 10-year life.

d. Insist that comparative income statements for prior years be restated and render an opinion qualified as to consistency. (AICPA Adapted)

CHAPTER 14

Audit of liabilities: Current, contingent, and long-term

A variety of current and noncurrent liabilities is encountered during the examination of financial statements. A comprehensive discussion of each potential liability account is beyond the scope of this book. This chapter concentrates on the suggested approach for accounts payable, accrued liabilities, contingent liabilities, and long-term liabilities. In general, the audit approach for liability accounts is different from the review of asset accounts. For assets the audit exposure focuses on the possibility of overstatement, whereas for liabilities the auditor is concerned with the possibility of understatement. Thus the thrust of the audit approach changes accordingly. In addition, the audit of liabilities is not concerned with the lower of cost or market or cost recoverability, which is an important element in the audit of assets. On the other hand, each liability account is somewhat unique, just like most asset accounts, as to the specific audit procedure to be employed and emphasized.

ACCOUNTS PAYABLE

Accounts payable refers to the incurrence of a liability associated with the purchase of inventory. Since this is a routine activity, an internal control system is established to process the transactions. Specifically, accounts payable are impacted by the inventory purchase accounting systems and the cash disbursements system. The inventory purchase system was discussed in Chapter 12, and the cash disbursements system was discussed in Chapter 10. These discussions included a description of the internal control models, the study and evaluation of the internal control systems, and the performance of compliance tests for each system. To avoid repetition, the current discussion is limited to the accounts payable substantive tests. Nonetheless, it is important to realize that the auditor structures the substantive audit program for accounts payable after these two systems have been analyzed and tested.

Substantive tests

The accounts payable substantive tests are performed after the date of the balance sheet. Unlike other audit procedures, these procedures cannot be performed at an interim date, since the audit risk focuses on the potentiality for unrecorded liabilities. The latter discussion, referred to as a *search for unrecorded liabilities,* confirms the need for the timing of the audit approach. The nature and extent of the audit procedures are dependent upon the auditor's evaluation of the internal control systems, the results of the compliance tests, and the materiality of the accounts payable amount. In the last-mentioned case, materiality refers not only to the unaudited balance that appears in the accounts payable account, but also to the importance of financing inventory purchases through the use of vendor credit. The timing, nature, and extent of audit procedures employed are discussed in the context of the four audit objectives—existence, valuation, cutoff, and classification and disclosure. A typical audit program, which embodies this approach, is presented in Figure 14-1.

Existence

One phase of the audit of accounts payable is to determine that the liabilities listed are obligations of the organization at the balance sheet date. To achieve this objective, the auditor utilizes the accounts payable trial balance and vendor statements and considers confirmation of accounts payable.

THE TRIAL BALANCE

The first step in the audit of accounts payable is to gain control of the universe that comprises the balance shown in the general ledger. This is done by acquiring a trial balance, a listing of accounts payable, from the client. The trial balance is footed by the auditor, and the total is traced to the general ledger control card. After the arithmetic accuracy of the listing has been proved, the individual balances contained on the listing are reviewed. The propriety of an individual balance is determined by tracing the amount to the appropriate accounts payable subsidiary ledger card or to the appropriate entry in the voucher register. In conjunction with this procedure, the voucher package—purchase order, receiving report, and vendor invoice—is reviewed to substantiate the liability. The data contained in the trial balance, subsidiary ledger card, and voucher package are reviewed for consistency. Of special interest is the date the goods were received, as shown on the receiving report. In addition to tracing from the trial balance to other supporting data, the auditor traces from the accounts payable subsidiary ledger or voucher register to the trial balance to ensure that obligations in the accounting records were not omitted from the trial balance.

In selecting items from the trial balance for substantiation, the auditor usually chooses those with relatively large balances. However, some of the small balances are audited to make certain there is no concentration of errors in the smaller accounts. In addition, any unusual vendor balances are selected for review. For example, accounts with a debit balance or accounts that appear to be nontrade items are vouched.

480
Audit of liabilities:
current, contingent,
and long-term

Figure 14-1

Audit program: accounts payable

PROCEDURES	DATE COMPLETED	WORK PERFORMED BY
1. Obtain and verify a trial balance for accounts payable.	_____	_____
2. Review vendor statements.	_____	_____
3. Consider confirming some accounts payable.	_____	_____
4. Perform a search for unrecorded liabilities.	_____	_____
5. Determine proper classification and disclosure for all open accounts.	_____	_____

VENDOR STATEMENTS

The validity of the accounts payable trial balance is enhanced by a review of vendor statements. Usually, on a monthly basis, the trade creditors of an organization mail out statements that are compared with amounts shown in the trial balance. When the two amounts do not agree, the client is asked to prepare a reconciliation between the vendor statement and an individual amount in the trial balance. Upon completion of the reconciliation, the auditor reviews the items for reasonableness. On a test basis, and for large or unusual items, the reconciling data are traced to the appropriate corroborative evidence. For example, the vendor invoice may contain a billing for an item shipped near the end of the accounting period but not received until after the close of the year. In this case the auditor obtains and reviews the receiving report for the shipment.

As evidential matter, the competency of the vendor statement is dependent upon how the auditor obtained the statement. In some cases he or she may receive the unopened vendor statement through the mail, or in many instances the statement is filed by the client in the vendor's correspondence file. Because the client has the opportunity to screen the data, the competency of the vendor invoice as evidential matter is reduced. Thus the vendor statement is not persuasive evidence in the audit of accounts payable.

CONFIRMATIONS

The limitation of use of the vendor statement as competent evidential matter can be overcome to some extent by use of the confirmation technique. The confirmation request is sent directly to the vendor with instructions to mail the signed confirmation directly to the auditor. In general the confirmation of accounts payable is no different from the confirmation of accounts receivable. In both cases the auditor makes an independent selection of confirmation requests to be mailed by, and returned directly to, him or her to ensure the integrity of the process. However, the specific application of the procedure and the strength of the evidence generated by its use are quite different.

In applying the confirmation procedure in the area of accounts receivable, the auditor is concerned with verifying the existence of an amount listed on the financial statements. For this reason, in the selection of amounts to be confirmed, the dollar balance is an important criterion for selection. On the other hand, in the audit of accounts payable the auditor is concerned with the omission of liabilities. Thus in the selection of accounts payable for confirmation, he or she considers verifying zero balances or small balances due to the vendor, especially in the case of vendors with a significant amount of activity as shown on their accounts payable subsidiary ledger card. In addition, the auditor's review of open purchase commitment contracts is used to identify important suppliers. Having selected an account for confirmation, he or she usually utilizes the opportunity to collect other data relevant to the audit. For example, year-end quotations for raw materials or commodities may be requested for use in testing the ending inventory for application of the lower of cost or market concept. Other data such as consigned goods and unfilled purchase commitment contracts are requested. Once the returned data are received by the auditor, they are reviewed and summarized. Differences are investigated to determine if they are significant.

The adequacy of evidence generated by the accounts payable confirmation process is less than complete. This point is emphasized by the fact that the confirmation of accounts payable, unlike that of accounts receivable, is not a required audit procedure. Again, the confirmation of accounts payable does not result in persuasive evidence, and for this reason the auditor must seek another audit procedure.

Existence, valuation, and cutoff

The crux of the audit of the year-end balance for accounts payable centers around the auditor's performing a search for unrecorded liabilities. The procedure is fundamental to determination of the existence and valuation of accounts payable, as well as to determination of a proper cutoff by the client. Since all three objectives are so intertwined with the performance of a search for unresolved liabilities, it is more useful to combine the discussion rather than to list and discuss each objective individually.

SEARCH FOR UNRECORDED LIABILITIES

In performing a search for unrecorded liabilities, the auditor obviously looks for amounts that have not been accrued on the financial statements. The review of vendor statements and the confirmation of individual accounts may produce some unrecorded liabilities, but the examination of transactions, documents, and records generated subsequent to the close of the fiscal year is far more likely to be productive. The following procedures are typically employed in the search for unrecorded liabilities.

Review the purchases journal or voucher register: The review of these two books of original entry focuses on items entered after the close of the year. The auditor selects items for review based upon their dollar value. Relatively large items are vouched, but some smaller balances are reviewed in a similar manner. In vouching these transactions, the auditor reviews the purchase order, vendor invoice, and receiving report. The critical information is the date of the receiving report and the shipping terms per the vendor invoice. If the data reveal the goods

482
**Audit of liabilities:
current, contingent,
and long-term**

were received after the end of the year, the item has been properly recorded in the purchase journal or voucher register.

Review of cash disbursements journal: If a voucher register is not used, the auditor reviews entries made in the cash disbursements journal after the end of the year. Again, he or she concentrates on large dollar items and vouches these transactions by using the voucher package. The review of this journal is especially useful, since most organizations prefer to pay their bills on a timely basis to avoid receiving a bad credit rating. In addition, the auditor performs this procedure toward the end of the audit so that the maximum number of days after the close of the year can be reviewed.

Review of the open-document files: The matching of the purchase order, vendor invoice, and receiving report occurs in the accounts payable section of the accounting department. Once matched, these documents become the basis for journalization of the liability. It is possible that all three documents were not matched but that a liability exists. For example, the unmatched receiving report file may document that goods were received but that for some reason a purchase order or vendor invoice has not been received or matched by the accounting department. Therefore the auditor reviews this file as well as the open invoice file to determine if a liability exists but is unrecorded.

Inventory cutoff: The search for unrecorded trade accounts payable includes the application of cutoff procedures during the inventory observation. Receipt of goods during the inventory count are segregated in the receiving area and counted by the client toward the latter part of the count. Once the inventory is counted and tagged, the auditor observes the inventory and records appropriate test counts. In addition, he or she records information from the last several receiving reports prepared on the observation day. With the information concerning inventory received, the auditor reviews the purchases journal or voucher register to see if the items are properly recorded.

Valuation

Under most circumstances the performance of a search for unrecorded liabilities results in adequate evidential matter to satisfy the audit objective of valuation. However, the auditor considers the possibility of imputing an interest factor for non-interest-bearing trade payables or interest-bearing trade payables in which the interest rate is different from the interest rate appropriate for the exchange at the date of transaction. *APB Opinion No. 21* provides guidelines for imputed interest where payables are generated. Since the opinion does not apply to "payables arising from transactions with customers or suppliers in the normal course of business which are due in customary trade times not exceeding approximately one year," most trade payables are exempt. Where trade payables exceed the one-year guideline, the auditor considers whether an imputed interest factor on these payables materially impacts the financial statements. If so, he or she collects sufficient and competent evidence as to the interest rate appropriate under the circumstances.

Classification and disclosure

Accounts payable result from the purchase of goods held for resale or to be used in production. During the vouching of the accounts payable as listed on the trial balance, the auditor determines whether other payables, such as amounts due to officers or affiliates, are listed as accounts payable. If material, these payables are removed from the accounts payable account and established as a separate liability or grouped with other nontrade payables. Also, the auditor's review of the accounts payable trial balance and subsidiary ledger may reveal accounts with debt balances. Again, if these are significant, they are listed as assets, and the auditor may confirm all or some of them. This is accomplished by making a reclassification entry on the working trial balance rather than proposing an adjusting journal entry that is actually "booked" by the client.

ACCRUED LIABILITIES

A variety of current liabilities result from an accrual entry at the end of the fiscal year. These accruals are made to achieve the accounting objective of matching revenues and expenses in the appropriate accounting period. They consist of accruals for wages, warranties, utilities, property taxes, payroll taxes, income taxes, and professional service contracts. For the most part, these accrued expenses are normally processed through the cash disbursements or other internal control systems. For example, wage expense is created and controlled through the payroll internal control system, which is discussed in Chapter 16. Utilities are paid and controlled through the cash disbursements internal control system. Thus routine transactions are controlled through the appropriate control system, but these systems are not designed to generate accruals at the end of the accounting period. The client's accounting staff makes an analysis of the data and generates the normal year-end adjusting journal entries. These entries result in an additional amount of expense being recognized and the creation of a short-term accrued liability account.

Since the internal control systems that process the routine transactions associated with accrued liabilities are discussed in other sections of this book, the current discussion is limited to performance of the substantive tests. Furthermore, only a few accrued liability accounts are discussed. Other accounts are encountered by the auditor, but the basic approach is the same. The audit emphasis is on the valuation objective, since the other three objectives are implied by recognition of the need to review the client's accruals. The auditor knows that there are almost always accrued expenses at the end of the year, so that the existence objective is apparent. The objective cutoff is the very essence of year-end accruals and is likewise apparent. Finally, by definition, accrued

484
Audit of liabilities:
current, contingent,
and long-term

expenses are disclosed and classified as current liabilities. This leaves valuation as the focal point of the audit of accruals, since the audit exposure centers around determination of the appropriate amount for the adjusting journal entry.

Accrued wages

Many organizations pay their employees in a manner that does not result in a payment on the last day of the fiscal year. Obviously, they need to make an adjusting journal entry to reflect the days worked by employees but not paid by the organization. The client may accumulate time cards and other work schedule documentation and make a detail analysis in determining the accrued liability. Alternatively, the client in most cases makes an estimate of the needed adjustment by relating the number of days unpaid to the normal dollar amount of the payroll. With this approach the auditor reviews the analysis for reasonableness rather than for penny accuracy. The number of days unpaid is verified by the auditor's knowledge of routine paydays and the counting of days since the last payment date. This of course is an extremely simple task for the auditor; however, he or she is careful to determine that the current pay period is not unusual for some reason. For example, if a significant amount of overtime has been worked during the current pay period, a simple pro rata amount of previous payrolls results in an understatement of the accrual. A review of production reports and time cards, and discussions with company personnel, are usually sufficient to determine the characteristics of the current pay period. Finally, the subsequent payroll costs are reviewed by the auditor and compared to previous payroll amounts.

Accrued warranty costs

Some companies sell their products with a commitment that certain repairs or replacements will be made within a stated period of time. To achieve the accounting objective of matching revenues and expenses, a provision for future warranty costs for current sales is made. Since the provision is an estimate, the auditor's review of the accrued liability is concerned with the reasonableness of the provision. In most cases the provision is simply a percentage of sales for a particular period. This percentage is the result of a historical analysis of the warranty cost. The auditor reviews this analysis, making tests where appropriate. Once he or she is satisfied with the historical percentage, the auditor remains alert to any changes that may have occurred in the current year that would have an impact upon the percentage. For example, changes in the warranty contract or the use of inferior goods must be evaluated by the auditor.

If the auditor accepts the warranty cost percentage, a simple recomputation is made using the percentage and sales made under the warranty agreement. If the client sells many products, some under warranty contracts and some not, the auditor reviews and tests the sales analysis made by product or product line. Charges against the accrued liability accounts made during the current year are tested. This involves a review of specific warranty claims, work orders, and relief of inventory for the replacement of parts or the entire unit.

Accrued utility costs

At the close of the fiscal year there are often various services that have been consumed by the client but have been neither paid for nor billed at that date. Among these items are telephone service, electricity and other fuel costs, and water and sewerage charges. In most cases these bills are received and paid in the month after the close of the fiscal year. When the cutoff date for the bill coincides with the last day of the fiscal year, the total amount of the bill is included as part of the accrued utility costs. When the two dates do not agree, an allocation of the cost is made. The auditor vouches the payment and reviews the allocation to see if it is reasonable. The allocation basis is usually a function of the number of days worked before and after the close of the fiscal year. Again, the auditor is not concerned with penny accuracy but rather with the reasonableness of the appropriation.

CONTINGENT LIABILITIES

FASB Statement No. 5, "Accounting for Contingencies," defines a contingency as follows:

> . . . an existing condition, situation, or set of circumstances involving uncertainty as to possible gain . . . or loss . . . to an enterprise that will ultimately be resolved when one or more future events occur or fail to occur.[1]

Although this statement refers to contingency gain, such gains are not recognized under current accounting principles, since to do so violates the realization concept. On the other hand, contingency losses may result in an adjusting journal entry or may require adequate disclosure in a footnote to the financial statements. Examples of contingency losses include pending or threatened litigation, endorsements on discounted notes, repurchase commitments, potential income tax assessments, and product warranty costs. The last item was discussed in the previous section and described as an estimated liability; however, *FASB Statement No. 5* classifies product warranty costs as contingent items.

Existence and cutoff

As suggested above there is a variety of contingent liabilities. The first step in the audit of these contingencies is to identify the existence of such contingencies at the balance sheet date. Unlike the situation in auditing other accounts, there is no list or control grouping which may be used as the starting point. On the contrary, contingent items may be associated with assets such as discounted notes receivable, liabilities such as pending assessments by the IRS, or executory contracts such as raw material purchase commitments. Thus the auditor is aware of the possibility of the existence of contingencies in the audit of all accounts

---

[1] "Accounting for Contingencies," *FASB Statement No. 5* (Stamford, Conn., FASB, 1975), p. 1.

486
**Audit of liabilities:
current, contingent,
and long-term**

and in the review of all contracts. Some of the more typical and standard audit procedures performed in the audit of contingencies are:

- Obtain a legal letter from each attorney employed by the client as outside counsel.
- Review the minutes of the board of directors meetings and other important committees.
- Review contract commitments.
- Review reports prepared by IRS agents since completion of the previous year's audit.

LEGAL LETTER

The independent auditor does not possess the legal expertise to evaluate the existence of and the possible loss from litigation. For this reason he or she relies heavily upon management as the primary source of information concerning litigation and potential litigation and upon the opinion of outside counsel. *SAS No. 12* suggests that the following procedures be followed in this situation:

- Inquire of and discuss with management the policies and procedures adopted for identifying, evaluating, and auditing for litigation, claims, and assessments.
- Obtain from management a description and evaluation of litigation, claims, and assessments that existed at the date of the balance sheet being reported on, and during the period from the balance sheet date to the date the information is furnished, including identification of those matters referred to legal counsel, and obtain assurances from management, ordinarily in writing, that they have discarded all such matters required to be disclosed by Statement of Financial Accounting Standards No. 5.
- Examine documents in the client's possession concerning litigation, claims, and assessments, including correspondence and invoices from lawyers.
- Obtain assurance from management, ordinarily in writing, that they have disclosed all unasserted claims that the lawyer has advised them are probable of assertion and must be disclosed in accordance with Statement of Financial Accounting Standards No. 5. Also the auditor, with the client's permission, should inform the lawyer that the client has given the auditor this assurance. This client representation may be communicated by the client in the inquiry letter or by the auditor in a separate letter.[2]

The above assertions by management must be corroborated. Generally, statements made by the client's in-house counsel are not considered competent evidential matter. If the client does not use outside counsel, the auditor may hire a lawyer. *SAS No. 11,* "Using the Work of a Specialist," which was discussed in Chapter 9, provides guidelines for such an approach. When the client employs outside counsel, the auditor sends a letter of audit inquiry to the lawyer which encompasses, but is not limited to, the following items:

---

[2] *SAS No. 12,* "Inquiry of a Client's Lawyer Concerning Litigation, Claims, and Assessments," (New York: AICPA, 1976), pp. 2–3. Copyright © 1976 by the American Institute of Certified Public Accountants, Inc.

a. Identification of the company, including subsidiaries, and the date of the examination.
b. A list prepared by management (or a request by management that the lawyer prepare a list) that describes and evaluates pending or threatened litigation, claims, and assessments with respect to which the lawyer has been engaged and to which he has devoted substantive attention on behalf of the company in the form of legal consultation or representation.
c. A list prepared by management that describes and evaluates unasserted claims and assessments that management considers to be probable of assertion, and that, if asserted, would have at least a reasonable possibility of an unfavorable outcome, with respect to which the lawyer has been engaged and to which he has devoted substantive attention on behalf of the company in the form of legal consultation or representation.
d. As to each matter listed in item B, a request that the lawyer either furnish the following information or comment on those matters as to which his views may differ from those stated by management, as appropriate:
   (1) A description of the nature of the matter, the progress of the case to date, and the action the company intends to take (for example, to contest the matter vigorously or to seek an out-of-court settlement).
   (2) An evaluation of the likelihood of an unfavorable outcome and an estimate, if one can be made, of the amount or range of potential loss.
   (3) With respect to a list prepared by management, an identification of the omission of any pending or threatened litigation, claims, and assessments or a statement that the list of such matters is complete.
e. As to each matter listed in item C, a request that the lawyer comment on those matters as to which his views concerning the description or evaluation of the matter may differ from that stated by management.
f. A statement by the client that the client understands that whenever, in the course of performing legal services for the client with respect to a matter recognized to involve an unasserted possible claim or assessment that may call for financial statement disclosure, the lawyer has formed a professional conclusion that the client should disclose or consider disclosure concerning such possible claim or assessment, the lawyers, as a matter of professional responsibility to the client, will so advise the client and will consult with the client concerning the question of such disclosure and the applicable requirements of Statement of Financial Accounting Standards No. 5.
g. A request that the lawyer confirm whether the understanding described in item f is correct.
h. A request that the lawyer specifically identify the nature of and reasons for any limitation on his response.[3]

The legal profession, through the board of governors of the American Bar Association, approved a document entitled "Statement of Policy Regarding Lawyers' Responses to Auditors' Requests for Information."[4] The guidelines set forth in this document are consistent with the guidelines established in *SAS No. 12*. In most cases the auditor views the legal letter as very competent

[3] Ibid, pp. 4–5.
[4] Reproduced in *SAS No. 12*, see pp. 19–42.

488
Audit of liabilities: current, contingent, and long-term

evidential matter. Therefore it is important that he or she understand clearly the financial reporting responsibilities mandated by *FASB Statement No. 5*.

REVIEW MINUTES

In the auditor's search for loss contingencies, the minutes of meetings of stockholders, the board of directors, and other key corporate committees are reviewed. During these proceedings it is likely that loss contingencies are discussed. References to pending litigation, certain contract provisions, or possible tax assessments are noted by the auditor. Such references are subsequently followed up through the use of other audit procedures to determine if the items are to be disclosed. The auditor's review of the minutes for these groups is not confined to the meetings held during the current year under audit but rather includes any meetings held subsequent to the balance sheet date but before the sign-off date of the report.

REVIEW CONTRACTS

A loss contingency due to the loss or impairment of an asset or the incurrence of a liability may result from a variety of contractural arrangements. However, in most instances the loss contingency arising from a contract is related to purchases and sales contracts. The auditor reviews these contracts carefully, perhaps with the aid of an independently contracted lawyer or other expert, to see if a loss contingency exists. Such contingencies include:

- Unfilled purchase commitments at a price in excess of market price at the balance sheet date
- Unfilled sales commitments at prices expected to result in a loss when delivery is made
- Agreements to repurchase property that has been sold
- Long-term construction contracts estimated to result in a loss

The auditor, upon review of the contract, evaluates sufficient evidential matter to determine whether a loss contingency exists. For example, for long-term construction contracts the auditor tests the buildup of cost accumulated. Also, he or she verifies estimates of future costs by referring to engineering and accounting reports. If the auditor believes the contract to be material it may be necessary to employ outside experts to validate cost estimates and the stage of completion of the item.

Loss contingencies arise from other contracts. Prominent among these are contingencies arising from the client's guarantee of indebtedness of others. Examples are the sale of accounts or other receivables with recourse and the guarantee of a leveraged lease where the client, acting as a lessee, guarantees a loan acquired by the lessor. The auditor notes these commitments as the contract is reviewed.

REVIEW OF REVENUE AGENT'S REPORT

There are many areas of tax law that remain ambiguous and subject to a variety of interpretations. The auditor reviews carefully the income tax provi-

sions, but the proper reporting of revenues and expenses may still remain **489**
uncertain. In most instances, these areas of controversy are not resolved until
Contingent liabilities
two or more years after the tax return is filed. Formally, this is accomplished by
the government's preparation and submission to the client of a revenue agent
report. Of course, the client may disagree with the government's findings, and
the disagreement may be appealed through the administrative court system as
well as the regular court system. Nonetheless, the auditor reviews the revenue
agent's report to determine if there is a loss contingency applicable to previous
years as well as to years subsequent to the period covered by the revenue agent's
report. If the assessment is not contested, the auditor, perhaps with the assistance
of a tax specialist with the firm of auditors, determines the total impact of the
ruling. However, if the assessment is contested, the auditor relies upon the
attorney's legal letter as well as the opinion of the tax experts employed by the
audit firm.

Valuation, classification, and disclosure

Having established the existence of a loss contingency at the balance sheet date
the auditor must determine the appropriate disclosure of the item on the financial
statements. *FASB Standard No. 5* states that an adjustment to income through
an accrual must be made if both of the following conditions are met:

- Information available prior to issuance of the financial statements indicates that
  it is probable that an asset had been impaired or a liability had been incurred at the
  date of the financial statements. It is implicit in this condition that it must be
  probable that one or more future events will occur confirming the fact of the loss.
- The amount of loss can be reasonably estimated.[5]

When one or both of the above conditions are not met, the loss contingency is
disclosed in a footnote or by the use of a parenthetical comment, if there is a
reasonable possibility that a loss has been incurred.

Differentiating between the need for an accrual entry for the loss contingency
and the need for disclosure in a footnote is no easy task. *FASB Standard No. 5*
attempted to establish a subjective frequency distribution for classifying and
accounting for a loss contingency. A summarization of this approach is presented
in Figure 14-2. By referring to this figure it can be seen that the statement defines
these key terms (''probable,'' ''reasonably possible,'' and ''remote''), but that
these definitions are too general to be helpful in a specific situation. Furthermore,
the amount of data the auditor can evaluate probably is very limited for such an
event. Thus the professional judgment of the auditor and perhaps the advice of
legal counsel are the dominant factors in determining the appropriate disclosure
of loss contingencies.

Because of the uncertainty and the inability to collect sufficient evidential
matter when loss contingencies arise, the auditor evaluates the impact of these
items on his or her report. If material, loss contingencies which cannot be

[5]''Accounting for Contingencies,'' *FASB Statement No. 5* (Stamford, Conn.: FASB, 1975), p. 4.

490
Audit of liabilities: current, contingent, and long-term

Figure 14-2

SUBJECTIVE PROBABILITY OF EVENT'S OCCURRENCE	DEFINITION PER FASB STANDARD NO. 5	ACCOUNTING TREATMENT	EXAMPLES
Probable	The future event or events are likely to occur.	Accrual of loss with appropriate explanation when the amount can be reasonably estimated. When an amount cannot be estimated, the loss contingency is disclosed in a footnote.	Estimated losses from foreign government's expropriation of a subsidiary's assets, where expropriation is imminent.
Reasonably possible	The chance of the future event occurring is more than remote but less than likely.	Loss is disclosed in a footnote stating the nature of the item and an estimate of the loss or possible range of the loss, or a statement that an estimate cannot be made.	Unresolved disagreements with the IRS.
Remote	The chance of the future event or events occurring is slight.	No accrual or disclosure is required.*	General business risks.

FASB Statement No. 5 notes that "certain loss contingencies are presently being disclosed in financial statements even though the possibility of loss may be remote. . . . Examples include (a) guarantees of indebtedness of others, (2) obligations of commercial banks under 'standby letters of credit,' and (c) guarantees to repurchase receivables (or in some cases, to repurchase the related property) that have been sold or otherwise assigned . . . the Board concludes that disclosure of those loss contingencies, and others that in substance have the same characteristics, shall be continued." "Accounting for Contingencies," *FASB Statement No. 5* (Stamford, Conn.: FASB, 1975), p. 6.

quantified may result in the issuance of a qualified opinion or a disclaimer. Report modifications due to uncertainties are discussed in depth in Chapter 17.

LONG-TERM LIABILITIES

The phrase "long-term liabilities" is used to identify obligations whose liquidation does not require the use of resources properly classified as current assets. Examples of long-term liabilities include mortgages, bonds, and notes payable. These forms of financing are discussed in this section of the chapter. Other forms of long-term liabilities, such as obligations based on pension agreements or capitalized leases, are beyond the scope of this book.

INTERNAL CONTROL MODEL

Transactions involving forms of long-term debt often significantly impact an organization's financial statements. The relative dollar value of the tranaction may be large, and there may be restrictions in the debt agreement that prohibit certain actions on the part of the organization. From the client's perspective, it is necessary to design an internal control system that closely reviews such transactions before they are approved. On the other hand, the auditor recognizes the need for strong internal control procedures in this area in order to be reasonably sure that significant unrecorded long-term liabilities do not exist and that important contractual restrictions imposed by the debt agreements, such as the payment of dividends, are adequately disclosed in the financial statements. An internal control system for long-term debt which meets the objectives of both the client and the auditor recognizes the need for an adequate plan of organization and an appropriate system of authorization and accountability.

Plan of organization

DEPARTMENTAL AUTONOMY

Once again, the key element in an adequate organizational scheme is the design and observance of the concept of departmental autonomy. The design of departmental autonomy is reflected in the organizational structure of the client as evidenced by the formal organizational chart and job descriptions. To complete the model system, the organization on a day-to-day basis needs to observe the autonomy of each department. Management intervention that circumvents the organizational structure cannot be tolerated. Listed here are the typical duties assigned to each department in a well-designed organization:

I. Accounting department
   1. Maintenance of accounting records, such as bond ledgers, that reveal the details of transactions and the holders of debt
   2. Maintenance of the general ledger
   3. Review of and accounting for all cash disbursements for payment of interest, repayment of principal, or early retirement of debt
   4. Review of and accounting for all cash receipts from the issuance of debt
II. Treasurer
   1. Custody control over cash, including proceeds from the issuance of long-term debt
   2. Signing and distributing of checks for payment of interest, repayment of principal, or early retirement of debt
III. Functions other than accounting and treasurer
   1. Authorization for the issuance of long-term debt, including interest rates, repayment schedules, conversion privileges, and covenants (board of directors)
   2. Authorization for the retirement or refinancing of long-term debt (board of directors)

System of authorization and accountability

EXECUTION OF TRANSACTIONS

The execution of a transaction involves the exchange of assets between two or more parties. In the area of long-term debt the transaction is executed in two

492
**Audit of liabilities:
current, contingent,
and long-term**

separate stages. In the first stage it is authorized, and subsequent to authorization it is carried out in a manner consistent with the authorization.

Authorization of transactions: Because of the potential for individual transactions involving long-term debt, the authorization for the transaction is explicit. The issuance of long-term debt is authorized by the board of directors, and its action is documented in the minutes of the meetings. The board's resolution usually refers to the terms of the debt, including the face amount, stated interest rate, and repayment strategy. Other factors, such as the means of marketing the debt, may be discussed. The resolution becomes the basis upon which the debt arrangements are made, and significant variations from the original resolution are submitted to the board for acceptance or rejection.

In the issuance of long-term debt the retirement date or repayment schedule is approved by the board of directors, and no other action on its part is needed at the maturity date of the debt. However, often debt agreements contain clauses whereby debt may be retired early or the repayment modified. In some instances the debt may be refinanced, or terms of the debt may be changed in the case of troubled debt restructuring. In the latter examples, since the original authorization by the board of directors did not approve the modification, the board is required to authorize the deviations before the change occurs. Again, such action is detailed in the minutes of the meeting of the board of directors.

Performance of debt commitments: Once the board of directors authorizes the issuance of long-term debt, it is the responsibility of the treasurer to market the debt and to fulfill the periodic commitments imposed by the debt agreement. The treasurer may obtain a creditor or creditors by negotiating the loan with a financial institution or issuance of the debt through a public sale. In the latter case, the treasurer's responsibilities include the preparation, in conjunction with the accounting department, of appropriate regulation statements required by the SEC or other regulatory authorities. After issuance of the debt, the treasurer's duties include the periodic payment of interest and principal in accordance with the debt agreement. In addition, the bond indenture may require that a sinking fund be established, in which case it is the duty of the treasurer to plan and make the periodic sinking fund payments.

RECORDING OF TRANSACTIONS

The recording of long-term transactions includes the initial journalization of issuance of the debt, interest payments and amortization of debt discount or premium. These duties rest with the accounting department. The initial issuance of the debt and the cash proceeds are recorded by the accounting department after it receives a copy of the board of director's resolution concerning the debt and the details of the actual placement of the debt are received from the treasurer. In a similar manner, early retirements of debt or the refinancing of debt is recorded by the accounting department upon receipt of the authorization from the board of directors and the detail data prepared by the treasurer's department. The initial sale and unusual retirement of debt are infrequent; however, there are transactions associated with long-term debt that are more recurring. The internal control system is somewhat dependent upon the nature of the debt. For this reason, control procedures for bonds, mortgages, and long-term notes are discussed separately.

Bonds: The internal control system for bonds depends upon the client's use of an independent registrar and transfer agent. These functions are usually performed by a financial institution. The purpose of an independent registrar is to determine that the amount of the bond issuance conforms to the board of directors' resolution and the bond indenture agreement. Thus it is the task of the registrar to see that each new bond certificate redeemed is canceled. The transfer agent's task is to record the sale of bonds between bondholders after the initial placement of the debt. Since bonds exchange hands on the open market, the client must know who owns the bonds at particular dates. Obviously, this relieves the client of a tremendous amount of clerical work if the bonds are actively traded. Also, the transfer agent usually acts as an interest-paying agent, so that the client draws only one check, payable to the transfer agent, at an interest payment date. The accounting department prepares the payment voucher based on data supplied by the registrar or transfer agent, and the treasurer signs the check after an appropriate review.

If the client operates as its own registrar and transfer agent, additional duties are imposed on the secretary of the corporation and the accounting department. The secretary's duties include custody control of all unissued bond certificates and a list of bonds issued, including the name of the bondholder, amount, and bond certificate number. If bonds are retired, it is the responsibility of the secretary to void or otherwise cancel the bond certificate. Basically the secretary functions as the independent registrar and, not surprisingly, the accounting department functions as the transfer agent. Specifically, the accounting department maintains the bond ledger, which lists the individual bondholders by accumulating the amount of the holdings of each bondholder on one ledger card. As sales and acquisitions occur among bondholders, the ledger cards are updated. At an interest date the accounting department prepares a voucher supported by a detailed list of bondholders and the interest due them, which is sent to the treasurer for preparation and mailing of the check. In addition, the secretary informs the treasurer of the total amount of bonds outstanding, which serves as a check against the data generated in the accounting department.

Mortgages: The internal control procedures for recording periodic mortgage payments are similar to those for any recurring cash disbursement. The accounting department prepares a mortgage voucher, probably on a monthly basis, which is sent to the treasurer. In the treasurer's department, the voucher is reviewed by comparing the payment request with the mortgate repayment schedule. If the amount is proper, the check is prepared, signed by the treasurer or other designated officer of the corporation, and mailed directly to the financial institution. The canceled voucher is returned to the accounting department for recording in the voucher register or cash disbursements journal.

494
Audit of liabilities: current, contingent, and long-term

Notes: Long-term notes refer to sources of general financing for the client. Trade notes payable, specifically used to finance the purchase of inventory, are short-term liabilities and are audited in the same way as trade accounts payable, the subject of the first part of this chapter. Once a long-term note is approved, the proceeds and the details of the note are recorded by the accounting department in a subsidiary ledger. The custody control of a copy of the note and of all unissued notes belongs to the secretary. In most cases a note calls for a single payment which includes the principal and interest. At this date, the accounting department prepares a voucher which is directed to the treasurer. The treasurer's department prepares, signs, and mails the check. The canceled note is returned by the holder and retained by the corporate secretary.

The above discussion of bonds, mortgages, and notes involved transactions that were the result of a cash receipt or a cash disbursement. Other noncash transactions are recorded and are the responsibility of the accounting department. For example, it may be necessary to accrue interest at the end of the accounting period, record the amortization of the bond discount or premium, or reclassify the current portion of long-term debt. The accounting department prepares these entries as part of the internal analysis of all accounting records, which results in adjusting journal entries.

STUDY AND EVALUATION

As in any internal control system, the auditor is required to evaluate the strengths and weaknesses of the system. In the long-term debt internal control system, the number of transactions processed tends to be relatively small, but they are often significant. In addition, the system is not complex and easily documented and understood. These factors result in an approach slightly different from the one described for previous accounts. First, since the system is rather simple, the extent of its documentation is usually limited to the preparation of an internal control questionnaire. An example of a questionnaire is presented in Figure 14-3. More importantly, the percentage of transactions tested is great, often 100 percent, since the dollar amounts involved are usually large. There is less of a differentiation between the compliance and substantive tests, and the following discussion emphasizes the point by combining the tests under one topic.

COMPLIANCE AND SUBSTANTIVE TESTS

In the audit of long-term debt, the auditor is still concerned with the familar objectives—existence, valuation, cutoff, and disclosure. An audit program that incorporates these four objectives is presented in Figure 14-4.

Existence and cutoff

An initial step in the audit of long-term debt is the preparation of an account analysis detailing the activity in the account for the current year. Balances at the beginning of the year are traced to the previous year's working papers. In the

Figure 14-3

Internal Control Questionnaire

	Answer		Answer based on		
Long-term Debt	Yes	No	Inquiry	Observation	Comments

1. Answer the following:
  a. Does the client employ an independent registrar?
  b. Does the client employ a transfer agent?					

2. If not —
  a. are unissued bonds, etc., prenumbered and in the hands of the the secretary?
  b. is a separate interest bank account maintained on an imprest basis?
  c. If a separate bank account is maintained, is proper internal control maintained in reconciling the bank account and in preparing, signing, and distributing the checks?					

3. Does the board of directors authorize borrowings?					
4. Are detailed registers for debt kept by employees who are not authorized to sign checks or debt agreements?					
5. Are registers balanced to the general ledger on a periodic basis?					
6. Are paid notes and cancelled bonds marked appropriately and retained by the secretary?					

case of a first-year audit, all debt transactions that impact the current financial statements are reviewed similarly to current year charges, which are described in the following discussion.

ADDITIONS

For new debt issued during the current accounting period, the auditor examines the minutes of the board of directors' meetings to determine that the transaction was authorized. The terms of the debt, as approved by the board of directors, are traced to the debt agreement. A copy of the debt agreement or a summary of important facts of the agreement is obtained by the auditor and placed in the permanent file of working papers. By referring to the board's action and the terms of the debt agreement, the auditor verifies the transaction by tracing the cash receipts to the cash records and the bank statement. In addition, comparison of the cash proceeds and the debt agreement is the basis for identifying the existence of a discount or a premium account or issuance cost that is capitalized as a deferred cost.

DELETIONS

Any reduction in debt outstanding during the year is audited in much the same way as debt additions. The authorization for the eventual retirement of

496
Audit of liabilities:
current, contingent,
and long-term

Figure 14-4

Audit program: long-term debt

PROCEDURES	DATE COMPLETED	WORK PERFORMED BY
1. Obtain an analysis of the long-term debt accounts.	_____	_____
2. Verify changes in the above accounts for the current year.	_____	_____
3. For outstanding debt, request confirmation of principal, maturity dates, date on which interest is paid, and other pertinent information.	_____	_____
4. Account for treasury bond certificates at the balance sheet date by inspection or by confirmation.	_____	_____
5. Determine that debt and related accruals are reported in the proper amount.	_____	_____
6. Determine the company's compliance with requirements specified in the long-term debt agreement.	_____	_____

debt is usually contained in the original resolution adopted by the board of directors. Also, the maturity date(s) are reflected in the debt agreement itself. These sources are reviewed by the auditor to determine that the transaction is executed as authorized. In the case of long-term notes or bonded debt, the auditor reviews the canceled note or bond certificate. For a mortgage, the mortgage repayment schedule and the periodic voucher prepared as a basis for the payment are examined. Finally, the cash disbursement is traced to the respective canceled check and bank statement.

In some cases debt may be retired before its maturity date. For example, bonds may be callable at a premium during a period of time designated by the bond agreement. The auditor traces such retirements to authorization granted by the board of directors and to the debt agreement to make sure the debt retirement is not in violation of corporate policy or the specific debt instrument. The cash disbursement for the retirement is traced by the auditor to the cash records and the bank statement. In addition, the book value of the debt at the time of retirement is compared to the cash disbursement to determine if a gain or loss on the retirement is appropriate.

CONFIRMATION

The auditor's use of corroborative evidence in the examination of long-term debt is not limited to internal documents. Details of the debt agreement are confirmed with the debt holder. In a letter prepared and signed by the client but mailed and otherwise controlled by the auditor, the following information at the date of the balance sheet is confirmed.

- Amount of debt held
- Stated interest rate
- Maturity date(s)
- Any interest or principal payments in arrears
- Any amendments to the original debt agreement

If the debt is registered, such as a bonded debt, the total amount of the debt outstanding is confirmed by the auditor. If no independent registrar is used, the

auditor is restricted to the review of internal documents accounting records. He **497**
or she reconciles the subsidiary ledger that shows the ownership of the bonds Valuation
with the control amount in the general ledgers. In addition, the unissued bond
certificates are reviewed and, by using data obtained from the printer, the auditor
determines the number of bond certificates issued. If bonds are held in the
treasury, but not retired, the auditor inspects them at the balance sheet date.
Treasury bonds held by a trustee are confirmed by the auditor.

VALUATION

APB Opinion No. 21 states that a note or similar instrument issued for cash is
to be recorded at the present value of the future cash flows. In determining
present value the cash flows are discounted at an appropriate market value rate
of interest. The auditor's most difficult problem in determining the value of the
debt at issuance date is verification of the market interest rate. If the debt is sold
in an established market, there are no grave problems, since the market forces
the debt to be sold at the market rate of interest by exchanging it at a discount
or premium. If an established market does not exist, the auditor evaluates the
appropriateness of the stated interest rate, taking into consideration "the credit
standing of the issues, restrictive covenants, the collateral, payment and other
terms pertaining to the debt, and, if appropriate, the tax consequences of the
buyer and seller."[6] To substantiate the interest rate, the auditor's working papers
document the procedures adopted to verify the interest rate.

The valuation of debt is further complicated if the exchange involves property,
goods, or services. It is the responsibility of the board of directors to assign a
value to the debt if the exchange is not restricted to the receipt of cash. However,
audit verification extends beyond the review of the board's action in such cases.
Generally accepted accounting principles require that such a transaction be
"recorded at the fair value of the property, goods, or service or at an amount
that reasonably approximates the market value of the note, whichever is the
more clearly determinable."[7] To validate such fair market values, the auditor
may find it necessary to use the services of an independent expert.

In the case of long-term debt, valuation is a verification problem for the
auditor at the transaction date. Conventional accounting rules do not require
determination of the present value of the debt at subsequent balance sheet dates.
Even in the case of modification of the debt agreement in a troubled debt
restructuring, the debtor does not change the carrying value of the debt unless
the total future cash payments, including interest, are less than the carrying
value of the debt.[8] Thus in most cases, the auditor simply tests the mathematical
calculation for amortization of the premium or discount account. Also, other
accounts related to the debt are reviewed for proper evaluation at the balance
sheet date. Prepaid interest or accrued interest payable is reviewed by the

[6] "Interest on Receivables and Payables," *APB Opinion No. 21* (New York: AICPA, 1971),
p. 42.

[7] *Ibid.,* p. 421.

[8] "Accounting by Debtors and Creditors for Troubled Debts Restructuring," *FASB Statement
No. 15* (Stamford, Conn.: FASB, 1977), p. 7.

498
Audit of liabilities: current, contingent, and long-term

auditor. By reference to the debt agreement and the last payment made, he or she determines if these amounts are properly stated.

DISCLOSURE

Basic information concerning long-term debt is disclosed on the financial statements. Such items as the maturity date, face value, interest rate, discount, and premium are shown on the face of the financial statement, in parenthetical comments, or in footnotes to the statements. Restrictions that may be useful to financial statement users are required to be disclosed. These may include dividend restrictions or working capital maintenance requirements. The basic characteristics of the debt, as well as special restrictions or other covenants, are determined by the auditor's reading of the debt agreement. A special consideration occurs when the client is in violation of debt covenants. If significant, these violations are disclosed in a footnote to the financial statements. Violations that result in uncertainties as to the continued existence of the corporation are considered for their potential impact on the auditor's report. Such report modifications are discussed in Chapter 17.

Included as an element of disclosure is the classification of long-term debt. Obviously, long-term debt is classified as a noncurrent liability. For debt that matures within the company's operating cycle or a year, whichever is longer, a current classification is required. The auditor's reference to the maturity date per the date agreement and the creditor's confirmation letter is the basis for classifying the debt. However, in some instances current-maturing debt may be classified with long-term debt when there is a refinancing of a short-term obligation on a long-term basis. FASB Standard No. 6 provides for such an approach, assuming the client's intent is to refinance the maturing debt on a long-term basis and the interest is supported by either (1) a post-balance-sheet-date issuance of a long-term obligation or equity securities for the purpose of refinancing the short-term debt, or (2) a refinancing agreement signed by the client and a third party that allows the client to refinance the debt. In the latter case, all of the following conditions must be met:

1. The agreement does not expire within one year (or operating cycle . . .) from the date of the enterprise's balance sheet, and during that period the agreement is not cancelable by the lender or investor (and obligations incurred under the agreement are not callable during that period) except for violation of a provision with which compliance is objectively determinable or measureable.
2. No violation of any provision in the financing agreement exists at the balance-sheet date, and no available information indicates that a violation has occurred thereafter but prior to the issuance of the balance sheet, or, if one exists at the balance sheet date or has occurred thereafter, a waiver has been obtained.
3. The lender or prospective lender or investor with which the enterprise has entered into the financing agreement is expected to be financially capable of honoring the agreement.[9]

---

[9] *FASB Standard No. 6,* Classification of Short-Term Obligations Expected to Be Refinanced, (Stamford, Conn.: FASB, 1977), pp. 5–6. Copyright © 1977 the Financial Accounting Standards Board, High Ridge Park, Stamford, Connecticut 06905, U.S.A. Reprinted with permission. Copies of the complete document are available from the FASB.

Verification of the post-balance-sheet issuance of debt is determined by the auditor's inspection of the records, bank statement, refinancing agreement, and the board of directors' refinancing resolution. If the actual cash is not received prior to issuance of the financial statements, the auditor reads the refinancing agreement to see if it meets the guidelines of *FASB Standard No. 6*. In determining if the prospective lender is financially sound, the auditor may refer to the general reputation of an established financial institution. In the absence of such an institution, it may be necessary to obtain the financial statements of the prospective lender or evaluations from financial rating services.

EXERCISES AND PROBLEMS

14-1. The substantive tests for accounts payable may be performed at an interim date or after the balance sheet date. Do you agree?

14-2. When an auditor uses the confirmation technique, it is necessary to select items from the audit population. How does the selection of accounts payable differ from the selection of accounts receivable?

14-3. Must accounts payable be confirmed? Explain.

14-4. In the auditor's application of the search for unrecorded liabilities, what sources of evidence are used?

14-5. Why is it more difficult to audit an estimated liability as opposed to a trade accounts payable?

14-6. Define a contingency. Is the auditor concerned with contingent losses or contingent gains?

14-7. What is the purpose of a legal letter? What is its content?

14-8. What procedures are employed by the auditor to determine whether a loss contingency from a lawsuit should be disclosed on the financial statements?

14-9. Describe the internal control model for long-term liabilities.

14-10. Comment on the following statement:

> In most audits accounts payable are not confirmed. It seems logical that this would also be true of long-term liabilities.

14-11. How does the audit approach for trade accounts payable differ from the approach for long-term liabilities?

14-12. Is there ever a valuation problem with long-term liabilities?

14-13. If a client violates a debt agreement which results in the possibility that the creditor may call the debt, what type of opinion should be issued by the auditor?

14-14. The accounting and internal control procedures relating to purchases of materials by the Branden Company, a medium-sized concern manufacturing special machinery to order, have been described by your junior accountant in the following terms:

> After approval by manufacturing department supervisors, material purchase requisitions are forwarded to the purchasing department supervisor who distributes such requisitions to the several department employees. These employees prepare prenumbered purchase orders in triplicate, account for all numbers, and send the original purchase order to the vendor. One

500
Audit of liabilities:
current, contingent,
and long-term

copy of the purchase order is sent to the receiving department where it is used as a receiving report. The other copy is filed in the purchasing department.

When the materials are received, they are moved directly to the storeroom and issued to the supervisor on informal requests. The receiving department sends a receiving report (with its copy of the purchase order attached) to the purchasing department and sends copies of the receiving report to the storeroom and to the accounting department.

Vendors' invoices for material purchases, received in duplicate in the mail room, are sent to the purchasing department and directed to the employee who placed the related order. The employee then compares the invoice with the copy of the purchase order on file in the purchasing department for price and terms and compares the invoice quantity with the quantity received as reported by the shipping and receiving department on its copy of the purchase order. The purchasing department employee also checks discounts, footings, and extensions and initials the invoice to indicate approval for payment. The invoice is then sent to the voucher section of the accounting department, where it is coded for account distribution, assigned a voucher number, entered in the voucher register, and filed according to payment due date.

On payment dates prenumbered checks are requisitioned by the voucher section from the cashier and prepared except for signature. After the checks are prepared they are returned to the cashier, who puts them through a check-signing machine, accounts for the sequence of numbers, and passes them to the cash disbursement bookkeeper for entry in the cash disbursements book. The cash disbursements bookkeeper then returns them to the voucher section which then notes payment dates in the voucher register, places the checks in envelopes, and sends them to the mail room. The vouchers are then filed in numerical sequence. At the end of each month one of the voucher clerks prepares an adding machine tape of unpaid items in the voucher register and compares the total thereof with the general ledger balance and investigates any difference disclosed by such comparison.

Required: Discuss the weaknesses, if any, in the internal control of Branden's purchasing and subsequent procedures and suggest supplementary or revised procedures for remedying each weakness with regard to

1. Requisition of materials
2. Receipt and storage of materials
3. Functions of the purchasing department
4. Functions of the accounting department (AICPA Adapted)

14-15. For each of the following liabilities, prepare a set of audit procedures to determine whether each is properly stated at the balance sheet date:

1. Accrued salaries and wages
2. Unclaimed wages
3. Accrued vacation pay
4. Excess of pension cost over amounts funded
5. Accrued property taxes
6. Accrued interest payable
7. Obligations under capital leases, long-term
8. Obligations under capital leases, short-term

14-16. When you arrive at your client's office on January 11, 1981, to begin the December 31, 1980 audit, you discover the client had been drawing checks as creditors' invoices became due but not necessarily mailing them. Because of a working capital shortage some checks may have been held for two or three weeks.

The client informs you that unmailed checks totaling $27,600 were on hand on December 31, 1980. He states that these December-dated checks had been entered in the cash disbursements book and charged to the respective creditors' accounts in December because the checks were prenumbered. Heavy collections permitted him to mail the checks before your arrival.

The client wants to adjust the cash balance and accounts payable on December 31 by $27,600 because the cash account had a credit balance. He objects to submitting to his bank your audit report showing an overdraft of cash.

Required

1. Submit a detailed audit program indicating the procedures you would use to satisfy yourself of the accuracy of the cash balance on the client's statements.

2. Discuss the propriety of reversing the indicated amount of outstanding checks.

(AICPA Adapted)

14-17. You have completed your review of current and long-term liabilities for the Harnow Company. However, during your review of the rent expense account you discover significant payments for the rent of several machines in Harnow's production process. As part of the audit of the rent expense account you examine the rental agreement for the machinery. The agreement is noncancelable and covers the period beginning January 1, 1979, and ending December 31, 1986. Rental payments are to be made on the first day of each year and they amount to $5000 for each of the 30 machines.

After reviewing the rental contract you ask the controller how the eight-year commitment is to be disclosed on the financial statements. The controller states that rent expense will be shown as a separate line item on the income statement because of its size.

Required

1. Have you collected enough evidence to determine whether the controller's suggested disclosure is appropriate? Why?

2. If your answer to part 1 is "no," explain (a) what additional evidence is needed, and (b) how you should collect the evidence.

3. Explain at least three separate disclosure approaches that may be appropriate for rental agreements.

4. It is apparent that you did not discover the disclosure problem during the review of liabilities. Does this suggest that your audit was deficient?

14-18. Compare the confirmation of accounts receivable with the confirmation of accounts payable under the following headings:

1. Generally accepted auditing procedures. (Justify the differences revealed by your comparison.)

2. Form of confirmation requests. (You need not supply examples.) (AICPA Adapted)

14-19. The Moss Company manufactures household appliances that are sold through independent franchised retail dealers. The electric motors in the appliances are guaranteed for five years from the date of sale to the consumer. Under the guaranty defective motors are replaced by the dealers without charge.

Inventories of replacement motors are kept in the dealers' stores and are carried at cost on the Moss Company's records. When the dealer replaces a motor, he or she notifies the factory and returns the defective motor to the factory for reconditioning. After the defective motor is received by the factory, the dealer's account is credited with an agreed-on fee for the replacement service.

When the appliance is brought to the dealer after the guaranty period has elapsed, the dealer charges the owner for installing the new motor. The dealer notifies the factory of the installation and returns the replaced motor for reconditioning. The motor installed is then charged to the dealer's account at a price in excess of its inventory value. In this instance, to encourage the return of replaced motors, the dealer's account is credited with a nominal value for the returned motor.

502
**Audit of liabilities:
current, contingent,
and long-term**

Dealers submit quarterly inventory reports on the motors on hand. These reports are later verified by factory salespeople. Dealers are billed for inventory shortages determined by comparison of the dealers' inventory reports and the factory's perpetual records of the dealers' inventories. The dealers order additional motors as they need them. One motor is used for all appliances in a given year, but the motors are changed in basic design each model year.

The Moss Company has established an account, estimated liability for product guaranties, in connection with the guaranties. An amount representing the estimated guaranty cost prorated per sales unit is credited to the estimated liability account for each appliance sold, and the debit is charged to a provision account. The estimated liability account is debited for the service fees credited to the dealers' accounts and for the inventory cost of the motors installed under the guaranties.

The engineering department keeps statistical records of the number of units of each model sold during each year and the replacements that were made. The effect of improvements in design and construction is under continuous study by this department, and the estimated guaranty cost per unit is adjusted annually on the basis of experience and improvements in design. Experience shows that, for a given motor model, the number of guaranties made good varies widely from year to year during the guaranty period, but that the total number of guaranties to be made good can be reliably predicted.

Required

1. Prepare an audit program to satisfy yourself as to the propriety of the transactions recorded in the estimated liability for product guaranties account for the year ended December 31, 1979.

2. Prepare the work-sheet format that would be used to test the adequacy of the balance in the estimated liability for product guaranties account. The work-sheet column headings should describe clearly the data to be inserted in the columns. (AICPA Adapted)

14-20. You are performing an audit of the Stamper Wholesale Company for the year ended December 31, 1979. Total assets of the company amount to about $10 million, and net assets are about $4 million. On April 6, 1980, a note payable of $700,000 matures. Although the company has the cash to meet the obligation, it has decided to refinance the note over a three-year period, paying $100,000 plus interest on October 1980 and each six months thereafter.

Since the company will not use current assets to meet the original obligation, the controller of the company believes the $700,000 should be listed as a long-term liability. The controller states that two banks have expressed an interest in the refinancing plan and sees no problem in obtaining the required funds.

Required

1. Do you believe the $700,000 debt should be classified as a long-term liability? Explain fully.

2. If the debt is shown as a long-term liability, what information must be disclosed? (AICPA Adapted)

14-21. During your examination of the financial statements of the Gary Manufacturing Company for the year ended December 31, 1979, you find that on January 1, 1979, the company had installed the following punched-card processing system for recording raw material purchases:

1. Vendors' invoices are sent directly to the accounts payable department by the mail department.

2. All supporting documents for the invoices are accumulated in the accounts payable

department and attached to the invoices. After being checked and cash discounts computed, the invoices are accumulated in batches and adding machine tapes are prepared of the net invoice amounts to provide predetermined totals. Then the batches of invoices and tapes are sent to the tabulating department.

3. In the tabulating department keypunch operators prepare for each invoice an accounts payable punched card and one or more punched cards for the related debit distribution to several departmental inventories.
4. The invoice register is prepared by tabulation runs of the distribution cards and accounts payable cards. In these runs, totals of distribution cards are compared by the tabulating machine with the amounts punched for the related accounts payable cards. Tabulation run subtotals by invoice batches are taken for checking with the predetermined totals.
5. The general ledger control account is posted monthly from the totals shown in the invoice register and all other journals.
6. By sorting, the distribution and accounts payable cards are separated. The distribution cards are filed for further processing. The accounts payable cards are sorted by due dates and tabulation runs prepared to determine cash requirements.
7. On the due dates the accounts payable cards are processed to prepare combined check and remittance statements.
8. At the end of the month the accounts payable cards in the unpaid file are tabulated for comparison with the general ledger control account.

Required

1. List the audit procedures you would employ in the examination of raw material purchases. Limit your discussion to procedures up to and including the preparation of the punched cards.

2. What audit procedures would you employ to satisfy yourself as to the reasonableness of the accounts payable balance on December 31, 1979.   (AICPA Adapted)

14-22. You were engaged to examine the financial statements of Ronlyn Corporation for the year ended June 30, 1979.

On May 1, 1979 the corporation borrowed $500,000 from Second National Bank to finance plant expansion. The long-term note agreement provided for the annual payment of principal and interest over five years. The existing plant was pledged as security for the loan.

Due to unexpected difficulties in acquiring the building site, the plant expansion had not begun at June 30, 1979. To make use of the borrowed funds, management decided to invest in stocks and bonds, and on May 16, 1979 the $500,000 was invested in securities.

Required

1. What are the audit objectives in the examination of long-term debt?

2. Prepare an audit program for the examination of the long-term agreement between Ronlyn and Second National Bank.

3. How could you verify the security position of Ronlyn at June 30, 1979?

4. In your audit of investments, how would you

a. Verify the dividend or interest income recorded?
b. Determine market value?
c. Establish the authority for security purchases?   (AICPA Adapted)

14-23. You are auditing the financial statements of The Goode Company for the year ended December 31, 1979. As part of your examination you have collected certain information concerning accounts payable. These data, in condensed form, are presented here:

504
**Audit of liabilities:
current, contingent,
and long-term**

12-31-79		DATA PER		
ACCOUNTS PAYABLE TRIAL BALANCE		PURCHASE JOURNAL		
VENDOR NAME	AMOUNT	ENTRY DATE	VENDOR NAME	AMOUNT
Alpha Corporation	$ 40,000	12-22-79	Moore Company	$12,000
Core Company	60,000	12-26-79	H & H Supplies	25,000
Gee Brothers	10,000	12-31-79	Roto Corporation	29,000
H & H Supplies	25,000	12-29-79	Gee Brothers	10,000
Moore Company	12,000	1-3-80	Friendly Corporation	16,000
Roto Corporation	29,000	12-30-79	Alpha Corporation	40,000
Salvo Company	26,000	12-30-79	Core Company	60,000
Accrued payroll	38,700	12-31-79	Salvo Company	26,000
	$240,700	1-4-80	Craig Shop	3,400

DATA PER RECEIVING REPORT		DATA PER VENDOR INVOICE			
VENDOR NAME	DATE RECEIVED	VENDOR NAME	AMOUNT	TERMS	DESCRIPTION
Moore Company	12-18-79	Gee Brothers	$10,000	FOB Dest.	Inventory
Roto Corporation	12-31-79	H & H Supplies	25,000	FOB S.P.	Supplies
H & H Supplies	12-24-79	Moore Company	12,000	FOB S.P.	Inventory
Gee Brothers	12-29-79	Roto Corporation	29,000	FOB S.P.	Inventory
Alpha Corporation	12-28-79	Salvo Corporation	26,000	FOB S.P.	Machinery
Davis Company	12-29-79	Alpha Corporation	44,000	FOB Dest.	Inventory
Friendly Corporation	12-30-79	Friendly Corporation	16,000	FOB Dest.	Inventory
Core Company	1-2-80	Core Company	60,000	FOB Dest.	Inventory
Salvo Company	12-31-79	T & J Service	6,400		December Service fee
Craig Shop	1-4-80	Craig Shop	3,400	FOB Dest.	(1)

(1) Represents the receipt of goods purchased from the Craig Shop under a bill-and-hold arrangement. The original purchase was for $24,000 and was made on July 1, 1979. Goode Company has received $18,000 worth of shipments as of 12/31/79. The contract requires a $2000 payment each month starting on July 1, 1979. Purchases are recorded when received.

Required

1. Based on the limited data available determine if the correct balance in accounts payable is $240,700.

2. Prepare a list of proposed adjusting journal entries.

14-24. Western Meat Processing Company buys and processes livestock for sale to supermarkets. In connection with your examination of the company's financial statements, you have prepared the following notes based on your review of procedures:

1. Each livestock buyer submits a daily report of his or her purchases to the plant superintendent. This report shows the dates of purchase and expected delivery, the vendor, and the number, weight, and type of livestock purchased. As shipments are received, any available plant employee counts the number of each type received and places a check mark beside this quantity on the buyer's report. When all shipments listed on the report have been received, the report is returned to the buyer.
2. Vendors' invoices, after a clerical check, are sent to the buyer for approval and returned to the accounting department. A disbursement voucher and a check for the approved amount are prepared in the accounting department. Checks are forwarded to the treasurer for his signature. The treasurer's office sends signed checks directly to the buyer for delivery to the vendor.
3. Livestock carcasses are processed by lots. Each lot is assigned a number. At the end of each day a tally sheet reporting the lots processed, the number and type of animal in each lot, and the carcass weight is sent to the accounting department, where a perpetual inventory record of processed carcasses and their weights is maintained.
4. Processed carcasses are stored in a refrigerated cooler located in a small building adjacent to the employee parking lot. The cooler is locked when the plant is not open, and a company guard is on duty when the employees report for work and leave at the end of their shifts. Supermarket truck drivers wishing to pick up their orders have been instructed to contact someone in the plant if no one is in the cooler.
5. Substantial quantities of by-products are produced and stored, either in the cooler or elsewhere in the plant. By-products are initially accounted for as they are sold. At this time the sales manager prepares a two-part form; one copy serves as authorization to transfer the goods to the customer, and the other becomes the basis for billing the customer.

Required: For each of the above notes state:

1. What the specific internal control objective(s) should be at the stage of the operating cycle described by the note.

2. The control weaknesses in the present procedures, if any, and suggestions for improvement, if any. (AICPA Adapted)

14-25. *FASB Statement No. 5* discusses the proper accounting for contingencies. Listed here are several situations that may be encountered by an auditor. Assume that each item is material and that the financial statements are being audited for the year ended December 31, 1979.

1. In January 1980, your client borrowed additional funds through the issuance of long-term bonds.
2. Your client has a long-term contract to purchase cotton, a raw material used in the production process, at $12 per unit. Similar cotton had a market price of $9 per unit on December 31, 1979. As of this date your client was committed to purchase 500,000 units.
3. A lawsuit against your client was settled on January 16, 1980, for $3 million. The litigation was a result of a patent infringement suit brought by a competitor in 1977. There was a $2 million appropriation of retained earnings in 1977, and the appropriation was not removed in 1979.

506
**Audit of liabilities:
current, contingent,
and long-term**

4. Your client has completed a study suggesting that significant technological changes may result in the development of a new industrial process in the latter part of 1980. If this is true, several pieces of machinery and a significant investment in a patented industrial process will be worthless.

5. It is expected that the business activity for the first and second quarters of 1980 will be moderately less than the activity for 1979. Since much of your client's expenses are fixed, it is likely that there will actually be a net loss from operations for the year 1980.

6. Your client suffered a fire on January 20, 1980. It is believed that only about 30 percent of the $2 million loss will be recovered from the insurance company.

7. Your client has sued a customer for lack of performance on a contract. Although the suit has not been settled, the client's independent legal counsel is certain that the client will be awarded at least $500,000 and possibly $1,500,000. It is apparent that the defendant wants to settle the lawsuit with as little publicity as possible.

Required
1. Which of the seven items are contingencies?
2. How should each item be disclosed on the 1979 financial statements?
3. What audit procedures are likely to bring the seven items to the auditor's attention?

14-26. During your audit of the Pientak Corporation for 1979 you find that it plans to install the following purchase order draft (POD) system for paying vendors:

1. The corporation will issue a draft in the form of a blank check attached to the purchase order for purchases. The POD form will combine a purchase order (upper half of form) with a blank check (lower half of form), and the two documents will be prenumbered with the same number and perforated so that the check can be easily detached.

2. The purchasing department will be responsible for issuance, and the PODs will be valid for a period of 90 days from the date of issuance. Each of eight buyers will maintain a supply of PODs. The supply will be replenished as needed.

3. The cashier's department will maintain a log of the numbers of the PODs given to each buyer. Unissued PODs will be kept in a safe in the cashier's office. The POD form will consist of five parts distributed as follows:

a. Copy 1 will be the purchase order and will be mailed to the vendor.
b. Copy 2 will be sent to the receiving department.
c. Copy 3 will be sent to the bookkeeping department.
d. Copy 4 will be filed numerically in the purchasing department.
e. Copy 5 will be kept by the buyer for follow-up purposes.

4. When the purchase order is issued, the buyer will enter the quantity, unit price, extended amount, and the total estimated amount of the order on the upper half of the POD form. The check will be made out in the vendor's name, dated, and signed by the buyer. The original of the five-part form will then be mailed to the vendor.

5. The vendor will enter his or her invoice number, quantity, unit price, and total amount of goods to be shipped in the space provided on the check. When the goods are shipped, the vendor will enter the total amount of the shipment on the face of the check and present the completed check to the bank for payment. No partially filled orders will be accepted. Vendors who deliver a quantity less than that ordered must receive a new purchase order for additional quantities to be delivered.

6. The bank will honor the check if it has not matured, stamp it "Paid," and charge the amount to the corporation's general cash account. The bank will send the paid checks to the cashier's department daily. After reviewing the paid checks the cashier's department

will prepare an adding machine tape of the amounts and enter the total each day in the **507** cash disbursements journal, debiting accounts payable. The paid checks will then be sent **Exercises and problems** to the purchasing department.

7. When the goods are received, the receiving department will compare the quantity of items received to copy 2 of the POD, indicate the date the goods are received, initial copy 2 and route it to the purchasing department. The purchasing department will match the receiving department's copy 2 with the paid POD received from the cashier's department and enter the account distribution in the description section of the check. The extensions of unit prices multiplied by quantities entered by the vendor will be checked, the receiving department's copy 2 attached to the paid check, and the documents sent to the bookkeeping department.

8. The bookkeeping department will charge the appropriate asset or expense accounts at the time the paid checks are recorded in the accounts payable register. The checks, together with the related receiving reports, will then be filed by vendor.

Required

1. The treasurer of the corporation requests your aid in preparing a memorandum informing the bank of the new POD procedures. List the instructions you would recommend be given to the bank regarding the POD bank account and the payment of POD checks.

2. The internal control procedures within the corporation with regard to purchases in general are excellent. Suggest additional internal control measures needed for the use of PODs and verification of paid and unpaid PODs. (AICPA Adapted)

14-27. You are in the final stages of your examination of the financial statements of the Ozine Corporation for the year ended December 31, 1979, when you are consulted by the corporation's president who believes there is no point to your examining the 1980 voucher register and testing data in support of 1980 entries. He states that (1) bills pertaining to 1979 which were received too late to be included in the December voucher register were recorded as of the year end by the corporation by journal entry, (2) the internal auditor made tests after the year end, and (3) he will furnish you with a letter certifying that there are no unrecorded liabilities.

Required

1. Should a CPA's test for unrecorded liabilities be affected by the fact that the client made a journal entry to record 1979 bills which were received late? Explain.

2. Should a CPA's test for unrecorded liabilities be affected by the fact that a letter is obtained in which a responsible management official certifies that to the best of his knowledge all liabilities have been recorded? Explain.

3. Should a CPA's test for unrecorded liabilities be eliminated or reduced because of the internal audit tests? Explain.

4. Assume that the corporation, which handled government contracts, had no internal auditor but that an auditor for a federal agency spent three weeks auditing the records and was just completing her work at this time. How would the CPA's unrecorded liability test be affected by the work of the auditor for a federal agency?

5. What sources in addition to the 1980 voucher register should a CPA consider to locate possible unrecorded liabilities? (AICPA Adapted)

14-28. To determine if all obligations are reflected in the liability accounts, the auditor performs a search for unrecorded liabilities. There is a variety of liabilities that may be overlooked by the client. Listed here are several examples of unrecorded liabilities for the year ended December 31, 1979:

508
**Audit of liabilities:
current, contingent,
and long-term**

- Several invoices applicable to 1979 were paid for by petty cash disbursements in January and February 1980.

- Inventory shipped FOB shipping point before 12/31/79 were not received until 1/6/80. They were omitted from the accounts payable listing.

- Inventory received before 12/31/79 was not recorded as purchases as of the report date, since no invoice had been received.

- Dividends declared by the board of directors of 12/19/79 were not recorded until payment was made on 1/19/80.

- The tax accrual was understated because recent rulings by the tax court disallowed certain deductions.

- The general bank account was overdrawn on 12/31/79.

- Several customers of the client had overpaid their bills, but the credits were treated as negative figures in the accounts receivable total.

- On 12/31/79 there was a significant reduction in the market price of a commodity which the company had committed itself to purchase under a long-term contract.

- On 12/26/79 the president of the company borrowed funds from a local bank, but the transaction was not recorded.

Required: For each unrecorded liability listed above determine what procedure the auditor should employ to discover the item.

14-29. Anthony, CPA, prepared the flowchart in Problem figure 14-29 which portrays the raw materials purchasing function of one of his clients, a medium-sized manufacturing company, from the preparation of initial documents through the vouching of invoices for payment in accounts payable. The flowchart was a portion of the work performed in the audit engagement to evaluate internal control.

Required: Identify and explain the systems and control weaknesses evident from the flowchart in Problem Figure 14-29. Include the internal control weaknesses resulting from activities performed or not performed. All documents are prenumbered.

(AICPA Adapted)

14-30. Mincin, CPA, is the auditor of the Raleigh Corporation. Mincin is considering the audit work to be performed in the accounts payable area for the current year's engagement.

The prior year's working papers show that confirmation requests were mailed to 100 of Raleigh's 1000 suppliers. The selected suppliers were based on Mincin's sample that was designed to select accounts with large dollar balances. A substantial number of hours was spent by Raleigh and Mincin resolving relatively minor differences between the confirmation replies and Raleigh's accounting records. Alternative audit procedures were used for suppliers who did not respond to the confirmation requests.

Required

1. Identify the accounts payable audit objectives that Mincin must consider in determining the audit procedures to be followed.

2. Identify situations in which Mincin should use accounts payable confirmations and discuss whether she is required to use them.

3. Discuss why the use of large dollar balances as the basis for selecting accounts payable for confirmation might not be the most efficient approach and indicate what more efficient procedures could be followed.

(AICPA Adapted)

Problem Figure 14-29

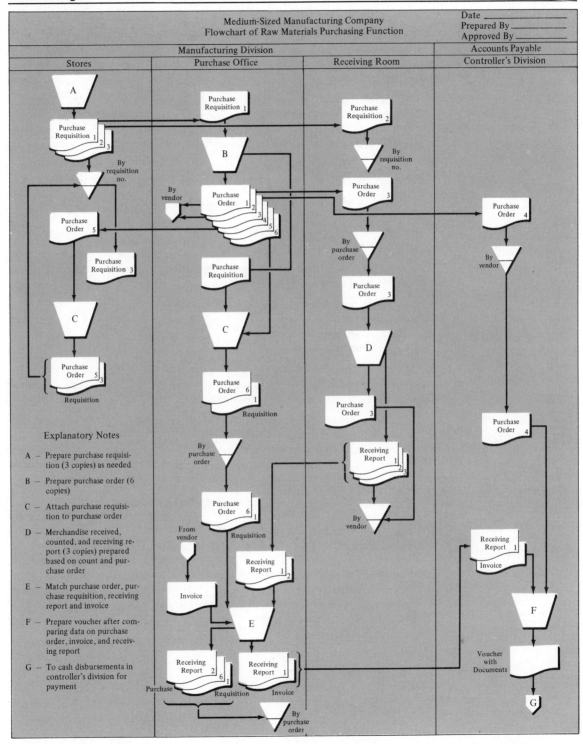

510
Audit of liabilities:
current, contingent,
and long-term

MULTIPLE CHOICE

1. Bell's accounts payable clerk has a brother who is one of Bell's vendors. The brother often invoices Bell twice for the same delivery. The accounts payable clerk removes the receiving report for the first invoice from the paid voucher file and uses it for support of payment for the duplicate invoice. The most effective procedure for preventing this activity is to

  a. Use prenumbered receiving reports.
  b. Mail signed checks without allowing them to be returned to the accounts payable clerk.
  c. Cancel vouchers and supporting papers when payment is made.
  d. Use dual signatures.

2. The audit step most likely to reveal the existence of contingent liabilities is

  a. A review of vouchers paid during the month following the year end.
  b. Accounts payable confirmations.
  c. An inquiry directed to legal counsel.
  d. Mortgage note confirmation.

3. Matching the supplier's invoice, the purchase order, and the receiving report normally should be the responsibility of the

  a. Warehouse receiving function.
  b. Purchasing function.
  c. General accounting function.
  d. Treasury function.

4. A CPA learns that her client has paid a vendor twice for the same shipment, once based upon the original invoice and once based upon the monthly statement. A control procedure that should have prevented this duplicate payment is

  a. Attachment of the receiving report to the disbursement support.
  b. Prenumbering of disbursement vouchers.
  c. Use of a limit or reasonableness test.
  d. Prenumbering of receiving reports.

5. On December 31, 1978, a company erroneously prepared an account payable voucher (debit cash, credit accounts payable) for a transfer of funds between banks. A check for the transfer was drawn January 3, 1979. This error resulted in overstatements of cash and accounts payable on December 31, 1978.

Of the following procedures, the least effective in disclosing this error is review of the

  a. December 31, 1978, bank reconciliations for the two banks.
  b. December 1978 check register.
  c. Support for accounts payable on December 31, 1978.
  d. Schedule of interbank transfers.   (AICPA Adapted)

CHAPTER 15
Audit of stockholders' equity

The stockholders' equity section of an organization's financial statement represents sources of assets either contributed by shareholders or earned and retained by the organization. Contributed capital may be composed of preferred stock, common stock, appraisal capital, donated capital, or a variety of other paid-in capital accounts. Earned capital consists of retained earnings, appropriated retained earnings and, in some cases, a contra account represented by a treasury stock account. This chapter deals with the more important and more common accounts found in the equity section of the balance sheet.

INTERNAL CONTROL MODEL

Stockholders' equities may account for a significant portion of the total sources of an entity's assets. To make sure these sources are properly accounted for, recognized internal control procedures must be adopted if an adequate internal control system is to exist. These procedures or guidelines are discussed in the context of a well-designed plan of organization and an adequate system of authorization and accountability.

Plan of organization

DEPARTMENTAL AUTONOMY
The specific responsibilities assigned to segments of an organization to ensure an adequate internal control system are consistent with the approach described for the cash receipts and disbursements system. The major duties in this area are:

    I. Accounting department
       1. Maintenance of accounting records, such as the capital stock ledger or another detail listing of holders of capital stock

511

512
Audit of stockholders' equity

2. Maintenance of the general ledger
3. Review of and accounting for all cash disbursements for payment of dividends or retirement of capital stock
4. Review of and accounting for all cash receipts from the issuance of capital stock

II. Treasurer
1. Custody control over cash, including proceeds from the issuance of capital stock
2. Signing and distributing checks for payment of dividends or retirement of capital stock

III. Functions other than accounting and treasurer
1. Authorization for the issuance of capital stock including dividend rates and covenants (board of directors)
2. Authorization for the retirement of capital stock or the repurchase of treasury stock (board of directors)
3. Approval of cash dividends, stock dividends, or stock-splits (board of directors)
4. Custody of blank stock certificates (secretary)

System of authorization and accountability

EXECUTION OF TRANSACTIONS

The internal control system for capital stock is designed in a manner to ensure that only authorized transactions are executed and that these transactions are processed in a manner consistent with corporate policies. Transactions in this area usually represent significant dollar amounts. Appropriately, authorization for these transactions is explicit and well documented.

Authorization for transactions: The issuance or retirement of capital stock requires the authorization of the board of directors. This authorization may be the basis for the execution of a single transaction, such as the issuance of a block of stock. In this case the board of directors approves the date of issuance, the approximate issue price, and other factors associated with the transaction. Alternatively the board of directors may delegate the authority to execute transactions within certain established guidelines. For example, it may designate a corporate official to purchase treasury stock if the company's stock falls within a certain price range. In either case the basis for the approval of the transaction is documented in the minutes of the directors' meetings. Furthermore, each instrument requires the signature of two designated employees, usually officers, of the corporation. These employees are designated by the board of directors.

RECORDING OF TRANSACTIONS

The internal control system includes procedures to encourage the recording of a transaction in a manner consistent with its execution. Entry in the proper

accounting period, in the correct amount, and in the appropriate account are **513**
elements of the recording of a transaction. Again, since long-term equity transactions tend to be relatively large, the omission of properly authorized items
from the financial statements represents an area of significant audit exposure.
Internal control procedures designed to ensure proper recording of the transaction are of interest to the auditor.

To determine that all transactions are recorded, an organization may employ
an independent registrar and transfer agent, or it may act as its own registrar and
transfer agent. The adequacy of a firm's internal control is enhanced if an
independent registrar and transfer agent are employed, since the task is performed
outside the control of the organization. Companies whose stock is traded on a
security exchange, such as the American Stock Exchange, must utilize an
independent registrar and transfer agent. Usually this task is performed by a
large bank.

Independent registrar: The role of an independent registrar is to make sure
stock is issued in accordance with the corporate charter. If 100,000 shares are
authorized, then the registrar's task is to see to it that the total number of shares
issued does not exceed this amount. In addition, the registrar is responsible for
control of the number of shares issued. Any new shares issued by the corporation
are registered, examined, and signed by the independent registrar. The registrar
controls the number of shares outstanding or held by the public. Each share of
stock repurchased or canceled by the corporation is examined and invalidated
by the registrar. When the ownership of a share of stock changes, the registrar
cancels the old certificate and issues a new certificate in its place.

Transfer agent: A transfer agent maintains up-to-date records as to the ownership of the corporation's shares of stock. As the ownership of the organization's
shares of stock changes, new shares are issued, or outstanding shares are
repurchased or canceled, and the transfer agent revises the records detailing
stock ownership. In effect, the transfer agent replaces the need for the corporation
to maintain a stock ledger. Periodically the transfer agent prepares and sends a
list of stockholders and the number of shares held by each to the corporation.
Among other things, this list is used in the preparation of individual dividend
checks. Many companies let the transfer agent also function as a dividend-paying
agent. By drawing a single check payable to the agent, an organization may
reduce the cost of performing such a task and in so doing strengthen the internal
control.

If an organization performs the tasks of the registrar and transfer agent
internally, the following control procedures are utilized to establish an adequate
internal control system.

Accounting and control of prenumbered documents: The stock certificates are
prenumbered, and unissued certificates are usually under the control of the
corporate secretary, an officer of the organization. The certificates are usually

514
**Audit of stockholders'
equity**

bound in a capital stock book which functions much like a checkbook. When a share of stock is issued, the name, date of issuance, number of shares issued, and so on, are recorded on the face of the stock as well as on the stub portion of the capital stock book. As shares of stock are canceled or otherwise remitted to the corporation, they are marked "Void" and stapled to the capital stock book or retained in a file. Thus at any particular time the certificate stubs that are not canceled represent the number of shares of stock outstanding.

Stock ledger: A stock ledger functions as a subsidiary ledger to the capital stock general ledger account. The stock ledger reveals the number of shares of stock owned by a particular individual. Maintenance of the stock ledger, as for any subsidiary ledger, is the responsibility of the accounting department. As transactions are executed, the stock ledger is updated in an appropriate manner.

COMPARISON OF RECORDED ACCOUNTABILITY

The comparison of recorded accountability, as shown in the capital stock general ledger account with supporting records, is made on a periodic basis. This task is performed by an individual who is not authorized to sign new stock certificates, is not responsible for custody of the stock certificate book, and is not responsible for maintenance of the capital stock ledger. Ideally, this function is performed by the staff of the internal audit department. In any case, the individual reviews the stock certificate book and reconciles it with the capital stock ledger. If the corporation employs an independent registrar and transfer agent, pertinent data are periodically confirmed and reconciled with the capital stock general ledger account.

STUDY AND EVALUATION

The study of the capital stock internal control system is conducted to provide the auditor with an opportunity to document and understand the system. As described above, the internal control system is generally not complex, and the necessary audit documentation consists of the preparation of an internal control questionnaire, such as the one presented in Figure 15-1. In most cases the preparation of a flowchart describing the system is unnecessary.

COMPLIANCE AND SUBSTANTIVE TESTS

In most engagements the auditor does not perform a partial test of transactions processed during the accounting period for one of two reasons. Typically, for a small organization there are very few capital transactions, and those that occur tend to be large. Thus the auditor audits every capital stock transaction rather than reviewing a representative sample. Also, where there are numerous capital stock transactions, it is highly likely that the client is a medium-sized or large corporation which employs an independent registrar and transfer agent. For these reasons, the compliance and substantive tests are discussed together. A combined audit program is shown in Figure 15-2.

Figure 15-1

Internal Control Questionnaire

	Answer		Answer based on		
Capital stocks	Yes	No	Inquiry	Observation	Comments

1. Answer the following:
  a. Does the client employ an independent registrar?
  b. Does the client employ a transfer agent?					

2. If not —
  a. are unissued stock certificates prenumbered and in the custody of an officer?
  b. is a stockholders' ledger kept for each class of authorized and outstanding capital stock, showing the name of each registered owner and the balance of shares owned?
  c. are surrendered stock certificates effectively canceled and attached to related issue stubs in the stock certificate books?
  d. In the case of capital stock transfers, does the officer authorized to sign new certificates inspect the surrendered certificates for proper assignment and comparison of the number of shares canceled?
  e. In the case of the issuance of additional capital stock (including exercised stock options), does the officer authorized to sign new certificates ascertain that the stock has been paid for in accordance with the board of directors' authorization?
  f. Are stockholders' ledgers and open stubs in the stock certificate books balanced periodically to the general ledger by persons who are not authorized to sign new certificates and who are not custodians of the stock certificate books?					

3. Does the client employ the services of the transfer agent for disbursing dividends?					

4. If not —
  a. are unclaimed dividend checks promptly set up in the accounts as liabilities and redeposited in the company's general bank account (or canceled if separate dividend bank account (or canceled if separate dividend bank
  b. is a separate dividend bank account maintained on an imprest basis?
  c. if a separate dividend bank account is maintained, is proper internal control maintained in reconciling the bank account and in preparing, signing, and mailing the dividend checks?					

5. Does the board of directors authorize the issuance and retirement of capital stock?					

Existence and valuation

An initial step in the audit of the capital stock account and the related paid-in capital in excess of par account is to obtain an analysis of activity in these accounts for the current year. An example of such an analysis is presented in Figure 15-3. Balances at the beginning of the period are traced to the previous year's working papers. If the audit occurs during the first year of the engagement,

516
Audit of stockholders'
equity

Figure 15-2

Audit program: capital stock

PROCEDURES	DATE COMPLETED	WORK PERFORMED BY
1. Obtain an analysis of the capital stock account and the related paid in capital in excess of par account.		
2. Verify changes in the above accounts for the current year.		
3. If an independent registrar and transfer agent is employed, confirm the number of shares of capital stock issued and outstanding at the balance sheet date.		
4. If an independent registrar and transfer agent are not employed, reconcile the stock certificate book, the stockholders' ledger, and the control account.		
5. Account for treasury stock certificates at the balance sheet date by inspection or by confirmation.		
6. Determine the company's compliance with stock option provisions and other restrictions, if any.		
7. Review modifications, if any, to the certificate of incorporation and corporate bylaws.		

the review of all capital transactions from the inception of the organization is similar to that for the current year charges, which are considered in the following discussion.

ADDITIONS

For additional shares issued during the current year, the auditor is concerned with the (1) authorization of the sale, (2) valuation assigned to the new shares, and (3) accounting for the transaction in accordance with state laws and generally accepted accounting principles.

Authorization: The corporate charter identifies the types of capital stock that may be issued and the number of shares authorized for each class of stock. Abstracts of the corporate charter are contained in the auditor's permanent working paper file. By reading the minutes of the board of directors and the stockholders' meetings, the auditor determines if the corporate charter has been amended during the current year. In addition to the general authorization provided by the charter, additional new shares issued are approved by the board of directors or stockholders, depending upon the laws of the state in which the organization is incorporated. The approval may be explicit for each new share issued. For example, Figure 15-3 illustrates the issuance of 15,000 shares of common stock for the purchase of another corporation. The transaction is specifically approved by the board of directors and, in most cases, the shareholders. On the other hand, the issuance of additional shares may require general approval rather than specific approval of any one transaction. Again with reference to Figure 15-3, 300 stock options were exercised at $22 per share. This specific transaction was not authorized, but rather the stock option plan was approved by the board of directors or the stockholders.

Figure 15-3

45-606 EYE-EASE
45-706 20/20 BUFF
NATIONAL · Made in U.S.A

Green Valley Corporation
Analysis of Capital Accounts
12-31-79

	Date		Common Stock Issued		Excess of Par Value	Treasury Stock		Options Outstanding	
			# of Shares	Amount		# of Shares	Cost	#	Price
1	1/1/79	Balances	75000 ⁴	$750000 ⁴	$375000 ⁴	4700 ⁴	$11500 ⁴	700 ⁴	$22 ⁴
3	2/15	Options Exercised	300 ⓨ	3000 C	3600 C			⟨300⟩	
5	6/30	Shares issued	15000 ⁴	150000 A	300000 A				
6		for purchase of							
7		Martin Corp.							
9	7/20	Disposition of				⟨4400⟩	⟨10766⟩ C		
10		Treasury Stock							
12	8/15	10% Stock Dividend	9000 ¢	90000 ¢	198000 ¢			40	20 ¢
14	12/31/79	Balances	99300 Y	$993000	$876600	300 Y	# 734	440	$20
15			✓	✓	✓	✓	✓		✓

⁴ Traced to previous year's working papers.
⁴ Approval traced to the board of directors' meeting on 3/15/79
    and the stockholders meeting on 4/2/79.
ⓨ Transaction examined to see if it was in accordance with
    the stock option plan adopted in 1975.
¢ Approved by Board on 7/1/79.
C Traced proceeds to cash records.
A Review appraisal and other analysis concerning value
    assigned to stock.
¢ Computation checked.
Y Confirmed — see working paper @ N-4.

518
Audit of stockholders' equity

Valuation and accounting: When the consideration received for the issuance of capital stock is cash, the proceeds are traced to the cash receipts journal and the bank statement. Furthermore, the auditor determines that the proceeds from the sale of stock are in agreement with the board of director's authorization. If the sale of capital stock involves the receipt of nonmonetary assets,[1] the board of directors is responsible for the assignment of a value to the property received as well as to the contributed capital amounts. Thus, when a company exchanges its capital stock for land and a building, the value assigned to the transaction is based upon the fair market value of the capital stock or the fair market value of the nonmonetary assets, whichever is the best measurement of the transaction. When the stock is actively traded on a stock exchange, the auditor's verification of the value of the transaction is very simple. However, if the corporation is closely held, the value assigned to the transaction is dependent upon the value of the building and land. The auditor examines the report and other documentation presented to the board of directors for approval and assignment of value. If the transaction is material and the auditor is not satisfied or is incapable of judging the value of the property, an independent appraisal may be obtained.

Capital stock additions may result from the declaration of a small stock dividend, a large stock dividend, or a stock split. The values assigned to these transactions are governed by generally accepted accounting principles. Stock dividends are classified as small or large based upon an arbitrary guideline established by the AICPA. Declared stock dividends less than 20 or 25 percent of the number of shares outstanding are considered small. In this case, the value assigned to the small stock dividend is equal to the fair market value of a share of stock on the date of the stock dividend declaration. For a corporation whose stock is actively traded verification of the fair market value at the declaration is determined by reference to newspapers or financial service publications. In the case of closely held companies, accounting procedures require that only an amount equal to the state's legal capital requirements be capitalized.[2] In a similar manner if a stock dividend exceeds the 20 to 25 percent threshold, retained earnings are capitalized at the required legal capital rate. Finally, if the board of directors declares a stock split, there is no impact on the total amount of the contributed capital amounts. Rather, the par value of the stock is decreased, and the number of shares outstanding is increased in accordance with the proportion of the stock split. Not only does this require the approval of the board of directors, but it also requires the corporate charter be amended to reflect the new par value of the stock and the number of shares authorized.

As the above discussion illustrates, the auditor needs to be aware of the laws that govern stock transactions in a client's state. If it is needed, the auditor solicits assistance from a lawyer.

---

[1] Nonmonetary transactions involve the receipt or disposition of nonmonetary assets or liabilities whose amounts are not fixed in terms of units of currency. Examples are property, plant, and equipment; inventories; and patents or other intangible assets.

[2] "Restatement and Revision of Accounting Research Bulletins," *Accounting Research Bulletin No. 43* (New York: AICPA, 1961), p. 52.

DELETIONS

Shares of stock may be retired, permanently or temporarily, by an organization. As with additions to capital stock, the auditor is concerned with (1) approval of the transaction, (2) valuation of the transaction, and (3) accounting for the transaction.

Authorization: Based upon approval by the board of directors or the stockholders and subject to restrictions imposed by state laws, an organization may repurchase its capital stock. The reacquired shares may be permanently retired or held by the company in the form of treasury stock. For each transaction the auditor reviews the appropriate minutes of the board of directors or stockholders' meeting and determines that the reacquisition was in accordance with guidelines established by one or the other. If the transaction results in the permanent retirement of capital stock, the auditor inspects the canceled stock certificates if an independent registrar and transfer agent are not used. If the shares are not permanently canceled, he or she inspects all treasury shares on hand at the balance sheet date.

Valuation and accounting: The dollar value assigned to the retirement transaction is easily verified by the auditor if the payment is in cash. The cash disbursement is traced to the cash records and the bank statement, and the canceled check or other documentation is inspected. Of course, the amount of the disbursement is compared to the amount authorized by the board of directors or stockholders. When payment is in the form of nonmonetary items, the value assigned to the transaction is determined by the board of directors. The auditor gathers competent evidential matter to determine if this valuation is reasonable.

Most states identify a portion of contributed capital as legal capital, which provides some protection to the creditors of the organization, since a capital distribution cannot impair legal capital. For example, a company that acquires its capital stock and holds it in the treasury usually must restrict retained earnings by the cost of the treasury stock. Other state laws may mandate the method of accounting for a capital stock dilution, and the auditor is therefore careful to stay abreast of the regulations or employ the service of a lawyer.

Existence and cutoff

By referring to Figure 15-3, it can be seen that the auditor verifies the beginning balances and all current transactions, so that in effect the ending balances in the capital stock accounts are verified. However, the auditor uses additional techniques to determine the existence of the number of shares of stock outstanding at the balance sheet date. The approach selected by the auditor depends upon whether or not the client uses the services of an independent registrar and transfer agent.

INDEPENDENT REGISTRAR AND TRANSFER AGENT

As suggested earlier, companies whose stock is traded on an exchange must retain an independent registrar and transfer agent. The auditor confirms the

520
Audit of stockholders'
equity

Figure 15-4

FIRST NATIONAL BANK
OF
PRINCETON

January 8, 1980

Portfield and Company
Certified Public Accountants
Albermarle Building
Richmond, Virginia 21002

     In accordance with your request dated December 31, 1979, we are furnishing the following data concerning The Green Valley Corporation.

Common stock, $10 Par	
Shares authorized	100,000
Shares outstanding	99,300
including 300 treasury shares	
held in the name of the corporation	
New shares issued during	
the year	24,300
Treasury shares purchased	
during the year	0
Treasury shares sold	
during the year	4,400

    If you should need additional data or further service, please let us know.
Sincerely,

D. Purdue
Vice-President

number of shares issued and outstanding at the balance sheet date, as well as other pertinent information. Like any confirmation it is sent by, and returned directly to, the auditor. An example of a confirmation is presented in Figure 15-4.

RECONCILIATION OF STOCK RECORDS

If the client does not employ an independent registrar and transfer agent, audit procedures are restricted to the review of internal documents and accounting records. Specifically the auditor reconciles the stock certificate book (maintained by the secretary), the stock ledger (maintained in the accounting department), and the capital stock general ledger account (also maintained in the accounting department but not by the same individual who keeps the stock ledger).

521
Retained earnings

The stock certificate book is reviewed by the auditor to determine the number of shares that is outstanding. The stubs for issued shares identify the number of shares outstanding. The auditor accounts for the numerical sequence of the prenumbered shares and stubs and reviews all unissued shares. Shares that are retired are also inspected by the auditor. The number of shares outstanding according to the review of the stock certificate book is compared to the number of shares represented in the capital stock ledger. If a difference exists, the auditor investigates each discrepancy. Finally, the number of shares verified by these procedures is multiplied by their par value and traced to the balance in the general ledger account.

Disclosure

Capital stock is shown in the stockholders' equity section of the balance sheet. The number of shares of stock authorized, issued, and outstanding is disclosed along with the par value of the stock. If an organization issues preferred stock, the same data are disclosed in addition to the dividend rate, liquidation value, whether the stock is participating, and other pertinent factors. For companies that retain treasury stock, disclosures depend upon whether the cost method or the par method is used to account for treasury stock transactions and the laws of a particular state.

Some companies adopt stock purchase plans for employees and key management officials. In addition to verifying transactions associated with the stock purchase plan, the auditor determines if the plan is properly described in a footnote to the financial statements. For example, proper disclosure for stock option and purchase plans includes the (1) status of the plan at the date of the balance sheet, (2) number of shares under option, (3) option price, and (4) number of shares exercised.[3]

RETAINED EARNINGS

Entries that impact the retained earnings account are likely to be few in number but significant in amount. For these reasons the account is audited in detail. The audit procedures include:

- Obtain an analysis of the retained earnings amount.
- Verify current charges in the account.
- Determine if there are any restrictions on the amount as a result of covenants in loan agreements or treasury stock transactions.

A typical working paper for an analysis of the retained earnings account is presented in Figure 15-5.

---

[3] "Restatement and Revision of Accounting Research Bulletins," *Accounting Research Bulletin No. 43* (New York: AICPA, 1961), p. 124.

Figure 15-5

Green Valley Corporation
Analysis of Retained Earnings
12-31-79

		Retained Earnings Unappropriated	Retained Earnings Appropriated	Total
Balances 1/1/79		4876921 13✓	500000 00✓	5376921 13
Current Net Income—See R100		376114 69		
Quarterly Dividends				
1st	35300 V			
2nd	35300 V			
3rd	49500 V			
4th	49500 V	⟨169600 00⟩		
Stock Dividend		⟨288000 00⟩ ✓		
Additional Appropriation for Replacement of Machinery		A⟨200000 00⟩	200000 00 A	
		4595435 82	700000 00	5295435 82

✓ – Traced to previous year's working paper.
V – Traced to board's approval; computations checked.
✓ – Traced to board's approval; computation checked.
A – Resolution passed by the board at their 8/15 meeting.

The beginning balance in the retained earnings account is traced to the previous year's working paper when the engagement is a continuous one. When the audit occurs during the first year of the auditor's involvement, the retained earnings account is reconstructed starting with the inception of the organization. However, if the company was audited by another public accounting firm in previous years, the current auditor may be able to use the work of his or her predecessors.

Net income (loss)

Obviously, retained earnings are increased or reduced based upon the amount of income earned or lost in the current accounting period. Net income or loss is the result of numerous transactions. Thus net income (loss) is not audited as a single figure, but rather the components that comprise the amount are reviewed. Many of the accounts that appear on the income statement are discussed in Chapter 15. At this point the auditor determines that the net income (loss) figure agrees with the amount shown in the trial balance for the current year.

Prior period adjustments

Rule-making bodies, such as FASB and the SEC, are taking an increasingly restrictive attitude concerning what items may be placed in the retained earnings account as a prior period adjustment. Until 1977, only items that met the following criteria were properly classified as prior period adjustments:

- Specifically identified with and directly related to the business activities of particular prior periods
- Attributable to economic events occurring subsequent to the date of the financial statements for the prior period
- Dependent primarily on determinations by persons other than management
- Not susceptible to reasonable estimation prior to such determination[4]

The FASB reconsidered the above criteria and adopted rules that remove a considerable degree of judgment as to what constitutes a prior period adjustment. Specifically, the FASB states:

> Items of profit and loss related to the following shall be accounted for and reported as prior period adjustments and excluded from the determintion of net income for the current period:
> a. Correction of an error in the financial statements of a prior period discovered subsequent to their issuance and
> b. Adjustments that result from realization of income tax benefits of pre-acquisition operating loss carry forwards of purchased subsidiaries.[5]

Thus a correction of an error, if material, is treated as a prior period adjustment to the current year's beginning balance for retained earnings, and the previous year's financial statements presented are restated.

[4] "Reporting the Results of Operations," *APB Opinion No. 9* (New York: AICPA, 1967), p. 115.

[5] "Prior Period Adjustments," *FASB Statement No. 16* (Stamford, Conn.: FASB, 1977), p. 5.

524
Audit of stockholders' equity

There is still a certain amount of judgment involved in determining whether an item is an error. For the time being *FASB Standard No 16* retained the definition of an error adopted by *APB Opinion No. 20*. This definition reads.

> Errors in financial statements result from mathematical mistakes, mistakes in the application of accounting principles, or oversight or misuse of facts that existed at the time the financial statements were prepared.[6]

If a transaction is suggested by management to be an error applicable to a prior year, the auditor researches the conditions under which the error was made to determine if it meets the above guideline. Also, he or she, in reviewing the current transactions, stays alert for the possibility of transactions that need to be reported on the retained earnings statement.

The other item that *FASB Statement No. 16* classifies as a prior period adjustment is concerned with loss carry-forwards. Recall that tax benefits from net loss carry-forwards are typically not recognized until future years when an organization generates taxable income. If a company purchases another company that has an unrecorded operating loss carry-forward, it is possible that goodwill is assigned an amount which is actually applicable to the unrecorded carry-forward. As the loss carry-forward benefits of an acquired company are realized as tax benefits, the acquiring corporation reduces the original amount of goodwill established when the acquired company was purchased.[7] This is to be treated as a prior adjustment.

Cash and other dividends

The most common form of a dividend is cash; however, there may be stock dividends, scrip dividends, and liquidating dividends, as well as other dividends. Irrespective of the type of dividend declared, the basic authority rests with the board of directors. The declaration of a dividend is documented in the minutes of the board's meeting, and the resolution contains three dates with which the auditor is concerned.

The date of declaration is the date upon which the corporation is legally bound to carry out the resolution passed by the board of directors. For example, if a cash dividend is declared, a current liability exists from the date of declaration. Individuals that hold the corporation's stock at the date of record receive the dividend when it is ultimately distributed. After the date of record, the stock trades without the dividend or exdividend. In most cases the number of shares of stock outstanding at the date of declaration and at the date of record are the same. However, if additional shares have been issued between the two dates, the number of shares at the date of record determines the total dividend to be distributed. To verify the dividend accrual, the auditor refers to the dividend rate per share declared by the board and multiplies this rate by the number of shares outstanding at the two dates. (Usually they are the same.) To determine

---

[6] "Accounting Changes," *APB Opinion No. 20* (New York: AICPA, 1971), p. 389.

[7] "Accounting for Business Combinations," *APB Opinion No. 16* (New York: AICPA, 1970), p. 320.

the number of shares outstanding, the auditor may confirm the number with the independent registrar and transfer agent at the appropriate date or review the capital stock certificate book and the capital stock ledger.

The third date of interest to the auditor is the date of payment. This is the date that the corporation meets its commitment through actual distribution of the dividend. In the case of a cash dividend, the auditor examines the canceled check(s). If the client uses a transfer agent for disbursing the dividends, a single disbursement to the transfer agent is involved. If the client makes the dividend disbursements, the auditor traces a sample of canceled checks to the cash disbursements records and the capital stock ledger to determine that the dividend payment is properly computed. When the balance sheet date falls between the date of declaration and the date of payment, the auditor determines that the liability is presented on the balance sheet. In most cases the payment date precedes the audit sign-off date, and the cash disbursements and assorted records are tested as described above.

In addition to the more-or-less mechanical verification of cash for other dividends, the auditor is concerned with the legality of the dividend declaration. In general the existence of retained earnings that are unencumbered usually suggests that an organization may declare a dividend. However, the appropriateness of a dividend is determined by state laws. For example, a corporation's creditors are protected to a degree by the statutory definition of legal capital. If a client repurchases its own stock, the auditor's familiarity with the state laws in this area becomes crucial.

Determining the legality of a dividend goes beyond the auditor's knowledge of appropriate state laws. Agreements between the client and its creditors often generate covenants or restrictions that impact the dividend policy of the client. Holders of long-term debt may require the client to maintain or expand its retained earnings or may completely restrict the payment of any dividends during the life of the debt. The existence of another form of senior securities, preferred stock, usually means that the payment of dividends is restricted to a certain degree. In the case of cumulative preferred stock, no cash dividend can be paid to the common shareholders until the current preferred dividend and any dividends in arrears are fully paid. Furthermore, if the preferred stock is participating preferred, the total amount of the dividend, both common and preferred, is determined by the preferred stock agreement. The auditor's review of bond indenture agreements, mortgages, and so on, is the basis for identifying contractual clauses that control or restrict the client dividend policy. If the client is in violation of a clause, the auditor considers whether the violation is to be disclosed in the financial statements. The disclosure is not required when the client obtains a written waiver from the aggrieved party. In the absence of a waiver, when the violation is considered important, the nature of the violation and its impact are disclosed on the financial statements. In the case of the assessment of a penalty, an appropriate accrual is made by the client. When the outcome of the violation cannot be reasonably predicted, the auditor may find it necessary to issue a qualified opinion or disclaim an opinion on the financial statements.

526
Audit of stockholders'
equity

Appropriated retained earnings

An organization may restrict the distribution of dividends simply by not making a declaration. However, management may decide to be more explicit in its desire not to distribute dividends by formally restricting the amount of dividends available for distribution. The reasons for such action include (1) the need to meet state laws, such as when treasury stock is purchased, (2) the recognition of a restriction imposed by contract, such as a requirement to establish a reserve for the retirement of long-term debt, or (3) the desire to identify a restriction for the expansion of operational assets. The creation of appropriated retained earnings is the responsibility of the board of directors, and its action is documented in the minutes of its meetings, which are read by the auditor. The appropriation remains in force until rescinded by the board. Again, such action is verified by the auditor's review of the minutes of the board's meetings.

This is the extent of activity that may impact an appropriation. *FASB Statement No. 5* states that "costs or losses shall not be charged to an appropriation of retained earnings, and no part of the appropriation shall be transferred to income."[8] The auditor's reconciliation of the beginning balance of the appropriation with the ending balance, and the action of the board as documented in the minutes of its meeting are the extent of the audit procedures necessary to determine if this standard is being observed. However, the promulgation does not prohibit the use of an appropriation amount as long as it is shown in the stockholders' equity section on the balance sheet and is clearly identified as an appropriation of retained earnings."[9]

EXERCISES AND PROBLEMS

15-1. What are the responsibilities of the accounting department in a well-designed system for stockholders' equities?

15-2. What is an independent registrar?

15-3. What is a transfer agent?

15-4. If an entity does not use the services of an independent registrar and a transfer agent, how does this impact accounting controls?

15-5. Why are the compliance tests and substantive tests usually combined in the audit of capital stock accounts?

15-6. If a transfer agent and independent registrar are used, is it necessary to reconcile the stock certificate book and the common stock ledger?

15-7. If capital stock is sold by an entity and payment is received in the form of a nonmonetary asset, what audit problem is encountered?

15-8. Differentiate between a large stock dividend and a small stock dividend.

---

[8] "Accounting for Contingencies," *FASB Statement No. 5* (Stamford, Conn.: FASB, 1975), p. 7.

[9] *Ibid.,* p. 7.

15-9. What audit problem is encountered when a closely held corporation declares a 5 percent stock dividend?

527
Exercises and problems

15-10. What audit problem is encountered when a company declares a property dividend?

15-11. Why may it be necessary for the auditor to use the services of a lawyer in the audit of capital accounts?

15-12. What information should be included in the confirmation letter received from the independent registrar and the transfer agent?

15-13. Is there an internal control system for processing transactions that impact the retained earnings account?

15-14. If a stock option plan is in existence, what are the disclosure requirements?

15-15. As part of the review of the retained earnings account the auditor may encounter a net loss figure. How does he or she review this part of the retained earnings analysis?

15-16. Which of the following two transactions is more difficult to audit:

	DEBIT	CREDIT
Retained earnings—prior period adjustment	$100,000	
Property, plant, and equipment		$100,000
Retained earnings—dividends declared	100,000	
Cash dividends payable		100,000

15-17. Which of the following two transactions is more difficult to audit:

	DEBIT	CREDIT
Marketable securities	$100,000	
Capital stock		$ 10,000
Paid-in capital in excess of par		90,000
Property, plant, and equipment	10,000	
Capital stock		100,000

15-18. In the review of dividend transactions is it necessary for the auditor to differentiate between the date of the cash dividend declaration and the date of record?

15-19. Why is it necessary for the auditor to read a bond indenture agreement as part of the review of retained earnings?

15-20. Which of the following two transactions is more difficult to audit:

	DEBIT	CREDIT
Retained earnings	$100,000	
Retained earnings—appropriated for pending lawsuit		$100,000
Loss contingency	100,000	
Estimated liability from pending litigation		100,000

15-21. You were engaged on May 1, 1980, by a committee of stockholders to perform a special audit as of December 31, 1979, of the stockholders' equity of the Major Corporation, whose stock is actively traded on a stock exchange. The group of stockholders who engaged you believe that the information contained in the stockholders' equity section

528
**Audit of stockholders'
equity**

of the published annual report for the year ended December 31, 1979, is not correct. If your examination confirms their suspicions, they intend to use the report in a proxy fight.

Management agrees to permit your audit but refuses to allow any direct confirmation with the stockholders. To secure cooperation in the audit, the committee of stockholders has agreed to this limitation, and you have been instructed to limit your audit in this respect. You have been instructed also to exclude the audit of revenue and expense accounts for the year.

Required

1. Prepare a general audit program for the usual examination of the stockholders' equity section of a corporation's balance sheet, assuming no limitation on the scope of your examination. Exclude the audit of revenue and expense accounts.

2. Describe any special auditing procedures you would undertake in view of the limitations and other special circumstances of your examination of the Major Corporation's stockholders' equity accounts.

3. Discuss the content of your audit report for the special engagement, including comments on the opinion that you would render. Do not prepare your audit report. (AICPA Adapted)

15-22. You are a CPA engaged in an examination of the financial statements of Pate Corporation for the year ended December 31, 1979. The financial statements and records of Pate Corporation have not been audited by a CPA in prior years.

The stockholders' equity section of Pate Corporation's balance sheet at December 31, 1979, follows:

Stockholders' equity:	
Capital stock—10,000 shares of $10 par value authorized; 5000 shares issued and outstanding	$ 50,000
Capital contributed in excess of par value of capital stock	32,580
Retained earnings	47,320
Total stockholders' equity	$129,900

Pate Corporation was founded in 1973. The corporation has 10 stockholders and serves as its own registrar and transfer agent. There are no capital stock subscription contracts in effect.

Required

1. Prepare the detailed audit program for examination of the three accounts comprising the stockholders' equity section of Pate Corporation's balance sheet. (Do not include in the audit program the verification of the results of the current year's operations)

2. After you have audited every other figure on the balance sheet, it might appear that the retained earnings figure is a balancing figure and requires no further verification. Why should you verify retained earnings as you have verified the other figures on the balance sheet? Discuss. (AICPA Adapted)

15-23. During your annual audit of the Claymore Company for the year ended December 31, 1979, you review the following stockholders' equity accounts:

CAPITAL STOCK		
	Balance 1/1/79	$100,000
	JE no. 4-19	2,000
	JE no. 6-12	1,000

PAID-IN CAPITAL IN EXCESS OF PAR			
		Balance 1/1/79	$400,000
		JE no. 4-19	6,000
		JE no. 6-12	3,500

TREASURY STOCK (AT COST)			
Balance 1/1/79	$16,000	JE no. 8-16	$6,000
JE no. 3-12	4,000		

RETAINED EARNINGS			
JE no. 4-19	$8,000	Bal. 1/1/79	$450,000
JE no. 8-16	4,000	JE no. 9-15	5,000

APPROPRIATED RETAINED EARNINGS			
JE no. 9-15	$5,000	Balance 1/1/79	$15,000

Required

1. From the limited information reconstruct the journal entries complete with explanations.

2. For each entry reconstructed, explain how you would verify the transaction.

15-24. You are auditing the financial statements of Mallory, Inc., for the year ended December 31, 1979. The company is 12 years old, and your firm has been its auditors for the past 5 years. As part of the examination you discover that the stockholders' equity section is comprised of the following six accounts:

ACCOUNT NO.	ACCOUNT NAME
700	Common stock
701	Additional paid-in capital
710	Executive stock options
800	Retained earnings
850	Deferred compensation expense
860	Unrealized losses on equity investments

To facilitate your examination you request the client to prepare an analysis of the accounts listed above. The client submits the analysis presented in Problem Figure 15-24.

Required

1. Explain, in general terms, how each account balance as of December 31, 1979, was generated.

2. Using the client's analysis, explain how each account would be audited as of December 31, 1979.

15-25. During your examination of the stockholders' equity accounts of a client you discover the following entry:

Retained earnings	$30,000	
Marketable securities		$20,000
Gain on distribution		10,000
To record the issuance of a property		
dividend on 8/3/79		

Problem Figure 15-24

Mallory, Inc.
Analysis of Stockholders' Equity
12-31-79

	$10 Par-Common Stock	Additional Paid-In Capital	Retained Earnings	Executive Stock Options	Deferred Compensation Expense	Unrealized Loss on Equity Investments
Balance - 1/1/79	200 000	600 000	800 000	50 000	30 000	15 000
Exchange of Stock for Garbor Corp.-Treated as a Purchase	24 000	65 000				
Shares issued under executive stock option plan	10 000	15 000		<20 000>		
Amortization of Deferred compensation expense					<6 000>	
Adjustment due to revaluation of equity investment						<6 000>
Cash Dividend			<15 000>			
Net Income			95 000			
Balance - 12/31/79	234 000	680 000	880 000	30 000	24 000	9 000

Required
1. Explain why the client made this entry.
2. Describe the procedures you would employ to verify the transaction.

MULTIPLE CHOICE

1. Mars Company has a separate outside transfer agent and outside registrar for its common stock. A confirmation request sent to the transfer agent should ask for

a. A list of all stockholders and the number of shares issued to each.
b. A statement from the agent that all surrendered certificates have been effectively canceled.
c. Total shares issued, shares issued in the name of the client, and unbilled fees.
d. Total shares authorized.

2. Braginetz Corporation acts as its own registrar and transfer agent and has assigned these responsibilities to the company secretary. The CPA primarily relies upon his or her

a. Confirmation of shares outstanding at the year end with the company secretary.
b. Review of the corporate minutes for data as to shares outstanding.
c. Confirmation of the number of shares outstanding at the year end with the appropriate state official.
d. Inspection of the stock book at the year end and accounting for all certificate numbers.

(AICPA Adapted)

CHAPTER 16

Audit of nominal accounts

The purpose of an audit is to issue an opinion on the client's financial statements, which include the balance sheet as well as the income statement.[1] Much of the discussion in the previous chapters tended to be balance sheet-oriented. A perceptive student may raise a question concerning the collection of sufficient and competent evidence as a basis for formulating an informed opinion about the income statement. The purpose of this chapter is to describe the audit approach used in the auditor's review of the income statement.

NOMINAL VERSUS PERMANENT ACCOUNTS: A CONTRAST

To contrast the audit approach adopted for the balance sheet and the approach used to review the income statement, it is useful to recall the nature of the two financial statements. The balance sheet measures assets, and the sources of these assets, at a particular date. Thus the auditor obtains a detail listing of the specific account and uses a variety of audit techniques to verify the existence and valuation of the items that comprise the account. On the other hand, the income statement accumulates data for a discrete period of time, usually a year. Items that appear in a nominal account do not represent a value at the balance sheet date but a summarization of numerous values assigned to the account throughout the income statement period. Nonetheless, this does not imply that the auditor cannot verify the collection of transactions in a manner somewhat similar to the procedures employed to verify balance sheet accounts. For example, an accounts receivable that appears on the balance sheet may be confirmed by the customer of the client. A single credit sale may be, but is usually not,

---

[1] A complete set of financial statements includes a statement of change in financial position; however, in preparing such a statement information impacting the balance sheet and income statement is utilized to a significant degree. Thus the auditor collects most of the evidence needed to review the statement of change in examination of the permanent and nominal account, and no specific audit approach must be described for the audit of this statement.

selected from the detail listing of sales for the period and confirmed with the customer. However, it is not the nature of a nominal account that prohibits the utilization of an audit approach similar to that used in auditing a permanent account. The primary reason for a different approach is the volume of detail transactions represented in the accounts. The sales account includes all the accounts receivable, except very old balances, at the balance sheet date, plus sales made on account during the year that were collected before the balance sheet date. To perform an efficient audit, an alternative approach is adopted by the auditor.

533
Nominal versus permanent accounts: a contrast

The audit approach used in reviewing the income statement cannot be described as a single audit approach. It encompasses the integrated audit approach described in previous chapters but includes additional phases. Specifically, the audit approach for the review of nominal accounts consists of the following steps:

- Determination of the consistency of data (investigation of client environmental conditions)
- Evaluation of internal controls
- Tests of transactions (compliance tests)
- Detailed testing of nominal accounts (substantive tests)
- Review of balance sheet allocations (substantive tests)

Consistency of data

As part of the analytic review, the auditor reviews the income statement accounts to determine their consistency with other data. This is a broad technique that usually results in the utilization of other, more specific, techniques. Data that appear to be inconsistent with other quantitative data, such as gross revenues, or other qualitative data, such as the business practices of a particular industry, are identified for more thorough investigation. Three procedures used by many auditors are (1) analysis of trends and ratios, (2) analysis of comparative amounts, and (3) analysis of interrelated accounts.

ANALYSIS OF TRENDS AND RATIOS

A variety of ratios may be computed by the auditor, such as an inventory turnover rate and a gross profit percentage, to name but two. In computing these ratios an experienced auditor evaluates the results in the context of the client's position. For a medium-sized or large client the computation of ratios is more useful if the data are disaggregated. For example, a single computation of the inventory turnover rate is less useful for a company that has several branches, subsidiaries, or divisions. However, the same ratio computation for each business segment is more likely to produce better insight into the propriety of the accounts used in the formulation of the ratio. *FASB Statement No. 14* requires that certain information about an "enterprise's operations in different industries, its foreign operations and export sales, and its major customers" be disclosed.[2] Such

---

[2] "Financial Reporting for Segments of a Business Enterprise," *FASB Statement No. 14* (Stamford, Conn: FASB, 1976), p. 1.

534
Audit of
nominal accounts

requirements ensure that a client will design its accounting system so that disaggregation, at least to a certain degree, is observed.

ANALYSIS OF COMPARATIVE AMOUNTS

The analysis of comparative amounts consists of a systematic comparison of current account balances with previous amounts and budgeted amounts. Such analysis may identify areas which suggest errors or omissions in the compilation of the data. For example, an analysis of a client's account for training and continuing education expenses is presented here:

	ACTUAL 1979	BUDGET 1979	ACTUAL 1978
Training and continuing education expense	$320,000	$900,000	$856,000

The above comparison obviously raises several questions about the current expense account. The apparent understatement of the expense may be explained by posting error(s), invoice coding error(s), or other errors. On the other hand, the deviation may be explained as the result of something other than the occurrence of an error. The client may have decided not to spend the discretionary amount budgeted in an attempt to improve its short-term profitability position. In any case the auditor adopts appropriate audit procedures to determine if errors or omissions are the reason for the inconsistency of the data.

In comparing current amounts with amounts generated in previous years, the auditor considers the nature of adjustments required in the previous year's audit. As part of the audit approach he or she reviews the previous year's working papers to determine if an adjustment was made or proposed. It is possible that errors or omissions made by the client in previous years may be repeated in the current year. The auditor considers adjustments proposed as well as those actually accepted as adjustments. In many cases a proposed adjustment is rejected because it is not material. The current error, if it does exist, may be significantly larger.

ANALYSIS OF INTERRELATED ACCOUNTS

Every transaction recorded in the accounting system impacts at least two separate accounts. A company buys merchandise on credit, and the purchases account and accounts payable are increased by a similar amount. Thus the processing of data through the accounting model (assets = equities) ensures a degree of consistency of many accounts. For example, a significant increase in credit sales during the accounting period suggests that the dollar value of accounts receivable will be greater at the end of the year, assuming no change in the cash collection pattern.

In addition to external transactions that activate the accounting model, internal analysis conducted by the controller's staff results in numerous adjusting journal entries. The results of this analysis are reviewed by the auditor for reasonableness based upon his or her understanding of the interrelationship of accounts and the operating characteristics of the firm. For example, a significant increase in sales covered by a warranty contract during the year impacts more than the sales account. The auditor expects to see an attendant increase in warranty expense for the year, as well as an increase in the estimated liability at the balance sheet date. If the relationships appear reasonable, he or she may perform a minimum amount of detail auditing of the accounts. However, if the data in the accounts are inconsistent, the auditor expands the degree of detail auditing.

In evaluating the interrelationship of accounts, the auditor is careful not to conduct the analysis in a mechanical manner. It may be that he or she can utilize a statistical technique, such as regression analysis, to determine the relationship of the independent variable (e.g., sales under warranty) and the dependent variable (e.g., warranty expense). However, any relationship between two or more accounts, whether determined statistically or by visual inspection, is evaluated in terms of the current circumstances of the client. Things seldom remain the same, and it is encumbent upon the auditor to be sensitive to these changes and be capable of placing them in perspective. To illustrate, the statistical analysis may confirm the reasonableness of the warranty expense account, but the auditor may be aware that the client switched to an inferior material in the manufacture of its inventory during the current year. This information may come to his or her attention during the review and test of the inventory account. In any case, the interrelationship of the accounts in the context of the total audit must be evaluated, not just the two accounts.

Evaluation of internal controls

The auditor's analytic review of nominal accounts encompasses evaluation of the client's internal control system. To determine the reliability of the system the auditor prepares the appropriate flowcharts, completes the internal control questionnaires, and performs other analytic procedures. He or she determines that the controls are being applied as prescribed by performing the compliance tests. Once this phase of the compliance tests is completed, the auditor determines the nature, timing, and extent of subsequent procedures to be employed in the audit of nominal accounts. The specific procedures employed depend upon the nature of the nominal account, as considered in the following discussion.

Tests of transactions (compliance tests)

The audit approach adopted for this book considers the tests of transactions to be part of the compliance tests. Technically, as explained earlier, the tests of transactions are part of the substantive tests, since the audit procedures substantiate a balance, or part of a balance, that appears on the financial statements. In practice the tests of transactions are performed as an integral part of the compliance tests since both are performed at an interim date in most audits.

Many accounts that appear on the income statement are a result of the processing of recurring transactions through an accounting subsystem. Also, these accounts are often related to balance sheet accounts. The latter fact is important, since a great deal of audit effort is directed toward the associated asset account. The most important accounts that possess this characteristic are:

NOMINAL ACCOUNT	ASSET ACCOUNT
Sales	Accounts receivable
Purchases	Accounts payable
Cost of sales	Inventory

The above accounts, which represent three distinct accounting subsystems, were extensively discussed in previous chapters. However, in these chapters the emphasis was directed toward the balance sheet accounts rather than the nominal accounts. It should be noted that other accounting subsystems exist, but because of their nature they are more appropriate for discussion in later sections of this chapter.

In the tests of transactions for the above three subsystems, a sample of transactions processed during the accounting period is selected for review. It is likely that a review of the sales–accounts receivable subsystem results in the selection of sales invoices prepared during the period. Once selected, these invoices are reviewed for authenticity and compliance with internal control procedures and are then traced through the accounting records. As part of this tracing the details per the invoice are compared to the listings in the book of original entry (the sales journal). The auditor tests the summarization of the book of original entry and traces the totals to the appropriate general ledger accounts which include the nominal account (sales). Thus in fact the tests of transactions substantiate major balances that appear in the income statement. Although many people characterize and criticize the contemporary audit as a balance sheet audit, this is certainly not true.

It is also important for the auditor to be concerned with discovering whether a proper cutoff is accomplished at the end of the year for the nominal accounts. Again, it appears that the cutoff is balance sheet-oriented. Although the cutoff procedures are usually performed as part of the audit program for a balance sheet account, the benefits of the analysis are just as useful in determining the propriety of the related nominal accounts. For example, the sales cutoff is part of the review of shipping notices, usually associated with accounts receivable and inventory, and the review of the bank cutoff statement (for cash sales) which is associated with the cash substantive tests. The determination of a proper cutoff at the beginning and ending of the fiscal year helps ensure proper measurement of the nominal accounts as well.

It is true that the auditor relies more heavily on internal documents to substantiate nominal accounts than to substantiate balance sheet accounts. For example, he or she usually confirms accounts receivable, inventories on consignment, and so on, but seldom confirms an entry in the sales journal or purchases journal. Likewise, audit procedures associated with balance sheet accounts usually generate more competent evidence. Inventory is observed, but a single purchase is not observed. This is not a weakness in the audit approach but rather a reaction to the type of evidence available to substantiate each balance. The ultimate test of the balances discussed in this section is their eventual validation through a cash flow. Most of the balance of a nominal account is usually validated in such a manner by a cash flow by the end of the period.

Most credit sales are collected by the end of the period. Their authenticity as a sale can be determined by tracing the sale to its eventual collection. If the internal control system is adequate, such reliance on internal documents is acceptable and generates competent evidence. The audit exposure is greater for sales that are not validated by a subsequent cash transaction at the end of the year. Obviously, such transactions are identified as accounts receivable, and the auditor must use stronger audit procedures to be reasonably certain of the existence and valuation of these collective transactions.

The auditor is not locked into the above approach. If the internal control is not adequate or fraud or management intervention in the system is suspected, the audit approach is modified. Specific sales or purchases may be confirmed by the auditor. He or she may attempt to observe the purchase of inventory items if a unique identification code is associated with the goods. Other procedures are selected for the nominal accounts to ensure they are properly stated. This of course is the exception rather than the rule.

Detail test of nominal accounts

While the three subsystems discussed above are tested in conjunction with the associated balance sheet accounts, other nominal amounts are associated with balance sheet amounts but the audit approach is different. The main difference is that there is no separate accounting subsystem for the related nominal and balance sheet accounts. These accounts are impacted, for the most part, by the cash disbursements or receipts system and the client's preparation of journal entries at the end of the fiscal year. Figure 16-1 lists some of the typical accounts that fit this description.

Some of the transactions that impact the accounts listed in Figure 16-1 are reviewed during the auditor's test of the cash disbursements subsystem. This test provides a basis to determine the reliability of the amounts generated. However, in most instances so few transactions for a particular account are reviewed that it is necessary to collect additional audit evidence. This may be accomplished by obtaining a detail listing of the account or by reviewing the general ledger account.

The auditor may ask the client to prepare an analysis of the nominal and balance sheet accounts. The account analysis is verified by the auditor by reviewing the client calculations, tracing amounts to approved invoices, reviewing canceled checks, and corroborating the data by reference to other relevant documentation. Figure 16-2 illustrates the approach used in auditing interest expense. The expense is verified in conjunction with two related accounts, notes payable and accrued interest payable. Usually a formal audit program is not prepared; rather, audit procedures are noted and explained on the work sheet. The specific audit procedures used are dependent upon the nature of the account. For example, the review of supplies expense may involve observation of supplies inventories, whereas the review of revenue earned and associated with customer advances may involve confirmation of advanced payments with the customer.

A specific cutoff test is not performed for each item listed in Figure 16-1.

Figure 16-1

NOMINAL ACCOUNT	BALANCE SHEET ACCOUNT
Rent expense	Prepaid rent
Insurance expense	Prepaid insurance
Utilities expense	Accrued utilities expense
Property tax expense	Accrued property tax expense
Professional fee expense	Accrued professional fee expense
Warranty expense	Estimated liability for warranties
Repairs and maintenance expense	Accrued repair and maintenance expense (if any)
Travel and entertainment expense	Accrued travel and entertainment expense
Supplies expense	Supplies
Interest expense	Accrued interest expense
Interest income	Accrued interest receivable
Dividend income	Accrued dividend income
Revenue	Unearned revenue (advances)

However, the items are subject to such a test when the auditor performs the typical search for unrecorded liabilities. By reviewing the vouchers register, cash disbursements journal, unpaid invoice file, and so on, the above accounts are subjected to a cutoff test.

Included in this group of nominal accounts, but excluded from Figure 16-1, is the payroll function, which deserves special attention.

For all organizations there is a need to process routinely payroll data and prepare and distribute the payroll. In any single accounting period the amount of payroll expense is a significant figure for most companies. For this reason the auditor evaluates and tests the payroll system as a single system similar to the other systems (cash receipts, etc.) discussed in this text. Also, the audit approach is very similar to that for the other systems.

INTERNAL CONTROL MODEL: PAYROLL

The features of an adequate internal control system for payroll relate to the plan of organization, especially the autonomy of departments. Also, the specific procedures associated with authorization of an element of payroll data and the responsibility for these tasks are important aspects of an adequate internal control system.

Plan of organization

DEPARTMENTAL AUTONOMY

Because of the volume of data involved in the payroll function and the numerous opportunities for errors in the commission of fraud, it is necessary to assign certain tasks to specific departments. Once assigned, these roles are not to be usurped by other departments. In the payroll system the following segregation of duties comprises part of a strong internal control system:

    I. Accounting department
        1. Maintenance of the payroll register

Figure 16-2

Green Valley Corp.
Analysis of Interest Expense & Related Accounts
12-31-79

Date		Notes Payable			Terms	1979 Interest Expense	Accrued Interest @ 12/31/79
		Balance 1/1/79	Additions Payments	Balance 12/31/79			
11-30-78	First State Bank	90000 ∅	(90000) +		60 days - 9%	6750 ∅ +	-0-
12-31-78	J. P. Walker	5000 ∅	(5000) +		120 days - 8%	1330 ∅	
6-30-79	Alliance Insurance	-0-	25000 C	25000	1 year - 7%	875 00 ∅	875 00
9-30-79	Farmers' Bank		80000 C	80000	1 year - 8%	1600 00 ∅	1600 00
11-30-78	G. X. Finance Co.		10000 C	10000	60 days - 9%	75 00 ∅	75 00
		95000 √	20000 √	115000		3358 00 √	2550 00 √

∅ Agrees with previous working paper balances.
+ Cancelled check inspected.
C Amount and terms confirmed with debtor.
∅ Calculation checked.

540
Audit of
nominal accounts

2. Preparation of individual payroll checks
3. Maintenance of earnings records
4. Responsibility for time cards (usually applicable to production personnel)

II. Treasurer
1. Signature of payroll checks (treasurer)
2. Distribution of payroll checks (paymaster)

III. Functions other than accounting and treasurer
1. Hiring of personnel (personnel department)
2. Maintenance of personnel files (personnel department)
3. Communication of the hiring of new employees, changes in pay rate, and the firing of employees to the payroll department (personnel department)
4. Authorization of hours worked (operating department heads and line supervisors)

A proper plan of organization segregates the elements of the payroll function so that no one department has complete authority over hiring, firing, and processing and distribution of payroll checks. A violation of the above structure invites fraudulent transactions and the occurrence of processing errors in the payroll function.

System of authorization and accountability

EXECUTION OF TRANSACTIONS

In the payroll system several authorizations occur before the eventual payroll check is prepared and distributed. The authorizations include initial authorization as well as current authorization. Even though the transactions are numerous, each individual transaction is specifically approved. This process generates several documents during the execution phase of the payroll procedures.

Authorization for hiring and firing: The hiring of new employees and the subsequent placement of their names on the payroll is centralized in the personnel department. Specifically, the personnel department, based upon requests from operating department heads, screens prospective employees for positions that are open. After the initial screening the strongest candidates are referred to the operating department head for the final selection. The candidates chosen for the position are formally hired and processed by the personnel department. A written notice is sent to the payroll department to place the individual on the payroll. It is important that the hiring function be centralized, so that there is no opportunity to ''pad'' the payroll. Payroll padding refers to the payment of nonexisting employees listed on the payroll.

Similar to the hiring phase the firing of individual employees is centralized in the personnel department. Thus only individual names submitted in writing to the payroll department are to be removed from the payroll. Concentration of the firing function is not as strong a procedure in the prevention of payroll padding as centralization of the hiring function. Obviously, it is difficult for the personnel department to know of every firing if the operating supervisor chooses not to communicate such action. However, other internal control procedures are employed to minimize the possibility of payroll padding.

541
Internal control model: payroll

Authorization of pay rates and deductions: At the initial hiring of an employee, the pay rate is determined and communicated to the payroll department in writing. In addition, other data needed to prepare the payroll are collected by the personnel department and communicated to the payroll department in a similar fashion. The new employee prepares Form W-4 to identify exemptions claimed for income tax purposes. Also, deductions for savings bonds, union dues, contributions, and the like, are formally authorized by the new employee and filed in his or her personnel folder. All these data, which constitute a large part of the information needed to prepare the periodic payroll, are sent to the payroll department. Changes in these basic data, such as a change in pay rate, come directly from the personnel department. The payroll department possesses no authority to make such changes on its own.

Authorization for hours worked: For each pay period, a responsible person approves the number of hours worked by an individual. The responsible person may be the head of an operating department, a manager, or other supervisory personnel. The form of approval varies depending upon the nature of the job performed. For production personnel, a job card, detailing the number of hours worked and the job or department that is to be charged, may be signed by a manager. Salaried employees may prepare a time report for the period, or their supervisor may prepare a payroll sheet indicating if the full salary is to be paid. In any case the approved payroll information is forwarded to the payroll department.

In many enterprises an employee is required to "clock in" and "clock out." If a time clock is employed, it is the responsibility of the timekeeping department, and this department is not involved in any other phases of the payroll function. To prevent abuses of the time clock system, a member of the timekeeping department observes the employees clocking in and out. At the end of the pay period the time cards are sent to the payroll department.

RECORDING OF TRANSACTIONS

The internal control system for payroll is designed to ensure reasonable recording of the payroll transaction in a manner consistent with its execution. The recording of the transaction occurs in the payroll department as part of the overall accounting function.

Consistency of data: The initial step in the payroll department is to determine the consistency of data supplied to the department. This may include the comparison of data per the time cards, obtained from the timekeeping department, and data per the job cards, obtained from managers and other supervisory personnel. The data from the two sources may be balanced for each employee,

542
Audit of
nominal accounts

or a few sample items may be tested. For these, as well as other employees, the names are compared by the payroll department to its lists of authorized employees received from the personnel department.

Preparation of payroll records: Once the propriety of the payroll input data is verified, the payroll, along with various payroll records, is prepared. The payroll department prepares a payroll journal which lists each employee, hours worked, pay rate, deductions, gross pay, and net pay. A cumulative earnings record for each employee is updated, showing payroll information from the beginning of the calendar year. The payroll checks and the payroll check register, showing net pay and payroll check number, are generated. Other payroll information may be generated depending upon the nature of the organization, showing the payroll distribution to various accounts.

The payroll process may be accomplished manually, mechanically, or by the use of a computer. In any case control totals are generated to make sure that only authorized transactions were processed and that no authorized transactions were omitted from processing. This is accomplished through the use of record counts, hash totals, and control totals. For example, in a computerized payroll system, the payroll department prepares the input data for submission to the data processing department. However, before transmitting the data appropriate totals and counts are recorded in the payroll department, which are used to review records generated by data processing and returned to the payroll department.

ACCESS TO ASSETS

Limiting access to assets in the payroll function is achieved through the proper segregation of duties as discussed in the previous sections, the control of documents authorizing the disposition of cash, and the control of distribution of the payroll. The last-mentioned two aspects are discussed at this point.

Once payroll data are collected in the accounting department and payroll records are prepared and updated, the individual payroll checks are prepared. These checks are sent to the treasurer for manual or mechanical signing and then given to the paymaster for distribution. The paymaster distributes each check to the appropriate employee. If the plant is large, it may be necessary for each employee to show identification before being paid. It is important to note that supervisors are not given the individual checks for distribution, even for individuals who may be absent. This internal control procedure prevents one form of payroll padding. Recall that it was stated that it is difficult to update payroll records for everyone that is fired or quits. This approach makes it impossible for the supervisor to omit the reporting of people who leave the company's employment and then obtain their checks.

COMPARISON OF RECORDED ACCOUNTABILITY WITH ASSETS

Except for costs that may be deferred as part of the inventory asset account in a manufacturing concern, the payroll function does not generate an asset.

However, just prior to the payroll distribution the net payroll determined represents a cash flow, and internal control procedures are adopted to compare the asset distribution with the recorded amount. This is achieved by a periodic review conducted by the internal auditing department. During this examination source documents, such as time cards and payroll deduction slips, are used to verify the payroll records generated. In addition, payroll calculations are mathematically checked. Finally, on a surprise basis, the internal audit staff witnesses the entire payroll distribution to make sure there is no payroll padding.

Periodically, usually monthly, the special payroll cash account is reconciled. Ideally this is done by the internal auditing department, but it may be done by someone in the accounting department that has no other payroll duties. For most companies the payroll account has a zero balance, since it is on an imprest basis. Nonetheless, the reconciliation is prepared. Unclaimed checks that show on the reconciliation as outstanding checks are transferred to a special account and after a reasonable period are canceled. Subsequently, if the former employee appears for the payment, a new check properly approved is prepared and charged against the special account.

STUDY AND EVALUATION OF THE PAYROLL SYSTEM

The study and evaluation of the payroll system is similar to the approach described earlier for the review of other systems. An internal control questionnaire, a flowchart, and a memorandum may be prepared. An internal control questionnaire for a payroll system is reproduced in Figure 16-3. A flowchart illustrating a strong internal control system is presented in Figure 16-4.

COMPLIANCE TESTS: PAYROLL

Subsequent to the auditor's study and evaluation of the payroll system, payroll compliance tests are performed. The compliance tests determine if the payroll system is functioning as described in the internal control questionnaire, flowchart, and narrative description. Also, the compliance tests encompass the detail tests of payroll transactions to determine if authorized transactions are properly processed through the accounting system. A typical audit program for the payroll compliance tests is presented in Figure 16-5.

Universe definition and sample selection

The primary objective of the payroll test is to determine that payroll disbursements are properly authorized, computed, and recorded in the accounting records. Probably the best universe definition for such an objective is the selection of the payroll checks processed during the period. The payroll checks are prenumbered, and the auditor determines that they are used in sequence by reviewing a few blocks of checks processed and returned by the bank. There is

Figure 16-3

Internal Control Questionnaire

Payrolls	Answer		Answer based on		
	Yes	No	Inquiry	Observation	Comments

1. Is a time clock system in use –
   a. for factory workers?
   b. for general office workers?					

2. If so, are the time cards –
   a. prepared and controlled by the payroll department, independent of supervisor?
   b. punched by the employees in the presence of the supervisor or other designated employees?
   c. signed by the supervisor at the close of the payroll period?					

3. Are piece-work production reports (if any) signed by –
   a. the employees?
   b. the supervisor?					

4. Are time cards and piece-work production reports checked to or compared with –
   a. production schedules?
   b. payroll distribution?					

5. Does preparation of the payroll require more than one employee?					
6. Are the duties of those preparing the payroll rotated?					
7. Are the names of employees hried reported in writing by the personnel office to the payroll department?					
8. Are the names of employees resigned or discharged reported in writing by the personnel office to the payroll department?					
9. Is the payroll checked at regular intervals against the personnel records?					
10. Are all wage rates fixed by union contract or authorized in writing by a designated official or employee?					
11. Are vacation and sick-leave payments similarly fixed or authorized?					
12. Is there adequate check against payments for vacation, etc., in excess of amounts authorized?					

a one-to-one correspondence between the payroll check universe and the payroll register (the list of checks written, employee names, etc.). The auditor verifies this relationship by tracing (1) from the payroll check universe to the payroll register and by tracing (2) from the payroll register to the payroll check universe.

Once the universe is determined, a sample is selected for testing. In many cases the sample is based on random selection, since there are numerous trans-

	Answer		Answer based on		
Payrolls (continued)	Yes	No	Inquiry	Observation	Comments
13. Is the payroll double-checked as to –					
a. hours?					
b. rates?					
c. deductions?					
d. extensions?					
e. footings?					
14. Are signed authorizations on file for all deductions being made from employees' wages?					
15. Is there a time department independent of the payroll department?					
16. Is the payroll signed prior to payment by –					
a. the employee preparing the payroll?					
b. the employee rechecking the payroll?					
c. the factory manager?					
17. Are salary payrolls approved by a responsible official prior to payment?					
18. Are all employees paid by check?					
19. If paid by check, are the checks prenumbered?					
20. Are checks drawn and signed by employees who do not –					
a. prepare the payroll?					
b. have custody of cash funds?					
c. keep the accounting records?					
21. Are checks distributed to employees by someone other than the supervisor?					
22. Are payroll disbursements made from a special Payroll Bank account?					
23. Is the Payroll Bank account reconciled by employees who do not prepare the payrolls, sign checks, or handle the pay-offs?					
24. If so, does the reconciliation procedure include the comparison of the paid checks with the payroll and the scrutiny of endorsements?					

actions and no one transaction significantly impacts the financial statements. For the same reason, a statistical sampling approach is appropriate for testing payroll transactions. After the sample is selected and a control sheet is prepared, the client may be asked to obtain supporting documents for the transactions. These documents include personnel folders, time cards, payroll checks, and approved payroll sheets.

Figure 16-4

Procedural Flowchart: Payroll. Procedural Flowchart Shown in Relation to Organization Chart to Portray the Control Obtained through Segregation of Functional Responsibility
SOURCE: AICPA, "Internal Control," 1949.

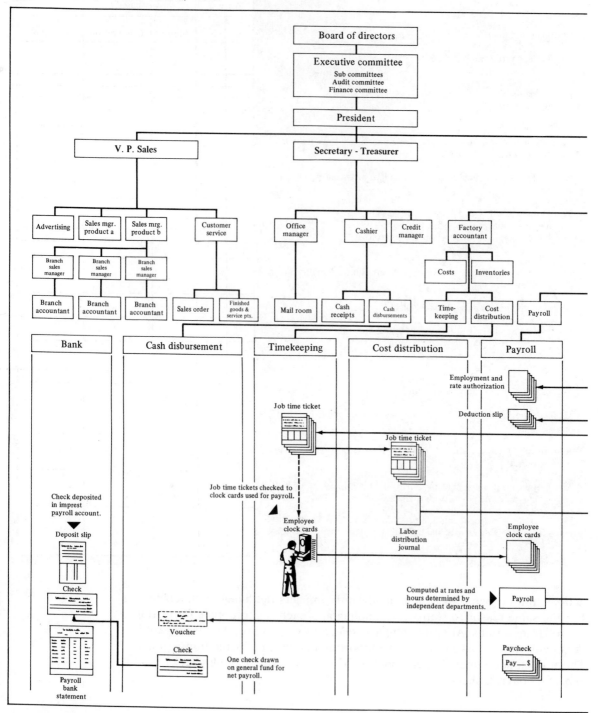

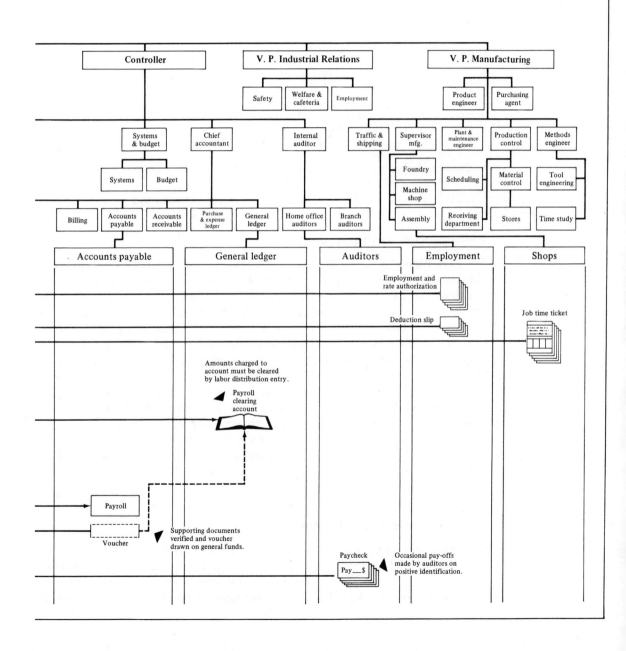

548
Audit of
nominal accounts

Figure 16-5

Audit program: payroll

PROCEDURES	DATE COMPLETED	WORK PERFORMED BY
1. The universe is defined as the prenumbered payroll checks used during the period under review. Each check is a sample item. Determine the size of the universe.	_____	_____
2. Randomly select 150 payroll checks for investigation.	_____	_____
3. For each sample item:		
a. Trace the pay rate to the appropriate authorization.	_____	_____
b. Trace the number of hours worked to the approved payroll forms.	_____	_____
c. Verify the gross pay.	_____	_____
d. Recompute the net pay by reference to authorized deductions contained in the personnel file.	_____	_____
e. Examine the canceled payroll check and compare to payroll records.	_____	_____
4. Account for the numerical sequence of payroll checks.	_____	_____
5. For three months chosen at random, foot the payroll journal and other payroll distribution journals and trace postings to the general ledger.	_____	_____
6. Consider witnessing a complete payroll distribution.	_____	_____
7. Review accounts impacted by the payroll function for unusual items.	_____	_____

Validation of authorization

The execution of a payroll transaction is reviewed to determine if it is properly authorized. For the sample items chosen for review, the auditor verifies the pay rate used by tracing this rate to information in the personnel folder. If the employee is covered by a union contract, the personnel folder contains the employee's rating, such as machinist-apprentice; the auditor reviews the union contract to establish the appropriate pay rate for such a rating. Nonunion employee rates are supported by salary authorizations, approved hourly rates or perhaps specific contracts. In addition to verification of the pay rate, audit procedures are adopted to authenticate the number of hours worked during the payroll period. For production personnel and other wage earners, it is probable that the hours worked are explicitly approved. The auditor reviews time cards and/or job tickets to substantiate the number of hours worked. For other employees, it is likely that the authorization is simply a list of employees and the number of hours worked, which is approved by the department head or other supervisory personnel.

Review of clerical accuracy

A number of computations is made by the client during the processing of the payroll data, and on a test basis these computations are verified by the auditor. The gross pay is verified by multiplying the approved rate by the approved number of hours worked. From this base figure a number of subtractions are made to arrive at the net or take-home employee pay. Each deduction is traced to the personnel folder which contains an appropriate authorization slip signed by the employee. Some deductions are not explicitly authorized but are the result of various tax provisions. For example, the federal income tax deduction is verified by referring to the employee's signed W-4 form and then using the tax deduction schedules supplied by the federal government. On the other hand, the social security tax (FICA) is a flat rate and is applied only up to a certain level of income. The auditor uses the cumulative employee payroll records to determine if the employee is subject to this tax.

After all deductions are verified and recomputed the net pay is verified. The net pay figure is traced to the payroll register for consistency. In addition, the returned payroll check is reviewed to see if the net pay, employee name, payroll check number, and date are consistent with the payroll records. The endorsement on the back of the check is inspected. The auditor is careful to investigate double endorsements, especially if the second signature is that of another employee.

Test of payroll summarization

The auditor tests the summarization of payroll journals that are posting sources for entries in the general ledger. He or she foots and cross-foots these books of original entry for one or more months. These records are scanned for unusual items, such as an unusually large amount. In a similar fashion, the general ledger accounts are reviewed for unusual items. For example, if the payroll is a monthly payroll, there should be 12 entries in the general ledger accounts. More or fewer entries in the records require investigation by the auditor.

SUBSTANTIVE TESTS: PAYROLL

As suggested earlier, the payroll accounting system does not generate significant balance sheet accounts. However, audit procedures are employed in this area. First, the payroll cash account usually carries a zero balance at any date, but at the close of the year the auditor reviews the account as if it were any other bank account. That is, the bank reconciliation is reviewed, and a cutoff bank statement is obtained. Other procedures employed were discussed in Chapter 10.

In most cases the client needs to prepare an adjusting journal entry to record accrued payroll. The auditor, based on the client's payday, reviews the accrual for reasonableness. At the same time, he or she may review the employer's payroll tax accrual. This accrual includes FICA provisions and federal and state unemployment insurance provisions. The auditor vouches all payments made to the federal and the state government and reviews reports prepared by the client for submission to the state and the federal government.

Review of balance sheet allocations

Many accounts appear on the income statement that are the result of internal analysis, that is, adjusting journal entries, made by the client. These are concerned with allocation of the cost of noncurrent assets to the statement as expenses.

550
Audit of
nominal accounts

Included in this category are natural resources; property, plant and equipment; intangible assets; and leases subject to capitalization. In reviewing these allocations the auditor is concerned with the following items:

- Historical cost
- Amortization period
- Amortization policy

HISTORICAL COST

The initial historical cost of an asset subject to amortization is the basis for determining subsequent allocation to the income statement. In general, only costs that benefit future periods are to be deferred in the asset account. Typically this includes the invoice or contract price and costs incidental to preparing the asset for production. Verification of most of these costs is relatively easy, since the auditor can usually review a vendor invoice, contract, freight bill, or the like. However, some costs may be the result of an internal allocation process which makes cost verification more difficult. For example, the salary of an engineer used to prepare a machine for initial production may be capitalized. For machinery or other assets constructed by the client, cost includes labor, materials, and perhaps a portion of factory overhead. With the use of internally generated documents, such as material requisition forms and labor distribution sheets, these costs are substantiated. In addition, new assets are inspected by the auditor on a test basis. For assets not subject to physical observation, existence is determined by reviewing documents that show legal title, registration, or other forms of ownership representation.

Once the initial cost of an asset subject to amortization is determined, it is not necessary to vouch these costs in subsequent audits. However, it is necessary to make sure the assets are being used in the business during subsequent periods. For tangible assets, the auditor inspects their utilization on a test basis. For intangible assets, he or she relies upon the testimony of key employees and on his or her knowledge of the client's business.

AMORTIZATION PERIOD

Assets subject to amortization encompass resources with asset lives subject to laws, contracts, formal promulgations, and economic conditions. For properties subject to depreciation, promulgations of the IRS play an important part in determining the amortization period. Obviously, a client is required to choose a life which is approximately the anticipated life of the asset. It appears that in many instances the IRS guidelines may be too conservative. That is, economic lives may in fact be longer than those allowed by the government. This has been somewhat substantiated by recent studies performed by the SEC in its research associated with replacement cost accounting. The studies are noted at this point because the auditing profession usually accepts the IRS guidelines and the critical evaluation of these guidelines seems to be lacking.

The above criticism of the auditing profession may be inappropriate for several reasons. First, the auditor is concerned with an asset life that is reasonable. Thus perhaps a machine life of five to eight years constitutes a reasonable range and, as long as the client chooses a life that falls within this range, the auditor is not too concerned. Also, the audit effort required to disallow a specific life may be too great in relationship to the benefits. The auditor may be required to review several years of asset records to substantiate an alternative life.

Whatever the explanation, the choice of an amortization period is management's prerogative, and little audit effort is expended to evaluate its assumptions.

AMORTIZATION POLICY

There are a number of acceptable methods that may be used in determining the annual amortization expense. Among them are straight-line, units-of-production, and so-called accelerated methods such as double-declining-balance. Theoretically, the amortization policy is chosen in a manner that reflects the characteristics of the asset. However, in practice it is unlikely that this is achieved. The accounting profession has been unable to establish guidelines that are useful in the selection of an amortization method. Without such guidelines it is very difficult for the auditor to seriously question a client's amortization policy and then sustain the objection. Unfortunately, as a result, the auditor is mainly concerned with the consistent application of amortization methods rather than the appropriateness of a particular method.

SUMMARY

This chapter emphasizes the audit of nominal accounts. It is obvious that contemporary auditing uses a variety of approaches to substantiate the balances that appear on the income statement. The emphasis of any one approach depends upon the nature of the audit environment and, to some degree, the personal preferences of the individual auditor.

EXERCISES AND PROBLEMS

16-1. Why does the approach for auditing a nominal account usually differ from the approach used to review a balance sheet account?

16-2. Is it correct to describe the audit of nominal accounts as being dominated by a single audit technique?

16-3. Is the integrated audit approach as described in this book appropriate for the audit of nominal accounts?

16-4. In the audit of nominal accounts, is the performance of a cutoff test necessary.

16-5. What department should be responsible for the distribution of payroll checks?

16-6. What duties should be performed by the personnel department in a well-designed payroll accounting system?

16-7. What is payroll padding?

16-8. Why does the auditor account for the numerical sequence of payroll checks?

16-9. How does the auditor determine that a payroll transaction has been properly authorized?

552
Audit of
nominal accounts

16-10. Does the auditor perform substantive tests for payroll accounts?

16-11. Prepare an audit program for prepaid insurance and insurance expense.

16-12. How does the auditor review the earnings per share figures that appear on the income statement?

16-13. How does the auditor use comparative analysis in the review of nominal accounts?

16-14. Should the issuance of *FASB No. 14* facilitate the auditor's use of comparative analysis?

16-15. Why does an auditor seldom confirm transactions that comprise the sales account?

16-16. You are engaged in auditing the financial statements of Henry Brown, a large independent contractor. All the employees are paid in cash, because Brown believes this arrangement reduces clerical expenses and is preferred by his employees.

During the audit you find in the petty cash fund approximately $200, of which $185 is stated to be unclaimed wages. Further investigation reveals that Brown has installed the procedure of putting unclaimed wages in the petty cash fund so that the cash can be used for disbursements. When the claimant appears, he or she is paid from the petty cash fund. Brown contends that this procedure reduces the number of checks drawn to replenish the petty cash fund and centers the responsibility for all cash on hand in one person inasmuch as the petty cash custodian distributes the pay envelopes.

Required
1. Does Brown's system provide proper internal control of unclaimed wages? Explain fully.
2. Because Brown insists on paying salaries in cash, what procedures would you recommend to provide better internal control over unclaimed wages? (AICPA Adapted)

16-17. Your client is the Quaker Valley Shopping Center, Inc., a shopping center with 30 store tenants. All store leases provide for a fixed rent plus a percentage of sales, net of sales taxes, in excess of a fixed dollar amount computed on an annual basis. Each lease also provides that the landlord may engage a CPA to audit all records of the tenant to ensure that sales are being properly reported.

You have been requested by your client to audit the records of the Bali Pearl Restaurant to determine that the sales totaling $390,000 for the year ended December 31, 1978, have been properly reported to the landlord. The restaurant and the shopping center entered into a five-year lease on January 1, 1979. The Bali Pearl Restaurant offers only table service. No liquor is served. During meal times there are four or five waitresses in attendance who prepare handwritten prenumbered restaurant checks for the customers. Payment is made at a cash register, to the proprietor, as the customer leaves. All sales are for cash. The proprietor is also the bookkeeper. Complete files are kept of restaurant checks and cash register tapes. A daily sales book and general ledger are also maintained.

Required: List the auditing procedures you would employ to verify the total annual sales of the Bali Pearl Restaurant. (Disregard vending machine sales and counter sales of chewing gum, candy, etc.) (AICPA Adapted)

16-18. You are auditing the financial statements of the Meyers Company for the year ended December 31, 1979. As part of your examination you ask your client to prepare an analysis of payroll taxes expense and accrued payroll taxes. In response the client prepares the analysis that appears in Problem Figure 16-18.

Problem Figure 16-18

Meyers Electric Company
Analysis of Payroll Taxes
December 31, 1979

	Balance 12-31-78	Additions	Payments	Balance 12-31-79
FICA Taxes	24836	629933	59263	595506
Withholding Taxes—Federal	39891	926839	894364	72366
State	2314	87272	85937	3649
State Unemployment Tax	1294	4812	4796	1310
Federal Unemployment Tax	1191	4486	4374	1303
	69526	1653342	1048734	674134

554
Audit of
nominal accounts

Required

1. Indicate, directly on the analysis, the audit procedures you would employ to verify the accounts mentioned above. (Assume that your firm audited the financial statements in 1978.)

2. Criticize the format of the client-prepared working paper.

16-19. You have been engaged to perform the audit of Marke Manufacturing Company for the year ended December 31, 1980. During your review of the payroll system you discover that Franklin, controller of the company, prepares the payroll and personally distributes the checks to all the company's 300 production employees. A brief review of payroll folders, files, and other data suggests that payroll transactions are properly documented, although no one has ever reviewed the work of Franklin.

In your review of the payroll system you are very concerned with Franklin's role. Furthermore, the company has never been audited during its seven years of existence.

As part of your audit approach you are considering witnessing of a payroll payoff.

Required

1. What is the purpose of witnessing a payroll payoff?

2. Should the procedure be performed as part of the interim work or the year-end work?

3. How should you prepare for such a procedure?

16-20. The Kowal Manufacturing Company employs about 50 production workers and has the following payroll procedures.

The factory interviews applicants and on the basis of the interview either hires or rejects them. When the applicant is hired he or she prepares a W-4 form (employee's withholding exemption certificate) and gives it to the supervisor. The supervisor writes the hourly rate of pay for the new employee in the corner of the W-4 form and then gives it to a payroll clerk as notice that the worker has been employed. The supervisor verbally advises the payroll department of rate adjustments.

A supply of blank time cards is kept in a box near the entrance to the factory. Each worker takes a time card on Monday morning, fills in his or her name and notes in pencil on the time card his or her daily arrival and departure times. At the end of the week the workers drop the time cards in a box near the door to the factory.

The completed time cards are taken from the box on Monday morning by a payroll clerk. Two payroll clerks divide the cards alphabetically between them, one taking the A to L section of the payroll and the other taking the M to Z section. Each clerk is fully responsible for his or her section of the payroll and computes the gross pay, deductions, and net pay, posts the details to the employee's earnings records, and prepares and numbers the payroll checks. Employees are automatically removed from the payroll when they fail to turn in a time card.

The payroll checks are manually signed by the chief accountant and given to the supervisor who distributes them to the workers in the factory and arranges for the delivery of checks to workers who are absent. The payroll bank account is reconciled by the chief accountant who also prepares the various quarterly and annual payroll tax reports.

Required: List your suggestions for improving the Kowal Manufacturing Company's system of internal control for factory hiring practices and payroll procedures.

(AICPA Adapted)

16-21. In many companies, labor costs represent a substantial percentage of total dollars expended in any one accounting period. One of the auditor's primary means of verifying payroll transactions is by a detailed payroll test.

You are making an annual examination of the Joplin Company, a medium-sized manufacturing company. You have selected a number of hourly employees for a detailed payroll test. The following work-sheet outline has been prepared:

COLUMN NUMBER	COLUMN HEADING
1	Employee number
2	Employee name
3	Job classification
	Hours worked
4	Straight time
5	Premium time
6	Hourly rate
7	Gross earnings
	Deductions
8	FICA withheld
9	Federal income tax withheld
10	Union dues
11	Hospitalization
12	Amount of check
13	Check and check number
14	Account number charged
15	Description of account

Required

1. What factors should you consider in selecting the sample of employees to be included in any payroll test?

2. Using the column numbers above as a reference, state the principal way(s) that the information in each column can be verified.

3. In addition to the payroll test, you employ a number of other audit procedures in the verification of payroll transactions. List five additional procedures which may be employed. (AICPA Adapted)

16-22. The Generous Loan Company has 100 branch loan offices. Each office has a manager and four or five subordinates who are employed by the manager. Branch managers prepare the weekly payroll, including their own salaries, and pay employees from cash on hand. The employee signs the payroll sheet compiled from time cards prepared by the employee and approved by the manager.

The weekly payroll sheets are sent to the home office along with other accounting statements and reports. The home office compiles employee earnings records and prepares all federal and state salary reports from the weekly payroll sheets.

Salaries are established by home office job evaluation schedules. Salary adjustments, promotions, and transfers of full-time employees are approved by a home office salary committee based upon the recommendations of branch managers and area supervisors. Branch managers advise the salary committee of new full-time employees and terminations. Part-time and temporary employees are hired without referral to the salary committee.

Required

1. Based upon your review of the payroll system, how might payroll funds be diverted?

2. Prepare a payroll audit program to be used in the home office to audit the branch office payrolls of the Generous Loan Company. (AICPA Adapted)

556
Audit of
nominal accounts

16-23. You are auditing the financial statements of the Soo Company for the year ended December 31, 1979. Following are transcripts of the company's general ledger accounts for salary expense and payroll taxes.

	SALARY EXPENSE				
DATE	EXPLANATION	FOL	DEBIT	CREDIT	BALANCE
12/31/79	Weekly payrolls (total of 12 monthly summary entries)	CD	$44,470		$44,470

	PAYROLL TAXES EXPENSE				
DATE	EXPLANATION	FOL	DEBIT	CREDIT	BALANCE
1/10/79	Quarterly remittance	CD	$ 4,100		$ 4,100
4/20/79	Quarterly remittance	CD	3,801		7,901
7/14/79	Quarterly remittance	CD	3,327		11,228
10/18/79	Quarterly remittance	CD	3,320		14,548

	PAYROLL TAXES WITHHELD				
DATE	EXPLANATION	FOL	DEBIT	CREDIT	BALANCE
1/1/79	Balance forward			$3,200	$ 3,200

	EMPLOYER PAYROLL TAXES PAYABLE				
DATE	EXPLANATION	FOL	DEBIT	CREDIT	BALANCE
1/1/79	Balance forward			$ 900	$ 900

The following additional information is available:

1. Copies of the quarterly tax returns are not available because the typist did not understand that the returns were to be typed in duplicate. The pencil drafts of the tax returns were discarded.
2. Your audit of the payroll records revealed that the payroll clerk properly computed the payroll tax deductions and the amounts of quarterly remittances. You develop the following summary:

		PAYROLL TAXES WITHHELD		
QUARTER	GROSS SALARIES	FICA	INCOME	NET SALARIES
First	$13,600	$425	$2,600	$10,575
Second	12,000	375	2,280	9,345
Third	12,800	325	2,400	10,075
Fourth	18,700	225	4,000	14,475

3. The Soo Company did not make monthly deposits of taxes withheld. You determine that the following remittances were made with respect to 1979 payrolls:

	4/20/79	7/14/79	10/18/79	1/12/80
FICA (6¼ percent)	$ 850	$ 750	$ 650	$ 450
Income tax	2,600	2,280	2,400	4,000
State unemployment insurance (2.7 percent)	351	297	270	162
Total	$3,801	$3,327	$3,320	$4,612

4. The effective federal unemployment tax rate for 1979 is 0.8 percent. The laws of the state in which Soo Company does business do not provide for employee contributions for state unemployment insurance.

557
Exercises and problems

Required

1. Prepare a worksheet to determine the correct balances on December 31, 1979, for the general ledger accounts, salary expense, payroll taxes expense, payroll taxes withheld, and employer payroll taxes payable. (Disregard accrued salaries at year end.)

2. Prepare the adjusting journal entry to correct the accounts on December 31, 1979. (AICPA Adapted)

16-24. You are auditing the financial statements of Beta Corporation for the year ended December 31, 1980. As part of your examination you ask your assistant to verify the cash payroll account as of the end of the year. The assistant makes the analysis and submits a working paper which is reproduced in Problem Figure 16-24.

Required

1. Since the asset balance is zero, is it necessary for you to analyze the account?

2. Suggest additional audit procedures that you should employ in reviewing the payroll cash account.

16-25. During your audit of the accounts of the Gelard Manufacturing Corporation, your assistant tells you that she has found errors in the computation of wages of factory workers and wants you to verify her work.

Your assistant has extracted from the union contract the following description of the system for computing wages in various departments of the company. The contract provides that the minimum wage for a worker is his or her base rate, which is also paid for any "down time," time when the worker's machine is being repaired or he or she is without work. The standard work week is 40 hours. The union contract also provides that workers be paid 150 percent of base rates for overtime production. The company is engaged in interstate commerce.

1. *Straight piecework:* The worker is paid at the rate of 20¢ per piece produced.
2. *Percentage bonus plan:* Standard quantities of production per hour are established by the engineering department. The worker's average hourly production, determined from total hours worked and production, is divided by the standard quantity of production to determine the efficiency ratio. The efficiency ratio is then applied to the base rate to determine the hourly earnings for the period.
3. *Emerson efficiency system:* A minimum wage is paid for production up to 66⅔ percent of the standard output or "efficiency." When the worker's production exceeds 66⅔ percent of the standard output, he or she is paid at a bonus rate. The bonus rate is determined from the accompanying table:

EFFICIENCY (%)	BONUS (%)
Up to 66⅔	0
66⅔–79	10
80–99	20
100–125	45

WORKER	WAGE INCENTIVE PLAN	TOTAL HOURS	DOWN TIME HOURS	UNITS PRO- DUCED	STAN- DARD UNITS	BASE RATE ($)	GROSS WAGES PER BOOKS ($)
Long	Straight piecework	40	5	400		1.80	82.00
Loro	Straight piecework	46	0	455 (1)		1.80	91.00

Problem Figure 16-24

Beta Corporation
Cash in Bank-Payroll
12-31-80

		1	2	3	4
1	Balance Per Bank 12-31-80			764 83 T	
2					
3	Add: Transfer to Payroll				
4	Account - 12-30-80			821 771 49	
5					
6					
7	Less: Payroll for the pay				
8	week ended 12/31/80			⟨821 771 49⟩	
9					
10	Check #				
11	1079		224 96		
12	8864		389 47		
13	11921		150 40	764 83	
14					
15	Balance Per Bank 12-31-80			-0-	
16				✓	
17					
18	✓- Footed.				
19	T- Traced to bank statement.				

WORKER	WAGE INCENTIVE PLAN	TOTAL HOURS	DOWN TIME HOURS	UNITS PRO-DUCED	STAN-DARD UNITS	BASE RATE ($)	GROSS WAGES PER BOOKS ($)
Huck	Straight piecework	44	4	420 (2)		1.80	84.00
Nini	Percentage bonus plan	40	0	250	200	2.20	120.00
Boro	Percentage bonus plan	40	0	180	200	1.90	67.00
Wiss	Emerson	40	0	240	300	2.10	92.00
Alan	Emerson	40	2	590	600 (3)	2.00	118.00

(1) Includes 45 pieces produced during the six overtime hours.

(2) Includes 50 pieces produced during the four overtime hours. The overtime, which brought about the down time, was necessary to meet a production deadline.

(3) Standard units for 40 hours production.

Required

1. Prepare a schedule comparing each individual's gross wages per books and his or her gross wages per your calculation. Computations of workers' wages should be in good form and labeled with the workers' names.

2. All the above errors, as well as others, were found in a weekly payroll selected for examination. The total number of errors was substantial. Discuss the courses of action you can take.

16-26. You are reviewing audit work papers containing a narrative description of the Tenney Corporation's factory payroll system. A portion of that narrative is as follows:

> Factory employees punch time clock cards each day when entering or leaving the shop. At the end of each week the timekeeping department collects the time cards and prepares duplicate batch control slips by department showing total hours and number of employees. The time cards and original batch control slips are sent to the payroll accounting section. The second copies of the batch control slips are filed by date.
>
> In the payroll accounting section payroll transaction cards are keypunched from the information on the time cards, and a batch total card for each batch is keypunched from the batch control slip. The time cards and batch control slips are then filed by batch for possible reference. The payroll transaction cards and batch total card are sent to data processing where they are sorted by employee number within each batch. Each batch is edited by a computer program which checks the validity of employee number against a master employee tape file and the total hours and number of employees against the batch total card. A detail printout by batch and employee number is produced, which indicates batches that do not balance and invalid employee numbers. This printout is returned to payroll accounting to resolve all differences.

In searching for documentation you found a flowchart of the payroll system which included all appropriate symbols (American National Standards Institute, Inc.) but was only partially labeled. The portion of this flowchart described in the above narrative appears in Problem Figure 16-26.

Required

1. Number your answers 1 through 17. Next to the corresponding number add the appropriate label (document name, process description, or file order) applicable to each symbol on the flowchart.

2. Flowcharts are one of the aids an auditor may use to determine and evaluate a client's internal control system. List the advantages of using flowcharts in this context. (AICPA Adapted)

Problem Figure 16-26

Tenney Corporation
Flowchart of Factory Payroll System

Timekeeping Department	Payroll Accounting Section	Data Processing

From factory
time clocks

(1)

(2)

By department:
- Total hours
- Number of
  employees

(3)

By
date

(4)

(5)

Batch
total
card

(9)

(6)

(7)

(8)

(10)

(11)

(12)

(13)

(14)

(15)

(16)

(17)

Problem Figure 16-27

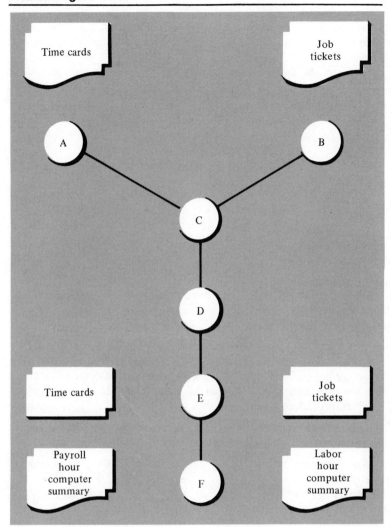

16-27. In connection with his examination of the financial statements of the Olympia Manufacturing Company, a CPA reviews procedures for accumulating direct labor hours. He learns that all production is by job order and that all employees are paid hourly wages, with time-and-a-half for overtime hours.

Olympia's direct-labor hour input process for payroll and job cost determination is summarized in the flowchart in Problem Figure 16-27.

Steps A and C are performed in timekeeping, step B in factory operations, step D in payroll audit and control, step E in data preparation (keypunch), and step F in computer operations.

Required: For each input processing step A through F:
1. List the possible errors or discrepancies that may occur.
2. Cite the corresponding control procedure that should be in effect for each error or discrepancy.

562
Audit of
nominal accounts

Note: Your discussion of Olympia's procedures should be limited to the input process for direct labor hours, as shown in steps A through F in the flowchart. Do not discuss personnel procedures for hiring, promotion, termination, and pay rate authorization. In step F do not discuss equipment, computer programs, and general computer operational controls.

Organize your answer for each input-processing step as follows:

STEP	POSSIBLE ERRORS OR DISCREPANCIES	CONTROL PROCEDURES

(AICPA Adapted)

MULTIPLE CHOICE

1. From the standpoint of good procedural control, distributing payroll checks to employees is best handled by the

    a. Accounting department.
    b. Personnel department.
    c. Treasurer's department.
    d. Employee's departmental supervisor.

Items 2 to 4 apply to a CPA's examination of the financial statements of the Mia Sal Corporation for the year ended December 31, 1981. An auditing procedure is described in each item and four potential errors or questionable practices are listed as answers. You are to choose the error questionable practice that has the best chance of being detected by the specific auditing procedure given.

2. The CPA reviews transactions in the repairs and maintenance account for the year and examines supporting documents on a test basis.

    a. Certain necessary maintenance was not performed during the year because of a shortage of workers.
    b. The cost of erecting a roof over the storage yard was considered maintenance.
    c. The annual painting of the company's delivery trucks was capitalized.
    d. Materials issue slips were not prepared for some of the maintenance supplies used.

3. The CPA compares 1981 revenues and expenses with those for the prior year and investigates all changes exceeding 10 percent.

    a. The cashier began lapping accounts receivable in 1981.
    b. Because of worsening economic conditions, the 1981 provision for uncollectable accounts was inadequate.
    c. Mia Sal changed its capitalization policy for small tools in 1981.
    d. An increase in property tax rates has not been recognized in Mia Sal's 1981 accrual.

4. The CPA analyzes the accrued interest payable account for the year, recomputes the amounts of payments and beginning and ending balances, and reconciles with the interest expense account.

a. Interest revenue of $52 on a note receivable was credited against miscellaneous expense.
b. A provision of the company's loan agreement was violated. Common dividends are prohibited if income available for interest and dividends is not three times interest requirements.
c. Interest paid on an open account was charged to the raw material purchases account.
d. A note payable had not been recorded. Interest of $150 on the note was properly paid and charged to the interest expense account.

5. The CPA reviews Pyzi's payroll procedures. An example of an internal control weakness is to assign to a department supervisor the responsibility for

a. Distributing payroll checks to subordinate employees.
b. Reviewing and approving time reports for subordinates.
c. Interviewing applicants for subordinate positions prior to hiring by the personnel department.
d. Initiating requests for salary adjustments for subordinate employees.

(AICPA Adapted)

CHAPTER

17

The audit report

The audit process culminates in preparation of the audit report. This report serves as the method of communication between the auditor and the user of the financial statements. To avoid misunderstandings, the wording of the audit report is carefully chosen. Since the information communicated is based upon technical subject matter, using generally accepted accounting principles, it is imperative that both the auditor and the user fully understand the nature of the audit reporting process. This chapter deals with the complexities of audit report preparation and the limitations of the reporting process.

COMPLETING THE AUDIT

Prior to preparation of the audit report, the auditor performs additional tasks which bridge the gap between the collection of evidence, as described in the previous chapters, and the actual preparation of the report. Two important phases of completion of the audit are:

- Review of subsequent events
- Review of all evidential matter

Review of subsequent events

The auditor is responsible for the discovery and reporting of significant events that occur after the balance sheet date but prior to the date of the audit report. The audit report date, often referred to as the sign-off date, is the date that the auditor completes the fieldwork. There is of course a time lag between the dates shown on the face of the financial statements and the date when a user can actually utilize the statements in the decision-making process. In most cases the minimum difference between the date of the statements and the date a user acquires possession of the statements is about 6 to 10 weeks. As suggested

564

above, during this period events may occur that significantly change the financial status of a particular company. Audit exposure can be great in this area; accordingly, the auditor adopts procedures to mitigate the possibility of the nonreporting of a significant event. The audit approach consists of procedures incorporated in the routine audit programs and procedures specifically used in a separate audit program.

ROUTINE PROCEDURES: SUBSEQUENT EVENTS

Much of the audit exposure in any engagement is due to the uncertainty of the cash realization or payment of a particular account. Once a transaction is validated by a cash flow, the collection of competent evidential matter is tremendously enhanced. Eventually all transactions are validated by a cash flow. Unfortunately for the auditor, timely financial information must be published and distributed and cannot wait for the cash flows to take place. It is not surprising that the auditor uses as much as possible events that occur after the close of the year to substantiate balances that appear on the financial statements. For example, a government contract, represented by a receivable on the balance sheet, may be validated by an actual cash flow after the close of the fiscal year but prior to the sign-off date. Subsequent events that generate evidential matter are not restricted to cash flows. In the case of the government contract, a report from the renegotiation board is utilized to substantiate the receivable balance.

Thus the auditor adopts procedures in almost every audit of a balance that utilize evidence generated after the balance sheet date. He or she reviews sales prices on the sales invoices after the close of the year to determine the likelihood of recovering the cost of inventory items. In the area of accounts receivable, subsequent cash collections are reviewed. The examination of subsequent transactions is a critical part of the audit of liabilities. In addition, cutoff data gathered in each area incorporate events that occur after the balance sheet date. Procedures adopted to determine that a proper cash cutoff was accomplished include the auditor's request for and utilization of a bank cutoff statement. It is obvious that the review of subsequent events permeates audit programs in a number of areas.

SPECIAL AUDIT PROGRAM: SUBSEQUENT EVENTS

In addition to the performance of procedures that are an integral part of other audit programs, the auditor usually prepares an audit program specifically designed to test for subsequent events. These procedures are performed at or near the completion of the audit. *SAS No. 1,* Section 560.12, lists the following procedures to be performed in the review for subsequent events:

a. Read the latest available interim financial statements; compare them with the financial statements being reported upon; and make any other comparisons considered appropriate in the circumstances. In order to make these procedures as meaningful as possible for the purpose expressed above, the auditor should inquire of officers and other executives having responsibility for financial and accounting matters as to whether the interim statements have been prepared on the same basis as that used for the statements under examination.

b. Inquire of and discuss with officers and other executives having responsibility for

566
The audit report

financial and accounting matters (limited where appropriate to major locations) as to:

(i) Whether any substantial contingent liabilities or commitments existed at the date of the balance sheet being reported on or at the date of inquiry.

(ii) Whether there was any significant change in the capital stock, long-term debt, or working capital to the date of inquiry.

(iii) The current status of items, in the financial statements being reported on, that were accounted for on the basis of tentative, preliminary, or inconclusive data.

(iv) Whether any unusual adjustments had been made during the period from the balance sheet date to the date of inquiry.

c. Read the available minutes of meetings of stockholders, directors, and appropriate committees; as to meetings for which minutes are not available, inquire about matters dealt with at such meetings.

d. Inquire of client's legal counsel concerning litigation, claims, and assessments. (See discussion in Chapter 14).

e. Obtain a letter of representation, dated as of the date of the auditor's report, from appropriate officials, generally the chief executive officer and chief financial officer, as to whether any events occurred subsequent to the date of the financial statements being reported on by the independent auditor that in the officer's opinion would require adjustment or disclosure in these statements. The auditor may elect to have the client include representations as to significant matters disclosed to the auditor in his performance of the procedures in subparagraphs (a) to (d) above and (f) below. (See Figure 17-1.)

f. Make such additional inquiries or perform such procedures as he considers necessary and appropriate to dispose of questions that arise in carrying out the foregoing procedures, inquiries, and discussions.

Procedure (e) above refers to the obtaining of a representation letter in which the client makes certain assertions about the occurrence of subsequent events. The purpose of the letter is to show that the auditor requested and received a written statement from the client concerning such events. This letter becomes part of the corroborative evidence acquired by the auditor. However, this evidence is considered rather weak and must be augmented by other audit procedures. Nonetheless, *SAS No. 19* requires that written representations from management be obtained as part of an examination made in accordance with generally accepted auditing standards. An example of a representation letter is shown in Figure 17-1.

NATURE OF SUBSEQUENT EVENT

The impact of a subsequent event on the financial statements is dependent upon the nature of the event. Using the audit procedures described above, the auditor may encounter two types of subsequent events.

The first type is defined by *SAS No. 1,* Section 560.03, as ". . . events that provide additional evidence with respect to conditions that existed at the date of the balance sheet and affect the estimates inherent in the process of preparing financial statements." These events result in adjusting journal entries if they are material. Again, with hindsight, an accountant can prepare financial statements that minimize the need for estimates. During the few weeks after the balance sheet date, events occur that may validate or invalidate an estimate at the balance sheet date. For example, the bankruptcy of a customer may result in the need to write off a large accounts receivable.

567
Completing the audit

The auditor is careful not to propose audit adjustments that do not reflect the measurement of an asset or liability at the balance sheet date. It is possible that assets and liabilities are correct at the balance sheet date but, as a result of economic events after the balance sheet date, an asset is impaired or a liability is incurred. In this case an adjustment to the account is not required, since the accounts are correct at the balance sheet date. It is often difficult to determine the date of the impact of an event and the need for an adjustment. The auditor is careful to recognize the informational lag between the economic impact of an event and the identification of the event. In reviewing subsequent events in the inventory area, the auditor may discover that a competitor's announcement of a clearly superior product makes part of the client's inventory obsolete. He or she must determine if the economic consequences existed at the date of the balance sheet, even though the actual announcement of the new product did not occur until after the balance sheet date. It appears that the AICPA encourages an adjustment in most of these cases, as evidenced by the following statement in *SAS No. 1*, Section 560.07:

> Subsequent events affecting the realization of assets such as receivables and inventories or the settlement of estimated liabilities ordinarily will require adjustment of the financial statements . . . because such events typically represent the culmination of conditions that existed over a relatively long period of time.

Clearly an uninsured casualty loss, such as damages from a flood, that occurs after the balance sheet date does not require an adjusting journal entry.

The second type of subsequent event is defined by *SAS No. 1 Statements on Auditing Standards,* Section 560.05, as "events that provide evidence with respect to conditions that did not exist at the date of the balance sheet being reported on but arose subsequent to that date." Such events do not require adjusting journal entries. However, when the events are significant to the interpretation of the financial statements, they are disclosed in footnotes to the financial statements. This is necessary to avoid making the financial statements misleading to the user. To illustrate, in the previous paragraph it was suggested that losses from a flood do not result in an adjustment to the financial statements if the flood occurred after the balance sheet date. If the productive capacity of the client is significantly impaired, it is necessary to disclose this event and its consequences to the user. This disclosure is achieved through the preparation of an appropriate footnote in most instances. Occasionally disclosure through the preparation of a *pro forma* balance sheet to supplement the historical cost financial statements is needed if the impact of the subsequent event on future periods is very great. One company explained the need for *pro forma* presentation under the following circumstances:

> The pro forma balance sheet presents the financial position of the company as it would have appeared at March 31, 1974, if the subsequent dispositions of segments of the business (Note B) and the subsequent sale of convertible debentures and the

568
The audit report

Figure 17-1

(Date of Auditor's Report)

(To Independent Auditor)

In connection with your examination of the (identification of financial statements) of (name of client) as of (date) and for the (period of examination) for the purpose of expressing an opinion as to whether the financial statements present fairly the financial position, results of operations, and changes in financial position of (name of client) in conformity with generally accepted accounting principles (other comprehensive basis of accounting), we confirm, to the best of our knowledge and belief, the following representations made to you during your examination.

1. We are responsible for the fair presentation in the financial statements of financial position, results of operations, and changes in financial position in conformity with generally accepted accounting principles (other comprehensive basis of accounting).

2. We have made available to you all—
   a. Financial records and related data.
   b. Minutes of the meetings of stockholders, directors, and committees of directors, or summaries of actions of recent meetings for which minutes have not yet been prepared.

3. There have been no—
   a. Irregularities involving management or employees who have significant roles in the system of internal accounting control.
   b. Irregularities involving other employees that could have a material effect on the financial statements.
   c. Communications from regulatory agencies concerning noncompliance with, or deficiencies in, financial reporting practices that could have a material effect on the financial statements.

4. We have no plans or intentions that may materially affect the carrying value or classification of assets and liabilities.

5. The following have been properly recorded or disclosed in the financial statements:
   a. Related party transactions and related amounts receivable or payable, including sales, purchases, loans, transfers, leasing arrangements, and guarantees.
   b. Capital stock repurchase options or agreements or capital stock reserved for options, warrants, conversions, or other requirements.
   c. Arrangements with financial institutions involving compensating balances or other arrangements involving

restrictions on cash balances and line-of-credit or similar arrangements.
d. Agreements to repurchase assets previously sold.

6. There are no—
    a. Violations or possible violations of laws or regulations whose effects should be considered for disclosure in the financial statements or as a basis for recording a loss contingency.
    b. Other material liabilities or gain or loss contingencies that are required to be accrued or disclosed by Statement of Financial Accounting Standards No. 5.

7. There are no unasserted claims or assessments that our lawyer has advised us are probable of assertion and must be disclosed in accordance with Statement of Financial Standards No. 5.

8. There are no material transactions that have not been properly recorded in the accounting records underlying the financial statements.

9. Provision, when material, has been made to reduce excess or obsolete inventories to their estimated net realizable value.

10. The company has satisfactory title to all owned assets, and there are no liens or encumbrances on such assets nor has any asset been pledged.

11. Provision has been made for any material loss to be sustained in the fulfillment of, or from inability to fulfill, any sales commitments.

12. Provision has been made for any material loss to be sustained as a result of purchase commitments for inventory quantities in excess of normal requirements or at prices in excess of the prevailing market prices.

13. We have complied with all aspects of contractual agreements that would have a material effect on the financial statements in the event of noncompliance.

14. No events have occurred subsequent to the balance sheet that would require adjustment to, or disclosure in, the financial statements.

(Name of Chief Executive Officer and Title)

(Name of Chief Financial Officer and Title)

SOURCE: "Client Representations," *Statement on Auditing Standards No. 19* (New York: AICPA, 1977), pp. 8–9.

570
The audit report

proposed application of proceeds therefrom (Note L) had been consummated at that date.

Events that normally require footnote disclosure are:

- Sale of senior securities or common stock
- Acquisition of a business
- Casualty losses occurring after the balance sheet date
- Settlement of lawsuits that resulted from events subsequent to the balance sheet date

DISCOVERY OF EVENTS SUBSEQUENT TO THE REPORT DATE

The auditor is not required to continue auditing after the date of the report. However, it is reasonable to expect that he or she may discover facts after the report date that impact the financial statements. The discovery of such facts may occur when the auditor performs interim audit work or other audit procedures for the client for the next year's audit. In addition, conversations with other business executives, such as bankers, may raise the auditor's suspicions. Irrespective of the source of the data, he or she determines whether the event is associated with the audited financial statements or with subsequent financial statements. If facts existed or an event occurred on or before the date of the report, then the auditor gathers additional evidence to evaluate the situation. For example, a client involved in litigation may disclose the problem in a footnote to the financial statement. After the report date the lawsuit may be resolved, requiring substantial payments by the client. Since the event, final determination of the contingency, occurred after the report date, the auditor is not required to perform additional investigation.

If the auditor believes that the event may impact the fairness of the previously issued financial statements, responsible personnel of the client is contacted. Through this conversation the auditor decides if there is a potential reporting problem. If he or she believes that such a problem exists, appropriate audit procedures are undertaken. Since time is critical and users rely on the financial statements, the auditor's course of action is dependent upon the circumstances. *SAS No. 1,* Section 561.06, identifies the following disclosure alternatives:

a. If the effect on the financial statements or auditor's report of the subsequently discovered information can promptly be determined, disclosure should consist of issuing, as soon as practicable, revised financial statements and auditor's report. The reasons for the revision usually should be described in a note to the financial statements and referred to in the auditor's report. Generally, only the most recently issued audited financial statements would need to be revised, even though the revision resulted from events that had occurred in prior years.

b. When the effect on the financial statements of the subsequently discovered information cannot be determined without a prolonged investigation, the issuance of revised financial statements and auditor's report would necessarily be delayed. In this circumstance, when it appears that the information will require a revision of the statements, appropriate disclosure would consist of notification by the client to persons who are known to be relying or who are likely to rely on the financial statements and the related report that they should not be relied upon, and that revised financial statements and auditor's report will be issued upon completion of an investigation. If applicable, the client should be advised to discuss with the Securities and Exchange Commission, stock exchanges, and appropriate regulatory agencies the disclosure to be made or other measures to be taken in the circumstances.[1]

The above approach assumes that the client cooperates with the auditor and agrees with the need for disclosure. If the client refuses to cooperate or to make the appropriate disclosures, the auditor informs the client and appropriate regulatory agencies that the auditor's report can no longer be associated with the financial statements. If a regulatory authority is not involved, the auditor is required to notify each individual known to the auditor to be relying on the financial statements. Since the auditor is disclosing information which the client may contest as being confidential, the former is in a very difficult position. Before such disclosures are made by the auditor, he or she is advised to discuss the matter thoroughly with an attorney.

Review of all evidential matter

A medium-sized or large audit is conducted with the assistance of several auditors. The specific tasks performed by the individuals may be limited to a few functional areas. One auditor may perform the audit work on receivables and cash, while another may be concerned with fixed assets and inventories. With such specialization it is necessary for one or more experienced auditors to capture a broad perspective of the audit. The old cliche, "One can't see the forest for the trees," is well worth remembering in an engagement. Auditors guard against becoming so involved in the details of the audit or an audit procedure that they overlook the potential impact of a particular situation. Additionally, they need to coordinate evidence gathered in one area of the audit with evidence gathered or needed to be gathered in another. In essence, at the conclusion of the engagement it is necessary to contemplate all the work done to that point and relate the results to the formulation of an opinion on the financial statements taken as a whole. The review process is concerned with (1) the review of working papers and (2) an independent review.

REVIEW OF WORKING PAPERS

The first phase of the review process is conducted by the auditors responsible for the engagement. This examination is characterized as a hierarchical process whereby each superior reviews the work of a subordinate. That is, the senior auditor reviews the working papers of the junior auditor, the audit manager reviews the working papers of the senior and junior auditors, and so on. In performing the review, the main objectives are to determine the completeness and relevance of the working papers.

[1] "Codification of Auditing Standards and Procedures," *Statement on Auditing Standards No. 1* (Copyright 1973 by the American Institute of Certified Public Accounts, Inc.), p. 129.

572
The audit report

There are many facets of the completeness objective. A partial list is:

- Audit programs are complete.
- Cross-referencing is complete.
- All working papers are signed and indexed.
- All working papers are logically arranged.
- All working papers are legible.

In general, the completeness objective is concerned with the clerical and mechanical correctness of the set of working papers.

In determining the relevance of the working papers, the auditor is concerned with the first phase of forming an opinion on the financial statements. He or she reviews the working papers to see if sufficient and competent evidential matter has been collected. Unlike the review for clerical and mechanical completeness, this part of the review is performed by someone with a thorough understanding of the client. In effect, the reviewer becomes a critic, reading the audit working papers and repeatedly using the standard of relevancy. For example, a weakness in the internal control system may have been identified by the auditor, but the modification of subsequent audit procedures to be employed may not be justified or logical. Perhaps a proposed audit adjustment is not properly supported by the working papers. Many other examples exist. In essence the auditor wants to make sure that a professional audit is performed and documented in the working papers.

Independent review

Many medium size and large accounting firms have established a special department that reviews the working papers before an opinion is expressed. The members of this department are usually not part of the regular audit staff. In fact, they tend to be highly technical and are appropriately referred to as specialists. Their job is to make an independent review to see if, among other things, all professional standards have been followed and the opinion expressed is a logical extension of the evidential matter collected.

Illegal acts by clients

During the performance of an audit, illegal acts that may have been committed by a client may be discovered. *SAS No. 17* suggests that illegal acts include, but are not limited to, "illegal political contributions, bribes, and other violations of laws and regulations." The auditor cannot be held responsible for the detection of all illegal acts, since the cost of conducting such an audit would be prohibitive. However, once an illegal act is discovered by an auditor, *SAS No. 17* states that he or she should

> . . . report the circumstances to personnel within the client's organization at a high enough level of authority so that appropriate action can be taken by the client with respect to—
> a. consideration of remedial actions;

b. adjustments or disclosures that may be necessary in the financial statements;
c. disclosures that may be required in other documents (such as a proxy statement).

It should be noted that the auditor is not required to notify external parties of an illegal act. This is the responsibility of management. If the illegal acts are pervasive, the auditor should consider withdrawing from the engagement.

FORMULATING AN OPINION

Once the auditor concludes that the audit working papers are complete, this evidence is the basis upon which an opinion is formulated and an audit report prepared. However, prior to the formal preparation of the report, the auditor meets with the client to discuss the findings. In this audit conference the auditor proposes audit adjustments and financial statement disclosures, and it is imperative that he or she be thoroughly prepared. In most cases the client does not passively accept the auditor's proposals, and it is necessary for the latter to present and explain the evidence. Management, with its accounting expertise, evaluates the proposals to determine if they are correct. It must be this way, since, first, the auditor is not infallible and, second, they are management's financial statements. Each group, knowing its responsibilities, comes to an agreement as to the need for additional adjustments and disclosures. This is the ideal conclusion of the audit conference. From a practical point of view, an auditor recognizes that the audit conference may on occasion result in a confrontation. In such a case, thorough preparation must be made and personal fortitude must be displayed.

The auditor's formulation of an opinion based on the review of the working papers must be communicated to the users of the financial statements. Since accounting is a technical discipline, the mode of communicating the auditor's findings must be chosen carefully. The professional standards that guide the wording of the audit report are detailed and voluminous. This is an obvious attempt to minimize the likelihood of misunderstanding the auditor's report. Unfortunately such an approach requires that the reader have a thorough understanding of the professional rules. The remainder of this chapter is concerned exclusively with the technical reporting requirements associated with the audit report.

Unqualified report

An auditor issues an unqualified report when all the following circumstances are prevalent:

- The three general standards of generally accepted auditing standards were observed.
- The three standards of fieldwork of generally accepted auditing standards were observed.
- The financial statements were prepared in accordance with generally accepted accounting principles.

574
The audit report

- The consistency principle was observed.
- No material uncertainties existed.
- Financial statements are fairly presented.

The four standards of reporting of generally accepted auditing standards are the basis for reporting the above circumstances. These four standards manifest themselves in the auditor's unqualified report. This is illustrated in Figure 17-2.[2]

Report modifications

A modification of the auditor's report as presented above is dependent upon the nature and extent of the circumstances. As discussed in Chapter 1, report modification can be the result of a deficiency in accounting, a deficiency in the scope of the audit, or the existence of a material uncertainty. In addition, recent changes now permit the auditor to emphasize a matter and still issue an unqualified opinion. Circumstances that may result in a departure from the auditor's standard report are:

1. Accounting circumstances
   a. The financial statements are affected by a departure from a generally accepted accounting principle.
   b. The financial statements are affected by a departure from an accounting principle promulgated by the body designated by the AICPA council to establish such principles.
   c. Accounting principles have not been applied consistently.
2. Scope circumstances
   a. The scope of the auditor's examination is affected by conditions that preclude the application of one or more auditing procedures he considers necessary in the circumstances.
   b. The auditor's opinion is based in part on the report of another auditor.
3. Uncertainty circumstance
   a. The financial statements are affected by uncertainties concerning future events, the outcome of which is not susceptible of reasonable estimation at the date of the auditor's report.
4. Emphasis of a matter
   a. The auditor wishes to emphasize a matter regarding the financial statements.

Before discussing these circumstances in detail it is first necessary to discuss the alternative report forms.

Once the circumstance is identified, the materiality of the item determines the type of audit opinion that is appropriate. The three alternative audit reports

---

[2] From a perusal of the items listed it is obvious to an accountant that the unqualified audit report communicates certain information. Although the precise meaning of the report may be obvious to an accountant, it is not so apparent to users without technical expertise in accounting. For this reason, the audit report is controversial. At the time of this writing the audit profession, through the AICPA Commission on Auditors' Responsibilities, is considering substantial changes in the auditor's report.

Figure 17-2

Impact of Reporting Standards on Unqualified Opinion.

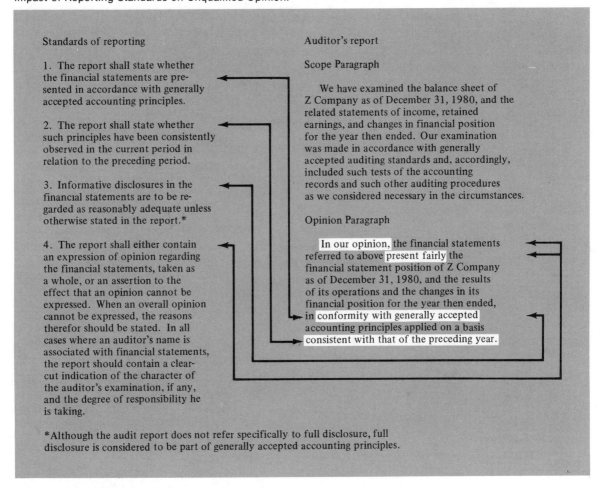

that may be issued are (1) a qualified opinion, (2) a disclaimer of opinion, and (3) an adverse opinion.

QUALIFIED REPORT

A qualified opinion is expressed when there are deficiencies in existence but even with these deficiencies the financial statements may be relied upon. Thus the financial statements, taken as a whole, fairly present the financial position, results of operations, and the changes in the financial position of the firm. A qualified report may be issued when there exists an accounting, scope or uncertainty deficiency. When a qualified opinion is issued, the deficiency is fully described in a separate paragraph(s) which is placed between the scope paragraph and the opinion paragraph. In preparing the opinion paragraph the auditor refers

576
The audit report

Figure 17-3

Examples of qualified reports

Accounting: An unacceptable accounting principle has been used in the preparation of the financial statements.

Scope paragraph: No change
Explanatory paragraph: The company has excluded from property and debt in the accompanying balance sheet certain lease obligations, which, in our opinion, should be capitalized in order to conform with generally accepted accounting principles. If these lease obligations were capitalized, property would be increased by $. . . , long-term debt by $. . . , and retained earnings by $. . . as of December 31, 19___, and net income and earnings per share would be increased (decreased) by $. . . and $. . . , respectively, for the year then ended.
Opinion paragraph: In our opinion, except for the effects of not capitalizing lease obligations, as discussed in the preceding paragraph, the financial statements present fairly. . . .

Scope: Auditor not able to observe inventory at the end of the year and was unable to be satisfied through the use of alternative procedures.

Scope paragraph: We have examined. . . . Except as explained in the following paragraph, our examination was made in accordance with generally accepted auditing standards and, accordingly, included such tests of the accounting records and such other auditing procedures as we considered necessary.
Explanatory paragraph: We did not observe the taking of the physical inventories as of December 31, 19___ (stated at $. . .), and December 31, 19___ (stated at $. . .), since those dates were prior to the time we were initially engaged as auditors for the company. Because of the nature of the company's records, we were unable to satisfy ourselves as to the inventory quantities by means of other auditing procedures.
Opinion paragraph: In our opinion, except for the effect of such adjustments, if any, as might have been determined to be necessary had we been able to observe physical inventories. . . .

Uncertainty: The outcome of pending litigation is not determinable.

Scope paragraph: No change
Explanatory paragraph: As discussed in Note X to the financial statements, the Company is a defendant in a lawsuit alleging infringement of certain patent rights and claiming royalties and punitive damages. The Company has filed a counter action, and preliminary hearings and discovery proceedings on both actions are in progress. Company officers and counsel believe the Company has a good chance of prevailing, but the ultimate outcome of the lawsuit cannot presently be determined, and no provision for any liability that may result has been made in the financial statements.

Fig. 17-3 Continued

577
Formulating an opinion

Opinion paragraph: In our opinion, subject to the effects, if any, on the financial statements of the ultimate resolution of the matter discussed in the preceding paragraph, the financial statements referred to above present fairly. . . .

SOURCE: "Reports on Audited Financial Statements," *Statement on Auditing Standards No. 2* (New York: Copyright 1974 by the American Institute of Certified Public Accountants), p. 11.

specifically to the explanatory paragraph. There is one exception to this. A qualification due to a consistency violation does not require the preparation of an explanatory paragraph.

The qualifying language used in the report is dependent upon the nature of the deficiency. Three examples are presented in Figure 17-3. When the deficiency is caused by a scope or accounting problem, the phrase "except for" is used as the qualifying language. When there is an uncertainty deficiency the phrase "subject to" is used.

DISCLAIMER

As implied by its name, a disclaimer of opinion is given when the auditor is unable to draw conclusions as to the fairness or lack of fairness of the financial statements. This occurs when he or she cannot gather sufficient and competent evidential material upon which to base an opinion. Scope or uncertainty deficiencies may account for this inability to collect appropriate evidence. The scope limitation may result from the inability to perform certain audit procedures, or may be the result of restrictions placed on the auditor by the client. In either case the auditor is unable to form an opinion on the financial statements because of the lack of evidence. Under no circumstances can an accounting deficiency lead to a disclaimer of opinion.

Determining whether a qualified opinion or a disclaimer of opinion is appropriate is dependent upon the materiality of the problem. Thus a particular deficiency is carefully analyzed to determine its impact on the overall fairness of the financial statements. For example, in Figure 17-3 a scope deficiency due to lack of observing inventories and employing alternative procedures resulted in the issuance of a qualified report. However, when the inventory accounts are so material as to make it unreasonable to rely upon the financial statements, a disclaimer of opinion is issued. Under these circumstances the scope and explanatory paragraphs shown in Figure 17-3 are not changed. The opinion paragraph is modified to read:

Since we did not observe the physical inventories and were unable to apply adequate alternative procedures regarding inventories, as noted in the preceding paragraph, the scope of our work was not sufficient to enable us to express, and we do not express, an opinion on the financial statements referred to above.

To avoid misunderstandings or unwarranted conclusions, the auditor does not disclose audit procedures employed when a disclaimer of opinion is issued.

578
The audit report

A disclaimer of opinion is also issued when the auditor is not independent. This circumstance was discussed in Chapter 3. The rationale for issuance of a disclaimer is that generally accepted auditing standards were not achieved, since the second general standard has been violated.

ADVERSE OPINION

As suggested earlier, an accounting deficiency may result in the issuance of a qualified opinion. However, when the deficiency is so material that the financial statements are misleading, an adverse opinion is issued. Thus the accounting deficiency that results in a qualified opinion or an adverse opinion is dependent upon the significance of the problem. The utilization of inappropriate accounting principles or the lack of adequate disclosure may result in the preparation of financial statements that cannot be relied upon. In preparing the adverse opinion, an explanatory paragraph(s) is used to describe fully the deficiency. Following the explanatory paragraph(s), the opinion paragraph explicitly states that the financial statements are not fairly presented. Language similar to the following may be used in the opinion paragraph:

> In our opinion, because of the effects of the matters discussed in the above paragraph(s), the financial statements referred to above do not present fairly, in conformity with generally accepted accounting principles, the financial position of X Company as of December 31, 19___, or the results of its operations and changes in its financial position for the year then ended.

In the above opinion paragraph, the adverse opinion covers all three basic financial statements. It is acceptable to "split" an opinion by offering a different opinion on each of the financial statements. For example, an unqualified opinion may be issued on the balance sheet, and a disclaimer of opinion may be issued on the income statement and on the statement of change in financial position.

Now that the four audit opinions have been described, it is possible to return to the original listing of circumstances resulting in departure from the auditor's standard report. Each of these is considered in the following discussion. Illustrations of the deficiencies are presented in the appendix to this chapter.

Accounting circumstances

Accounting Circumstances   Departure from a generally accepted accounting principle.

Generally accepted accounting principles include formal rules promulgated by the FASB and the APB and conventions that have not been formalized but through general acceptance are recognized as part of generally accepted accounting principles. When these rules are not followed in the preparation of financial statements, the auditor decides whether the issuance of a qualified opinion or an adverse opinion is appropriate.

Selection of the appropriate opinion is dependent upon the significance of the departure. When the deviation from accounting principles is material but the usefulness of the financial statements taken as a whole is not impaired, a qualified opinion is issued. If the financial statements are considered by the auditor to be misleading because of a departure from generally accepted accounting principles, an adverse opinion is issued. The selection of a qualified opinion or an adverse opinion is a matter of professional judgment. Factors to be considered are (1) the relative dollar amount involved, (2) the significance of the departure in qualitative terms, and (3) the ability to isolate the impact of the departure on the financial statements. The first element obviously refers to materiality. Thus the auditor considers the impact of the deficiency on net income from operations, total assets, current assets, and other bases that may be distorted by the error. Evaluating the departure in qualitative terms is not so obvious. In general, the auditor considers factors that are not subject to a dollar measurement but whose disclosure is important to the understanding of the financial statements. Finally, the departure's impact on individual accounts contributes to the selection of a qualified opinion or an adverse opinion. When several accounts are materially impacted, it is harder to issue a qualified opinion. For example, a decision by a manufacturer not to capitalize fixed assets impacts fixed assets, inventories, cost of goods sold, net income, and perhaps the deferred income tax credit account.

The issuance of a qualified opinion or an adverse opinion does not change the scope paragraph of the auditor's report. However, an explanatory paragraph(s) which fully explains the departure from generally accepted accounting principles and its impact on the financial statement is included in the report. The amount of the detail in the explanatory paragraph(s) may be reduced by referring to a footnote in the financial statements. When a qualified opinion is issued, the opinion paragraph reads:

> In our opinion, except for the impact of capitalizing certain depreciable properties, as described in the preceding paragraph, the financial statements fairly present. . . .[3]

When the deficiency results in an adverse opinion, the opinion paragraph is modified:

> In our opinion, because of the effects of the matter discussed in the preceding paragraph, the financial statements referred to above do not present fairly, in conformity with generally accepted accounting principles, the financial position of the Company as of December 31, 19—, or the results of its operations and changes in its financial position for the year then ended.[4]

Inadequate disclosure on the financial statements is an example of a departure from generally accepted accounting principle. When a disclosure deficiency exists, the auditor decides whether a qualified or an adverse opinion is to be issued. In an explanatory paragraph(s), included in the report, he or she details the data that the client refused to disclose in the financial statement footnotes. A special type of disclosure problem exists when a client omits the statement

---

[3] For an illustration of a qualified opinion due to a departure from generally accepted accounting principles, see Example I in the appendix.

[4] See Example II in the appendix.

580
The audit report

of change in financial position. The auditor is not required to prepare the statement, but the opinion paragraph must be qualified.[5]

Accounting Circumstance: Departure from an accounting principle promulgated by the body designated by the AICPA council to establish such principles.[6]

In the previous section generally accepted accounting principles were described as those formally issued by an authoritative body and those that have gained acceptance but have not been formally adopted. When an accounting principle is formally adopted, the degree of flexibility is substantially reduced. This is obvious, since the rule is written. However, if the rule is not formally adopted, there is more flexibility in adapting it to a particular reporting problem. There is a danger that when rules are written they will not be flexible enough to accommodate every situation adequately. Narrow application of the rule may result in the financial statements being prepared in accordance with generally accepted accounting principles, but the results may not be a fair presentation of the facts. In an attempt to remedy this problem, Rule 203 of the AICPA professional code of ethics was adopted. The rule states:

> A member shall not express an opinion that financial statements are presented in conformity with generally accepted accounting principles if such statements contain any departure from an accounting principle promulgated by the body designated by Council to establish such principles which has a material effect on the statements taken as a whole, unless the member can demonstrate that due to unusual circumstances the financial statements would otherwise have been misleading. In such cases his report must describe the departure, the approximate effects thereof, if practicable, and the reasons why compliance with the principle would result in a misleading statement.

When the auditor determines that unusual circumstances dictate a deviation from a codified rule, the audit report is modified. An explanatory paragraph(s) describes the departure, the reason for the departure and, if practicable, the impact on the financial statements of the departure. The opinion paragraph is not modified, and no reference is made to the explanatory paragraph. The position taken by the AICPA is that the auditor's best judgment in applying an accounting principle to a specific situation takes precedence over the mechanical application of an accounting principle. This places an enormous responsibility on the auditor, since in effect he or she is "promulgating" an accounting rule for a particular circumstance. It is not surprising that there are few examples of the application of Rule 203.[7]

Accounting Circumstance: Departure from a consistent application of accounting principles.

---

[5] See Example III in the appendix.

[6] Currently the FASB is the body designated by the council. See page 31 for the resolution.

[7] See Example IV in the appendix.

APB Opinion No. 20, "Accounting Changes," states that "a change in accounting principle results from adoption of a generally accepted accounting principle different from the one used previously for reporting purposes." Generally speaking, management is relatively free to change accounting principles from period to period. When a change in an accounting principle is made, the nature and justification for the change is disclosed in a footnote along with its effect on income. Since such a change is a violation of the consistency standard, the auditor's report is modified. The nature of the report modification depends upon whether the change in the accounting principle resulted in the restatement of prior financial statements contained in the audit report.

581
Formulating an opinion

Normally a change in an accounting principle does not require the restatement of comparative prior years' financial statements. The effects of the change are shown by a cumulative adjustment on the income statement and the presentation of *pro forma* amounts. Under such circumstances, the auditor qualifies only the opinion paragraph of the report in the following manner:

> In our opinion . . . in conformity with generally accepted accounting principles which, except for the change, with which we concur, in the method of computing depreciation as described in Note X to the financial statements, have been applied on a basis consistent with that of the preceding year.

The auditor makes an explicit statement as to whether he or she concurs with the change.[8] If the change is not adequately disclosed in the financial statements, the deficiency is no longer a consistency violation and the auditor considers whether a qualified or adverse opinion is required due to a departure from generally accepted accounting principles.

In some instances accounting changes result in the restatement of prior years' financial statements presented in the audit report. Specifically, the following changes are accounted for in this manner:

1. A change from the LIFO method of pricing inventory to another method
2. A change in the method of accounting for long-term construction-type contracts
3. A change to or from the full-cost method of accounting used in the extractive industries
4. A change in the reporting entity

Since the financial statements for the previous year(s) are restated, the statements are comparable and no consistency violation exists. However, the opinion paragraph states that the statements are consistent "after giving retroactive effect to the change." An example of the opinion paragraph is:

> In our opinion . . . in conformity with generally accepted accounting principles applied on a consistent basis, after giving retroactive effect in the method of accounting for long-term construction contracts, with which we concur, as explained in Note X to the financial statements.[9]

[8] See Example V in the appendix.
[9] See Example VI in the appendix.

582
The audit report

Scope circumstances

Scope Circumstance: Departure from the performance of one or more audit procedures considered necessary.

An auditor issues an opinion on the client's financial statements based upon evidence he or she has collected. If evidential matter critical to the formulation of an opinion is not collected, the engagement suffers from a scope deficiency. Scope deficiencies are classified as those resulting from restrictions imposed by the client and those which practical circumstances preclude the auditor from performing.

Client-imposed restrictions usually result from the client's desire to minimize the engagement fee. The client may ask that inventory not be observed, accounts receivable not be confirmed, or a particular branch not be visited by the auditor, and so on. It is the responsibility of the auditor to determine independently the audit procedures to be used and the scope of the audit. For these reasons the auditor should be wary of restrictions imposed by management. When restrictions that significantly limit the scope of the audit are imposed by management, it is usually necessary for the auditor to disclaim an opinion on the financial statements.

The circumstances of the engagement may preclude the performance of audit procedures. For example, if the auditor is appointed after the year-end inventory is taken, it is obviously impossible for him or her to observe the inventory at that date. When the auditor is able to use alternative audit procedures and is satisfied with the evidence generated from their use, the audit report is not modified in any way. However, when alternative procedures cannot be satisfactorily applied, the auditor modifies the audit report.[10] The scope paragraph notes the audit restriction, and an explanatory paragraph(s) fully explains the restriction. An illustration is:

> We have examined . . . our examination was made in accordance with generally accepted auditing standards, and accordingly included such tests of the accounting records and such other auditing procedures as we considered necessary in the circumstances, except as explained in the following paragraph.

> We did not observe the taking of the physical inventories at December 31, 19—, since we were appointed as auditors subsequent to this date. Furthermore, we were unable to satisfy ourselves as to the inventory quantities at that date through the use of alternative audit procedures.

The opinion paragraph that follows the two paragraphs above may be either a disclaimer of an opinion or a qualified opinion. If the financial statements taken as a whole, may be relied upon, a qualified opinion is issued. Two factors to be considered by the auditor are (1) the maximum potential dollar impact on the financial statements that may result from misstatement of the account or transaction, and (2) the number of accounts on the financial statements that may be

---

[10]See Example VII in the appendix.

impacted. When a qualified opinion is appropriate, wording similar to the following example is required:

> In our opinion, except for the effects of such adjustments, if any, as might have been determined to be necessary had we observed the physical inventories. . . .

When it is appropriate to disclaim an opinion, the opinion paragraph may read:

> Since the company took its physical inventories prior to our appointment and we were unable to apply adequate alternative procedures regarding inventories, as noted in the preceding paragraph, the scope of our work was not sufficient to enable us to express, and we do not express, an opinion on the aforementioned financial statements.

Scope Circumstance: Part of the audit was performed by another auditor.

Many engagements involve the auditing of an accounting entity comprised of numerous operating units such as subsidiaries, divisions, investees, and the like. Also, it is not unusual to find that these operating units are audited by two or more separate public accounting firms. In such situations, the principal auditor, the auditor concerned with issuing an opinion on the consolidated or combined entity, is faced with two questions:

- Has sufficient work been done by the firm to justify its role as the principal auditor?
- If the role of principal auditor is justified, is the audit report modified so that the scope of the secondary auditor(s)' role is adequately described?

In deciding if the auditor can serve as the principal auditor, the significance of the work performed by the secondary auditor is considered. An important criterion used in making this decision is the materiality of the financial statements or combined accounts audited by the secondary auditor in relationship to the financial statements taken as a whole. The professional literature contains no quantitative guidelines; materiality is usually measured by referring to total assets, total revenue, and total net income for the consolidated or combined entity. It is not unusual to find such financial statements where the secondary auditor's work accounts for a majority of one or more of these bases.

The quantitative significance of the work performed by the secondary auditor is not the sole criterion used to determine if the auditor can serve as the principal auditor. Initially the potential principal auditor determines if the secondary auditor is reputable and independent of the client. The professional reputation of the secondary auditor may be established by directing inquiries to the AICPA, the state society of CPAs, local practitioners, or other appropriate sources. In determining independence, the secondary auditors are asked to make a representation that their firm meets the definition of independence as defined by the AICPA or, if appropriate, the SEC. The secondary auditors are informed that their work is to be used in the combining or consolidating process. Other procedures to coordinate the efforts of the two audit firms are discussed.

584
The audit report

When the auditor decides that it is improper to function as the principal auditor, the audit report is modified. Depending upon the significance of the work performed by the secondary auditor, a qualified opinion or a disclaimer of opinion is issued. In either case an explanatory paragraph is used to describe the nature of the scope deficiency.

If the auditor concludes that it is proper to serve as the principal auditor, he or she decides whether to make reference in the audit report to the work performed by the secondary auditor. When the principal auditor decides to assume responsibility for the work of the secondary auditor, the audit report is not modified. *SAS No. 1,* Section 543.05, identifies four instances where reference is not required.

    a. Part of the examination is made by another independent auditor which is an associated or correspondent firm and whose work is acceptable to the principal auditor based on his knowledge of the professional standards and competence of that firm; or

    b. The other auditor was retained by the principal auditor and the work was performed under the principal auditor's guidance and control; or

    c. The principal auditor, whether or not he selected the other auditor, nevertheless takes steps he considers necessary to satisfy himself as to the other auditor's examination and accordingly is satisfied as to the reasonableness of the accounts for the purpose of inclusion in the financial statements on which he is expressing his opinion; or

    d. The portion of the financial statements examined by the other auditor is not material to the financial statements covered by the principal auditor's opinion.

When the principal auditor decides to make reference to the secondary auditor's work, the audit report is modified.[11] Although the audit report is modified, technically this does not result in a scope deficiency. It is referred to as an indication of the division of responsibility taken by each participating audit firm. This division of responsibility is clearly described in the scope and the opinion paragraphs. The scope paragraph describes the proportion of the audit performed by the secondary auditor. The scope paragraph may read:

> We have examined . . . considered necessary in the circumstances. We did not examine the financial statements of Z Company, a consolidated foreign subsidiary, which statements reflect total assets, total revenues and consolidated net income constituting 8 percent, 20 percent, and 15 percent, respectively, of the related consolidated totals. These statements were examined by other auditors whose report thereon has been furnished to us, and our opinion expressed herein, insofar as it relates to the amounts included in Z Company, is based upon the report of the other auditors.

As implied in the above paragraph, the financial statements audited by the secondary auditor are not included in the principal auditor's report. Furthermore, the name of the secondary auditor is not disclosed.

If the principal auditor refers to the work of the secondary auditor, the opinion paragraph is written in a manner similar to the following:

---

[11] See Example VIII in the appendix.

In our opinion, based upon our examination and the report of other auditors, the accompanying consolidated balance sheet . . . presents fairly. . . .

585
Formulating an opinion

If the secondary auditor issued a qualified opinion on the financial statements, the principal auditor considers the impact of the qualification on the financial statements taken as a whole. When the qualification is not material in relation to the total financial statement, the opinion paragraph, as illustrated, is not modified. However, if the qualification is material, the auditor includes an explanatory paragraph(s) and a qualified opinion is issued.

Uncertainty circumstance

Uncertain Circumstance: Uncertainties concerning the outcome of future events exists.

The preparation of financial statements requires that many estimates be made. The estimated life of an asset subject to depreciation, the provision for uncollectible accounts, and the estimated profit on a long-term contract are but a few examples. Accounting estimates are characterized as being subject to reasonable estimation. However, there are instances in the financial reporting process when it is not possible to estimate reasonably the outcome of an event. The auditor is in this case unable to collect sufficient evidential matter to feel confident about the outcome of a future event. Under these circumstances, he or she modifies the audit report if the uncertainty is material. A material uncertainty may result in a qualified opinion or the auditor may disclaim an opinion on the financial statements.

A qualified opinion is issued when the uncertainty is related to a specific matter and its potential impact on the financial statements can be isolated and readily understood by the user. The financial statements are believed to be useful on an overall basis under these circumstances. Such an uncertainty may be the result of (1) the uncertainty of cost recoverability under a governmental contract where significant contract violations are in question, (2) the outcome of a lawsuit or (3) the outcome of a proposed additional income tax assessment. If these problems are material, the auditor includes an explanatory paragraph(s) in the audit report and the opinion paragraph includes a ''subject to'' qualification by referring to the explanatory paragraph(s).[12] For example, the opinion paragraph may read as follows:

In our opinion, subject to the effects of such adjustments, if any, as might have been required had the outcome of the uncertainty referred to in the preceding paragraph been known, the financial statements referred to above present fairly. . . .

Due to the nature of some uncertainties, it may be difficult to assess their potential impact on the financial statements. This situation may result from (1) an inability to secure adequate financing, (2) recurring operating losses, and (3) violations of loan agreement terms. In such cases the continued existence of the

[12] See Example IX in the appendix.

586
The audit report

firm may be in question. Since the auditor cannot predict the future of the firm, the general concern for the uncertainty is communicated through the auditor's report. The difficult question that the auditor decides is whether a qualified opinion is sufficient warning to the potential user. Obviously the issuance of a disclaimer of opinion is more dramatic and is carefully considered by the auditor. Nonetheless, if the "going concern" appears to be in jeopardy, a disclaimer may be issued.[13] The disclaimer is necessary because the recoverability and classification of accounts are in question. For example, it may be appropriate to question whether fixed assets are to be listed at book value or at liquidation value. If this question arises, an explanatory paragraph(s) is added to the auditor's report in which the uncertainty problem is fully explained. The disclaimer of opinion may read as follows:

> Because of the material uncertainties referred to in the preceding paragraph(s), we are unable to and do not express an opinion on the aforementioned financial statements.

The auditor is careful not to confuse an uncertainty deficiency with an accounting deficiency. The ability to differentiate between the two is often dependent upon the availability of competent and sufficient evidential matter. In other words, the client may prefer a "subject to" qualification rather than an "except for" qualification or an adverse opinion. For example the client may claim that there is not enough data upon which to write an asset down or off. However, the auditor may conclude that data is sufficient and the adjustment is required. If the client refuses, an accounting deficiency, not an uncertainty deficiency, exists. Also, in the previous paragraph the going-concern concept was discussed as a basis for a disclaimer. When evidence is adequate to support the contention that the going-concern concept is not appropriate for this client, then adjustments reducing historical cost values to liquidating values are proposed by the auditor. In practice, the distinction between an uncertainty and an accounting deficiency is not always clear. Furthermore, if an uncertainty deficiency is identified, it is often difficult to determine whether a qualified opinion or a disclaimer of opinion is appropriate.[14]

Emphasis of a matter

Emphasis of a matter: The auditor may wish to emphasize a matter regarding the financial statements.

From the discussion in this chapter it can be seen that there are numerous rules and guides for the preparation of an audit report. Such a structural approach introduces the possibility that a particular circumstance may not be subject to precise classification as prescribed by professional standards. To provide some flexibility, the auditor is allowed to comment in the auditor's report on a significant item and still issue an unqualified report. In effect the item does not result in a

---

[13] See Example X in the appendix.

[14] In 1974 several accounting firms were faced with this problem. The student may wish to refer to an article in the *Wall Street Journal* (April 17, 1975).

technical deficiency, but it is considered by the auditor to be so important that users need to be told of the event in a manner they are unlikely to overlook. Audit reports may emphasize:

- Evaluation of an accounting principle
- Change in the reporting entity
- Related party transactions
- Change in an accounting estimate
- Reference to prior period adjustments
- Change in operating conditions

When a matter is to be emphasized, an explanatory paragraph(s) is added to describe the significant item. The scope paragraph and the opinion paragraph are not modified.[15] For example, it is inappropriate to use a phrase in the opinion paragraph, such as ''with the foregoing explanation,'' that implies qualification of the opinion.

Piecemeal opinions

Prior to 1975, it was acceptable to issue an adverse opinion or a disclaimer of opinion but state that some of the accounts in the financial statements were fairly stated in accordance with generally accepted accounting principles. Because of the potential for misunderstanding the audit report, piecemeal opinions are no longer allowed.

Negative assurances

In the preparation of an audit report, the auditor is careful not to use language which may encourage users to place unwarranted reliance on the financial statements. To this end scope deficiencies that result in a qualified opinion or a disclaimer of opinion are not to be tempered with phrases such as ''. . . nothing came to our attention which would indicate that these financial statements are not fairly stated.'' Nonetheless, there are some limited cases where the professional rules allow the use of negative assurances. *SAS No. 1,* Section 518.03, identifies the following occasions:

Letters required by security underwriters. Special reports relating to
a. the results of applying agreed-upon procedures to one or more specified elements, accounts, or items of a financial statement and
b. compliance with aspects of contractual agreements or regulatory requirements related to audited financial statements.

CONCLUSION

This chapter was concerned with the technical nature of the auditor's report, however, it was only an introduction to the subject. Some additional aspects of the audit report are considered in Chapter 18.

[15] See Example XI in the appendix.

APPENDIX   Audit Report Illustrations

EXAMPLE I: QUALIFIED OPINION DUE TO A DEPARTURE FROM GENERALLY ACCEPTED ACCOUNTING PRINCIPLES.

SOURCE: *Illustrations of Departures from the Auditor's Standard Report* (New York: AICPA, 1975), p. 96. Copyright © 1975 by the American Institute of Certified Public Accountants, Inc.

WESTERN MARYLAND RAILWAY COMPANY
Auditor's Opinion
To the Shareowners and the Board of Directors
Western Maryland Railway Company:

We have examined the consolidated balance sheets of Western Maryland Railway Company and subsidiaries as of December 31, 1974 and 1973 and the related consolidated statements of earnings, earnings reinvested in the business and changes in financial position for the years then ended. Our examination was made in accordance with generally accepted auditing standards, and accordingly included such tests of the accounting records and such other auditing procedures as we considered necessary in the circumstances.

As more fully described in note 3 to the consolidated financial statements, a net provision for loss on abandonment of track of $13,600,000 after related income taxes has been presented as an extraordinary charge against earnings for 1974. In our opinion, generally accepted accounting principles require that the gross amount of such provision be included in the determination of earnings before income taxes and that the per share amount of the provision not be separately presented in the consolidated statement of earnings.

In our opinion, except for the effect of the matter described in the preceding paragraph, the aforementioned consolidated financial statements present fairly the financial position of Western Maryland Railway Company and subsidiaries at December 31, 1974 and 1973 and the results of their operations and the changes in their financial position for the years then ended, in conformity with generally accepted accounting principles applied on a consistent basis after restatement for the change, with which we concur, in the method of accounting for deferred income taxes described in note 2 to the consolidated financial statements.

Notes to Financial Statement
(3) Investment in Properties

The investment in properties consists of the following (in thousands of dollars):

	1974	1973
Transportation properties:		
Road	$ 75,736	$ 94,832
Equipment	97,010	101,277
Miscellaneous physical property, at cost	11,934	16,122
	184,680	212,231
Accumulated depreciation	59,706	60,965
Net investment	$124,974	$151,266

A trackage agreement was made during 1973 between the Company and B&O which, upon approval of applications filed with the Interstate Commerce Commission, would permit the Company to operate over B&O main line tracks in Maryland,

Pennsylvania and West Virginia and to abandon 116 miles of parallel tracks (22% of its main line). A hearing has been held before the Interstate Commerce Commission and approval of the applications is expected. The agreement with B&O provides that certain benefits resulting from the abandonment, principally income tax savings, be shared equally between the companies. The provision for loss on abandonment of $13,600,000, which reflects the sharing of benefits with B&O (a charge of $3,866,000) and related income taxes (a credit of $8,777,000), has been presented as an extraordinary charge against earnings for 1974. However, in the opinion of the Company's independent public accountants, this provision for loss does not meet the criteria for presentation as an extraordinary charge under generally accepted accounting principles.

EXAMPLE II: ADVERSE OPINION RESULTING FROM A DEPARTURE FROM GENERALLY ACCEPTED ACCOUNTING PRINCIPLES

SOURCE: *Codification of Statements on Auditing Standards* (New York: AICPA, 1977), Section 509.43. Copyright © 1977 by the American Institute of Certified Public Accountants, Inc.

(Standard Scope Paragraph)

(Explanatory Paragraph)

As discussed in Note X to the financial statements, the Company carries its property, plant and equipment accounts at appraisal values, and provides depreciation on the basis of such values. Further, the Company does not provide for income taxes with respect to differences between financial income and taxable income arising because of the use, for income tax purposes, of the installment method of reporting gross profit from certain types of sales. Generally accepted accounting principles, in our opinion, require that property, plant and equipment be stated at an amount not in excess of cost, reduced by depreciation based on such amount, and that deferred income taxes be provided. Because of the departures from generally accepted accounting principles identified above, as of December 31, 19___, inventories have been increased $. . . by inclusion in manufacturing overhead of depreciation in excess of that based on cost; property, plant and equipment, less accumulated depreciation, is carried at $. . . in excess of an amount based on the cost to the Company; and allocated income tax of $. . . has not been recorded; resulting in an increase of $. . . in retained earnings and in appraisal surplus of $. . . . For the year ended December 31, 19___, cost of goods sold has been increased $. . . because of the effects of the depreciation accounting referred to above and deferred income taxes of $. . . have not been provided, resulting in an increase in net income and earnings per share of $. . . and $. . . respectively.

In our opinion, because of the effects of the matters discussed in the preceding paragraph, the financial statements referred to above do not present fairly, in conformity with generally accepted accounting principles, the financial position of X Company as of December 31, 19___, or the results of operations and changes in its financial position for the year then ended.

EXAMPLE III: QUALIFIED OPINION RESULTING FROM A LACK OF FULL DISCLOSURE

SOURCE: *Codification of Statements on Auditing Standards* (New York: AICPA, 1977), Section 545.02. Copyright © 1977 by the American Institute of Certified Public Accountants, Inc.

590
The audit report

(Standard Scope Paragraph)

(Explanatory Paragraph)

On January 15, 19_2, the company issued debentures in the amount of $. . . for the purpose of financing plant expansion. The debenture agreement restricts the payment of future cash dividends to earnings after December 31, 19_1.

In our opinion, except for the omission of the information in the preceding paragraph, the aforementioned financial statements present fairly. . . .

EXAMPLE IV: UNQUALIFIED OPINION BASED ON RULE 203

SOURCE: *Illustrations of Departures from the Auditor's Standard Report* (New York: AICPA, 1975), p. 97–98. Copyright © 1975 by the American Institute of Certified Public Accountants, Inc. Note that the qualification is due to the certainty deficiency and is not the result of the departure from promulgated generally accepted accounting principles.

AERONCA, INC.
Auditor's Opinion
Board of Directors and Shareholders
Aeronca, Inc.
Torrance, California

We have examined the consolidated balance sheet of Aeronca, Inc. and subsidiaries as of December 31, 1973 and 1972 and the related statements of operations. stockholders' equity and changes in financial position for the years then ended. Our examination was made in accordance with generally accepted auditing standards, and accordingly included such tests of the accounting records and such other auditing procedures as we considered necessary in the circumstances.

In October, 1973, the Company extinguished a substantial amount of debt through a direct exchange of new equity securities. Application of Opinion No. 26 of the Accounting Principles Board to this exchange requires that the excess of the debt extinguished over the present value of the new securities should be recognized as a gain in the period in which the extinguishment occurred. While it is not practicable to determine the present value of the new equity securities issued, such value is at least $2,000,000 less than the face amount of the debt extinguished. It is the opinion of the Company's Management, an opinion with which we agree, that no realization of a gain occurred in this exchange (Note 1), and therefore, no recognition of the excess of the debt extinguished over the present value of the new securities has been made in these financial statements.

The accompanying financial statements have been prepared on the basis of the continuation of the Company as a going concern and requires continued profitable operations, adequate financing of the L-1011 program by the customer and continued adequate financing by the credit grantors (Note 4).

In our opinion, subject to the comments in the preceding paragraph and the recovery of investments in certain aerospace programs (Note 3), the aforementioned consolidated financial statements present fairly the financial position of Aeronca, Inc. and subsidiaries at December 31, 1973 and 1972, and the results of their operations and the changes in their financial position for the years then ended, in conformity with generally accepted accounting principles which, except for the change, with which we concur, in the method of presenting losses arising from the disposition of segments of the business (Note 2), have been applied on a consistent basis.

Notes to Financial Statements
Note 1—Summary of Accounting Policies:

591
Example V:
qualified opinion
due to consistency
violation

Extinguishment of Debt: In October, 1973, the Company issued 50,000 shares of 6% Prior Preferred Shares, par value $100, in exchange for the outstanding $5,000,000 of 6% Senior Subordinated Notes. It also issued 18,040 shares of convertible $6 Serial Preference Shares, Series A, stated value $100 a share, in exchange for $1,300,000 and $504,000 of outstanding 6% convertible subordinated debentures and 5¾% convertible subordinated debentures, respectively. The Company expensed the unamortized balance (approximately $148,000) of the deferred financing costs associated with the issuance of each of the three classes of subordinated debt to the extent that such unamortized balances were allocable to the debt so extinguished.

Opinion No. 26 of the Accounting Principles Board of the American Institute of CPA's states that the excess of the carrying amount of the extinguished debt over the present value of the new securities issued should be recognized as a gain in the statement of operations of the period in which the extinguishment occurred. While it is not practicable to determine the present value of the new equity securities issued, such value is at least $2,000,000 less than the face amount of the debt extinguished. However, the terms and provisions of these new equity securities are substantially similar to those of the debt securities extinguished, both on the basis of the Company's continuing operations and in the event of liquidation. It is the opinion of the management, therefore, that no gain as a result of this exchange has been realized or should be recognized in the financial statements.

EXAMPLE V: QUALIFIED OPINION DUE TO CONSISTENCY VIOLATION

SOURCE: *Illustrations of Departures from the Auditor's Standard Report,* (New York: AICPA, 1975), pp. 61–62. Copyright © 1975 by the American Institute of Certified Public Accountants, Inc.

GENERAL PUBLIC UTILITIES CORPORATION
Auditor's Opinion
To the Board of Directors and Stockholders,
General Public Utilities Corporation,
New York, New York

We have examined the consolidated balance sheet of General Public Utilities Corporation and Subsidiary Companies as of December 31, 1974 and the related consolidated statements of income, retained earnings and sources of funds used for construction for the year then ended. Our examination was made in accordance with generally accepted auditing standards, and accordingly included such tests of the accounting records and such other auditing procedures as we considered necessary in the circumstances. We previously examined and reported upon the consolidated financial statements for the year 1973.

In our opinion, the aforementioned statements (pages 24 through 32) present fairly the consolidated financial position of General Public Utilities Corporation and Subsidiary Companies at December 31, 1974 and 1973 and the consolidated results of their operations and the consolidated sources of funds used for construction for the years then ended, in conformity with generally accepted accounting principles consistently applied, except for the change, with which we concur, in accounting for energy costs as described in Note 1 to Financial Statements.

592
The audit report

Notes to Financial Statements
Note 1

Deferred Energy Costs:

Prior to 1974, the Corporation's subsidiaries recorded the cost of fuel used for generation and of net interchange purchased in the period of such use and purchase, even though part of such cost was recouped in subsequent periods under the subsidiaries' fuel adjustment clauses because such amounts were not material in any of those years. Subsequent to the Arab oil embargo, when fuel costs increased dramatically and in order to achieve a better matching of costs and revenues, the Corporation's subsidiaries effective January 1, 1974, adopted a policy of providing for the recognition of such costs in the period in which the related revenues are billed. The tariffs under which the subsidiary companies' excess fuel and energy costs are billed provide for the automatic recovery of such costs within a period of four months from the incurrence of such costs. There are no indications that the regulatory bodies governing the subsidiary companies' rates will not permit the recovery of such costs, including those deferred, in the future.

As a result of this accounting change, at December 31, 1974, energy costs of $40,246,000 have been deferred and related income taxes of $20,323,000 have been accrued. The net effect of the deferral of energy costs incurred during 1974 ($40,-246,000) less energy costs incurred prior to January 1, 1974 ($18,124,000) and billed during 1974 was to increase net income by $10,956,000. The cumulative effect of such change for periods prior to January 1, 1974, is $8,967,000. If such accounting had been employed from the initial operation of the fuel adjustment clauses, net income for the year 1973 would have increased by $916,000 and earnings per share would have been $2.27 as compared to $2.25 in 1974.

EXAMPLE VI: UNQUALIFIED OPINION AFTER RETROACTIVE EFFECT OF A CHANGE IN ACCOUNTING PRINCIPLES

SOURCE: *Illustrations of Departures from the Auditor's Standard Report* (New York: AICPA, 1975), p. 53. Copyright © 1975 by the American Institute of Certified Public Accountants, Inc.

CHRISTIANA SECURITIES COMPANY
Auditors' Opinion
To the Stockholders and Board of Directors,
Christiana Securities Company:

We have examined the statement of assets and liabilities of Christiana Securities Company as of December 31, 1974, and the related statements of operations and changes in net assets for the two years then ended. Our examination was made in accordance with generally accepted auditing standards, and accordingly included such tests of the accounting records and such other auditing procedures as we considered necessary in the circumstances. We have examined the securities owned at December 31, 1974 by count and inspection thereof in the vaults of Wilmington Trust Company and Bankers Trust Company.

In our opinion, the accompanying financial statements present fairly the net assets of Christiana Securities Company at December 31, 1974, and the results of its operations and the changes in its net assets for the two years then ended, in conformity with generally accepted accounting principles applied on a consistent basis after giving retroactive effect to the change, with which we concur, in the method of reporting investment values described in Note 1 to the financial statements.

Notes to Financial Statements
1. Summary of Significant Accounting Policies
Investments

The American Institute of Certified Public Accountants' Industry Audit Guide for Investment Companies became effective for fiscal years beginning after December 31, 1973 and accordingly the Company has adopted the Guide's recommendations that investment securities be reported at quoted values at December 31, 1974; prior to that time investment securities were carried at the Federal income tax basis (book value). In accordance with provisions of the Audit Guide, the change in the accounting method has been applied retroactively in the accompanying financial statements. The effect of the change on the accompanying financial statements was an increase in net assets of $2,332,381,770 and $2,083,760,106 as of December 31, 1972 and 1973, respectively, over the amounts previously reported under the old method; and an increase in the carrying value of investments at December 31, 1974 of $1,187,053,986.

EXAMPLE VII: QUALIFICATION DUE TO SCOPE LIMITATION

SOURCE: *Codification of Statements on Auditing Standards* (New York: AICPA, 1977), Section 509.40. Copyright © 1977 by the American Institute of Certified Public Accountants, Inc.

We have examined the balance sheet of X Company as of December 31, 19___, and the related statements of income, retained earnings and changes in financial position for the year then ended. Except as explained in the following paragraph, our examination was made in accordance with generally accepted auditing standards and, accordingly, included such tests of the accounting records and such other auditing procedures as we considered necessary in the circumstances.

(Explanatory Paragraph)

We did not observe the taking of the physical inventories of December 31, 19___ (stated at $. . .), and December 31, 19___ (stated at $. . .), since those dates were prior to the time we were initially engaged as auditors for the Company. Due to the nature of the Company's records, we were unable to satisfy ourselves as to the inventory quantities by means of other auditing procedures.

In our opinion, except for the effects of such adjustments, if any, as might have been determined to be necessary had we been able to observe the physical inventories, the financial statements referred to above present fairly the financial position of X Company as of December 19___, and the results of its operations and the changes in its financial position for the year then ended, in conformity with generally accepted accounting principles applied on a basis consistent with that of the preceding year.

EXAMPLE VIII: UNQUALIFIED OPINION WITH PART OF THE AUDIT PERFORMED BY ANOTHER CPA FIRM

SOURCE: *Illustrations of Departures from the Auditor's Standard Report* (New York: AICPA, 1975), p. 72. Copyright © 1975 by the American Institute of Certified Public Accountants, Inc.

STONE & WEBSTER INCORPORATED
Auditor's Opinion
To the Stockholders and Board of Directors of
Stone & Webster, Incorporated:

We have examined the consolidated balance sheet of Stone & Webster, Incorporated and Subsidiaries as of December 31, 1974, and the related consolidated statements of income and retained earnings and of changes in financial position for the year then ended. Our examination was made in accordance with generally accepted auditing standards, and accordingly included such tests of the accounting records and such other auditing procedures as we considered necessary in the circumstances. We previously examined and reported upon the consolidated financial statements for the year 1973. We did not examine the financial statements of certain consolidated foreign subsidiaries, which statements reflect total assets and gross earnings constituting 8% and 10%, respectively, of the related consolidated totals in 1974 and 4% and 7%, respectively, in 1973. These statements were examined by other auditors whose reports thereon have been furnished to us and our opinion expressed herein, insofar as it relates to the amounts included for such foreign subsidiaries, is based solely upon the reports of the other auditors.

In our opinion, based upon our examination and the reports of the other auditors, the aforementioned financial statements present fairly the consolidated financial position of Stone & Webster, Incorporated and Subsidiaries at December 31, 1974 and 1973, and the consolidated results of their operations and the consolidated changes in their financial position for the years then ended, in conformity with generally accepted accounting principles applied on a consistent basis.

EXAMPLE IX: QUALIFIED OPINION DUE TO UNCERTAINTY

SOURCE: *Illustrations of Departures from the Auditor's Standard Report,* AICPA, 1975, p. 43.

ARTHUR D. LITTLE, INC.
Auditor's Opinion
The Board of Directors and Stockholders
Arthur D. Little, Inc.
Cambridge, Massachusetts

We have examined the consolidated statement of financial condition of Arthur D. Little, Inc., and subsidiaries as of December 31, 1974 and the related consolidated statements of income and retained earnings and changes in financial position for the year then ended. Our examination was made in accordance with generally accepted auditing standards and, accordingly, included such tests of the accounting records and such other auditing procedures as we considered necessary in the circumstances. We previously examined and reported upon the consolidated financial statements for the year 1973.

The company is currently engaged in litigation with the Manitoba Development Corporation as described in Note C to the financial statements. The outcome of this proceeding and its effect, if any, on the financial statements of the company cannot presently be estimated, and accordingly no provision therefor has been made.

In our opinion, subject to the effect, if any, on the financial statements of the outcome of the litigation described in the preceding paragraph, the afore-mentioned consolidated financial statements present fairly the financial position of Arthur D. Little, Inc. and subsidiaries at December 31, 1974 and 1973, and the results of their operations and changes in their financial position for the years then ended, in conformity with generally accepted accounting principles applied on a consistent basis.

Notes to Financial Statements
C. Commitments and Contingencies
Litigation

As reported last year, the Manitoba Development Corporation filed a claim against the company and its Canadian affiliate, Arthur D. Little of Canada Limited, for unspecified damages arising from services rendered in connection with the construction of a forest products complex at The Pas, Manitoba. In April, 1974, the court directed the plaintiff to revise its statement of claim for greater particulars. The plaintiff has not yet filed this revised statement with the court. The company believes that it has meritorious defenses against the suit and intends to contest it vigorously.

595
Example X:
disclaimer of an
opinion due to
uncertainty

EXAMPLE X: DISCLAIMER OF AN OPINION DUE TO UNCERTAINTY

SOURCE: *Illustrations of Departures from the Auditor's Standard Report* (New York: AICPA, 1975), pp. 8–9. Copyright © 1975 by the American Institute of Certified Public Accountants, Inc.

FIDELITY MORTGAGE INVESTORS
Auditor's Opinion
The Trustees and Shareholders
Fidelity Mortgage Investors (Debtor-in-Possession):

We have examined the balance sheets of Fidelity Mortgage Investors (Debtor-in-Possession) as of October 31, 1974 and 1973 and the related statements of earnings (loss), shareholders' equity and changes in financial position for the years then ended. Our examination was made in accordance with generally accepted auditing standards, and accordingly included such tests of the accounting records and such other auditing procedures as we considered necessary in the circumstances.

Our opinion dated January 15, 1974 on the 1973 financial statements was subject to the Trust's ability to continue as a going concern. However, we can no longer express that opinion because of the matter discussed in the following paragraph.

The accompanying financial statements have been prepared in conformity with generally accepted accounting principles which contemplate continuation of the Trust as a going concern. However, on January 30, 1975, the Trust filed a petition for an arrangement under Chapter XI of the Federal Bankruptcy Act. As more fully explained in note 2(b) of notes to financial statements, the filing of that petition may negate or substantially alter the underlying assumptions upon which the accompanying financial statements, particularly the allowance for possible losses, are based. If these assumptions are negated or substantially altered, the accompanying financial statements may be affected materially.

At October 31, 1974, non-income producing loans, loans in process of foreclosure and real estate acquired through foreclosure represented approximately 69.5% of the Trust's total investments. The ultimate realization of the carrying value of the investments is dependent upon, in addition to the matter discussed in the preceeding paragraph, the successful completion and marketing of the underlying properties. Present depressed conditions in the general economy and, in particular, the real estate industry and the uncertainty of future conditions are such that the amounts and timing of such ultimate realization cannot be reasonably determined at this time.

The Trust is a defendant in numerous legal proceedings as described in note 9 of notes to financial statements; the final outcome of these proceedings is not presently determinable.

Because the matters discussed in the four preceding paragraphs may have a material effect on the financial statements of Fidelity Mortgage Investors (Debtor-in-Possession) as of October 31, 1974 and 1973 and for the years then ended, we express no opinion on them.

Notes to Financial Statements
(1) Bankruptcy Proceedings

On January 30, 1975, Fidelity Mortgage Investors (the "Trust") filed a petition for an arrangement under Chapter XI of the Federal Bankruptcy Act with the United

596
The audit report

States District Court for the Southern District of New York. On January 31, 1975, the Court authorized the Trust to operate its business and manage its property as debtor-in-possession.

The petition states that the Trust intends to propose an arrangement with its senior and junior creditors which will provide for the satisfaction of their respective claims under terms to be agreed upon with each class of creditor.

(2) Accounting Policies and Financial Statement Presentation

(b) Allowance for Possible Losses: The Trust maintains an allowance for possible losses which relates to all investments. The adequacy of the allowance is evaluated by management by means of periodic reviews of the investment portfolio on an individual investment basis. Net investments are thereby stated at the lower of cost or "estimated net realizable value" which is defined as the estimated sales value upon subsequent disposition reduced by the sum of the following estimates:

(1) Direct selling expenses

(2) Costs of completion or improvement

(3) Direct holding costs during the projected holding period, including taxes, maintenance and insurance (net of rental or other income), and in some cases

(4) The cost of money, representing an allocation of financing costs for the period to the expected date of disposition (discount factor). When problem investments are estimated to be disposed of within two years, no provision for the discount factor is made. However, in situations which are estimated to involve a protracted period of disposition, consideration is given to the discount factor. In such protracted situations, when the estimated net realizable value (including the discount factor) is less than the Trust's investment, an amount equal to the difference is included in the allowance for possible losses. The Trust generally charges the allowance when actual losses are realized upon ultimate disposition of the property.

The accompanying financial statements have been prepared in conformity with generally accepted accounting principles which contemplate continuation of the Trust as a going concern. Accordingly, the evaluation of the adequacy of the allowance for possible losses was predicated on the assumption that the Trust would be able to dispose of its investments in the ordinary course of business and not on a liquidating basis. It was also assumed that adequate funds would be available to the Trust to finance the completion of partially completed projects. However, the bankruptcy proceedings referred to in note 1 may invalidate the above assumptions. If that should occur, ultimate losses may substantially exceed the allowance for possible losses at October 31, 1974.

(9) Contingencies

The Trust is a defendant in numerous legal proceedings relating to various of its borrowers, investments and lenders. Many of these suits involve claims by mechanics lien holders against projects with which the Trust is associated as lender or owner. In addition, there is one lawsuit in which the plaintiff has claimed actual damages of approximately $11,951,000 and exemplary damages of approximately $23,903,000 as a result of alleged breach of contract, fraud and misrepresentation. The plaintiff in this suit is a former borrower to whom the Trust had advanced approximately $2,300,000 under two mortgage loan commitments aggregating $3,550,000 prior to instituting foreclosure proceedings against the underlying security. Because of the many complexities surrounding this and the other proceedings, it is not possible to determine the effect, if any, of such litigation on the accompanying financial statements.

EXAMPLE XI: UNQUALIFIED OPINION WITH THE EMPHASIS OF A MATTER

SOURCE: *Illustrations of Departures from the Auditor's Standard Report* (New York: AICPA, 1975), p. 84. Copyright © by the American Institute of Certified Public Accountants, Inc.

ROWAN COMPANIES, INC.

Auditor's Opinion

The Stockholders and Directors of
Rowan Companies, Inc.:

We have examined the consolidated balance sheet of Rowan Companies, Inc. and subsidiaries as of December 31, 1974 and 1973, and the related statements of consolidated income, changes in stockholders' equity, and changes in consolidated financial position for the years then ended. Our examination was made in accordance with generally accepted auditing standards, and accordingly included such tests of the accounting records and such other auditing procedures as we considered necessary in the circumstances.

As explained in Note 3, the Company in 1974 assigned salvage value to certain of its drilling equipment. Assigning salvage value to the equipment in our opinion does not represent a change in the consistent application of accounting principles but does affect the comparability of the financial statements.

In our opinion, the consolidated financial statements referred to above present fairly the financial position of the companies at December 31, 1974 and 1973, and the results of their operations and changes in their financial position for the years then ended, in conformity with generally accepted accounting principles applied on a consistent basis.

Notes to Financial Statements

3. Property and Depreciation

Estimated useful lives used to compute depreciation of property and equipment are as follows:

Drilling equipment	2 to 12 years
Aircraft and related equipment	2 to 8 years
Other property and equipment	3 to 33 years

In 1974, the Company, based on its operating experience assigned salvage value to certain of its drilling equipment. The effect of this change was to increase the Company's consolidated net income for the year ended December 31, 1974 by approximately $308,000 ($.14 per share).

EXERCISES AND PROBLEMS

17-1. Why is it necessary for the auditor to review events that occur subsequent to the balance sheet, especially since his or her opinion explicitly refers to the balance sheet date?

17-2. List the typical procedures that are part of the audit program for the review of subsequent events.

17-3. Describe two ways that subsequent events may impact the financial statement. Give an example of each.

598
The audit report

17-4. Can the auditor be held responsible for detecting significant subsequent events that occur after the audit report date?

17-5. Why is it advisable to have an internal independent review of all the working papers before the audit report is prepared?

17-6. Under what circumstances may it be necessary to modify the standard auditor's report? Give an example of each.

17-7. Differentiate between an adverse opinion and a disclaimer of an opinion. Which do you believe is more useful to the user?

17-8. What is the purpose of Rule 203 of the AICPA's code of professional ethics?

17-9. When part of the audit is performed by another CPA firm and this fact is disclosed in the auditor's report, is this considered a qualification?

17-10. Why do you believe professional standards allow the auditor to emphasize a matter in the audit report although such emphasis does not constitute a qualification?

17-11. What are negative assurances? Why do professional standards prohibit the use of negative assurances in most cases?

17-12. When may negative assurances be used?

17-13. You have assigned your assistant to the examination of the Cap Sales Company's fire insurance policies. All routine audit procedures with regard to the fire insurance register have been completed (i.e., vouching, footing, examination of canceled checks, computation of insurance expense and prepayment, tracing of expense charges to appropriate expense accounts, etc.). Your assistant has never examined fire insurance policies and asks for detailed instructions.

Required

1. In addition to examining the policies for the amounts of insurance and premium and for effective and expiration dates, to what other details should your assistant give particular attention as she examines the policies? Give the reasons for examining each detail. (Confine your comments to fire insurance policies covering buildings, their contents, and inventories.)

2. After reviewing your assistant's working papers, you concur with her conclusion that the insurance coverage against loss by fire is inadequate and that if loss occurs the company may have insufficient assets to liquidate its debts. After a discussion with you management refuses to increase the amount of insurance coverage.

    a. What mention will you make of this condition and contingency in your short-form report? Why?

    b. What effect will this condition and contingency have upon your opinion? Give the reasons for your position. (AICPA Adapted)

17-14. Go the library or other resource center and review several current annual reports. For each audit report modification found, list the type of deficiency and the type of opinion issued.

17-15. Presented below are three independent, unrelated auditor's reports. The corporation being reported on, in each case, is profit oriented and publishes general-purpose financial statements for distribution to owners, creditors, potential investors, and the general public. Each of the following reports contains deficiencies.

Auditor's Report I

599
Exercises and problems

We have examined the consolidated balance sheet of Belasco Corporation and subsidiaries as of December 31, 1980, and the related consolidated statements of income and retained earnings and changes in financial position for the year then ended. Our examination was made in accordance with generally accepted auditing standards and accordingly included such tests of the accounting records and such other auditing procedures as we considered necessary in the circumstances. We did not examine the financial statements of Seidel Company, a major consolidated subsidiary. These statements were examined by other auditors whose report thereon has been furnished to us, and our opinion expressed herein, insofar as it relates to Seidel Company, is based solely upon the report of the other auditors.

In our opinion, except for the report of the other auditors, the accompanying consolidated balance sheet and consolidated statements of income and retained earnings and changes in financial position present fairly the financial position of Belasco Corporation and subsidiaries at December 31, 1980, and the results of its operations and the changes in its financial position for the year then ended, in conformity with generally accepted accounting principles applied on a basis consistent with that of the preceding year.

Auditor's Report II

The accompanying balance sheet of Jones Corporation as of December 31, 1980, and the related statements of income and retained earnings and changes in financial position for the year then ended were not audited by us; however, we confirmed cash in the bank and performed a general review of the statements.

During our engagement, nothing came to our attention to indicate that the aforementioned financial statements do not present fairly the financial position of Jones Corporation at December 31, 1980, and the results of its operations and the changes in its financial position for the year then ended, in conformity with generally accepted accounting principles applied on a basis consistent with that of the preceding year; however, we do not express an opinion on them.

Auditor's Report III

I made my examination in accordance with generally accepted auditing standards. However, I am not independent with respect to Marvic Corporation because my wife owns 5 percent of the outstanding common stock of the company. The accompanying balance sheet as of December 31, 1980, and the related statements of income and retained earnings and changes in financial position for the year ended were not audited by me; accordingly, I do not express an opinion on them.

Required: For each auditor's report describe the reporting deficiencies, explain the reasons therefor, and briefly discuss how the report should be corrected. Each report should be considered separately. When discussing one report, ignore the other two. Do not discuss the addressee, signatures, and date. Also do not rewrite any of the auditor's reports. Organize your answer sheet as follows:

REPORT NO.	DEFICIENCY	REASON	CORRECTION

(AICPA Adapted)

17-16. Pace Corporation, an audit client of yours, is a manufacturer of consumer products and has several wholly owned subsidiaries in foreign countries which are audited by other independent auditors in those countries. The financial statements of all subsidiaries were properly consolidated in the financial statements of the parent company, and the foreign auditors' reports were furnished to your CPA firm.

600
The audit report

You are now preparing your auditor's opinion on the consolidated balance sheet and statement of income and retained earnings for the year ended June 30, 1979. These statements were prepared on a comparative basis with those of last year.

Required

1. How would you evaluate and accept the independence and professional reputations of the foreign auditors?

2. Under what circumstances may a principal auditor assume responsibility for the work of another auditor to the same extent as if he had performed the work himself?

3. Assume that both last year and this year you were willing to utilize the reports of the other independent auditors in expressing your opinion on the consolidated financial statements but were unwilling to take full responsibility for performance of the work underlying their opinions. Assuming your examination of the parent company's financial statements would allow you to render an unqualified opinion, prepare (1) the necessary disclosure to be contained in the scope paragraph, and (2) the complete opinion paragraph of your audit report.

4. What modification(s), if any, would be necessary in your auditor's opinion if the financial statements for the prior year were unaudited? (AICPA Adapted)

17-17. Lancaster Electronics produces electronic components for sale to manufacturers of radios, television sets, and phonographic systems. In connection with his examination of Lancaster's financial statements for the year ended December 31, 1979, Don Olds, CPA, completed fieldwork two weeks ago. Mr. Olds now is evaluating the significance of the following items prior to preparing his auditor's report. Except as noted none of these items has been disclosed on the financial statements or in footnotes.

Item 1

Recently Lancaster interrupted its policy of paying cash dividends quarterly to its stockholders. Dividends were paid regularly through 1978, discontinued for all of 1979 in order to finance equipment for the company's new plant, and resumed in the first quarter of 1980. In the annual report the dividend policy is to be discussed in the president's letter to the stockholders.

Item 2

A ten-year loan agreement, which the Company entered into three years ago, provides that dividend payments may not exceed net income earned after taxes subsequent to the date of the agreement. The balance of retained earnings at the date of the loan agreement was $298,000. From that date through December 31, 1979 net income after taxes has totaled $360,000 and cash dividends have totaled $130,000. Based upon these data the staff auditor assigned to this review concluded that there was no retained earnings restriction at December 31, 1979.

Item 3

The company's new manufacturing plant building, which cost $600,000 and has an estimated life of 25 years, is leased from the Sixth National Bank at an annual rental of $100,0000. The company is obligated to pay property taxes, insurance, and maintenance. At the conclusion of its 10-year noncancelable lease, the company has the option of purchasing the property for $1. In Lancaster's income statement the rental payment is reported on a separate line.

Item 4

A major electronics firm has introduced a line of products that will compete directly with Lancaster's primary line now being produced at the specially designed new plant. Because of manufacturing innovations, the competitor's line will be of comparable quality but priced 50 percent below Lancaster's line. The competitor announced its new line during the week following the completion of fieldwork. Olds read the announcement in the newspaper and discussed the situation by telephone with Lancaster executives. Lancaster will meet the lower prices which are high enough to cover variable manufacturing and selling expenses but will permit recovery of only a portion of fixed costs.

Required: For each item above discuss:

1. Any additional disclosure on the financial statements and in the footnotes that the CPA should recommend to his client.

2. The effect of this situation on the CPA's report on Lancaster's financial statements. For this requirement assume that the client did not make the additional disclosure recommended in part a.

Complete your discussion of each item (both parts 1 and 2) before beginning discussion of the next item. The effects of each item on the financial statements and on the CPA's report should be evaluated independently of the other items. The cumulative effects of the four items should not be considered. (AICPA Adapted)

17-18. Presented here is the auditor's report from the annual report of a company.

```
We have examined the consolidated balance sheet (name of
company) and subsidiaries as of October 31, 1974 and 1973, and the
related statements of operations and retained earnings (deficit)
and changes in financial position for the years then ended. Our ex-
amination was made in accordance with generally accepted auditing
standards, and accordingly included such tests of the accounting
records and such other audit procedures as we considered necessary
in the circumstances.

     The accompanying financial statements have been prepared on
the basis of the continuation of the Company as a going concern,
which contemplates the realization of assets and liquidation of li-
abilities in the normal course of operation. However, the Company
is in default of two provisions of its bank credit agreement, has
encountered difficulty in meeting its obligations on a timely ba-
sis, and has incurred operating losses during each of the past two
years. The continuation of the business as a going concern is con-
tingent upon continued forebearance by the bank, the maintenance of
adequate financing, and ultimately upon future profitable opera-
tions.

     Because of the material uncertainties referred to in the pre-
ceding paragraph, we are unable to and do not express an opinion on
the aforementioned financial statements.

                              Certified Public Accountants
                              Philadelphia, Pennsylvania
                              January 6, 1975
```

Required

1. Why did the material uncertainty explained in the middle paragraph of the auditor's report result in a disclaimer of opinion rather than a qualified opinion?

2. In the preparation of the above audit report, is the auditor making a judgment on the ability of the company to earn future profits? Is this a requirement of a typical engagement?

3. Assume the auditor decides to issue a qualified opinion because of the uncertainty. Prepare the opinion paragraph under this circumstance.

17-19. You are newly engaged by the James Company, a New England manufacturer with a sales office and warehouse located in a western state. The James Company audit must be made at the peak of your busy season when you will not have a senior auditor available

602
The audit report

for travel to the western outlet. Furthermore, the James Company is reluctant to bear the travel expenses of an out-of-town auditor.

Required

1. Under what conditions would you, the principal auditor, be willing to accept full responsibility for the work of another auditor?

2. What would your requirements be with respect to the integrity of the other auditor? To whom would you direct inquiries about the other auditor?

3. What reference, if any, would you make to the other auditor in your report if you were:

    a. Assuming full responsibility for his or her work?

    b. Not assuming responsibility for his or her work?   (AICPA Adapted)

17-20. The net assets of Westinghouse Electric Corporation for the year ended December 31, 1976, were approximately $750 million dollars. The following footnote accompanied the 1976 annual report of Westinghouse.

Note 17: *Uranium Litigation*

The Corporation is defending 17 lawsuits by 27 public utility customers alleging breach of uranium supply contracts. Two of these lawsuits allege violations of the antitrust laws. Three of the lawsuits are in Sweden, one is in a Pennsylvania state court and the rest have been consolidated for pretrial proceedings in the United States District Court for the Eastern District of Virginia. These suits followed a notification by the Corporation to its customers in September 1975 that performance was excused under the legal doctrine of commercial impracticability. Trial of the suit filed in the Pennsylvania state court commenced in October 1976, and is continuing.

The alleged contracts, based on the Corporation's analysis, call for the delivery of approximately 80 million pounds of uranium over the next 20 years at an average price of $10 per pound, including price escalation to date, which is based on industrial indices and is not keyed to changes in the market price of uranium. Recent spot market price quotations for uranium have been in the $40–45 per pound range. Industry marketing information indicates that purchases of uranium for long-term delivery may require large down payments and specify that the price will be the world market price at the time of delivery or a stated minimum, whichever is the higher at the time of delivery.

Under an arrangement affirmed by court order in February 1976 in the consolidated action, the Corporation became obligated to deliver, subject to a later determination of the proper price, the approximately 15 million pounds of uranium it had in inventory or under contract to the extent received by the Corporation, leaving a shortfall of approximately 65 million pounds. A portion of the 15 million pounds has since been delivered to certain plaintiff utilities under the court ordered allocation plan. Plaintiffs in the consolidated action have filed a motion contending that under the arrangement, the Corporation has an unconditional obligation to deliver uranium under its supply contracts regardless of the extent to which uranium is received under the contracts. The Corporation has controverted plaintiffs contention. In October 1976, a uranium supplier filed suit asking for a declaratory judgment that it is not required to perform its contract for the delivery of 450,000 pounds of uranium. Two other uranium suppliers under contract for about seven million pounds have suggested they may be entitled to price relief. One has completed delivery under protest; the other has continued delivery to date under protest.

The court arrangement also provides for the establishment of a utility committee to enter into discussions and negotiations with the Corporation, looking toward a possible amicable resolution of the disputes beyond the 15 million pounds and related financial matters.

Certain of the contracts in litigation are also included in a group of fuel fabrication contracts that may require the Corporation to supply, starting about 1982, an additional 3.7 million pounds of uranium for use as diluent in making plutonium fuel. As to diluent uranium required by these certain contracts, the Corporation has not asserted the doctrine of commercial impracticability.

If the plutonium fabrication option in each of those certain contracts should not be exercised for some reason (e.g., government prohibition), the Corporation may be obligated under those certain contracts to supply sufficient uranium to provide equivalent energy, i.e., an estimated nine million pounds. (There would be no such additional requirement under the other contracts in the group.) This would increase the Corporation's uranium shortfall to approximately 74 million pounds. There continues to be uncertainty as to the need for an additional nine million pounds.

Until the suits are resolved, there will continue to be major uncertainties as to the financial impact on the Corporation. One possibility is that the lawsuits may be settled under the court-directed negotiating arrangements noted above, in which case the cost of settlement to the Corporation could well be substantial. In the meantime, the Corporation will continue vigorously to assert its defenses under the Uniform Commercial Code. If the Corporation is not wholly successful and is granted only partial relief from its alleged contractual obligations, the financial impact could be severe. If the Corporation is required to fulfill all the contracts under current market conditions, the financial impact will, of course, be extremely adverse.

The Corporation is also defending against several purported shareholder class actions alleging securities law violations for failure to make proper disclosure of, among other things, the uranium situation. On January 26, 1977 the court ordered that one of such actions should proceed as a class action. All allegations of wrongdoing have been denied. In addition, a stipulation dismissing a uranium shareholder class and derivative action without prejudice has been filed with the court.

Because of the uncertainties pertaining to the foregoing matters, the eventual outcome cannot be predicted and potential financial effect cannot reasonably be estimated and, accordingly, no provisions have been recorded in the consolidated financial statements.

Required

1. Assume there were no other deficiencies in the audit. Prepare the 1976 auditor's report.

2. Go to your school's library or other resource center and obtain the auditor's report actually issued in the 1976 annual report. Contrast your report with the one issued. If there are any differences explain fully why you believe your audit report is preferable.

17-21. Nancy Miller, CPA, has completed fieldwork for her examination of the financial statements of Nickles Manufacturers, Inc., for the year ended March 31, 1979, and now is preparing the audit report. Presented here are four independent, unrelated assumptions concerning this examination:

Assumption 1

The CPA was engaged on April 15, 1979, to examine the financial statements for the year ended March 31, 1979, and was not present to observe the taking of the physical inventory on March 31, 1979. Her alternative procedures included examination of shipping and receiving documents with regard to transactions during the year under review as well as transactions since the year end, extensive review of the inventory count sheets, and discussion of the physical inventory procedures with responsible company personnel. She has also satisfied herself as to inventory valuation and consistency in valuation method. Inventory quantities are determined solely by means of physical count. (Note: Assume that the CPA is properly relying upon the examination of another auditor with respect to the beginning inventory.)

Assumption 2

During the year ended March 31, 1979, Nickles' new pollution control systems division incurred development costs which are material to the company's financial statements and are presented in the balance sheet as deferred research and development expense. The pollution control equipment developed thus far has performed well in controlled laboratory simulations, but it has not been tested in a practical setting. Nickles cannot afford to proceeds further with this project, but in management's opinion sufficient government funds can be obtained to

604
The audit report

develop fully functioning equipment that can be sold at a price that will permit recovery of these costs. There is support for management's optimism, but no commitment of government funds has been received to date. Nickles' board of directors refuses to amortize development costs applicable to the pollution control systems division.

Assumption 3

As of April 1, 1979, Nickles has an unused balance of $1,378,000 of federal income tax net operating loss carryover that will expire at the end of the company's fiscal years as follows: $432,000 in 1980, $870,000 in 1981, and $76,000 in 1982. Nickles' management expects that the company will have enough taxable income to use the loss carryover before it expires.

Assumption 4

On February 28, 1979, Nickles paid cash for all the outstanding stock of Ashworth, Inc., a small manufacturer. The combination was consummated as of that date and has been appropriately accounted for as a purchase.

Required: For each assumption described above discuss:

1. In detail, the appropriate disclosures, if any, on the financial statements and in accompanying footnotes.

2. The effect, if any, on the auditor's short-form report. For this requirement assume that Nickles makes the appropriate disclosures, if any, recommended in part 1.

Note: Complete your discussion of each assumption (both parts 1 and 2) before beginning discussion of the next assumption. In considering each independent assumption, assume that the other three situations did not occur. Organize your answer sheet as follows:

ASSUMPTION NUMBER	A. FINANCIAL STATEMENTS AND FOOTNOTES	B. AUDITOR'S REPORT
		(AICPA Adapted)

17-22. Various types of accounting changes can affect the second reporting standard of the generally accepted auditing standards. This standard reads: "The report shall state whether such principles have been consistently observed in the current period in relation to the preceding period."

Assume that the following list describes changes which have a material effect on a client's financial statements for the current year.

1. A change from the completed contract method to the percentage-of-completion method of accounting for long-term construction-type contracts.
2. A change in the estimated useful life of previously recorded fixed assets based on newly acquired information.
3. Correction of a mathematical error in inventory pricing made in a prior period.
4. A change from prime costing to full absorption costing for inventory valuation.
5. A change from presentation of statements of individual companies to presentation of consolidated statements.
6. A change from deferring and amortizing preproduction costs to recording such costs as an expense when incurred because future benefits of the costs have become doubtful. The new accounting method was adopted in recognition of the change in estimated future benefits.

7. A change to including the employer share of FICA taxes as retirement benefits on the income statement from including it with other taxes.
8. A change from the FIFO method of inventory pricing to the LIFO method of inventory pricing.

Required: Identify the type of change described in each item above, state whether any modification is required in the auditor's report as it relates to the second standard of reporting, and state whether the prior year's financial statements should be restated when presented in comparative form with the current year's statements. Organize your answer sheet as shown.

For example, a change from the LIFO method of inventory pricing to the FIFO method of inventory pricing would appear as shown.

ITEM NO.	TYPE OF CHANGE	SHOULD AUDITOR'S REPORT BE MODIFIED?	SHOULD PRIOR YEAR'S STATEMENTS BE RESTATED?
Example	An accounting change from one generally accepted accounting principle to another generally accepted accounting principle	Yes	No

(AICPA Adapted)

17-23. Presented here is the auditor's report from the annual report of Meridian Industries, Inc.:

Board of Directors
Meridian Industries, Inc.
Southfield, Michigan

We have examined the consolidated balance sheet of Meridian Industries, Inc. and subsidiaries as of March 31, 1974 and 1973, and the related consolidated statements of operations, deficiency in assets, and changes in financial position for the years then ended. Our examinations were made in accordance with generally accepted auditing standards, and accordingly included such tests of the accounting records and such other auditing procedures as we considered necessary in the circumstances, except that, because of deficiencies in internal controls and records of the discontinued Andy Gard and Equipment Divisions of the Company, we were limited in the performance of certain auditing procedures with respect to the liquidation of residual assets of these Divisions having an approximate carrying amount of $450,000 prior to disposition (see the last paragraph of Note B).

As explained in Notes B, C, D, F, G, and J, the pending settlement of receivables related to a terminated merger, the disposal of several segments of the business as a going concern is dependent upon the Company's ability to attain profitable operations and/or to restructure its indebtedness (see Note E) or obtain additional capital.

606
The audit report

Corporate administrative office expenses, approximating $750,000 in both 1974 and 1973, have been charged entirely to continuing operations, since it is not possible to reasonably estimate the amount of the subsequent reduction in such expenses, principally staff salaries and related costs, which may be directly attributed to the discontinuance of segments of the business, as described in Note B.

In our opinion, subject to (1) a final resolution of the uncertainties and contingencies referred to in the second paragraph and (2) the Company's ability to attain profitable operations and/or to successfully restructure its indebtedness or obtain additional capital, and except for the effect, if any, of the limitation in the scope of our examination referred to in the first paragraph, the accompanying consolidated financial statements identified above present fairly the consolidated financial position of Meridian Industries, Inc. and subsidiaries at March 31, 1974 and 1973, and the consolidated results of their operations and changes in financial position for the years then ended, in conformity with generally accepted accounting principles applied on a consistent basis, after giving retroactive effect to the change, with which we concur, in the form of presentation of the financial statements, as described in Note A.

Further, in our opinion, except as affected by the qualifications described in the preceding paragraph, the accompanying pro forma balance sheet presents fairly the consolidated financial position of the Company and its subsidiaries as it would have appeared at March 31, 1974, if the subsequent dispositions of segments of the business, described in Note B, and the subsequent sale of convertible debentures and the proposed application of proceeds therefrom, described in Note L, had been consummated at that date.

Ernest & Ernst
Certified Public Accountants

Detroit, Michigan
November 7, 1974

Required

1. Classify the type of deficiencies identified in the above report.

2. What type of audit opinion was issued on the financial statements for the years ended March 31, 1974 and 1973?

3. Do you agree with the type of opinion that was issued? Why or why not?

4. In the last paragraph the auditor's opinion covers the *pro forma* balance sheet. What is meant by a *pro forma* balance sheet? Is this a violation of professional rules that prohibit issuing of an opinion on forecasted financial statements?

5. Why do you think the auditor's report was dated November 7, 1974, more than seven months after the date of the balance sheet?

17-24. Charles Burke, CPA, has completed fieldwork for his examination of the Willingham Corporation for the year ended December 31, 1973, and now is in the process of determining whether to modify his report. Presented here are independent, unrelated situations which have arisen.

Situation I

In September 1973, a lawsuit was filed against Willingham to have the court order it to install pollution control equipment in one of its older plants. Willingham's legal counsel has informed Burke that the cost of the pollution control equipment is not economically feasible and that the plant will be closed if the case is lost. In addition, Burke has been told by management that the plant and its production equipment would have only minimal resale value and that the production that would be lost could not be recovered at other plants.

Situation II

During 1973, Willingham purchased a franchise amounting to 20 percent of its assets for the exclusive right to produce and sell a newly patented product in the northeastern United States. There has been no production in marketable quantities of the product anywhere to date, and neither the franchiser nor any franchisee has conducted any market research with respect to the product.

Required: In deciding the type of report modification, if any, Burke should take into account such considerations as:

· Relative magnitude

· Uncertainty of outcome

· Likelihood of error

· Expertise of the auditor

· Pervasive impact on the financial statements

· Inherent importance of the item

Discuss Burke's type-of-report decision for each stiuation in terms of the above and other appropriate considerations. Assume each situation is adequately disclosed in the notes to the financial statements. Each situation should be considered independently, and in discussing each situation, ignore the other. It is not necessary for you to decide the type of report which should be issued. (AICPA Adapted)

17-25. The complete set of financial statements for the Maumee Corporation for the year ended August 31, 1979, is presented here:

The Maumee Corporation Balance Sheet (in Thousands of Dollars) August 31, 1979

ASSETS		
Cash		$ 103
Marketable securities, at cost which approximates market value		54
Trade accounts receivable		
(net of $65,000 allowance for doubtful accounts)		917
Inventories, at cost		775
Property, plant, and equipment	$3,200	
Less accumulated depreciation	1,475	1,725
Prepayments and other assets		125
		$3,699

608
The audit report

LIABILITIES AND STOCKHOLDERS' EQUITY

Accounts payable	$ 221
Accrued taxes	62
Bank loans and long-term debt	1,580
Total liabilities	1,863
Capital stock, $10 par value (authorized 50,000 shares, issued and outstanding 42,400 shares)	424
Paid-in capital in excess of par value	366
Retained earnings	1,046
Total stockholders' equity	1,836
Total liabilities and stockholders' equity	$3,699

The Maumee Corporation Statement of Income and Retained Earnings (in Thousands of Dollars) for the Year Ended August 31, 1979

Product sales (net of $850,000 sales returns and allowances)		$10,700
Cost of goods sold		8,700
Gross profit on sales		2,000
Operating expenses:		
Selling expenses	$1,500	
General and administrative expense	940	2,440
Operating loss		(440)
Interest expense		150
Net loss		(590)
Retained earnings, September 1, 1978		1,700
		1,110
Dividends:		
Cash $1 per share	40	
Stock 6 percent of shares outstanding	24	64
Retained earnings, August 31, 1979		$ 1,046

Required: List deficiencies and omissions in the Maumee Corporation's financial statements and discuss the probable effect of the deficiency or omission on the auditor's report. Assume that the Maumee Corporation is unwilling to change the financial statements or make additional disclosures therein.

Consider each deficiency or omission separately, and do *not* consider the cumulative effect of the deficiencies and omissions on the auditor's report. There are no arithmetical errors in the statements.

Organize your answer sheet in two columns as indicated and write your answers in the order of their appearance within the general headings of balance sheet, statement of income and retained earnings, and other.

FINANCIAL STATEMENT DEFICIENCY OR OMISSION	DISCUSSION OF EFFECT ON AUDITOR'S REPORT

(AICPA Adapted)

17-26. When an auditor issues a qualified opinion or a disclaimer of opinion because of an uncertainty, it is often suggested that he or she is making a judgment about the outcome of a future event. For example, it may be suggested that in many cases the probability of a future event is so great that the financial statements should be adjusted for the anticipated loss of assets or the likely incurrence of a liability.

The AICPA Commission on Auditors' Responsibilities recommended the following solution to the problem:

> . . . the audit requirement to express a "subject to" qualification when financial statements are affected by material uncertainties should be eliminated. In combination with improvements in financial accounting standards for the disclosure of uncertainties, eliminating the requirement should improve understanding of both the effect of uncertainties on financial statements and the auditor's responsibility when certainties exist. (Page 29 of *Report of Tentative Conclusions*)

Required

    1. Why do you believe the commission suggested the above approach?

    2. Does this reduce the degree of subjectivity involved in the reporting process?

    3. Do you believe the suggested approach is superior to the present reporting requirements?

17-27. Upon completion of all fieldwork on September 23, 1979, the following short-form report was rendered by Timothy Ross to the directors of the Rancho Corporation.

To the Directors of
The Rancho Corporation:

    We have examined the balance sheet and the related statement of income and retained earnings of the Rancho Corporation as of July 31, 1979. In accordance with your instructions, a complete audit was conducted.

    In many respects, this was an unusual year for the Rancho Corporation. The weakening of the economy in the early part of the year and the strike of plant employees in the summer of 1979 led to a decline in sales and net income. After making several tests of sales records, nothing came to our attention that would indicate that sales have not been properly recorded.

    In our opinion, with the explanation given above, and with the exception of some minor errors that are considered immaterial, the aforementioned financial statements present fairly the financial position of the Rancho Corporation at July 31, 1979, and the results of its operations for the year then ended, in conformity with pronouncements of the Accounting Principles Board and the Financial Accounting Standards Board applied consistently throughout the period.

Timothy Ross, CPA
September 23, 1979

Required: List and explain deficiencies and omissions in the auditor's report. The type of opinion (unqualified, qualified, adverse, or disclaimer) is of no consequence and need not be discussed.

    Organize your answer sheet according to each paragraph (scope, explanatory, and opinion) of the auditor's report.   (AICPA Adapted)

610
The audit report

17-28. Specific rules have been promulgated concerning the disclosures that must be made when an audit is performed by two or more accounting firms.

When the primary CPA firm refers to the other CPA firms in the auditor's report, there may be some confusion on the part of the user as to the degree of responsibility assumed by each firm.

To avoid this confusion two alternative reporting schemes have been suggested. They are:

1. Require the primary auditor to do enough work, including supervisory work, so that there is no need to refer to the work performed by the other auditor.
2. Require that the other auditor's report and a summarization of the financial statements audited by the other auditor be included in the overall annual report.

Required

1. Do you believe that present reporting requirements are adequate?
2. What are the advantages and disadvantages of each of the two alternatives?
3. Do you believe it would be feasible to require that only one accounting firm be involved in the audit of a set of financial statements?

17-29. In connection with her examination of Flowmeter, Inc., for the year ended December 31, 1979, Hirsch, CPA, is aware that certain events and transactions that took place after December 31, 1979, but before she issues her report dated February 28, 1980, may affect the company's financial statements.

The following material events or transactions have come to her attention.

1. On January 3, 1980, Flowmeter, Inc., received a shipment of raw materials from Canada. The materials had been ordered in October 1979 and shipped FOB shipping point in November 1979.
2. On January 15, 1980, the company settled and paid a personal injury claim of a former employee as the result of an accident which occurred in March 1979. The company had not previously recorded a liability for the claim.
3. On January 25, 1980, the company agreed to purchase for cash the outstanding stock of Porter Electrical Company. The acquisition is likely to double the sales volume of Flowmeter, Inc.
4. On February 1, 1980, a plant owned by Flowmeter, Inc., was damaged by a flood, resulting in an uninsured loss of inventory.
5. On February 5, 1980, Flowmeter, Inc., issued and sold to the general public $2 million in convertible bonds.

Required: For each of the above events or transactions, indicate the audit procedures that should have brought the item to the attention of the auditor, and the form of disclosure in the financial statements including the reasons for such disclosures.

Arrange your answers in the following format.

ITEM NO.	AUDIT PROCEDURES	REQUIRED DISCLOSURE AND REASONS

(AICPA Adapted)

17-30. The Robert Corporation commenced doing business on January 1, 1979. It produces **611** one product which is sold to a single customer, Brown Corporation. Mr. Robert Brown Exercises and problems is president of both corporations and owns all the outstanding stock except for a few qualifying shares.

You have been the CPA for Brown Corporation for several years and accepted the engagement of examining the Robert Corporation financial statements presented here:

Robert Corporation Statement of Operations for Year Ended December 31, 1979

Sales	$150,000
Cost of sales	75,000
Gross profit	75,000
Selling and administrative expenses	55,000
Net profit before taxes	20,000
Provision for federal income taxes	6,000
Net profit	$ 14,000

Robert Corporation Balance Sheet December 31, 1979

ASSETS

Current assets:		
Cash	$ 8,000	
Accounts receivable	15,000	
Inventory	16,000	
Total current assets		$ 39,000
Fixed assets:		
Land	20,000	
Building	$50,000	
Allowance for depreciation	2,000	48,000
Machinery and equipment	20,000	
Allowance for depreciation	2,000	18,000
Total fixed assets		86,000
Total assets		$125,000

LIABILITIES

Current liabilities:		
Accounts payable	$11,800	
Liability for federal income taxes	6,000	
Total current liabilities		$ 17,800
Long-term liabilities:		
Mortgage payable		43,200
Stockholders' equity:		
Capital stock, authorized and issued, 100 shares at $100 par value	10,000	
Retained earnings	54,000	
Total stockholders' equity		64,000
Total liabilities and stockholders' equity		$125,000

Management cooperated in every respect during the audit. You did not confirm the accounts receivable. All other generally accepted auditing procedures were followed, and no items of importance were revealed by the audit except the following:

612
The audit report

1. The selling and administrative expenses included Brown's salary of $35,000.
2. The client had made a $1000 write-down to adjust the finished goods inventory to the lower of average cost or market.
3. Land, building, machinery, and equipment are recorded at current market values determined as of January 1, 1979, by a qualified appraiser. Brown purchased the assets from Brown Corporation at net book value and contributed them as part of his investment in Robert Corporation. The net book values on the records of Brown Corporation were:

Land	$10,000
Building	25,000
Machinery and equipment	10,000
	$45,000

4. Depreciation was computed by the straight-line method.
5. The mortgage payable is the balance due on a 10-year, 5 percent, $48,000 mortgage payable to the First National Bank in equal annual installments. The mortgage is secured by the company's fixed assets and is guaranteed by Brown.
6. The company customarily contracts for raw materials on a quarterly basis. An audit of post-balance-sheet events revealed that the quarterly raw material contract for the first quarter of 1980 calls for a price increase of 10 percent.
7. The sales prices to Brown Corporation were approximately 25 percent above competitive prices.
8. The usual inventory and liability certificates were signed by Brown.

Required: (Disregard the income tax problems arising from the intercorporate relationship and the control by a single stockholder.)

1. State briefly the adjustments you would suggest that the client make to his financial statements. Formal journal entries are not required.
2. Prepare the footnotes you would suggest for the financial statements.
3. Assuming that the client adopts your suggested adjustments and footnotes, prepare the auditor's opinion. The scope paragraph should be omitted. If your report is in any way modified or qualified as to opinion, give your reasons. (AICPA Adapted)

MULTIPLE CHOICE

1. Your independent examination of the Dey Company reveals that the firm's poor financial condition makes it unlikely that it will survive as a going concern. Assuming that the financial statements have otherwise been prepared in accordance with generally accepted accounting principles, what disclosure should you make of the company's precarious financial position?

    a. You should issue an unqualified opinion, but in a paragraph between the scope and the opinion paragraphs of your report direct the reader's attention to the poor financial condition of the company.

    b. You should insist that a note to the financial statements clearly indicate that the company appears to be on the verge of bankruptcy.

    c. You need not insist on any particular disclosure, since the company's poor financial condition is clearly indicated by the financial statements themselves.

    d. You should provide adequate disclosure and appropriately modify your opinion because the company does not appear to be a going concern.

2. Jackson, CPA, is the principal auditor for the Jones Corporation. He requests

another CPA to perform the examination of a subsidiary corporation located in a distant **613** state. Jackson has satisfied himself as to the independence, professional reputation, and **Multiple choice** conduct of the examination of the other auditor. What reference, if any, must Jackson make to the work of the other CPA, assuming that he is willing to accept responsibility for his work?

    a. He should indicate the extent of the other auditor's work in the scope paragraph of his report and state in the opinion paragraph that he accepts full responsibility for the work.
    b. He need not make any reference to the examination or report of the other CPA.
    c. He should make certain that the report of the other CPA accompanies his own.
    d. He should indicate the extent of the other auditor's work in the scope paragraph of his report, but he need not make any reference to it in the opinion paragraph.

    3. In reporting on the consolidated financial statements of a parent company and its subsidiaries, if the principal auditor decides to assume responsibility for the work of another CPA insofar as the other CPA's work relates to the principal auditor's expression of an opinion on the financial statements taken as a whole, the principal auditor should

    a. Make reference in his audit report to the other CPA's examination.
    b. Not make reference to the other CPA's examination.
    c. Make reference in his audit report to the other CPA's examination and responsibility and include the report of the other CPA.
    d. Not make reference to the other CPA's examination, but include the other CPA's report.

    4. A CPA rendered an unqualified opinion on the financial statements of Beemster Company for the year ended December 31, 1970. Beemster is now preparing to issue common stock. The prospectus for the common stock issue includes year-end statements and an auditor's opinion, together with unaudited financial statements for the three months ended March 31, 1971. The CPA has performed only a limited review of Beemster's financial statements for the three months ended March 31, 1971. Nothing came to her attention in this review which would indicate that the March 31 statements were not fairly presented.

    The underwriters of the common stock issue have requested that the CPA furnish them with a comfort letter giving as much assurance as possible relative to the March 31 financial statements. Her response to this request should be to

    a. Give negative assurance as to the March 31 financial statements but disclaim an opinion on the statements.
    b. Furnish to the underwriters a piecemeal opinion covering only the first three months of 1971.
    c. Furnish to the underwriters an opinion that the March 31 statements were fairly presented subject to year-end audit adjustments.
    d. Inform the underwriters that no comfort letter is possible without an audit of the financial statements for the three months ended March 31, 1971.

    5. Subsequent to rendering an unqualified report on the financial statements of Rosenberg Company for the year ended December 31, 1970, a CPA learns that property taxes for the year 1970 have been significantly underaccrued. This resulted from the company's disregard of a taxing authority ruling that was made prior to completion of the CPA's examination but was not brought to his attention. Upon learning of the ruling the CPA's immediate responsibility is

614
The audit report

a. Advisory only, since he did not learn of the ruling until after completion of his examination.
b. To make certain that the 1970 income statement is restated when the December 31, 1971, financial statements are prepared.
c. To issue immediately a disclaimer of opinion relative to the 1970 financial statements.
d. To ascertain that immediate steps are taken to inform all parties to whom this information would be important. (AICPA Adapted)

CHAPTER 18

Additional aspects of the audit report and other reports

In the previous chapter a general introduction to the audit report and report modifications were discussed. This chapter focuses on additional ramifications of the attest function. However, the latter part of the chapter attempts to put the attest function into proper perspective by discussing the limitations and possible need for improvements in the audit report.

Reports on comparative statements

In most cases the audit report is contained in an annual report that presents a set of financial statements for two or more years. Prior to 1976, it was customary for the audit report to refer only to the current set of financial statements. Under such circumstances it was difficult to determine if the auditor was attesting to the prior years' financial statements. To remedy this ambiguity, *SAS No. 15*, "Reports on Comparative Financial Statements," was issued to clarify the relationship of the current auditor to the previous years' financial statements.

CONTINUING AUDITOR

Typically, the auditor functions as a *continuing auditor* in most engagements. A continuing auditor is one who has audited the current year's financial statements as well as the previous year's statements. The language of the scope and the opinion paragraphs is slightly modified when this is the case. Basically the report refers to and reports on both sets of financial statements. For example, language similar to the following is used for the two years if unqualified opinions are appropriate:

> We have examined the balance sheets of the X Company as of December 31, 1978 and 1979, and the related statements of income, retained earnings, and changes in financial position for the years then ended. Our examinations . . . necessary in the circumstances.

616
**Additional aspects of
the audit report
and other reports**

In our opinion, the financial statements referred to above present fairly the financial position of the X Company as of December 31, 1978 and 1979, and the results of its operations and the changes in its financial position for the years then ended, in conformity with generally accepted accounting principles applied on a consistent basis.

When different opinions are appropriate for the set of two or more financial statements, the auditor constructs the report so that it is clear which opinion is associated with which set of statements. Each deficiency, whether applicable to the current year's financial statements or to prior financial statements, is fully described in an explanatory paragraph(s). In effect, the guidelines discussed in Chapter 17 are used in the preparation of the report. Thus a number of combinations may occur, such as an unqualified opinion on the current year's financial statements and a qualified opinion on the prior year's financial statements. *SAS No. 15* suggests the following illustrative report when the current year's financial statements are qualified due to an uncertainty deficiency and the prior year's financial statements contain no deficiencies:

(Explanatory Paragraph)

As discussed in Note X, during 19_2 the company became a defendant in a lawsuit relating to the sale in 19_2 of a wholly owned subsidiary. The ultimate outcome of the lawsuit cannot be determined, and no provision for any liability that may result has been made in the 19_2 financial statements.

(Opinion Paragraph)

In our opinion, subject to the effects on the 19_2 financial statements of such adjustments, if any, as might have been required had the outcome of the uncertainty referred to in the preceding paragraph been known, the financial statements referred to above present fairly the financial position of ABC Company as of December 31, 19_2 and 19_1, and the results of its operations and the changes in its financial position for the years then ended, in conformity with generally accepted accounting principles applied on a consistent basis.

During the current year's engagement the auditor may discover facts, or subsequent events may occur, that impact his or her original opinion on the previous year's financial statements. Under such circumstances it is necessary to update the previous opinion. This is accomplished in the current year's audit report. The reason for the change in the original report is fully explained in an explanatory paragraph(s). The explanatory paragraph(s) discloses (1) the date of the auditor's prior report, (2) the type of opinion originally expressed, and (3) the reasons for changing the original opinion. When the revised opinion is other than an unqualified opinion, the opinion paragraph covering the comparative financial statements is appropriately modified and there is a reference to the explanatory paragraphs.

The need to update a previous opinion may occur as a result of (1) the discovery of an uncertainty in a subsequent period that impacts the previous financial statements, (2) the discovery of inappropriate accounting methods used in the preparation of previous financial statements, or (3) restatement of financial statements previously prepared not in accordance with generally accepted accounting principles. *SAS No. 15* illustrates the last example:

(Explanatory Paragraph)

In our report dated March 1, 19_2, we expressed an opinion that the 19_1 financial statements did not fairly present financial position, results of operations, and changes in financial position in conformity with generally accepted accounting principles because of two departures from such principles: (1) the Company carried its property, plant, and equipment at appraisal values, and provided for depreciation on the basis of such values, and (2) the Company did not provide for deferred income taxes with respect to differences between income for financial reporting purposes and taxable income. As described in note X, the Company has restated its 19_1 financial statements to conform with generally accepted accounting principles. Accordingly, our present opinion on the 19_1 financial statements, as presented herein, is different from that expressed in our previous report.

The opinion paragraph for the above example does not refer to the explanatory paragraph since the revised report contains an unqualified opinion on both years.

NONCONTINUING AUDITOR

When the auditor has not audited the previous year's financial statements, the relationship of the predecessor auditor to the comparative financial statements is considered. Typically, the predecessor auditor can reissue the previous audit report so that it can be part of the current annual report. Before reissuance he or she reads the current year's financial statement, comparing these data with the previous year's report. In addition, the predecessor auditor obtains a representation letter from the successor auditor in which the latter states whether evidence was discovered in the current year that may require the predecessor's previous opinion or the previous financial statements to be revised. If the predecessor decides that the previous opinion needs to be modified, the report issued conforms to the guidelines discussed above for the case in which an updated opinion different from a previous opinion is issued. If the predecessor auditor decides that the previous opinion need not be revised, the original report is reissued, and the date of the original report is retained to demonstrate that subsequent significant fieldwork was not performed by the predecessor auditor. Thus the report on comparative financial statements under these circumstances may contain two sets of auditors' reports.

When the predecessor auditor updates the prior report but the report is not included in the current report the current year's audit report is modified. The successor auditor discloses in the scope paragraph that the previous year's financial statements were examined by another auditor. Also, in the scope paragraph the type of opinion issued by the predecessor is disclosed. If the previous opinion is other than an unqualified opinion, a complete description of the report modifications is contained in the scope paragraph. The opinion paragraph is not modified but refers only to the current year's financial statements.

Other data in financial reports

The audit report and financial statements often are not presented alone. For example, a typical annual report may contain a message from the president, a summary of operations, management's discussion and analysis of the summary of operations, and a variety of graphs and charts, as well as the audit report and

618
**Additional aspects of
the audit report
and other reports**

set of financial statements. A casual reader of an annual report may conclude that the entire report is reviewed by the auditor and subjected to certain audit procedures. This is a current problem with the reporting process and will continue to be a problem as long as audited financial statements are published with other information.

Current professional standards do not require the auditor to perform procedures to verify information not contained specifically in the financial statements and the associated footnotes. However, he or she is required to read the other information to determine if it is materially inconsistent with the information presented in the audited financial statements. For example, the income statement may report a significant extraordinary gain as part of the determination of net income. In the president's message the net income figure, which includes the extraordinary gain, may be described as net income from operations. Since this presentation is inconsistent with the information contained in the audited financial statements, the client is asked to revise the president's statement. If the client refuses, the auditor considers whether the inconsistency is significant enough to warrant an explanatory paragraph in the audit report. When an explanatory paragraph describing the inconsistency is deemed appropriate, the scope and the opinion paragraphs are not impacted. In an extreme case the auditor may decide not to allow the audit report to be part of the total report or may withdraw from the engagement.

In the above case it is fairly easy to identify an inconsistency between the audited statements and other documents. However, the auditor may question the client's interpretation or evaluation of the data when there appears to be a material misstatement of fact. Since judgment is involved in this case, the auditor's position is usually far more difficult to substantiate. For this reason he or she questions only statements that are within his or her expertise and subject to some standard of measurement and where valid differences of opinion are not likely to materialize. For example, it would be inappropriate for the auditor to question statements made by the president of the company concerning the likely impact of government-imposed energy conservation regulation on future operations. Nonetheless, if the auditor concludes that there is a misstatement of fact, the situation is fully described in writing and communicated to the client. Futhermore, the auditor may consider consulting with legal counsel to consider an appropriate course of action. The appropriate course of action may include the alternatives discussed in the previous paragraph concerning discovery of an inconsistency.

Unaudited financial statements

The role of the independent auditor often requires that he or she be associated with financial statements that are unaudited. The defining of this role and the responsibility assumed by the auditor has proven to be a difficult and delicate task for the profession. On the one hand, the auditor does not perform audit procedures to the extent necessary to render an opinion on the financial statements. On the other hand, the mere fact that the auditor's name is associated with a set of unaudited financial statements may be interpreted by some users to mean the statements possess some degree of reliability. This situation is typically encountered by the auditor when unaudited financial statements are prepared for small clients and when larger clients prepare and distribute interim financial information.

ANNUAL UNAUDITED FINANCIAL STATEMENTS

The clientele of many auditing firms includes companies that need an accounting service often referred to as write-up work. That is, the auditor may be asked to post transactions, prepare and post adjusting and closing entries, and prepare financial statements and tax returns. These companies lack the accounting expertise to accomplish these tasks. In such situations, the auditor is not required to perform any auditing procedures to determine if the data being processed are valid. However, many auditing firms believe that some minimum audit procedures and inquires should be made even when unaudited financial statements are prepared. This is a result of the 1136 Tenants' Corporation case, discussed in Chapter 4, and the desire by the firm to perform high-quality service. A checklist for the preparation of unaudited statements is presented in Figure 18-1.

A key factor in determining the auditor's reporting requirements in relationship to unaudited financial statements is the matter of association. An auditor is associated with unaudited financial statements when he or she (1) prepared or assisted in the preparation of the statements or (2) consented to the use of his or her name in the report or document containing the financial statements. Association does not exist if the auditor simply reproduces, rather than prepares, the unaudited statements.

If the auditor is associated with unaudited financial statements, each page of the financial statements is clearly and conspicuously marked "Unaudited." In addition, he or she disclaims an opinion on the financial statements using language similar to the following example:

> The accompanying balance sheet of X Company as of December 31, 19__, and the related statement of income and retained earnings and changes in financial position for the year then ended were not audited by us and accordingly we do not express an opinion on them.

The audit report illustrated above is expanded when the auditor is aware that the statements are not prepared in accordance with generally accepted accounting principles. This does not imply that he or she is required to make such a determination; rather, during the course of the engagement such facts may come to his or her attention. In such a case, a paragraph(s) disclosing the accounting deficiency and the effects of the deficiency, if known by the auditor, is included in the audit report. The paragraph(s), such as the following example, appears after the disclaimer of opinion paragraph:

> Under generally accepted accounting principles, land is ordinarily stated at cost. Management has informed us that the company has recorded its land at appraisal value and that if generally accepted accounting principles had been followed, the land account and stockholders' equity would have been decreased by $150,000.

620
Additional aspects of the audit report and other reports

Figure 18-1

General
1. Prepare engagement letter before starting engagement.
2. Whether trial balance is supported by general ledger account balances.
3. Whether subsidiary ledgers have been reconciled with general ledger control accounts.
4. Whether accounting principles have been applied consistently.
5. At the completion of the engagement, some CPAs obtain from the client a representation letter that covers significant aspects of the financial statement contents and presentation and that acknowledges management's responsibility for the financial statements.

Cash
1. Whether bank reconciliations have been prepared.

Receivables
1. Whether a reasonable allowance has been provided for doubtful accounts.
2. Whether receivables from employees, shareholders, affiliated organizations, etc., are separately disclosed.
3. Whether receivables have been discounted, pledged, or factored.

Inventory
1. The method of determining inventory quantities.
2. The basis for pricing inventory.
3. Other considerations:
   a. Possible obsolescence.
   b. Inventory that is unrecorded (located at client's premises or elsewhere).
   c. Inventory owned by others (consigned, bill-and-hold, etc.).
   d. Whether inventories are encumbered.

Property, Plant, and Equipment
1. Whether stated at cost.
2. The depreciation method used; the amount of depreciation expense for the period; consistency in computing depreciation.
3. Possible unrecorded additions, retirements, abandonments, sales, or trade-ins.
4. Property mortgaged or otherwise encumbered.
5. The policy of capitalizing or expensing repairs and betterments.

Other Assets
1. The basis for stating prepayments, deferred charges, investments, etc.
2. Amortization methods.
3. Assets pledged.

Liabilities
1. Unrecorded payables.
2. Whether assets are pledged as collateral.
3. Whether payables to employees, shareholders, affiliated companies, etc., are classified separately.
4. Whether accruals have been properly recorded.
5. Contingent liabilities such as discounted notes, drafts, endorsements, warranties, litigation, unsettled claims, taxes in dispute, etc.
6. Reasonableness of income tax accruals.
7. Whether debt is properly classified as to current portion and long-term portion.
8. Long-term liability maturities, interest rates, collateral, conversion rate, restrictions, if any; possible defaults with respect to any convenant; review disclosure for adequacy.
9. Contractual obligations for construction or purchase of real property, equipment, etc.; commitments to purchase or sell company securities, options, lease commitments, etc.

Equity Accounts
1. Changes in equity accounts.
2. Matters that require disclosure (descriptions and details of capital stock, stock options, warrants, dividend restrictions, etc.).

Revenue and Expenses
1. Whether proper cutoffs of sales and purchases, etc., were made.
2. Abnormal variations between periods in income and expense accounts.
3. Method of recognizing income and the proper matching of costs and revenues.

SOURCE: "Guide for Engagements of Certified Public Accountants to Prepare Unaudited Financial Statements," (New York: AICPA, 1975), pp. 19–21. Copyright © 1975 by the American Institute of Certified Public Accountants, Inc.

INTERIM UNAUDITED FINANCIAL STATEMENTS

In a dynamic economy reporting financial information on an annual basis is often untimely. For this reason, interim financial statements prepared on a monthly, quarterly, or semiannual basis may be distributed to user groups. There are many theoretical and practical problems associated with interim reporting. One of the most important is concerned with the quality of the data being presented. As described in Chapter 1, an independent review of the data enhances user acceptability of the material. Of course, an independent audit of information is expensive and, at this point in its development, the financial reporting community has not demanded that interim financial statements be audited. However, there is a definite trend toward requiring the auditor to be associated in some way with regular interim reports. Such a trend seems to be introducing a "secondary level of assurance" of financial statements.[1] That is, the interim financial statements are not audited, but some procedures or reviews have been conducted by the auditor. This area of responsibility is not settled, and the description that follows is based upon the profession's limited experience with such an approach.

The objective of a limited review of interim financial statements is to provide the auditor with a basis for reporting to user groups significant matters affecting interim financial information. It does not provide assurance that the auditor's approach was sufficiently extensive to identify all significant matters. In the performance of a limited review the auditor is not required to achieve the standards of fieldwork of generally accepted auditing standards, and the procedures employed are not corroborative in nature. For the most part the approach consists primarily of analytic procedures supplemented by auditor inquiries directed toward key management personnel.

SAS No. 10, "Limited Review of Interim Financial Information," lists the following as procedures that may be employed by the auditor in a limited review of interim financial information:

a. Inquiry concerning (i) the accounting system, to obtain an understanding of the manner in which transactions are recorded, classified and summarized in the

[1] See Larry P. Bailey, "Secondary Level Assurances," *The CPA Journal* February 1978, pp. 27–31.

622
**Additional aspects of
the audit report
and other reports**

preparation of interim financial information, and (ii) any significant changes in the system of internal accounting control, to ascertain their potential effect on the preparation of interim financial information.

b. Analytical review of interim financial information by reference to internal financial statements, trial balances or other financial data, to identify and inquire about relationships and individual items that appear to be unusual. An analytical review consists of (i) a systematic comparison of current financial information with that anticipated for the current period with that of the immediately preceding interim period, and with that of the corresponding interim period of the previous fiscal year, (ii) a study of the interrelationship of elements of financial information that would be expected to conform to a predictable pattern based on the entity's experience, and (iii) a consideration of the types of matters that in the preceding year or quarters have required accounting adjustments.

c. Reading the minutes of meetings of stockholders, board of directors and committees of the board of directors to identify actions that may affect the interim financial information.

d. Reading the interim financial information to consider on the basis of information coming to the accountant's attention whether the information to be reported conforms with generally accepted accounting principles.

e. Obtaining letters from other accountants, if any, who have been engaged to make a limited review of the interim financial information of significant segments of the reporting entity, its subsidiaries or other investees.

f. Inquiry of officers and other executives having responsibility for financial and accounting matters concerning (i) whether the interim financial information has been prepared in conformity with generally accepted accounting principles consistently applied, (ii) changes in the entity's business activities or accounting practices, (iii) matters as to which questions have arisen in the course of applying the foregoing produces, and (iv) events subsequent to the date of the interim financial information that would have a material effect on the presentation of such information.

While making the review the auditor may discover events or circumstances that require additional investigation. For these events he or she employs analytic as well as corroborative audit procedures to determine whether the interim financial information is to be modified.

The audit report on the interim financial information discloses the nature of the limited review and contains a disclaimer of opinion. On the assumption that the auditor does not discover significant items or that the significant items are appropriately accounted for, a report similar to the following is issued:

We have made limited reviews, in accordance with standards established by the American Institute of Certified Public Accountants, of the balance sheets of XYZ Company as of June 30, 19_2 and 19_1, and the related statements of income, retained earnings, and changes in financial position for the three-month and six-month periods then ended. Since we did not make an audit, we express no opinion on the interim financial statements referred to above.

In the limited review of interim financial information, reporting deficiencies are usually limited to accounting problems resulting from the use of an unacceptable accounting principle or the client's failure to give the effect of an adjustment or disclosure prepared by the auditor. Under these circumstances the auditor includes an explanatory paragraph(s) to explain the nature of the deficiency.

623
Special reports

Special reports

The attest function is not confined to the auditor's determination of whether financial statements are prepared in accordance with generally accepted accounting principles. A compliance audit environment exists when there (1) is a set of standards that function as a norm, (2) are economic events recorded and subject to verification, (3) is a defined and acceptable method of reporting the results of the investigation, and, (4) is an adequately trained auditor. There are many situations where it is necessary to review a particular set of events and present an independent evaluation of the matter. *SAS No. 14,* "Special Reports," identified four such situations:

1. Financial statements that are prepared in accordance with a comprehensive basis of accounting other than generally accepted accounting principles.
2. Specified elements, accounts, or items of a financial statement.
3. Compliance with aspects of contractual agreements or regulatory requirements related to audited financial statements.
4. Financial information presented in prescribed forms or schedules that require a prescribed form of auditor's report.

COMPREHENSIVE SET OF PRINCIPLES

Generally accepted accounting principles are not the only basis upon which financial statements may be prepared. A comprehensive set of accounting rules for recording, processing and reporting financial events may be based upon (1) promulgations of a regulatory agency (the state insurance commission), (2) promulgations of an income tax authority, (3) cash receipts and disbursements principles, and (4) criteria which have substantial support, such as price-level accounting as described in the APB Statement No. 3. The above examples, while at variance with generally accepted accounting principles, fully describe an alternative accounting model.

SAS No. 14 provides the following guidelines for preparation of the audit report:

a. A paragraph identifying the financial statements examined and stating whether the examination was made in accordance with generally accepted auditing standards.
b. A paragraph that
   i. States, or preferably refers to the note to the financial statements that states, the basis of presentation of the financial statements on which the auditor is reporting.
   ii. Refers to the note to the financial statements that describes how the basis of presentation differs from generally accepted accounting principles. (The monetary effect of such differences need not be stated.)
   iii. States that the financial statements are not intended to be presented in conformity with generally accepted accounting principles.

624
Additional aspects of
the audit report
and other reports

c. A paragraph that expresses the auditor's opinion (or disclaims an opinion) on whether:

   i. The financial statements are presented fairly in conformity with the basis of accounting described. If the auditor concludes that the financial statements are not presented fairly on the basis of accounting described, he or she should disclose all the substantive reasons for that conclusion in an additional explanatory paragraph(s) of his/her report and should include in the opinion paragraph appropriate modifying language and a reference to the explanatory paragraph(s).

   ii. The disclosed basis of accounting used has been applied in a manner consistent with that of the preceding period.

These reporting principles are illustrated in Figure 18-2.

REPORT ON SPECIFIED ELEMENTS, ACCOUNTS, OR ITEMS

An auditor may be engaged to determine whether part of the financial statements is prepared in accordance with generally accepted accounting principles. As suggested in the previous chapter, he or she is precluded from issuing a piecemeal opinion. Thus such a request encompasses only elements that do not constitute a major portion of the financial statements. When the auditor makes this conclusion, the relevant elements are audited to an extent necessary to form an opinion on the data. The general standards, the standards of fieldwork, and the third and fourth reporting standards are applicable to the limited engagement. The auditor is careful to recognize the interrelationship of accounts, which probably requires the auditing of other accounts not reported upon. For example, an examination of purchases from a particular vendor may require the auditor to review cash disbursements journals and accounts payable subsidiary records, as well as other accounts. An example of the audit report appropriate to this type of engagement is presented in Figure 18-3.

CONTRACT COMPLIANCE ASSOCIATED WITH AUDITED STATEMENTS

Contractual arrangements between the client and a third party may require the client to meet certain conditions or be in violation of the contract. For example, a creditor may require that the client maintain a certain current ratio during the year. To determine the client's compliance with such specifications, the third party may ask the auditor to see if the agreement is being observed. Notice that this is incidental to the engagement, for the primary purpose of the audit is to issue an opinion on the financial statements. The auditor communicates the findings through the utilization of negative assurances. Recall that normally the auditor is prohibited from using negative assurance. However, in this case such assurances are allowed if (1) they accompany the auditor's report on the financial statements, or (2) they are included in a separate report and that report refers to the original audit conducted which serves as a basis for the negative assurance.

PRESCRIBED FORMS OR SCHEDULES

Regulatory agencies or other authorities may prescribe that accounting data be presented in a particular manner and that certain statements be made by the

Figure 18-2

625
Special reports

Financial statements prepared on a basis prescribed by a regulatory agency solely for filing with that agency

We have examined the statement of admitted assets, liabilities, and surplus-statutory basis of XYZ Insurance Company as of December 31, 19___, and the related statements on income-statutory basis and changes in surplus-statutory basis for the year then ended. Our examination was made in accordance with generally accepted auditing standards and, accordingly, included such tests of the accounting records and such other auditing procedures as we considered necessary in the circumstances.

As described in Note X, the Company's policy is to prepare its financial statements on the basis of accounting practices prescribed or permitted by the Insurance Department of Pennsylvania. These practices differ in some respects from generally accepted accounting principles. Accordingly, the accompanying financial statements are not intended to present financial position and results of operations in conformity with generally accepted accounting principles. This report is intended solely for filing with regulatory agencies and is not intended for any other purpose.

In our opinion, the financial statements referred to above present fairly the admitted assets, liabilities and surplus of XYZ Insurance Company as of December 31, 19___ and the results of its operations and changes in its surplus for the year then ended, on the basis of accounting described in Note X, which basis has been applied in a manner consistent with that of the preceding year.

SOURCE: "Special Reports," *Statement on Auditing Standards No. 14* (Copyright 1976 by The American Institute of Certified Public Accountants), pp. 6–7.

Figure 18-3

Report relating to amount of sales for the purpose of computing rental

Board of Directors
ABC Company

We have examined the schedule of gross sales (as defined in the leases agreement dated March 4, 19—, between ABC Company, as lessor, and XYZ Stores Corporation, as lessee) of XYZ Stores Corporation as its Main Street store, (City), (State), for the year ended December 31, 19—. Our examination was made in accordance with generally accepted auditing standards and, accordingly, included such tests of the accounting records and such other auditing procedures as we considered necessary in the circumstances.

In our opinion, the schedule of gross sales referred to above represents fairly the gross sales of XYZ Stores Corporation at its Main Street store, (City), (State), for the year ended December 31, 19—, on the basis specified in the lease agreement referred to above.

SOURCE: "Special Reports," *Statement on Auditing Standards No. 14* (Copyright 1976 by The American Institute of Certified Public Accountants), p. 10.

626
Additional aspects of
the audit report
and other reports

independent auditor concerning these data. Furthermore, these requirements may be formalized by the use of preprinted forms or schedules issued or approved by the authority. To avoid violating disclosure requirements the auditor may revise the schedules, inserting appropriate terminology or observing an acceptable classification scheme. If the schedule includes assertions that the auditor believes are not justified or are inconsistent based upon the role of the independent auditor, then it may be necessary to attach a separate audit report that conforms to the reporting guidelines described in the above section concerning the reports on financial statements prepared in accordance with a comprehensive basis of accounting other than generally accepted accounting principles.

Reports on internal control

The objective of an audit is to perform the tasks necessary to enable the auditor to form an opinion on the financial statements. He or she is not required to make any statement in the audit report that refers to an evaluation of the internal control system, even though such an evaluation is an integral part of the audit approach. However, there may be parties that are interested in the internal control system and, more important, want the independent auditor to make a definite statement as to its adequacy. The problem that arises when such a request is made involves the user's understanding of the role of the internal control system in an organization. A statement by the auditor that the system is adequate may be interpreted by some interested parties to mean that material errors or fraud cannot occur. As suggested in other sections of this book, such an inference is inappropriate, since no system, no matter how elaborate its design, can meet such a test.

To avoid or minimize the possibility of misinterpreting the auditor's assertions concerning the internal control system, the profession designates two groups presumed to possess the ability to utilize such a report properly. They are management and government regulatory agencies. Furthermore, the report on the internal control system may be circulated to other user groups if management or the regulatory agency decides that the user group is capable of using it properly. Under no circumstances does the auditor allow the report on a client's internal control system to be distributed to a user group other than management or regulatory authority if the report is contained in a document that includes the client's unaudited financial statements.

If the auditor concludes that an internal control report can be issued, he or she is careful to word the report in a manner that identifies the limitations and assumptions inherent in an internal control system. Section 640.12 of *SAS No. 1* proposes a model for the internal control report which is reproduced in Figure 18-4. Any deviations from this guide are carefully considered by a prudent auditor to avoid the possibility of changing the precise meaning of the report.

The last sentence in Figure 18-4 states that " . . . such study and evaluation disclosed the following conditions that we believe to be material weaknesses." At this point, in a separate paragraph, the auditor describes the weakness and corrective action taken or to be taken by the client. If corrective action is

Figure 18-4

627
Long form reports

We have examined the financial statements of ABC Company for the year ended December 31, 1980, and have issued our report thereon dated February 23, 1981. As a part of our examination we reviewed and tested the Company's system of internal accounting control to the extent we considered necessary to evaluate the system as required by generally accepted auditing standards. Under these standards the purpose of such evaluation is to establish a basis for reliance thereon in determining the nature, timing, and extent of other auditing procedures that are necessary for expressing an opinion on the financial statements.

The objective of internal accounting control is to provide reasonable, but not absolute, assurance as to the safeguarding of assets against loss from unauthorized use or disposition, and the reliability of financial records for preparing financial statements and maintaining accountability for assets. The concept of reasonable assurance recognizes that the cost of a system of internal accounting control should not exceed the benefits derived and also recognizes that the evaluation of these factors necessarily requires estimates and judgments by management.

There are inherent limitations that should be recognized in considering the potential effectiveness of any system of internal accounting control. In the performance of most control procedures, errors can result from misunderstanding of instructions, mistakes of judgment, carelessness, or other personal factors. Control procedures whose effectiveness depends upon segregation of duties can be circumvented by collusion. Similarly, control procedures can be circumvented intentionally by mangement with respect either to the execution and recording of transactions or with respect to the estimates and judgments required in the preparation of financial statements. Further projection of any evaluation of internal accounting control to future periods is subject to the risk that the procedures may become inadequate because of changes in conditions and that the degree of compliance with the procedures may deteriorate.

Our study and evaluation of the Company's system of internal accounting control for the year ended Decemeber 31, 1980, which was made for the purpose set forth in the first paragraph above, would not necessarily disclose all weaknesses in the system. However, such study and evaluation disclosed the following conditions that we believe to be material weaknesses.

SOURCE: "Codification of Auditing Standards and Procedures," *Statement on Auditing Standards No. 1* (New York: AICPA, 1973), pp. 177–178

---

impractical, because of excessive costs or the peculiarities of the client's business, the description of the weakness may be excluded from the report. In such a case the last sentence of the fourth paragraph in Figure 18-4 is changed to read, "However, such study and evaluation disclosed the following conditions that we believe to be material weaknesses for which corrective action by management may be impractical under the circumstances."

Long-form reports

For the most part conventional auditing involves the issuance of a short-form report which contains the client's financial statements, footnotes to these statements, and the auditor's report. However, there may be situations in which a more voluminous report is appropriate and professional standards allow the issuance of a long-form report. The long-form report contains the same basic statements that comprise a short-form report, but a variety of other data may be added. These additional data may include a summarization of the aged accounts receivable, ratios and trend analysis, explanatory comments, and a description of the audit procedures employed, as well as other accounting and

628
**Additional aspects of
the audit report
and other reports**

nonaccounting data. This type of analysis is usually requested by small companies that lack the financial expertise to develop it internally.

If the audit report is part of a long-form report, the auditor is careful to describe the responsibility he or she has assumed in relationship to the supplemental data. The standard language of the scope and the opinion paragraphs is used, but the auditor states whether the supplemental analysis has been subjected to appropriate audit procedures. If this analysis has been subjected to audit, the auditor states whether the data are fairly stated in all material respects in relation to the basic financial statements. The auditor's statements may be made in a separate paragaraph of the audit report, or may be presented as a preface immediately preceding the supplemental data.

Evaluation of the audit report

This chapter and previous chapters demonstrate the highly technical nature of the audit report. It may be recalled from Chapter 1 that the audit report serves as the basis for communication between the auditor and user groups. Many feel that the audit report in its present form does not adequately achieve this goal. Some of the typical criticisms that support this position are:

- The language used in the report is too technical, that is, "generally accepted accounting principles," "consistency," and so on.
- The term "fairly stated" is not subject to meaningful interpretation, *SAS No. 5* notwithstanding.
- The report does not make it clear that the financial statements are management's representations.
- A "clean" opinion implies that the company is efficiently managed.
- The scope paragraph does not adequately describe the nature of the auditor's work.

These criticisms are in part due to a lack of user education, and are also the result of an attempt to communicate data generated by a complex process. There are no easy answers to this problem; however, two encouraging developments or trends seem to be materializing.

One development relates to the identification of the user group. There has always been a debate in accounting as to whether the user group possesses the abilities of a sophisticated financial analyst or those of a layperson. Obviously, unless the target group is identified and adequately characterized, the success of communicating with the user group will be less than optimal. It appears that the profession is ready to cope with this problem. For example, the FASB's discussion memorandum on the conceptual framework of accounting reached the following tentative conclusions:

> Financial statements of business enterprises should provide information, within the limits of financial accounting, that is useful to present and potential investors and creditors in making rational investment and credit decisions. Financial statements should be comprehensive to investors and creditors who have a reasonable under-

Figure 18-5   **629**

Evaluation of the audit report

Illustration of the revised auditor's report

Financial Statements

The accompanying consolidated balance sheet of XYZ Company as of December 31, 1980, and the related statements of consolidated income and changes in consolidated financial position for the year ended, including the notes, are the representations of XYZ Company's management, as explained in the report by management.

In our opinion, those financial statements in all material respects present the financial position of XYZ Company at December 31, 1980, and the results of its operations and changes in financial position for the year then ended in conformity with generally accepted accounting principles appropriate in the circumstances.

We audited the financial statements and the accounting records supporting them in accordance with generally accepted auditing standards. Our audit included a study and evaluation of the company's accounting system and the related controls, tests of details of selected balances and transactions, and an analytical review of the information presented in the statements. We believe our auditing procedures were adequate in the circumstances to support our opinion.

Other Financial Information

We reviewed the information appearing in the annual report (or other document) in addition to the financial statements, and found nothing inconsistent in such other information with the statements or the knowledge obtained in the course of our audits. (Any other information reviewed, such as replacement cost data, would be identified.)

We reviewed the interim information released during the year. Our reviews were conducted each quarter (or times as explained) and consisted primarily of making appropriate inquiries to obtain knowledge of the internal accounting control system, the process followed in preparing such information and of financial and operating developments during the periods, and determining that the information appeared reasonable in the light of the knowledge we obtained from our inquiries during the current year, from any procedures completed to the interim date in connection with our audit for such year, and from our audits for preceding years. Any adjustments or additional disclosures we recommended have been reflected in the information.

Internal Accounting Controls

Based on our study and evaluation of the accounting system and related controls, we concur with the description of the system and controls in the report by management (or, Based on our study and evaluation of the accounting system and controls, the following uncorrected material weaknesses not described in the report by management. . .) (or other disagreements with the description of the system and controls in the report by management) (or a description of uncorrected material weakness found if there is no report by mangement). Nevertheless, in the performance of most control procedures, errors can result from personal factors, and also, control procedures can be circumvented by collusion or overridden. Projection of any evaluation of internal accounting control to future periods is subject to the risk that changes in conditions may cause procedures to become inadequate and the degree of compliance with them to deteriorate.

Other Matters

We reviewed the company's policy statement on employee conduct, described in the report by management, and reviewed and tested the related controls and internal audit procedures. While no controls or procedures can prevent or detect all individual misconduct, we believe the controls and internal audit procedures have been appropriately designed and applied during the year.

We met with the audit committee (or the board of directors) of XYZ Company as often as we thought necessary to inform it of the scope of our audit and to discuss any significant accounting or auditing problems encountered and any other services provided to the company (or indication of failure to meet or insufficient meeting or failure to discuss pertinent problems).

SOURCE: *The Commission on Auditors' Responsibilities: Report, Conclusions, and Recommendations* (Copyright 1978 by The Commisison on Auditors' Responsibilities), pp. 77–79.

630
Additional aspects of
the audit report
and other reports

Figure 18-6

Illustration of report by management

Financial Statements

We prepared the accompanying consolidated balance sheet of XYZ Company as of December 31, 1980, and the related statements of consolidated income and change in consolidated financial position for the year then ended, including the notes (or, The named statements have been prepared on our behalf by our independent auditor from the company's records and other relevant sources.). The statements have been prepared in conformity with generally accepted accounting principles appropriate in the circumstances, and necessarily include some amounts that are based on our best estimates and judgments. The financial information in the remainder of the annual report (or other document) is consistent with that in the financial statements.

Internal Accounting Controls

The company maintains an accounting system and controls over it to provide reasonable assurance that assets are safeguarded against loss from unauthorized use or disposition and that financial records are reliable for preparing financial statements and maintaining accountability for assets. There are inherent limitations that should be recognized in considering the potential effectiveness of any system of internal accounting control. The concept of reasonable assurance is based on the recognition that the cost of a system of internal control should not exceed the benefits derived and that the evaluation of those factors requires estimates and judgments by management. The company's systems provide such reasonable assurance. We have corrected all material weaknesses of the accounting and control systems identified by our independent auditors, Test Check & Co., Certified Public Accountants (or, We are in the process of correcting all material weaknesses . . .) (or, We have corrected some of the material weaknesses but have not corrected others because)

Other Matters

The functioning of the accounting system and controls over it is under the general oversight of the board of directors [or the audit committee of the board of directors]. The members of the audit committee are associated with the company only through being directors. The system and controls are reviewed by an extensive program of internal audits and by the company's independent auditors. The audit committee [or the board of directors] meets regularly with the internal auditors and the independent auditors and reviews and approves their fee arrangements, the scope and timing of their audits, and their finding.

We believe that the company's position in regard to litigation, claims and assessments is appropriately accounted for or disclosed in the financial statements. In this connection we have consulted with our legal counsel concerned with such matters and they concur with the presentation of the position.

The company has prepared and distributed to its employees a statement of its policies prohibiting certain activities deemed illegal, unethical, or against the best interests of the company. (The statement was included in the 197_ annual report of the company; copies are available on request.) In consultation with our independent auditors we have developed and instituted additional internal controls and internal audit procedures designed to prevent or detect violations of these policies. We believe that the policies and procedures provide reasonable assurance that our operations are conducted in conformity with the law and with a high standard of business conduct.

[If applicable—The Board of Directors of the Company in March 1980 engaged Supers, Sede & Co., Certified Public Accountants, as our independent auditors to replace Test Check & Co., following disagreements on . . . Test Check & Co. agrees with that description of disagreements.]

SOURCE: *The Commission on Auditors' Responsibilities: Report, Conclusions, and Recommendations* (Copyright 1978 by The Commission on Auditors' Responsibilities), pp. 79–80.

standing of business and economic activities and financial accounting and who are willing to spend the time and effort needed to study financial statements.[2]

Thus, it appears that information will be constructed for distribution to individuals with a reasonable background in financial reporting.

The profession is not trying to place all the burden of improvement on those outside the profession. The AICPA Commission on Auditors' Responsibilities has made some recommendations that it hopes will improve the audit report so that the user may better understand what the auditor is attempting to communicate. The commission suggests that the audit report go into more detail as to the role of management in preparation of the statement, the nature of an audit, and the role of an internal control system in an organization. Their suggested audit report is presented in Figure 18-5. In addition, the commission recommended that management include a report to supplement the audit report. An example is presented in Figure 18-6.

Whether these proposals will be accepted by the profession is unclear at this point. However, it is clear that auditing and the attendant reporting responsibilities are changing. This is but one bit of evidence indicating that auditing is a dynamic discipline. There will always be problems and hopefully the profession will strive to solve these problems in order to serve the community better. This is what makes being a part of the profession truly exciting and challenging. Although this book serves only as an introduction to the discipline, we hope it has provided the serious student with a foundation for understanding the professional challenge and has whetted the student's appetite for learning more about the profession.

EXERCISES AND PROBLEMS

18-1. What are the reporting requirements when comparative financial statements are presented?

18-2. When comparative financial statements are presented, what is the effect if the current auditor did not audit the previous year's financial statements?

18-3. Assume the current auditor did not audit the previous year's financial statements. What should the current auditor do if the predecessor auditor refuses to reissue the previous audit report?

18-4. Since the annual report includes a variety of data, is the auditor responsible for the validity of these other data?

18-5. With respect to other information in documents containing audited financial statements, differentiate between (1) a material inconsistency and (2) a material misstatement of fact.

---

[2] *Tentative Conclusions on Objectives of Financial Statements of Business Enterprises* (Stamford, Conn.: FASB, 1976), p. 3. Copyright © 1976 by the Financial Accounting Standards Board, High Ridge Park, Stamford, Connecticut 06905, U.S.A. Reprinted with permission. Copies of the complete document are available from the FASB.

632
**Additional aspects of
the audit report
and other reports**

18-6. If the auditor determines that there is a material inconsistency between information contained in the audited financial statements and other unaudited information, what course of action should he or she take?

18-7. Unaudited financial statements must be noted as such, and the auditor must issue a disclaimer of opinion on these statements. With such a caveat, do users rely upon these financial statements?

18-8. When is an auditor associated with unaudited financial statements?

18-9. Is it proper for the auditor to issue a disclaimer of opinion on unaudited financial statements and, assuming no problems, include negative assurances?

18-10. Differentiate between unaudited financial statements and interim financial statements?

18-11. With respect to a limited review of interim financial statements, what is meant by the phrase "secondary level of assurance"?

18-12. What is a limited review of interim financial information? Must the auditor review every set of interim financial statements?

18-13. What conditions are the basis for a compliance audit environment?

18-14. *SAS No. 14* describes four types of special reports. Give an example of each.

18-15. Why is the internal control letter so carefully structured?

18-16. How does the long-form report differ from the short-form report?

18-17. What are some of the criticisms of the present auditor's report?

18-18. The audit report proposed by the Cohen Commission (see Figure 18-5) may be described as an attempt to "educate" the user of the financial statements. Comment on this statement.

18-19. The limitations on the CPA's professional responsibilities when he is associated with unaudited financial statements are often misunderstood. These misunderstandings can be substantially reduced by carefullly following professional pronouncements in the course of his work and taking other appropriate measures.

Required: The following list describes seven situations the CPA may encounter, or contentions he may have to deal with in his association with and preparation of unaudited financial statements. Briefly discuss the extent of the CPA's responsibilities and, if appropriate, the actions he should take to minimize any misunderstandings. Number your answers to correspond with the numbering in the following list.

1. The CPA was engaged by telephone to perform write-up work including the preparation of financial statements. His client believes that the CPA has been engaged to audit the financial statements and examine the records accordingly.

2. A group of business people who own a farm managed by an independent agent engage a CPA to prepare quarterly unaudited financial statements for them. The CPA prepares the financial statements from information provided by the independent agent. Subsequently, the businesspeople refuse to pay the CPA's fee and blame him for allowing the situation to go undetected, contending that he should not have relied on representations from the independent agent.

3. In comparing the trial balance with the general ledger the CPA finds an account

labeled "Audit fees" in which the client has accumulated the CPA's quarterly billings for accounting services including the preparation of quarterly unaudited financial statements.

633
Exercises and problems

4. Unaudited financial statements were accompanied by the following letter of transmittal from the CPA.

> We are enclosing your company's balance sheet as of June 30, 1980, and the related statements of income and retained earnings and changes in financial position for the six months then ended which we have reviewed.

5. To determine appropriate account classification, the CPA reviewed a number of the client's invoices. He noted in his working papers that some invoices were missing but did nothing further because he felt they did not affect the unaudited financial statements he was preparing. When the client subsequently discovered that invoices were missing he contended that the CPA should not have ignored the missing invoices when preparing the financial statements and had a responsibility to at least inform him that they were missing.

6. The CPA has prepared a draft of unaudited financial statements from the client's records. While reviewing this draft with his client, he learns that the land and building were recorded at appraisal value.

7. The CPA is engaged to review without audit the financial statements prepared by the client's controller. During this review, he learns of several items which by generally accepted accounting principles would require adjustment of the statements and footnote disclosure. The controller agrees to make the recommended adjustments to the statements but says that he will not add the footnotes because the statements are unaudited.

(AICPA Adapted)

18-20. You were appointed auditor for Clay Corporation on January 17, 1979. The controller of Clay explained that you were appointed early in the year so that you would be able to issue an opinion on the 1979 financial statements. The 1979 financial statements will be used by Clay Corporation in attempts to secure long-term financing sometime in late 1979 or early 1980. Clay Corporation has never been audited by a CPA firm during its five-year history.

With this understanding you immediately begin some preliminary work on January 20, 1979. As part of this preliminary work you analyze and test the company's perpetual inventory system. After appropriate testing you conclude that the system is very adequate. On January 23, 1979, you perform test counts of the inventory and trace these counts to the updated perpetual inventory cards. No discrepancies are discovered. You estimate that your test counts amounted to approximately 65 percent of the total inventory. Using the updated perpetual inventory cards and documentation generated by January sales and purchases you are able to reconcile to the inventory quantity count made by the client on December 31, 1978. Again, no errors are found. Finally, you perform other inventory tests and conclude that the inventory figure of December 31, 1978, was determined in accordance with generally accepted accounting principles.

You perform appropriate audit procedures during your interim work in October 1979. Other audit procedures are completed on or after December 31, 1979, and you conclude that an unqualified opinion is to be issued on the balance sheet, income statement, statement of retained earnings, and statement of change in financial position.

On January 28, 1980, Clay Corporation applies for a loan from the Third National Bank and submits the set of 1979 audited financial statements along with other unaudited financial information. After reviewing the material, the bank states that it cannot process the loan unless comparative financial statements for 1978 and 1979 are presented. Immediately, the controller asks you to perform an audit of the 1978 financial statements.

634
**Additional aspects of
the audit report
and other reports**

On February 3, 1980, you return to Clay Corporation and begin an audit of the 1978 financial statements. You complete your fieldwork on March 8, 1980, and conclude that the 1978 financial statements are prepared in accordance with generally accepted accounting principles, except that you were not able to satisfy yourself regarding inventory quantities as of December 31, 1977. The inventory is a material asset.

Required

1. Prepare the auditor's report for the years ended December 31, 1978 and 1979.

2. Why do you believe that you were unable to satisfy yourself as to the inventory quantities as of December 31, 1977, but had no reservations about the count as of December 31, 1978?

3. Wouldn't you have a similar problem with accounts receivable, since confirmations as of December 31, 1977, would be impossible? Explain fully.

18-21. The major written understandings between a CPA and his or her client, in connection with an examination of financial statements, are the engagement (arrangements) letter of the client's representation letters.

Required:

  1.a. What are the objectives of the engagement (arrangements) letter?
     b. Who should prepare and sign the engagement letter?
     c. When should the engagement letter be sent?
     d. Why should the engagement letter be renewed periodically?
  2.a. What are the objectives of the client's representation letters?
     b. Who should prepare and sign the client's representation letters?
     c. When should the client's representation letters be obtained?
     d. Why should the client's representation letters be prepared for each examination?
    3. A CPA's responsibilities for providing accounting services sometimes involve his or her association with unaudited financial statements. Discuss the need in this circumstance for:
     a. An engagaement letter
     b. Client's representation letters   (AICPA Adapted)

18-22. The financial statements of the Tiber Company have never been audited by an independent CPA. Recently Tiber's management asked Alice Burns, CPA, to conduct a special study of Tiber's internal control; this study will not include an examination of Tiber's financial statements. Following completion of her special study, Burns plans to prepare a report that is consistent with the requirements of *SAS No. 49*, "Reports on Internal Control."

Required

1. Describe the inherent limitations that should be recognized in considering the potential effectiveness of any system of internal control.

  2. Explain and contrast the review of internal control that Burns might make as part of an examination of financial statements with her special study of Tiber's internal control covering each of the following:

    a. Objectives of review or study
    b. Scope of review or study
    c. Nature and content of reports

Organize your answer for part 2 as follows:

EXAMINATION OF FINANCIAL STATEMENTS	SPECIAL STUDY
Objective	Objective
Scope	Scope
Report	Report

3. In connection with a loan application, Tiber plans to submit the CPA's report on her special study of internal control, together with its latest unaudited financial statements, to the Fourth National Bank. Discuss the propriety of this use of the CPA's report on internal control. (AICPA Adapted)

18-23. *SAS No. 8* requires that the auditor read other information in documents containing audited financial statements. In reading this information the auditor must determine if the other information is presented in a manner inconsistent with its presentation or representation in the audited financial statements. In addition, he or she must determine whether the other information is a material misstatement of fact. In the latter case, the auditor must consider whether he or she has the expertise to assess the validity of the client's statements or whether the statement is simply an opinion by management not subject to validation.

The following are several statements taken from annual reports:

1. The Federal Power Commission took a step in the right direction during 1976 with an order allowing producers to increase their wellhead prices for certain vintages of gas sold in interstate commerce.
2. The agricultural equipment market is expected to remain strong worldwide, although down slightly in 1980 in North America because of expected reductions in exports and lower grain prices.
3. Consolidated operating revenues rose for the 38th consecutive year, totaling $6.4 million, for a 14% increase over 1979 revenues of $5.6 million.
4. The 1980 oil income declined from the record 1979 levels because of increasingly competitive conditions which produced lower profit margins on refined products.
5. Sales to the U.S. government increased by $39 million in 1979 to $830 million from $791 million in 1978, while the ratio to total sales dropped to 37%.
6. Aerospace was a strong market for us last year and showed a 20% sales gain that offset the decline in our machinery business.
7. For the past four years, the Company's sales have grown at an average compounded rate of 44%. Earnings, however, have grown at a rate of 77% during those four years; earnings per share, including the dilution of the 1979 equity offering, have grown at a rate of 61%.
8. Had the Company opted to develop its own end-user marketing, leasing and support capabilities of like size, rather than acquire them, it would have taken approximately $20 to $30 million in cash and future profits.

Required

1. For each statement listed above classify it as either

a. Subject to an auditor's evaluation since it can be verified as consistent or inconsistent with data presented in the financial statements.
b. Subject to an auditor's evaluation since it can be determined whether it is a material misstatement of fact.

636
Additional aspects of the audit report and other reports

c. Not subject to an auditor's evaluation.

2. For each item fully explain how it is verified. If it can not be verified, explain why.

18-24. A CPA was engaged by the Alba Nursing Home to prepare, on the CPA's stationary and without audit, financial statements for 1979 and its 1979 income tax return. From the acounting and other records he learned the following information about the nursing home:

1. The Alba Nursing Home is a partnership that was formed early in 1979. The nursing home occupies a large old mansion that stands on a sizable piece of ground beside a busy highway. The property was purchased by the partnership from an estate that out-of-state heirs wanted to settle. The heirs were unfamiliar with the local real estate market and sold the property at the bargain price of $10,000 for the house and $5000 for the land.
2. A few weeks after the purchase the partnership employed a competent independent appraisal firm that appraised the house at $100,000 and the land at $50,000.
3. The property was then written up on the partnership books to its appraisal value, and the partners' capital accounts were credited with the amount of the write-up.
4. Additional funds were invested to convert the mansion to a nursing home, to purchase the necessary equipment and supplies, and to provide working capital.

Required

1. Assume that the CPA prepared the financial statements of the Alba Nursing Home from the accounting records, placed them on his stationary, and labeled each page "Prepared without audit." In accordance with the client's preference, the assets were reported only at appraisal values. Under the circumstances presented, what is the CPA's responsibility, if any, to discuss the method of valuation of the assets? Discuss.

2. In this situation, how does the CPA's responsibility for disclosure of the valuation basis of the assets differ, if at all, from the responsibility he would have had if he had made a typical examination of the financial statements?

3. In this situation, would it be proper for the CPA to prepare, and sign as preparer, the 1979 federal income tax return of the partnership if the mansion is shown on the income tax return at its appraisal value? Discuss.　　　　　(AICPA Adapted)

18-25. You are engaged by the Sono Company to prepare its tax return and unaudited financial statements for the year ended December 31, 1979. In preparing for the engagement you read the AICPA latest guide for engagements of CPAs to prepare unaudited financial statements. During this engagement you follow some of the suggestions made in the guide. At the conclusion of this work you prepare the following report:

I have examined the balance sheet of Sono Company as of December 31, 1979, and the related tax return, statement of income, and statement of changes in financial position for the year then ended. My examination was made in accordance with generally accepted auditing standards and, accordingly, included such tests of the accounting records and such other auditing procedures as I considered necessary in the circumstances except as explained in the following paragraph.

Since the financial statements were unaudited, as noted on the face of each one, I did not perform many of the routine audit procedures. However, I did perform the procedures outlined in the AICPA's "Guide for Engagement of Certified Public Accountants to Prepare Unaudited Financial Statements (1975)," except that none of the procedures suggested for the review of liabilities was employed.

Since the company limited the scope of my audit, I am unable to express, and I do not express, an opinion on the financial statements referred to above. However, nothing came to my attention which would indicate that these statements are not fairly presented, except that ending inventories are stated at replacement cost.

Required
1. Identify and explain the deficiencies of your report.
2. Prepare a revised auditor's report.
3. Relative to your answer in part 1, what is the purpose of the AICPA guide for the preparation of unaudited financial statements?

18-26. As part of your annual audit of Call Camper Company, you have the responsibility for preparing a report to management on internal control. Your work papers include a completed internal control questionnaire and documentation of other tests of the internal control system which you have reviewed. This review identified a number of material weaknesses; for some of these corrective action by management is not practicable in the circumstances.

Required
1. Discuss the form and content of the report on internal control to management based on your annual audit and the reasons or purposes for such a report. Do not write a report.
2. Discuss what differences there would be in the form and content of the report if it were based on a special study for the purpose of reporting to a regulatory agency. (AICPA Adapted)

18-27. Jiffy Clerical Services is a corporation which furnishes temporary office help to its customers. Billings are rendered monthly based on predetermined hourly rates. You have examined the company's financial statements for several years. Following is an abbreviated statement of assets and liabilities on the cash basis as of December 31, 1980.

ASSETS:	
Cash	$20,000
Advances to employees	1,000
Equipment and autos, less allowance for depreciation	25,000
Total assets	46,000

LIABILITIES:	
Employees' income taxes withheld	8,000
Bank loan payable	10,000
Estimated federal income taxes on cash basis profits	10,000
Total liabilities	28,000
Net assets	$18,000

REPRESENTED BY:	
Common stock	$ 3,000
Cash profits retained in the business	15,000
	$18,000

Unrecorded receivables were $55,000, and payables were $30,000.

Required
1. Prepare the opinion you would issue covering the statement of assets and liabilities as of December 31, 1980, as summarized above, and the related statement of cash income and expenses for the year ended that date.
2. Briefly discuss and justify your modifications of the conventional opinion on accrual basis statements. (AICPA Adapted)

638
Additional aspects of the audit report and other reports

18-28. The AICPA Commission on Auditors' Responsibilities, in its *Report, Conclusions, and Recommendations* expressed the feeling that the standard auditor's report has become a symbol which may be reducing its communicative potential. In response to this possibility the commission suggested an alternative report structure which was presented in Figure 18-5 of this chapter.

Required

1. What does the commission mean when it refers to the current auditor's report as a "symbol"?

2. Do you believe the auditor's report should be interpreted as a symbol?

3. Read the commission's suggested auditor's report. Assume that an alternative course of action is simply to revise the auditor's report to read:

> The accompanying financial statements are prepared in accordance with generally accepted accounting principles.

What are the advantages and disadvantages of each alternative? Which one do you believe is superior?

18-29. Following are the financial statements of the Young Manufacturing Corporation and the auditor's report of their examination for the year ended January 31, 1980. The examination was conducted by John Smith, an individual practitioner, who has examined the corporation's financial statements and reported on them for many years.

Young Manufacturing Corporation Statements of Condition January 31, 1980 and 1979

ASSETS	1980	1979
Current assets:		
Cash	$ 43,822	$ 51,862
Accounts receivable pledged less allowances for doubtful accounts of $3,800 in 1980 and $3,000 in 1979 (see note)	65,298	46,922
Inventories, pledged at average cost, not in excess of replacement cost	148,910	118,264
Other current assets	6,280	5,192
	264,310	222,240
Fixed assets:		
Land at cost	38,900	62,300
Buildings at cost, less accumulated depreciation of $50,800 in 1980 and $53,400 in 1979	174,400	150,200
Machinery and equipment at cost, less accumulated depreciation of $30,500 in 1980 and $25,640 in 1979	98,540	78,560
Total fixed assets	311,840	291,060
Total assets	$576,150	$513,300

LIABIILTIES AND STOCKHOLDERS' EQUITY	1980	1979
Current liabilities:		
Accounts payable	$ 27,926	$ 48,161
Other liabilities	68,743	64,513

	1980	1979
Current portion of long-term mortgage payable	3,600	3,600
Income taxes payable	46,840	30,866
Total current liabilities	$147,109	$147,140
Long-term liabilities:		
Mortgage payable	90,400	94,000
Total liabilities	237,509	241,140
Stockholders' equity:		
Capital stock, par value $100, 1,000 shares authorized, issued, and outstanding	$100,000	$100,000
Retained earnings	238,641	272,160
Total stockholders' equity	338,641	272,160
Total liabiities and stockholders' equity	$576,150	$513,300

Note: I did not confirm the balances of the accounts receivable but satisfied myself by other auditing procedures that the balances were correct.

Young Manufacturing Corporation Income Statements for the Years Ended January 31, 1980 and 1979

	1980	1979
Income:		
Sales	$884,932	$682,131
Other income	3,872	2,851
Total	888,804	684,982
Costs and expenses:		
Cost of goods sold	463,570	353,842
Selling expenses	241,698	201,986
Administrative expenses	72,154	66,582
Provision for income taxes	45,876	19,940
Other expenses	12,582	13,649
Total	835,880	655,999
Net income	$ 52,924	$ 28,983

March 31, 1980

To: Mr. Paul Young, President
Young Manufacturing Corporation

I have examined the balance sheet of the Young Manufacturing Corporation and the related statement of income and retained earnings.

These statements present fairly the financial position and results of operations in conformity with consistent generally accepted principles of accounting. My examination was made in accordance with generally accepted auditing standards, and accordingly included such tests of the accounting records and other such auditing procedures as I considered necesary in the circumstances.

(Signed)
John Smith

640
Additional aspects of
the audit report
and other reports

Required: List and discuss the deficiencies of the auditor's report prepared by John Smith. Your discussion should include justifications that the matters you cited are deficiencies.(Do not check the addition of the statements but assume that the addition is correct.)

(AICPA Adapted)

18-30. Professional standards recognize that an auditor may be asked to issue an opinion on a set of financial data other than the typical statements prepared in accordance with generally accepted accounting principles. Thus a CPA may issue an opinion on (1) statements prepared in accordance with a comprehensive set of accounting rules, (2) specific data which are part of a financial statement, (3) compliance with a contractual agreement or regulatory requirement, or (4) financial data presented in prescribed form. Listed here are several statements or analyses that may warrant the auditor's issuance of a specific report:

1. A report relating to the amount of sales made to a foreign government
2. A report on whether a client has complied with certain financial covenants contained in the bond agreement with bondholders
3. A statement of changes in owners' equity
4. A capital budgeting analysis identifying the internal rate of return of a project
5. A report to determine the effectiveness of the management team at a major subsidiary
6. Financial statements based on price level accounting rules
7. A set of financial statements prepared to comply with rules and regulations established by the SEC.
8. A *pro forma* balance sheet
9. A report designating the amount of expenditures devoted to advertising and public relations
10. Financial statements prepared in accordance with the client's income tax basis
11. Cash basis financial statements
12. A schedule of estimated cash receipts for the next five years for a new branch
13. A report identifying the amount of home office expenses allocated to a government contract
14. Financial statements of a municipality

Required

1. Of the items described above, identify which ones may be the basis for the auditor's preparation of a special report.

2. Classify those identified in part 1 according to the four categories described in *SAS No. 14.*

MULTIPLE CHOICE

Items 1 through 4 are based on the following information:

The Mastermind Security Company has asked you to prepare a report on its internal control. The report is to be based on your study and evaluation of the company's control system made in conjunction with your recently completed annual audit of Mastermind. Mastermind is considering the inclusion of the report on internal control in a document that will be sent to stockholders. Mastermind's stock is widely held and actively traded.

1. Under which of the following conditions would the inclusion of the internal control report in a document to stockholders be prohibited?

a. If the document contains only the internal control report and unaudited interim financial statements

b. If only a select class of stockholders receives the document

c. If Mastermind has requested the internal control report because of a ruling by a regulatory agency

d. If the internal control report indicates a management negligence

2. If the report on internal control is distributed to the general public, it must contain specific language describing several matters. Which of the following must be included in the specific language?

a. The distinction between internal administrative controls and internal accounting controls

b. The various tests and procedures utilized by the auditor during his or her review of internal control

c. The objective of internal accounting controls

d. The reason(s) Mastermind's management requested a report on internal control

3. If the report on internal control will be distributed to Mastermind's stockholders, the opening paragraph of the internal control report should indicate its timeliness by including which of the following pair of dates?

a. The date on which your review of internal control was completed and the date on which you agreed to prepare the internal control report

b. The date of the audit report issued on Mastermind's financial statements and the date on which you agreed to prepare the internal control report.

c. The date of Mastermind's financial statements and the date on which your review of internal control was completed

d. The date of Mastermind's financial statements and the date of the audit report issued on these financial statements

4. How should the report on internal control deal with the possibility that some stockholders might use it for speculation about the future adequacy of Mastermind's internal control system?

a. The report should contain an opinion as to whether the present internal control system can be relied upon for the next accounting period.

b. The report should make no mention of the possibilty of making such projections.

c. The report should disclose management's opinion about the number of future accounting periods during which the present internal control system can be relied upon.

d. The report should discuss the risk involved in making such projections.

5. An auditor should avoid expressions of negative assurance except in

a. Internal control letters.

b. Letters to underwriters.

c. Piecemeal opinions.

d. Reports containing an adverse opinion. (AICPA Adapted)

Index

Access controls, EDP internal control system and, 222–223
Access to assets
cash disbursement system and, 330–331
cash receipts system and, 318
credit sales system and, 363
fixed-assets system and, 448
internal control and, 185
inventory purchase system and, 404–405
payroll system and, 542
Accountability. *See also specific topics*
cash receipts system and, 317–318
comparison of assets with recorded. *See* Assets, comparison of recorded accountability with
fixed-assets system and, 446–449
internal control and system of, 183–185
inventory purchase system and, 403
Accountancy Law Reporter Service, 35
Accounting controls, 117–179. *See also* Internal control
Accounting deficiencies. *See* Deficiencies
Accounting department
cash disbursements system and, 329
cash receipts system and, 316–317
credit sales system and, 360
EDP function and, 219
fixed-assets system and, 446
inventory purchase system and, 402–403
long-term liabilities and, 491
payroll system and, 538, 540
Accounting firms. *See* Public accounting firms
Accounting manual, 187
Accounting principles and policies
adverse opinion based on deficiencies in, 578–581

changes in, 42–43, 581
disclosure of, 304–305
generally accepted. *See* Generally accepted accounting principles
special reports based on comprehensive set of, 623–626
Accounting Principles Board, 4
Accounting Series Releases, 33, 80
Accounting structure, internal control and, 186–188
Accounts payable, 478–483
vendors' statements reconciled with, 331
Accounts receivable
confirmation of, 107
credit sales system and access to, 363
substantive tests for, 374–387
aged trial balances, 374–376
audit program, 374, 375
classification and disclosure, 385
confirmation at an interim date, 385
confirmation process, 375, 377–383
cutoff of sales and credit allowances, 384
valuation of, 383–384
Accrued liabilities, 483–485
Accumulated depreciation, analysis of, 454–455
Accumulation of cost, in fixed-assets system, 447–448
Activity, evidence based on observation of, 139
Adjustments in working trial balance, 159
Adverse opinion, auditor's, 14–15, 578–587
Advertising, AICPA rule on, 75–76
Aged trial balance for accounts receivable, 374–376
Allowances
authorization for, 362
purchase, 413

643

644
Index

Alpha risk, 274–275
American Institute of Certified Public Accountants (AICPA), 7
  Auditing Standards Executive Committee, 30, 33
  code of ethics of. *See* Code of ethics, AICPA's
  Commission on Auditor's Responsibilities, 29
  Committee on Auditing Procedures, 36
  Continental Vending case and, 111
  on EDP systems, 218
  examination for CPA, 34–35, 37
  fairness of financial standards as defined by, 12
  industry audit guides, 45
  internal control as defined by, 176–177
  on liability of auditor
    to clients, 99
    fraud detection, 100
    to third parties, 101
  on materiality of evidence, 142
  objective of audit as described by, 6
  peer review and, 118
  on planning phase, 151
  professional corporations and, 7, 8
  on promulgation of accounting principles, 31
  role of, 30
  Statements on Auditing Standards (SAS), 36. *See also* Generally accepted auditing standards
  Trial Board, 71, 75, 78–79
American National Standards Institute, 227
Amortization period, 550–551
Amortization policy, 551
Annual reports
  data other than auditor's report and financial statements in, 617–618
  SEC requirements, 32
Application controls in EDP internal control system, 223–226
  in-depth review of, 235, 236
Assets
  access to. *See* Access to assets
  comparison of recorded accountability with, 185–186
    cash receipts and disbursements systems, 319, 331
    credit sales system, 363
    fixed assets system, 448–449
    inventory purchase system, 405
    payroll system, 542–543
  fixed. *See* Fixed assets internal control system
  observation and verfication of, 143
Assistants, supervision of, 39, 40
Attestation, definition of, 26
Attribute sampling. *See* Frequency estimation
Audit(s)
  completing, 564–572
    events subsequent to balance sheet date but prior to report date, 564–570
    events subsequent to report date, 570–571
    evidential matter, review of, 571–572
  compliance, 4

  financial compliance, 4–5
  objective of, 6
  operational, 5–6
  procedural compliance, 5
  scope of, 192
Audit approach, compliance tests and, 293–296
Audit committee in internal control model, 191–193
Audit firms. *See* Public accounting firms
Audit plan, 156
Audit report. *See* Auditor's report
Audit staff, internal, 190–191
Audit trial, following the, 294, 295
Audit working papers. *See* Working papers
Auditing
  defensive approach to, 118–119
  definition, 26
  economic justification of, 27–28
  history of, 1–3
  planning process in, 39–40
  role in society, 26–27
  societal controls on, 29–34
  timing of, 39
Auditing standards, generally accepted. *See* Generally accepted auditing standards
Auditing Standards Executive Committee (AICPA), 30, 33
Auditor. *See also* Certified Public Accountant; Public accounting firms
  assignation to engagements, 37
  change in, 73–74
  continuing, 615–617
  due professional care of, 38–39
  education of, 116, 118
  efficient utilization of resources by, 39–40
  entry-level requirements for, 34–35
  hiring of, AICPA standards, 37
  independence of. *See* Independence of auditors
  liability of. *See* Liability of auditor
  nomination of, as audit committee function, 191–192
  noncontinuing, 617
  personal characteristics of, AICPA standards, 36–39
  professional development of, 37–38
  professional standards of, 35–36
  proficiency of, 37
  social role and responsibilities of, 26–29
  in tax practice. *See* Tax practice
  technical training of, 36–37
  who should fill the role of, 28–29
Auditor's report, 10–16
  addressee of, 11
  adverse, 14–15, 578–587
    accounting circumstances, 578–581
    scope circumstances, 582–585
    uncertainty circumstances, 585–586
  AICPA standards for, 42–44
  comparative statements, reports on, 615–617
  completion of audit prior to preparation of, 564–573
  criticisms of, 628

disclaimer of opinion in. *See* Disclaimer of opinion

emphasis of matter in, 586–587

illustrations of, 588–597

on internal control system, 626–627

long-form, 627–628

management's report to supplement, 629

modifications of, 13–16, 574–575
  lack of independence of auditor, 66–67

negative assurances in, 587

opinion paragraph in, 12–13

piecemeal opinions in, 587

qualified, 15, 575–577

in registration statement, liability for, 103–104

scope paragraph, 12

signature, 13

sign-off date, 13

special, 623–626

unqualified, 11–14, 44, 573–575

user group and, 628–629

Authority to sign checks, 330
  compliance test, 333

Authorization (of transactions)
  for billing, 361
  for capital stock transfers, 512
    additions, 516
    deletions, 519
  for cash disbursements, 329–330
    review of, 333–334
  cash receipts system and, 317–318
  compliance tests and, 294
  for credit, 361, 372
  for credit allowances, 362
  in credit sales system, 361–362
    validation of authorization, 370, 372
  for disposition of fixed assets, 447
  EDP internal control model and, 220–221
  fixed-assets system and, 446–449
  for hiring and firing, 540–541
  for hours worked, 541
  internal control and system of, 183–185
  inventory purchase system and, 403–404
  for long-term liabilities, 492
  of pay rates and deductions, 541
  for payroll transactions, 540–541
    validation, 548
  for purchase, 403
  for purchase of fixed assets, 447
  for receipt and storage, 403–404
  for sales, 361, 370, 372
  for shipment, 361, 372
  validation of. *See* Validation of authorization
  for write-offs, 362

Autonomy, departmental. *See* Departmental autonomy

Balance
  substantive tests of. *See* Substantive tests
  working trial, 157–159

Balance sheet approach to auditing, 289, 290

Bank accounts, cash in. *See* Cash, in bank accounts

Bank confirmation for cash account, 338, 340–341

Bank reconciliation, 319
  substantive tests of cash in bank and, 335–338
  year-end, 335–337

Bank statements
  cash disbursements traced to, 334
  cutoff, 335–338
  as documentary evidence, 138
  reconciliation of. *See* Bank reconciliation

BarChris case, 107–109

Beta risk, 275

Bidding, competitive, by auditors, 77

Billing, authorization for, 361

Bill of lading, 361, 362, 372, 373

Board of directors, 183
  long-term debt and, 491, 492, 495
  minutes of meetings of, 149
  review minutes of meetings of, 488

Bonding, fidelity, 189

Bonds. *See also* Long-term liabilities
  investment in, 465
  recording of transactions involving, 493

Budget, capital, 447

Business cycle, integrated audit approach and, 148, 149

Capital budget, 447

Capital expenditures, recording of, 448

Capitalism, 28

Capitalization policy, 448

Capital stock. *See also* Investments; Securities; Stock
  general ledger, 514, 520–521

Cardozo, Benjamin, 102

Cash
  in bank accounts
    cutoff bank statements, 335–338
    existence, 335, 337
    extended procedured, 341
    substantive audit procedures for, 325, 334–342
    valuation, classification, and disclosure, 338–341
  petty. *See* Petty cash
  proof of, 341, 342
  substantive tests for, 341. *See also* in bank accounts *above*
    petty cash, 343
    results of tests and auditor's opinion, 345
    undeposited cash receipts and near-cash items, 344–345

Cash disbursements for petty cash, 343

Cash disbursements journal
  comparison of checks to, 333
  preparation of, 330
  review of, 482
  testing the summarization of, 334

Cash disbursements system, 328–345. *See also* Checks, disbursements by
  compliance tests for, 331–334
  internal control model and, 328–331

646
Index

Cash disbursements system (*Continued*)
  study and evaluation of, 331
  substantive tests for. *See* Cash, in bank accounts
Cash dividends, 524
Cashier, cash receipts system and, 317, 318, 327
Cash receipts, accounts receivables' existence and, 380
Cash receipts journal, 326, 327
  testing the summarization of, 328
Cash receipts listing, 318, 325
Cash receipts system, 315–328
  authorization and accountability system and, 317–319
  compliance tests of, 321, 325–328
  in internal control model, 315–319
  plan of organization and, 316–317
  study and evaluation of, 319–321
  substantive tests for. *See also* Cash, in bank accounts
  undeposited cash receipts, 344
Certificates of deposit, 465
Certified Public Accountants (CPAs). *See also* Auditor; Public Accounting firms
  academic preparation for, 35, 37
  code of professional ethics of. *See* Code of ethics
  continuing-education requirements for, 35
  entry-level requirements for, 34–35
  examination for, 35–37
  experience required for, 35
  professional development of, 35, 37–38
  responsiblities of, 59
  state licensing of, 34, 35
Chart of accounts, 186–187
Check(s). *See also* Bank reconciliation; Bank statements
  canceled, as documentary evidence, 138
  disbursements by
    all disbursements to be made by checks, 331
    compliance tests, 333–334
    mailing of checks, 330
    preparation of checks, 330
    recording of checks in cash disbursement journal, 330
    signing of checks, 330
  endorsement of. *See* Endorsement of checks
  restrictive endorsement of, 318
Check writer, mechanical, 330
Classification
  of accounts payable, 483
  of accounts receivable, 385
  of cash balance, 338, 340
  of inventory, 429
  of inventory purchases, 411
  of investments, 464
Clerical accuracy, payroll system and, 548–549
Clients, responsiblities of CPAs to, 59. *See also* Liability of auditor
  confidentiality, 71–72
Code of ethics, AICPA's, 58–83
  concepts of professional ethics in, 59–60

  enforcement of, 78–79
  rules of conduct, 60–78
    advertising and solicitation, 75–76
    competence, 67–69
    discreditable accounts, 75–78
    form of practice and name of firm, 77–78
    incompatible occupations, 77
    independence, 60–67
    responsibilities to clients, 71–72. *See also* Liability of auditor
    responsibilities to colleagues, 72–74
    technical standards, 69–71
  SEC and, 79–80
Commissions to obtain clients, AICPA rule on, 77
Committee on Accounting Procedure, 4
Common law
  liability of auditor based on
    clients, 99–100
    detection of fraud, 100–101
    third parties, 101–103
Common stock. *See* Stock
Companies Act of 1862, 3
Comparative accounts, analysis of, 147, 534
Comparative financial statements, reports on, 615–617
Comparison routine, 306
Competence
  AICPA rules concerning, 67–69
  of CPA, 59
  of evidence, 41–42, 135–136, 141
Competitive bidding by auditors, 77
Completing the audit. *See* Audit(s) completing
Compliance tests, 290–297
  audit approach and, 293–296
  for cash disbursements system, 331–334
  for cash receipts system, 321, 325–328
  for credit sales system, 364, 366, 370–374
  EDP impact on, 296–297
  EDP internal control system and, 234, 236–237
  frequency estimation used in. *See* Frequency estimation
  integrated audit approach and, 151, 152, 154
  objectives of, 290–291
  for payroll system, 543–545, 548–549
  size of sample for, 292–293
  techniques used for, 292
  timing of, 291–292
Computational evidence, 137
Computational routine, 206
Computer equipment (EDP equipment). *See also* EDP internal control system
  controlling access to, 222–223
  controlling malfunctions of, 222
  Equity Funding fraud and, 112–113
  protection of, 223
Confidence interval in variable estimation, 270
Confidence level
  frequency estimation and, 253–254
  variable estimation and, 266–267
Confidentiality, principle of, 71–72
Confirmation, 143–144, 299

of accounts payable, 480–481
of accounts receivable, 377–383
  alternative audit procedures, 380
  clearing of exceptions, 380–381
  control of process, 375, 377
  form for confirmation request, 378–380
  interim date, confirmation at an, 385
  limitations of process, 381, 383
  returned, 161
  selection of accounts, 377
  summary of findings, 381
  bank, for cash account, 338, 340–341
  credit sales system and direct, 363
  of long-term debt, 496–497
  of securities, 461
Confirmation forms for accounts receivable,
  378–380
Confirmation routine in file analyzer, 306
Conflict of interest. *See* Independence
Consignment sales, 150
Consistency of data, 146–147
  credit sales system and, 362–363
  in inventory purchase system, 405
  of nominal accounts, 533–535
  payroll system, 541
  standard of, 42–43
Consolidated financial statements, 463–464
Consultation with other auditors who possess
  specialized skills, 74
Continental Vending case, 74, 110–112
Contingent fees, 72
Contingent liabilities, 303, 485–490
  classification of, 489, 490
  definition of, 485
  disclosure of, 489–490
  existence of, 485–489
  legal letter on, 486–488
  valuation of, 489
Contracts
  audited statements associated with, compli-
    ance with, 624
  review of, for contingent liabilities, 488
Control accounts in internal control model, 187
Control group
  in EDP department, 221
  output controls, 226
Controller (controller's department)
  EDP function and, 219
  functions of, 180–181
Control totals, 219, 224
Corporations, professional, of CPAs, 7, 77
Corroborative evidence, 135
Counting, 143
Credit allowances
  authorization of, 361
  cutoff of, accounts receivable and, 384
Credit manager, credit sales system and, 360–362
Credit policies and guidelines, 361
Credit sales system, 359–387
  authorization and accountability system for,
    361–363
  compliance tests for, 364, 366, 370–374

departmental autonomy and, 360
internal control model for, 360–363
study and evaluation of, 363–366
Cross-indexing of working papers, 157
Current file, working papers included in, 156
Current report, SEC requirements for, 32–33
Customer order, credit sales system and, 361
Customer statements
  cash receipts system and, 319
  credit sales system and, 363
Cutoff
  of fixed-asset transaction, 456
  inventory, 429
  for investments, 464
  for nominal accounts, 536
  substantive audit approach and, 304
Cutoff bank statements, 335–338

Data input controls in internal control model,
  188
Data processing. *See also entries starting with*
  EDP
  in internal control model, 188
Debit memos, 413
Debt. *See* Liabilities
Decision tables in EDP internal control systems,
  232, 233
Deductions, payroll, 541
  review of clerical accuracy, 549
Defense Contract Audit Agency, 4–5
Defensive auditing, 118–119
Deficiencies
  accounting, 14–15
  opinion of auditor on, 44
  scope of, 15
  uncertainty of, 15–16
Departmental autonomy (segregation of functional responsibility), 180–181
  cash disbursements system and, 329
  cash receipts system and, 316–317
  credit sales system and, 360
  of EDP department, 219
  fixed-assets system and, 446
  inventory purchase system and, 402–403
  long-term liabilities and, 491
  payroll system and, 538, 540
Departmental structure. *See also* Organizational
  structure
  internal control model and, 181–183
Deposit slips, 318, 325
Deposits of cash receipts, 318
Depreciation
  accumulated, 454–455
  disclosure of, 456
  IRS guidelines for, 455
  recomputation of, 455
Detail audit schedules, 161
Detail test of nominal accounts, 537–538
Difference estimates, 273
Direct labor costs, inventory valuation and, 427
Direct materials cost, inventory valuation and,
  426

647
Index

648
Index

Disbursements, cash. *See* Cash disbursements system
Disclaimer of opinion, 15, 44, 577–578
  lack of independence and, 66–67
  unaudited statements and, 114
Disclosure
  of accounts payable, 483
  of accounts receivable, 385
  adequate, 43
  cash accounts and, 338, 340
  of confidential information, 71
  of fixed-asset valuation, 456–457
  full, 43, 44
  inventory, 429–430
  of investments, 464
  of long-term debt, 498–499
  of loss contingencies, 489–490
  of stock transactions, 521
  of subsequent events. *See* Subsequent events
  substantive audit approach and, 304–305
Discounts, cash purchase, 413
Discovery sampling, 273
Discreditable accounts, AICPA rules on 75–78
Disposition of fixed assets
  authorization for, 447
  review of, 453–454
Dividend income account, 465
Dividends
  declaration of, 524–525
  stock, 518
Dividends receivable account, 465
Documentary evidence
  confirmation of, 143–144
  vouching and, 144–145
Documentation
  credit sales system and review of, 362
  frequency estimation, 263
  operations, 221–222
  program, EDP internal control system and, 221–222
  systems, 221
  of variable estimation, 271–272
Due professional care, 67

Economic conditions
  general, 148–149
  industry, 149
Economics, 28
EDP department
  control group in, 221
    output controls, 226
  internal organizational structure of, 220–221
  relationship to user departments, 219–220
EDP internal control system, 217–240
  compliance tests of, 296–297
  model, 217–226
    access controls, 222–223
    application controls, 223–226
    general controls, 218–223
    hardware controls, 222

    input controls, 224–225
    output controls, 225–226
    plan of organization, 219–222
    processing controls, 225
  study and evaluation of, 226–240
    assessment of in-depth review, 236
    assessment of preliminary review, 233–234
    auditing around the computer, 237–238
    auditing through the computer, 238–239
    compliance tests, 234, 236–237
    decision tables, 232, 233
    EDP service centers, 239–240
    final evaluation, 239
    flowchart, 228–229
    in-depth review, 234–235
    preliminary review, 227–233
  substantive tests for, 305–307
EDP questionnaire, 227
EDP service centers, audit of, 239–240
EDP software, protection and reconstruction of, 223
Education of auditors, 116, 118
Effectiveness, definition, 5
Efficiency, 6
  of auditor, 39
  definition, 5
Electronic data processing. *See* EDP department; EDP internal control system
1136 Tenants' Corporation case, 115–116
Emphasis of matter, 586–587
Employees. *See also* Personnel department; Personnel policies
  fraud by, auditor's responsibility for detecting, 100–101
  observation of, 143
  selection of, 188–189
  supervision of, 189–190
  training of, 189
Employment offers to employees of other accounting firms, 74
Encroachment, AICPA rule on, 73–74
Endorsement of checks
  disbursements system and review of, 334
  restrictive (for deposit only), 318
Engagement letters, 116, 117
Entry-level requirements for CPAs, 34–35
Environmental conditions
  confidence level in frequency estimation and, 254
  integrated audit approach and, 148–151, 154
Equity Funding Life Insurance Company case, 112–113
Ernst and Ernst v. *Hockfelder,* 101n, 106
Error rate
  expected, 252–253
  maximum potential, 261–263
Errors
  definition, 203–204
  sample testing definition of, 260–261
Estimation
  difference, 273

frequency. *See* Frequency estimation
ratio, 273
variable. *See* Variable estimation
Evidence, audit, 134–164
activity and testimonial, 139
collection of sufficient amount of, 41
competency of, 41–42, 135–136
sufficiency of evidence and, 141
completing the audit and review of, 571–572
computational, 137
corroborative, 135
cost of obtaining, 141
definition of, 134
documentary, 137–138. *See also* Documentary
evidence
documentation of. *See* Working papers
gathering techniques, 142–147
confirmation, 143–144
consistency of data, 146–147
environmental conditions, 148
inquiry, 145–146
observations, 143
recomputation, 145
vouching, 144–145
general sources of, 134–135
internal control, 139
integrated audit approach and collection of,
147–153
compliance tests, 152
environmental conditions, 148–151
internal controls, 151–152
substantive tests, 153
materiality of, 108, 141–142
physical, 137
risk and amount of, 140–141
sufficiency of, 140–142
competency of evidence and, 141
types of, 137–139
underlying accounting data, 135
validity of, 135
Execution of transactions
capital stock, 512
cash disbursements system and, 329–330
cash receipts system and, 318
compliance tests and, 294
credit sales system and, 361–362
validation of authorization, 370, 372
fixed-assets system, 446–447
in internal control model, 184
in inventory purchase system, 403–404
long-term liabilities, 491–492
payroll system, 540–541
Existence
of accounts payable, 479–481
of accounts receivable amounts, 374–383
of capital stock, 515, 519
of contingent liabilities, 485–489
of fixed assets, 450–454
of inventory, 415–424, 458–461. *See also* Inventory, physical observation and counting of

of long-term liabilities, 494–497
substantive audit approach and, 302–303

Factory overhead, inventory valuation and,
427–429
Fairness of financial standards, 12
False or misleading statements by auditor,
104–106
Federal Register, 33
Federal Taxation Executive Committee, AICPA,
71
Fees
advertising of, 76
contingent, 72
Fieldwork. *See also* Evidence, audit standards
of, 39–42
FIFO (first in first out) costing method, 424
File analyzer (generalized audit software pack-
age), 305–308
Files, reconstruction of, 223
Financial Accounting Standards Board (FASB),
4, 13, 28
function of, 30, 31
role of, 33
Financial compliance audits, 4–5
Financial statements
comparative, reports and, 615–617
fairness of, 12
unaudited. *See* Unaudited financial statements
Financial structure of a client, integrated audit
approach and, 150–151
Finished goods, inventory valuation and, 426
Finite correction factor, 258
Firing, authorization for, 540–541
Fixed asset changes, summary of, 450
Fixed assets internal control system, 445–457
audit program for, 450
authorization and accountability system for,
446–449
compliance tests for, 449
plan of organization and, 446
study and evaluation of, 449
substantive tests for, 449–457
classification and disclosure, 456–457
existence, 450–454
valuation, 454–456
Flowchart
for cash receipts system, 321
credit sales, 368–369
of inventory purchase system, 408–409
for payroll system, 546–547
program, 227, 232
for study and evaluation of EDP internal control system, 228–229
symbols used in, 197, 227, 230
understanding the internal control system and,
195–199
EDP system, 227–232
Forecasts, AICPA rule of conduct on, 67, 69
Fraud
by auditor, 101

650
Index

Fraud (*Continued*)
    liability to third parties, 102, 104–106
      Securities Act of 1933, 104
      Securities Exchange Act of 1934, 105–106
    Equity Funding case, 112, 113
    responsibility of auditor for detection of, 100–101, 106
Frequency estimation, 252–263
    confidence level, 253–254
    documentation of, 263
    evaluation of sampling results, 261–263
    expected error rate, 252–253
    flowchart of steps in, 253
    precision, 254–255
    random sampling, 258–260
    size of the sample, determination of, 255–258
    testing sample items, 260–261

General Accounting Office (GAO), 5–6
General economic conditions, 148–149
General EDP internal controls, 218–223
    in-depth review of, 235, 236
Generalized audit software package, 305–308
Generally accepted accounting principles
    adverse opinion based on departure from, 578–579
    AICPA rule on, 70
    definition, 42
    FASB and, 30, 31, 33
    SEC and, 33
Generally accepted auditing standards, 36–46
    in auditor's report, 10–13
    Equity Funding fraud and, 112
    fieldwork standards, 39–42
    general standards, 36–39
    interpretations of, 44–45
    monitoring quality of an accounting firm's auditing practice, 45–46
    reporting standards, 42–44
    rule of conduct concerning, 69–70
    unqualified opinion and, 574, 575
Government. *See also* Regulatory agencies
    trade policy of, 149
Grandfather-father-son procedure, 223
Guides, 45

Hardware controls, EDP internal control system and, 222
Hash total, 224
Hiring, authorization for, 540
Historical cost, 303, 550
Hours worked, authorization for, 541

Illegal acts by clients, auditor's responsibilities regarding, 572–573
Imprest petty cash fund, 343
Income statement. *See* Nominal accounts
Income tax. *See also* Internal Revenue Service
    review of revenue agent's report concerning, 488–489
Independence of auditors, 38, 59
    accounting services (write-up work), 64–66

definition of, 61
incompatible occupations, 77
lack of independence and report modifications, 66–67
loans, 60–62
management advisory service, 63–65
monitoring, 66
nomination of auditor by auditing committee, 191–192
rules of conduct, 60–67
SEC rule on, 79–80
tax service, 62–63
Independent registrar. *See* Registrar, independent
Independent review, 572
Indexing of working papers, 156–157
Industrial Revolution, 2
Industry, financial condition of, 150–151
Industry audit guidelines, 45
Industry economic conditions, integrated audit approach and, 149
Information. *See* Disclosure; Evidence
Information for CPA Candidates, 35
Injuction, SEC, 113
Input controls in EDP internal control system, 224–225
Inquiry technique, 145–146
    general economic conditions and, 149
    in in-depth review of EDP internal control system, 235
    industry conditions and, 149
Intactness
    compliance tests and criterion of, 293
      credit sales system, 364, 366
    of deposits of cash receipts, 318
Integrated audit approach, 148–153, 289, 290
    collection of evidence, 147–153
    compliance tests in, 152
    environmental conditions in, 148–151
    internal control evaluation in, 151–152
    substantive tests in, 153
Integrated test facility (ITF) technique, 238
Integrity of CPA, 59
    definition, 61
    rules of conduct, 61
Interest accounts, notes receivable and, 387
Interest rate, valuation of accounts receivable and, 384
Interim report, SEC requirements, 32
Internal audit. *See also* Control group
    in internal control model, 190–191
    substantive tests and, 301–302
Internal audit department, internal control model and, 190–191
Internal control system
    accounting, 178–179
    administrative, 177
    compliance tests and, 151, 152
    cost-effectiveness of, 193
    definition of, 176–177
    EDP. *See* EDP internal control system
    evaluation and study of, 40–41

evaluation of, 203–207
  analysis of system weaknesses, 204, 205
  communication of material weaknesses, 206–207
  identification of material weaknesses, 203–204
  recommendation letter, 204, 206
evidence generated and processed by, 139
  validity of, 135, 136
fraud-detection responsiblity of auditor and, 100, 101
integrated audit approach and evaluation of, 151–152, 154
limitations of, 193
model of, 179–193
  accounting structure, 186–188
  audit committee, 191–193
  authorization and accountability systems, 183–186
  cash disbursements, 328–331
  cash receipts system, 315–319
  credit sales, 360–363
  EDP internal control model. *See* EDP internal control system
  internal audit staff, 190–191
  investments, 458
  limitations, 193
  observation and evaluation of, 143
  personnel policies, 188–190
  plan of organization, 179–183
  study and evaluation of, 193–207. *See also* evaluation of *above and* understanding of *below*
reports on, 626–627
understanding of, 194–203
  flowcharts, 195–199
  questionnaires, internal control, 194–196
vouching and, 144–145
Internal Revenue Code, positions contrary to Treasury Department or IRS interpretations of, 83
Internal Revenue Service (IRS)
  depreciation guidelines of, 455
  financial compliance audits by, 4
Interrelated accounts, analysis of, 534–535
Interrelationship of data, 147
Inventory
  access to, 404
    credit sales system, 363
  cutoff, 482
  definition of, 401
  observation of, 107
  periodic counting of, 405
  physical observation and counting of, 415–424
    alternative audit procedures, 423–424
    control of inventory-counting process, auditor's, 417–418
    inventory held by others, 421
    movement of inventory during count, 418, 429
    observation of inventory by auditor, 418, 420–421

procedures for taking physical inventory, client's, 417
test of summarization, 421–423
timing of physical inventory by client, 416
substantive tests for, 415–430. *See also* physical observation and counting of *above*
  audit program, 415, 416
  classification and disclosure, 429–430
  cutoff, 429
  existence, 415–424
  valuation, 424–429
valuation of
  costing methods, 424–425
  direct labor, 427
  direct materials, 426
  factory overhead, 427–429
  lower of cost or market, 425
  raw materials, 426
  work in process and finished goods, 426
Inventory cost methods, 424–425
Inventory purchases, test of summarization of, 411–412
Inventory purchase system, 401–430
  compliance tests for, 406, 410–415
  study and evaluation of, 406
Inventory tags, 418, 420
Investment changes, summary of, 458–459
Investments, 457–465
  substantive tests for, 458–464
    classification and disclosure, 464
    cutoff, 464
    existence, 458–461
    valuation, 461–464
Invoices. *See* Sales invoice; Vendor's invoice
Irregularities, definition of, 204

Job descriptions in internal control model, 187
Joint ventures, 465
Judgement sampling, 250–251

Key punch verification, 225

Labor costs, direct, inventory valuation and, 427
Lantell v. *Lybrand,* 102
Lapping, 327
Lead schedule, 159–161
Legal letter, 149–150
  on litigation against client, 486–488
Letter of representation, 566, 568–569
Liabilities
  accrued, 483–485
  common law
    client's liability to, 99–100
    fraud, detection of, 100–101
    third parties, liability to, 101–103
  contingent. *See* Contingent liabilities
  estimated, 303
  existence of, 302
  fixed, 303
  legal cases, 106–113
  long-term. *See* Long-term liabilities

652
Index

Liabilities (*Continued*)
  professional response to recent litigation involving question of, 116–119
  search for unrecorded, 479, 481
  unaudited statements and, 114–116
  valuation of, 303–304
Liability of auditor, 98–119
  to third parties. *See* Third parties, liability of auditors to
Library, EDP department, 221
LIFO (last in first out) costing method, 424
Limit checks, 297
Litigation. *See also* Liability of auditor
  on contingent liability, 485–488
  professional response to recent, 116, 118–119
Loans, independence of CPAs and, 60–61
Long-term liabilities, 490–499
  authorization and accountability systems for, 491–494
  confirmation of, 496–497
  departmental autonomy and, 491
  disclosure of, 498–499
  existence and cutoff of, 494–496
  study and evaluation of internal control system for, 494
  valuation of, 497–498
Loss carry-forwards, 524
Loss contingencies, 485–490
Lower of cost or market, 303, 425

Machine operation, in EDP department, 220
Mailing of checks, 330
Mailroom clerk, 318
Maintenance expenses, 454
Management, administrative controls and, 177
Management Advisory Services Committee, AICPA's, 71
  independence of auditor in, 63–65
  Yale Express Systems case, 109
Marketing function, integrated audit approach and, 150
Materiality
  of deficiencies, 14
  definition, 108
Material weaknesses. *See* Weaknesses, material
Maximum potential error rate, 261–263
McKesson and Robbins case, 107
Mean-per-unit variable estimation. *See* Variable estimation
Memoranda
  for cash receipts system, 321–322
  debit, 413
  internal control system described in, 199–203
  for preliminary review of EDP internal control system, 232–233
  in working papers, 161
Minutes of meetings, review of, for contingent liabilities, 488
Missing data, EDP compliance testing and, 297
Mortgages. *See also* Long-term liabilities
  recording of transactions involving, 493

Narrative descriptions. *See* Memoranda
Near-cash items, cash system audit and, 344–345
Negative assurances, 587, 624
Negligence
  auditor's, 99–100
    gross negligence, 102, 106
    Securities Act of 1933, 104
    unaudited statements: 1136 Tenants' Corporation Case, 115
  contributory, 100
Nominal accounts, 532–538
  consistency of other data with, 533–535
  detail test of, 537–538
  evaluation of internal controls and, 535
  permanent accounts contrasted to, 532–538
  tests of transactions for, 535–537
Notes, long-term, 494
Notes payable. *See* Long-term liabilities
Notes receivable, 385, 387

Objectivity of CPA, 59
  definition, 61
  rules of conduct, 61
Observation of evidence, 143
Observation technique in substantive tests, 299
Occupations, incompatible with auditor's independence, 77
Offers of employment, to employees of other accounting firms, 74
Open-document file, review of, 482
Operational audits, 5–6
Operations documentation, EDP internal control system and, 221–222
Opinion of auditor, 43–44
  adverse. *See* Adverse opinion, auditor's; Auditor's opinion, adverse
  disclaimer of. *See* disclaimer of opinion
  independent review before expression of, 572
  piecemeal, 587
  qualified, 15, 575–577
  unqualified, 11–14, 44
Opinion paragraph of auditor's report. 12–13, 44
Organizational chart
  credit sales flowchart shown in relation to, 368–369
  inventory purchase system flowchart shown in relation to, 408–409
  payroll flowchart shown in relation to, 546–547
Organizational plan. *See* Plan of organization
Organizational structure, 150. *See also* Plan of organization
  cash disbursements system and, 329
  departmental, cash receipts system and, 317
  of EDP department, 220–221
  in internal control model, 181–183
Output controls in EDP internal control system, 225–226
Ownership, substantive audit approach and, 302–303

Partnership of CPAs, 7
Payables. *See* Accounts payable

Pay rates
authorization of, 541
verification of, 548
Payroll. *See also* wages
authorization and accountability system and, 540–543
compliance tests for, 543–545, 548–549
departmental autonomy and, 538, 540
internal control system for, 538–551
study and evaluation of, 543–547
Payroll deductions, 549
authorization of, 541
Payroll records, preparation of, 542
Payroll system, substantive tests for, 549
Peer review, 46, 118
Permanent file, type of information in, 155–156
Personnel department, payroll system and, 540–542
Personnel policies, internal control model and, 188–190
Petty cash
accountability for, 183
testing system of, 343
Physical evidence, 137
Piecemeal opinions, 587
Plan, audit, 156
Planning of audit, 39, 151
review of working papers, 163
Plan of organization. *See also* Organizational structure
cash disbursements system and, 329
cash receipts system, 316–317
for credit sales system, 360–363
EDP system, 219–222
fixed-assets internal control system and, 446
internal control model, 179–183
for inventory purchase system, 402–403
payroll system and, 538, 540
Precision level, frequency estimation and, 254–255
Preferred stock, 525
Preliminary review of EDP internal control system, 227–233
assessment of, 233–234
Prenumbered internal documents
compliance tests and, 293
credit sales system and, 362
internal control model and, 187–188
in inventory purchase system, 403–405
Prepayments, lead schedule for, 159–161
Prior period adjustments in retained earning account, 523–524
Problem definition, EDP internal control system and, 221
Procedural compliance audit, 5
Processing of authorized transactions by EDP department, 219–220
Processing controls, EDP internal control system and, 225
Production function, integrated audit approach and, 150

Professional competence. *See* Competence
Professional corporations of CPAs, 7
Professional development of auditors, 35, 37–38
Professional ethics. *See* Code of ethics
Professional standards, auditor's, 35–36
Pro forma balance sheet, 567
Program documentation, EDP internal control system and, 221–222
Program flowcharts, 227, 232
Programming, EDP departmental structure and, 220
Promissory notes, 465
Proof of cash, 341, 342
Property, plant, and equipment. *See* Fixed assets
Public accounting firms. *See also* Auditor
"big eight," 8n
functional division of, 9–10
internal structure of, 7–9
monitoring auditing standards in, 45–46
name of, 77–78
objective of audit by, 6
partnership and professional corporation forms of, 7
review procedure in, 40
Public Utility Holding Company Act of 1935, 31
Purchase commitments, as contingency, 488
Purchase memos, 413
Purchase of fixed assets
authorization for, 447
vouching additions, 453
Purchase orders
cash disbursements and, 330, 333
in inventory purchase system, 403–405, 410–411
unrecorded liabilities and, 482
Purchase returns and allowances, 413
Purchases, inventory. *See* Inventory purchases; Inventory purchasing system
Purchases journal, 411–412
review of, 481–482
Purchasing department (or agent)
authorization validation and, 410–411
inventory purchase system and, 402, 403

Qualified opinion, auditor's, 15, 575–577
Questionnaires, internal control, 194–196
cash receipts system and, 319–320
for credit sales system, 364–366
EDP system and, 227
for inventory purchase system, 406, 407
for long-term debt, 494, 495
for payroll system, 544–545
for property, plant, and equipment, 451

Random numbers table, 258–261
Random sampling, 258–260
Ratio estimates, 273
Ratios, analysis of, 146–147, 150
nominal accounts, 533–534
Raw materials, inventory valuation and, 426
Reasonable assurance, concept of, 193

654
Index

Receipts, cash. *See* Cash receipts system
Receivables. *See* Accounts receivable
Receiving department, 360
    inventory purchase system and, 402–404
Receiving reports
    cash disbursements and, 330
    inventory purchase system and, 403–405, 410–411
    review of, 482
Reclassifications in working trial balance, 159
Recommendation letter, internal control, 204, 206
Recomputation, 137, 145
    as compliance test, 292
    of depreciation of fixed assets, 455–456
    in substantive testing, 300, 303
Reconciliation of stock records, 520–521
Record count, 224
Recording of transactions
    capital stock, 512–513
    cash disbursement system and, 330
    cash receipts system and, 317, 318
    compliance tests and, 294
    credit sales system and, 362–363
        compliance test, 373
    in fixed-assets system, 447–448
    in internal control model, 184–185
    in inventory purchase system, 404
        compliance tests, 411
    long-term liabilities, 492–494
    payroll system, 541–542
Records, accounting, comparison of assets with, 185–186
Registrar, independent, recording of stock transactions and, 513, 519–520
Registrar of bonds, 493
Registration of securities, 31–34
Registration statement (SEC), 31–32
    effective date of, 104–105
    liability of auditor for, 103–105
    S-1 review of, 105, 108–109
Regulatory agencies, special reports based on requirements of, 623–626
Related party transactions, 113, 119
Reliability
    alpha risk and, 275
    frequency estimation and, 253–254
Repair of fixed assets, 448
    review of, 454
Replacement cost
    disclosure of, 457
    of inventory, 424, 425, 430
Report, auditor's. *See* Auditor's report
Reporting standards, 42–44
Report modifications. *See* Auditor's report, modifications of
Representation letter, 566, 568–569
Repurchase agreements as contingency, 488
Responsibilities to clients, 59. *See also* Liability of audit
    confidentiality, 71–72
Responsibilities to colleagues, 72–74

Retained earnings, 521–526
    appropriated, 526
Retirement of fixed assets, 447
    review of, 453–454
Returned confirmations, 161
Returns, purchase, 413
Revenue, recognition of, 359
Revenue agent's report, review of, 488–489
Revenue expenditures, recording of, 448
Review (review procedures), 46. *See also* Internal control system
    AICPA standards for, 40
    of audit results, as audit committee function, 192
    of documantation, credit sales system and, 362
    of EDP internal control system
        assessment of in-depth review, 236
        assessment of preliminary review, 233–234
        in-depth review, 234–235
        preliminary review, 227–233
    of one firm by another, 113
    peer, 46, 118
    of working papers, 163
Risk
    consistency and data and, 146
    sufficiency of evidence and degree of, 140–141
Rules of conduct. *See* Code of ethics
Rusch factors, Inc. v. *Levin,* 103
Ryan v. *Kanne,* 102

Safe deposit box, near-cash items in, 344
Sale(s). *See also* Marketing function
    authorization for, 361, 370, 372
    of fixed assets, 447
Sales commitments, as contingency, 488
Sales department, 360
    authorization for sale by, 361
Sales invoice
    credit sales system and, 361
        compliance tests, 372, 373
    review of, 362
Sales order, 361
Sales summarization, test of the, 373
Sample selection (for compliance tests)
    cash disbursements system, 332
    cash receipts system, 327–328
    credit sales system, 266
    for confirmation of accounts receivable, 377
    in frequency estimation, 258–260
    for inventory purchase system, 406
    payroll system, 544–545
    in variable estimation, 269
Sample selection routine, 306
Sample size
    for compliance tests, 292–293
    for confirmation of accounts receivable, 377
    determination of
        in frequency estimation, 255–258
        in variable estimation, 268–269
Sample testing
    in frequency estimation, 260–261

in variable estimation, 269–270
Sampling, 250–280
discovery, 273
evaluation of results of, 261–263
frequency estimation (attribute sample). *See* Frequency estimation
judgment (nonstatistical), 250–251
random, 258–260
random numbers table, 258–261
ratio and difference estimates, 273
risk, identifying and controlling, 274–276
stratification, 273–274
systematic, 259–260
testing sample items, 260–261
variable estimation (mean per unit). *See* Variable estimation
Scanning, 146
Scope
adverse opinion concerning, 582–585
definition of, 15
Scope paragraph of auditor's report, 12
Securities. *See also* Investments; Stock
confirmation of, 461
count of, 459, 461
registration of, 31
registration with SEC, 31–34
valuation of, 461–464
Securities Act of 1933, 30–31
registration statement under. *See* Registration statement
third-party liability of auditor and, 103–105
BarChris case, 107–109
Securities Exchange Act of 1934, 31
Securities and Exchange Commission (SEC), 46
change in principal auditors, 73
code of ethics and, 79–80
function and powers of, 30–34
injunction of a firm or individual, 113
registration of securities with, 31–34
suspension of a firm or auditor from practicing before the, 113
third-party liability of auditors
McKesson and Robbins Case, 107
Rule, 10b-5, 106
sanctions, 113
Segregation of functional responsibility. *See* Departmental autonomy
Shipment
authorization for, 361, 372
during inventory, 418, 429
Shipping department, credit sales and, 360, 361
Signature
on auditor's report, 13
on checks
cash disbursement system, 330
compliance test, 333
of tax return preparer, 80
of tax return reviewer, 80–81
Sign-off date of auditor's report, 13
Sign test in EDP compliance testing, 297
Society, auditings role in, 26–27
Software package, generalized audit, 305–308

Solicitation, AICPA rules on, 75–77
S-1 review, 105, 108–109
Specialists
substantive testing and, 300–301
using the work of, 68
Specialized auditors
consultation with, 74
self-designation as, 76
Standard deviation, 252
State boards of accountancy, 78
Statements on Auditing Standards (SAS), 36, 37. *See also* Generally accepted auditing standards
Statements on Auditing Standards, 44–45
Statements on Management Advisory Services, 64, 65
Statement on Responsibilities in Tax Practice, 63
State Street Trust Company v. *Ernst,* 102
Stock
authorization and accountibility system and, 512–514
departmental autonomy and, 511–512
internal control system for, 511–526
retained earnings, 521–526
appropriated retained earnings, 526
cash and other dividends, 524–525
net income or loss, 523
prior period adjustments, 523–524
study and evaluation of, 514
Stock certificate, 520–521
Stock dividends
capital stock additions resulting from, 518
small or large, 518
Stockholders, review of minutes of meetings of, 488
Stock ledger, 514, 520–521
Stock purchase plans, 521
Stock split, 518
Stratification, 273–274
Stratification routine, 306
Structure, organizational. *See* Organizational structure
Structure of the firm, integrated audit approach and, 150–151
Subsequent events, 564–572
after report date, 570–571
nature of, 566–567
routine procedures in review of, 565
special audit program for review of, 565–566
Subsidiary ledger in cash receipts system, 325–328
Substantive tests, 297–307
for accounts payable, 478–483
for accounts receivable. *See* Accounts receivable, substantive tests for
audit approach in, 302–305
for cash, 341
in bank accounts. *See* Cash in bank accounts
for cash
petty cash, 343
results of tests and auditor's opinion, 345

656
Index

Substantive tests (*Continued*)
undeposited cash receipts and near-cash items, 344–345
EDP impact on, 305–307
extent of, 298–299
for fixed-assets system. *See* Fixed-assets system, substantive tests for
integrated audit approach and, 153, 154
internal audit function and, 301–302
for inventories. *See* Inventories, substantive tests for
for investments, 458–464. *See also* Investments, substantive tests for
for long-term debt, 494–499
for payroll system, 549
purpose of, 297
for stock transactions, 514–521
techniques and procedures used in, 299–301
timing of, 298, 299
variable estimation procedures for. *See* Variation estimation
Summarize routine, 306
Supreme Court, U.S. *See specific cases*
Supervision of auditor's assistants, 39, 40
Supervision of employees, 189–190
System analysis, EDP departmental structure and, 220
Systematic sampling, 259–260
Systems approach to auditing, 41, 289–290
compliance tests
audit approach and, 293–296
EDP impact on, 296–297
objectives of, 290–291
size of sample for, 292–293
techniques used for, 292
timing of, 291–292
substantive tests. *See* Substantive tests
Systems documentation, EDP internal control system and, 221
Systems flowcharts, 227, 231
EDP documentation and, 221, 227

Tax practice
AICPA's Statement on Responsibilities in, 80–82
independence of CPA and, 62–63
Technical standards, 59. *See also* Generally accepted accounting procedures
AICPA rule on, 70–71
Technology, industry economic conditions and, 149
Test deck (or tape), 296–297
Testimonial evidence, 139
Tests
compliance. *See* Compliance tests
substantive. *See* Substantive tests
of transactions, 152
nominal accounts, 535–537
Third parties
confirmation of evidence by, 143–144

liability of auditor to
civil cases, 107–110
common law, 101–103
criminal cases, 110–113
Securities Act of 1933, 103–105
Securities Exchange Act of 1934, 105–106
SEC Rule 10b-5, 106
unaudited statements, 114–116
Trade policy, 149
Transactions
authorization of. *See* Authorization of transactions
execution of. *See* Execution of transactions
recording of, 184–185
tests of, 152
nominal accounts, 535–537
Transfer agent
for bonds, 493
recording of stock transactions and, 513, 519–520
Treasurer (treasurer's department)
cash disbursements system and, 329
cash receipts system and, 316
credit sales system and, 360
fixed-assets system and, 446
functions of, 180–182
long-term liabilities and, 491, 492
payroll system and, 540
Trend analysis, 146–147
of nominal accounts, 533–534
Trial balance
accounts payable, 479–480
working, 157–159
Trial Board, AICPA, 71, 75, 78–79

Ultimate risk, 275–276
Ultramares Corporation v. *Touche,* 102
Unaudited financial statements, 618–623
annual, 619–621
interim, 621–623
legal liability and, 114–116
Uncertainty
adverse opinion because of, 585–586
deficiencies resulting from, 15–16
Underlying accounting data, 135
Universe definition
compliance tests for cash disbursements and, 332–333
compliance tests for cash receipts system and, 326–327
for credit sales system, 364, 466
for inventory purchase system, 406
payroll system, 543–544
Unqualified opinion, 11–14, 44
Utility costs, accrued, 485

Validation of authorization for payroll transactions, 548
credit sales system, 370, 372
inventory purchase system, 410–411
Validity of evidence, 135–136

Valley Commercial Corporation, 110–111
Valuation
  of accounts payable, 482–483
  of accounts receivable, 383–384
  of capital stock additions, 518
  of capital stock deletions, 519
  for cash account, 338
  of fixed assets, 454–456
  of inventory. *See* Inventory, valuation of
  of investments, 461–464
  of long-term debt, 497–498
  substantive audit approach and, 303–304
Variable estimation (mean per unit) 263, 265–271
  confidence level and, 266–267
  documentation, 271–272
  evaluation of sampling results, 270–271
  flowchart of steps in, 266
  precision and, 267–268
  selection of sample, 269
  size of sample, determining, 268–269
  standard deviation estimate, 265
  testing sample items, 269–270
Vendor's invoice, 411
  cash disbursements and, 330
Vendor's statements
  accounts payable trial balance and, 480
  reconciliation of accounts payable records
    with, 331
Verification, key punch, 225
Voucher package, 330
Voucher register, review of, 481–482
Vouching, 144–145
  in compliance testing, 292
  in substantive testing, 299–300

Wages, accrued, 484
Warehouse department (stores department),
  credit sales system and, 360, 361
Warranty costs, accrued, 484
Weaknesses, material
  in internal control system, 203–207
    analysis of, 204, 205
    communication of, 206–207
    definition, 206
    identification of, 203–204
    recommendation letter concerning, 204,
      206
Weighted-average costing method, 424
Wheat Commission, 30
Working papers, 153–164
  for cash receipts system, 321, 323
  completing the audit and review of, 571–572
  in current file, 156–157
  detail audit schedules, 161
  format of, 156–157
  guidelines for items to be included in, 155
  indexing and cross-indexing of, 156–157
  lead schedule, 159–161
  memorandum, 161
  other, 161
  in permanent file, 155–156
  review of, 163
  working trial balance, 157–159
Working trial balance, 157–159
Work-in-process inventory, valuation of, 426
Write-off, authorization for, 362

Yale Express Systems case, 109–110

80 9 8 7 6 5 4 3